Kohlhammer

International Exegetical Commentary on the Old Testament (IECOT)

Edited by:

Walter Dietrich, David M. Carr,

Adele Berlin, Erhard Blum, Irmtraud Fischer, Shimon Gesundheit, Walter Groß, Gary Knoppers, Bernard M. Levinson, Ed Noort, Helmut Utzschneider and Beate Ego (Apocrypha/Deuterocanonical books)

Cover:
Top: Panel from a four-part relief on the "Black Obelisk of Shalmaneser III" (859–824 BCE) depicting the Israelite king Jehu (845–817 BCE; 2 Kings 9f) paying obeisance to the Assyrian "King of Kings." The vassal has thrown himself to the ground in front of his overlord. Royal servants are standing behind the Assyrian king whereas Assyrian officers are standing behind Jehu. The remaining picture panels portray thirteen Israelite tribute bearers carrying heavy and precious gifts.
Photo © Z.Radovan/BibleLandPictures.com

Bottom left: One of ten reliefs on the bronze doors that constitute the eastern portal (the so-called "Gates of Paradise") of the Baptistery of St. John of Florence, created 1424–1452 by Lorenzo Ghiberti (c. 1378–1455). Detail from the picture "Adam and Eve"; in the center is the creation of Eve: "And the rib that the Lord God had taken from the man he made into a woman and brought her to the man." (Gen 2:22)
Photograph by George Reader

Bottom right: Detail of the Menorah in front of the Knesset in Jerusalem, created by Benno Elkan (1877–1960): Ezra reads the Law of Moses to the assembled nation (Neh 8). The bronze Menorah was created in London in 1956 and in the same year was given by the British as a gift to the State of Israel. A total of 29 reliefs portray scenes from the Hebrew bible and the history of the Jewish people.

Luca Mazzinghi

Wisdom

W. Kohlhammer

Translation: Michael Tait
Redaction: Jonathan M. Robker

1. Edition 2019

Production: W. Kohlhammer GmbH, Stuttgart

Print:
ISBN 978-3-17-022425-4

E-Book-Formats:
pdf: ISBN 978-3-17-033649-0
epub: ISBN 978-3-17-033650-6
mobi: ISBN 978-3-17-033651-3

Content

Editors' Foreword

The International Exegetical Commentary on the Old Testament (IECOT) offers a multi-perspectival interpretation of the books of the Old Testament to a broad, international audience of scholars, laypeople and pastors. Biblical commentaries too often reflect the fragmented character of contemporary biblical scholarship, where different geographical or methodological sub-groups of scholars pursue specific methodologies and/or theories with little engagement of alternative approaches. This series, published in English and German editions, brings together editors and authors from North America, Europe, and Israel with multiple exegetical perspectives.

From the outset the goal has been to publish a series that was "international, ecumenical and contemporary." The international character is reflected in the composition of an editorial board with members from six countries and commentators representing a yet broader diversity of scholarly contexts.

The ecumenical dimension is reflected in at least two ways. First, both the editorial board and the list of authors includes scholars with a variety of religious perspectives, both Christian and Jewish. Second, the commentary series not only includes volumes on books in the Jewish Tanach/Protestant Old Testament, but also other books recognized as canonical parts of the Old Testament by diverse Christian confessions (thus including the Deuterocanonical Old Testament books).

When it comes to "contemporary," one central distinguishing feature of this series is its attempt to bring together two broad families of perspectives in analysis of biblical books, perspectives often described as "synchronic" and "diachronic" and all too often understood as incompatible with each other. Historically, diachronic studies arose in Europe, while some of the better known early synchronic studies originated in North America and Israel. Nevertheless, historical studies have continued to be pursued around the world, and focused synchronic work has been done in an ever greater variety of settings. Building on these developments, we aim in this series to bring synchronic and diachronic methods into closer alignment, allowing these approaches to work in a complementary and mutually-informative rather than antagonistic manner.

Since these terms are used in varying ways within biblical studies, it makes sense to specify how they are understood in this series. Within IECOT we understand "synchronic" to embrace a variety of types of study of a biblical text *in one given stage of its development*, particularly its final stage(s) of development in existing manuscripts. "Synchronic" studies embrace non-historical narratological, reader-response and other approaches along with historically-informed exegesis of a particular stage of a biblical text. In contrast, we understand "diachronic" to embrace the full variety of modes of study of a biblical text *over time.*

This diachronic analysis may include use of manuscript evidence (where available) to identify documented pre-stages of a biblical text, judicious use of clues within the biblical text to reconstruct its formation over time, and also an examination of the ways in which a biblical text may be in dialogue with earlier biblical (and non-biblical) motifs, traditions, themes, etc. In other words, diachronic study focuses on what might be termed a "depth dimension" of a given text – how a text (and its parts) has journeyed over time up to its present form, making the text part of a broader history of traditions, motifs and/or prior compositions. Synchronic analysis focuses on a particular moment (or moments) of that journey, with a particular focus on the final, canonized form (or forms) of the text. Together they represent, in our view, complementary ways of building a textual interpretation.

Of course, each biblical book is different, and each author or team of authors has different ideas of how to incorporate these perspectives into the commentary. The authors will present their ideas in the introduction to each volume. In addition, each author or team of authors will highlight specific contemporary methodological and hermeneutical perspectives – e.g. gender-critical, liberation-theological, reception-historical, social-historical – appropriate to their own strengths and to the biblical book being interpreted. The result, we hope and expect, will be a series of volumes that display a range of ways that various methodologies and discourses can be integrated into the interpretation of the diverse books of the Old Testament.

Fall 2012 The Editors

Preface

The book of Wisdom is the object of renewed interest. Although deeply rooted in the Scriptures of Israel, it forms an interesting bridge between the Jewish and Hellenistic worlds.

This commentary presupposes two previous works which both constitute solid points of reference for the exegesis of Wisdom: the three volumes of C. Larcher (*La Sagesse de Salomon ou le livre de la* Sagesse, 1983-1985) and the three of G. Scarpat (*Libro della Sapienza,* 1989-1999). Begun in 1969 with his pioneering *Etudes sur le livre de la Sagesse*, Larcher's work constitutes the best existing work on Wisdom carried out in light of the criteria of traditional historical-critical exegesis. For its part, Scarpat's work offers a monumental philological analysis of our book which it would be hard to surpass. However, the studies of the last twenty years have contributed to the highlighting of some fundamental aspects which complete and develop these works. First of all, there has been a discovery of a careful literary structure through which the author of the book intends to communicate a precise theological message (M. Gilbert, P. Bizzeti). Then, a broader and more complete view of the style and literary genre of the book has developed. These too are seen to serve the message which the author is intending to offer to his readership. Secondly, there has been a broader and deeper assessment of the relationship which the book displays with the biblical and Jewish world, on the one hand, and with the Hellenistic world, on the other. There has also been a more accurate view of the historical context in Alexandria towards the end of the first century BCE. Finally, there has been closer attention to the particular theological standpoint of our sage. Although taken into consideration in the studies of Larcher, this has not been highlighted sufficiently by the other commentators, however illustrious (Scarpat, but also D. Winston). That is especially the case of the third part (Wis 10-19) which has been rediscovered only since the 1990s. All of this leaves room for a new commentary on Wisdom, certainly one that is more concise than the majority of its predecessors, but also one that seeks to unite exegetical analysis properly so called with the three factors indicated above: structure and literary genre; relationship with the biblical (and Jewish) world and with Hellenism; and the theological perspective of the author.

General Introduction[1]

A Unique Book

Written directly in Greek, the book of Wisdom displays novel characteristics which render it a unique book in comparison with other texts of its time. Composed towards the end of the first cent. BCE by an Alexandrian Jew well-versed in the Bible and faithful to the tradition of Israel, the book of Wisdom forms an important point of contact between the biblical world and the vast world of Hellenism.

The book also shows itself to be rich in novelties with regard to its content. The strong eschatological perspective, opened up by the announcement of the future fate of the just and the ungodly (Wis 1-6), is bound together with a vision of the past of Israel to which the final part of the book refers (Wis 10-19). There, eschatology is linked to history by means of the role of the cosmos. At the heart of the book stands the praise of wisdom (Wis 7-9), mediator between God and humanity.

The Book's Title

The book is known in the Greek manuscripts as ΣΟΦΙΑ ΣΑΛΟΜΩΝΟΣ (S*), or else ΣΟΦΙΑ ΣΑΛΟΜΩΝ (B^c), or even ΣΑΛΟΜΩΝΤΟΣ (A).[2] In the codices of the *Vetus Latina*, the inscription *Liber Sapientiae Salomonis* appears or sometimes *Sapientia Salomonis*, or, more simply, *Liber Sapientiae.* The book is entered in the Latin Vulgate and, thereafter, in the modern translations more simply as "book of Wisdom". On account of the fact that in the central part of the book (Wis 7-9) the author seems to identify himself with King Solomon – although this identification is never explicit – it is not improbable that it was he himself who called his own text "Wisdom of Solomon". This would accord with a practice that was not rare in antiquity and frequent in the Jewish tradition which tended to place under the aegis of Solomon a good part of the sapiential *corpus*: Proverbs, Qoheleth and the Song of Songs. However, already from the patristic period, it was clear that the attribution to Solomon was only pseudepigraphic. That is recognised by Origen, Augustine, and Jerome among others.[3]

Text and Versions[4]

Greek Text

The Greek text of the book of Wisdom has been transmitted to us in a good state in the three most important uncial codices which, according to Ziegler, represent the best text possible: Vaticanus (B), Sinaiticus (S) and Alexandrinus (A). The other

1 For a complete introduction to the book of Wisdom, the point of departure is still represented by Larcher, *Etudes sur le livre de la Sagesse* (1969). More summary, but complete, is the introduction of Gilbert ("Sagesse de Salomon") which dates from 1986.

2 Cf. the critical apparatus in Ziegler, *Sapientia*, 95.

3 Origen, *Comm. Jo.* 20.4 (PG XIV, 581); Jerome, *Praef. in libros Salomonis* (PL XVIII, 1307); Augustine, *Civ.* 18.20 (PL XLI, 554).

4 Cf. Larcher, *Sagesse,* I:53-74; Ziegler, *Sapientia*, 7-64; Gilbert, "Sagesse", 58-65. A pioneering work is that of Feldman, *Textkritische Materialien zum Buch der Weisheit* (Freiburg i.B. 1902).

uncials (V and C in particular) and the various minuscules are of less importance. Some fragments of the book of Wisdom also exist in papyrus. The patristic quotations and the *florilegia* take on a certain interest for textual criticism.[5] The edition of J. Ziegler has ironed out most of the problems of the text which is thus one of the most accessible books of the Old Testament.[6]

Vetus Latina and Vulgate

The most important of the ancient versions is the *Vetus Latina* which originated in North Africa, probably towards the end of the second century CE, and was inserted into the *Vulgate* towards the fifth century.[7] Jerome did not translate the book of Wisdom himself because he did not recognise it as canonical.[8] The Latin translation is earlier than the oldest Greek manuscript available to us (B) by at least two centuries and turns out to be very useful for the reconstruction of passages that are particularly difficult. It seems probable that the *Vetus Latina* was translated from a Greek text different from that of the great uncials, more similar to that of S* (cf., for example, the reading preserved in 2:9a: *nullum pratum* which is probably the original reading).[9] The other ancient versions – the *Peshitta*, the various Coptic versions, the Armenian, Arabic and Ethiopian versions – are all later than the great uncials and offer little interest for textual criticism.

Original Language

We must regard as completely eclipsed the opinion of those who speculated that the book of Wisdom was originally written in Hebrew (or Aramaic) and subsequently translated into Greek.[10] The book does not lack Hebraisms, such as the constant use of *parallelismus membrorum*,[11] but such an argument does not appear sufficient for considering the Greek of Wisdom as the translation of a Semitic original. In this connection, J. Reider writes that "[the book of Wisdom] is written in the purest form of Alexandrinian Greek, free from the Hebraisms and anomalies of the Septuagint and full of passages which combine the richest vocabulary with

5 Cf. Ziegler, *Sapientia*, 10-11; Gilbert, "Sagesse", 58-59. For the Cologne papyrus containing the text of Wis 17:5-20b, cf. Mazzinghi, *Notte di paura e di luce*, 310.

6 For some small problems raised by Ziegler's text, see Gilbert, "Sagesse", 59. Cf. also the whole study of Engel, "Sophia Salomonos".

7 Gribomont, Jean, "L'édition Vaticane de la Vulgate et la Sagesse de Salomon dans sa recension italienne", *Rivista di Storia e Letteratura Religiosa* 4 (1968) 472-496.

8 Cf. *Praefatio Hieronymi de translatione graeca: Biblia Sacra*, XI (Roma: PIB 1957), 6 (PL XXIX,427-428).

9 In an appendix to each of the three volumes, Scarpat's commentary records the entire Latin text of Wisdom with an appropriate philological commentary and constitutes the best point of reference in this connection. Cf. De Bruyne, Donatien D., "Etude sur le texte latin de Sagesse"; *RBén* 41 (1929) 100-133. According to the opinion of De Bruyne, the Latin translator was not at the peak of his profession (cf. p. 130). Cf. also Skehan, Patrick W., "Note on the Latin text of the Book of Wisdom"; *CBQ* 4 (1942) 230-243. The text of the *Vetus Latina* of Wisdom can be found in Thiele, Walter, *Vetus Latina* XI,1, (Freiburg i.B.: Herder 1977-1985).

10 Larcher, *Sagesse*, I:91-95; Gilbert, "Sagesse", 61-65. Outstanding pioneers of this study are Gärtner, *Komposition und Wortwahl des Buches der Weisheit* (1912), and Focke, *Die Enstehung der Weisheit Salomos* (1913). However, the latter held that Wis 1-5 was originally composed in Hebrew (cf. pp. 65-66).

11 Cf. Winston, *Wisdom of Solomon*, 15.

genuine rhetorical eloquence. Compared with the Septuaginta, Wisdom appears to be an original and independent work"[12].

The Unity of the Book[13]

Already towards the middle of the nineteenth cent., C.L.W. Grimm held that the question of the literary unity of the book had been definitively resolved. For the great German commentator, the book of Wisdom was undoubtedly the work of a single author, even if there were some opposing voices which made themselves heard as late as the beginning of the twentieth century.[14] Some contemporary authors do indeed presuppose the unity of the work but think of a composition of the book in successive stages. In particular, Wis 11-19 would have been composed later, even if by the same author as the rest of the book.[15] The stylistic unity of the book, as well as the use of the same literary genre (see below), are excellent arguments for postulating not only unity of authorship but also of composition. In the light of the studies of Wright, Bizzeti and Gilbert, however, the main argument in favour of the unity of the book of Wisdom is the discovery of a careful literary structure (see below) which renders it very difficult to think of a composition which is not unitary. In addition, some authors have wanted to find precise numerical correspondences within the book itself, even if, in the case of Wright, the calculations do not seem entirely convincing.[16]

Two further reasons in favour of the unity of author and composition are the discovery of the so-called *flashbacks* and the presence of themes and *motifs* common to the book as a whole. Within the third part of the book (Wis 11-19), J.M. Reese points out the presence of verbal references and themes typical of the first Flashbacks

12 Reider, *The Book of Wisdom*, 25-26. On the other hand, it is this Reider who claims that Wisdom is characterised by "some ignorance and poverty of diction" (27). Cf. a similar judgement by Larcher, *Sagesse*, I, 102. For the problems of the original language of the book, cf. Larcher, *Sagesse*, I, 95, but, above all, Gilbert, "Sagesse", 62-63. However, the latter notes that it is difficult to prove that the Greek is not in fact a brilliant translation from an author who knew the language perfectly. The work of Reese, *Hellenistic Influence on the Book of Wisdom and its Consequences* (1973) seems, however, to leave few doubts about a text composed directly in Greek. Another problem, almost impossible to solve, is that of proving the existence of possible Hebrew or Aramaic sources employed by our author.

13 Vílchez Líndez, *Sapienza*, 22-29; Gilbert, "Sagesse", 87-91. H. Engel emphasises the current consensus relating to the unity of the book of Wisdom, cf. *Die Sapientia Salomonis als Buch*, 135-137.

14 Grimm, *Weisheit*, 9-15 For the history of the problem in the eighteenth and nineteenth cents., cf. Vílchez Líndez, *Sapienza*, 21-24.

15 Cf. Skehan, "Text and Structure", 5; Larcher, *Sagesse*, 1:95-119.

16 Cf. Skehan, "Text and Structure", *passim*. In Wis 1-9, he counts a total of 500 stichs; Wis 10:1-11:1 a total of 60 stichs; and Wis 11:2-19:22 a further 561 stichs. Cf. Gilbert, "Sagesse", 89-90 who confirms Skehan's calculations. Wright, Addison G. ("Numerical Patterns in the Book of Wisdom", *CBQ* 29 [1967]: 524-538) claims that the book of Wisdom is constructed according to the principle of the so-called "golden number", represented by the ratio x/y = y/x+y; cf. a critical discussion in Gilbert, "Sagesse", 89.

two sections of Wisdom. Reese describes these texts as *flashbacks*, that is, as "a short repetition of a significant words or groups of words or distinctive ideas in two different parts of Wis".[17] Reese notes the presence of a good 45 *flashbacks*, a list which could, however, be extended.[18] We observe that it is not just a question of simple literary references. Very often, in the third part of the book, our sage takes up again a thematic element of the first or second part, broadening its significance (cf., e.g., Wis 17:20-21 as a *flashback* to Wis 7:29-30; see the comment on 17:20-21).[19] All this confirms a profound compositional unity which characterises the whole of the book of Wisdom.

Themes Common to the Whole of the Book

Finally, a careful analysis of the book of Wisdom reveals the presence of common themes which are repeated in a coherent way throughout the book. This supports the idea of a strong internal unity.[20]

One of these themes is undoubtedly that of justice which, for some authors, constitutes the real pillar of the whole work. In this key, the book of Wisdom actually could be read as a treatise of political theology.[21] The wisdom that is praised in the central part of the text (7-9) becomes the means made available to rulers for learning about justice (Wis 1 and 6). The judgement of God is ready to strike the unjust, particularly idolaters (Wis 13-15) but offers salvation to the just. The compass of the theme of justice within the book of Wisdom is not to be undervalued, although the addressees of the book are not actually pagan rulers (cf. below) and although it is wisdom that emerges instead at the centre of the book.

A second theme which runs throughout the book is that of the cosmos. This plays a fundamental role throughout the book. God created everything for life (1:13-14). Wisdom, craftsman of the world, is the point of contact between God and people, precisely because of its presence in the cosmos (cf. 7:1, 6, 21, 24, 27). The cosmos itself will intervene as an instrument at God's side to reward the just and punish the ungodly (5:17-20), as has already happened in the past (16:17, 24). Finally, the book of Wisdom closes with the view of a renewed creation (19:18-21).

Literary Structure[22]

The book of Wisdom displays a very careful literary structure. Through the use of hook-words, inclusions, concentric constructions that are often polished, and other stylistic devices, our sage offers his public a pleasing work in which the literary structure is at the service of a precise theological design. Here, for the

---

17 Reese, *Hellenistic Influence*, 124; cf. pp. 122-145 for a complete list of *flashbacks*.

18 Gilbert, "Sagesse", 89-90.

19 "The flashbacks reminded his readers that the past wonders of God's providence are an assurance that future rewards are awaiting the just"; Reese, *Hellenistic influence*, 124.

20 Gilbert, "Sagesse", 90-91.

21 Along these lines are the commentaries of Alonso Schökel, *Sabiduría* and Vílchez Líndez, *Sapienza*, 114-119. Cf. Bretón, Santiago, "¿Libro de la Sabiduría o libro de la justicia? El tema de la justicia en la interpretación del libro de la Sabiduría", *Cuadernos Biblicos* 1 (1978): 77-104.

22 Cf. a *status quaestionis* of the whole problem in Gilbert, "The literary structure".

most part, we are following the proposals of P. Bizzeti and M. Gilbert.[23] We shall offer, first of all, a general outline of the book. A detailed treatment of the literary structure will be given in the commentary to the individual sections of the text.

The book of Wisdom can be subdivided into three large sections. First, up to chapter 6 (see the introduction to Wis 6 for the problem represented by 6:22-25), we have what we could describe as the "book of eschatology".

The second part of the book, Wis 7-9, we can consider as the "book of wisdom" properly so called. After the praise of wisdom (7-8), the heart of the whole book is the prayer of "Solomon" to obtain the gift of wisdom (ch. 9).[24]

The third part, Wis 10-19, we could call the "book of history". Here, our sage reflects on the presence of wisdom in the history of his people (Wis 10) and, in particular, on the events of the Exodus in seven antithetical sketches in which the Israelites are contrasted with the Egyptians. What emerges is the action of God who makes use of his creation to punish the latter and save the former. Two extended digressions appear in this part: Wis 11:15-12:27, on divine philanthropy, and Wis 13-15, on idolatry.

A Theological Project

The general subdivision of the book follows an order that is neither logical nor chronological but rather *theological*. In fact, the book is introduced by the triumphal proclamation of the salvation which awaits the just (Wis 3-4; but also 1:13-15; 2:21-24). Right from the beginning, the reader is invited to be open to a future full of hope. This future is bound up with the reception of the gift of wisdom (Wis 7-9). This, in turn, is guaranteed by the certainty of the divine interventions in Israel's history (Wis 10-19). Past, present, and future come together in a brilliant synthesis. Hope in the future provides the motor for the life of the just, but, at the same time, it is history which is the basis of this hope. The link between past and future is wisdom, given by God and present in the cosmos. In fact, salvation moves out from creation.

Language and Style

Language

The vocabulary of Wisdom is indicative of the special nature of the Greek employed by our author. In all, 1734 words appear in the book. Of these, a good 1303 appear once only. Of these, 335 words, approximately 20%, are *hapax legomena* of the LXX (315, according to Larcher).[25] However, we must add a further 126 which appear in the LXX only in late texts such as Sir and 3-4 Macc. There also exist some twenty *hapax totius graecitatis* which lead us to consider our author as a real creator of language.[26]

---

23 Bizzeti, *Il libro della Sapienza*; Gilbert, "Sagesse", 65-77.

24 Cf. the introduction to Wis 10-19 for ch. 10 as belonging to the third part of the book.

25 All the Greek terms in the book of Wisdom that are ἅπαξ λεγόμενα of the LXX will be marked in the commentary with a preceding asterisk (*).

26 Cf. Scarpat, "Ancora sull'autore"; Gilbert, "Sagesse", 63; Mazzinghi, *Notte di paura e di luce*, 274 (δυσδιήγετος, 17:1; περικομπέω, 17:4; ἐφύβριστος, 17:7; φυλακίζω, 18:4).

Many of the terms employed by Wisdom hail from a vocabulary of a learned character: philosophical, poetic, sometimes even medical and scientific. Our author is a lover of compound words which are very numerous in the book.[27] There are a good 59 adjectives which are rare, poetic or composed with an α–privative.[28]

If some stylistic aspects could make us think of a Hebrew original (cf. the use of the causal ὅτι, especially in Wis 1:1-2:5[29]), others instead, such as the use of the infinitive[30] or of personal pronouns,[31] differ notably from the style of the LXX and show themselves to be genuinely Greek.

Style

History of Research

As far back as antiquity, commentators were aware of the special nature of the style on this book, so different from the majority of the other books of the LXX, and so profoundly Greek. Jerome wrote: "ipse stylus graecam eloquentiam redolet [the style itself is redolent of Greek eloquence]".[32] His judgement has been taken up again by the moderns: Brook Foss Westcott claimed that Wisdom is typical "of the style of composition which would be produced by the sophistic schools of rhetoric".[33] Henry Barclay Swete states that "no other book in the Greek Bible is so manifestly Alexandrian in tone and style".[34] Already, Carl L.W. Grimm provided a first list of typically Greek stylistic usages in Wisdom.[35]

Until now, James M. Reese has been the one who has devoted particular attention to the question of style.[36] His conclusion in this respect is clear: "this survey of the vocabulary and style of Wis shows that the sacred writer was trained in Greek rhetoric and was subject to a wide variety of Hellenistic influences".[37] The commentaries of Larcher and Scarpat confirm Reese's conclusions; but research on the style of the book of Wisdom remains a field that is still open. Only recently (2011) was the first study entirely devoted to Wisdom's style published, that of

---

27 Focke, *Enstehung*, 61; Winston, *Wisdom*, 14-15, with many examples.

28 Focke, *Entstehung*, 60-61.

29 Sollamo, Raija, *Renderings of Hebrew Semipropositions in the Septuagint*, AASF B Diss 19 (Helsinki: Helsinki Academia Scientiarum Fennica / Suomalainen Tiedeakatemia 1979), 296. Ruppert still upholds the existence of a Semitic original for Wis 2:12-20; 5:1-7: cf. "Gerechte und Frevler (Gottlose) im Weish 1,1-6,21".

30 Soisalon-Soininen, Ilmari, *Die Infinitive in der Septuaginta*, AASF B 132,1 (Helsinki: Helsinki Academia Scientiarum Fennica / Suomalainen Tiedeakatemia 1965), 193.

31 Wifstrand, Albert, *Die Stellung der enklitischen Personalpronomina bei der Septuaginta*, Lund University Press: Lund 1950, 63.

32 *Praef. in libros Salomonis* (PL XXVIII, 1242).

33 Westcott, Brooke Foss, "Wisdom of Solomon", in *Smith's Dictionary of the Bible* 4 (Cambridge: Cambridge University Press 1872), 3547.

34 Swete, Henry Barclay, *An Introduction to the Old Testament in Greek*, Cambridge: Cambridge University Press 1914[2] (repr. New York: KTAV 1968, 268). Swete adds that "in the *style* of the originally Greek books [of the LXX] there is little to remind us of the Semitic origin of the writers" (313).

35 Grimm, *Weisheit*, 6-9.

36 Reese, *Hellenistic Influence*, 25-31.

37 Reese, *Hellenistic Influence*, 30.

Alexis Léonas, who discovers a conscious attempt to imitate the style and idiom of the Septuagint, rejecting it when it does not conform to Greek literary use.[38]

The style of the book is clearly affected by the typical devices of classical rhetoric. Word order is one of the basic characteristics of Greek style. Without doubt, the most significant element in this connection is the use of well-crafted periodic sentences, such as, for example, in 12:3-7:27; 13:11-5; 15:7; and 17:16-19. Prominent in this area is the repeated stylistic use of *hyperbaton*, which is rather rare in the LXX but present a good 240 times in Wisdom, especially in Wis 10-19. At times, as in Wis 14:18, this is in the form of a double *hyperbaton*.[39] The use of *hyperbaton* is not dictated by stylistic reasons alone but also by those of content, for example, when it is a question of highlighting a specific term: cf. 17:2a (νύκτα); 17:21b (σκότους).

Our author intends to address his audience by the additional means of the beauty of literary form which he employs. The careful style and the closeness to Greek rhetoric and poetry render the book of Wisdom attractive precisely to those Jews of Alexandria who feel themselves drawn to the Greek world. In this way, the tradition of Israel is re-presented to such readers in more congenial language.

Rhetorical Figures

The author of the book demonstrates a good knowledge of the classical figures of ancient rhetoric. The frequency of such devices is considerably greater compared with the books of the LXX translated from the Hebrew.[40]

- Metaphor: let us take note of a single example, the metaphor of darkness employed throughout the fifth diptych (17:1-18:4) which takes on simultaneously a cosmological, psychological, moral and eschatological value.
- Litotes (the replacement of a term with the negation of its antonym in order to strengthen what is meant: Wis 1:2a (τοῖς μή πειράζουσιν); 1:11b; 3:11bc; 11:7b; 12:9a, 10, 13b; 17:4a; 18:2a.; 19:22b (οὐχ ὑπερεῖδες).
- Anaphora (the repetition of the same word or group of words at the beginning of multiple successive sentences or clauses): Wis 10 (repetition of αὕτη); 11:18a-d; 17:18c-19d.
- Paronomasia (the repetition of the same lexical root in different syntactical functions): Wis 5:3b, 10c; 6:10a; 12:25-26; 13:19b; 14:5a.
- There are also many cases of plays on words: 11:14-15; 17:12-13a, 21; 18:4).
- Isocolia (ἰσοκωλία identical clauses or similar sounding clauses): Wis 18:1b.
- Antithesis (juxtaposition of contrary elements): Wis 3:5a; 4:16; 7:6; 9:16; 18:7b.
- *Accumulatio* (the accumulation of multiple terms of the same category): cf. the compilation of the 22 attributes of wisdom listed in Wis 7:22-23.
- Asyndeton (words or phrases in successive order without the use of conjunctions that are regarded as equal and not comparative grammatically and in terms of content): asyndetic construction is used frequently to indicate a new point of view: cf. 4:10, 20; 10:12.

---

38 Léonas, "The Poetics of Wisdom. Language and Style in the Book of Wisdom", 124.

39 Reese, *Hellenistic Influence*, 26-27; Mazzinghi, *Notte di paura e di luce*, 278.

40 Rowe, Gregory O., "Style", in Porter, Stanley E., *Handbook of Classical Rhetoric in the Hellenistic Period. 330 B.C. - A.D. 400* (Leiden – New York – Cologne: Brill 1997), 121-157; cf. also Denniston John Dewar, *Greek Prose Style*, Oxford: Clarendon Press, 1952.

- *Homoioteleuton* (the repetition of the same or similar final syllables of words in uninterrupted succession, here in successive stichs): Wis 1:1, 4; 2:3-4; 4:10.
- Wisdom uses the figure of *sorites* (σωρείτης: chain syllogism) in 6:17-20.[41]

A final aspect of the style typical of the book of Wisdom is the use of clauses which recall classical metre. Examples of iambics or hexameters had already been discovered by Gregg (1906) and, with more care, by Thackeray (1909), the only one till now who has studied the poetic aspect of Wisdom, albeit in outline. A good example is Wis 17:1-18:4, where, in addition to a literary style that is typically Asianic, it is possible to recognise, on occasions, the use of the classical metre even if this is not systematic.[42]

The Literary Genre: Between the Epideictic Genre and Midrashic Style[43]

Wisdom: A Protreptic

Among the arguments in favour of the unity of the book of Wisdom, discussion of the literary genre has gained important weight. This debate is not without importance when it comes to the interpretation of the text. To identify the literary genre of a book means to see things from the point of view of the author and to have a better understanding of the purpose behind his work.

Taking up a proposal of Friedrich Focke,[44] James M. Reese has suggested associating the book of Wisdom with the literary genre of the *logos protreptikos*, well known to Aristotle, and, subsequently, to the Fathers. The *logos protreptikos* combines the deliberative and epideictic genres. It appears as an exhortation to follow a particular line of conduct by proving the validity and the advantage of following the orator's suggestion.[45] However, Reese hypothesises the existence of lesser literary genres within the various parts of Wisdom.[46]

---

41 Further examples in Winston, *Wisdom*, 15-17; Reese, *Hellenistic Influence*, 27-28; Larcher, *Sagesse*, 1:107-108.

42 Cf. Gregg, *The Wisdom of Solomon*, xv; Thackeray, "Rhythm in the Book of Wisdom". For Wis 17:1-18:4, see Mazzinghi, *Notte di paura e di luce*, 277-280 and *ibid.* 163-165 for an analysis of the poetic dimension of Wis 17:16-21.

43 The debate on the literary genre of Wisdom culminated in the work of Bizzeti, *Il libro della Sapienza*, 113-180 who takes up and refines the insights of Gilbert, "Sagesse", 77-87. Cf. Larcher, *Le livre de la Sagesse*, 109-114, who suggests that, actually, there are different literary genres for the different parts of Wisdom.

44 Cf. Focke, *Entstehung*, 86.

45 Cf. van der Meeren, Sophie, "Le protreptique en philosophie: essai de définition d'un genre", *REG* 115 (2002) 595.

46 Cf. *Hellenistic Influence*, 90-121. Winston (*Wisdom of Solomon*, 18-20) accepts Reese's idea, albeit with some reservations; cf. Winston's observations on the book of Bizzeti in his review in *CBQ* 48 (1986) 525-527. Cf. also Engel, *Die Sapientia Salomonis als Buch*, 138-142 who does not exclude the idea of Wisdom as a protreptic and so as a text devoted to the education of the young Jews of Alexandria.

The greatest problem is the fact that we do not have complete examples of a *logos protreptikos* for this period nor do we have a complete treatise about it. Winston concludes, therefore, in a more nuanced way that "it is thus extremely difficult to determine whether Wis is an epideictic composition with an admixture of protreptic, or essentially a protreptic with a considerable element of epideictic".[47]

Wisdom: An *Encomium*

Starting with the studies of Paul Beauchamp (1963) and, above all, thanks to the work of Paolo Bizzeti and Maurice Gilbert, research has turned in the direction of the epideictic genre in an increasingly convincing way.[48]

According to the canons of classical rhetoric, it possible to distinguish the "forensic" (*genus dikanikon*), "deliberative" (*genus symbouleutikon*, lat: *genus deliberativum*) and "demonstrative" (*genus epideicticum*; lat: *genus demonstrativum*, or *laudativum*) genres (cf. Aristotle, *Rhet.* 1358b). The forensic genre deals with the past and is used in law courts to establish the innocence or guilt of the accused. The deliberative genre, on the other hand, targets the future, what we ought or ought not do. From Aristotle's *Rhetoric* up to the treatises on rhetoric of Cicero and Quintilian, the "epideictic" or "demonstrative" genre is described, as a discourse which is situated instead in the present and has the aim of praising a specific virtue or criticising some vice; cf. the *Paradoxa Stoicorum* of Cicero, the *Quod omnis probus liber est* and *De nobilitate* of Philo, and the *De clementia* of Seneca. The epideictic genre has a pedagogic and scholastic character, and so is addressed to the young. It seeks to persuade them by the force of demonstration and, above all, by the *encomium* of the virtue which it is intended to celebrate. The fictitious "Solomon" who speaks in Wis 7-8 insists heavily on his youth as we see, for example, in 8:10, but also in the reference to the dream of Gibeon (1 Kgs 3) implicit in Wis 9. The emphasis on the metaphor of royalty, which points to a clear Stoic background, presupposes a youthful audience (cf. below).

A comparison between the classical *encomium* and the book of Wisdom tells us still more about the author's project. The *encomium* generally opens with an *exordium* in which the listeners are exhorted to follow a specific virtue, and – at the same time – the opponents are refuted. Pitted against them are examples of those who have lived out the same virtue. This is the procedure in the first part of Wisdom (Wis 1-6) which opens with an appeal addressed to the listeners that they embrace justice and wisdom (Wis 1 and 6). It follows with a refutation of the points made by the opponents (Wis 2 and 5), and with a series of antithetical examples which serve to illustrate the main thesis, that is, the fate of the just and of the ungodly in Wis 3-4, a text which confirms the soundness of following wisdom and justice.

---

47 "A Century of Research on the Book of Wisdom", 5.

48 Cf. n. 43. For Beauchamp, cf. *De libro Sapientiae Salomonis*, 1-40, a theory taken up again in: Id., "Epouser la Sagesse", 358-360. Cf. Reese's criticism of Bizzeti, "A Semiotic Critique". Reese mentions the difficulty of confining the book of Wisdom within a single literary genre.

The classical *encomium* then continues with the *elogium* proper in which the virtue which is the subject of the treatise is celebrated. There has to be a highlighting of the origin (τὸ γένος), nature (ἡ φύσις), and actions (ἡ πράξις) of the virtue, in our case, wisdom. This is what happens in the central part of the book of Wisdom: from 6:22-25 our author will deal with the origin and nature of Wisdom (Wis 7-8); its actions will be portrayed in Wis 10. With regard to the text of Wis 7-8, Alexis Leproux has proposed that these two chapters should be read in the light of the rhetorical *elogium* dedicated to a particular person, something that was widespread at the start of the imperial period, especially for works of the Second Sophistic.[49]

The final part of the classical *encomium* comprises the σύγκρισις (*comparatio*). Through a series of examples drawn from the past, the orator wishes to convince his public of the advantage of his thesis. Not infrequently, there is recourse to digressions on themes related to the main one. This is the case with the third part of Wisdom (Wis 10-19) which deals with the just/ungodly contrast (Israel and Egypt). This is read against the background of the events of the Exodus and animated by two large digressions, on the philanthropy of God (11:15-12:27) and, above all, on idolatry (13-15). Finally, the *encomium* closes with an *epilogue* in which the author recapitulates his arguments and draws his conclusions from them. This is what happens at the end of the book, in Wis 19:10-22.

The *Midrashic* Style

The subject of the *encomium* within Wisdom is not so much a moral quality or a human virtue, as in the classical *encomium*, but is rather the wisdom that comes from God. Moreover, at the centre of the book, there appears a text which does not find any echoes in the classical *encomia*: the prayer to obtain Wisdom (Wis 9) in which Solomon addresses the Lord directly. Furthermore, within the comparison of chapters 11-19, beside the two antagonists, Israel and Egypt, there intervenes a third element of comparison, the cosmos. It too is absent from the classical *encomium*. In Wis 9, the subject addressed by the author is no longer his audience but God directly, who is also addressed several times in the second person in the course of chapters 11-19. Joseph Heinemann has already indicated the differences between Wis 11-19 and the classical Greek σύγκρισις in which the analogy is internal to the comparison and not external as happens instead in Wis 11-19. This is achieved precisely by means of the *tertium quid* of the cosmos.[50]

Let us observe again that the constant background of the book of Wisdom is Scripture (see below), which our author continually rereads and re-presents for his audience even if through the lens of the Hellenistic culture of his time. In this way, the typically Greek literary genre of the *encomium* is embellished with a process which is more characteristic of Jewish literature: what we know by the name of *midrash*.

---

49 Cf. Leproux, *Un discours de Sagesse*, 73-116. In Leproux's proposal, a little difficulty is created by the fact that the examples he adduces are mostly of the first cent. CE (cf. his thoughts on the dating of the book of Wisdom, pp. 81-82).

50 Cf. Heinemann, "*Synkrisis* oder äußere Analogie". Heinemann points out that, in Wis 11-19, the Jewish influence is undoubtedly more evident and ought not to be diminished for the benefit of the Greek influence.

It is impossible to give an exact definition for *midrash*. We could describe it as an attitude, a way of thinking, which betrays itself in a way of writing in a style proper to Judaism, one which characterises the approach it has to Scripture.[51] *Midrash* is the "search" for the meaning of Scripture which starts out from the conviction that it is contemporary with its readers and that it retains a perennial relevance. It is this relevance that the authors of *midrash* are striving to search for, bringing the biblical text into the situation in which they and their listeners are living. The perception of the unity of Scripture and its perennial relevance for whomever is listening to it constitute, therefore, the peculiar features of every *midrashic* commentary which thus has a character at once popular and homiletic.

In these circumstances, it is possible to speak of the *midrashic* character of the book of Wisdom, particularly in the book's third part (Wis 10-19), which takes up again the events of the Exodus. However, already in the first part (Wis 1-6), there is some attestation of the presence of this midrashic style.[52] In fact, the aim of our author is to demonstrate the unity of Scripture together with its relevance for the readers of his time, thus creating what Roger Le Déaut has felicitously described as a "sonorisation of history".[53] What makes the book of Wisdom a work that is absolutely original is precisely this close connection between the *midrashic* style and the use of a Greek literary genre, that is, the *encomium*. The brilliance of the Alexandrian sage consists in having known how to express in a Hellenistic literary form a content that is profoundly Jewish. The author of the book thus succeeded in setting before his listeners a text which, though remaining faithful to the biblical tradition, succeeded in expressing it in a language that was much more accessible to them.[54] We can, therefore, conclude that in the book of Wisdom we find a kind of Greek *midrash* on Israel's Scriptures.[55]

Author, Date, and Place of Composition

Author

The author of the book conceals himself under the Solomonic mask. That transpires from chapters 7-8 and, in particular, from the prayer of Wis 9, even if Solomon is never explicitly mentioned. Some Fathers of the Church still thought

---

51 Cf. Le Déaut, Roger, "A propos d'une définition du Midrash", *Bib* 50 (1969) : 395-413.

52 Cf. Schaberg, "Major Midrashic Traditions in Wisdom 1,1-6,25".

53 "A propos d'une définition", 406 (cf. n. 50).

54 "He (the Sage) employs what Ricoeur calls distanciation because he was able to 'de-contextualize' the biblical text and to 're-contextualize' it in a way that would appeal to readers in a different culture. In a sense he did for a group of Jews what early Christian preachers did for their fellow believers by reinterpreting figures received from the written Hebraic and Hellenistic cultures in regard to Jesus"; Reese, "Can Paul Ricoeur's Method Contribute to Interpreting the Book of Wisdom?", 390.

55 Already, Jacob Freudenthal (*Hellenistische Studien: Alexander Polyhistor* [Breslau: Barth und Comp. 1875], 65-68) spoke of a Hellenistic *midrash*; cf. Jacob Weingreen, *From Bible to Mishna: The Continuity of Tradition*, Manchester: Manchester University Press 1976.

of the historical figure of Solomon. The Muratorian fragment (lines 69-71) thinks rather of the friends of Solomon: *ab amicis Salomonis in honorem eius scripta* [written by the friends of Solomon in his honour].[56] Although not seeming to accept it, Jerome records the opinion that Philo was the author of Wisdom. This is the origin of a legend about a hypothetical Christian Philo.[57] The position of Wisdom in the canon makes one think also, and perhaps more naturally, of Ben Sira, or his grandson who translated his book, a theory already advanced by Augustine in *Doctr. chr.* 2.8.13 though subsequently retracted (*Retract.* 2.30[4].2).[58] Later thoughts turned also to the priest Onias, the philosopher Aristobulus, and to Apollos, the Alexandrian mentioned in the Acts of the Apostles (cf. Acts 18). All of these are purely hypothetical attempts at identification.[59]

In reality, a precise identification of the author is impossible. We must content ourselves with thinking of an anonymous Greek-speaking Jew from Alexandria with a deep knowledge of Scripture, well anchored in the tradition of his ancestors but, at the same time, linked to the Hellenistic cultural environment which characterised the city of Alexandria.

Date

Time of Caligula?

For a long time, the period of the composition of the book of Wisdom has remained a further enigma for scholars.[60] In the past, the date proposed has oscillated from the beginning of the second cent. BCE to the time of Caligula (37-41 CE).[61] The linguistic arguments do not appear conclusive for dating Wisdom to the time of Caligula.[62] The possible connections with Philo play a role in this late dating of Wisdom. If it is admitted that the author of Wisdom knew Philo, the book obviously must be situated in a

56 For a list of patristic texts which identified Solomon as the author of Wisdom, cf. Vílchez Líndez, *Sapienza*, 53 n. 8; Horbury, "Christian Use", 189.

57 Cf. Jerome, *Praef. in libros Salomonis* (PL XXVIII, 1308). Cf. Bruns, Peter E., "Philo Christianus: The Debris of a Legend", *HTR* 66 (1973): 141-145. For the Muratorian fragment, cf. Horbury, "The Wisdom of Solomon in the Muratorian Fragment", *JTS* 45 (1994): 149-159.

58 Cf. La Bonnardière, *Biblia Augustiniana*, 46-57; 144-145.

59 Cf. Larcher, *Sagesse*, 1:125-139; Winston, *Wisdom*, 12-14.

60 Cf. Larcher, *Sagesse*, 1:141-161. He thinks of different dates of composition for the different parts of Wisdom. These go from 31/30 BCE as far as 15-10 BCE for the third part of the book. A more up to date view can be found in Gilbert, "Sagesse", 91-93 and Vílchez Líndez, *Sapienza*, 59-70. Vílchez Líndez provides three appendices which help to place Wisdom against the background of the situation in Alexandria at the end of the first cent. BCE (*Sapienza*, 544-607).

61 Cf. Winston, *Wisdom of Solomon*, 20-25; Scarpat has strongly defended a dating of Wisdom to the time of Caligula: cf. "Ancora sull'autore", especially pp. 180-184. Scarpat returned to the subject later in: "Ancora sulla data di composizione della Sapientia Salomonis. Il termine *diágnôsis* (Sap 3,18; At 25,21)".

62 Cf. Scarpat, "Ancora sull'autore", *passim*; Scarpat notes that these arguments prove only that Wisdom should be placed *no earlier* than the principate of Octavian; cf. similar observations in Winston, *Wisdom*, 22-23, who lists a good 35 words in Wisdom (cf. note 33 p. 22) which do not appear in Greek usage before the first cent. BCE.

time close to him. The period of Caligula's rule constitutes a plausible background on account of the anti-Jewish persecutions to which the text of Wis 2 seems to intend to allude. Wis 14:15-17, a text relating to the divinisation of the sovereign, could also be a precise allusion to Caligula.[63] Passages such as Wis 5:16-23 would presuppose a really desperate historical situation which could have occurred only in the time of Caligula.[64] However, we observe that the contacts between Wisdom and Philo could be explained by recourse to the hypothesis of a common cultural environment. In fact, the book of Wisdom does not seem to have been familiar with the works of Philo. As for the allusions to possible anti-Jewish persecutions, we should observe that Wis 2 seems to presuppose a *typical* situation relating to the just man persecuted by the ungodly rather than a real persecution in progress. Alternatively, perhaps our sage intends to refer to previous anti-Jewish persecutions, either in Egypt itself or in Judaea (cf. below).

Augustan age

Within the book we can find clues which lead us to confirm a date during the time of Octavian Augustus, that is, between 30 BCE and 14 CE, probably towards the last phase of his principate. Until now, study of the vocabulary has prevented us from placing the composition of the book before the Augustan period. The classic argument is the presence, in Wis 6:3, of the term κράτησις, "dominion", a technical term to indicate the taking possession of Egypt by the Romans in 30 BCE after the battle of Actium. However, as Maurice Gilbert has shown, the expression τῆς καίσαρος κρατήσεως, used with reference to the conquest of Egypt by Octavian, appears to have been completely abandoned after the death of the emperor, which happened in 14 CE. The use of κράτησις, therefore, not only constitutes a *terminus a quo,* but should also be considered as a *terminus ad quem* for the dating of the book.[65]

Further clues which bring the book close to the Augustan period are the text of Wis 14:22, which could be an ironic allusion to the *pax romana* proclaimed by Octavian Augustus in 9 CE, while the entire section of 14:16-22 could refer to the nascent cult of the emperor which was already current in the time of Augustus, not only in that of Caligula. The hostility displayed by the book in its dealings with the Egyptians could be read as a sign of the changed social situation created in Alexandria after the arrival of the Romans, but, above all, of the discontent widespread among the Alexandrian Jews following the institution of the so-called *laographía*. This was the poll tax already instituted by Rome in the first years of the rule of Augustus for all those who, like the Jews, did not enjoy the totality of Alexandrian citizenship.

Wis 19:13-17 and the question of civil rights

Here we have a polemic which is well reflected in Wis 19:13-17, a text which presupposes that Alexandrian Jews did not enjoy full civil rights. The problem of the struggle for civil rights causes the emergence of a deeper question: the Jews of Alexandria are striving simultaneously both for integration and for the recognition of their own particular identity. If the rich and prosperous Philo feels himself very close to the Greeks and seeks forcefully for equality between the Jews of Alexandria and the Greek element of the population, the author of the Third Book of the Maccabees regards the seeking of Alexandrian citizenship or even the

63 Cf. the historical picture sketched by Perdue, *The Sword and the Stylus*, 292-309.

64 "A desperate historical situation"; so Winston, *Wisdom*, 23.

65 Gilbert, "Your sovereignty comes from the Lord. Wis 6,4"; in: Id., *La Sagesse de Salomon*, 121-140 [especially 127-129].

search for any kind of integration on the political and social level as a betrayal of the faith, done "for the sake of the belly" (3 Macc 7:11). In fact, the Jews are a λαός ἐν ξένει γῇ ξένος, a foreign people in a foreign land (3 Macc 6:3).[66] In 3 Macc 3:3-4, the Jews considered truly faithful are those who, though maintaining their loyalty in their dealings with their rulers (εὔνοιαν καὶ πίστιν ἀδιάστροφον), conduct themselves (πολιτευόμενοι) according to the law of their God "and for this reason appeared hateful to some".

It is clear that full integration with the Greek population, beginning with access to the gymnasium, would have set insurmountable problems of faith for the majority of Jews. Is it possible, then, to look for integration with the Greek world and, at the same time, preserve one's own faith? With various nuances, and with solutions that are often opposed (at the two extremes, Philo and the Third Book of the Maccabees), the Jews of Alexandria want to be, at one and the same time, *citizens* and yet *different*. Our sage intends to place himself half-way between the polemical view of the Third Book of the Maccabees and the overtures which characterise Philo a little later. The attitude defended by the book of Wisdom in relation to the problem of the rights of the Jews of Alexandria is that of a Judaism which is conscious of its own special nature but which, at the same time, is seeking a certain amount of integration.[67]

As in the rest of the book, in Wis 19:13-17 also, our author never yields to the temptation of renouncing his own faith. Even the Egyptians, although pagans, have benefited from the presence of the Israelites and, if there is anyone who has hated guests and foreigners, it has been precisely them. There is undoubtedly some idealism in this position: we would like to maintain our full religious identity, our sage seems to be saying, and, at the same time, receive the recognition of the rights common to the Greek part of the city. For the Greeks, the Jews would remain so privileged as to be hated, as Josephus will write, putting the phrase in the mouth of Apion: "Why, then, if they are citizens, do they not worship the same gods as the Alexandrians?" (*C. Ap.* 2.65). For the book of Wisdom, on the other hand, it is a question of keeping up good relations with the Greeks although remaining faithful to the law of Moses.[68]

Place

That Egypt was the environment of the composition of the book of Wisdom seems indisputable. Together with the Israelites, the Egyptians are the key protagonists of the whole of the third part of the book which, although basing itself on a *relecture* of the texts of the Exodus, continually alludes to the historical situation

66 For the problem of ἰσοπολιτεῖα in 3 Macc, cf. Passoni Dell'Acqua, Anna, "Terzo Libro dei Maccabei", in: Sacchi, Paolo (ed.), *Apocrifi dell'Antico Testamento* (Brescia: Queriniana 2000), 605-609.

67 "To ask for the advantages of Greek citizenship and then to repudiate some of its obligations as incompatible with their national religion was to attempt to make the best of both worlds", Smallwood, E. Mary, *The Jews under Roman Rule. Studies in Judaism in Late Antiquity* (Leiden: Brill 1981^2), 14.

68 Cf. Mazzinghi, "Wis 19,13-17 and the Civil Rights of the Jews of Alexandria", *passim*.

of Greco-Roman Egypt. The text of Wis 19:13-17, just mentioned, leaves few doubts about the Egyptian origin of our author. The figure of the ungodly presented in Wis 2 finds its most natural explanation if set against the background of life in the city of Alexandria. With its famous institutions, the Library and the Museum, Alexandria was a cultural and religious crossroads. From the time of its foundation, it was the site of the most numerous and important Jewish colony outside the land of Israel. It is thus the best candidate for the place of composition of the book.[69]

The Book of Wisdom and the Scriptures[70]

The author of Wisdom displays a great familiarity with the Scriptures of Israel and presupposes his audience's deep knowledge of them. The book of Wisdom often follows the Greek translation of the LXX closely, even if direct recourse to the Hebrew text is not to be precluded entirely.[71] A peculiar characteristic of our author is that of never citing any biblical book explicitly but only suggesting it or alluding to it. He thus hands over to his audience the effort (but also the joy) of discovery.[72]

We offer here a general overview which can serve as a first orientation to the way in which our sage makes use of the sacred text.

In the first part of the book (Wis 1-6), the author keeps firmly in mind the questions posed by Job and by Qoheleth on the problem of retribution. What is the justice of God about if the just suffer and die while the ungodly seem to have success?[73] The response offered by the book of Wisdom, namely, the eternal happiness of the just and the sad fate of the ungodly in the last judgement, arises Wis 1-6

69 On Egyptian Alexandria, see Fraser, Peter Marshall, *Ptolemaic Alexandria*, 1-2, Oxford: Clarendon Press 1972; Haas, Christopher, *Alexandria in Late Antiquity. Topography and Social Conflict*, The John Hopkins University: Baltimore (MD) 1997; Engster, Dorit, "Alexandria als Stadt der Forschung und Technik", *BN* 147 (2010): 50-66; Nesselrath, H.-G., "Das Museion von Alexandria", *BN* 147 (2010) 66-82; Tanaseanu-Döbler, I., "Philosophie in Alexandria. Der Kreis um Ammonios Sakkas", *BN* 147 (2010): 82-103. On the Jewish presence in Alexandria, Tcherikover Victor A. in: Tcherikover, Victor A. – Fuks, Alexander (eds.), *Corpus Papyrorum Judaicarum* (Harvard University Press, Cambridge (Mass.) 1957, I), 2-93; Id., *Hellenistic Civilization and the Jews*, Philadelphia: The Jewish Publications Society of America 1962; Kasher, Ariel, *The Jews in Hellenistic and Roman Egypt*, Tübingen: J.C.B. Mohr 1985; Barclay, John M.G., *Jews in the Mediterranean Diaspora from Alexander to Trajan* (323 BCE – 117 CE), Edinburgh: T&T Clark 1996; Mélèze Modrzejewski J., *Les Juifs d'Egypte de Ramses II à Hadrien*, Presses Universitaires de France: Paris 1997.

70 For a general sketch of the problem, cf. Larcher, *Etudes*, 85-103; Gilbert, "Sagesse", 93-95; Id., "Wisdom of Solomon and Scripture"; Adinolfi, "Il senso dell'economia paleotestamentaria"; Skehan, *Studies in Israelite Poetry and Wisdom*, 143-236.

71 Fichtner, "Der At-Text der Sapientia Salomonis", *passim*.

72 "L'auteur ne facilite pas l'enquête ...": Gilbert, "Sagesse", 93.

73 D'Alario, "La réflexion sur le sens de la vie en Sg 1-5. Une réponse aux questions de Job et de Qohélet".

from a bold *relecture* of the text of Gen 1-3.[74] God's original plan for man as expressed in the Genesis text is reread, in the key of incorruptibility, especially in Wis 1:13-15 and 2:23-24. We note how the texts of Gen 1-3 are scattered throughout the book. That reveals our sage's fundamental interest in the theology of creation: the cosmos is destined for life (Wis 1:13-14; 2:23-24); salvation (cf. Wis 19:6-12) will consist precisely in a creation that has been renewed. Idolatry is an overturning of the meaning of creation (Wis 13:13; 15:8, 11).

The presentation of the ungodly in Wis 2:1-20 takes up many biblical themes (cf. Job and the Psalms); but, already in Wis 1:10-11, the Exodus theme of murmuring had emerged. In the theme of the suffering just man (Wis 2:10-20), our author is rereading Ps 22 and especially Isa 53, the Fourth Servant Song.[75] In the announcement relating to the happiness of the just (cf. Wis 3-4), we discover the presence of texts of an eschatological character such as Ps 2 (utilised as early as Wis 1:1) in addition to Dan 7 and 12. The Daniel texts are reproduced within a sapiential dimension and deprived of their messianic content, transforming them into a real sapiential anthropology.[76] Finally, in chapters 3 and 4 of Wisdom, the book of Isaiah is well and truly present for our sage (cf. also Wis 5:17-20 in comparison with Isa 59:16-17). Isaiah is one of the principal sources for our sage whereas Jeremiah and Ezekiel are present to a much lesser extent.[77] The novelty of Wisdom's teaching concerning the immortality of the just arises particularly from the deep reflection our sage makes on the Isaiah texts (cf. Wis 2:23 and Isa 54:16-17).

Wis 7-9

In the second part of the book (Wis 7-9), the point of departure is furnished, first of all, by two classic texts on Solomon's prayer to obtain wisdom: 1 Kgs 3:5-15 and 2 Chr 1:7-12 (cf. 1 Kgs 5:13). These are especially the basis of Wis 9. Here, echoes of texts from Genesis, Exodus, and the prophets also return. In the description of Solomon's love for wisdom, use is also made of various passages from Proverbs,[78] in addition to many other biblical texts. The presentation of wisdom in Wis 7-8 echoes, among other places, Prov 8:22-30 (cf. Wis 7:12, 21; 8:6) but also Sir 24.

Wis 10-19

In the third part of the book (Wis 10-19), the list of the eight just men, from Adam to Moses, in Wis 10 is a careful and sweeping résumé of many passages from Genesis and Exodus. This list in chapter 10 recalls the praise of the ancestors in Sir 44-50.[79]

---

74 Gilbert, "La relecture de Genèse 1 à 3 dans le livre de la Sagesse".

75 Suggs, "Wisdom of Solomon: A Homily based on the Fourth Servant Song".

76 "Apocalypse is transformed into a philosophical stance and an offering of a revelation of the ultimate structure of reality, of the basic plan of God for humanity": Schaberg, "Major midrashic traditions", 90.

77 Skehan, "Isaiah and the teaching of the Book of Wisdom"; Beentjes, "Wisdom of Solomon 3,1-4,19 and the Book of Isaiah".

78 Clifford, "Proverbs as a source for the book of Wisdom". Cf. also Skehan, "The literary relationship", *passim*. We note how, with regard to the sapiential literature, the Song of Songs forms an exception: a "surprising" absence, Gilbert, "Wisdom of Solomon and Scripture", 617.

79 Cf. Gilbert, "The Review of History in Ben Sira 44-50 and Wisdom 10-19"; for a comparison between Sir and Wis, cf. also Di Lella, "Conservative and Progressive Theology: Sirach and Wisdom".

The seven antitheses (Wis 11:1-14; 16:1-19:9) follow the Exodus traditions closely (in particular Exod and Num)[80] but also the rereading of these traditions which is already present in Psalms 78, 105, and 107. These psalms do not contribute as such to the general architecture of the book. However, the whole of the book of Wisdom is continually threaded through with allusions to and citations from the Psalms.[81]

Less present in the book are Leviticus (in fact, our author does not have any great interest in the cult) and Deuteronomy (cf., however, Wis 6:7ab and Deut 1:7; Wis 16:26 and Deut 8:3). Our sage does not award primary importance to the *Torah* understood as a legislative text. Even with Exod-Num, it is the narrative texts that are privileged. The texts of the Exodus tradition, then, are presented by means of a constant work of actualisation and reread in the light of the situation of the Alexandrian Jews at the end of the first cent. BCE.

In the first digression, Wis 11:15-12:27, the book of Wisdom reflects on why God did not punish the Egyptians as severely as he later did the Canaanites. The stories of the Pentateuch and the book of Joshua are utilised to highlight the divine "philanthropy".

In the digression on idolatry (Wis 13-15), our author has recourse to the texts of the prophetic and psalmic traditions which polemicise against the worship of idols. Particularly prominent is the use of the texts against the idols typical of Isa 40-55; cf. Isa 44:9-20 but also Ps 113:1-16.

The concluding section (Wis 19:10-22) is largely a bold rereading of the account of the creation in Gen 1:1-2:4a and serves to set out the principal thesis of our author: the profound link between the history of salvation and the creation. Thus, the events of the Exodus are re-presented against the background of the account of the creation in Gen 1. This reading, combined from Exodus and from the narratives of the creation, becomes exemplary in view of a future marked by a creation that has been renewed.[82]

In conclusion, the book of Wisdom appears to be thickly woven with continual references to biblical texts. This is not simply a mosaic of allusions placed where they could be helpful. Precisely because he never cites a text directly, our author leaves primarily to his audience the freedom to place every reference he makes within its original context. In this way, they can penetrate still more deeply into the sense of what the text wishes to communicate.

Our sage is profoundly convinced of the unity of the Scriptures. Hence his anthological style: one biblical text immediately recalls another. Scripture is perceived by him as a divine word which produces a coherent meaning. In his use of the biblical texts, our sage shows himself to be respectful of their context and, at the same time, particularly creative in the direction of a pronounced actualisation of these very texts. In this way, the sage shows his readers that the Word of God is always living and relevant for them if one knows how to read it in new contexts

---

80 Schwenk-Bessler, *Sapientia Salomonis als ein Beispiel frühjüdischer Textauslegung. Die Auslegung des Buches Genesis, Exodus 1-15 und Teilen der Wüstentradtion in Sap 10-19*; Cheon, *Exodus in the Wisdom of Solomon*; Enns, *Exodus Retold.*

81 Skehan, "Borrowings from the Psalms in the Book of Wisdom".

82 Cf. the conclusions of Gilbert, "La relecture de Genèse 1-3", 343-344.

such as the one in Alexandria. All this explains our sage's peculiar use of the Scriptures.[83]

The Book of Wisdom and the Ancient Jewish Tradition[84]

Part of the biblical tradition, the book of Wisdom similarly belongs to the Jewish tradition of its time. A comparison with contemporary texts, such as some parts of the book of Enoch and the manuscripts of Qumran, reveals that our sage is aware of traditions present in these works or, in some cases, perhaps, also of the works themselves.

Wisdom and Enoch

1. *The Enochic tradition.*[85] Our sage could have known the so-called Epistle of Enoch (cf. 1 En. 91-105; cf. also 1 En 108), probably written in the same period. A good part of the text of the Epistle is focused on the revelation of the "mystery" of the eschatological reward of the just (cf. 1 En 104:2) and punishment of the wicked. Perhaps the book of Wisdom also knew the introduction to the book of Enoch (1 En 1-5) where there is already an announcement of the judgement of God which involves the punishment of the wicked contrasted with the glory of the just. The Epistle of Enoch is significant for its capacity to integrate a typically sapiential perspective with a theological vision that is clearly apocalyptic. The book of Wisdom, on the other hand, offers us a sapiential eschatology, but not one bound up with apocalyptic, and far distant from the dualism, the determinism and the pessimism typical of the Enochic tradition.

Wisdom and Qumran

2. *Qumran.* As for the Qumran literature, the book of Wisdom reveals the presence of common themes: concentration on the eschatological dimension; the theme of the glory of the just and the punishment of the ungodly; the idea of resurrection; and the divine "mystery" that has been revealed.[86] Today, the growing interest of scholars in the Qumran texts belonging to the sapiential/apocalyptic vein, the so-called "Sapiential works" or "Instructions" (1Q26; 4Q415-418a; 4Q423; cf. also 4Q419 and 4Q424 to which we must add the texts of 1Q27 and 4Q299-301, known also as 4QMysteries) have offered us the opportunity to study more deeply the possible relationship between the book of Wisdom and a form of "apocalyptic" wisdom now attested by these Qumran texts.[87]

---

83 Cf. Dimant, Devorah, "Use and Interpretation of Mikra in the Apocrypha and Pseudepigrapha" in Mulder, Martin Jan (ed.), *Mikra: Text, Translation, Reading and Interpretation of the Holy Bible in Ancient Judaism and Early Christianity* (Assen: Van Gorcum 1988), 409-415. Cf. also Mazzinghi, "La figura di Abramo in Sap 10,5".

84 Gilbert, "Sagesse", 95-98; Larcher, *Etudes*, 103-112; 302-305 (Wis and Enochic literature); 112-132 (Wis and Qumran); 132-151 (Wis and Hellenistic Judaism).

85 Grelot, "L'eschatologie de la Sagesse et les apocalyptiques juives"; Grelot puts the eschatology of Wisdom close to that of Qumran. Cf. also Collins, *Jewish Wisdom*, 182-185.

86 Mazzinghi, "I misteri di Dio: dal libro della Sapienza all'Apocalisse". While the Dead Sea community reserves knowledge of the mysteries solely to the members of the community, the book of Wisdom proclaims that the mysteries of God are accessible to all (cf. Wis 2:21; 6:21-25).

87 Cf. Collins, "The Mysteries of God", *passim.*

Our sage could certainly have known the milieu and the theology of the Dead Sea community and, perhaps, some of its texts as well. One thinks of the Qumran view of the fate of the just and of the resurrection; cf. 4Q521 5 II 7: "... when he who gives life will [raise] the dead of his people ..."; cf. also the text of 4Q418 69 II 4-15 (belonging to the *Sapiential Instructions*) in which the eternal fate of the just is clearly distinguished from that of the ungodly, precisely as happens in Wisdom. Noticeable is the theme of the eschatological battle contained in Wis 5:17-23, compared with the vision offered by 1QH XIV, 32-39.[88] At Qumran too, there is evidence of the use of the history of Israel – the Exodus in particular – as a theme in a sapiential instruction; cf. 4Q185, 1-2 I 14-15.[89] However, the theological viewpoint of Wisdom is clearly different from that of Qumran. In fact, in Wisdom, there is an absence of all trace of dualism and determinism, and the vision of creation offered to us by our sage is wholly positive, without any pessimism (cf. 1:14).

Wisdom and the Palestinian-Jewish Traditions

3. *The Palestinian-Jewish traditions.* What is surprising in an Alexandrian text like Wisdom is its closeness to the traditions of Palestinian Judaism which are known to us from the Targumic, midrashic, and rabbinical literature of the following centuries. In Wis 10-19 the interpretations of the texts from Genesis and Exodus coincide, not infrequently, with the choices made by the Targums and subsequently attested in the midrashic tradition. In some cases, Wisdom also seems to be the oldest witness of biblical interpretations that are characteristic of the Targumic and midrashic literature (cf. the connection made between the story of Abraham and the episode of Babel in 10:5; the tradition in 10:21 about the infants who praise God during the crossing of the sea;[90] and the traditions concerning the plague of darkness in Exod 10:21-23, reread in Wis 18:1-4 in the optic of the "light of the Law"). The book of Wisdom shows itself to be really well rooted in the tradition of the Fathers at the very moment in which it is open to Hellenism.

Wisdom and Greek-Language Judaism

4. *The literature of Greek-language Judaism.* There are very close connections between Wisdom and the Alexandrian-Jewish literature in Greek owing to the origin of the book within that same cultural context. Wisdom shows itself to have known the Letter of Aristeas, sharing its universal and dialogic perspective but with a much more solid link with the biblical tradition and without ever such a clear apologetic style as Aristeas. On the level of vocabulary, there are notable connections with 3 Macc and 4 Macc, although it is difficult to prove a real dependence in one direction or the other. There are notable contacts between the book of Wisdom and the Testaments of the Twelve Patriarchs, but, in this case too, it is difficult to prove in which direction any possible dependence lies.

To speak of Alexandrian Judaism means speaking first of all of Philo. The problem of the relationship between the book of Wisdom and Philo is resolved for the most part negatively, unless one admits a dating for Wisdom later than

88 Puech, "The Book of Wisdom and the Dead Sea Scrolls", *passim.*

89 This Qumran testimony reflects a stage in the sapiential tradition in which the appeal to the traditions of Israel is united with ideas of an apocalyptic character, and where the whole fits as part of an instruction of a sapiential nature. Cf. Collins, *Jewish Wisdom*, 117.

90 Grelot, "Sagesse 10,21 et le Targum de l'Exode".

the Alexandrian-Jewish philosopher (thus D. Winston and G. Scarpat).[91] There are thematic links and a common vocabulary between Wisdom and Philo owing to their being part of the same religious and cultural environment. Like Philo, Wisdom too shows a concern with the political situation of the Alexandrian Jews (cf. 19:13-17).

However, the book of Wisdom follows a path that is quite different from that of Philo. Our sage does not employ the allegorical interpretation of biblical texts so characteristic of Philo nor does he seem to know of such a method.[92] At the heart of the book of Wisdom is, rather, the rereading of the events of the Exodus through the filter of the sapiential theology of creation and, at the same time, within a perspective that has a clear eschatological stamp. Moreover, although there is a dialogue with Greek philosophy, its influence is much less marked than in Philo's work. The book of Wisdom is free from the emphasis on the Platonic doctrine of ideas that is so frequent in Philo and from the Philonic reflection of the powers (δυνάμεις) of God.

The Book of Wisdom and Hellenism

Speaking of the city of Alexandria, Philo describes it as a μεγαλόπολις or also a πολύπολις (*Flacc.* 163). It is a cosmopolitan city, but he never calls it a μετρόπολις. Alexandria is, therefore, a city where many peoples live together, but Philo never looks on it as the "mother" city for the Jews who live there. Thus, the relationship between Jews and Greeks in Alexandria is complex.

Immersed as it was in a world that was totally different, Alexandrian Judaism could not be other than tolerant. To speak of adaptation does not mean *per se* to speak of apostasy. However, Philo records the presence of apostates from the Jewish faith (cf. *Virt.* 182; *Spec.* 1.54-57; *Mos.* 2.193-208); so, the problem existed even if the phenomenon of apostasy need not have been predominant among the Alexandrian Jews.[93] In this connection, we must ask ourselves how the book of Wisdom situates itself in the face of the Hellenistic world. In the past, some authors (Paul

---

91 Cf. a general view in Larcher, *Etudes*, 151-178, who accepts a knowledge of Wisdom on the part of Philo. Cf. Winston (*Wisdom*, 59-63), who, because of the dating he proposes, tends to acknowledge a dependence of Wisdom on Philo although he underlines the absence of an allegorical reading of the biblical texts in Wisdom.

92 On the use of allegory in Philo, cf. Laporte, Jean, "Philo in the Tradition of Biblical Wisdom Literature" in Wilken, Robert L., (ed.), *Aspect of Wisdom in Judaism and Early Christianity* (Notre Dame [IN]: University of Notre Dame 1975), 103-143 (Laporte assumes a knowledge of Wisdom on Philo's part); Cazeaux, Jacques, "Philon: l'allégorie et l'obsession de la totalité", in Kuntzmann, Raymond – Schlosser, Jacques (edd.), *Etudes sur le judaïsme hellénistique* (Paris: Cerf 1984), 267-320.

93 On Greek-speaking Judaism, see the classical work of Hengel, Martin, *Judentum und Hellenismus*, Tübingen: J.C.B. Mohr 1969; cf. Momigliano, Arnaldo D., *Alien Wisdom. The Limits of Hellenization*, Cambridge: Cambridge University Press 1969; cf. also Kunztmann – Schlosser (edd.), *Études sur le judaïsme ellénistique*; Baslez, Françoise-Marie, *Bible et histoire. Judaïsme, hellénisme, christianisme*, Paris: Fayard 1999.

Henisch; Johannes Fichtner) inclined towards a minimum influence of Hellenism on Wisdom. Still now, there are those who maintain that the author of Wisdom was an opponent of Hellenism.[94] Present day studies, however, have clarified that the relationship between Wisdom and the Hellenistic world is actually very complex and undoubtedly more positive.[95]

Wisdom and Greek Philosophy

The relationship of Wisdom with Greek philosophy is profound and reveals that our sage was much more than an eclectic author.[96] In the praise of wisdom (Wis 7-8 in particular), the use of Stoic categories is evident, cf. Wis 7:22b-24 and 8:1. The Stoic idea of a cosmic *pneuma* helps our sage to describe the presence of wisdom in the world (cf. also 1:6-7; 9:17). In 7:25-26, the use of Platonism is added to that of Stoicism and is present also elsewhere in the book (cf. 8:19-20; 9:15).[97] In Wis 18:4, the idea of *nomos* is introduced in a way that is not opposed to the Stoic concept but, on the contrary, recalls it. The polemic against the philosophers in 13:1-9 reveals an approach that is not entirely negative to Stoicism. We note again the use of Stoic categories like that of kingship (cf. the comment on Wis 1:1); the use of concepts well known in the neo-Pythagorean treatises on kingship (cf. in connection with 6:1-21); and the recourse to the category of "philanthropy", familiar to the Hellenistic world (cf. Wis 1:6).

The relationship with the Hellenistic world concerns not only the world of philosophy. Already the use of a typically Greek literary genre, like that of the *encomium*, is a clear indication of a positive relationship with this world. This is not to mention the style and vocabulary which reveal a positive and profound relationship with Hellenism. If Philo intends to offer his readers a real *interpretatio*

---

94 Cf. Barclay, *Jews in the Mediterranean Diaspora*, 181-192. With regard to Wisdom, he speaks of "cultural antagonism". Cf. the judgement of Hanhart: "Hellenistische Judentum bedeutet darum nicht Israels Offnung für die hellenistische Welt und die Umgestaltung seines Wesens (...), sondern die kritische, leidende Auseinandersetzung mit dieser Welt auf Grund dessen, was Israels schon war und jenseits dieses Grenzen bleiben musste"; in: Hanhart, Robert, "Die Bedeutung der Septuaginta für die Definition des 'Hellenistische Judentums' ", in Kratz, Reihnard Gregor (ed.), *Studien zur Septuaginta und Hellenistische Judentum* (FAT 24, Tübingen: Mohr Siebeck 1999), 76.

95 For a *status quaestionis*, cf. Larcher, *Études*, 179-201 (Wis and Greek culture); 201-223 (Wis and Greek philosophy); 222-236 (Wis and the Hellenistic sources); Vílchez Líndez, *Sapienza*, 76-86; Gilbert, "Sagesse", 98-100; Id., "La Sagesse de Salomon et l'hellénisme"; Mazzinghi, "Il libro della Sapienza: elementi culturali". On the problem of the influence of Hellenism in Wisdom, the work of Reese remains fundamental. Cf. *Hellenistic Influence on the Book of Wisdom*, in particular pp. 32-89. Cf. also Kepper, *Hellenistische Bildung*.

96 Cf. Larcher, *Etudes*, 201-236 and Gilbert, "Sagesse de Salomon", 100. A similar judgement is that of Focke, *Die Entstehung*, 90-92. Cf., by contrast, the judgement of Collins, *Jewish Wisdom*, 202: "The author of Wis. Sol. was not a philosopher (...). Nevertheless there is enough correspondence with Philo to debunk the idea that he was an idiosyncratic amateur making his own superficial use of philosophical terms".

97 On the Platonism of Wisdom, cf. Winston, "A Century of Research", 9 An opposing position can be found in Scarpat, *Sapienza*, 2, 8. On the other hand, Hübner reaches the conclusion that our sage is offering his own combination of ideas, both Stoic and Platonic, for example, neutralising the Stoic materialism relating to the divine *pneuma* through the introduction of the idea of transcendence which is of Platonic origin. Cf. "Die Sapientia und die antike Philosophie", 55-83.

judaica of Stoic philosophy, the book of Wisdom, rather, makes use of some ideas circulating in its time – in large part those which Philo will take up again later – to express his own conception relating to the wisdom of Israel in a way that is in harmony with the needs of his audience.

Wisdom and Greek Religion

Finally, our sage is well aware of the multi-aspect religious view proper to the Alexandrian world. In Wis 14:16b-21, for example, he polemicises against the imperial cult. In many passages of Wisdom (cf. 2:21-22; 6:22; 8:2; 9:4, 9-10; 12:4; 14:1-10; 17:1-18:4), there is clear evidence of the polemic being conducted by our sage in relation to the mystery cults, especially the Isis cults that were so widespread in Alexandria. The wisdom described in Wis 7-9 is really being re- presented in Isiac dress, not only to show the Alexandrine Jews that, in the wisdom of Israel, they could find everything that Isis offered to her initiates but also to revitalise the figure of the wisdom of the Fathers in clothing – that of Isis – much more familiar to the author's public.[98]

Our sage shows himself much harsher in his dealings with the magic which was so widespread in his time; cf. 12:4 and, in particular, the comment on Wis 17:1-18:4.

The Eschatological Perspective

As for eschatology, the thesis of the book of Wisdom appears particularly new when compared with the concept which the Hellenised Egyptian Jews are known to have had of death. An analysis of the Jewish funerary inscriptions found at Leontopolis confirms this.[99] In fact, the faith expressed by these inscriptions, appears to be more Greek than Jewish and expresses a generic belief in some form of survival in Hades. The Leontopolis inscriptions often leave room for a bitter lament for the life which is fleeting, for the acceptance of death as an unavoidable fact, and for no distinction between the final fate of the just and the unjust. The *motif* of premature death is really very frequent (we shall return there below in connection with Wis 4:7-17, the premature death of the just man).[100] From these inscriptions, it appears that death is *the* problem of life. The tone is always very sad, and material that is specifically Jewish rarely makes an appearance. This is not the case in the book of Wisdom where the lament over fleeting life is placed in the mouth of the ungodly (cf. Wis 2:1-6). In the light of the Leontopolis inscriptions, they seem to be expressing the opinion of the *majority* of contemporary

---

98 On the connections between the book of Wisdom and the mysteries of Isis, cf. Reese, *Hellenistic Influence*, 36-50; Kloppenborg, "Isis and Sophia". Cf. also Mack, Burton L, *Logos und Sophia*, Göttingen: Vandenhoeck & Ruprecht 1973, 62-95; Engel, in relation to Wis 7-8: "Was Weisheit ist und wie Sie entstand"; Mazzinghi, "La barca della Provvidenza" (on Wis 14:1-10); Id., "La Sapienza, presente accanto a Dio" (on Wis 9:9-10); Dumoulin, *Entre la Manne et l'Eucharistie*, 136-142 (in relation to Wis 16:15-17:1); Mazzinghi, *Notte di paura e di luce* (in relation to Wis 17:1-18:4).

99 Cf. Blischke, *Eschatologie*, 233-263. For the inscriptions of Leontopolis, cf. Noy, David, "The Jewish Community of Leontopolis and Venosa" in van Hente, Jan Wilhelm – van der Horst, Pieter Willem (edd.), *Studies in Early Jewish Epigraphy* (Leiden: Brill 1994), 162-182. For the texts, cf. van der Horst, Pieter Willem, *Ancient Jewish Epitaphs. An Introductory Ssurvey of a Millennium of Jewish Funerary Epigraphy (300BCE-700CE)*, Kampen: Koh Pharos 1991.

100 Cf. Griessmair, Ewald, *Das Motiv der Mors Immatura in den griechischen Grabinschriften*, Innsbruck: Wagner 1966.

Jews! Death is seen as an intrusion into God's plan, and the final fate of the just is quite different from that of the ungodly.

State of Research

The book of Wisdom appears something more than a simple apology for Judaism. By contrast with the apologetic Jewish literature (Demetrius, Artapanus, Eupolemus...), Wisdom is not limited to re-presenting Judaism in the clothing of Greek categories to a cultural environment which is accusing it of being asocial and hostile to foreigners, a people ἀπάνθρωπος and μισόξενος.[101]

Thomas Finan

Thomas Finan emphasises that the fundamental difference between the Greek and Jewish worlds is anthropocentrism contrasted with the theocentrism typical of Israel. "In the single concept of universally active Wisdom, at once transcendent in its nature and immanent in its effects, the author of Wisdom has found a principle which, while affirming Jewish universalism (...) so guarantees the unity of truth in its origins and of history in its progress, that the Hebrew sage is justified in fusing his theocentric wisdom with Greek anthropocentric *paideia*".[102] God, the author of the universe, is unique with his principle of order and reason in the cosmos, which is wisdom. In this optic, one can state that the book of Wisdom is describing the biblical God, transcendent and Creator, in the light of the immanent *Logos* of Stoicism.

James M. Reese

James M. Reese observes that Wisdom is not limited to "speaking Greek", that is, to expounding the Jewish faith in a language accessible to the Greek world. The use of a philosophical, literary and religious vocabulary that is typically Hellenistic is all too clear. In reality, the use which Wisdom makes of Hellenism is much more profound. Reese recognises that Wisdom's inspiration is primarily biblical. Hellenism and biblical revelation are never put on the same level. However, Wisdom's aim is to address the young Jews of Alexandria to help them and urge them to express their faith in a particular cultural context, that of the Greeks. "By incorporating Hellenistic learning so thoroughly into his work the author intended to actualize revelation in the way that would best encourage them to carry out their responsibilities as believers in a cosmopolitan society".[103]

According to Reese, the use that Wisdom makes of Hellenism is primarily "strategic".[104] The book of Wisdom is really open to the propositions coming from the Greek world, but these propositions are being inserted into the frame of the tradition of Israel. In fact, it is the law of Israel that gives light to the world (18:4), and, although they are only "to be blamed lightly", the philosophers have not succeeded in finding God (cf. 13:1-9). Wisdom wishes to demonstrate that the values of the Greek *paideia* are truly present and recapitulated in the faith of Israel which is founded on the Scriptures. Thus, our sage is reacting against the tendency of Alexandrian Judaism to close in on itself in the face of a hostile world, but, at the same time, he does not renounce his own faith. It is this attempt to

---

101 Thus Hecataeus of Abdera, cited by Diodorus Siculus (*Bibl.* 40.3.4). Cf. Stern, Menahem, *Greek and Latin Authors on Jews and Judaism*, I-III, Jerusalem: Israel Academy of Science and Humanities 1974-1984; cf. vol. I, 26-35. For the Jewish apologetic literature, cf. Sterling, Gregory E., *Historiography and Self-definition. Josephus, Luke-Acts and Apologetic Historiography* (NT Supp. 64, New York – Leiden – Cologne: Brill 1996), 137-225.

102 Finan, "Hellenistic Humanism in the Book of Wisdom", 47.

103 Reese, *Hellenistic Influence*, 155.

104 *Ibid.*, 156.

take the Hellenistic culture seriously and utilise it to advance the understanding of revelation that makes Wisdom a text that is extremely topical.

M. Gilbert and the Concept of "Incultura-tion"

In this connection, Maurice Gilbert goes so far as to speak of real "incultura-tion", showing how the relationship between Wisdom and the Greek world is a real and profound one and not limited to the surface of the problems.[105] Wisdom succeeds in not repudiating anything from the biblical patrimony but in re-expressing it and amplifying it by the use of Greek categories.

> "How, then, should one seek to open the eyes of those who are distant and of those who, within this community, are subject to the temptation and fascination of pagan Hellenism? How, then, speak unless having recourse to the very means of this Hellenistic culture, using its methods and schemes of expression and thought yet without denying anything of the religious content received from the Fathers? This seems to have been our author's plan. His inculturation seems to have been motivated by an authentic care for the community and for its unity in the faith". "The author never seems obliged to defend his own way of doing things, excusing himself, so to speak, for speaking like the Greeks. He proceeds as if it were natural. In so doing, he is aware of writing a work in the service of God: in Wis 7:15, he asks for the grace to express himself according to the very desires of God. He thus becomes exemplary. With his positive attitude, he is also demonstrating, perhaps, that inculturation experienced like this is wholly natural and is an obligation on the one who is called to transmit the authentic message of faith".[106]

The Book of Wisdom and the Christian Tradition

The Links with the New Testament

The problem of the links between the book of Wisdom and the New Testament has not yet been satisfactorily resolved. After a long period of scepticism in which the main tendency was to deny a direct knowledge of Wisdom on the part of the authors of the New Testament, more recent studies lean towards paying greater attention to the possible clues which could testify to a use of the book of Wisdom within the Christian Scriptures, especially Paul and John.[107]

Wisdom and Paul

Within the Pauline corpus, there is no lack of possible points of contact with the book of Wisdom. A text as theologically important as Wis 13:1-9 resembles Rom 1:18-23 without it being possible, however, to prove Paul's real reliance on Wisdom. According to S. Lyonnet, the Letter to the Romans actually contains a series of important references to the book of Wisdom.[108] In particular, it is possible to compare the view of paganism in Rom 1 with the perspective opened up by Wis 13-15. The way in which Paul rereads the events of the Exodus in 1 Cor 10:1-

105 Cf. Gilbert, "Inculturazione"; Id., "La Sagesse de Salomon et l'héllenisme".

106 *Ibid.*, 15.22; cf. also Colzani, "Il popolo di Dio fra tradizione giudaica e cultura greca", 47.

107 Mazzinghi, *Notte di paura e di luce*, 298-304, with bibliography. Cf. the general presentation of the problem in Larcher, *Etudes*, 11-36.

108 Cf. Lyonnet, Stanislas, *Épître aux Romains*, in *Dictionnaire de la Bible. Supplément*, 7:536; Linebaugh, *God, grace, and righteousness in Wisdom of Solomon and Paul's Letter to the Romans.*

4 is very close to the *midrashic* method in Wis 11-19. Passages like 1 Thess 5:1-11 demonstrate the existence of many points of contact with the fifth and sixth diptychs (Wis 17:1-18:4 and 18:5-25). These connections would find their natural explanation in the acknowledgement that Paul actually knew the book of Wisdom.

Wisdom and John

Greater attention has been devoted to the relationship with the Gospel of John. Both John and Wisdom mention the miracles of the Exodus as a model for the signs operated by wisdom (in Wis) and by Jesus (in John). Both John and Wisdom present these signs in the same order, which is not that of Exodus. John 2:1-11, the marriage at Cana, recalls the first antithesis of Wis 11:4-14, underlining the theme of thirst. John 4:43-54 and 5:1-9a, are centred on the theme of healing which appears in the third diptych of Wis 16:4-14. The diptych of the manna (Wis 16:15-28) finds its correspondence in John 6 (the bread of life). Finally, the diptych of the darkness (Wis 17:1-18:4) can be set in relation to John 9 (the man born blind) while John 11, the resurrection of Lazarus, corresponds to Wis 18:5-25, the death of the firstborn and the saving of the Israelites. To conclude, in John as in Wisdom, the historical facts become symbolic, signs, that is, of spiritual and eschatological realities. Thus, the darkness of the Egyptians in Wis 17:1-18:4 is the sign of the darkness of Hades which will strike the ungodly (Wis 17:21). In its turn, the cure of the man born blind is the sign of the spiritual blindness of the Pharisees. The light which illuminates the world (Wis 17:20) is the light of the law (18:4), just as Jesus himself is the light of the world (John 8:12; 9:39). It is certainly possible to hypothesise the existence of a common *midrashic* tradition, but it is equally legitimate to think that the Gospel of John knew and made use of the book of Wisdom.

The Problem of Canonicity and the Use of the Book in Christian Antiquity[109]

The Church Fathers knew and made use of the book of Wisdom. It seems to have been used as Scripture that was considered inspired (Irenaeus, Cyprian, Eusebius). In any case, Wisdom seems to have been the most utilised deuterocanonical book in the first three centuries of the Christian era.[110] In the ancient Jewish world too, Wisdom does not seem to have encountered much opposition, even if was not received as a canonical text.[111]

The first to have used Wisdom seems to have been Clement of Rome (1 Clem 3:4, which alludes to Wis 2:24a; 1 Clem 27:5, which alludes to Wis 11:20-21) together with Melito of Sardis (*peri Pascha,* 22-23, which alludes to Wis 17,[112] followed, later, by Irenaeus of Lyons (*Haer.* 4.38.3 which alludes to Wis 6:19) and by Clement of Alexandria, who cites Wisdom as Scripture (*Strom.* 5.108.2 [Wis 2:12];

109 Cf. Larcher, *Études*, 36-85; Horbury, "The Christian Use", 185-194.

110 Cf. Stuhlhofer, Franz, *Der Gebrauch der Bibel von Jesus bis Euseb* (Wuppertal: R. Brockhaus 1988) 147; Larcher, *Etudes*, 36-63.

111 Wisdom represented "an acceptable 'outside book'"; cf. Horbury, "The Christian Use", 187.

112 On the connections between Melito and Wisdom, cf. Mazzinghi, *Notte di paura e di luce*, 308.

6.92.3 [Wis 9:17-18]). It has been hypothesised that the book of Wisdom was read not only as a sapiential book but also as a real Solomonic prophecy, a type of reading which perhaps already had a Jewish origin.[113]

At Alexandria, Origen made use of the book, particularly texts like Wis 7:25-26, applying it to the generation of Christ (*Comm. Jo.* 13.25; PG 14,444). Christ is the image of God as wisdom is the mediation of God. This is a key passage in Origen's theology.[114]

From the end of the third century, however, discordant voices were raised. Already, Origen mentions some doubts on the canonicity of the book (*Princ.* 4.4.6; PG XI, 407). The reasons seem to have been bound up with fidelity to the Hebrew canon but probably also with perplexity relating to the authenticity of the Solomonic authorship. Cyril of Jerusalem forbade the reading of it because he did not consider the Wisdom of Solomon a canonical text (PG XXXIII, 497-501). Athanasius speaks of Wisdom as a non-canonical text (cf. PG XXVI, 1436-1440) even if elsewhere he considers it Scripture.[115]

Among the Latin Fathers, Jerome pronounces clearly against the canonicity of the book. Bound to the *hebraica veritas*, Jerome limits himself to the Hebrew books of the Palestinian canon, excluding Wisdom from the canon of inspired Scriptures (*Praef. in libros Ps.* PL XXVIII, 1241-1242; XXIX, 404-405). The Muratorian fragment seems to indicate a non-canonical status for Wisdom.[116] In the great uncials (B, S, A), Wisdom is placed after Prov – Qoh – Song and before Ben Sira, so after the books of the Hebrew canon.[117]

It was Augustine, above all, who was to make a powerful defence of the canonicity of the book of Wisdom, appealing chiefly to the apostolic tradition, to liturgical usage, and to the continuity of the ecclesial tradition.[118] Among the Fathers, Augustine is the one who seems to make most use of our book, though with the third part (Wis 10-19) much less in evidence. One of the texts most used by Augustine is Wis 9:15 which, instead of being read pessimistically, expresses for Augustine an established fact of the human condition, that it derives from sin. For Augustine, Wisdom is primarily a theological, Christological, and pneumatological treatise as we see from his interpretation of 7:27 and 9:17 (cf. *Trin.* 4.20).[119]

Writing in 405 to the Bishop of Toulouse, Pope Innocent I sided with the Augustinian position. However, the weight of Jerome's authority continued to make itself felt. In fact, we do not have any patristic commentary on the book of

113 Cf. Horbury, "The Christian Use", 193.

114 It is a text much used also by other Alexandrian theologians. Cf. Grant, "The Book of Wisdom at Alexandria", *passim*.

115 Cf. Larcher, *Etudes*, 48-49.

116 Horbury, "The Wisdom of Solomon in the Muratorian Fragment".

117 "In the broader context of the Solomonic corpus, the new book of Wisdom had redeemed Solomon from the appearance of supporting the Sadducees [cf. Qoh and Hebrew Ben Sira, *author*] and had enrolled him as a partisan of Pharisaic martyrs, an ardent prophet of righteousness, immortality and judgment to come", Horbury, "The Christian Use", 196.

118 Cf. the texts cited in La Bonnardière, *Biblia Augustiniana*, 56-57.

119 La Bonnardière, Anne-Marie, "Le livre de la Sagesse dans l'oeuvre de Saint Augustin", *Revue des études Augustiniennes* 17 (1971) :171-175.

Wisdom, and the debate over its canonicity remained open until the decision of the Council of Trent in 1546 with regard to all the books which would thereafter be called *deuterocanonical*, among them the book of Wisdom itself (cf. DS 784). The Catholic Church has never neglected to make use of the book of Wisdom within its liturgy. The lectionaries in use today in the Roman rite are evidence of an extensive use of the book, with the significant exception of the texts of the third part.[120]

As for the Orthodox Churches, they have never pronounced on the canonicity of the book of Wisdom although it is usually included in the Orthodox editions of the Bible in view of its being part of the LXX. Following Luther's choice of limiting himself to the Hebrew canon, the Reformed Churches excluded the book of Wisdom from the canon of Scripture although they have always regarded it with great esteem. One of the first great modern commentators on the book of Wisdom was actually a Protestant author, Carl Grimm (*Das Buch der Weisheit,* Leipzig 1860), but non-Catholic commentators on Wisdom remain rather rare. The commentary of Hans Hübner (1999) is the first after that of Johannes Fichtner which was published in 1938.[121]

120 Cf. Engel, Weish [NSK] 316-317.

121 According to Hübner, the Reformation Churches' criterion of the *hebraica veritas* is not a sufficient criterion for canonicity: "Ich gehe davon aus, dass die sogenannten Apocryphen essentielle Teile des AT sind und als biblische Bücher zu exegesieren sind" (Hübner, *Weisheit,* 15).

Introduction to the First Part (Wis 1–6)

The protagonists of the first part of the book of Wisdom are the just and the ungodly, but only the latter appear as active characters. The just appear to be totally passive: they undergo the violence of the ungodly and experience only death (Wis 2). Our sage is thus reflecting on the eternal reality of violence and evil which had already led to Job's courageous rebellion and to the bitter and disenchanted conclusions of Qoheleth and wishes to offer a response.[1] Human life appears as a drama in which the ungodly seem to emerge as protagonists.[2] However, in the heart of this first part of the book (Wis 3-4), a wholly new perspective opens up, one which neither Job nor Qoheleth imagined: the just have the prospect of eternal life. The immortality given to the just is immediately transformed into the defeat of the ungodly. Their plans, expounded and so criticised in 1:16-2:24, are contrasted with their knowledge of their own tragic failure (Wis 5). In both cases, speech is given to the ungodly. In the outer frame (Wis 1:1-15 and 6:1-25), the author addresses his audience, the Alexandrian Jews, exhorting them to follow justice and to learn wisdom in order to find life. Justice, wisdom, and life thus become a triad which runs through the whole of the book: "Justice, Wisdom and Life are the universe offered by God whereas injustice, error and death are the way of the ungodly. Not for nothing, the author sets his hand to dramatic forms and speaks in a pathetic tone".[3]

Literary Structure

We limit ourselves here to some general observations, noting first of all that Wis 1-6 offers an elegant concentric structure:

A – *Initial exhortation* (1:1-15): the pericope is identified by a double *inclusio*: δικαιοσύνη (vv. 1a, 15) and γῆς (vv. 1a and 14c). The book opens with an appeal to listen, addressed to those who "govern" so that they may embrace justice and wisdom.

---

1 Cf. V. D'Alario, "La réflexion sur le sens de la vie en Sg 1-5. Une réponse aux questions de Job et de Qohélet".

2 In connection with Wis 1, McGlynn (*Divine Judgment*, 54-88) speaks of an "apocalyptic drama".

3 Alonso Schökel, *Sabiduría*, 83. Schmitt compares the dramatic structure of Wis 1:1-6:21 to the traditional structure of Greek tragedy: 1:1-15 is the exposition; 1:16-20 and 4:20-5:23 the drama proper; 3:1-4:19 the kind of commentary which Greek tragedy would have entrusted to the chorus; 6:1-21, the conclusion, that is, the "epilogue": cf. "Zur dramatischen Form von Weisheit 1,1-6,21".

B – *Life project of the ungodly* (1:16-2:24): cf. the *inclusio* on the term μερίς, "part / party" (1:16 and 2:24), the only occurrences of the term in the whole of the book of Wisdom except for 2:9 at the centre of this passage. Wis 2:1-20 presents the reasoning of the ungodly surrounded by the negative judgement of the author in 1:16 and 2:21-24 which, at the same time, recalls God's plan for creation (cf. 1:13-15).

C – Wis 3:1-4:20 forms the centre of the first part of the book and contains four antithetical diptychs which highlight the different destiny of the just and the ungodly:

C1. The eternal bliss of the just with God (3:1-9) is contrasted with the misery of the ungodly (3:10-12); the key word "hope" (ἐλπίς), in vv. 4 and 11, binds the two parts of the passage together.

C2. The bliss of the sterile but virtuous woman and of the eunuch who is also virtuous is contrasted with the misery of the children of the adulterers (3:13-19).

C3. The sterile person without children is worth more than someone who has many children but is without virtue (4:1-6).

C4. For the just, premature death is the passage to eternal life (4:7-16; cf. the *inclusio* on γῆρας, "old age", in vv. 8 and 16), while the misery of the ungodly is assured even if they live a long time (4:17-20).

B' – *Final account of the ungodly* (5:1-23); the author's thought is laid out in the frame represented by vv. 1-3 and 14-23. Verse 14 and v. 23 are characterised by the repetition of the rare word λαῖλαψ, "hurricane", present only here in the book. This frame encloses a second discourse of the ungodly (5:4-13) similar to that of chapter 2, but relating, this time, to their miserable destiny at the moment of judgement.

A' – *Concluding exhortation addressed to the "governors" that they may follow wisdom* (6:1-21). A good example of the keyword is "all the earth" (πᾶσα ἡ γῆ), which links 5:23 with 6:1. Two *inclusios* with the beginning of the book, "examine" (ἐξέτασις: 1:9 and ἐξετάσει: 6:3) and "seek" (ζητέω in 1:1 and 6:12, 16) link this final exhortation with the opening one (1:1-15).

The text of Wis 6:22-25 makes up the conclusion of the first part as well as the announcement of the second. The author is preparing to speak of wisdom, its nature, its origin, and its history. The term "wisdom" (σοφία; 6:21 and 22) and the verb παιδεύω, "educate" (6:11 and 25) link the introduction to the previous section.

Literary Genre: Wis 1-6 and the Encomium

Transumptive Narration

From a perspective of the literary genre employed, David Seeley has an interesting proposal: Wis 1-5 would constitute a "Transumptive Narration",[4] that is, a new narration, which is based on previous stories and which intends to respond to the great questions of life. In fact, our sage is combining the Servant Songs of Isaiah, as well as other biblical sources (cf. Introduction, p. 31-32), with themes from the Graeco-Roman

4 Seeley, "Trasumptive Narration"; "Narrative, the Righteous Man and the Philosopher".

philosophical sphere. A common *topos* in the philosophy of the time is the accusation made against Epicureanism of leading from hedonism to violence (cf. the comment on Wis 2:10). Another *topos* is that of the philosopher who is opposed because of observing the laws (cf. the comment on 2:12). Our sage is thus constructing a story relating to a pious Jew which is actually following Hellenistic philosophical models.[5]

Wis 1-6 as *Exordium*

Within the literary genre of the *encomium*, chapters 1-6 have the precise function of representing the *exordium* of the *encomium* itself.[6] Wis 1:1-11 constitutes the *exordium* as such. There is an appeal to the listeners (1:1-2), and the subject (wisdom associated with the spirit) is introduced, incorporated (1:3-5, 6-11) within a polemical warning against the opponents. Wis 1:(12)13-15 contains the first announcement of the theme which will be at the heart of this *exordium*: God did not create death, and justice is immortal. Then, the opponents, the ungodly, come into the scene (2:1b-20), as happens in the *exordium* of some classical *encomia* (in his *De amicitia*, Cicero fields the Epicureans). The author's judgement (2:21-24) closes the presentation of the ungodly, returning to what was anticipated in 1:13-15. The rejection of the opposing theses is illustrated by four paradoxical antitheses presented in Wis 3-4. The paradox is typical of the literary genre of the *encomium* and is introduced by our sage here precisely at the heart of the exordium. Chapter 5, with its presentation of the ungodly *post mortem*, is not part of the literary genre of the *encomium* but forms a logical pendant to chapter 2 within a concentric literary structure (cf. below).

The text of Wis 6:1-11 takes up the same themes as 1:1-11, introducing more clearly the basic theme of the book: wisdom.

In 6:12-21, we are once again in language typical of the *exordium*, but there are beginning to appear themes which will form part of the following *elogium* of wisdom. The text of Wis 6:22-25, a bridge between the first and second parts (see below) announces that the author will be speaking of the nature of wisdom (τί δέ ἐστιν σοφία; 6:22a) and of its origin (πῶς ἐγένετο) along the lines of the classical style of the *encomium* which takes its inspiration from the ἀρχή and the γένος of a person.[7]

5 However, it appears excessive to conclude, with Seeley, that Wisdom "becomes a syncretistic story for a syncretistic age" ("Transumptive Narration", 248).

6 Bizzeti, *Sapienza*, 163-168, with a detailed comparison with the classical *encomium*.

7 Burgess, Theodore C., "Epideicteic Literature", *Studies in Classical Philology* 3 (1902): 220-222.

Wis 1:1-15: Love Justice!

Literary Structure of Wis 1:1-15[1]

Introduction to the Work

Here we have the introduction to the whole work, an initial appeal addressed to the recipients of the book (those who "govern on earth"). It will be taken up again in Wis 6 in accordance with the concentric structure which we have outlined above. It is not strange, therefore, to find anticipated here many themes which run through the entire book: justice, the wisdom associated with the spirit of God, the presence of this spirit in the world, the contrast between the just and the ungodly, death and immortality, and the cosmos. Despite the presence of polemical points, the general tone is positive and, towards the end, almost joyful. Everything that exists has a salvific value, and there is no dominion of death on the earth.

Verse 1 opens with three imperatives in positive form (ἀγαπήσατε, φρονήσατε, ζητήσατε). The same verbal form is taken up again in vv. 11-12 where there appears a second series of four imperatives, in negative form or with a negative sense (φυλάξασθε, φείσασθε, μὴ ζηλοῦτε, μηδὲ ἐπισπᾶσθε). Verses 1-12 thus constitute a fairly unitary section. Its internal arrangement can be outlined as follows:

Wis 1:1-5 An urgent invitation to seek wisdom and justice. Cf. the quasi-*inclusio* δικαιοσύνη – ἀδικία (v. 1a, 5c). In 4a and in 5a, the two terms σοφία and πνεῦμα appear separately while in 6a they are associated with each other, something that suggests the existence of a certain caesura between v. 5 and v. 6.

Wis 1:6-10 The emphasis is shifted on to the theme of the word, something which gives unity to this short pericope. The terms γλώσσης (v. 6e and 11b) and γογγυσμῶν / γογγυσμόν (v. 10b and 11a) constitute two keywords with the following section.

Wis 1:11-12 With its four imperatives, this concluding exhortation recalls the text of 1:1 (cf. above). Two imperatives urge the avoidance of wrong behaviour (v. 11), and two are openly negative (v. 12).

Wis 1:13-15 These verses present characteristics which distinguish them from the rest of the pericope: between v. 12 and v. 13, there exists a certain break, even one of a thematic character[2]. This short section attests the existence of notable contacts with Wis 2:23-24 at the end of the discourse of the ungodly (cf. 1:16-2:20). Like 2:23, v. 13 also opens with the expression ὅτι ὁ θεός followed by the verb ποιέω, which does not appear again before 6:7, and by κτίζω, which does not reappear before 10:1. Further points of contact are the presence of κόσμος (only used before 5:2) and of θάνατος (only used before 12:20). We note, however, that 1:13 is also linked with the previous verse (1:12) precisely by the presence of θάνατος which thus acts as a hook-word with the preceding material, and, at v. 14, by the repetition of ὄλεθρ-. We can therefore consider Wis 1:13-15 as the conclu-

---

1 Perrenchio, "Struttura e analisi letteraria di Sap I,1-15"; Bizzeti, *Sapienza*, 52-53; Gilbert, "Sagesse", 65-66; Kolarcik, *The Ambiguity of Death*, 34-38.

2 Gilbert, "Sagesse", 66.

sion of the section which began in Wis 1:1 (namely, Wis 1:1-12) and, at the same time, as a preparation for the following section, that is, 1:16-2:24.[3]

Wis 1:1-5: Justice, Wisdom, and Spirit

1 Love justice, you who govern on earth,
reflect on the Lord with a soul that is well-disposed
and seek him with simplicity of heart,
2 for he allows himself to be found by those who do not test him
and he reveals himself to those who do not lack faith in him.
3 For devious thoughts separate one from God,
so that, when put to the test, divine power punishes the foolish.
4 Because wisdom will not enter a soul that is plotting evil
and it cannot dwell in a body that is the slave of sin.
5 For the holy spirit of discipline will flee from the deceitful one
and will take itself off from foolish thoughts
and will be driven away at the arrival of injustice.

Notes on the Text and Translation

v. 1. The three aorist imperatives ἀγαπήσατε, φρονήσατε, ζητήσατε are stronger than the simple present imperative. The three aorists suggest a punctual and ingressive aspect, and so express "the realisation of an action by contrast with that which lasted up to that moment";[4] the nuance is that of "begin, at last, to love...!".

v. 2. The two stichs are constructed in clear parallelism. The form εὑρίσκεται should be translated with the intransitive nuance proper to the middle voice, "allows to be found", and corresponds to the *niph.* of the Hebrew מצא. The use of the present underlines the perennial value of the maxim: the Lord always allows himself to be found by those who seek him.

Εμφανίζεται is used with a reflexive/passive nuance (cf. Wis 16:21; 17:4; 18:18), chosen with care to avoid the use of ἀποκαλύπτειν which would have had clear echoes of the mysteries in an Alexandrian context. Cf. Philo who, in *Leg.* III, 27, employs ἐμφανίζω precisely in relation to the manifestation of God to the faithful soul.[5]

As for τοῖς μὴ ἀπιστοῦσιν αὐτῷ, the reading of codex A should be rejected since it seems to be a *lectio facilior* or else a theological correction: τοῖς μὴ πιστεύουσιν.[6] The verb ἀπιστέω here takes on the nuance of "not believing", "not trusting", "distrusting" (cf. Wis 10:7; 12:17; 18:13). It is absent from the LXX (8x, on the other hand, in the NT), with the exception of 2 Macc 8:13, a passage which is very useful for understand-

3 Raurell, "From δικαιοσύνη to ἀθανασία", 337 n. 18.
4 Blass/Debrunner/Rehkopf, *Grammatik,* § 335. 337,1; cf. also Scarpat, *Sapienza,* 1:108-109.
5 Scarpat, *Sapienza*, 1:74.
6 Larcher, *Sagesse,* 1:169; Vílchez Líndez, *Sapienza,* 146.

ing the sense of the verb in a context analogous to this one: "those who did not trust (ἀπιστοῦντες) in the justice of God".

v. 5. The verbal form ἐλεγχθήσεται created difficulties for the ancient interpreters.[7] It is not necessary to correct the text (cf. Ziegler, critical apparatus); Larcher leans towards a provisional solution giving the passive form ἐλεγχθήσεται a middle sense ("transforms itself into a judge") and referring the verb to the action of the spirit which disciplines man. Vílchez proposes to translate with "will be accused", in the sense that the holy spirit is being accused by the ungodly.[8] However, Scarpat's solution seems better: he preserves the force of the middle voice of ἐλεγχθήσεται as in v. 3 (where he renders it with "confuse") and translates with "will be rejected", "will be driven away".[9] The idea is that the spirit of God is driven away by human wickedness.

Synchronic Analysis

1:1: Love Justice

"Love justice". No other book in Scripture opens with an imperative. Our author chooses to open his work with two terms the first of which (ἀγαπάω) is typical of the LXX, the other (δικαιοσύνη), rich with resonances for Hebrew ears as well as Greek ones.[10] In Wisdom, the verb ἀγαπάω always has a religious nuance, indicating the fundamental attitude of God towards people (cf. Wis 11:24)[11]. The imperative ἀγαπήσατε thus introduces us within a dynamism of reciprocal love between God and humanity.

The *incipit* of the book presents itself as a reference to the texts of Ps 44:8 LXX (ἠγάπησας δικαιοσύνην) and Isa 61:8 LXX (ἐγὼ γάρ εἰμι κύριος ὁ ἀγαπῶν δικαιοσύνην); cf. 1 Chr 29:17 (δικαιοσύνην ἀγαπᾷς). Wis 1:1a also contains a reminiscence of Ps 2:10 LXX where κρίνοντες translates the Hebrew שפטי הארץ, synonym of "governors". In our case too, οἱ κρίνοντες indicates "governors" according to LXX usage. From its very beginning, therefore, Wisdom presents itself as a collection of delicately interwoven allusions to Scripture. However, no biblical text is cited explicitly. Our sage presupposes an excellent "biblical memory" on the part of his readers as well as the ability to recognise the texts which he employs.

In Wis 6:21, in a great *inclusio* at the close of the first part of the book, the invitation to the rulers "to love justice" is transformed into that of "to love wisdom", and it is precisely the latter, wisdom, which is the protagonist of the central part of the book (Wis 7-10). It is thus possible to claim that in our book we have a reflection on wisdom which is made concrete as "justice" in the daily life of the wise.

---

7 Cf. an extended discussion in Larcher, *Sagesse*, 1:176-178 who ends up declaring that he has no satisfactory solution.

8 Vílchez Líndez, *Sapienza*, 155.

9 Scarpat, *Sapienza*, 1:116-117.

10 Scarpat, *Sapienza*, 1:47-48 and 56-57, for the differences from the vocabulary of Philo who prefers to use δίκη when speaking of justice in the biblical sense

11 Wis 4:10; 6:12; 7:10, 28; 8:3, 7; 11:24; 16:26 Cf. Ceresa Gastaldo, Aldo, "Ἀγάπη nei documenti anteriori al Nuovo Testamento", *Aegyptus* 31 (1951): 296-306; De Carlo, "Ami, infatti, gli esistenti tutti"; with an extended bibliography on ἀγαπάω (cf. in connection with Wis 11:24).

Addresses of the Book

Who are those whom the sage is addressing? Some think of the Roman rulers.[12] In this case, "justice" would be considered as a political virtue. In fact, Wis 1:1 forms part of that "royal" metaphor typical of biblical wisdom which, not infrequently, is presented as the art of good governance (cf. Prov 8:15-16). Thus we are faced with a *royal fiction*, an interesting variation of that same royal fiction which opens the book of Qoheleth (Qoh 1:12-2:26). The rulers, therefore, are the actual recipients of the book of Wisdom, those Jewish young men of Alexandria who are being invited to live out a "political" virtue, that is, justice. This is necessary for them if they are to take on their responsibility as leaders of their local Jewish community. There is more. From the typical standpoint of Stoicism, there is a common idea that the sage is the only true king because he is free and is his own master.[13] From this perspective, the addressees of the book are being called to be sages and, for this very reason, to be "kings" as well.

In 1:1b, the theme of justice moves on to that of faith. The syntagma φρονήσατε περὶ refers to the sphere of man's mental activity: "form thoughts for yourself", that is, "reflect". This expression is generally followed by an adverb but here by the form ἐν ἀγαθότητι, a Semitism with modal value (cf. also ἐν ἁπλότητι). This is an invitation to reflect on who is truly Lord (περὶ κυρίου): the God of the faith of Israel (cf. Wis 14:30) who, in v. 3, alternates with θεός according to a use typical of the LXX (cf. also vv. 6, 7, 9, 13). Ἀγαθότης is generosity of soul, and is recalled with reference to God in Wis 7:26 and 12:22. For Philo, it is one of the supreme attributes of the divinity (*Cher.* 27). Referring to people, ἀγαθότης can be understood as a good disposition of the soul in its relations with God.[14]

Seeking the Lord

The addressees of the book are invited to "seek" the Lord (1c). The stich is constructed in a close parallel with the previous one: (1b) φρονήσατε (verb) περὶ τοῦ κυρίου (object of the verb) ἐν ἀγαθότητι (modality) // (1c) καὶ ἐν ἁπλότητι καρδίας (modality) ζητήσατε (verb) αὐτόν (object of the verb).

Here, the verbal form "seek him" (ζητήσατε αὐτόν) has the whole import of the "seeking God" that is so frequent in the Scriptures. Cf. Deut 4:29; Zeph 2:3 LXX; Amos 5:4-6 LXX; 1 Chr 28:9; 29:17; see ζητέω in Wis 6:12, 16; 8:2, 18; 13:6: 19:17, always with a religious tone.

The mention of ἁπλότης καρδίας is striking. It is understood as the right attitude for seeking the Lord.[15] Ἁπλότης indicates something that is not double. In the LXX, the term often translates the Hebrew תם and refers to rectitude of life, understood in both a cultic and a legal sense, to the characteristics of one who wishes to fulfil only the will of God: cf. 1 Macc 2:37; Noah in Gen 6:9; Abraham in Gen 17:1 (δικαιοσύνην ἀγαπᾷς); and Job in Job 1:1. In the prayer of David (1 Chr 29:17-19 LXX, a text already echoed in v. 1), ἁπλότης is close to the idea of rectitude of heart, moral integrity, the inability to think or act in a calculating way. Outside the LXX, ἁπλότης is described as the principal virtue characterising the

12 "The author is clearly addressing the pagan world rulers"; Winston, *Wisdom*, 101. Cf. also Vollger, "Die Adressaten des Weisheitsbuches".

13 Cf. *SVF* III, 155 frag. 597/2; III, 156 frag. 599.603; III, 158 frag. 617; III,159 frag. 620; III, 170 frag. 681.

14 Larcher, *Sagesse*, 1:166. In the LXX of outside Wisdom, the term appears only in Sir 45:23.

15 Spicq, *Notes*, 1:125-130. Cf. also Scarpat, *Sapienza,* 1:57-61.

patriarchs (T. Reu. 4:1; T. Levi 13:1) and refers to a life lived with simplicity, in obedience to the Torah. The mention of the "heart" should be understood within the frame of biblical anthropology. The heart is equivalent to the seat of reason, the will, and the conscience. It is the place where people take their most intimate decisions.

The progression of the ideas contained in v. 1 is clear. The addressees of the book are invited to adopt a voluntary and preferential inclination towards the value of divine justice ("love") which has, at the same time, a human and political dimension. They are thus being invited to turn to a benevolent reflection about the one who is really the Lord ("reflect") and, finally, they are being called to a "simple" opening of themselves to his will, adopting the attitude of "seeking". Right from the beginning of the book, then, the κύριος of Israel appears at the centre of our sage's reflection.

The initial tone of the book also suggests a polemical point. The Jewish leaders are being invited to seek the true God, the Lord, with simplicity and without following the speculations and the ideas coming from the Hellenistic world. The background to v. 1 is biblical. Even so, the acceptance of the Stoic category of wisdom understood as something royal is already a prime example of how, in the face of Greek culture, our author has a standpoint which is also dialogic in character.

Verse 2 is closely linked to the previous one by the particle ὅτι which here 1:2
corresponds well to the Hebrew כִּי.[16] From v. 2 to v. 5, there is a predominance of negative reasons relating to the obstacles which could be encountered by the addressees of the book in following justice. Two positive reasons appear only in v. 6, and later in v. 15.

God allows himself to be found (εὑρίσκεται) by those who seek him. The double rhetorical use of *litotes* ("those who do not test him"; "those who do not lack faith in him") highlights the fact that possible obstacles arise only from people. This is the case for the people of Israel who repeatedly put the Lord to the test in the desert. Wisdom employs πειράζω on seven occasions (1:2; 2:17, 24; 3:5, 11:9; 12:26; 19:5). In all these texts, the idea is always present that the moment of testing reveals the true dispositions of people in their relations with God. Here, however, we have the only case where the subject of the verb is human and the object God, and the verb has the sense of "putting to the test", "tempting". It is the Israelites, therefore, who are putting the Lord to the test. It is they and not the pagan rulers who are the real addressees of the book.

The Lord reveals himself, then, to those who do not refuse to believe in him (2b). The use of ἀπιστέω is mentioned to emphasise the need for a relationship of faith understood as trust in God without which the link with the Lord cannot exist. To know God, or rather to believe in him, appears to be the most important thing for our sage. Faith trumps ethics.[17]

---

16 On ὅτι as a particle which structures the entire chapter, cf. Reiterer, "Philosophische Lehre", 132-135.

17 Gilbert, "La connaissance de Dieu", especially 312-314. Cf. Keller, "Glaube", with different conclusions.

1:3 Verse 3 acts as the proof of what has been affirmed in the previous verses and represents the centre of the whole argument of 1:1-5. The initial γὰρ links it directly with what goes before. The first stich places the emphasis on the interior nature of a person, on his "thoughts" (λογισμοί), rather than on his actions. It is the first indication of the importance that Wisdom awards to human reason. On the other hand, it is precisely reason that is not upright, "devious" (σκολιός), which separates people from God, thus representing the antithesis of everything which a faithful Jew is called to live. This statement, placed at the beginning of the book, appears to be categorical. But what kind of devious thoughts does our sage have in mind? We do not yet have a clear picture. However, our sage does seem to be concerned with the purity of the faith of his community.

In 1:3b, "power" (ἡ δύναμις) comes on the stage, presented as a personified attribute of God's activity or rather as a kind of divine energy in action according to a perspective that is certainly more Hellenistic than biblical.[18]

This "power" of God, if put to the test (δοκιμαζομήνη),[19] punishes (ἐλέγχει) whoever does not follow the Lord. The text of 3b appears to be linked to the previous stich by the particle τε which takes on a consecutive nuance ("so that"). The author's thought seems to be as follows: devious thoughts separate from God *so that* divine power confounds the foolish. Ἄφρονες is a play on φρονήσατε (1b). The term is frequent in the LXX, especially in Proverbs, and is mostly a translation of the Hebrew כסיל, a person who is unreasonable, obtuse, capable of devious thoughts and thus morally perverse (cf. ἄφρονες in Wis 3:2, 12; 5:4; 12:24; 14:11; 15:5, 14).

1:4 The allusion to the "foolish" (1:3b) prepares for the appearance of the figure of wisdom (σοφία), placed in emphatic position at the end of the first stich and set in relation with the divine "power" of the previous verse by the particle ὅτι which opens the verse.

Σοφία, the Hebrew חכמה, is a phenomenon well known to the Jews of the time. Continuing on the lines marked out by the discourses of personified wisdom in Prov 1-9, where it appears to be something closely linked with God and, at the same time, with human beings, our sage places σοφία immediately in relation to God, connecting it with the divine power that has just been mentioned. At the same time, wisdom appears as something which also concerns peoples' interior nature. The two verbs which describe its action ("enter" and "dwell") confirm its twofold character.

The fact remains that it is not the presence of wisdom in people that is being described in this verse but rather its absence. Wisdom does not enter the one who rejects it. It does not dwell with one who lives in sin.

Soul and Body

Verse 4 represents a first approach to the particular anthropological concepts of our sage. With "soul" and "body", he intends to refer to the human being as a whole. The ψυχή seems to be conceived of as an active principle, the subject of specific moral

---

18 Larcher, *Sagesse*, 1:171-172. The doctrine of the divine powers will be developed by Philo in particular.

19 On δοκιμάζω, cf. Spicq, *Notes*, Supp. 160-161. Here, the verb seems synonymous with πειράζω and has the sense of "putting to the test". For the Latin version (*probata autem virtus*), which misinterprets the meaning of the verb, cf. Scarpat, *Sapienza*, 1:414.

activities. Here, it is associated with the adjective κακότεχνος, a poetic and learned term (cf. Homer, *Il.* 15.14) which, in Greek use, indicates someone who works badly at his trade. In the LXX, κακότεχνος occurs only in 4 Macc 6:25 (cf. Wis 15:4), but with reference to things. Here, used with reference to the soul, κακότεχνος indicates the soul itself inasmuch as it makes a conscious decision to do evil. In Stoic philosophy, the ψυχή has a role of primary importance and is sometimes placed in relation to the τέχνη which is described as a system of understanding coordinated with experience and aimed at the good use of the events of life.[20]

The highly rare κακότεχνος thus acquires the flavour of an oxymoron. The system of understanding which lies at the basis of Greek thought is "wicked" (κακός) if it is not accompanied by a clear ethical perspective. The following stich is a clear introduction to the theme of sin (ἁμαρτία).

The body is seen as a passive reality, even if it too is the object of the dwelling of wisdom (κατοικέω). The σῶμα is described with the term κατάχρεως,[21] to be understood in the sense of "slave" or else of "debtor", here, obviously, in a metaphorical sense. The "debt" is that of sin (ἁμαρτία; in Wisdom only again in Wis 10:13) which oppresses the body, making it just that, a slave. Our author does not specify what sin he is concerned with, but the immediate context makes us suppose it is wrong thoughts about the deity, lack of faith in God.

The whole person, therefore, body and soul, appears to be subject to the power of sin. However, under Hellenistic influence, our author tends to distinguish the two elements and to give the soul a certain pre-eminence. Yet, this is of a nature that is more psychological than ontological. If the soul is able to commit evil, the body appears rather as the slave of sin. The text also allows us to think of some kind of personification of sin along the lines which will be particularly developed by some NT texts such as Rom 7:14 or John 8:34. However, sin does not seem to be a reality bound up with the fact that the soul is somehow a Platonic prisoner of the body.

In introducing a new figure, that of the ἅγιον πνεῦμα παιδείας, v. 5 acts as the 1:5
explanation (ἅγιον γάρ) for the possibility of the absence of wisdom described in the previous verse. The "holy spirit of παιδεία" is placed in parallel with σοφία. The theme of the spirit appears in three consecutive verses: in 1:5 and in 1:7 on its own, in v. 6 in connection with the figure of wisdom.

In associating wisdom with the spirit, our sage is insisting with greater emphasis on the relationship between wisdom and God and, at the same, underlining the presence of wisdom in people. Thus, the fact that this holy spirit does not tolerate the deceitful one (δόλος) and shuns foolish thoughts and injustice (5bc) emphasises the presentation of wisdom in a moral key. The theme of "foolish thoughts" (λογισμοί ἀσύνετοι) takes up the "devious thoughts" mentioned in 1:3a. The expression λογισμοί ἀσύνετοι is resumed in Wis 11:15, precisely in connection with ἀδικία. In 11:15, the foolish thoughts refer to idolatry, confirming the idea that here too, as already in 1:3a, the devious or foolish λογισμοί of people are to be understood as wrong conceptions of God.

In the book of Wisdom, the use of παιδεία in Wis 3:11 and 7:14 comes close to the Greek idea of "education". In 2:12 and 17:2, however, the connection is rather that of παιδεία and the law. The ἀπαίδευτοι of Wis 17:1 are those Jews who have rejected discipline, the education offered by Wisdom, that is, the Mosaic law.

---

20 Cf. *SVF* II, 30, frags. 94, 95, and 96.

21 Note the use of alliteration: κακότεχνον; κατοικήσει; κατάχρεῳ.

Cf. Wis 2:12, where παιδεία and νόμος are set in a reciprocal relationship. In the book of Wisdom, behind the idea of παιδεία, there lies a biblical-sapiential vision rather than the humanistic Greek ideal, even if the latter does not seem to be excluded *a priori*.[22] The true formation of a person is that imparted by the Lord himself by means of his holy spirit of discipline present in wisdom. In the context of the book as a whole, the "holy spirit of discipline" is what teaches the discernment of the will of God expressed in the law, as in Wis 9:17. It is for this reason that the spirit shuns injustice and all false thoughts about God.

Diachronic Analysis

1:1a The reference to those who "govern on earth" right at the beginning of the book (1:1a) could lead to the thought of human justice as conceived by the Greek world. However, the religious background of the use of ἀγαπάω points us rather in the direction of the justice of *God*, that צדקה (righteousness) which the biblical tradition very often connects with salvation, truth, and mercy.[23] This is the same "immortal justice" mentioned in the *inclusio* in 1:15, a justice that is clearly divine. If someone loves it, he obtains with it all the other virtues, including "justice" understood as a political virtue (cf. 8:7).

1:1c If the reference to "simplicity of heart" in 1:1c can seem a touch Greek, the theme of the search for God leads us into a dimension that is profoundly biblical. God is never an object, a truth that is offered to humanity from on high. God is rather a living and real person who has to be sought.

1:2 In v. 2 also, the theme of "seeking God" is biblical: cf. Isa 55:6; 65:1; Jer 29:13; Hos 10:12; 1 Chr 28:9; 2 Chr 15:2, 4, 15. As for the verb πειράζω, it refers to the context of Exod 17:1-7 and, in particular, to v. 7, where the subject is represented by the Israelites and the object by the Lord: διὰ τὸ πειράζειν κύριον λέγοντας εἰ ἔστιν κύριος ἐν ἡμῖν ἢ οὔ; (cf. also Pss 77:41, 56 LXX and 105:14 LXX).

1:3 In confirmation of the Exodus background, Wis 1:3b adds δοκιμάζω, which is found precisely with πειράζω in Ps 94:9 LXX, again with reference to the episode at Massah and Meribah: οὗ ἐπείρασαν οἱ πατέρες ὑμῶν ἐδοκίμασαν καὶ εἴδοσαν τὰ ἔργα μου. Moreover, ἐμφανίζω (cf. Wis 16:21) confirms the Exodus context. Cf. Exod 33:13 LXX: "If I have found favour in your eyes, show yourself to me" (ἐμφάνισόν μοι σεαυτόν). Together with our verse, this passage is the only text in the LXX in which ἐμφανίζω appears with God as subject.

1:4 In Wis 1:4, in referring, albeit negatively, to an "entrance" of wisdom into the soul and its dwelling in the body, our sage is developing an idea present in germ in Proverbs: in Prov 2:10; 3:13; 4:7; 7:4; 8:17, wisdom is presented as a feminine

---

22 "Der Paideia-Begriff des Weisheits-buches bleibt ganz im Rahmen des Alten Testaments" (Ziener, *Begriffsprache*, 103). The aim of παιδεία is that of bringing men into a correct knowledge of God. It is not an education with anthropocentric aims as it was with the Greeks. On the other hand, in Jewish texts in Greek, like the Letter of Aristeas, παιδεία becomes a clear meeting point between the Greek and Jewish worlds. Cf. Boccaccini, *Medio Giudaismo*, 138-142.

23 Cf. an excellent discussion in Scarpat, *Sapienza*, 1:47-48 and 51-57.

figure who is available to all who seek her.[24] Nor is there an absence of some aspects belonging to Hellenistic religiosity. The theme of wisdom's "dwelling" in people could be actually of Stoic origin.[25]

1:5 In presenting the figure of the holy spirit in v. 5, after mentioning justice (v. 1), the divine power (v. 3) and wisdom (v. 4), the author is aware that he is speaking of something well known to the biblical tradition. Cf. Ps 50:13 LXX; Dan 4:5 LXX [8 Th], 6 LXX [9 Th], 15 LXX [18 Th]; 5:12 LXX; and 6:4 LXX. Here, the "holy spirit" is probably being introduced in the light of Isa 63:10-14 where the spirit of God is described as the one who flees on account of the sins of Israel. What is new in this presentation of the "holy spirit" when compared with the biblical texts which mention him is the description of him as the "spirit of παιδ-εία". In v. 6, he becomes, instead, the "spirit of wisdom".

Paideia

In Greek usage, παιδεία refers to everything that belongs to human education.[26] In the LXX, however, παιδεία translates a concept which is typically sapiential, מוסר, a term that contains within itself a double idea:[27] first of all, that of "punishing", "correcting", with reference to the pedagogical methods typical of antiquity (cf. Prov 13:24; 22:15; 23:13; Job 5:17). In this sense, מוסר appears in the book of Proverbs paired with תוכחת, "reproof" (Prov 3:11; 5:12; 6:23). A second idea is that of "instructing", "educating". As in Prov 1:2, מוסר appears in connection with חכמה (Prov 3:8 and 4:1, 13; 8:10). In Prov 1:8, מוסר is linked with תורה understood in the sense of "instruction" and not so much as of "law". Therefore, the term מוסר carries within itself what we could call "education" or "formation". The text of Prov 1:2a LXX is significant: τοῦ γνῶναι σοφίαν καὶ παιδείαν Wisdom and sapiential education seem to be connected with each other, as in Wis 1:5a, 6a.

Wis 1:6-10: Wisdom is a Philanthropic Spirit

6 For wisdom is a spirit, the friend of humanity,
but will not leave unpunished the one who blasphemes with his own lips,
because God is the witness of his feelings [kidneys]
and the true searcher of his heart
and hears what the tongue says.
7 For the spirit of the Lord fills the earth
and the one who holds all things together knows every voice.
8 Therefore no one who speaks unjust things can remain hidden from him,
and accusing justice will not pass him by without notice.

24 At the same time, our sage seems to betray the influence of some currents of Jewish piety attested at Qumran. Cf. Larcher, *Etudes*, 123 n. 5.

25 Larcher, *Etudes*, 253 and n. 7; Winston, *Wisdom*, 102. Cf. Larcher, *Sagesse*,1:174 for the notable patristic resonances of this verse. Cf. also the critical apparatus of Ziegler, *sub loco*.

26 Jäger, Werner *Paideia. Die Formung des griechischen Menschen*, I-III, Berlin-Leipzig: De Gruyter 1934-1947.

27 Branson, Robert D., *jāsar, mûsār, TDOT* 6:129-134.

9 For on the plots of the ungodly an inquest will be opened,
the sound of his words will reach the Lord,
in condemnation of his iniquities;
10 because an ear full of jealousy hears everything,
not even the whisper of murmurings remains secret.

Notes on the Text and Translation

v. 6a. Codices A and V and some minuscules, as well as the Latin version (cf. Ziegler, apparatus), read: πνεῦμα σοφίας, a probable *lectio facilior* which arose to harmonise the text with that of v. 5a where we find a similar form: πνεῦμα παιδείας. On the other hand, the reading of the majority of the witnesses (πνεῦμα σοφία) makes wisdom the subject of the entire phrase and brings wisdom still closer to the spirit: "wisdom is a spirit ...".

v. 7b. In the language of Stoicism, συνέχειν is a technical term for indicating the power of the divine *Logos* which "contains", "embraces" or, better, holds together the universe (cf. the translation of Lat: *hoc quod continet omnia*). Cf. *SVF* II, 137, frag. 416; II, 144, frag. 439.26; II, 144-145, frag. 440; II, 146, frag. 444; and II, 147, frag. 448. In all these texts, συνέχειν indicates the activity of the *pneuma* which guarantees unity and internal cohesion to the cosmos. Cf. *SVF* II, 144, frag. 439.26: τὴν μὲν γὰρ πνευματικὴν οὐσίαν τὸ συνέχον ...: "the pneumatic substance is that which holds together...", that is, it is the force of cohesion which pervades the world. However, by associating it with πληρόω, our author shows that he does not intend to give συνέχειν a pantheistic sense as in the Stoic usage. In fact, the spirit of the Lord is something quite distinct from the creation, something which fills the creation which, although being present in it, is nonetheless distinguished from it.

Synchronic Analysis

1:6a "Wisdom (is) a spirit ...". This has the flavour of a definition. The association between wisdom and the spirit is one of the most significant theological novelties put forward by our sage. Wisdom and spirit are here attributed to God himself insofar as he reveals himself to people; and yet it seems as though our sage does not wish to make a full identification of the two realities. Rather, he seems to be suggesting that to welcome the φιλάνθρωπον spirit of God leads one to possess wisdom also.[28]

In the light of what he already knows of the Scriptures, the Israelite who listens to this text – φιλάνθρωπον γὰρ πνεῦμα σοφία –understands that the wisdom which was put forward by the sages and praised as a companion of life (cf. Prov 8:32-36) is not different from that "holy spirit of discipline" introduced in Wis 1:5 and well known to the biblical tradition as the "spirit of God" present in man.

---

28 Contra Hübner: "Weisheit und heiliger Geist werden demnach identifiziert"; *Weisheit*, 32. Cf. Engel, *Weisheit*, 53-54, who notes the close link in 1:1-5 on the level of internal structure and so considers wisdom and spirit as manifestations of God himself. Cf. again Van Imschoot, "Sagesse et esprit"; Larcher, *Etudes*, 361-376; Gilbert, "L'Esprit Saint dans le livre de la Sagesse"; Mazzinghi, "La sapienza è uno spirito che ama l'uomo".

This association between wisdom and spirit causes the author to attribute to wisdom many characteristics of the spirit of God contained in the Bible of Israel. Wisdom thus acquires a cosmic role (Wis 1:7; 7:22b-23) and becomes a sign of the presence of God in the world, and the active principle in creation (8:1) and in people, a source of the moral life (7:24, 27). Wisdom becomes an interior power which enables a person to understand the will of God expressed in the law, just like the spirit announced in Ezekiel 36 (cf. Wis 9:17).

Between 6a and 6b, there exists an apparent variance between the "spirit 1:6b
friend of humanity" and the mention of the same spirit as one who will not leave the blasphemer unpunished (ἀθῳόω means "consider innocent"). The καὶ in 6b has adversative force, just as in Num 14:18 LXX.[29] Thus, the sense of v. 6ab is that wisdom is a spirit, the friend of humanity, *but* that he will not leave the blasphemer unpunished. The βλάσφημος is primarily one who is sceptical about the divine action, in this case the philanthropy of God. For this person, there is no pardon despite the kindness of wisdom. Our sage has in mind those Alexandrian Jews who were putting the action and the presence of the God of Israel in doubt.[30] This is the first appearance of that close connection between the mercy and justice of God which characterises the whole work. This was a problem that was very alive in the Judaism of the time. It had already been observed by Ben Sirach, even if the "mercy-justice" dichotomy was not resolved by him but only stated: the mercy of God does not annul his punitive justice (cf. Sir 16:11-12).

However, our author does not seem to wish to tackle a real problem of theodicy. For him, it appears wholly natural that divine philanthropy can also have a punitive aspect. In fact, he does not concern himself with attenuating the negative impact which the idea of the wrath of God and of punishment could have on his listeners. On the contrary, precisely the awareness that the blasphemer will not remain unpunished is a clear sign of the fact that the "spirit" is really the "friend of humanity". As already in Isa 63:10-14, the spirit of the Lord both saves and punishes (cf. Prov 1:23). Thus, philanthropy does not exclude justice. On the contrary, the spirit becomes the mirror of the goodness and mercy of God even when it is punishing men.

In these three stichs, the context is still that of judgement. Starting with 6c, 1:6c–e
there is a sudden change of subject: it is no longer wisdom or the spirit but God himself who is described with three substantives (μάρτυς, ἐπίσκοπος, ἀκουστής). In this way, wisdom and the spirit are brought back to God as aspects of his activity and as realities that are closely connected with him.

God is here called "witness" (μάρτυς) (cf. Gen 31:44; Jer 36:23 LXX [29:23 MT]). God is also called ἐπίσκοπος, to be understood as true or rigorous (ἀληθής) "searcher" or "inspector" of the "heart", that is, of the conscience. Finally, God is described as "hearer of the tongue", or careful listener to what man says. Here, ἀκουστής is employed in an etymological sense as "one who listens". If God knows a person's interior ("heart and kidneys"), *a fortiori* he listens to what he is saying,

29 Cf. Blass/Debrunner/Rehkopf, *Grammatik*, 442,1; contra Larcher, *Sagesse*, 1:179-181.

30 "In this statement of our author, it is difficult not to hear a criticism of his fellow citizens of Alexandria who, having been subjected to oppression by the pagans (Egyptians and Romans), have given vent to words which were blasphemies against Providence..." (Scarpat, *Sapienza*, 1:118).

knows what he is speaking. The mention of the tongue refers directly to the "blasphemer" cited in 6b whose wicked speech cannot escape from God.

1:7 Verse 7a opens with a ὅτι explicative and continues the reasons for v. 6: a universal presence of the "spirit", subject of the entire verse,[31] who "fills" τὴν οἰκουμένην, a term which in itself indicates the inhabited earth but which can be extended to the entire world, the universe.

It is not impossible that our author had in mind Gen 1:2 where the mention of the πνεῦμα θεοῦ is along the lines of a benevolent divine presence in its relations with the entire creation.

With the expression τὸ συνέχον τὰ πάντα, our author is referring to an influence of the spirit of God in the cosmos which guarantees its cohesion and its harmony. The activity of the spirit is extended particularly to human beings and is a conscious activity which emphasises still further the significance of this personification. In fact, the spirit γνῶσιν ἔχει φωνῆς: "knows (every) voice". Since, in recording the figure of the blasphemer, the previous verse (1:6) referred to human speech, the concluding expression of 7b does not seem to be out of place. Precisely on account of its cosmic presence, the spirit knows what someone can say and so is linked with the divine activity described in 6e (τῆς γλώσσης ἀκουστής).

In this way, the book of Wisdom can deal with a problem that is not only of a cosmic but also of an anthropological character, namely, that of the presence of God in people (cf. 7:24, 27 and 9:17). Indeed, the spirit that holds all things together knows every voice (1:7b).

1:8-10 Verses 8-10 go deeper into the theme of *speech* contained in 7b.[32] Verse 8 is closely linked to the previous text by the initial διὰ τοῦτο. No one who utters unjust things (φθεγγόμενος ἄδικα) can claim to be able to hide from the spirit of the Lord (cf. Wis 17:3a).

The divine judgement will be not only on the speech of the ungodly man but also on his thoughts which are at their root (v. 9). The term διαβούλιον is used *in malam partem* (Hos 4:9; 7:2) and emphasises the plots of the ungodly (ἀσεβοῦς). This is the first explicit reference to the ungodly in Wisdom. On the part of God (κύριος cited in 9b), there will be an inquest into the thoughts of the ungodly. The term ἐξέτασις has an eschatological nuance, as is the case with ἐξετασμός in Wis 4:6 and ἐξετάζειν in 6:3.

The thoughts of the ungodly (9a) are followed by his words (9b), and his words by his actions (ἀνόμημα; 9c). The book of Wisdom is alert to the interior processes of sin. The speech of the ungodly does not escape the Lord (9b) in order that his sins (ἀνόμημα; 9c; cf. Wis 3:14; 4:20) may be punished. In 9c, the eschatological nuance of ἐξέτασις is strengthened by the expression εἰς ἔλεγχον, "in condemnation" which is also used in the book of Wisdom in eschatological contexts (cf. 2:14; 18:5). Cf. ἐλέγχω which has already been used in 1:8b. Thus, at the beginning of the book, there is introduced, albeit with discretion, another of the great leading themes of the work: reflection on the final destiny of people. However, in the

31 This is a text much used by the Fathers of the Church as well as in the Catholic liturgy of Pentecost. Cf. Larcher, *Sagesse*, 1:184.

32 Reiterer, "Philosophische Lehre", 138-139.

light of v. 9 alone, it is impossible to say whether, in speaking of "inquest" and condemnation, our author is thinking of a personal judgement or a collective one.

Verse 10 contains the reason for the two preceding verses. The initial ὅτι has an explicative value. The use of γογγυσμός, "murmuring", reinforces the idea that our author sees in the ungodly those Israelites of his time who have lost their faith in the God of Israel. These murmurings do not remain hidden from God (οὐκ ἀποκρύπτεται). The verse closes with another allusion to the divine judgement. Thus, the vocabulary employed in 1:6-10 is characterised by its judicial aspect,[33] creating a dramatic contrast with the description of the spirit of wisdom which loves people and which pervades the whole world with his presence.

Diachronic Analysis

In the Jewish Scriptures, the theme of the "holy spirit" which is introduced in Wis 1:6 1:6
refers to a dynamic reality that characterises the relationship between people and God, and which, in many cases, expresses the presence of God in people, often in relation to a specific mission that they are called on to carry out (cf. Isa 11:2; 61:1; Ezek 36:26-27). In the sapiential tradition, the "holy spirit" appears in connection with wisdom only in Prov 1:23. There, personified wisdom is presented as the one who possesses the very spirit of God and is ready to pour it out on the one who listens: "Behold, I will pour out my spirit on you and reveal my words to you".[34] Ben Sirach (Sir 1:8-10) seems to apply to wisdom what the prophets (cf. Joel 3:1) had said of the spirit of God. Whereas the prophets waited for the future for such a gift, for Ben Sirach, wisdom is something which has already been granted to the man of God.

In 1:6a, we find a still more important novelty: the holy spirit is described as φιλάνθρωπος, "the friend of humanity". Wisdom is accepting a humanistic ideal that is typically Greek, namely, philanthropy, seen here, as already in Plato, as a divine quality which also becomes a political quality that, for Wisdom, can come to belong to everyone.[35] In fact, the God of Israel possesses a "philanthropic spirit", which loves people. However, in order to realise this ideal of friendship, the only way accessible is that marked out by wisdom.

In 1:6b, the term βλάσφημος is rare in the LXX and appears there always in religious contexts and with reference to God: 2 Macc 9:28; 10:4, 36; Sir 3:16; Is

---

33 Kolarcik, *The Ambiguity of Death*, 63-68.

34 In fact, in Prov 1:23, the theme of the spirit can be understood *in malam partem* as the expression of the divine wrath which strikes whomever does not listen to the words of wisdom Cf. Gilbert, Maurice, "Le discours menaçant de la Sagesse en Proverbes 1,20-33" in: Garrone Daniele – Israel Felice (edd.), *Storia e Tradizioni d'Israele. Scritti in onore di J.A. Soggin* (Brescia: Paideia 1991), 102-106.

35 Cf. Spicq, *Notes*, 2:922-926; Id., "La Philanthropie hellénistique, vertu divine et royale [à propos de Tite III,4]", *ST* 12 (1958): 169-191; Le Déaut, Roger, "*Philanthropia* dans la littérature grecque jusqu'au Nouveau Testament [Tite III,4]", in *Mélanges E. Tisserant. Ecriture Sainte. Ancient Orient*, vol. I, Città del Vaticano: Biblioteca Apostolica Vaticana 1964, 255-294; George, S., "Philantropie im Buche der Weisheit", *Bibel und Leben* 11 (1970): 189-198. Cf. also Scarpat, *Sapienza*, 1:82-87.

66:3. An analogous use is found in Philo: for those who τῶν εἰς τὸ θεῖον βλασφημούντων, there is no forgiveness (*Fug.* 84).

In 1:6c, the pair "kidneys and heart" is a biblical expression present in various texts of the LXX. Cf. Pss 7:10; 25:2; 72:21; Jer 11:20; 17:10; 20:12. Except for Ps 72:21, in all these cases, the reference is to God who searches and knows the kidneys and heart of man, that is, his inner being. As for the idea of the divinity as "witness", on the other hand, it seems to be Greek in origin. Cf. Pindar, *Pyth.* 4.297; Sophocles, *Trach.* 1248. Appeal is made to the witness of the gods in relation to pacts or oaths because the gods know the real intentions of men. Philo make use of this concept in *Cher.* 17; *Ios.* 265; *Migr.* 115.

The term ἐπίσκοπος (1:6d) appears in the LXX as referring to God only in Job 20:29 while it is more frequent in the Greek environment to indicate the divinity which knows and is concerned with human affairs.[36] The idea is already in Homer (cf. *Il.* 22.225), where we find the expression μάρτυροι καὶ ἐπίσκοποι used with reference to the gods. Philo employs both terms to speak of God (cf. *Leg.* 3.43). Indeed, God is the ὁ τῶν ὅλων ἐπίσκοπος (*Somn.* 1.91), the God who sees everything and from whom wickedness cannot escape (cf. also *Migr.* 81, 115, 135, etc.). In Wis 2:20; 3:7, 13, our sage will introduce the theme of the ἐπισκοπή, the eschatological visitation of God.

Finally, in relation to 1:6ce, we observe that the mention of three parts of the human body, the kidneys, the heart, and the tongue is typical of the language of the Bible. Biblical too is the idea that God knows every person and is the true judge of them, whereas the three terms referring to God – μάρτυς, ἐπίσκοπος, ἀκουστής – betray the Greek influence.

1:7 In Wis 1:7, the idea that the Lord fills the earth is not a new one for Scripture. Cf. Jer 23:24 LXX: μὴ οὐχὶ τὸν οὐρανὸν καὶ τὴν γῆν ἐγὼ πληρῶ; λέγει κύριος (cf. Isa 6:3). It is possible that our sage is inspired by both these texts (Jer 23:24 and Gen 1:2; see above, the synchronic analysis), not to mention Ps 103:30 LXX, where there is emphasis on the activity of the spirit *vis à vis* the creation, as well as Ps 138:7 LXX, which highlights the omniscient activity of the spirit (ποῦ πορευθῶ ἀπὸ τοῦ πνεύματός σου;).

In Philo, the verb πληρόω characterises a philosophical reflection on the presence of God, but never in relation to the πνεῦμα.[37] Thus, the thought expressed in 7a seems biblical even if no text of Scripture speaks explicitly of the spirit of God who "fills" created reality. Our sage is probably extending an idea that is already implicit in Gen 2:7. Not only does God breathe the πνοὴ ζωῆς into the human but the presence of God's spirit is extended to the entire creation (cf Wis 7:22-23 and 12:1).

If the first part of v. 7 can be explained well by reflection on a series of biblical texts, Greek influence appears a good deal more marked in 7b. The use of συνέχω adds an idea of unity and cohesion. Such a reflection on the cosmic role of the spirit derives largely from the openness of our text to the cultural contributions of Stoicism (cf. above).

---

36 Beyer, Hermann Wolfgang, ἐπίσκοπος, *TDNT* 2:608-622.

37 Larcher, *Sagesse,* 1:183 and the texts cited there. We note that the perfect πεπλήρωκεν indicates a past action, the effects of which last into the present. We should reject the variant of codex A, ἐπλήρωσε, which probably arose on the basis of a reference to Gen 1:2.

Here, we find a brilliant way of giving dynamic expression to the activity of God in the world. By uniting biblical concepts (7a) with ideas that are Greek in origin (7b), the author of Wisdom wished to evoke divine activity in the world in this way, as a kind of immanent energy, as a spirit which remains nonetheless in contact with its own transcendent source, God. In 1:7b, seeking to explain what was stated in 7a concerning the universal presence of the spirit, Wisdom is precisely intending to avoid the pantheism of the Stoics even while making use of their concepts. The biblical figure of the spirit, reread through Stoic categories, allows our author to express a presence of God in the world without confusing the two.

In 1:8b, there appears the personified figure of divine justice (ἡ δίκη), intro- 1:8
duced in Greek fashion (cf. Add Esth E,4 = 8:12d; Acts 28:4). Noticeable also is the play on words ἄδικα – δίκη. Our sage could also have been inspired by Isa 59:13-14 LXX, in a not dissimilar context. Divine justice assumes here a punitive aspect. For the verb ἐλέγχω, cf. 1:3. The verb παροδεύω is used here. It occurs in the LXX only in Wisdom (cf. 2:7; 5:14; 6:22; 10:8, apart from in Ezek 36:34).

The biblical background of v. 10 is clear, beginning with the Semitism οὖς 1:10
ζηλώσεως, "jealous ear" (cf. the πνεῦμα ζηλώζεως recorded in Num 5:14 and 30). In this case also, our sage constructs plays on words, like that on οὖς and θροῦς. This last term is present in the LXX only in 1 Macc 9:39 and is to be understood as "murmur", "whisper". It is right to see in the expression οὖς ζηλώσεως not so much the biblical theme of the "jealous God", as rather that of a God who is very alert and zealous, who does not allow any murmuring to go unpunished.

The theme of murmuring confirms the reprise of the Exodus background with which the book opened. Γογγυσμός, in fact, comes from texts such as Exod 16:7, 9, 12; Num 17:20, and 25 (cf. also Exod 15:24; Num 14:2; and 17:6) where it is employed with reference to the murmurings of the Israelites in the desert, and it is used here almost as a synonym of "blasphemy".

Wis 1:11-12:
Do Not Seek Death!

11 Keep yourselves, therefore, from useless murmuring,
and avoid the tongue of slander,
because not even a word spoken in secret will escape without consequences
and a lying mouth slays the soul.
12 Do not strive to seek death by the error of your life,
nor bring ruin upon yourselves by the works of your hands!

Notes on the Text and Translation

v. 11. Φυλάξασθε (middle) should be translated here as „keep yourselves from...! Protect yourselves from!". Φυλάσσω in the active and middle voices in the LXX is bound with the accusative, meaning „regard, maintain, adhere", particularly regarding the

observation of the law (cf. Wis 6:4, 10). With the meaning „protect oneself from“ in the LXX, the middle-voiced φυλάσσομαι appears in statements with the prepostion ἀπό (e.g., Jdg 13:13; Jer 9:3; Mic 7:5; Sir 4:20; 12:11; 22:13, 26; 32:22). However, as in Classical Greek, the simple accusative is possible, as found here.
Φείδομαι is bound here, as in Classical Greek, with a genitive object (γλώσσης), but nonetheless also in a Hebraising manner with a prepositional phrase (ἀπὸ καταλαλιᾶς); cf. Job 33:18 LXX; Ps 18:14 LXX; 77:50 LXX: „c'est là un exemple caractéristique de la double personalité littéraire de l'auteur“, zugleich griechisch und hebräisch (Larcher, *Sagesse* I, 191).

Synchronic Analysis

1:11 This verse draws the conclusions (τοίνυν) from the previous reflection on the theme of speech, increasing the tension between the goodness of God and human sin. The text opens with a double imperative (φυλάξασθε ... φείσασθε) to be linked with the other two in v. 12 μὴ ζηλοῦτε ... μηδὲ ἐπισπᾶσθε. With this new series of imperatives, our author intends to indicate the moral consequences which his listeners are warned they will be taking on themselves if they do not wish to accept his words.

The term γογγυσμός constitutes a hook-word with the previous section and prolongs the Exodus background of these verses. Beside the murmurings against God, here described as "useless", ἀνωφελῆ, there appears a new term, *καταλαλιά. In light of the καταλαλεῖν present in Num 21:5, 7; and Ps 77:19 LXX, it is possible to understand καταλαλιά as malicious speech spoken against God. From this point of view, it could simply be considered a synonym of γογγυσμός. In the light of Ps 100:5 LXX (τὸν καταλαλοῦντα λάθρᾳ τοῦ πλησίον αὐτοῦ), it is possible also to think of slander proper. Just as previously (cf. vv. 6-10), the book of Wisdom does not have in mind only a fault in relations with God but also in dealings with one's neighbour. It is from these murmurings and this slander that one must keep oneself (φυλάξασθε, φείδεσθαι). In this way, there is indirect preparation for the speech of the ungodly (Wis 2:1-20).

The importance given to the theme of speech is such that, in 1:11c, our sage notes again that "a word spoken in secret (*λαθραῖος)" κενὸν οὐ πορεύσεται. This expression is an idiotism: "it does not go away empty from it (from man's mouth: understood here: ἐκ τοῦ στώματος)", "does not escape without consequences", that is, human speech is never neutral on the moral plane.

The text of 1:11d then introduces the figure of the calumniator (στῶμα *καταψευδόμενον, the "lying mouth"), to be understood as one who speaks against God, uttering lies against him, but, at the same time also, against his neighbour: whoever does not think of the Lord in a way that is well disposed (1:1), who puts him to the test (1:2), who thinks in a devious manner (1:3-5), and who blasphemes (1:6).

In 11d, our sage begins to prepare the theme of death which he will develop in 1:13-15 and to which the whole of chapter 2 will be devoted. The result of lying is so serious that it "slays the soul" (ἀναιρεῖ ψυχήν). The use of the present after the future (cf. 11c) should not be a surprise, given that πορεύσεται has a gnomic value. The present refers to an immediate consequence of the lying.

In 11d, ἀναιρέω is to be understood in its proper sense of "slay, murder" as in Wis 14:24. An analogous expression is found in Sir 21:2 with the proper sense of "kill": ὀδόντες λέοντος οἱ ὀδόντες αὐτῆς ἀναιροῦντες ψυχὰς ἀνθρώπων. In this case, it is fairly clearly the Hebrew נפש that is intended with ψυχή. However, in our context, ψυχή could simply mean "life", despite the use which our author has already made of it in 1:4 (cf. Wis 14:5).[38] However, it is precisely in the light of 1:4 that it is preferable also to think of ψυχή as the soul understood as a spiritual principle, in this sense contrasted with the "body". Perhaps the text is being deliberately ambiguous. Of what death, then, is v. 11d speaking?

Some authors prefer to leave the text vague, while many think of *spiritual* death, loss of friendship with God, a death of the soul which in some way anticipates that of the body.[39] Scarpat thinks of the death of the soul understood as the loss of immortality: "The true life, that of the soul, is killed by lying which is considered among the major sins, so much so that the verb used is typical of murderers".[40] Winston thinks of an idea derived from Philo, the spiritual death of the soul of the ungodly: "the wicked, even when alive, are called dead", cf. *Det.* 49; *Spec.* 1.345; *Fug.* 55. For Philo, there exist living persons who are dead but also dead people who are living. The foolish are dead, even if they attain a ripe old age, because they are deprived of life lived according to virtue. The just, on the other hand, even if deprived of the body, live for ever.[41] In a little-noticed study, H. Engel claims, contrary to current opinion, that 11d refers without any doubt to the death of *others* caused by the ungodly.[42]

In my opinion, the data offered us by the text appears to be as follows. There exists a very close link between the different kinds of lying. Lying directly against God assumes the aspect of blasphemy or murmuring; lying directly against the neighbour is slander. The use of ἀναιρέω leaves no doubts in this regard: even lying against one's neighbour results in death. In the light of v. 11 alone, one could think of the death of one who is "killed" by the lying word of another. Yet v. 16 leads to the thought that the death in question could also be the death of the ungodly man himself (cf. below). In conclusion, our author is undoubtedly ambiguous, and his ambiguity will not wholly disappear in what follows. The term θάνατος, introduced in 1:12 for the first time, makes us think of *physical* death, but, on the other hand, it is precisely v. 12 which seems to exclude it. The reading

---

38 Taylor, "Eschatological meaning", 84-98.

39 Larcher, *Sagesse*, 1:194-195. Thus, with different nuances, Cornely, *Commentarius*, 61 and 70-73; Heinisch, *Das Buch der Weisheit*, 21-23; Feldmann, *Das Buch der Weisheit*, 28; Taylor, "Eschatological meaning", 106-111; Weisengoff, "Death and Immortality", 112; Ziener, "Weisheitsbuch und Johannesevangelium", 2:43-45. Alonso Schökel (*Sabiduría*, 88) prefers to leave the text in its ambiguity, while Vílchez Líndez (*Sapienza*, 162-163) tends towards a reference to the loss of friendship with God as a consequence of sin.

40 Scarpat, *Sapienza*, 1:96. Cf. also p. 127.

41 Winston, *Wisdom*, 106. For this Philonian concept which, in my view, is not wholly absent from Wisdom, cf. also the comment on Wis 17:21.

42 Cf. "Wem nimmt unrechtes Denken". Following a suggestion of N. Lohfink, Engel readopts the ancient interpretation of the monk Malachy. Engel emphasises how the presentation of the ungodly, especially in Wis 2:1-20, leads to placing the stress, first, on their thoughts against God, then, on their wrong behaviour in their dealings with others which results in violence and murder.

of vv. 13-14 will orient us further towards the idea of an ambiguous death. We can, therefore, conclude that if, on the one hand, the strange expression ἀναιρεῖ ψυχήν refers to death caused by the ungodly with their conduct, on the other hand, the idea of the actual death of the ungodly is not to be wholly excluded.

1:12 Verse 12 is constructed in perfect parallelism:

μὴ ζηλοῦτε	θάνατον	ἐν πλάνῃ	ζωῆς ὑμῶν
μηδὲ ἐπισπᾶσθε	ὄλεθρον	ἐν ἔργοις	χειρῶν ὑμῶν

We have here two negative imperatives in the second person plural which complete those of v. 11; two object complements placed in synonymous parallelism (θάνατον, ὄλεθρον); and a double reference to the moral activity of man (ἐν + dative + genitive + ὑμῶν). The use of the present imperative is an indication of continuous action: "do not continue to strive ..."; ζηλόω has its usual sense of "striving" for something. Verse 12a is targeted at people seen in their interior conduct: πλάνη indicates error – the loss of way in life (ἐν πλάνῃ ζωῆς ὑμῶν) in one's dealings with God and what is good – and refers to the verb πλανάω which is used in 2:21 and 5:6.[43]

Thus, the text of 12a refers to man considered in his interior conduct and exhorted not to lose his way in useless strivings which only lead him far from God.

In mentioning "the works of your hands", on the other hand, v. 12b, takes into consideration external conduct in parallel with the interior conduct mentioned in the previous stich. The idea contained in 1:12b, that people brings upon themselves ruin with their own hands (cf. Wis 1:16a),[44] leads us to understand that death (θάνατος) is something which actually concerns only the ungodly. It would be rather difficult for our sage to be thinking simply of physical death which, in fact, touches all without distinction, both just and ungodly.

Diachronic Analysis

1:12 In Wis 1:12a, the use of the term πλάνη could make us think of Jer 23:17 or Ezek 33:10, but it also suggests a classical background. In fact, the term is employed by Plato (cf. *Resp.* 4.444b; *Phaedr.* 81a) to indicate a life that is far from virtue and it has, as we shall see in connection with πλανάω in Wis 17:1b, echoes of the mysteries.

The idea of the person who brings his death upon himself by his own hand (1:12b) is traditional. See Sir 15:11-17, a text very close to our passage. Cf. also

43 The text of Jas 5:20 seems very close to our passage, not only in vocabulary but also in content: "whoever brings back a sinner from the way of his error (ἐκ πλάνης ὁδοῦ αὐτοῦ) will save him from death".

44 The verb used is ἐπισπάομαι; cf. Isa 5:18 LXX, but the whole of the context of Isa 5 was probably in our sage's mind. So Engel, *Weisheit*, 57. Ὄλεθρος, that is, the end, the ruin of life. Cf. *Il.* 22.325; here, in clear parallel with θάνατος.

Philo, *Det.* 122: "God is not the cause of evils, as some of the ungodly think, but our own very hands"; cf. also 1 En. 98:4: "sin was not sent on the earth, but men alone created it".

Wis 1:13-15: God Did Not Create Death!

13 Because God did not create death,
and he takes no delight in the destruction of the living.
14 For he created everything for existence,
the generations of the cosmos are bearers of salvation
and there is no poison of ruin in them
nor is the dominion of Hades over the earth;
15 for justice is immortal.

Synchronic Analysis

Verse 13 contrasts human conduct (vv. 11-12) with that of God (θεός, in emphatic position), both in its external ("he did not create death") and interior ("he does not delight in the destruction of the living") aspects. Thus, in some ways, what is being emphasised is the *humanity* of God.[45] The use of ἀπώλεια, "destruction, ruin", frequent in the LXX, points us in the direction of an eschatological context (cf. Wis 5:7; 18:7). That goes also for ὄλεθρος ("ruin, destruction") employed in the previous verse. In Wis 1:12, 14, ὄλεθρος is placed in parallel with "death" and "Hades". Wisdom 18:13 could constitute an exact *flashback* to our passage. 1:13

The whole of the inspiration of v. 13 is biblical, then, with its explicit reference to creation. Thus, v. 13a reconnects with the basic theme of Gen 1-3. God did not wish death; therefore, it is not to be considered as a "creature" of God. We find ourselves before a negative paraphrase of the statement in Genesis "God made the heaven and the earth".[46] However, the book of Wisdom elaborates what is not yet so explicit in Gen 1-3: there is a salvific will of God which does not wish death precisely because there is present in the world a "spirit, the friend of humanity" (1:7).

Ambiguity of Death

Wisdom is playing with an idea of death which is *ambiguous and ambivalent*.[47] On the one hand, it seems that the text of v. 13 is speaking of *physical* death, also because of the close relationship with the texts of Gen 1-3; but, on the other hand, in light of v. 12 and, later, v. 16, the death, the ruin in question, only affects the ungodly.

Verse 14 is the positive expression of what v. 13 expressed negatively: God's plan for creation and humanity is a project of life and not of death. The back- 1:14

45 Raurell, "From ΔΙΚΑΙΟΣΥΝΗ", 344.
46 Gilbert, "La relecture de Genèse 1 à 3", 324.
47 Larcher, *Sagesse*, 1:198. The author is offering a complex idea of death.

ground is always that of Gen 1-3. Κτίζω, in particular, (cf. also Wis 2:23) recalls expressly the ברא of Genesis. With τὰ πάντα our author is offering a Greek translation of the Genesis expression "the heaven and the earth". The expression εἰς τὸ εἶναι recalls the intention (εἰς) of the Creator. Wisdom is expressing itself here with a more philosophical kind of language which refers to the notion of eternity and of the existence of the world. Perhaps for this reason, the author prefers to use εἶναι with the nuance of "remain in being", rather than the γίνεσθαι "come into existence" of the text of Gen 1:3 (where the Hebrew text uses a form of the verb היה).[48] The expression εἰς τὸ εἶναι should then be understood without doubt in the light of Wis 11:17. God brings individual creatures into existence starting from material without form.

Salvific Value of the Creation

This statement of Wisdom has been variously interpreted. According to Winston, what we have here is the Stoic principle of self-preservation;[49] according to Larcher, the creatures, or – better – the generations of the world, "keep" the world itself in existence by reproducing themselves.[50] It seems that the text wishes to affirm that the creation is "good", taking up the theme of the "blessing" and goodness of creation present in Gen 1. There could also be a polemic here against concepts of Platonic origin which tended to devalue the goodness of earthly reality in favour of "another" world (the Ideas), or else against Gnostic tendencies claiming that this world is corrupt and poisoned.[51]

This is not enough: our sage is aiming to propose to us that the creation has in itself a salvific value. As the whole of the third part of the book will demonstrate, the cosmos is allied with God in favour of the just (cf. 16:24). In any case, Wis 1:14 is one of the most important statements of principle made by Wisdom: *salvation comes through creation.* The cosmos has a fundamental role in the salvific plan of God. This verse is thus an anticipation in germ of a good part of the content of the third section of the book (Wis 11-19).

In the second part of v. 14, the term βασίλειον (cf. Wis 5:16) has an active value and refers to the idea of "rule", emphasising in particular the idea of sovereignty. The text refers to a precise power of Hades over the earth which is here expressly denied. "Hades" is not simply a metaphor for death nor is it just the biblical *she'ôl.* The "dominion of Hades" is here an almost personified reality behind which one begins to glimpse hell as a place of eternal punishment for the ungodly.[52]

1:15 In its brevity, v. 15 seems not to have any apparent connection with the text which immediately precedes it. Perhaps it was such a consideration that gave rise to the addition of a supplementary stich in the Latin version.[53] Be that as it may, the γάρ connects our text with the previous section in some way.

---

48 Gilbert, "La relecture de Genèse 1 à 3", 325; Fabbri, *Creazione e salvezza*, 102-104.

49 "All that has come into existence preserves its being", Winston, *Wisdom,* 108-109.

50 Larcher, *Sagesse*, 1: 199-200.

51 On this last point cf. Winston, *Wisdom*, 109-110.

52 Mazzinghi, "Non c'è regno dell'Ade", 244-245. Cf. the comment on Wis 17:14.

53 "Iniustitia autem mortis est acquisitio". Cf. Scarpat, *Sapienza*, 1:131f who rightly rejects the Latin addition for reasons of scant attestation and on account of the perfect *inclusio* between 1:1a and 1:15. Cf. also Raurell, "From ΔΙΚΑΙΟΣΥΝΗ", 348 n. 47.

In the light of Wis 8:7d, it could be thought that the justice spoken of here is the human variety, one of the four cardinal virtues that were already known to Plato. In this case, our text would be suggesting that the way of the ungodly leads to death (vv. 11-12) but that the way of the just to immortality. In Wis 8:7, in fact, this justice is at the same time that of God, expressed in God's law. Notice the verb ἀγαπάω which links 8:7 with 1:1. The text of 1:15 reinforces this idea. Our sage wishes to claim that only a world regulated by this divine justice is immortal. Everything that is contrary to the justice of God (which, in this case, is transformed from δικαιοσύνη into the punitive δίκη, cf. Wis 1:8) will be destroyed (cf. Wis 5:6). It is, therefore, by "loving" (1:1) this "immortal" justice of God that a person obtains immortality. Cf. the ἀθανασία mentioned in Wis 3:4 (cf. the comment); see also Wis 15:3.[54]

Diachronic Analysis

The idea that God does not delight in the death of a sinful person (1:13) is biblical 1:13
(cf. Ezek 18:32: διότι οὐ θέλω τὸν θάνατον τοῦ ἀποθνήσκοντος λέγει κύριος).[55] However, our sage goes beyond the ideas expressed by Ezekiel. Not only does God not delight in the death of the sinner, but God's deep intention, bound up with God's very act as Creator (cf. the use of ποιέω with God as subject) is that of giving life to people.

As for ὄλεθρος, it is used in an eschatological sense in the prophets: cf. LXX- 1:14
Jer 31:3, 8, 32 (cf. MT-Jer 48:3, 8, 32) in relation to the ruin of the nations; Ezek 6:14 LXX in relation to the ruin of Israel; in the NT, cf. 1 Thess 5:3 and 2 Thess 1:9.

Double Death

A solution to the dilemma represented by the ambiguity of death (cf. above in connection with 1:13) comes to us from Philo's idea of double death.[56] For Philo, true death is not that of the body but that of the soul (cf. *Leg.* 1:105-106). In fact, there exist living people who are as if they were dead, and dead people who are as if they were alive (*Fug.* 55). Reflecting on Gen 1-4, Philo observes that the fact that Adam and Eve did not die after their sin is the proof that the true death is that of the soul. In a typically Hellenistic perspective, this concept serves to explain some serious exegetical problems arising from Gen 1-4: why did Adam and Eve not die despite their sin, and why was Cain punished by God and not killed? The use of the verbal form συναπολέτω in Wis 10:3-4 with reference to Cain leads us to think precisely of the death of the soul.

The book of Wisdom does not follow the configuration of Philo's philosophy directly, but it does offer the impression of utilising two different and complementary aspects in relation to the idea of death, an ambiguity, therefore, that was *deliberate* on the part

---

54 Cf. Fabbri, *Creazione e salvezza*, 245-246, who highlights the close relation between 1:13-15 and 15:1-3. See also Scarpat, *Sapienza*, 1:102-107 with observations of great topicality (cf. p. 104).

55 Fabbri, *Creazione e salvezza*, 59 n. 151 and 152 who takes up the observations of Larcher, *Sagesse*, 1:198-199. Cf. p. 199 for the patristic use of 1:13-14.

56 Scarpat, *Sapienza*, 1:95-102; Fabbri, *Creazione e salvezza*, 54-55 and, above all, Scarpat, "La morte seconda". On the idea of life, death and resurrection in the Judaism of the time, cf. Avery-Peck Alan J. – Neusner, Jacob, *Judaism in Late Antiquity. Death, Life-after-death, Resurrection and the World-to-Come in the Judaism of Antiquity*, Leiden: Brill 2000.

of the author himself. It is the ungodly, in fact, who are the first to deceive themselves on the subject of death, regarding it as the irremediable end of life (2:1-5). In chapters 3 and 4, our author will refute this false view held by the ungodly (cf., in particular, 3:1-9): for the just, death is a passage to life. Thus, it is necessary to distinguish between *the natural condition of human mortality, physical death which is ambiguous, and the eternal death of the ungodly which is to be seen as punishment.*

The natural condition of human beings is that of being mortal (Wis 7:1-2). It does not seem as if Wisdom connects this idea with a possible primordial human sinfulness (cf. 10:1-2) nor does our author ever give the idea of speaking of the natural condition of human mortality as a punishment consequent on such a sin. *Physical* death assumes the character of a divine punishment only for the ungodly. However, physical death is such only because, for the ungodly, it is the sign of a death that is even more serious, *eternal* death, that is, destruction and separation from God. This, ultimately, is the death which God did not create (1:13-14) and which entered the world through the envy of the devil (2:24).[57]

In conclusion, physical death is really *ambiguous*: it is a passage to eternal life for the just ("it seemed that they had died"; cf. 3:2) and, at the same time, a prelude to eternal ruin for the ungodly (cf. Wis 5). The mortal condition of man is not to be considered as a punishment but as a datum of creaturely existence. However, the just experience physical death in a way that is completely different from the ungodly. The only punishment per se is the eternal death of the ungodly of which physical death becomes the sign and anticipation.

In Wis 1:14, with αἱ γενέσεις τοῦ κόσμου, we are faced with an expression that had become technical in the Hellenistic period in the area of philosophical debates on the origin of the world. Cf. Plato, *Tim.* 27a, where γένεσις τοῦ κόσμου stands for the formation of the world by the Demiurge. In the Stoic conception, this terminology indicates rather the beginning of a new period in the life of the cosmos (*SVF* II, 180, frags. 581. 582). Instead, our author has in mind the Hebrew תולדות, the successive "generations" of the world which contribute to keeping it in life.[58] With αἱ γενέσεις τοῦ κόσμου, therefore, it is necessary to understand the "generations" in the sense of the different creatures of the world (cf. Wis 16:26, the various species of fruits; 19:11, a new generation of birds), namely, the "production" of creatures according to Gen 1 which contribute to keeping the world in life. Thus, the more common translation, "creature", is to be rejected. The term σωτήριοι has an active significance, according to a sense well known also to secular Greek: "salvific, bearer of salvation".[59]

If the generations of the world are bearers of life, if the "poison of death" is not in them, if Hades, the kingdom of the dead, has no dominion over the earth, then where does death itself come from? Perhaps from the power of Hades which has just been denied or from the διάβολος who will be mentioned later in Wis 2:24? In classical mythology, there often returns the idea of the kingdom of Hades as a power which no one can escape. In the *Papyri graecae magicae* in particular there are numerous references to the magus who, with his arts, succeeds in over-

57 Kolarcik, *The Ambiguity of Death*, 148-151; 169-170; Collins, *Jewish Wisdom*, 187-189.

58 Larcher, *Sagesse*, 1:203; Fabbri, *Creazione e salvezza*, 118-120.

59 Scarpat, *Sapienza*, 1:129; *salutares*, in Jerome's interpretation; Larcher prefers to translate with "conserving/preserving" (cf. 1:202). Cf. also Fabbri, *Creazione e salvezza*, 121-126.

coming the power of Hades (*PGM* I,177-180; IV,358, 3009-3087; etc.). According to v. 14, however, such an infernal dominion has no power over the earth (cf. Wis 17:14), except over those human beings who seek it and find it because of their wicked conduct.

Summary of Wis 1:1-15

The *inclusio* between 1:1 and 1:15 governs the whole of the initial section of the book. It is necessary to love the justice [of God]. The initial exhortation, addressed to the leaders of the Jewish community, is based on the memory of the journey of the people of Israel in the desert. Israel is not to lack faith in God, nor to attempt to put him to the test (v. 2), avoiding useless murmurings and outright blasphemies which lead to death (vv. 11-12). By contrast, only the man of simple heart can receive wisdom. In v. 4, wisdom appears as an interior power which cannot dwell along with sin. By means of the association with the holy spirit (v. 4), this wisdom is a philanthropic spirit (1:6) which fills the entire created reality (1:7). The cosmos, therefore, is not something negative but is, as it were, the home of wisdom. In order to express the presence of wisdom in the world (especially in v. 7), our author is not afraid to have recourse to Stoic categories, thus actualising and developing a message which arises from Scripture through a careful use of Greek philosophy.

However, the death which strikes those who distance themselves from wisdom is not part of God's plan. Recalling the texts of Gen 1-3, the concluding verses of this section (vv. 12, 13-15) affirm that God did not create death but that, on the contrary, every created reality has in itself a salvific value. Death and Hades have no power over the earth. Death has, therefore, in itself an aspect of ambiguity. It is a sign of the creaturely nature of humanity which has become a punishment for the ungodly.

Responding to the unfaithfulness of humanity is the plan of God who offers salvation and life. In this way, the book opens on a note that is wholly positive, despite the negative and dramatic appearances that run through it (cf. also vv. 8-10).[60] It is in this perspective that we must reflect on the discourse of the ungodly which opens immediately (Wis 1:16-2:24). Only the justice of God, which is immortal, can save the ungodly from death (cf. 1:15).

60 McGlynn (*Divine Judgment*, 54-88) speaks, in connection with Wis 1, of "apocalyptic drama".

Wis 1:16–2:24: The Godless Summon Death through Their Words and Deeds

Literary Structure of Wis 1:16–2:24

Suddenly, after the wholly positive close to the introduction (cf. 1:13-15), the ungodly enter the scene. With great poetic and rhetorical ability, our author introduces them in a dramatic way which catches the attention of the listener. The ungodly are introduced by means of their own words.[1]

The dramatic nature of the text is accentuated by the constant use of *irony*. The ungodly believe in boasting, describing their own way of life (2:1-9), but they do not realise that they actually are rushing towards death. Their apparent joy hides a deep despair, their complete existential failure. The text also plays on the contrast between *appearance and reality*. The appearance is the search for pleasure and the enjoyment of a life which seems to be empty of meaning, but the reality is quite different. Such a way of life is a source of death and ruin for those who practise it. Salvation is there, instead, for those who are persecuted by the ungodly. The latter believe in disparaging the just man (2:10-20), but the evil which they speak of him and the violence to which they subject him are transformed into an *elogium* for the just man himself. Thus, the death of the just is in fact life; the life of the ungodly, on the other hand, leads only to death.

Finally, in reproducing the discourse of the ungodly, our sage makes stylistic use of the *diatribe* in which fictional adversaries are often quoted.[2] A certain analogy can be found with the discourse of the sinners in 1 En. 102:6-11.

The text is structured in the following way:

1:16–2:1a: Introduction to the Words of the Godless
    2:1b-5.6–9: The Speech's First Part
    2:10–20: The Speech's Second Part
2:21–24: The Author's Judgement of the Speech of the Godless

Wis 1:16-2:1a; 2:21-24: Introduction to the Words of the Godless and The Author's Judgement

The literary structure of the text is very clear and coherent.[3] At the extremities of the discourse of the ungodly (Wis 2:1b-20), we find a double value judgement of the author (1:16-2:1a and 2:21-24); noticeable are the *inclusio* on the term μερίς, "part, party" (1:16 and 2:24) and the repetition of λογίζομαι, "reasoning" (2:1a and 2:21). The term μερίς is taken up again at the end of v. 9; these are the

---

1 For the Hellenistic tendency to favour discourse rather than action, cf. Schmitt, Armin, *Wende des Lebens. Untersuchungen zu einem Situations-Motiv der Bibel* (Berlin – New York: De Gruyter 1996), 30.

2 Cf. Reese, *Hellenistic Influence*, 90-121 and the clarifications of Gilbert who notes that it is not possible to speak of the diatribe as a true literary genre ("Sagesse", 78-79).

3 Bizzeti, *Sapienza*, 54-56; Gilbert, "Sagesse", 66; Kolarcik, *The Ambiguity of Death*, 39-41.

only occurrences of this word within the book. We have previously observed (cf. *Literary Structure of Wis 1:1-15*) the verbal and thematic contacts between 1:13-15 and 2:21-24, two passages which are densely theological and which should, therefore, be read in close connection with each other.

Wis 2:1b-5, 6-9: The Speech's First Part

The discourse of the ungodly (2:1b-20) can be easily subdivided into two sections which, in their turn, can be further subdivided into two short pericopes, more on thematic grounds than on account of precise literary indications. The first section of the discourse is in 2:1b-9 where the ungodly expound their life-plan. In vv. 1b-5, they outline their disillusioned and bitter view of life (*inclusio*: ἐν τελευτῇ / τῆς τελευτῆς ἡμῶν, vv. 1c, 5b and ὁ βίος ἡμῶν, 1b, 4c.). In vv. 6-9, on the other hand, they draw the practical consequence (οὖν) of this view: let us, then, enjoy this life which is so fleeting!

Wis 2:10-16, 17-20: The Speech's Second Part

The second part of the discourse of the ungodly comprises 2:10-20 and contains two further sections: the decision to persecute the just because they are a nuisance (vv. 10-16) and the final decision to destroy them in order to prove the validity of their own actions (vv. 17-20; *inclusio*: οἱ λόγοι αὐτοῦ – ἐκ λόγων αὐτοῦ).

The just person is seen as wholly passive (δίκαιος as object in 2:10a, 12a, 16c – in the plural – and 2:18a, the only example where δίκαιος is subject). It is noticeable again that, in 2:1b-20, a good twenty-one times, one finds the plural pronoun of the first person, "we": the ungodly are occupying centre stage.

Wis 1:16-2:5: The Party of Death: A Life without Meaning

1:16 With their deeds and words, however, the ungodly summon [death],
they pine for it, believing it to be a friend,
and they make a pact with it,
because they deserve to belong to its party!
2:1 For, reasoning falsely, they said to one another:

1b "Short and sad is our life,
there is no cure for person's end
and no one is known who can free from Hades.
2 By chance we were born
and afterwards we shall be as though we had never been.
Because the breath of our nostrils is steam,
thought, a spark which comes from the beating of our heart.
3 When it is extinguished, the body becomes ash
and the spirit vanishes like thin air.
4 Even our name will be forgotten with time
and no one will remember our deeds.
Our life will pass away like the trail of a cloud

and will be scattered like the mist,
chased by the rays of the sun
and overcome by its heat.
5 For the time of our life is the fleeting of a shadow
and our end is without return;
once the seal has been fixed, no one turns back.

Notes on the Text and Translation

2:1. The expression ἐν ἑαυτοῖς could have the force of ἐν ἀλλήλοις, "to one another", a solution preferable in view of the context,[4] or else, as happens in the LXX, ἑαυτοῖς is equivalent to αὐτοῖς and so to the Hebrew בלבו, "to speak to oneself".

v. 1d. The ancient versions understand ὁ ἀναλύσας in an intransitive sense (cf. Wisd 5:12; Lat: *qui sit reversus ab inferis*).[5] If we translate the aorist participle "no one exists who has returned from Hades", it is necessary to give the clause an ironic sense; if the kingdom of the dead exists, no one has ever come back to describe it to us! Classical Greek knows only a transitive use of ἀναλύω. Moreover, the parallelism with the previous stich ("there is no cure for man's end") suggests rather an active sense:[6] "no one is known who can free from Hades". This theme is not infrequent in classical literature.[7] We get a confirmation of this interpretation from the biblical texts which our author could have had in mind, especially Ps 48 [49 MT]:8-10 and Job 33:23-25. Both texts contain the idea that no one exists who can save anyone from the world of the dead.

v. 2a. The adverb *αὐτοσχεδίως corresponds to the more common αὐτομάτως, which, in Epicurean teaching, describes the birth of man as originating in a chance encounter of atoms. For the Epicurean idea of life as the chance aggregation of atoms, cf. Lucretius, *Rer. Nat.* V, 419-431. Josephus polemicises against the belief of the Epicureans who, according to him, claim that that the world runs by chance (αὐτομάτως), without knowing a guide or another's care" (*A.J.* 10.278). The ungodly described by Wisdom actually do not seem to be true followers of Epicurus but, rather, deniers of the meaning of life, absolute nihilists. Human beings are dominated by chance. They disappear without leaving any trace.

Synchronic Analysis

Wis 1:16-2:1a The initial δέ has an adversative force which contrasts the ungodly with the "justice" mentioned in v. 15 and, more generally, creates an opposition with Wis 1:1-15. However, it is not the "unjust" who are contrasted with "justice" but the "ungodly". Why? With the term ἀσεβής, our author intends to emphasise not

4 Cf. BDF § 297; cf. Mark 9:50.

5 Cf. Larcher, *Sagesse*, 1:214-215; Winston, *Wisdom*, 115; Mazzinghi, "Non c'è regno dell'Ade", 240-242.

6 Cf. Scarpat, *Sapienza*, 1172-173 and 332-333. Cf. already Grimm, Weisheit, 67: "der aus der Unterwelt Befreiende ist nicht bekannt geworden".

7 See the texts cited by Winston, *Wisdom*, 115-116 and the use of ἀναλύω in Wis 16:14.

only the moral aspect but also, considering the religious nuance of the word, the opposition of the ungodly in their relations with God.

The pronoun αὐτόν which closes 1:16a could refer to Hades, but, more correctly, it should be understood in relation to the "death" (θάνατος) mentioned in vv. 12-13 and recalled *ad sensum* by the adjective "immortal" in v. 15. With their deeds and their words (ταῖς χερσὶν καὶ τοῖς λόγοις), the ungodly summon death. Death, therefore, is something which the ungodly seek on their own, which touches them alone. This is the return of the idea of an *ambiguous* death and, at the same time, the concept of a *double death* (cf. 1:14; 2:24): physical death is true death only for the ungodly.

The three gnomist aorists of v. 16abc (cf. the present εἰσίν in 16d)[8] indicate a progression in the attitude of the ungodly. After having invited death and desired it, they are, as it were, in love with it and conclude a pact with it.

The verb τήκω is used in Wis 16:22, 27, and 29 in the sense of "melt", like wax; here and in 6:23, in an ironic sense, it indicates the pining of the lover for his lady. The ungodly live under the illusion of being able to escape the death and yet they appear to desire it with all their might.[9]

The ungodly have become worthy (ἄξιοι) members of the party (μερίς) of death. In the LXX, μερίς is not infrequently employed to describe Israel as the "portion" (חלק) of the Lord (Deut 39:2; Zech 2:16; 2 Macc 1:26). By contrast, the ungodly are described here, polemically, as the "portion" of death. On the other hand, used in a political sense, μερίς indicates the "party" with which the ungodly are registered![10] Death, therefore, strikes only those who are members of this lethal "party". Again, we have the idea that death strikes only those who seek it. The use of ἄξιος, dear to our author, is an indirect suggestion of divine intervention: the ungodly *deserve* death.[11]

The text of 2:1a constitutes the introduction to the discourse of the ungodly: "reasoning falsely, they said to one another". The "false reasoning" of the ungodly refers to the σκολιοὶ λογισμοί of Wis 1:3. Even before the deeds of the ungodly, our sage is concerned with their devious way of reasoning: the concept that the ungodly have of life (2:1-9) and the idea that they have of God and of the just man who believes in him (2:10-20).

After the initial statement on the brevity of life, the text places the formula 2:1b-d
οὐκ ἔστιν ἴασις in the mouth of the ungodly. The term ἴασις is to be understood in the sense of "remedy, cure", here with the nuance of "salvation". According to biblical understanding, the just will be healed by God; according to the opinion of the apostates, on the other hand, there is no possibility of recovering from the sickness of death, which is called "the end" (τελευτή) here. We should note that

8 The translation of these gnomic aorists with the present makes it impossible to think of some kind of allusion in the text to an "historic" sin like that of Gen 3. Cf. Sisti, *Sapienza*, 107.

9 Dodson ("Locked-Out Lovers") believes he has discovered in this sequence of an erotic character an ironic adoption of the literary form of the *paraklausithyron*: the lover calls his loved one as he stands beside her closed door.

10 Cf. Winston, *Wisdom*, 113, who suggests some Philonian echoes also; Scarpat, *Sapienza*, 1:133. Cf. Amir, "The Figure of Death", 157.

11 For the use of ἄξιος in Wisdom, cf. Mazzinghi, *Notte di paura e di luce*, 218.

the ungodly never call death by its name, θάνατος, but by various euphemisms. They fear it!

"No one is known who can free from Hades". In the light of texts like Job 7:9-10 LXX and Hos 13:14 LXX, θάνατος and ᾅδης appear interchangeable. Hades is used here more traditionally as a synonym for the world of the dead, the "netherworld". In Hos 13:14, God appears as the only one who can free humanity from death. It is precisely that which the ungodly deny. After death, there is nothing more. There is no God who can free humanity from the kingdom of the dead (cf. Wis 2:13-18).

2:2 Here, the ungodly deny any form of personal survival and think of human beings as the fruit of a blind and incomprehensible destiny, thus denying one of the hinges of the biblical faith: the existence of a creator God who is caring.

2:3 When the heart stops beating, when that spark is extinguished, all that remains of a person is the "ash": τέφρα is a literary word, often used in Greek for the decomposition of the corpse, but the idea is biblical (Gen 3:19), although the "dust" (γῆ) of Genesis, the element of which the human is composed, is reduced here to "ash".

2:4 In the first two stichs of v. 4, the ungodly state that, after death, both the "name" and the "deeds" of men are forgotten. However, what the ungodly say in 4ab will show itself to convey an ironic truth: of the ungodly there is really no memory whereas the just will be remembered by God (cf. 3:1-9).

For the ungodly, human life will pass like the trail of a cloud (4c), it will be dissolved like mist (4d; for the use of διασκεδάννυμι, cf. above) chased by the rays of the sun (4e) and overcome by its heat (4f). The negative context of these images, very beautiful in themselves, makes us think that the interest in science actually seems to be dominating the poetry.[12] The images of the cloud and mist which vanish in the heat of the sun emphasise for the ungodly the absolutely fleeting, transitory, and ephemeral character of human life.

2:5 This verse concludes the bitter and disillusioned reflection of the ungodly on the brevity of life. The use of καιρός in place of βίος (cf., however, 4c) is deliberate, and serves to underline the brevity of life considered as a fixed time which has no reversal.[13]

The image of the shadow to indicate the shortness of life is topical (see below). Moreover, this image serves to give further emphasis a certain determinism inherent in the words of the ungodly. Life passes like a shadow, like something that depends on an already predetermined path, that of the sun.

Verse 5 closes with the theme that opened the discourse of the ungodly: after death, there is nothing. There is no possibility of return (cf. Sir 38:21 with regard to the underworld). As in 1c, death is once more referred to euphemistically as the "end" (τελευτή). Not even the possibility remains of a miracle like that recounted in 2 Kgs 20:9-11, when according to the words of Isaiah the shadow on the sundial went back, just as King Hezekiah had sought from the Lord (cf. the allusion to this episode in Sir 48:23 LXX. where the verb ἀναποδίζω is employed).[14]

---

12 Cf. Larcher, *Sagesse*, 1:223-225, for the details.

13 Many authoritative codices also read βίος instead of καιρὸς as *lectio facilior*; cf. Ziegler.

14 The term *ἀναποδισμός is *hapax totius graecitatis*; cf. Scarpat, *Sapienza*, 1:177-178.

Death is thus a final "seal". Noticeable is the use of the aorist: κατεσφραγίσθη (cf. Rev 20:3 and Matt 27:66). No one can return (οὐδεὶς ἀναστρέφει) from death. The verb reappears in Wis 16:14, always in a context of death. In both cases, it has an intransitive sense. This is a confirmation of the idea already present in 2:1d. For the ungodly, any other talk about the afterlife is a fable, totally without substance.

Diachronic Analysis

"Loving death" (1:16) is a theme present in the sapiential literature: cf. Prov 8:36 LXX: "those who sin against me harm their own lives (ἀσεβοῦσιν τὰς ἑαυτῶν ψυχάς); all who hate me love death (ἀγαπῶσιν θάνατον)". 1:16

The ungodly have concluded a pact (συνθήκη) with death. The text alludes to Isa 28:15 LXX: ἐποιήσαμεν διαθήκην μετὰ τοῦ ᾅδου καὶ μετὰ τοῦ θανάτου συνθήκας. The wicked inhabitants of Samaria think they can escape death precisely because they have concluded a pact with it while the ungodly seek it openly. The description of the drunkards of Ephraim (Isa 28:1-6) and the hedonistic priests and prophets (Isa 28:7-15) could also have inspired the account of the lifestyle of the ungodly. However, our author goes beyond the context of Isaiah in the light of the lifestyle of the Jews of Alexandria. The link between the ungodly and death is also frequent in Proverbs: cf. Prov 2:18-20; 7:27; 9:18; and 11:19. In 1:16, Wisdom takes up this idea and develops it: the ungodly have *already* chosen death.[15] A more exact point of reference may come from the cultural environment of the Alexandrian *élite*. Our author could be alluding to the "association of death", founded at Alexandria by Anthony and Cleopatra after the battle of Actium.[16]

Biblical or Greek Sources for Wis 2:1b-20?

Within the discourse of the ungodly, which continues from 2:1b as far as 2:20, it is important to grasp which sources have inspired the book of Wisdom: biblical, Greek, or both? And, in any case, to what extent?[17] Declarations similar to those of the ungodly are topical in the Hellenistic world: "the *carpe diem* based on the insecurity of the future seems to be the theme of this hymn of the Jews of the Diaspora".[18]

The idea that life is "short" (2:1b) is a commonplace both in the Bible and in classical literature (cf. Job 10:20 LXX [ἦ οὐκ ὀλίγος ἐστὶν ὁ χρόνος τοῦ βίου μου]; Job 14:1). In the Bible, there also appears, not infrequently, a note of sadness (here: λυπηρός) which accompanies the description of the shortness of life (cf. Gen 47:9; 2:1b

15 Cf. Clifford, "Proverbs as a source", 262.

16 Plutarch, *Ant.* 71.4-5, reports that Anthony and Cleopatra, after their defeat at the battle of Actium (31 BCE), disbanded the "club of the inimitable" (σύνοδος Ἀμιμητοβίων) and founded a "club of those mutually waiting for death" (σύνοδος συναποθανουμένων), that lacked nothing of its predecessor's luxury and festivity. Cleopatra supposedly sought the quickest working and least painful mortal poisons at this time and tested them on those sentenced to death. For information about such organisations in Alexandria in which life was not taken seriously, but rather in which enjoyment was sought as a salve against the fear of death, cf. Larcher, *Etudes*, 289; Baslez, „The Author of Wisdom", 40–41.

17 Cf. Kolarcik, *The Ambiguity of Death,* 114-123.

18 Scarpat, *Sapienza*, 1:136-137.

Job 10:18-22; 14:1-2, as well as various psalmic texts: Pss 36[37 MT]:35-36; 38[39 MT]:5-6; 89[90 MT], etc.). Both in Job and in the Psalms, however, the tone is never despairing and irremediably bitter as it is in these declarations of the ungodly. This can be seen from what "Solomon" says in Wis 9:5b when he reflects on the brevity of life, but with quite different results. If, on the one hand, like Job, the ungodly seem to be lamenting on the shortness of life, on the other hand, they are totally unable to turn to God as happens with Job and as is the case in the Psalms.

2:1c The formula οὐκ ἔστιν ἴασις (2:1c) is frequent in the LXX, often with a religious meaning (cf. Prov 29:1 LXX and Jer 17:14 LXX, where the prophet turns to God to be cured: ἴασαί με κύριε καὶ ἰαθήσομαι; cf. also Jer 14:19 LXX and, in our book, Wis 16:12). According to the message of Scripture, the just are healed by God. According to the ungodly, on the other hand, there is no possible cure from the malady of death which is here called the "end" (τελευτή).

2:2 The first two stichs of v. 2 combine a Greek expression of Epicurean flavour (αὐτοσχεδίως; cf. above)[19] with one that is more clearly biblical (ἐσόμεθα ὡς οὐκ ὑπάρξαντες; cf. Ps 38[39 MT]:14; 102[103 MT]:16; Obad 16 LXX; Job 10:19a; Sir 44:9 LXX).

The last two stichs of v. 2 present a further combination of biblical and Greek *motifs*. πνοή is taken from Gen 2:7 LXX (cf. also Job 27:3 and Isa 42:5), and the basic idea is biblical (Ps 101[102 MT]:4; Job 27:3; cf. הבל in Qoheleth), even if the ungodly radicalise it: we are only breath and smoke. The image of the soul that flees like smoke is Greek. Cf. Plato,, *Phaed.* 70a: "the soul is ruined and perishes on the same day that a man dies; as soon as it is separated from the body and goes out like breath or smoke, it is dispersed (ὥσπερ πνεῦμα ἢ καπνὸς διασκεδασθεῖσα[20]), goes out and vanishes, and ceases completely to exist".

The ungodly reveal that they are aware of the roots of biblical anthropology. However, they reread it in an ironic key in light of the materialist theories attaching to some of the medicine of the time and some aspects of Greek philosophy without any particular theory being recognisable. The mechanistic connection between "thought" and "heart" in 2d belongs, in fact, to a part of Stoicism and the medical theories.[21] "Thought" (λόγος) is described as a warm breath which goes out from the "heart". Life is nothing more than a process of combustion set in motion by the air, inhaled by the organism, and mixed in the heart with the blood. It is this which sets in motion the thought which is none other than a "spark" which is destined soon to be extinguished. The image of the spark does not seem to have parallels in the classical world and can be considered as a poetic insight of our author.[22]

---

19 Cf. Winston, *Wisdom*, 116; Larcher, *Sagesse*, 1:215-216. However, the sense of "chance" (פגע) is not absent. Cf. Qoh 9:11 (D'Alario, "La réflexion sur le sens de la vie", 317-318).

20 (περὶ τῆς ψυχῆς) ἐπειδὰν ἀπαλλαγῇ τοῦ σώματος οὐδαμοῦ ἔτι ᾖ ἀλλ' ἐκείνῃ τῇ ἡμέρᾳ διαφθείρηταί τε καὶ ἀπολλύηται ᾗ ἂν ὁ ἄνθρωπος ἀποθνῄσκῃ εὐθὺς ἀπαλλαττομένη τοῦ σώματος καὶ ἐκβαίνουσα ὥσπερ πνεῦμα ἢ καπνὸς διασκεδασθεῖσα οἴχηται διαπτομένη καὶ οὐδὲν ἔτι οὐδαμοῦ ᾖ. Wis 2:4d uses the same Platonic verb διασκεδάννυμι.

21 Cf. Larcher, *Sagesse*, 1:218.

22 Cf. Kolarcik, *The Ambiguity of Death*, 117 and n. 77.

In v. 3, the extinction of thought and the body's becoming ash could seem strange. 2:3
The ungodly are underlining their more radical materialism. Thought is nothing more than one of the many "physical" aspects of human life. What others call πνεῦμα is only a "breath" for the ungodly (cf., above, *Phaed.* 70a). In Epicurean thinking, the soul escapes after death: "tenuis enim quaedam moribundos deserit aura mixta vapore" (Lucretius, *Rer. Nat.* 3.232-233).

The theme of the immortality of memory, introduced in v. 4, is one of the 2:4
commonalities of both the Greek and the biblical worlds. Remembrance in the memory of another after death is the reward which comes to the just (Ps 111[112 MT]:6; Sir 37:26); being forgotten, on the other hand, constitutes the punishment of the ungodly. All this recalls some texts from Qoheleth (Qoh 2:16; 8:10; 9:5, and 14-15), but the context is quite different. In Qoheleth, in fact, the absence of any "remembrance" of the just is proof that after death there is nothing. For the ungodly of our text, however, it is much more: the absence of remembrance is proof that there is not even a God who remembers people. The passage of Wis 2:4ab is also, perhaps, a parody of Amos 8:7 LXX where the Lord swears that he will not forget the wicked deeds of Jacob and where we find the same verb ἐπιλησθήσεται. The absence of other-worldly sanctions is a full justification of the lifestyle of the ungodly.

In the second part of the verse (4c-f), the biblical background continues to be present, always linked with references to Greek thought (cf. Job 7:9 together with Job 9:26; 14:2; 30:15; Ps 38:7 LXX [39:7 MT], etc.).

In Wis 2:5 there is, perhaps, a reference to that astral determinism which 2:5
circulated in Hellenised Egypt and which also excluded the immortality of the soul.[23] Behind the expression σκιᾶς πάροδος, the "fleeting of a shadow", there is a probable reminiscence of Pindar: σκιᾶς ὄναρ ἄνθρωπος, "a person is a dream of a shadow" (*Pyth.* 8.133). Cf. also Job 14:2, 3, 5; Ps 101(102 MT):12.

Wis 2:6-9:
Let Us Enjoy Life!

6 Come, then, let us enjoy present pleasures
and take advantage of created things with the ardour of youth!
7 Let us take our fill of costly wine and perfumes
and not allow the flower of spring to escape us!
8 Let us crown ourselves with rosebuds before they wither,
let no meadow be safe from our orgy.
9 Let us leave the signs of our pleasure everywhere,
because this is our role, this our heritage.

---

23 Cf. Larcher, *Etudes*, 260n8.

Notes on the Text and Translation

v. 6b. The codices record different variants for ὡς νεότητι (cf. Ziegler's edition) which nonetheless remains the best attested reading; ὡς ἐν νεότητι (Rahlfs) is *lectio facilior*; ὡς νεοτῆτος is a stylistic correction (a genitive with temporal meaning); νεοττίδι, "like a daughter of joy", is an improbable conjecture by J. K. Zenner (1898), in relationship with the personal name Νοσσίς. All the other variants can be explained as starting out from ὡς νεότητι.[24] The sense of ὡς νεότητι is "as in youth", that is, as one does when one is young and not, therefore, as Larcher would like, with a comparative force: "let us use creatures *like* youth". Indeed, the invitation of the ungodly is addressed to all, and not solely to the young.

v. 7a. Πολυτελής, rare in the LXX, is used in relation to precious stones (cf. Prov 3:15; 8:11; 31:10). The adjective appears, precisely in connection with wine, in some descriptions of the Alexandrian luxury of the time.[25] The ἰταλικὴ πολυτέλεια, the "Italian luxury" is the lifestyle introduced by the Romans. Philo inveighs against this luxury: πολυτέλεια is the lifestyle typical of the fool (*Opif.* 164) to which, under the influence of the Cynic-Stoic diatribe, Philo opposes the asceticism of the Therapeutae who renounce wine. Also not to be excluded, perhaps, is an implied condemnation by our sage of the banquets which accompanied the mystery rites, above all those of Dionysius.

v. 8a. The mention of the rose is a typically Greek touch.[26] We are choosing the reading ἔαρος instead of the rival and better attested ἀέρος.[27] As for the connection ἄνθος ἔαρος, it is not attested elsewhere in Greek literature, but, in this context, it acquires the sense well known to classical literature of "bloom of youth". The "spring" is to be understood, therefore, as a reference to the pleasure connected with youth, especially the sexual variety. We must not forget that the rose, mentioned immediately afterwards, is traditionally the *flos Veneris.*[28]

v. 8b. The majority of manuscripts read ἡμῶν: "let none of us fail ..."; some manuscripts read ὑμῶν, "none of you". The Latin version has *nullum pratum sit quod non pertranseat luxuria nostra* which supposes a reading λειμών that is not preserved by any Greek codex, but which is accepted by Ziegler. Independently of each other, Scarpat and Busto Saiz have demonstrated a possible connection of the Latin text of Wis 2:9a with the *Cyclops* of Euripides. We can conclude that "meadow" is a metaphor for the female sexual organ, according to language known in Alexandrian erotic lyrics. The ungodly intend to give free rein to their every sexual desire.[29]

In Greek, the term ἀγερωχία would have a positive sense (boldness, or else honour), but, in this context, the meaning is clearly negative (cf. in the LXX, only in 2 Macc 9:7 and 3 Macc 2:3). With slight semantic stretching it is some kind of "debauchery", but along the lines of the sense we have given to "meadow", one could think of an orgy.

---

24 Larcher, *Sagesse*, 1:229. Cf. the long discussion in Scarpat, *Sapienza*, 1:179-180.

25 Cf. Scarpat, *Sapienza*, 1:147-152 and 181; Larcher, *Etudes*, 223 and n. 1.

26 Winston, *Wisdom*, 119. With a little imagination, Hübner (*Weisheit*, 41) thinks of the equation roses = women.

27 Larcher, *Sagesse*, 1:231.

28 Cf. Rosa, "Note a *Sap* 2,6-9", who hypothesises also emending ἄνθος ἔαρος into ἄνθος ὥρας, something which would explain the Latin translation, *flos temporis*, better. For this translation, cf. Scarpat, *Sapienza*, 1:427.

29 Cf. Scarpat, *Sapienza*, 1:182-183; Busto Saiz, "The meaning of Wisdom 2:9a". See also Gilbert, "Sagesse", 61-62; Rosa, "Note a Sap 2,6-9"; Tait, "Crudités à l'anglaise". Cf. Larcher, *Sagesse*, 1:232-233, for an opposing opinion.

Synchronic Analysis

The verse opens with an invitation (δεῦτε οὖν) followed by ἀπολαύνω, in the aorist subjunctive with ingressive force ("come, then, let us enjoy ..."), like the aorist subjunctives of vv. 7-8. These are all exhortations which contrast with the imperatives that characterise chap. 1. In the case of the ungodly, it is a question of enjoying "present pleasures" (τῶν ὄντων ἀγαθῶν), those which are available here and now. The following stich clarifies that it is a matter of creation itself. The verb χράομαι, "use, make use of", is to be understood *in malam partem*, with the sexual nuance of "abuse", as in Gen 19:8 LXX (an episode which our author has clearly employed in Wis 19:13-17). The ungodly intend to abuse, do violence to the creation, behaving with youthful ardour, considering themselves, that is, as eternal youths. 2:6

The use of κτίσις placed in the mouth of the ungodly might seem strange. In Wisdom, κτίσις indicates the "creation", always in a religious sense (cf. 5:17; 16:24; 19:6). The use here is ironic. The ungodly are essentially denying that the reality which they are abusing is "creation" and think that it is only a possession to be taken advantage of and enjoyed in an unbridled way. As the third part of the book will show, it is creation itself which will turn against those ungodly people who have denied it.

The use of luxury wine (cf. above) and perfumes during banquets is another commonplace of the ancient world. The reference to not letting the flower of spring escape, that is, the spring of youth, could be another commonplace, as also the custom of crowning oneself with buds (*κάλυξιν) of roses. The background is certainly sexual (cf. v. 9). 2:7-8

In 2:7-8, all the anxiety of the ungodly emerges for the shortness of life, a reality to be seized "before it withers", just as happens with the wreaths of roses, used while still budding so that they fade less quickly. By contrast, wisdom is ἀμάραντος, which never withers (Wis 6:12a). Cf. also Wis 19:21.

"Let us leave the signs of (our) pleasure everywhere". The "signs" of pleasure are contrasted with the "signs" of virtue mentioned in Wis 5:13b in the "posthumous" discourse of the ungodly. 2:9

For the theme of the "heritage" (μερίς) cf. 1:16.

Diachronic Analysis

The use of ἀπολαύνω in Wis 2:6 refers to "enjoying" with a very negative nuance. Philo (*Spec.* 3.113) reproaches those who, in marriage, copulate with their wives not in order to have children but, as the pigs and goats do, seeking the pleasure of coitus (θηρώμενοι συῶν ἢ τράγων τρόπον τὴν ἐξ ὁμιλίας ἀπόλαυσιν). Cf. also Prov 7:18 LXX, where the prostitute invites the inexperienced youth to copulate with her: ἐλθὲ καὶ ἀπολαύσωμεν φιλίας ... (cf. Heb 11:25). As for the invitation to *carpe diem* which the ungodly address to themselves, it is a frequent *topos* in the literature both of the Ancient Near East and of Hellenism, although the theme is 2:6

not absent from Scripture. Cf. Isa 22:13 and, in a positive key, many passages of Qoheleth.[30]

2:7-8 Crowning oneself with roses (Wis 2:8) is a custom of cultic origin common in the *symposia*, although openly opposed by the Epicureans (Lucretius, *Rer. Nat.* 3.912-915). Horace (*Carm.* 2.3, and 13-16) presents a similar combination of wine, roses and perfume. In the biblical texts, Sir 32:3 [35:2] mentions the use of crowns in banquets. 2 Macc 6:7 records that the Jews were forced to wear crowns (κισσοὺς ἔχοντες) of ivy in honour of Bacchus.

2:9 The use of εὐφροσύνη (Wis 2:9) is polemical. According to Sir 1:11, true εὐφροσύνη is that offered by the fear of God and wisdom offer. In Sir 4:12, those who rise early to seek wisdom will be full of εὐφροσύνη. In Isa 25:9 LXX, εὐφραίνω occurs in relation to God. Cf. also Isa 61:7 and 10 LXX (εὐφροσύνη αἰώνιος ὑπὲρ κεφαλῆς αὐτῶν ... εὐφροσύνῃ εὐφρανθήσονται ἐπὶ κύριον); Bar 4:27-29 (εὐφροσύνην αἰώνιον μετὰ τῆς σωτηρίας ὑμῶν); Pss. Sol. 10:8; 14:10. Εὐφροσύνη occurs also in Qoheleth's texts relating to joy. Cf. Qoh 2:26; 5:19; 8:15; and 9:7. According to the ungodly, on the other hand, the only possible joy is that which a man can experience in the most licentious banquets and in unbridled sex![31] To this joy, so different from that experienced by the just, everything is sacrificed, starting from the very life of the just, which prevents the ungodly from the full enjoyment of theirs (cf. Wis 2:10-20).

Μερίς is here connected with κλῆρος which has a clear theological background in the LXX: cf. Jer 13:25 LXX; Isa 57:6 LXX (connected precisely with μερίς). In the Deuteronomic vocabulary, κλῆρος indicates the promised land as part of the heritage which belongs to the people of Israel. The term occurs several times in this sense in Deut-Josh. In the light of Ps 15:5 LXX (κύριος ἡ μερὶς τῆς κληρωνομίας μου), one could note that the ungodly are distorting the biblical language in a blasphemous way: their "part/share" and their "heritage" is quite different from that "part/share" and that "heritage" which the Lord promised to the faithful.

Wisdom and Qoheleth

This type of vocabulary is typical of Qoheleth: μερίς, in fact, is found in the LXX as the translation of חלק. Cf. Qoh 2:10, 21; 3:22; 5:17; and 9:9. In Qoheleth too, there is a strong irony in relation to the sense that חלק normally has in the biblical vocabulary.[32] Yet, when Qoheleth speaks of the "share/lot" that belongs to people, he does not intend a materialistic enjoyment of life but refers to the joy understood as God's "gift". It is unlikely that the author of Wisdom is depicting the ungodly as disciples of Qoheleth. The fact remains that Qoh 9:7-9 seems to be the biblical passage which is closest to Wis 2:6-9. Only here, in fact, is the brevity of life associated with the theme of enjoyment (εὐφροσύνη) and above all with the theme of the "part/share/lot" (μερίς)

---

30 Cf. the many texts cited in Winston, *Wisdom*, 118-119, and Scarpat, *Sapienza*, 1:147. As for Qoheleth, Skehan's observation is valid: "Ecclesiastes is not, therefore, the typical hedonist whom Wis is arraigning; nor is there any real warrant from language employed for supposing that Wis is concerned with deliberate misuse of the doctrine of Eccl." ("The Literary Relationship", 228).

31 For the "playfulness" which characterised the Alexandrine *clubs*, cf. Baslez, "The Author of Wisdom", 42-45. The σύμβολα would be precisely the badges of the Dionysian *clubs* (*ibid.*, p. 46).

32 Cf. Mazzinghi, Luca, *Ho cercato e ho esplorato*. Studi sul Qohelet (Bologna: EDB 2009²), 401-403.

which belongs to people. Our sage puts into the mouth of the ungodly, on the one hand, the words of Job who laments over the brevity of life (cf. Wis 2:8a = Job 14:2; Wis 2:9c = Job 20:29; 27:13; 31:2-3) and, on the other, the idea expressed in Isa 22:13, together with the idea of the "part/lot" suggested by the texts of Qoheleth. Thus, the ungodly are Jews who know Scripture but distort its message, beginning precisely with that of Qoheleth![33]

Wis 2:10-16:
Let Us Oppress the Just Man!

10 Let us lord it over the poor man who is just,
let us not spare the widow,
no respect for the white hairs of the old, laden with years.
11 Let our might be the law of justice,
because weakness is no use for anything.
12 Let us set snares for the just man, because he is troublesome to us
and opposes our actions.
He rebukes us for sins against the Law
and accuses us of sins against the traditional discipline.
13 He proclaims that he possesses knowledge of God
and declares himself to be son of the Lord.
14 He has become for us a reproof to our way of thinking,
the very sight of him is a burden to us,
15 because his life is different from that of others
and his ways are totally alien.
16 We are considered counterfeit coin by him
and he avoids our ways as something impure.
He proclaims the final destiny of the just to be happy
and he boasts of having God as his father.

Notes on the Text and Translation

v. 10c. Πρεσβύτου πολιὰς πολυχρονίους. For the textual variants πρεσβύτερους and πολυχρονίου, cf. Ziegler *sub loco*, and Larcher, *Sagesse*, 1:237, who rightly rejects both. The expression πολιὰς πολυχρονίους should be taken as a kind of hypallage: "the white hairs laden with years" even if, *ad sensum*, πολυχρονίους refers to the old man.

v. 16a. For εἰς κίβδηλον, cf. Scarpat, *Sapienza*, 1:189-190. In secular use, κίβδηλος indicates "counterfeit (coin)"; in the LXX (Lev 19:19; Deut 22:11), it indicates something "false", connected with pagan and impure practices (Cf. also 1 En. 10:9, 15). The

33 Cf. D'Alario, "La réflexion sur le sens de la vie", 322-323. Skehan observes that Wis 2:1-9 makes greater use of the words of Job than those of Qoheleth (cf. n. 31).

term is used in this sense in Wis 15:9 in relation to idols. The reference to impurity is present in 2:16b: the ungodly are alluding ironically to the Jewish practice of separating oneself from what is "impure" (cf. the accusations recorded by Tacitus, *Hist.* 5.5). The ungodly perceive that the just man regards them as "false", Jews who are no longer Jews, with something fake about them, connected with pagan and idolatrous institutions.

Synchronic Analysis

With great psychological depth, the author presents here a further aspect of the thought of the ungodly. After having laid out their materialistic view of life (vv. 1b-5), the ungodly have expressed their true desire: to enjoy life without restraints (vv. 6-9). Now, the passage to violence seems sudden, but it is not. Actually, it is a question of eliminating the just man who is hindering us from enjoying life as we would like (vv. 10-16). Whoever is opposed to our view of life does not have the right to live (2:17-20). In these final verses, the text takes on a strong theological depth.

2:10 The use of καταδυναστεύω refers to the oppression which someone powerful exercises over an inferior (κατά). The oppression of the "poor man who is just" (δίκαιον should be understood as in apposition) is the sign of an ironic reversal of the profoundest biblical values. The rewards which the Lord promises to the just in Scripture (cf. Pss 1:1-3; 36[37 MT]:25; 111[112 MT]:1-3; Prov 12:21) do not exist.

To the poor are added (10bc) the widow and the old. In fact, the more traditional triad of Scripture is represented by the poor, the widow, and the orphan (cf., for example, Isa 10:2), the "weak" classes of the population which ought to be protected. The mention here of lack of respect for the old could be a sign that the ungodly of which our author is thinking are young or, at least, in view of vv. 6-9, adults who *think* that they are young! In any case, it is the "mighty" who are under consideration, people of high rank or those who can let themselves use their power with arrogance.

2:11 "Let our might be the law of justice". For the ungodly, the just person is "useless" (ἄχρηστος) and "troublesome" (δύσχρηστος), and so must be eliminated. He or she does not have the right to exist. Furthermore, the use of the expression νόμος τῆς δικαιοσύνης is deliberate. For the ungodly, the true law is not, in fact, the Torah, but their own might. God, on the other hand, acts differently. Precisely because he is "strong", he is also merciful (cf. Wis 12:16b).

2:12 With another acute psychological observation, the book of Wisdom notes how the ungodly do not have the courage to tackle the just face to face, but do so in secret, by surprise, setting traps for them.

Beginning with this verse, the "just" takes on an importance of the first order. The use of the article (τὸν δίκαιον) shows that our author has in mind a particular "just" person (see below). The ungodly regard a just person like this as a living reproof to their lifestyle (2:12b) because he or she reproaches them for their sins committed against the law (ἁμαρτήματα νόμου) and against the traditional discipline (ἁμαρτήματα παιδείας ἡμῶν). Ἁμαρτήματα expresses a biblical theme. In fact, the idea of a sin against the law does not correspond to the Greek mentality where, for the most part, sins were considered as the fruit of ignorance.

The law is probably the Mosaic Torah. In addition to the lack of the article, it is chiefly the parallel with παιδεία which points us in this direction, recalling the sapiential מוסר (cf. the comment on 1:5). What seems decisive is the possessive "our" (παιδείας ἡμῶν). The just person, the faithful Israelite, will reprove the ungodly, fellow Jews, for their sins committed against "our" Law, that is, against the Torah and against the traditional sapiential education.

The "knowledge of God" (γνῶσιν θεοῦ) which the just person "proclaims" (ἐπαγγέλλεται) is not to be understood as the theoretical recognition of the existence of God which, strictly speaking, the ungodly have never denied. The context orients us towards a practical, vital knowledge of God on the part of people. The ungodly have never "experienced" God. We do not have here even an esoteric kind of knowledge, reserved to a few chosen ones, as the choice of γνῶσις could lead us to think (cf. 2:21). The mysteries of God (and those of wisdom; cf. Wis 6:22) are accessible to all and not only to an elite. Knowledge of God is recognising the divine "judgements", namely, the action of God in history (cf. 17:1a). From this γνῶσις, knowledge of the future is not excluded (cf. 2:16cd and the whole passage of 2:21-24). 2:13

In addition to "knowing" God, the just person "declares himself to be son of the Lord". Κύριος refers directly to YHWH, the God of Israel. The just boast that they are his "sons". In light of vv. 16 and 18, παῖς should certainly be understood as "son" and not "servant" (cf. Wis 12:7 and 19:6; cf. also the translation of 2:13 in the ancient versions). However, it is not to be excluded that our sage used παῖς here and υἱός only in v. 18 precisely because of the double sense of the term παῖς, something which could lead us to think not only of "son" but also of "servant". In this way, our sage obtains a twofold result: reading the figure of the just person in the light of the Fourth Servant Song of Isaiah and at the same time showing that this "servant" is in reality "son" of God.[34]

The just person is a βαρύς, a "burden", unbearable (cf. Wis 17:20) This applies even to the sight of him (καὶ βλεπόμενος). The reason is of an elaborate psychological nature. For the ungodly, the very presence of the just becomes a living accusation and constant protest against their wicked deeds. 2:14-15

The behaviour of the just appears different (*ἀνόμοιος) from that of others. It is behaviour that is "alien", according to the use of the term ἐξηλλαγμένος, which is to be understood in the sense of something that arouses astonishment. Cf. Plato, *Gorg.* (513ab), where we read that it is not possible to be ἀνομοίοι if one wants to be successful in politics. This is a clear reference to the way of life of the Jewish people which arouses astonishment and which appears strange to the eyes of non-Jews. In the same way, precisely what annoys the ungodly is the disciplined and honest life of the just person who observes that law which the godless no longer follow, a life which renders the just different from the others and, thus, the object of astonishment.

The idea of the just who separate themselves from the ungodly is biblical (cf. Ps 25[26 MT]:4-5. As we observed in our textual note in connection with εἰς 2:16

---

34 For a possible interpretation of παῖς as "servant" cf. Larcher, *Sagesse*, 1:245-246, and Scarpat, *Sapienza*, 1:188; cf. Giménez González, *"Si el justo es hijo de Dios"*, 260-269. Cf., also, below.

κίβδηλον, the reference to Jewish practices is increasingly being emphasised, here, the laws of purity.

The final part of v. 16 opens up a new perspective: the just "proclaim happy" (μακαρίζω, cf. 3:13) their own ἔσχατα. In Greek usage, ἔσχατα can indicate "extreme evils". In this case, the ungodly would be speaking in a highly ironic way: the just man has the nerve to boast of those sufferings which we are inflicting on him! However, in the light of Sir 7:36; 28:6; 38:20, ἔσχατα can indicate what awaits people after their death. Elsewhere too, τὰ ἔσχατα appears with this significance (cf., in the LXX, Isa 41:22; 46:10; and 47:7). Here, we can understand τὰ ἔσχατα in the sense that the just person is thinking generically of being "happy" at the end of his or her life. What for the ungodly is only an *appearance*, the just declare to be *real*, namely, happiness at the end of one's life. Thirdly, it is possible to see a reference to Job 42:12 LXX: ὁ δὲ κύριος εὐλόγησεν τὰ ἔσχατα Ιωβ. We do not rule out that our sage is drawing a parallel between the "just" person of whom he is speaking and Job who is suffering but blessed at the end.

God as Father Finally, the just man boasts of having God as his father. In itself, ἀλαζονεύω has a negative sense (cf. Wis 17:7b). In fact, for the ungodly, what the just person says is foolish boasting, but ironically the verb acquires a contrary value. What the just man is boasting of is true. The parenthood of God is to be seen in connection with the theme of the end of the just. Despite his sufferings he knows that he will be received by a father who, as in Prov 3:12, corrects his son because he loves him (cf. Wis 11:10).

Diachronic Analysis

2:10-16 In Wis 2:10-16, force and violence are seen as the direct result of an exclusively materialistic configuration of life. This is a *topos* of the contemporary philosophy, especially in the accusations mounted against the Epicureans. Epictetus makes a good deal of use of the idea that a life of pleasures leads to violence (cf. the case of Socrates; *Diatr.* 2.2.15-20, etc.). The true philosopher avoids both a life of pleasures and one of violence. It is for this reason that he faces opposition.

2:10 The verb καταδυναστεύω is frequent in the LXX and could have been suggested by Hab 1:4 (ὅτι ὁ ἀσεβὴς καταδυναστεύει τὸν δίκαιον); Ezek 22:7; or Exod 1:13 (καὶ κατεδυνάστευον οἱ Αἰγύπτιοι τοὺς υἱοὺς Ισραηλ βίᾳ) which our sage calls to mind in Wis 17:2, a possible *flashback* to 2:10.

Still in Wis 2:10, for the persecution of the poor, cf. Exod 23:6; Deut 15:12; and Ezek 18:12; of the widow, Exod 22:22 and Deut 14:28-29; of the old, cf. Isa 47:6 and Lam 5:12. Cf. also Lev 19:32 and Sir 25:6.

2:11 The idea that the law of the strongest becomes the only rule of justice is well known to Plato who places similar considerations in the mouth of the Sophist Callicles: "I think that it is nature itself which indicates that it is just that the better imposes itself on the worse, the stronger on the weak" (*Gorg.* 483bcd). However, the ungodly are also opposed, ironically, to ideas well rooted in the prophetical texts. See Hos 14:10 LXX[35]: "the ways of the Lord are right; the just

---

35 Cf. Scarpat, *Sapienza*, 1:153.

go forward in them, but the ungodly show themselves weak (ἀσθενήσουσιν) in them".

Verse 12a is a probable quotation of Isa 3:10 LXX (δήσωμεν τὸν δίκαιον ὅτι 2:12
δύσχρηστος ἡμῖν ἐστιν),[36] the only other occurrence in the LXX of the adjective δύσχρηστος which must necessarily have an active sense: he is an embarrassment, an obstacle to us (the Old Latin prefers a passive sense: *insuavis*, pathetic, unpleasant). The only difference of Wis 2:12a from Isaiah lies in the use of ἐνεδρεύω which is to be understood in the sense of "set ambushes", "set snares", and this is undoubtedly stronger than Isaiah's δήσωμεν. For this verb one can think of Ps 9:30 LXX[10:9 MT] where it refers to the ungodly who lays traps for the poor (cf. also Job 24:11 LXX; 38:40 LXX).

In connection with the mention of the "law", the book of Wisdom could be bearing in mind another philosophical *topos*: the philosopher is one who observes the laws (cf. Plato, *Crit.* 50a); has a strange lifestyle which is difficult to tolerate (Plutarch, *Mor.* 90e; Epictetus, *Diatr.* 4.8.5-12); and his lot is happy after his death (Cicero, *Tusc.* 1.29.71, in relation to Socrates).

In a personal sense, in relation to an individual and not to a people, speaking 2:16
of God as "father" is a rare usage in biblical Hebrew, one which begins to be seen only within the Judaism of the Hellenistic period (cf. Sir 23:1 and 4 and, for our author above all, the text of Wis 14:3).[37] That which for the just has the flavour of a joyful achievement is for the ungodly only the product of useless boasting.

Wis 2:17-20: Let Us See If the Just One Is the Child of God ...!

17 Let us see if his words are true
and let us put to the test what will happen at his end,
18 for if the just man is son of God, he will take care of him
and deliver him from the hand of his adversaries.
19 With insults and tortures, let us put him to the test,
to discover his meekness
and try his forbearance.
20 Let us condemn him to a shameful death,
because, he claims, God will come to him at the end".

---

36 Cf. Larcher, *Sagesse*, 1:140-141, who hypothesises instead a dependence of the LXX of Isa 3:10 precisely on this text of Wisdom. Isa 3:10 LXX is different from the MT which is usually considered a gloss. The LXX then places the words of Isa 3:10 in the mouth of the ungodly. It is very difficult to come to a decision on this, and even Larcher shows himself uncertain.

37 Cf. Giménez González, "*Si el justo es hijo de Dios*", 271-325.

Notes on the Text and Translation

v. 17. The rare expression τὰ ἐν ἐκβάσει (cf. Wis 8:8 and 11:14; *ἔκβασις is *hapax* of the LXX and of the NT) indicates the end result of something, to be understood here as "what will happen at his end", that is, the final stages of the life of the just man (cf. 1 Cor 10:13; Heb 13:7). Noticeable is the difficulty of the Latin translator who doubles the stich (*et temptemus quae ventura sunt illi / et sciemus quae erunt novissima illius*).

v. 19a. The use of ὕβρις is heavy with Greek resonances. The term, chosen by the LXX to translate the Hebrew גאון, indicates in classical Greek the tragic arrogance of the man who turns against the gods. In this context, it indicates more precisely the "scorn" with which the ungodly torment the just and which will fall on them in the day of judgement (cf. 4:18).

v. 19b. The term ἐπιείκεια returns in Wis 12:18 with reference to the action of God (cf. 2 Macc 2:22; 10:4), just as in the NT (2 Cor 10:1) it is an attribute of the activity of Christ and refers also to the mercy which tempers justice (Acts 24:4) (Spicq, *Notes*, 1:263-268). In a moral sense, ἐπιείκεια also indicates composure (1 Tim 3:3). Sometimes, the term assumes the nuance of sweetness and moderation, of gentleness, especially in relation to insults that have been suffered. It is a "meekness", therefore, which is something that goes well beyond due politeness.

v. 20. The term ἐπισκοπή, "visit/come to", returns in Wis 3:13; 4:15; 14:11; 19:15. In the LXX, the word is used to translate the Hebrew פקדה, very often in relation to God's intervention on behalf of his people (cf. Gen 50:24; Exod 3:16; 13:19), not infrequently, especially in the language of the prophets, with eschatological force, be it salvific or punitive (Jer 6:15; 10:15; and Isa 10:3; cf. Wis 14:11). In the context of the book of Wisdom, ἐπισκοπή indicates "visit" in the sense of the last, eschatological judgement of God. At the end, he will visit the just (referred to by the pronoun αὐτοῦ) who will be the object of favourable judgement on the part of the Lord; cf. Beyer, Hermann Wolfgang, ἐπισκοπή, *TDNT* 2:606-608.

Synchronic Analysis

2:17-18 The initial asyndeton of v. 17 marks the passage to a new resolution on the part of the ungodly. It is now a question of seeing whether all that the just person boasted about is true. As clearly appears from their plan of life (2:1-9), for the ungodly, only what can be demonstrated is real. The entire passage of 2:17-20 is an ironic reflection of the style of the philosophical discourses of the period in which the student was urged to verify what he had learned in theory: "the final examination which every school demands".[38]

The "words" (λόγοι) of the just referred to in v. 17 are those of v. 16 which are repeated in v. 18: boasting of having God for one's father and of having a happy final destiny. The expression τὰ ἐν ἐκβάσει refers to the previous ἔσχατα δικαίων (16c). The argument of the ungodly is clear: if God is really father of the just (cf. 16d), God will take care of them (ἀντιλήμψεται) and deliver them (ῥύσεται; 18b) from the hand of their adversaries. The response which our sage will offer

---

38 Cf. Scarpat, *Sapienza*, 1:159; Premstaller, *"Gericht" und "Strafe" im Buch der Weisheit*, 78-79.

in 2:21-24 will undoubtedly be surprising and will shift our attention on to the future lot of the just "son of God".

In v. 18, the statement of divine paternity contained in 2:16 is succeeded by the logical claim that follows from it: the just person is God's child (ὑιὸς θεοῦ).

In our text, speaking of the *individual* just person as "child of God" represents a certain novelty for the Jewish tradition (cf. Sir 4:10), a novelty of which our sage is well aware. In fact, the just person "boasts" (2:16d) of being God's child. Being a child refers here, primarily, to a profound and personal relationship, a relationship of protection and trust which characterises the just in relation to God.

The problems raised by our text are complex and refer to the identity of the "just" person introduced in these verses. If the influence of texts like 2 Sam 7:14 and Ps 2:7 could lead us to think of the "son of God" as an individual figure with messianic traits, the clear relationship with the innocent and oppressed just man of Ps 21[22 MT] and with the "sons of God" of the third part of the book seems to us to confirm a collective reading of "son", along the lines of a figure who represents the faithful Israelites, the protagonists of the third part of the book (cf. Wis 9:7; 12:19-21; 16:10, and 26). However, as we have seen in connection with v. 16, a "personal" reading of the theme of divine sonship cannot be excluded *a priori*. The "son of God, therefore, is also the individual just person, the protagonist of Wis 3-4 who experiences the closeness of the Father in time of difficulty and, above all, at the hour of death. The latter, in this text of Wisdom, represents as it were the test of his sonship.[39]

For the ungodly, the testing of the truth of the just man's words comprises 2:19
scorn (ὕβρις) or insults and torture (βάσανος). A little further on, the lot of the just will be described with a similar vocabulary: no βάσανος will touch them. For the ungodly, on the other hand, who wished to put the just man to the test (ἐτάσωμεν; v. 19), there will be exactly that ἐξέτασις already mentioned in 1:9.

The just person's virtues which the ungodly want to put to the test with their insults and their tortures are ἐπιεικεία ("meekness") and ἀνεξικακία, which is to be understood as forbearance, the ability to endure evils, one of the characteristics proper to the sage (the term is rare and late. Cf. Plutarch, *Mor.* 90E and, in the NT, the adjective ἀνεξίκακος in 2 Tim 2:24).

The transition carried out in this verse is striking. The preoccupation of the 2:20
ungodly with enjoying life, because at its end there awaits only death, results in the death inflicted on the weaker ones. This is the definitive test to which the ungodly subject the just which will expose their false nature and illusions. What we have here is a "shameful" death (ἀσχήμων; *mors turpissima*: Lat). One can think of a form of death that was particularly shameful, like crucifixion, or else of a death inflicted on the just as a result of shameful accusations which destroy one's moral stature before others. Or, again, the death of the just will be shameful because, according to their words, God ought to have assisted, but did not do so.

The discourse of the ungodly concludes with an ironic reference to the future. In the face of death, there will not be any "visitation" (ἐπισκοπή) on the part of God, any salvation for the just. It is difficult to say whether the reference to ἐπισκοπή put into the mouth of the ungodly indicates a physical salvation or is

39 Cf. Giménez González, *"Si el justo es hijo de Dios"*, 135-137.

already alluding to a salvation that is eternal. It seems easier to understand ἐπισκοπή as an irony on the visitation *ante mortem* which God reserves for God's people and the faithful (cf. 1 Sam 2:21; Jer 15:15), saving them from the danger of death. A further possibility is that of interpreting ἐπισκοπή in its etymological sense of "examination", the final test to which the ungodly subject the just (in this sense, cf. Job 31:14; Sir 18:20; and 23:24). This "examination" will be death itself. In this case, however, the use of the preposition ἐκ is unusual.

From the words of the ungodly, there emerges an important fact: the truth of what the just person claims will be proved by death. One question remains in suspense: are the ungodly correct? What response can be made to their accusations against the just? This is what our sage is preparing for in the final verses of the chapter.

Diachronic Analysis

2:17-18 In 2:18b, the verb ῥύομαι refers to the text of Ps 21[22 MT]:9 (ῥυσάσθω αὐτόν). The text of 18b can be suitably read as an ironic comment by the ungodly on this passage. Cf. also Sir 2:6 (πίστευσον αὐτῷ καὶ ἀντιλήμψεταί σου). Matt 27:43 is probably using this passage in connection with Jesus (ῥυσάσθω νῦν εἰ θέλει αὐτόν· εἶπεν γὰρ ὅτι θεοῦ εἰμι υἱός). In both cases, there is a reprise of Ps 21[22 MT]:9.

The Just Son of God

In the OT, the divine sonship of Israel is a fundamental aspect in the description of the relation between God and God's people, often viewed in connection with the event of the Exodus (Exod 4:22; Deut 14:1; Jer 38[31 MT]:9). They are a people called by God out of Egypt (Hos 11:1) whom God considers God's favourite (Jer 38[31 MT]:20). For Israel, the state of "son" underlines their distance from God (Mal 1:6), but at the same time also God's fatherly love (Ps 102[103 MT]:13). The "son" *par excellence* is the king-messiah (2 Sam 7:14; cf. Ps 2:7 which our sage could have had in mind).
In the texts of the Hellenistic period, the theme of the divine sonship of Israel appears to be increasingly widespread. Being "sons" of God also acquires an eschatological nuance and is related to faithfulness to the law (cf. T. Levi 18:8, etc.; and below in connection with Wis 18:4). In texts like 3 Macc 6:28; Est E,16 (8:12q), "sons" appear also in relation to the oppression exercised by the ungodly, just as happens in Wis 17:2 and 18:4.[40]

2:20 As the background to v. 20, one can think of the famous text of Plato which describes the death of the just man in the strongest terms (cf. *Resp.* 361e–362a)[41] or else another reprise of the Fourth Servant Song (cf. Isa 53:2-3, 8, and 12).

It is more difficult to know whether v. 20 is referring to real events. The sources available to us do not permit us to claim that in Ptolemaic Egypt there were times of anti-Jewish persecution in which the Jews were condemned to death, still less by fellow-Jews. One could also think that there lingered in Alexandria echoes of the scandalous killings which took place in Judaea under the Hasmonean dynasty from the time of Alexander Jannaeus up to that of Herod the Great. The possibility remains that our sage is taking up here an ideal *motif.* Not infrequently, in the Psalter, the ungodly seek to cause the death of the just (cf. Ps 93:21 LXX [94:21 MT]).

---

40 Cf. Mazzinghi, *Notte di paura e di luce,* 219-221 and n. 38; Larcher, *Sagesse*, 1:252-255.

41 Larcher, *Sagesse*, 1:256-257.

Wis 2:21-24: The Mysteries of God

21 They reason thus, but they deceive themselves;
for their wickedness has blinded them,
22 since they have not known the mysterious plans of God,
nor hoped in a reward for holiness
nor looked for a reward for souls without fault:
23 for God created humanity in incorruption,
and made it the image of his own nature.
24 But, through the devil's envy, death entered the world
and those who belong to its party experience it.

Notes on the Text and Translation

v. 21. The aorist ἐλογίσαντο has gnomic rather than historic force (cf. also in 3:10). For the use of πλανάω, cf. Mazzinghi, *Notte di paura e di luce*, 4-5. The verb indicates a mistake that is more of a religious and moral type than the purely physical variety. In Plato, πλανάω assumes a theoretical and moral nuance. In the LXX, the verb is often used with reference to idolatry (cf. Wis 5:6; 11:15; 12:24; 14:22; 15:4; 17:1).

v. 22a. The term μυστήριον is present in the LXX only in texts of the Hellenistic period. Other than in Wisdom, it appears in Tob 12:7, 11; Jud 2:2; Sir 3:18 (S); Sir 22:22; 27:16, 17, 21; 2 Macc 13:21; and eight times in Dan 2. In that context, the "secret mysteries" (μυστήρια κρυπτά; Dan 2:47) represent God's plan for history and for the world which is being revealed to the seer.

v. 22b. The term ὁσιότης is rare in the LXX (Deut 9:5; 1 Sam 14:41; 1 Kgs 9:4; Prov 14:32; cf. Wis 5:19; 9:3; 14:30; on the other hand, the adjective ὅσιος occurs seven times). The source is probably Plato: "whoever does what he ought with men does just things (δίκαια) with the gods, pious ones (ὅσια)" (*Gorg.* 507ab); so too Philo: ὁσιότης μὲν πρὸς θεόν, δικαιοσύνη δὲ πρὸς ἀνθρώπους (*Abr.* 208). Wis 9:3 also links ὁσιότης with δικαιοσύνη. "Piety/holiness" is thus the correct disposition in dealings with God as "justice" is in dealings with people. Cf. Scarpat, *Sapienza*, 1:197.

v. 23a. The initial ὅτι is not to be understood in a causal sense ("because"), as suggested in Ziegler's edition which places a point at the end of the previous stich. Rather, it is to be understood as a declarative ὅτι which introduces an objective statement (for some examples of ἐλπίζειν with declarative ὅτι, cf. BDF § 397.2 n5).

Scarpat (*Sapienza*, 1:162) suggests giving ἐπί final force ("*for* incorruption"; cf. 4 Macc 9:22); Reese notes, however, that in the 22 times that ἐπί is used with the dative in Wisdom (cf. Wis 3:9a; 10:5c; 16:24c, and above all 1:13, ἐπ' ἀπωλείᾳ) what is indicated is rather a *state*. We, therefore, have to translate "*in* incorruptibility". "He [Wis] conceives 'incorruption' not as a man's goal but as the positive quality granted to his nature, enabling him to enter into a special, personal relationship with his Creator" (*Hellenistic Influence*, 66).

The term ἀφθαρσία returns in Wis 6:18, 19; ἄφθαρτος in 12:1 and 18:4. Ἀφθαρσία appears in the Hellenistic period in relation to the Epicurean disputes on the nature of the gods and should not be understood as a simple synonym for ἀθανασία. Philodemus, the Epicurean, states that ἀφθαρσία is a positive power, proper to the gods, able to hold the atoms together and so preserve them from physical corruption

(Reese, *Hellenistic influence*, 64-69, especially n. 156). The term will be used by Plutarch to describe the essence of divinity. God is "incorruptible" in the sense that God is permanent, lasting, eternal: ὡς ἄφθαρτος ὁ θεός (*E Delph.* 388F). Plutarch's definition of the divine is that of being a μακαρία καὶ ἄφθαρτος φύσις (cf. *Is. Os.* 358E). God is incorruptible in the sense that God is permanent, lasting, opposed to that which is corrupted and so to that which is subject to φθορά (cf. *Corpus Herm.* 12.16). Philo makes indifferent use of the combinations ψυχὴ ἄφθαρτος and ψυχὴ ἀθάνατος (cf. *Somn.* 1.137; *Opif.* 119-120). In *Somn.* 1.181, the incorruptibility of the soul (ἀφθαρσία ψυχῆς) is considered a doctrine present in Scripture (in light of Gen 28:15 LXX). Cf., in 1 Cor 15, the Pauline use of ἄφθαρτος in relation to the body, perhaps even in opposition to Philo. With ἄφθαρτος, Wisdom wishes to indicate something that is incorruptible and eternal, and at the same time something that can come only from God.

v. 23b. Some versions (cf. Lat) presuppose the reading κατ' εἰκόνα, which arises under the influence of Gen 1:26-27. For the absence of the preposition κατά in Wis 2:23, cf. Larcher, *Sagesse*, 1:268. If our author has before him the Hebrew text of Gen 1:26, perhaps he is reading the *beth* of בצלמנו as a *beth essentiae.* Man was not created "in" the image of God but "as" the image of God. In this way, the meaning of εἰκών goes rather in the direction of that of "copy", "reproduction", as happens also in Wis 7:26.

The textual witnesses alternate ἰδιότητος with ἀιδιότητος (Rahlfs) and ὁμοιότητος (Ziegler). Rejecting the last as an accommodating reading of a difficult text and one that is sparsely attested, the editors and commentators are divided between the first two. However, in addition to giving a sense to the text that is hardly clear, the reading "eternity" has perhaps been suggested by the presence of ἀφθαρσία in the previous stich. The play on words with the same roots (ἰδίας ἰδιότητος) is not unusual in Wisdom. The term ἰδιότης indicates what is proper to a particular being, in this case, what is proper to God. Humanity has thus been created an image of the very nature of God.

v. 24. The exegesis of this text has long been disturbed by the idea that it refers to the Christian doctrine of original sin. Cf. Lyonnet, "Le sens de πειράζειν en Sap 2,24". Larcher, *Sagesse*, 1:270-271: those who belong to the "party of the devil" are the ungodly who "experience" (πειράζειν) death. Leaving aside some more debatable interpretations (cf. Gilbert, "Sagesse", 105), we should take note of Scarpat's proposal (*Sapienza*, 1:164-167). Death strikes only those who belong to the "party of the devil". It is, therefore, eternal death: "but through the envy of the devil, death entered into the world: it is put to the test by those who belong to it". In the light of the use of μερίς in 1:16, I hold that Scarpat is right in maintaining that it is the ungodly who belong to the "party of death" and – precisely for this reason (*contra* Scarpat) – experience it. The verb πειράζω is to be understood of the experience of death undergone by the ungodly, just as intended by Lyonnet. Ἐκείνου is to be referred to death and not to the devil.

Synchronic Analysis

2:21-22 The reasonings (ταυτᾶ ἐλογίσαντο; cf. 2:1a) of the ungodly lead them to an error which is both moral and religious (ἐπλανήθησαν). The ungodly are blind because of their wickedness (κακία). Verse 21 sees the emergence of one of the *motifs* which has characterised the chapter as a whole: the dichotomy between appearance and reality. The paradox is clear: the ungodly believe only in what they see; they do not perceive that reality is very different from what they have imagined.

Verse 22 describes what the ungodly are not able to see: they do not know the μυστήρια θεοῦ, that is, the secret plans of God. Right reasoning (Wis 1:2-3 compared with Wis 1:16 and 2:21), a life led according to justice, and faith in God are all conditions for the successful understanding of the "plans of God". But how are they revealed to the just? Although anchored in the sapiential tradition of Israel, the book of Wisdom does not seem to wish to base knowledge merely on the experience of life, as happens for example in Qoheleth. Although awarding much importance to reason and not excluding the value of the human sciences (cf. 7:17-21), Wisdom introduces the category of "mystery" precisely to avoid the impression of carrying out an argument that is exclusively philosophical or simply ethical. The "mysteries of God" relating to "incorruptibility", and so to man's eschatological destiny, can undoubtedly be known to all, but nonetheless they are called "mysteries". In other words, they are connected with some higher form of revelation. A first answer to this question comes to us from the fact that, in Wis 2:23-24, our sage refers very naturally to the texts of Gen 1-3 in order to justify his own statements about "incorruptibility". Although affirming things that are clearly new within the panorama of contemporary Judaism, the book of Wisdom seems to want to say that such affirmations are already contained in the biblical texts.[42] The "Mysteries" of God

Verse 22 is built up in a progression. The ungodly have not known the mysterious plans of God; they have not hoped in a reward (μισθός) for holiness (ὁσιότης). The use of ἐλπίζω (the only occurrence in Wisdom) is to be understood in a weak sense. The ungodly have not expected a reward for holiness, in other words, for the right attitude of people in their dealings with God (cf. notes to the text). Μισθός here has an eschatological force.

The ungodly, then, have not made good judgement (ἔκριναν) about the recompense (γέρας) which belongs to souls without fault (ψυχῶν ἀμώμων). With the term ψυχαί, read in light of Wis 3:1-3, we have to understand, not the soul separated from the body but the entire human being (cf. the comment on 1:4). The term ἄμωμος, *hapax* in Wisdom, indicates in the LXX the quality of the victims reserved for sacrifice ("pure"); cf. 1 Pet 1:19 in connection with Christ. The use of a sacrificial vocabulary is interesting precisely because it is found in a non-sacrificial context. The "souls" of the just are the true sacrifice that is pleasing to God (cf. further in connection with 3:6).

The mysteries of God, therefore, are to do with the recompense which God grants to the just man as a reward for his holiness. The text gives no explicit indication as to the nature of such a reward, but v. 23 and especially Wis 3:1-9 suggest to us with clarity that this reward is to be seen along the lines of a life without end. It is interesting to note that eternal life is presented as a recompense for morally just behaviour (cf. also 3:15). Elsewhere (cf. 3:5 and 9), however, it is presented as a free gift. However, there is no contradiction in this juxtaposition of grace and reward, a juxtaposition, moreover, which is typically biblical.

God's plan did not envisage death. What Wis 1:13-15 put in negative terms is here expressed in a positive form. 2:23-24

42 Collins, "The Reinterpretation of Apocalyptic Traditions". For the polemical thrust of this text against the mysteries, cf. Mazzinghi, "I misteri di Dio", 151-161.

Incorruptibility The use of ἀφθαρσία, "incorruptibility", instead of ἀθανασία, makes us think of a qualified immortality. In 6:18–19, incorruptibility is described as a "being close to God". Ἀφθαρσία does not make us think of the soul but rather of the body which is not corrupted, of the idea of a *life* that involves the entire human being. Our sage is probably thinking of the resurrection of the body.

The text of v. 24 states that death entered the world through the jealousy of the devil. According to Wis 1:13-15, God created everything for existence. Indeed, God loves everything which God has created (cf. 11:24). Whence then comes the διάβολος, and whom or what does he represent? This figure does not appear any further in the book and the theme of the devil's jealous, just hinted at here, will be developed further only in later traditions. In any case, Wisdom does not seem to establish any explicit relationship between the sin of the human couple recounted in Gen 3 and the entrance of death into the word (cf. also the comment on 10:1). Rather, death appears to be bound up with personal sin. In fact, those who experience it are those who belong to its party (cf. 1:16). There exists a "party of death" with which the ungodly are registered, thus finding paradoxically exactly what they are seeking to hold distant by their lifestyle.

Ambiguity of Death As for death, which "entered the world through the devil's envy", it seems at first glance to be physical death as in 1:13, since both Wis 1:13 and 2:24 refer explicitly to the Genesis account and in particular to Gen 2:17 and 3:19.[43] In this case too, however, the notion of death is ambiguous. It is a death which causes humanity to lose the state of incorruptibility in which it was created. Thus, it is not so much physical death, which touches the just as well, though this is without their losing this incorruptibility. Here, the death which "entered the world" is eternal death of which physical death is an ambiguous representation. It is not to be considered as a punishment but as a passage, to life for the just (3:1-9) but to eternal ruin for the ungodly.[44]

Diachronic Analysis

2:22 In Wis 2:22, the background for this terminology is to be sought in Dan 2 LXX, but here the context is different, and the divine "mysteries" are actually not those which are revealed to the seer alone.

In the light of Wis 6:22b, it seems difficult to exclude an allusion to the mystery cults which promised the initiate immortality through the knowledge of se-

43 Cf. Gilbert, "La relecture de la Genèse", *passim.* See an up-to-date summary of the question in Giménez Gonzalez, *"Si el justo es hijo de Dios"*, 143-147. Giménez Gonzalez defends the idea that in Wis 2:23-24 our sage is referring also to the idea of physical death.

44 Cf. Kolarcik, *Ambiguity of Death*, 152-156 for a reflection on the theological consequences of such exegesis for the Christian doctrine of "original sin". In the book of Wisdom, physical death as such cannot be considered as the result of sin (cf. also Wis 10:1-2) but as a fact connatural to humanity. What changes with sin is the relationship of man with death. Cf. also pp. 147-148 and 187-188 for an actualisation of these themes: present day society rejects death but then undergoes it, just as happens to the ungodly in Wisdom.

crets reserved to the elect alone. Wisdom, on the other hand, is accessible to all (cf. Wis 6:22-25). Those mysterious plans of God which apocalyptic reserved to the knowledge of the seers, those mysteries which, in the various mystery rites, were unveiled solely to the initiate are instead for our sage available to all those who are capable of seeing them, except for the ungodly. The book of Wisdom excludes every type of mediation, whether prophetic or angelic, such as happens in the apocalyptic tradition.

Behind v. 23 undoubtedly stands Gen 1:26-27. However, being "image" of the divine nature is understood by our author in a much more extended sense than in Gen 1:26-27. In fact, it is to do with the participation in the very nature (ἰδιότητος) of God, a "nature" associated with the incorruptibility (ἀφθαρσία) proper to God. 2:23-24

In this verse, Wisdom carries out a complex exegetical operation. The text of Gen 1:26-27 is being reread in the light of Gen 3:2b: before this sin, humanity was able to eat of the tree of life. Wis 2:23 explains the theme of humanity in the image of God in Gen 1:26-27 in the light of the account of Gen 2-3. It is as if the author wished to tell us that *God's plan of life for people remains in force even after the sin which provoked the introduction of death into the world.* Humanity was created "in incorruptibility", which does not appear as a preternatural gift then lost as a result of sin, but rather a *state* in which humanity was created. However, humanity does not possess incorruptibility but is the image of the nature of God because God exists *in* incorruptibility. Death does not, then, form part of God's plan concerning humanity (cf. 1:14). Our sage is developing here an idea which was already present in germ in some texts of the LXX: Isa 54:16, "I have not created you for destruction" (ἐγὼ δὲ ἔκτισά σε οὐ εἰς ἀπώλειαν φθεῖραι); and Isa 44:7 (ἐποίησα ἄνθρωπον εἰς τὸν αἰῶνα, a text which could be understood as "I fashioned humanity for eternity"). Our sage does not intend to speak of a "natural" immortality of humanity in the Greek sense of an immortal soul, for example, but of an orientation of humanity – understood as a unitary being – to *life*, as a gift of the Creator.

Finally, we note that Wis 2:24 is one of the first attestations of διάβολος identified with the serpent of Gen 3 (cf. Rev 12:9 and 20:2).[45]

Summary of Wis 1:16 – 2:24: The Identity of the Ungodly and That of the Just

Life (ὁ βίος ἡμῶν; cf. 1b and 4c) and death (τελευτὴ; cf. 1c and 5b) constitute the great guiding theme of this first part of the discourse of the ungodly, who are the deniers of life but frozen by the fear of death. This is the theme against which the contest between the just and the ungodly is played out. The contemporary relevance of this text will thus not escape present day readers of Wisdom, given

45 According to Collins, it is the oldest attestation; cf. 1 En. 31:6; LAE 10-17. This figure does not find any room in the Philonian corpus. Cf. Collins, *Jewish Wisdom*, 190; Winston, *Wisdom of Solomon*, 121-123; Martin – Hogan, "The Exegetical Background", 19-21.

that it tackles a set of problems that are perennially topical: the meaning of life and the fear of death.

But who are the ungodly presented in this chapter? Are they disciples of Qoheleth? Sadducees? Persecutors of the Teacher of Righteousness of Qumran? Epicureans? None of these identifications appears decisive. At most, the ungodly can be considered popularisers of some teachings of Epicurean origin which, however, cannot be used to justify the violence with which the ungodly are depicted in the second part of the discourse (2:10-20). Nor is it possible to think with certainty of the Epicurean philosophy as such as something which urges extreme, unbridled pleasure.[46]

In 2:1-9, the starting point for the reasoning of the ungodly is represented not so much by Hellenistic philosophy or culture but, on the contrary, precisely by Scripture of which the ungodly show themselves to be so knowledgeable.[47] At the same time, the discourse of the ungodly is packed with allusions to the Hellenistic cultural environment, to the medical theories that were then fashionable, and – not infrequently – to philosophy. Above all, this is the Epicurean variety, without disdaining Platonic ideas, yet without wishing to be seen as adopting a particular philosophical tendency. In conclusion, the ungodly are apostate Jews who have reread Scripture and their own faith experience in the light of the most fatalistic and pessimistic aspects of contemporary Greek philosophy and culture.

It is difficult to assess the phenomenon of apostasy in Alexandrian Judaism.[48] However, one could think that the ungodly of Wis 2 are those apostate Jews who are also found in the works of Philo (cf. *Praem.* 126; *Virt.* 182), those who have abandoned the παιδεία and the νόμος, in other words, the *mûsar*, the sapiential education, and the *Torah* (cf. Wis 2:12). From our sage's point of view, the error of the ungodly lies in not having known how to form a synthesis between the biblical faith, the profundity of which they have not grasped, and the rationality of the Hellenistic culture, though this is never condemned as such in the book of Wisdom. In this sense, they are truly the *ungodly*, ἀσεβεῖς, people without God. It is conspicuous how our sage avoids making the ungodly utter the divine name.[49]

---

46 For a discussion of the various positions, see Larcher, *Études*, 99-101 (disciples of Qoheleth?); 114-115; 127-129 (persecutors of the "teacher of Righteousness" of Qumran?); 213-216 (Epicureans?); Id., *Sagesse*, 1:115-117, and150 (Sadducees?). For the interpretation of the ungodly as Jewish apostates, cf. Gilbert, "Sagesse", 103; Kolarcik, *The Ambiguity of Death,* 120-123; Scarpat, *Sapienza*, 1:138; Vílchez Líndez, *Sabiduría*, 154. Cf. also Conti, "L'umanesimo ateo", 438-439; Dupont – Sommer, "Les 'impies' du Livre de la Sagesse sont-ils des Epicuriens?"; Fichtner, "Die Stellung", 120-122; Weisengoff, "The Impious of Wisdom 2".

47 Cf. Kolarcik, *The Ambiguity of Death*, 114-131. Chapter 2 "is a mosaic of biblical terms and thoughts turned on their heads and contradicted. Our "Epicurean" is an Alexandrian Jew, a discouraged defector, who reasons, writes, and sings his hymn, laughing at those principles which the just man observes and celebrates" (Scarpat, *Sapienza*, 1:138).

48 Cf. Mazzinghi, *Notte di paura e di luce,* 8 n. 27 and 36 n. 107. According to Barclay (*The Jews,* 102-112), Wis 3-4 would be evidence of the existence of Jews who marry pagan women and do not educate their children in Judaism. But where are the borders with apostasy? In fact, it was never a dominating factor in Alexandrian Judaism, and living as Greeks was felt more of as a necessity than as a real betrayal.

49 Dante does the same in his *Divine Comedy*: in hell, the damned do not utter the name of God.

In the light of the works of Philo, it is possible to advance a further hypothesis. Philo often enters into debate with some Alexandrian Jews. They too were involved in commenting on Scripture but in an entirely rationalistic way, inspired by Aristotelianism. They proposed a critical reading of Scripture in support of a policy of greater cultural openness to the Hellenistic world. Philo does not hesitate to describe these exegetes as "ungodly" (cf. *Mut.* 61-62; *Conf.* 2). His polemic is evidence at least of the existence of a group of Alexandrian Jews with a knowledge of the Scriptures but with a much more Greek approach than authors like Philo and, *a fortiori*, than the author of Wisdom.[50]

Who, then, is the just person of this chapter? The first element which characterises this figure is its lack of definition, its general nature. It does not seem as though our sage had in mind a particular "just" person, such as, for example, the prophet Jeremiah or the "Teacher of Righteousness" of Qumran. Study of the sources which our sage could have used is shown to be important. Platonic influence is present, but it is not enough to explain the entire text of Wisdom 2. Commentators have repeatedly highlighted the importance of the Fourth Servant Song.[51] Then, the study of J. Schaberg has pointed out the importance of Ps 2 in combination with Dan 7; 11:32-35; and 12:1-3, but also with Ps 21[22 MT]. Wis 2:13 speaks of a παῖς κυρίου who recalls once more the figure of Isa 52:13.[52] Schaberg concludes that the figure of the just person in the book of Wisdom, taken as a whole, is a sapiential reinterpretation of Dan 7, with greater weight given to the sufferings of the just man himself. The eschatological expectations are transformed into a kind of sapiential anthropology. However, an important difference between the just person of Wis 2:10-20 and the servant of Isa 53 lies in the fact the book of Wisdom is completely lacking in the aspect of the just person's expiatory suffering. The just person does not suffer for others nor does some suffering appear to be a source of salvation. Nickelsburg, for his part, maintains that the book of Wisdom and the text of 1 En. 62-63, which refers to the judgement of the kings before the son of man, show themselves to hark back to a common tradition which is linked also to Isa 53. Moreover, the scheme, which is present in particular in Wis 2 and 5, would be typical of the so-called "wisdom tales". Wisdom would, therefore, be making use of both the Isaiah tradition and the sapiential account of the persecuted just person.[53]

There again, one thinks of the figure of the just who are suffering in the Psalter. Cf. Pss 3:6; 16[17 MT]:7 and, again, 21[22 MT]:9, and 20-21. However, none of these texts exhausts completely the depth of the figure of the just person as presented in Wisdom. It is certainly the image of an innocent just person being persecuted, recalling the similar figures of Isa 53 and of Ps 21[22 MT]. He is the son of God, as in Ps 2, though without royal features. To a certain degree, he recalls the figure of the "son of man" of Dan 7, though without heavenly characteristics.

---

50 Cf. Nihan, Cristophe, *Jewish Exegesis and Homeric Scholarship in Alexandria* (Cambridge (UK): Cambridge Univ. Press 2011), 76-129.

51 Cf. Suggs, "Wisdom of Solomon: A Homily based on the Fourth Servant Song".

52 Cf. Schaberg, "Major midrashic traditions in Wisdom 1,1-6,25".

53 "The story of the righteous man in Wisdom is a variation on the model of the wisdom tale, with the framework of the Isaianic exaltation scene". Cf. Nickelsburg, *Resurrection, Immortality and eternal life in intertestamental Judaism*, 48-92. The quotation is on p. 66.

We must also pay some attention to the figure of the just as presented in Wis 3 and 4. In these two chapters, our sage presents the just who have been glorified (in the plural: cf. 3:1-9) and two “individual” examples of the just, the sterile woman (3:13-15) and the eunuch (4:7-14). P. Bizzeti has demonstrated that the text of 3:1-9 in particular displays literary contacts precisely with 2:17-20.[54] The faithful just who live forever are thus set in a close relationship with the just person who is oppressed and, finally, killed by the ungodly.

In conclusion, gathering from a broad biblical tradition, our sage creates a very rich and really original picture in which the individual “just” person of Wis 2:10-20 becomes a figure of all those just people who are none other than the faithful Israelites being persecuted and even killed by their own co-religionists but who ultimately find from God that life which has been taken away from them.[55]

---

54 Cf. Bizzeti, *Il libro della Sapienza*, 55.

55 Giménez González, “*Si el justo es hijo de Dios*”, 333. For the question of the messianic interpretation of the “just” man of Wis 2, cf. Adinolfi, “Il messianismo”; Gilbert, “Il giusto perseguitato”; La Bonnardière, “Le ‘juste’ défié”; Sisti, “La morte violenta del giusto”. Larcher, *Sagesse*, 1:258-263, offers a reasoned and balanced summary of the history of the exegesis of Wis 2:17-20.

Wis 3-4: The Just and the Godless between Life and Death: Four Contrasts

Literary Structure of Wis 3-4[1]

In his conclusion to the previous section (2:23-24), the author refuted the thinking of the ungodly. They have not understood the plan of life which was involved in God's creating humanity. The strongest argument of the ungodly was the uselessness of justice. The just man is simply an obstacle to be removed from their midst so that they can live according to the law of pleasure and that of force (2:10-20). In Wis 3-4, at the literary centre of the first part of the book, the author responds to the objections of the ungodly along the lines laid out in 1:13-15 and 2:21-24, giving an antithetical description of the destiny of the just and that of the ungodly, and employing metaphorical rather than philosophical language.

Why do the just suffer while the ungodly enjoy success? Such a question runs intermittently throughout Scripture (cf. Jer 12:1; Job 24; Hab 1; Qoh 4:1; Ps 72 LXX [73 MT]; etc.) and had long been resolved by Israel through the idea of retribution, collective or personal. Human suffering is caused by sin. The ungodly will be punished but the just rewarded (cf. Ps 36:22 LXX [37:22 MT]). The books of Job and Qoheleth highlighted the impossibility of such an explanation. The law of retribution does not seem to function on the earth (cf. Qoh 8:11-14). The experience of life seems to prove the thinking of the ungodly who have just been mentioned. They always have success whereas the good suffer. Thus, it is not nearly worth the effort to be just!

The great novelty of these two chapters is the announcement of the reward which is promised to the just: eternal life with God. In this connection, the author chooses some symbolic examples: the suffering just man, the barren woman and the eunuch, and the just person who dies prematurely. Now, in Israel's Scriptures, suffering, sterility, and brevity of life are generally considered signs of divine punishment whereas children and fertility are God's gifts, like a long life.[2] In Wisdom, on the other hand, the true value is virtue, and it guarantees immortality to the just, to the barren woman and the eunuch, and to the youth dying before his time. It is in relation to eternal life that a person's success is measured.

We can identify a first literary unit in 3:1-12 from the clear *inclusio* ἀφρόνων – ἄφρονες (vv. 2a, 12a) together with the play on words between 3:4b and 3:11b: ἡ ἐλπὶς αὐτῶν ... πλήρης; καὶ κενὴ ἡ ἐλπὶς αὐτῶν. Thus, the theme of hope is immediately prominent. Wis 3:1-12

This first literary unit can be divided easily into two further sections with a caesura in 10a (οἱ δὲ ἀσεβεῖς). The first section of the diptych (3:1-9) describes the destiny of the just in antithesis to the reasonings of the ungodly which were

1 Cf. Bizzeti, *Libro della Sapienza*, 56-60; Gilbert, "Sagesse", 66-67.

2 Cf. Vílchez Líndez, *Sapienza*, 213-214, for a series of biblical references in this connection.

presented in the previous chapter (v. 1a: δικαίων **δὲ** ...). The particular contrast is with 2:24 (the ungodly belong to the party of death). The initial δὲ has adversative force and creates a powerful contrast with the previous section.

The first part of this section comprises vv. 1-6 which play upon the *appearance/reality* contrast. Noticeable is the antithetical construction which characterises vv. 2-4 and the references to "seeing" in 3:2a, 4a. Verses 1-6 are an ironic adoption of the theme opened in 2:17 (cf. below 4:17-18). This contrast is reinforced by the careful use of tenses: *the past* (3:2ab-3a) *seems to want to deny the present* (3:1a, 3b, 4ab), but, if one really knows how to read it (3:5b-6b), it is actually shown to be a salvific past. *The future*, then, *will be antithetical to the past, as the ungodly see it* (3:1b, 5a). This temporal contrast characterises both chapters 3 and 4.

We observe further how, starting from v. 7, the verbs are all in the future (cf. also 4:17-20). The possible *inclusio* with the term ἐπισκοπή (vv. 7-9d) thus identifies a new subsection in vv. 7-9,[3] wholly centred on the future of the just.

The presence of the preposition ἐν confers additional unity on the entire section and serves to emphasise further the presence of a dramatic reversal of situation which attends the just in the future:
3:1 ἐν χειρὶ θεοῦ
3:2 ἐν ὀφθαλμοῖς ἀφρόνων
3:3 ἐν εἰρήνῃ
3:4 ἐν ὄψει ἀνθρώπων

3:6 ἐν χωνευτηρίῳ
3:7a ἐν καιρῷ ἐπισκοπῆς
3:7b ἐν καλάμῃ
3:9 ἐν αγάπῃ

Other important details: the use of ὁράω and of the already cited references to "seeing" in 2:17; 3:2, 4; 4:14, 17, 18; and 5:2 constitute a further element of unity, not only for this section but for the entire passage of Wis 2-5. The ungodly wanted to see whether the just man had spoken the truth (2:17). The just seemed dead to the eyes of the foolish (3:2, 4), but, in the end the ungodly had to make an about-face (cf. 4:17; 5:2).[4] On the one hand, we have the tragic illusion of the ungodly, on the other, the glorious reality of the life of the just.
Next, we note that 3:1-9 takes up the vocabulary of 2:17-20 in an antithetical way. Βάσανος in 3:2b recalls 2:19a, but in 2:19 it is a question of the tortures inflicted by the ungodly on the just, whereas in 3:2 these torments are excluded for the just person who has been glorified. In 2b, the verbal form ἐλογίσθη (with God as implicit subject) recalls ἐλογίσαντο in 2:21a (referring instead to the ungodly) while ἐπείρασεν in 5b recalls πειράσωμεν in 2:17b and πειράζουσιν in 2:24b. Δοκίμαζω appears in 3:6a and 2:19c. In the two cases, both the ungodly and God, respectively, put the just to the test, but with very different results. The theme of ἐπισκοπή appears in 2:20b in an ironic sense, but in 3:7 and 9, there will really take place that visitation of God which the ungodly wished to exclude. Finally, while the ungodly doubt the truth of the words

3 Cf. below the textual problem regarding the authenticity of 9d. According to Vílchez Líndez (*Sapienza*, 201), we have here in fact a small concentric structure, namely: A: vv. 1-3; B: vv. 4-6; A': vv. 7-9. This is possible, even if it is preferable to consider vv. 1-6 as a unit (see above concerning the analysis of the verbal tenses).

4 Cf. Beauchamp, *De libro Sapientiae*, 63.

of the just (εἰ οἱ λόγοι αὐτοῦ ἀληθεῖς; cf. 2:17), they will understand precisely the ἀλήθεια (3:9a) of God.

The second part of the diptych (3:10-12) is an antithetical description of the destiny of the ungodly. Verse 12 constitutes the hook with the following section, announcing its theme (πονηρά in 3:14b and πονηρίας in 4:6b; τέκνα in 3:16 and 4:6 and ἀτεκνία in 4:1; for γένεσις, cf. γενεᾶς in 3:19).

Wis 3:13-19

The existence of a second literary unit is more debated. According to Wright, the text of Wis 3:13-4:6 constitutes an independently standing literary unit.[5] In fact, the text of Wis 3:13-4:6 is well constructed according to series of internal cross-references: ἀμίαντος and ἀμιάντων (3:13a; 4:2d); καρπόν and καρπός (3:13c; 3:15a; 4:5b); πονηρά and πονηρία (four times, two in relation to the ungodly – 3:12b; 4:6b – and two to the just – 3:14b; 4:14b). We note further ῥίζα and ῥίζαν (3:15b; 4:3b); τέκνα, ἀτεκνία and, again, τέκνα (3:6a; 4:1; 4:6a); ἀτέλεστα and ἀτέλεστοι (3:16a; 4:5a; only here in the LXX). Each of these words recalls an important theme: purity contrasted with wickedness, the root and fruit of good works, and the theme of progeny. This confirms the fundamental theme of Wis 3-4: the final destiny of the just contrasted with that of the ungodly.

These links invite us to consider 3:13-4:6 as a distinct literary unit; and yet there are indications which help us to subdivide it into a second and into a third diptych, namely, 3:3-19, the contrast between the virtuous barren woman and eunuch versus the numerous children of the adulterers, and 4:1-6, virtue counts for more than having many children.

The *inclusio* with καρπός (3:13c, 15a) invites us to isolate vv. 13-15 as the first half of the second diptych (3:13-19) concerning the barren woman and the virtuous eunuch. In v. 16, a sudden change of subject and the use of the plural (τέκνα δέ) introduce seven stichs which present the antithetical picture (3:16-19): the children of the ungodly and their sad fate.

In its solemn rigidity and in its rhythmical imitation of classical clauses, the sentence of v. 19 forms an evident closure to this section. One sees again the keyword κοίτη which binds together the two parts of the diptych (13b, 16b); but also the mention of "visitation" in v. 13c finds a reprise in the theme of the διάγνωσις in v. 18b. Finally, we notice how both parts of the diptych are constructed by first presenting a development of the theme (3:13-14; 3:16-18) followed by a conclusion (3:15 and 3:19).

Wis 4:1-6

In 4:1-6, it is possible to identify a third diptych. The text of 4:1-2 constitutes a first section, seven stichs focused on the theme of virtue, something more important than having children. The term ἀτεκνία (4:1a) takes up the τέκνα of v. 16.

Verses 3-6 constitute the antithesis: cf. the quasi-*inclusio* between πολύγονον (v. 3a) and γεννώμενα – γονέων (v. 6). Verse 3 is marked by the change of subject and by an adversative (πολύγονον δὲ ἀσεβῶν πλῆθος). Compared with the previous diptych, the contrast is not between sterility and fertility but, more precisely, between the lack and abundance of children.

---

5 Cf. Wright, "The Structure" 171, but also Bizzeti, *Sapienza*, 56, who emphasises that the identification of a literary unit in 3:3-4:6 does not undermine the existence of two distinct diptychs: 3:13-19 and 4:1-6.

After the initial statement of 4:1a and the immediate reason for this statement in 4:1b, the five stichs which follow develop the theme through a series of contrasts: παρὰ θεῷ ... παρὰ ἀνθρώποις (1c); παροῦσαν – ἀπελθοῦσαν (2ab); στεφανηφοροῦσα πομπεύει (in eternity) – (in the present) ἀγῶνα (2cd). The scholastic construction, together with the use of vocabulary of an athletic character, give this passage the flavour of a demonstration which has as its centre not so much the theme of children as that of virtue and its eternal remembrance.

Wis 4:7-20 The fourth diptych (4:7-20) is less characterised by precise literary indications, but it constitutes a clear literary unit focused on the theme of the just man who dies prematurely. A quasi-*inclusio* is that between τίμιον and ἄτιμον (4:8a and 19a). It is easier to identify the first part of the diptych with its clear *inclusion*. Cf. δίκαιος (7a) which identifies a different subject (δίκαιος δέ) compared with the previous section and, in the following stich (8a), γῆρας, both terms repeated in v. 16. We can add, in 7a, the presence of τελευτῆσαι, echoed by τελεσθεῖσα in 16b (cf. τελευτήν in 17a). See again πολυχρόνιον in 8a and πολυετές in 16b.

In this way, we can identify 4:7-16 as the first part of the diptych relating to the just man who dies prematurely. Verbs in the passive predominate. A more precise internal subdivision does not seem to be demonstrable, even if the first part can be subdivided *ad sensum* into three shorter pericopes: 4:7-9, 10-12, and 13-15.

Starting from v. 17 and as far as v. 20, the text of the diptych tackles the theme of the sad fate of the ungodly who live for a long time. This concluding section is marked by the presence of a good thirteen verbs in the future. An key expression, μὴ νοήσαντες (14c) – οὐ νοήσουσιν (17b), links it to the previous section. Verse 20 in particular constitutes the announcement of the theme belonging to Wis 5:1-23.

This last diptych recalls the first, thus giving a profound cohesion to chapters 3-4. The "soul of the just" of 3:1 becomes the "soul of the just person" (ἡ ψυχὴ αὐτοῦ) who has died prematurely (4:14a). The "ungodly" (3:10 and 4:16a) are those who despise (ἐξουθενέω) wisdom and education (3:11a) and also scoff at the just (4:18a). Cf. also the relationship between 3:9 and 4:15 (cf. the notes on the text).
Next, the fourth diptych takes up the appearance-reality contrast already noted in connection with 3:1-9. The theme, which was announced in 2:17, will be concluded in 5:2. In particular, vv. 17 and 18 again employ the verb "see" (ὄψονται) in relation to those who will see the end of the just. They will see what they wanted to see, but they will not understand. The theme will be repeated also in the following chapter. In 5:2, the ungodly will find themselves in a new situation. Only *post mortem* will they understand the glorious end of the just.
The links of the fourth diptych with the beginning of the following section (Wis 5) are closer still.[6] We observe τελευτή in 4:17a and 5:4d; κύριος in 4:17c and 5:7c; ἐκγελάσεται in 4:18c and εἰς γέλωτα in 5:4a; ἄτιμος in 4:19a and 5:4d; ἀπολεῖται in 4:19g and ἀπωλείας in 5:7a. These are literary cross-references with a precise theological significance: the ungodly who had scorned the just and thought that his end was contemptible (5:4) will themselves have a contemptible end (4:19), and the Lord will laugh at them (4:18). The ungodly will be filled with condemnation (5:7). They will see their memory fall into perdition (4:19). At the centre of both scenes, in 5:7 and 4:17, there

6 Cf. Bizzeti, *Il libro della Sapienza*, 59.

emerges the presence of the Lord whose activity in favour of the just (cf. 4:17) is not understood by the ungodly (5:7).

According to the canons of Greek rhetoric, the examples of the barren woman and the eunuch belong to the literary genre called παραδείγματα which are employed within a demonstration (ἀπόδειξις). According to Aristotle, the example should be regarded as a convenient epilogue for a demonstration (cf. *Rhet.* 1.2). If we consider the diptych of 3:1-12 as an initial demonstration relating to the destiny of the just and the ungodly, the three diptychs that follow can be considered exactly as *exempla* relating to the thesis that has been stated. The barren woman, the eunuch, and the youth who dies prematurely are a plastic and dramatic illustration of the author's basic thesis relating to the final destiny of the just and the dramatic end of the ungodly.

The First Diptych: The Destiny of the Just and the Ungodly (Wis 3:1-12)

The first diptych consists in itself of two antithetical pieces, presented independently in the following.

Wis 3:1-9: The Just Are in the Hand of God and Will Govern Nations

1 The soul of the just is in the hand of God,
no torture will touch them.
2 In the eyes of the foolish, it seemed that they were dead
and their end was considered a punishment
3 and their going from us destruction;
but they are in peace.
4 And though, in the eyes of people, they have been punished
their hope was full of immortality.
5 In return for a slight correction, they will receive great benefits,
because God has put them to the test
and found them worthy of himself.
6 He has proved them like gold in the crucible
and has accepted them like a perfect offering.

7 As a result, in the day of their visitation, they will shine
and run like sparks through a thicket.
8 They will govern nations and rule peoples
and the Lord will reign over them forever.

[9] Those who have trusted in him will understand the truth;
those who are faithful in love will remain close to him,
because grace and mercy are for his holy ones
and a visitation for his elect.

Notes on the Text and Translation

v. 1. We translate the expression δικαίων ψυχαί with the singular, "the soul of the just", taking ψυχαί as a distributive plural. The stress falls on the "just", as appears from the masculine article οἱ (with pronominal force) in 3:3b. To them, therefore, and not to their "souls", the pronoun αὐτῶν in 1b is to be referred. For the concept of ψυχή, cf. the comment on 1:4. We should not insist too much here on "souls", as if our author considered them as separate and autonomous entities, even if he seems to wish to attribute the "I" of the person to the ψυχή. It is, rather, the just, considered in their totality as persons, who are in the hands of God.

For the sense of βάσανος as "torment, torture", here with a strong eschatological force, cf. 2:19 and Mazzinghi, *Notte di paura e di luce,* 119.

vv. 2-3. The form of the perfect τεθνάναι does not indicate an action ("it seems that they died"), but a state now completed and permanent ("it seems that they were dead"). Thus, the text does not mean to deny either the physical death or the sufferings of the just but rather the value which all these take on in the eyes of the foolish.

The term κάκωσις has perhaps been suggested by Isa 53:4 LXX, where it has active force ("punishment, affliction"). The context is similar: the servant of the Lord was held to be ἐν πόνῳ, ἐν πλέγει, ἐν κακώσει, oppressed by men and punished by God. Cf. also Exod 3:7 and 17 LXX where the Greek modifies the Hebrew עני, replacing the idea of "affliction" with that of "ill treatment" (κάκωσις). Larcher (*Sagesse,* 1:276) prefers to think instead of a passive sense ("malheur").

The term σύντριμμα, "destruction, ruin", has a very strong sense in the LXX. Cf. the examples in Scarpat, *Sapienza,* 1:231, and Larcher, *Sagesse,* 1:277. The verb συντρίβω in particular is often used by the LXX in connection with the destruction of enemies. In Lev 21:19 σύντριμμα indicates a fracture; in Ps 2:9, a destruction of pots.

vv. 4-5. The preposition ἐάν with the aorist subjunctive (κολασθῶσιν) can indicate a repeated action (cf. BDF § 373): "every time that they are punished" (Scarpat), or else a reference to a punctual fact without precise temporal determination (cf. BDF § 373,2): "although they were punished" in relation to the death of the just understood as a fact that has already happened. What interests the author here is not so much the temporal frame of the hope as its content. In this case, we find ourselves with a concessive clause in the apodosis which has a verb that should be understood in the imperfect: "their hope (was) full of immortality", and not: "their hope of immortality was full".

v. 6. The aorist ἐδοκίμασεν has gnomic value. The sense is that of "proving metals", according to a usage that was widespread both in the classical world and in the LXX, especially in sapiential contexts: Job 34:3; Ps 65:10, 12 LXX [Ps 66:10, 12 MT]; Prov 17:3; Sir 2:5; Zech 13:9; cf. Wis 1:3; 2:19. The term χωνευτήριον, "foundry", "crucible", is proper to the LXX (cf. 1 Kgs 8:51; Zech 11:13; Mal 3:2).

The expression ὁλοκάρπωμα θυσίας is not easy. The first term indicates a vegetable offering (καρπός) destined to be a holocaust, but in the LXX ὁλοκάρπωμα is used in alternation with ὁλοκαύτωμα (cf. the variant in codices V and 46). The second term, θυσία, refers to the idea of sacrifice. We could then translate "the complete offering of a sacrifice", that is, a perfect sacrifice. The genitive θυσίας should be understood as a genitive of identity, as in Wis 1:10; 1:12; 2:12; etc. On the sole basis of the text of the Latin (*quasi holocausta hostiam accepit illos*), Scarpat (*Sapienza*, 1:234) prefers to read the accusative θυσίαν, "he has accepted them in sacrifice, as a holocaust", instead of the more attested genitive θυσίας. Although such an emendation simplifies the text, it does not seem necessary. Cf. Schenker, "Le sacrifice de l'holocauste", 352 n. 6.

v. 7. The verb ἀναλάμπω, *hapax* in Wisdom, has an eschatological force, as happens in the NT in Matt 13:43. For 7b, we reject the conjecture of Dupont Sommer, André, "De l'immortalité astrale dans la Sagesse de Salomon", *REG* 62 (1949) 80-87, who proposed reading γαλαξίῃ instead of καλάμῃ, (cf. Larcher, *Etudes*, 319 n. 2).

v. 9. The perfect participle preceded by the article (οἱ πεποιθότες) has a substantivised value and, at the same time, indicates a past action with effects which last into the present: "those who have trusted and continue to trust". The expression οἱ πεποιθότες is illuminated also by οἱ πιστοί which is one of the first examples of a usage which will become classical, that is "the faithful". According to Larcher (*Sagesse* I, 290-291), however, it is preferable to retain for οἱ πιστοί a less specific sense and think of those who remain strong, faithful in trials. Cf. Sir 44:20; 1 Macc 2:52. For the contrary, see Scarpat, *Sapienza*, 1:238: οἱ πιστοί is here joined with ἐν ἀγάπῃ as demanded by the parallelism with the previous stich. Then it becomes a question not of the "faithful" in general, but of those who are faithful in love.

The verb προσμένω (present in the LXX only in $Judg^{A}$ 3:25; Tob^{S} 2:2; 3 Macc 7:17) followed by the name of a person, can mean "remain close, united to someone" (πρός); cf. Acts 11:23: προσμένειν τῷ κυρίῳ.

A more complex textual problem is represented by the text of 9c(d). The textual tradition oscillates between a short text and a long one:

ὅτι χάρις καὶ ἔλεος ἐν τοῖς ἐκλέκτοῖς αὐτοῦ (B, 7 mss, Lat, *quoniam donum et pax electis eius*, Sah, Eth; cf. Rahlfs);

ὅτι χάρις καὶ ἔλεος ἐν τοῖς ἐκλέκτοῖς αὐτου καὶ ἐπισκοπὴ ἐν τοῖς ὁσίοις αὐτοῦ (A, 16mss, Syr, Ar);

ὅτι χάρις καὶ ἔλεος ἐν τοῖς ὁσίοις αὐτοῦ καὶ ἐπισκοπὴ ἐν τοῖς ἐκλέκτοῖς αὐτοῦ (S, V, 8 mss, O, Luc, Arm; cf. Ziegler).

It is necessary to observe that the text proposed by Ziegler is repeated (varied) in 4:15 where, however, the same Ziegler places it within square brackets. Larcher (*Sagesse*, 1:292-293) prefers to consider 9c as original and 9d as an addition based on 4:15 (namely as a copyist's attempt to create a parallel stich to 3:9a) so he adopts the short text. Furthermore, Larcher regards as suspect the mention of "visitation" after v. 7a. Scarpat is of the same opinion (*Sapienza*, 1:289) and adds his choice of retaining 4:15 as original, expunging only 3:9d. However, in favour of Ziegler's text (chosen, among others, by Winston, Vílchez Líndez, and Hübner), there is the possibility of considering ἐπισκοπή precisely as an *inclusio* with 3:7a. With some hesitation, therefore, we accept the text of Ziegler which is partly confirmed also by the reading of Codex Alexandrinus. In this way, while 9c refers to the whole of 3:1-9; the final stich, 9d, refers more precisely to the glorification of the just which is presented in 3:7-9b. Cf. also the note to 4:15.

Synchronic Analysis

In v.1, the reflection of 2:21-24 is met with the contrast of a declaration that is joyful 3:1
and full of hope: the just are in the hands of God; no torture will touch them. In the light of vv. 2-3, clearly it is the just who have died that are being spoken of. The men-

tion of "souls" does not refer to the existence of an autonomous entity which survives death (cf. above). The whole person (οἱ δὲ; cf. v. 3) is in the hands of God. On the other hand, our sage remains vague concerning the final destiny of the just. Such reserve characterises the entire text of Wis 1-9. Next, one observes that the "just" individual who was oppressed by the ungodly of the previous chapter passes here into the "just" understood as a collective entity. This confirms that the "just" person portrayed in the second chapter is a symbolic figure who represents an entire group of the "just", that is, faithful Israelites.

The second stich describes the divine protection afforded to the just as the absence of every "torture" (βάσανος). To what tortures does this refer, those of the present life or the *post-mortem* ones inflicted by God on the ungodly? In light of Wis 2:19, one could think of the torments and tortures to which the ungodly subject the just. The latter, now in the hands of God, are finally snatched from their power. However, in Wis 17:12, βάσανος appears as in 3:1-9, in an eschatological context. One could therefore think also of the infernal torments which await the ungodly in Hades (cf. Wis 4:19; Luke 16:28), torments which the just will be able to avoid. In fact, the verbal form οὐ μὴ ἅψηται (οὐ μή with aor. subj.) must be understood as a future : no torment *will touch them*. This is perhaps already the interpretation of the Latin text which translates βάσανος with *tormentum mortis* which is probably an explanatory gloss.[7]

3:2-3 In these two verses, the play on appearance and reality is very clear. The two verses are carefully constructed, arranged in chiastic form: in the eyes of the foolish it seemed that they were dead / and their *end* was considered a *punishment* // and their *going* from us *destruction* [appearance] / but they are in peace (reality).

In the eyes of the foolish, physical death appears as a punishment, as ruin. The terms κάκωσις and σύντριμμα refer not only to the idea of death understood as definitive ruin but also as a paradoxical punishment which the just undergo notwithstanding their reputed justice (cf. Isa 53:4b). Moreover, ἔξοδος and πορεία are not chosen by chance. Words like "end" and "going" are still used today in a euphemistic sense to cover over a tragic event like "death". However, this is where all the irony of our sage emerges. For the ungodly, death is a "passing away". They do not believe, in fact, in a life which goes beyond death itself. For the just, on the other hand, death is rather a "departure", a "going away", in other words, an *exodus* which is not focused on nothing, but which has its destination in God.

The ungodly have become here the "foolish" (ἄφρονες. Cf. Wis 1:3; 5:4; 12:24; 14:11; 15:5, and 14), that is, those who stand by the opinion (ἔδοξαν) that they have formed starting from the materiality of what is seen (ἐν ὀφθαλμοῖς), and who thus abandon themselves to false reasonings (ἐλογίσθη). Λογίζομαι recalls the foolish reasonings of the ungodly recorded in 1:16 and 2:21, closely binding this text with the whole of the previous section.

The reality of the death of the just is unveiled by our sage at the end of v. 3: they are in peace. The use of the present (εἰσίν) after the aorists of v. 2 refers to a permanent and stable state which the just securely possess.

---

7 For the patristic interpretation of this stich, cf. Larcher, *Sagesse*, 1:275. The Catholic liturgy has often applied it to Christian martyrs. Cf. Sisti, *Sapienza*, 136-137. There are famous musical settings by, among others, William Byrd and Orlando di Lassus.

Verse 4a emphasises (καὶ γάρ) a nuance that, once again, highlights the theme of appearance/reality. To the superficial glance of people (ἐν ὄψει ἀνθρώπων), the just dead were considered the object of punishment, precisely by the God in whom they had placed all their trust. The use of κολάζω is significant. Apart from in this text, in Wis 11:5, 8, 16; 12:14, 15, 27; 14:10; 16:1, 9; 18:11, and 22, κολάζω is used systematically to indicate the punishment of the unjust by God. The ungodly are claiming, therefore that, for all his reputed justice, the just individual is punished by that God in whom he or she trusted so much. 3:4

These verses tackle the great enigma of the suffering of the just. It appears under a triple aspect: as divine correction, modest in comparison with the benefits received (3:5a), as a trial (5b-6a), but also as a sacrifice (6b). 3:5-6

With the verb παιδεύω, we encounter a theme already seen from the very beginning of the book (cf. the comment on 1:5a): παιδεία. In this context, however, παιδεύω refers rather to the correction which God offers to his people, quite different from the κωλάζειν, the punishment of the ungodly (cf. Wis 11:8-9 and 12:20-22). The idea of a "slight" (ὀλίγα) correction recalls Isa 26:16b LXX (ἐν θλίψει μικρᾷ ἡ παιδεία σου ἡμῖν). What the ungodly regard as a punishment, that is, the death of the just, becomes, from the point of view of God, an act of salvation. The suffering of the just is presented as a slight, necessary correction which is, however, the prelude to a greater benefit, namely, immortality. Cf. the use of εὐεργετέω (cf. the comment on Wis 11:5, 13; 16:2). 3:5a

An aspect of this correction is the "test" which God reserves for his faithful in order to try their faith (cf. Gen 22:1; Exod 15:25; Judg 8:25-26 etc.), a "test" which contrasts with the one set by the enemy (cf. Wis 2:17). In both cases, there is a recurrence of πειράζω (cf. also 2:24b, although with different significance). 3:5b-6a

In Wis 3:5c, the result of the test of the just is being found "worthy" of God. The term ἄξιος is dear to our author[8] and acquires here a nuance of resemblance rather than of merit. The just person is "worthy" of entering into an intimate relationship with God, of participating in some way in the very life of God (cf. 3:9).

Verse 6a prolongs the theme of v. 5bc. The suffering is described with the image of the proving of metals, a common one in Scripture (cf. the textual notes). The just are described in a passive way whereas the action of God on their behalf emerges strongly.

In 6b, the life of the persecuted just individual is described as a holocaust, a sacrifice pleasing to God. In many ways, this is a new idea (cf. the textual notes and, below, the diachronic analysis). 3:6b

Here, the verb προσδέχομαι, "accept", assumes the nuance of "admitting to the presence of someone". Cf. Hos 8:13; Amos 5:22; Mic 6:7; Mal 1:10, 13 where it is used in relation to the acceptance of sacrifices. The aorist indicates an action already completed following the death of the just. With his death, the persecuted just individual performs an act of worship that is pleasing to the Lord.[9]

---

8 Cf. Mazzinghi, *Notte di paura e di luce*, 218.

9 On this connection between sacrifice and the martyrdom of the just which has been little observed by commentators, cf. Schenker, "Et comme le sacrifice de l'holocauste il les agréa". Cf. a possible closeness with *Martyrium Polycarpi* 14.1-2.

3:7 Starting from v. 7 and up to v. 9, the verbs are in the future tense. Following the intervention of God, the passivity of the just will cease and they will enter into a new, glorious phase of their life whereas, in 3:1-6, our sage described their death (verbs in the past tense) or their state immediately after death (verbs in the present tense). Cf. the literary structure.

We have already come across ἐπισκοπή in 2:20 (cf. the comment). The expression ἐν καιρῷ ἐπισκοπῆς αὐτῶν occurs in Jer 6:15 and 10:15 in a non-eschatological context in connection with the judicial intervention of God with regard to the ungodly. In Wis 3:7, the pronoun αὐτῶν refers very clearly, however, to the just of Wis 3:1-6. Our sage could be alluding to Isa 24:22, where the divine "visitation" is shifted instead on to the eschatological plane. In our context, therefore, the "visitation" refers to an eschatological intervention of God in favour of the just after their death (cf. also Wis 3:13: ἐν ἐπισκοπῇ ψυχῶν), an intervention which vv. 7-9 in particular are seeking to explain. They do this with some suggestive images which have to be interpreted by the careful study of the possible biblical sources employed (and possibly modified) by the author. See below.

3:8 The destiny of the glorified just is described as a kingship exercised over the peoples and nations. The terms λαοί and ἔθνη are synonyms. Κρίνω (cf. Wis 1:1) and κρατέω should be understood in a positive sense: governing and ruling, in relation to the kingship of God over the just (8b).[10] The text does not clarify the exact import of this dominion of the just over other peoples, a dominion closely connected with the kingship God exercises over the just (cf. Dan 7:18 and 27).

Some problems remain that are difficult to solve. Are the just here identical with the people of Israel who will have a role of the first rank in God's plan for the world's future? Is Israel, then, the mediator of God's kingship to the other peoples? What type of kingdom of the just is being presented here? Totally eschatological or still with some earthly element? It is difficult to give a precise reply. Our sage probably intends to claim that human history will know a new phase: the rule of God over the world, exercised by the reign of the just, who will share to some degree in the divine kingship. That allows us to think that the "visitation" spoken of in these three verses is not only the individual judgement which God carries out on people at the moment of each one's death, but a much greater reality which comes close to the idea of a last judgement.

3:9 At the conclusion of the first section devoted to the destiny of the just, Wisdom here makes a very close connection between the earthly life of the just (their faithfulness) and the happiness which they will receive as a gift from God after death.

Those who have trusted in him will understand the truth.[11] The just are first and foremost those who have always trusted in the Lord. Their reward will be to understand (grasp, penetrate; that is the sense of συνίημι) the truth. The term ἀλήθεια is not to be understood within a gnostic or Platonic context but is profoundly biblical.[12] One could think of the "truth" of what the just man was declar-

---

10 Scarpat (*Sapienza*, 1:236) sees here a polemical allusion to Roman rule.

11 For the use of ἀλήθεια without article as happens with abstract substantives, cf. Scarpat, *Sapienza*, 1:237.

12 Cf. De La Potterie, Ignace, "La verità in san Giovanni", in *San Giovanni: Atti della XVII Settimana Biblica* (Brescia: Paideia 1964), 123-144.

ing when he was accused by the ungodly of claiming to be "son of God". From this point of view, understanding the truth means understanding that one is in the right. Close to the idea of faithfulness and justice (cf. Wis 5:6), truth is here set in relation to love, grace, and mercy (9bc). Understanding the truth can also be seen in relation to the knowledge of the mysterious ways of the divine mercy which are revealed to the just. This is a truth, therefore, of a more existential than ontological order.[13] Understanding the truth means leaving the logic of the ungodly, which is based on appearances, and grasping the "mysteries" of God (cf. 2:20). These relate precisely to the salvation of the just.

Those who are faithful in love will remain close to him. The term ἀγάπη, rare in the LXX with the exception of the Song of Songs, returns in Wisdom only in 6:17-18. On nine other occasions, Wisdom employs the verb ἀγαπάω instead (cf. the comment on 1:1). The context is always strongly theological. The "faithful" are those who trust in the love that God has for them and who remain firm in this love (cf. the textual notes). However, the ambiguous position of ἀγάπη, placed exactly at the centre of the verse, could also make us think of an allusion to faithfulness in that love which people ought to have *towards* God, the love, that is, required by the faith of Israel (Deut 6:4-5).

In addition to the ἐπισκοπή mentioned in 7a, verse 9 closes by recording the grace and mercy of God, χάρις καὶ ἔλεος, with regard to the "holy ones" (ὅσιοι) and the "elect" (ἐκλέκτοί). In our context, the former pair of words makes clear the content of the divine "visitation": the action of God with regard to the just is a gratuitous and merciful action, a sign of the divine fidelity in God's dealings with God's people. It is these same just who are here called ὅσιοι, a term which, in Wisdom, refers to the faithfulness of God rather than that of people.[14] Here, they are also called "elect", a term which is not intended to underline the just's membership of a particular people chosen by God (Israel) or to suppose that the just belong to a special group within this people. Our sage's intention is, rather, to highlight the free initiative of God who "chooses" the just and makes them the object of divine love.[15] In this way, both v. 9c and the final stich (if it is authentic. See above) wish to remove the impression that salvation is ultimately a product of human effort. It is, rather, a free gift of God.

Diachronic Analysis

In biblical language, "being in the hand of God" simply indicates being under 3:1
divine protection: Isa 51:16; Ps 88:22 LXX [89:22 MT] and Job 12:10; cf. Wis 7:16; 19:8. In some texts, however, it could be understood with a negative nuance, as in 2 Chr 32:13-15 (in the hands of Sennacherib); Job 19:21; Qoh 9:1a (meaning disputed). Our sage is not more specific, although this declaration could be seen as an indirect response to the hope expressed by the text of Ps 48:16 LXX [49:16

13 Cf. Hübner, *Weisheit*, 53-54.

14 Cf. Mazzinghi, *Notte di paura e di luce*, 205-206, and the comment on Wis 18:1.

15 Under this eschatological profile, the use of ἐκλεκτοί is common in an apocalyptic setting. Cf. Schrenk, Gottlob, ἐκλεκτός, *TDNT* 4:181-192; Larcher, *Sagesse*, 1:294.

MT] where the psalmist hopes to be delivered "from the hands of Hades". The just are, instead, in the hands of God and protected by him.

3:2-3 As for the description of death as ἔξοδος, cf. Wis 7:6 and Sir 38:23; Luke 9:31; 22:22; 2 Pet 1:15; the first term, πορεία, "journey, voyage" could have classical resonances (cf. Plato, *Phaed.* 115a: τὴν τοῦ ἅδου πορείαν), but expressions related to the journey or the departure are present also in the LXX (cf. Qoh 12:5 (ἐπορεύθη); Gen 15,15 (ἀπελεύσῃ); see also πορεύεται in Luke 22:22).

In Wis 2:3b, behind εἰρήνη, we should certainly see all the depth of the Hebrew שׁלום, a term which indicates a state of repose, harmony, well-being, and prosperity that God grants to people and which not infrequently assumes tones of an eschatological character (cf. the already mentioned text of Isa 57:1-2 LXX; cf. again Ps 4:9 LXX; Sir 44:14). However, it is difficult to specify further the whole import of this peace in which the just find themselves, for our sage continues to display great reserve.

3:4 By contrast with the ungodly, the just have an ἐλπὶς ἀθανασίας πλήρης. The text of v. 4b highlights primarily the term ἐλπίς which, in the LXX, bears a very positive sense and which frequently translates the Hebrew root קוה. The reference is, thus, on the one hand, to the expectation of material goods, an expectation that is often frustrated, and, on the other hand, to a profound relationship with God.[16]

The book of Job often highlights man's lack of hope: cf. Job 17:15: ποῦ οὖν μου ἔτι ἡ ἐλπίς; see also Job 14:7 and 19:10. In these passages, the suffering Job denies being able to have hope again in this life. In Job 17:16, his only alternative seems to be descent into Hades, the world of the dead from which there is no return. The text of Wis 3:4b could be properly read as a response to the doubts and questions of Job. The just have a "hope" which is really "full of immortality", a real, authentic hope of life.

Larcher holds that our author made use of a term (ἐλπίς) which, already in Platonic usage, indicates a straining towards immortality (the philosopher is εὔελπις in the face of death; cf. *Phaed.* 64a), but loaded it with the religious sense which the word acquires in the LXX; for example, Ps 13[14 MT]:5: κύριος ἐλπὶς αὐτῶν.[17] That happens also in Philo where hope is described as ἀγαθῶν προσδοκία (*Abr.* 14); that is, it is the ἀγαθὴ ἐλπίς of the Greeks, but reinterpreted as the expectation of the divine reward, as the expectation of the salvation which God offers to his people (cf. *Legat.* 196). For Philo, hope has an explicitly religious content which is still more accentuated in the book of Wisdom. Hope is, in fact, the expectation of the divine eschatological intervention which is contrasted with the empty hope of the ungodly (cf. Wis 3:11, 18; 5:14; 16:29) who confide in dead idols (Wis 13:10; 15:6).

Immortality It remains to clarify the meaning of ἀθανασία in relation to hope.[18] The theme of ἀθανασία mirrors precise concepts proper to Greek philosophy. Found as far

16 Cf. Larcher, *Sagesse*, 1:279-280, and for קוה, cf. Waschke, Ernst-Joachim, קו, *TDOT* 12:562-573. Cf. also E. Bons, Eberhard, "ἐλπίς comme l'ésperance de la vie dans l'au-delà dans la littérature juive hellénistique", in Kuntzmann, René (ed.), *Ce Dieu que vient.* Mélanges offertes à Bernard Renaud (LeDiv 159, Paris: Cerf 1995) 345-370.

17 Cf. Larcher, *Sagesse*, 1:279-280; Scarpat, *Sapienza*, 1:208-209.

18 Cf. a good summary of the problem in Dalla Corte, *Il Dio vivente, Dio dei viventi*; cf. also Fabbri, *Creazione e salvezza*, 217-235.

back as Homer with reference to the gods (cf., for example, *Od.* 24.47), only with Plato is the term ἀθανασία referred to the natural immortality of the soul. Not only are the gods immortal but every human soul by its very nature is so too whereas the body decays. Aristotle and then the Stoics are opposed to this idea of the natural immortality of the soul. The use of ἀθανασία is unusual in the LXX. In fact, it is found only in 4 Macc 14:5-6 and 16:13 in relation to the martyrdom of the seven brothers. In 4 Macc 14:6 and 18:23, there appears for the first time in Jewish literature written in Greek the Platonic combination ψυχὴ ἀθάνατος;[19] cf. Jos. Asen. 15:6-7. In Philo, the combination ψυχὴ ἀθάνατος or ψυχὴ ἄφθαρτος is frequent (*Somn.* 1.137; *Opif.* 119-120; *Conf.* 176; *Virt.* 9-10), just as in Josephus, who attributes this belief to the Essenes (cf. *B.J.* 2.154; *A.J.* 18.4). In Wisdom, ἀθανασία appears in six texts: 3:4; 4:1; 8:13, 17; 15:3; cf. the adjective ἀθάνατος, already encountered in 1:15.

The book of Wisdom carefully avoids linking immortality with the ψυχή.[20] Our author's message turns not so much on "souls" that are separate from the body as rather on the *content* of the hope of the just. It is "full", that is, solid, founded on God. Our sage prefers to link ἀθανασία with hope (3:4), with justice (1:15; 15:3) and with memory (4:1; 8:13 and 17).

The immortality spoken of in Wis 3:4 could, therefore, simply be the expectation of those goods which God gives to the souls of the just.[21] However, in light of Wis 8:13 and 17, immortality undoubtedly appears something greater: a divine prerogative which is given to people through wisdom, relating to the "peace" (3:3b) in which the just find themselves after their death. In light of Wis 3:1-9, immortality is also morally qualified. See the reference to hope (v. 4), to faith, and to love (v. 9).

The avoidance of the Platonic-sounding combination ψυχὴ ἀθάνατος has another important consequence. The *post mortem* existence of the just is not guaranteed by a natural human property but by God himself. It is in the order of a gift, not a condition inherent in human nature itself. In light of 2:23, immortality is a kind of participation in the very nature of God, a state in which humanity was created.[22] Wisdom's originality, therefore, lies in having employed a Greek concept

---

19 Cf. *Phaed.* 73a: ἀθάνατος ἡ ψυχή. For the Fourth Book of Maccabees, cf. G. Scarpat, *Quarto libro dei Maccabei*, Brescia 2006, 238. The context of the passages of 4 Macc where this vocabulary occurs is topical and rhetorical, with the exception of 18:23, exactly at the end of the book, where there is certainly the expression of faith in the existence of an immortal soul (ψυχὰς ἁγνὰς καὶ ἀθανάτους ἀπειληφότες παρὰ τοῦ θεοῦ).

20 Cf. already Lagrange, "Le livre de la Sagesse", 94: "On voit comment cette immortalité est distincte de l'immortalité platonicienne, à laquelle on la compare souvent. Nulle part elle est regardée comme une conclusion philosophique. Jamais l'âme n'est répresentée comme ayant dans sa nature même une raison suffisante de subsister, qu'elle soit le principe du mouvement, ou que la pensée soit, de son essence, immatérielle".

21 Cf. Scarpat, *Sapienza*, 1:216-218.

22 "Immortality for man is not a quality of his nature as such, but of a particular condition, whether he receives it as a gift or as a recompense"; Reese, *Hellenistic Influence*, 64. Cf. Scarpat, "Una speranza", 491-494, but, especially, Puech, "The Book of Wisdom", 127-129 (against Winston, *Wisdom of Solomon*, 26-28) and the bibliography cited on p. 128 n. 44.

within thought that is typically biblical and, above all, within a substantially unitary conception of the human person. The use of the term ἀφθαρσία alongside ἀθανασία (cf. 2:23) makes us think, then, of an immortality which also involves the body.

3:5-6 The theme of suffering understood as a test (3:5b-6a) appears in Sir 2:1-6. The just spoken of by Wisdom have learned the lesson put forward by Ben Sira. They were faithful in the time of misfortune (cf. Sir 2:2) and accepted their trial as true divine correction (Sir 2:4). They thus showed themselves to be like real gold that is tested by fire (Sir 2:5). This does not counterfeit the metal but highlights its full value. Thus, God likens the just to the most precious of metals. Although generic, the trial spoken of by Ben Sirach is something which tests the whole person and which, therefore, demands an attitude of total trust in God. Without this trust and without the help of God, the disciple will not emerge from the trial victorious.[23]

The idea expressed in 6b, the description of the life of the just who have been persecuted as a holocaust, is a theme prepared for by Ps 50:19 LXX [51:19 MT] (although the psalm does not mention the martyrdom of the just nor does Wisdom mention the forgiveness of sins) and inspired perhaps also by Isa 53:10 and Dan 3:38-40 LXX and Th, but not MT. It will be taken up again only in the NT (cf. Rom 12:1; Heb 13:15-16). Wis 3:6 is thus one of the first attestations of a real "theology of martyrdom".

3:7 Grimm's commentary already discussed various opinions about the interpretation of ἀναλάμπω and of the whole of the following stich (7b).[24] We could have here a symbolic interpretation of an earthly event relating to the victory of Israel over its enemies. That could be confirmed by the biblical references underlying v. 7. On the other hand, we could have a symbolic representation of the *post mortem* revenge of the just over their own enemies. Grimm thinks rather of a description of the eschatological resurrection of the dead and the coming of the messianic kingdom (cf. τότε οἱ δίκαιοι ἐκλάμψουσιν ὡς ὁ ἥλιος ἐν τῇ βασιλείᾳ τοῦ πατρὸς αὐτῶν; Matt 13:43; cf. also Dan 12:3 Th; 1 En. 104:2). We note that, by itself, the verb ἀναλάμπω is insufficient to resolve the question. It is possible to think, in fact, of the just who are illuminated by a reflection of the divine glory when they are finally introduced into the sphere of God after the "visitation of souls" (cf. 3:13).

Our sage is probably referring to Dan 12:3, and so it is the tradition of Israel which is his primary source of inspiration. The wise who have been raised shine like the firmament (καὶ οἱ συνιέντες ἐκλάμψουσιν ὡς λαμπρότης τοῦ στερεώματος; Dan 12:3 Th). Here we have another indication that leads us to think that our sage is intending to allude to the resurrection of bodies, a real transformation of the person of the just after their death. If we read "shining" in this sense, then the following reference to the activity of the glorified just becomes even clearer.

The images of the sparks, the thicket, and the running to and fro are borrowed from some prophetic texts. The image of the "sparks" (σπινθῆρες) has already appeared in Wis 2:2 and is inspired by Isaa 1:31: the ungodly and sinners will burn

---

23 Calduch-Benages, Nuria, *En el crisol de la prueba. Estudio exegético de Sir 2,1-18* (Estella, Navarra: Verbo Divino 1997) 33-94.

24 Grimm, *Weisheit*, 88-90.

without any deliverance. The "thicket" (καλάμη) is an image which is probably derived from Obad 18 and Zech 12:6. Our author is thus applying to individual eschatology two texts which speak of the future role of Israel. Cf. also Isa 1:31; 5:24; Joel 2:5; Mal 3:19, all of them texts that speak of a context of judgement. The verb διατρέχω is used in connection with fire in Exod 9:23 and of torches which run here and there in Nah 2:5.

Some authors continue to think that the image of Wis 3:7b intends to indicate a possible participation of the glorified just in the eschatological battle of God and his creation against the ungodly (cf. 1QH XIV, 32-39; but also 1QH XI, 20-37).[25] It is strange, however, that such a battle takes place *after* the glorification of the just.[26] Only in Obad 18 and Zech 12:6 do we find the idea of a purified Israel which destroys its enemies. In the other texts mentioned, the punishment of the ungodly is rather the work of God. The only real contact of Wis 3:7b with these prophetic texts is the comparison between the ungodly and the straw or the thicket (καλάμη). In Wisdom, the punishment of the ungodly comes rather from the creation itself as instrument in God's hand to save or to punish (cf. Wis 5:17-20; 16:24), and not from any activity of the just. Verse 7b is intended only to describe with poetic images known already in prophetic texts (sparks, thicket, running to and fro...) the glorious state of the risen just after the divine visitation.

As for the "grace" and "mercy" reserved for the elect, we observe that the 3:9
first term, χάρις, had not yet taken on in the LXX the theological sense which it would have in the NT. Translating mostly the Hebrew חן, χάρις, it usually indicates a favour, a gift granted freely.[27]

Behind the term ἔλεος in the LXX lies all the wealth of the vocabulary of the covenant, often translating the Hebrew חסד. In the book of Wisdom, ἔλεος appears in 3:9; 4:15; 6:6; 9:1; 11:9; 12:22; 15:1; and 16:10, always in connection with God's faithfulness in his dealings with his people.[28] In the LXX, χάρις and ἔλεος appear together only in Gen 39:21; Ps 83:12 LXX [84:12 MT] and Sir 45:1; in the NT, they appear in the initial salutations of three apostolic letters (χάρις, ἔλεος, εἰρήνη, 1 Tim 1:2; 2 Tim 1:2; 2 John 3; cf. Heb 4:16).

Wis 3:10-12: The Ungodly and Their Descendants

[10] But the ungodly will receive a punishment worthy of their reasonings,
they who have disregarded the just and abandoned the Lord;

---

25 Cf. Puech, *La croyance des Esséniens*, 2:354-355, criticised by John J. Collins in his review, *DSD* 1 (1994) 250. Cf. again Puech, "The Book of Wisdom", 132-133.

26 Cf. Gilbert, "Sagesse 3,7-9", 312, who claims that it is impossible to give further precision to the meaning of this text.

27 Cf. Conzelmann, Hans-Georg, χάρις, *TDNT* 9:372-402; Spicq, *Notes*, 2:260-305. On the Hebrew חן cf. Ina Willi-Plein, "חן. Ein Übersetzungsproblem. Gedanken zu Sach XII 10", *VT* 23 (1973): 90-99. In Wisdom, the term occurs in 3:9, 14; 4:15; 8:21; 14:26; and 18:2.

28 Cf. Bultmann, Rudolph, ἔλεος, *TDNT* 2:477-487.

[11] – for unhappy is the one who despises wisdom and discipline! –
empty is their hope, vain are their labours,
useless are their deeds.
[12] Their wives are foolish,
their children evil
and their offspring cursed.

Notes on the Text and Translation

v. 10. The term ἐπιτιμία acquires a sense different from that which it has in classical Greek, that is, the condition of the citizen who enjoys his rights. According to Winston (*Wisdom*, 129) it is used here for the first time with the meaning of punishment. Cf. Lat *correptionem habebunt*. In the NT, cf. 2 Cor 2:6.
Larcher (*Sagesse*, 1:296) defends the translation of τοῦ δικαίου, in v. 10, with the neuter they neglected *what is just*, following Augustine: *qui neglexerunt iustitiam* (PL 34.947). Larcher's arguments are weak. In the light of the whole of the previous chapter, the idea of the ungodly who neglect the just seems to dictate itself. Moreover, in 10b, "the Lord" corresponds to the "just" and, here too, ἀμελέω requires a personal object.

v. 11. The change in person is frequent in sapiential literature, and v. 11a assumes the characteristic of a proverbial expression which our sage suddenly inserts into the text.
The three adjectives used in 11b (κενή - ἀνόνητα - ἄχρηστα) draw the picture of uselessenes; the last two are synonyms, and both refer to the idea of uselessness: ἀνόνητος is rare and refined, poetical in character (cf. 4 Macc 16:7, 9); ἄχρηστος is a term dear to our author (Wis 2:11; 4:5; 13:10; 16:29).

Synchronic Analysis

Verses 10-12 constitute the second part of the diptych. The joyful destiny of the just is contrasted with the tragic fate of the ungodly (οἱ δὲ ἀσεβεῖς). Whereas, in 3:1-9, even the negative elements were transformed into positive ones, here, everything is negative, even what ought to be positive, like family and children.

3:10 The fate of the ungodly is labelled as a punishment (ἐπιτιμία) which is not explained more precisely and which is postponed into the future (ἕξουσιν). Κατά has adverbial force and establishes a certain relationship between the punishment and the thoughts of the ungodly. The verb λογίζομαι recalls closely the "devious thoughts" of 1:3 and the erroneous thoughts of the ungodly (2:1; 2:21; 3:2b). It is a question of wrong thoughts in dealings with God, and, in this context, in relation to the destiny which God awards to the just.

The second part of the verse specifies the faults of the ungodly: they are primarily those who have disregarded the just man. Ἀμελέω was, perhaps, suggested to our author by Jer 4:17 LXX (ἐμοῦ ἠμέλεσας) and Jer 38:32 LXX, where it has a strong religious import (cf. Matt 22:5).

A further fault of the ungodly is their abandoning the Lord: τοῦ κυρίου ἀποστάντες; cf. Isa 30:1 and Jer 3:14 LXX. At the time of Wisdom, as Philo attests, one can already speak of a technical use of the expression. It refers to those "apostate" Jews who have abandoned the law of the fathers; τοὺς τῶν ἱερῶν νόμων ἀποστάντες (*Virt.* 182). It is worth noting that, here, disregarding the just is set in parallel with having abandoned the Lord.

Verse 11a constitutes a sentence of a proverbial character: the ungodly is one who despises wisdom and sapiential education (the מוסר); cf. Wis 1:5. For this reason, the ungodly will never be able to be happy. One is aware, on the contrary, of the blessed state of the barren woman, who is undefiled, which opens the following diptych in 3:13. 3:11

In 11b, we read about the ungodly, that "their hope is empty". The contrast is clearly with the "full hope" of the just evoked in 3:4b. Without hope, the ungodly live immersed only in the present, as people without a future. However, in reality, even their present is empty. In fact, their labours (κόποι) and their deeds (ἔργα) are vain (ἀνόνητοι) and useless (ἄχρηστα). Whoever lacks hope loses also the value of everything that he seeks to do.

Verse 12 is really very harsh, and not infrequently, commentators, betraying a certain embarrassment, seek to minimise such harshness.[29] The asyndetic construction reveals a new phase in the punishment of the ungodly. The subjects now are their wives, described as "foolish" (ἄφρονες), and their children, described as "evil" (πονηρά), perhaps because they are the product of an erroneous education. Such offspring of the ungodly (ἡ γένεσις αὐτῶν) are, therefore, cursed (ἐπικατάρατος). 3:12

Diachronic Analysis

Our author takes the proverbial sentence of 11a from the text of Prov 1:7: σοφίαν δὲ καὶ παιδείαν ἀσεβεῖς ἐξουθενσνουσιν. Our sage adds the adjective ταλαίπωρος, "unfortunate, unhappy, wretched", a word with a strongly tragic flavour which transforms the statement of Prov 1:7 into a kind of lament on the sad fate of the ungodly. 3:11

In 11b, our sage seems to wish to respond to Job 7:6: what the suffering Job regarded as belonging to everyone, that is, having hope that is empty, is actually the fate which affects only the ungodly.

Our sage is certainly influenced by the perspective of collective retribution; cf. Exod 20:5 and, for an idea that is not dissimilar, Sir 41:5. In Isa 65:23 LXX, an opposite idea is expressed, *à propos* of the children of the elect. Moreover, Wisdom achieves the result of introducing the theme of children which will characterise the following pericope (the barren woman) and, at the same time, begins to introduce the understanding that the procreation of children no longer constitutes an absolute value. This is unlike the whole of Israel's tradition. There remains the fact that the harshness of v. 12 is not completely foreign to the style of our author. It serves to highlight the extreme gravity of the situation of the ungodly and, by contrast, the greatness of the blessing reserved for the just (cf. the diptych which follows). 3:12

29 Thus, Larcher, *Sagesse*, 1:299.

The Second Diptych: The Barren Woman, the Eunuch and the Infertility of the Ungodly (Wis 3:13-19)

13 Happy, rather, is the woman who is barren but undefiled
and who has not experienced a sinful union:
she will have her fruit at the time of the visitation of souls.
14 Happy too is the eunuch who has not committed iniquity with his hand
and has not thought wicked things against the Lord:
for he will be given a special reward for his faithfulness
and a most favourable place of honour in the temple of the Lord.
15 For glorious is the fruit of good labours
and the root of understanding is without flaws.

16 The children of adulterers, however, will never reach maturity;
the seed of an illegitimate union will vanish.
17 Even if they have a long life, they will be regarded as nothing,
and, at the end, their old age will be without honour.
18 If they die early, they will have no hope,
no comfort, in the day of judgement,
19 for hard is the end of an unjust generation.

Notes on the Text and Translation

v. 13. The term ἀμίαντος, in connection with κοίτη, refers to sexual purity (cf. Heb 13:4). It recurs in Wis 4:2 and 8:20 with the sense of "without defects", "without stain", in a moral sense. For its use in the LXX, cf. 2 Macc 14:36 and 15:34.
Although omitted by the majority of codices (cf. Ziegler), the γάρ of 13c should be reinserted because it probably fell out as a result of haplography (καρπόν instead of γὰρ καρπόν).

v. 14. The insertion of ἐν χειρί appears to Larcher (*Sagesse*, 1:303) to depend on Isa 56:2 MT, where the "hand" refers to committing evil. Mattioli thinks rather of eunuchs who have become such at their own hands for reasons of money or prestige, a reference to the practice of voluntary emasculation which was widespread in some areas of the Graeco-Hellenistic world (cf. "Felicità e virtù", 31).

v. 15. The term ἀδιάπτωτος is an erudite word which was used in the Hellenistic period in an etymological sense: α-, δια, πίπτω: something or someone who does not fall, who is without defects (cf. Scarpat, *Sapienza*, 1:245).
The term φρόνησις appears here for the first time in the book where it will appear a further eight times: 4:9; 6:15; 7:7, 16; 8:6, 7, 18, 21; and 17:7. In this case, the sense is positive, contrary to 17:7 (cf. Mazzinghi, *Notte di paura e di luce*, 68). In Stoicism, φρόνησις indicates wisdom as the ability to discern what one ought and ought not to do (cf. *SVF* I 86, frag 375), the ability, therefore, to discern good from evil (*SVF* I 85-86, frag. 374), a moral virtue relating to man's actions, the knowledge (ἐπιστήμη) of good and evil. Cf. *SVF* III 63, frag. 262. For Philo, φρόνησις is the virtue which concerns action and which places limits on it (cf. *Leg.* 1:63). In Wis 7:16b, φρόνησις is associated precisely with ἐπιστήμη. In Wis 6:15, it is clear that φρόνησις is distin-

guished from σοφία and is close to the virtues of discernment and prudence (cf. Larcher, *Etudes*, 358-360), the practical side of the virtue of wisdom.

v. 16. The term *ἀτέλεστος occurs only here and in Wis 4:5. In Greek usage, it can sometimes indicate "one who has not been initiated in the mysteries" (cf. Euripides, *Bacch.* 40: Plato, *Phaed.* 69), but this does not seem to be the case here. Ἀτέλεστος is to be understood rather in connection with the mention of τὰ τέλη in v. 19, rare in the plural (cf. v. 19) so to be understood as the "end", the final destiny of a person. Discussion on the τέλος of a person is typical of the Hellenistic schools of philosophy. Already, Socrates and Plato discuss the τέλος of people (cf. *Theaet.* 176b; but Plato prefers to use the term σκόπος: *Gorg.* 507d. Cf. Des Places, Edouard, *Lèxique de la langue philosophique et religieuse de Platon*, Paris: Les Belles Lettres 1964, *sub voce*), and Aristotle does the same. Later, debate about the τέλος is very lively in Stoicism. For the Stoics, the τέλος of human life consists in being happy (τὸ εὐδαιμονεῖν) and in the virtuous life (*SVF* III 6, frag. 16), that is, in living according to nature which, for the Stoics, is identical with living according to virtue (*SVF* I 125, frag. 552). Given also the use of τελέω in 4:16, one could think that our sage is taking up this scholastic discussion in his own way. The ungodly are ἀτέλεστοι. They lack precisely the τέλος, the ultimate destiny of their life, something which is reached by the virtuous man (cf. 4:16). However, if the language reflects philosophical problems, the background of vv. 16-19 remains, as always, profoundly biblical.

v. 18. The term διάγνωσις has here the technical sense which this word acquired in the Roman period. Scarpat has shown that it has to do with the so-called *cognitio extra ordinem*, namely, that juridical process with which the emperor resolves a legal problem in person without recourse to judges. Thus, in Acts 25:21 (cf. Scarpat, *Sapienza*, 1:17-21 and 247-248). We observe, however, that the Latin text has *in die agnitionis* rather than *cognitionis*. The term is important to be able to date Wisdom in the Roman period. On the basis of Philo's text of *Flacc.* 100, Scarpat claims that this term is one of the proofs for dating Wisdom in the time of Caligula (cf. the Introduction, p. 28-29). In our context, διάγνωσις is an indication that, in the day of judgement, God will intervene in a personal way, directly and decisively, and that, for the ungodly, there will be no possibility of mercy or of mitigation of their punishment (παραμύθιον).

Synchronic Analysis

Wis 3:13-15: Praise for the Childless and the Eunuch

The use of μακάριος is significant (cf. 2:16 with regard to μακαρίζω).[30] Our author 3:13
is linking up with the numerous macarisms in the Scriptures, especially in the psalmic and sapiential texts, that is, with those literary forms which are used to congratulate those who possess a particular reality which renders them happy, a reality always related to God, such as the gift of wisdom (Prov 3:13; 8:34 LXX). However, to call the barren woman "blessed/happy" constitutes a statement that is certainly critical of the whole of whole received tradition (see below).

We have observed (cf. the textual notes) that ἀμίαντος ought to be understood as purity in a sexual sense. The commentators discuss the meaning of 13b. We should

30 Cf. Mattioli, "Felicità e virtù", 27-28, with further bibliography.

undoubtedly reject the idea that was once widespread that the book of Wisdom is praising virginity. In fact, the στεῖρα, is clearly a married woman, as the reference to adultery (cf. v. 16a) makes clear, and is not a woman who has remained a virgin through her own choice. The text does not even suppose the idea that the "sin" (παράπτωμα; cf. Wis 10:1) lies in having enjoyed sexual relations with a purpose different from that of procreation (cf. Wis 7:2 where sexual union is presented in a positive context). The explanation comes from v. 16 where παράνομος κοίτη indicates a sexual union forbidden by the law of Moses, such as adultery, or else a marriage contracted with a pagan or with someone who was not of the woman's kin (cf. also "illicit unions" mentioned in 4:6). It is difficult, however, to be more precise.

What constitutes the happiness of a person is not so much their physical condition (in the case of a woman, having many children), but their moral stature. It may be a cause of surprise that our sage is not more precise in describing the "transgressions" to which he refers and does not enter into more detailed examples. He is not a moralist, however, and it is not his purpose to discuss questions of sexual morality. It is enough for him to have recalled human beings to the root of their own personal duties: the exercise of virtue.

The result of the life of the barren woman will be "to have her fruit" (καρπός). In the usage of the LXX, the term refers to the result of particular actions (cf. Prov 1:31; Ps 1:3). If the image of fruit suggests a close connection between the conduct of the barren woman and its result, the verb ἕξει and the mention of the divine "visitation" (ἐπισκοπή; cf. 3:7) refer rather to the action of God and God's future judgement. We are faced here with a dialectic, not rare in Scripture, between grace and merit, between the action of God and that of people. The mention of the ἐπισκοπὴ ψυχῶν makes us understand that the "fruit" obtained by and at the same time given to the barren woman is clearly to be understood in the eschatological order.[31]

3:14 The first part of v. 14 is given over to illustrating the blessedness/happiness of the virtuous eunuch ("eunuch" is undoubtedly to be understood here in a physical sense) whereas the second part v. (14cd) describes his reward. Verse 14c introduces the theme of the eunuch's πίστις. This is the only occurrence of the term in Wisdom. Cf. πιστός already encountered in 3:9 and πιστεύω in 12:2; 14:5; 16:26 and 18:6 (and ἀπιστέω in 1:2; 10:7; 12:17; and 18:13). It is inappropriate to load this term with resonances from the New Testament. Here, πίστις is the Hebrew אמונה, the "faithfulness" a person has to God. In this sense, πίστις is used also in the secular field, with the meaning of "sworn faith", faithfulness to an agreement that has been established (τὴν πίστιν τηρεῖν, "keeping one's word").

The reward promised to the eunuch for his faithfulness has a twofold aspect: Wisdom promises him a choice "reward" (χάρις), which is special (ἐκλεκτή), and "a most favourable place (κλῆρος)[32]" in the "temple of the Lord". Sharing in the

---

31 The "visitation of souls" is further illustration of the fact that Wisdom considers ψυχή as a term that is adequate to express the personal "I" of a person. We note in passing that our author is far from the Philonian allegory which, in *Leg.* 1.75-76, speaks of sterility and fertility as allegories of wisdom or folly.

32 The adjective *θυμηρής has the meaning of "pleasant, delectable". It is a poetic term that is rarely used in prose. Grammatically, θυμηρέστερος is a comparative but should probably be understood as a weakened superlative. Cf. Mattioli, "Felicità e virtù", 37 n. 73.

life of God is worth far more than having children and being physically fertile. The temple (ναός) is probably the heavenly temple hinted at in Wis 9:8c, but the text remains deliberately generic. Used here without the article, χάρις refers simply to a benefit granted freely by God, but, in this case too, our sage remains vague. However, the use of κλῆρος in interesting. If read in the light of 2:9, what the ungodly denied with such fierce irony becomes true for the just. Despite everything, there is a κλῆρος for people, and – for the just – it is God himself!

Constructed chiastically (genitive – subject – attribute / attribute – subject – 3:15
genitive), v. 15 presents itself as a sapiential conclusion of a general nature which applies both to the barren woman and the eunuch. The "good labours" have a strenuous character, implicit in the term πόνοι, a positive effort which makes for the increase of virtue itself. Their fruit is glorious (εὐκλεής). Without doubt, our sage is thinking of the eschatological reward mentioned in 3:1-9. This idea will be developed more extensively in Wis 8:7.

In 15b, the image of the root prolongs that of the fruit. The root of understanding (φρόνησις) is without flaws (ἀδιάπτωτος); or, if we are reading this term in an etymological sense, it does not fall, it is firm, it does not decrease. Thus, φρόνησις (see above) is set as the foundation of the moral life. Just as the plant is born from the root and the fruit comes from the plants, so from understanding (15b), from the ability to discern good and evil, good labours arise. The image of the root and the fruit has a particular significance precisely because it is applied to the barren woman and the eunuch: what is not fruitful in the order of nature is so in the order of grace.[33]

Wis 3:16-19: The Children of the Godless

The second part of the diptych (3:16-19) is constructed very carefully. Verse 16 constitutes a general declaration on the fate of the sons of the ungodly. Verse 17 contains a first theory about their children who have a long life. The verse is constructed with a protasis (ἐάν τε, common in the LXX), followed by a double apodosis. The same construction returns in v. 18 which puts forward a second theory, this time about the children who die young. Verse 19 is a general concluding sentence, antithetical to that of v. 15 but more incisive and rhythmic, imitating classical clauses.

Who are the "children of adulterers"? Many commentators have thought of 3:16
the children of the Jewish apostates, following the sense which "adultery" assumes in some prophetic texts: cf. Isa 57:3 LXX: ὑμεῖς ... σπέρμα μοιχῶν, a text which Wisdom could well have had in mind. In the following stich, it is made clear that we have here the children of an illegitimate union, namely, the children of marriages forbidden by the law (cf. v. 13b).

However, the use of the term "adulterers" gives the text a more general dimension, considering the many prophetic texts which attribute the image of adultery to the entire people of Israel. By means of the literary figure of synecdoche, our sage mentions the children of adulterers and the seed of illegitimate unions,

---

33 Cf. Sisti, *Sapienza*, 153.

thinking globally of all the ungodly. It is necessary, therefore, to be careful not to force the text excessively. Otherwise, we would have to admit that our author is contradicting himself. In fact, the children of the adulterers would be paying for faults which were not their own (cf. instead Wis 1:16). Thus, v. 16 has in mind all the descendants of the ungodly. These descendants will not attain the end of life (ἀτέλεστοι; cf. the textual notes) and will disappear very quickly. The same verb ἀφανίζω is employed in relation to the ruin of the ungodly in the texts of Prov 10:25; 12:7; 14:11; and 1 Macc 9:73; cf. Pss 93:23 LXX [94:23 MT] and 145:9 LXX [146:9 MT].

3:17-18 Verse 17 relativises also the value of long life and old age, a theme which will be taken up more extensively in the fourth diptych. Even if the descendants of the ungodly were to live a long time (μακρόβιοι), it would serve no purpose, and their old age would not be held in honour. If, moreover, these children were to die young (v. 18), they would have no hope. The mention of ἐλπίς takes us back directly to 3:1-12 (cf. vv. 4 and 11). By contrast with the just, the future of the ungodly is marked by nothingness, by the total absence of hope. Even if they are the values most esteemed by tradition, such as many children and a long life, material goods serve for nothing if they are not accompanied by virtue. The second part of v. 18 returns to the theme of the divine "visitation", here called διάγνωσις (see the textual notes). At the time of judgement – and once more the modality is left vague – the ungodly will not have any consolation, no comfort (according to the most probable sense of *παραμύθιον).

3:19 What makes an impression on many commentators is the harshness of our author's judgement on the adulterers' children.[34] The end (τὰ τέλη) of the unjust is hard (χαλεπός). The adjective returns in Wis 17:10 and 19:13 in eschatological contexts (cf., in the NT, 2 Tim 3:1). The expression "unjust generation" should be understood as the same reality as v. 16, that is, the entire body of the unjust and ungodly, and not only their children.

The sentence of v. 19 is certainly a rhetorical simplification which serves to highlight, by contrast, the reward promised to the just as opposed to the total ruin of the ungodly and their descendants. The idea of a collective retribution is not yet wholly excluded by our sage, and he does not seem to perceive any contradiction around his statements on the death which affects only the ungodly (cf. 1:16) and, at the same time, on the ruin which falls on all their descendants.

Diachronic Analysis

3:13 Our sage seems to be recalling here the text of Ps 127 LXX [128 MT] which he engages in dialogue: it is no longer children and a wife's fertility which render the just man happy but his own virtue.

Μακαρία στεῖρα! As was said, the beginning of the diptych appears polemical. The barren woman actually belongs to a category of women considered unhappy in the biblical texts. ("Sterile, barren" here refers to married women who cannot have children.) Fertility is a gift of God and infertility a punishment. The Jewish tradition expresses this idea in texts that are even harsher: "barrenness has not

34 "Cruel indeed", so Goodrick, *Wisdom*, 134.

been given to a woman, but because of the deeds of her hands she dies without children" (1 En. 98:5). But does happiness really depend on fertility, as suggested by the culture and faith of the time, and not only within Judaism?

Ben Sirach (cf. Sir 16:1-3) distinguishes between children who have the fear of God and children who do not. As a result of this, he concludes that it is better to die without children than to have children who are apostate (16:3). However, we are still far from the ideas expressed in Wisdom. A possible biblical background to our text could be sought rather in Isa 54:1-8. Applying nuptial imagery to Jerusalem, this prophetic text suggests that a barrenness also exists that is fertile and in the end blessed by the Lord with the gift of a new motherhood. Our sage takes up Isaiah's images and applies them to each individual: blessed/happy is the woman who is barren but undefiled and who has not experienced a sinful union.

In 13c, the image of the "fruit" was perhaps suggested by Gen 30:2, but, above all, by Ps 126[127 MT]:3 where καρπὸς τῆς γαστρός refers to the fruit of the womb, namely, children. In our case, however, the barren woman's "fruit" is left undetermined, shifted into the future and seen as a divine reward.

The figure of the eunuch does not have a good reputation in Judaism (cf. Deut 3:14
23:2). The beatitude here is a clear reworking of Isa 56:3-5, but Isaiah's text, which in the Greek version does not differ much from the Masoretic Text, is reused in an original way:

> For thus says the Lord:
> "To the eunuchs who keep my sabbaths,
> choose the things that please me
> and remain fast in my covenant,
> I will give a place and a name in my house and within my walls
> better than sons and daughters; I will give them an everlasting name, and it shall not fail".

Wisdom also exacts from the eunuch conditions: two, but different ones from those in the Greek text of Isaiah which asks the eunuchs to keep the sabbaths and "choose the things that please me". The latter are to be understood as a reference to the observing of the law, as is clear from the following mention of "remaining fast in my covenant". Law, covenant, and sabbath disappear completely in the text of Wisdom, and the moral demands required of the eunuch are deliberately generic: one external, avoiding iniquity (ἀνόμημα; cf. Isa 56:2), and one internal, not thinking wicked things (πονηρά) against the Lord; not having negative sentiments against God.[35] By itself, the use of ἀνόμημα could make us think also of a violation of the law, but the same term was already employed in Wis 1:9 precisely in its generic sense of "iniquity". The general nature of the moral requests made of the eunuch demonstrates in this case too that our sage does not wish to speak as a moralist. The book of Wisdom does not insist so much on observance of the law as an instrument of salvation,[36] but is open to a humanism of a universalistic character which is unafraid of entering into dialogue with the Greek culture.

In the description of the reward which belongs to the virtuous eunuch (14cd), the text of Isa 56:3-5 is modified once again. Instead of a prominent place in the

35 The verb ἐνθυμεῖσθαι returns in Wis 6:15; 7:15; and 9:13.
36 Mazzinghi, "La memoria della Legge", *passim.*

assembly of the Lord, from which he was excluded, and of a "name", that is, a posterity granted by God, as in the text of Isaiah, the eunuch is promised (cf. above) a "special reward" and "a most favourable place of honour" in the temple of the Lord. In this case too, Wisdom loosens the promise made to the eunuch from the cultic institutions of Israel by contrast with the text from Isaiah.

3:15 In 3:15, the image of the fruit is inspired again perhaps by Isa 56:3 (the eunuch who compares himself to a dry tree), but also by Ps 1:3 (cf. also above regarding 3:13c).

3:16-19 The fate of the ungodly described in 3:16-19 is inevitably disastrous. Despite the originality of his reflections, our sage does not detach himself from the form of thought which he has inherited from the Scriptures. Once again, our author makes use of Isa 40-66, in particular of Isa 48:22 LXX ("there is no reason to rejoice for the ungodly, says the Lord") and 57:21 LXX ("there is no reason to rejoice for the ungodly, says the Lord God"); cf. also Isa 66:24, precisely at the end of the prophetic book.

3:16 The success of the children of the ungodly – challenged in 3:16 – had probably become a problem that was discussed in sapiential circles. Cf. Job 21:7-34 and 24:1-25. In this verse, the author's intention is that of relativising still further the value of having many children which, from the traditional point of view, was a sure sign of divine blessing.

The Third Diptych: Virtue and Children (Wis 4:1-6)

1 Better to be childless and have virtue,
for it finds immortality in the memory,
because it is acknowledged by both God and people.
2 They imitate it when it is present,
they weep for it when it is distant.
In eternity, it triumphs, crowned,
victor in the contest for prizes that are undefiled.

3 But the prolific brood of the ungodly will be no good for anything
and, born from bastard shoots, they will not put forth deep roots
or be established on a firm foundation.
4 Even if, for a time, the shoots put forth buds on the branches,
not being firmly planted, they will be shaken by the wind
and uprooted by the violence of the gales.
5 Their shoots will be torn off while they are still young
and their fruit will be useless, unripe to eat,
and will not serve any purpose,
6 because children born of illicit unions
are witnesses to the evil of their parents,
when the inquest on them is opened.

Notes on the Text and Translation

v. 1. Some Latin manuscripts read: *o quam pulchra est casta generatio cum claritate* "how beautiful is chaste procreation together with glory", thus insinuating the idea of generation given by God. This is completely absent, however, from the Greek text, although it is a theme introduced into some patristic rereadings of the text and supported by some ancient commentators. Cf. Larcher, *Sagesse,* 2:313-314, and Scarpat, *Sapienza,* 1:445.
The second stich of v. 1 could also be translated: "in the memory of this [*viz.* virtue] there is immortality". Some mss and ancient versions (cf. Ziegler, apparatus) read: ἡ μνήμη αὐτῆς instead of ἐν μνήμῃ αὐτῆς, that is, "its memory is immortality", but this is a poorly attested, unconvincing correction. In fact, there is no opposition in the text between immortality of the memory and personal immortality (cf. below).

v. 2. Instead of μιμοῦνται, some manuscripts offer the reading τιμῶσιν. This is perhaps an intentional variant of someone who had in mind consecrated virginity (cf. the Latin text of 4:1a) or else an error arising from a false reading of τε μιμοῦνται. We note that μιμέομαι appears in the LXX only here and in 4 Macc 9:23 and 13:9. On the other hand, it is frequent in Philo. In the present, the verb acquires the nuance of an effort or an attempt: "they strive, they seek to imitate virtue".

v. 3. Πολύγονος (here linked through hypallage with πλῆθος) is a technical term, *hapax* in Wisdom (cf. in the LXX, only in 4 Macc 15:5). In Greek usage, "prolific" is used almost exclusively of animals and so has a pejorative sense. We translate it with "the prolific (πλῆθος) brood". *Μοσχεύμα is another technical term; it indicates the "shoots" of a tree.
The expression οὐ δώσει ῥίζαν is unusual: δώσει does not have an explicit subject. *Ad sensum*, the subject is πλῆθος. Larcher proposes reading οὐ ῥίζα (on the basis of some minuscules) δύσει (on the basis of *Arab*), that is, "a deep root will not take root" with the expression ἐκ μοσχευμάτων understood as a complement of origin. Without having to emend the text, there remains the possibility of reading πολύγονον πλῆθος as subject of οὐ δώσει: the prolific brood of the ungodly will not put forth deep roots (εἰς βάθος).
The verb ἑδράζω, "establish firmly", is rare in the LXX and found only in Prov 8:25; Sir 22:17.
The term νόθος indicates what is corrupt, faulty, "bastard". In Greek usage, different from the biblical conception, a "bastard" is a son born of a slave or a concubine to the master of the house. Here, our author is probably using the term in its broader sense as happens in Philo who also applies it (*Mos.* 2.193; *Spec.* 3.29) to children born of mixed marriages.

v. 4. κἂν introduces a conditional, concessive clause. The expression πρὸς καιρόν underlines the "right moment", here, the moment of blooming. In classical Greek, the combination is typical of Sophocles (Scarpat, *Sapienza*, 2:281).
The term ἐπισφαλῶς recalls through antithesis ἀσφαλῆ of the previous verse. What is "not firm" is contrasted with what is "firm". Larcher (*Etudes*, 183) thinks of a possible reminiscence of Archilochus (frag. 114,4 West.).

v. 5. ἄωρος indicates what is premature. In Prov 11:30 LXX, ἄωρος refers to the premature death of the ungodly. Premature death is a very common *topos* in the funerary inscriptions, even in the Jewish ones at Leontopolis. Cf. Griessmair, Ewald, *Das Motiv der Mors Immatura in den griechischen metrischen Grabsinschriften*, Innsbruck: Universitätsverlag Wagner 1966; Blischke, *Eschatologie*, 223-263.

v. 6. For ἐξετασμός, cf. ἐξέτασις in 1:9; cf. also 3:18. The term indicates the divine inquest. The present εἰσίν could make us think also of a form of earthly judgement, but the general context of chapters 3 and 4 leads rather to the thought of the divine inquest *post mortem*.

The pronoun αὐτῶν is difficult to interpret. It could refer to both the children and the parents. Grimm (*Weisheit*, 101) defends the first reading: as an attenuating factor in their judgement, the children will invoke the wickedness of their parents. However, the presence of μάρτυρες points us in the direction of thinking of the children as further witnesses for the prosecution in the divine judgement against their own parents.

Synchronic Analysis

4:1 By contrast with the wholly earthly lifestyle of the ungodly, the idea returns that spiritual goods (here, virtue) are superior to material ones, in this case, to the abundance of children.

Verse 1 opens with a comparative, κρείσσων, which in fact lacks a term of comparison. One could think *ad sensum* of the descendants of the ungodly, the subject of the immediately preceding passage (3:16-19) as of that which follows (4:3-6).

Better than having many children is ἀτεκνία accompanied by virtue. Virtue is the true focus of 4:1-2. In the memory of virtue, there is ἀθανασία, that is, immortality. The seemingly strange formulation of 4:1b is perhaps due to the influence of Greek ideas which precisely bound up immortality with the memory of the just.[37] However, Wis 3:4b has already made use of ἀθανασία in relation to the future life of the just, and, in 4:1c, memory of virtue is linked with God himself. Therefore, the sense of ἀθανασία is certainly more pregnant. The "memory" spoken of here is thus not only that of people but, above all, that of the just on the part of God. There is in fact a difference in being remembered by God or by people (cf. 4:1c). Thus, ἀθανασία is not simply the memory of a virtuous life which does not fade. It is, rather, the content itself of the memory. Indeed, ἀθανασία consists ἐν μνήμῃ αὐτῆς. We could also say that virtue leaves a positive memory which, before God and through God's works, becomes ἀθανασία for the one who has practised virtue. In this connection, we note that in 4:19g, precisely at the end of the chapter, the theme of memory returns: the μνήμη of the ungodly will perish, that is, they will be destroyed forever by contrast with the just who are destined to a life without end.

4:2 To remember virtue means to live it and imitate it. Verse 2ab refers to human action (cf. the "men" mentioned at the end of 1c) whereas v. 2cd refers to the divine action (cf. "God, mentioned" first in 1c). The text of 2a is constructed with great skill, chiastically and with refined language:

παροῦσαν τε	μιμοῦνται αὐτὴν
καὶ ποθοῦσιν	ἀπελθοῦσαν

37 Larcher, *Sagesse*, 2:315 notices Xenophon, *Mem.* 2.1.33. Imitation of the virtuous man is a common *topos* in the Greek world (cf. Scarpat, *Sapienza*, 1:258-259). Scarpat (*Sapienza*, 1:254) also thinks of a possible reminiscence of Sophocles (*Phil.* 1417ff). Hercules claims to have received an ἀθάνατος ἀρετή, eternal virtue, in the sense of a reward, eternal glory. However, our sage employs ἀρετή in a sense that is certainly moral but ἀθανασία in a theological sense.

Imitated and followed by people, virtue never decreases and is rewarded by God (2cd); rather, it triumphs, victorious as an athlete in a competition. This victory of virtue takes place ἐν τῷ αἰῶνι. Rather unusual and unique in Wisdom, this expression should not be understood only in a temporal sense ("in eternity"), but also, perhaps, in a sense that is vaguely spatial, in reality, that is, in the world of God.[38]

The final stich of v. 2 records the victory of virtue in a competition for "prizes that are undefiled". Here, ἀμίαντος (cf. Wis 8:20 and, with a sexual nuance, Wis 3:13) is to be understood by contrast with earthly rewards which are tainted by competition and jealousy (cf., in the NT, 1 Pet 5:4: ἀμίαντος κληρονομία). Perhaps here too, there is an indication of polemic against those Jews who took part naked in the athletic games, often in honour of pagan divinities and so defiling themselves. The "reward" here seems to be ἀθανασία, the life without end which God grants to those who live according to virtue.

With the initial δέ, our sage is underlining the antithesis with vv. 1-2 and 4:3a
introducing the second part of the diptych. For the second time (cf. Wis 3:16-19), the text returns to the relative nature of the value attributed by the biblical tradition to having many children, here described in pejorative language ("brood"; cf. the textual notes). For the ungodly, having many children is no good at all: χρησιμεύω is used in an absolute sense (cf. Sir 13:4) to indicate radical uselessness. It thus recalls, in a quasi-*inclusio*, ἄχρηστος in v. 5b.

For a good eight stichs (3b-5), the text develops images drawn from the vege- 4:3b-5
table world and applies them to the children of the ungodly. What is the sense of all this? On a first level of significance, one could think of an allegory. The bastard children, born of illicit unions (cf. 3:16), are like shoots without firm roots (3bc). Sometimes, their life seems successful, that is, the branches appear green (4a), but, as they have not been firmly planted, they are really shaken by the wind and torn up by the gales (4bc). Outside the metaphor, in the end, the life of the ungodly does not enjoy true success even if their beginnings seem to be promising. On the contrary, the ungodly (and their children) will be like immature buds (5a) and, if the fruit actually grows, it will really be good for nothing (5bc).

However, some of these terms had already been used previously in a non-metaphorical sense. Thus the "root" of the ungodly is contrasted with the root of "understanding" (ἀδιάπτωτος ἡ ῥίζα τῆς φρονήσεως; cf. 3:15b) which never decreases. The buds of the ungodly are ἀτέλεστοι, just as the children of the adulterers were described in 3:16a. The theme of "fruit" had already been introduced in 3:15a in connection with the "fruit of good labours" which is undoubtedly "glorious". Thus, the long plant-related comparison serves to give a clearer illustration of our sage's basic thesis: the children of the ungodly will not succeed in gaining full moral maturity because they are lacking in virtue (cf. 4:1-2). They do not acquire that "fruit" of a virtuous life which is, ultimately, life without end with God (cf. the contact with 3:15). We note again that ἀτέλεστοι (5a) can have existential import: the children of the ungodly will not attain the end, the τέλος, of their existence. They are exactly like plants which produce only unripe fruit, good for nothing (5bc; cf. also the comment on 3:16a).

38 Gärtner, *Komposition und Wortwahl*, 119.

The use of ἄωρος, "unripe", points us already in the direction of the topic of the following section of the chapter, 4:7-16: the youth who died prematurely, but after having reached the maturity of his existence.

A final detail: our author's judgement on the children of the ungodly is again very hard but reflects similar ideas that were widespread in both the Greek and Jewish worlds.[39] It arises from an observation of an experiential character: it is difficult for good fruit to come from rotten roots.

4:6 The concluding verse of this section emphasises more the fault of the parents than that of the children born from "illicit" unions (cf. the comment on 3:16). The inquest (ἐξετασμός) on the parents alluded to in 6b (cf. the textual notes) is the divine judgement which was already introduced in 1:9 and 3:18, even if it is difficult to be precise whether this is a judgement *post mortem* or a divine act which also concerns the present life. The ambiguity is, perhaps, deliberate.

However, v. 6 tells us that when God judges the wicked parents, their children, with their very existence and their corrupt life, will be the first witnesses for the prosecution. According to our sage, it appears that it is evident that the children will follow the footsteps of their parents. In this way, Wisdom expresses the strong conviction, one, moreover, that is profoundly biblical, that the guilt of the ungodly inevitably falls on their descendants. Finally, we should not undervalue the contact between v. 6 and 4:1-2 of which v. 6 constitutes the antithesis: whereas virtue is recognised publicly by God and people (cf. 4:1c), wickedness too is recognised, but through the very children of the ungodly (4:6b).

Diachronic Analysis

4:1 Ἀτεκνία is not to be understood in the sense of Isa 47:9, that is, having been deprived of one's children, but in that of Ps 34:12 LXX where, instead, it signifies not having (or not having had) children, and so infertility, regardless of the cause.

Our sage could have in mind the aforementioned text of Sir 16:3: κρείσσων γὰρ εἷς ἢ χίλιοι καὶ ἀποθανεῖν ἄτεκνον ἢ ἔχειν τέκνα ἀσεβῆ. However, the thought here is more developed and, in many aspects, innovative. In fact, in the biblical world children are a gift of God, which is being relativised here in favour of a virtuous life. Fecundity is no longer the highest gift that a woman can desire.

"At first sight, the combination μετὰ ἀρετῆς turns out to be less biblical".[40] The term ἀρετή is not very frequent in the LXX with the exception of Wis and 2-4 Macc (cf. 4 Macc 9:18; 10:10). As is well known, living according to virtue is one the central ideas of Stoic ethics. In the light of Wis 8:7, ἀρετή is closely connected with δικαιοσύνη but also includes the other three virtues typical of Stoicism: σωφροσύνη, φρόνησις, ἀνδρεία (cf. the comment on 8:7). In Wisdom (cf. also 5:13), however, virtue is not the heroism of the Maccabees but rather a moral *habitus* bound up first of all with the practice of justice (cf. the comment on 1:1). In 4:1, it is this general, though elevated, idea of virtue that our sage has in mind. A more restricted interpretation, therefore, of a sexual nature or virtue understood as the woman's faithfulness in marriage is to be excluded.

---

39 Cf. the texts quoted in Winston, *Wisdom*, 134-135.

40 Scarpat, *Sapienza*, 1:252.

The text of v. 2 repeats with variation a proverb transmitted to us by Horace among others: "virtutem incolumem odimus sublatam ex oculis quaerimus invidi [We hate virtue when it is flourishing but when it is taken from our eyes, we seek it with envy]" (*Carm.* 3.24.31).[41] Virtue is a very lofty phenomenon which people make an effort to imitate when they see it and search for it when they do not find it. Better still, virtue is admired and followed as if it were a beautiful woman, regretted when it is no longer there. Perhaps our sage is drawing here on a passage of Xenophon (*Mem.* 3.11.3).[42] 4:2

In 4:2c, however, the language is taken from the world of sport. Cf. the reference to the crown and the use of πομπεύω in the sense of "celebrate the victory". In the Greek world, ἀγών is the competition in which there is a prize (ἆθλον). For similar images within the NT, cf. 1 Cor 9:24-27; Phil 3:13-14, and, for the crown, 2 Tim 4:8; Jas 1:12; 1 Pet 5:4; Rev 2:10; 3:11.

We note that the idea of life understood as ἀγών returns, in an Alexandrian setting, in 4 Macc 17:11-16, but it is a classical image which will be taken up later in the NT (Heb 12:1; 2 Tim 2:5; 4:7).[43] The text of 1QS IV, 6-8 is interesting in that it presents some points of contact with Wisdom:

"These are the plans of action of the spirit concerning the sons of truth on the earth. The divine visitation in favour of all those who walk according to this spirit brings health and great peace with long life and fecundity, accompanied by all the eternal blessings; it brings eternal joy in life without end, that is, a crown of glory and with great splendour in the eternal Light".[44]

This Qumran text shows us that the Dead Sea community were living the expectation of a divine "visitation" (פקודה) which reminds us closely of the ἐπισκοπή of the book of Wisdom. The beneficiaries of this visitation are found to live with long life, fecundity, peace, and health in this world, and in eternal joy (cf. Wis 3:3b) where the just will be crowned with glory (Wis 4:2c). In the Qumran text, however, there is a recovering of the traditional values of fecundity and longevity, but the eschatological perspective shows that in the Judaism of its time the book of Wisdom is certainly not isolated in its announcement of a future life.

In Wis 4:3b-5, the symbolism of the roots (3bc), the shoots, buds and branches (4), and the shoots and the fruit (5) seen in relation to human life and – in particular – to children is a topic drawn from Scripture (cf. Isa 11:1; Ps 127:3 LXX [128:3 MT]; Job 8:16-19). Our sage could also have been inspired by texts like Job 30:32-33 and Sir 23:25, the latter *à propos* of the children of the adulteress. Cf. also Sir 40:15, but in our case the details are undoubtedly developed a good deal further. 4:3b-5

To the ear of Wisdom's public, on the other hand, the term ἄωρος sounds like a clear reference to the funerary *topos* of the *mors immatura* which here seems to affect only the ungodly (cf. the textual note).

---

41 Cf. Scarpat, *Sapienza*, 1:255.

42 Cf. Scarpat, *Sapienza*, 1:256-257.

43 Winston, *Wisdom*, 134; Scarpat, *Sapienza*, 1:279. Cf. Larcher, *Sagesse*, 2:318, who observes that the contrast between the virtuous struggle of the sage and the profane struggles in sport are a typical theme of the diatribe.

44 Cf., with some changes, Paolo Sacchi, *Regola della Comunità* (Paideia: Brescia 2006), 107-108.

The Fourth Diptych: The Premature Death of the Just and the Sad Death of the Ungodly (Wis 4:7-20)

7 But even if he dies prematurely, a just person will be at rest,
8 for an honoured old age is not one which lasts a long time
nor is it reckoned by the number of years.
9 For humans, discernment is fitting for white hair,
a life without stain for advanced age.

10 Having found favour with God, he was loved
and, while he lived in the midst of sinners, he was translated.
11 He was carried off, lest wickedness corrupt his mind
and deceit seduce his soul.
12 The attraction of vice obscures what is noble,
and the whirl of passion overwhelms a mind without guile.

13 Having attained perfection in a short time, he fulfilled a long life,
14 because his soul was pleasing to the Lord.
Therefore, he hastened to leave this place of wickedness,
while the people saw but did not understand
and did not concern themselves to reflect on such a thing,
15 that grace and mercy are for his elect
and a visitation for his holy ones.
16 The just person who has died condemns the ungodly who are still alive,
and the youth that has reached the end so quickly
will condemn the old age, the load of years, of the unjust.

17 For they will see the end of the wise person,
but they will not understand what he had decreed for him,
nor for what purpose the Lord had kept him safe.
18 They will see and scoff,
but it is at them that the Lord will laugh
19 so that they will become a ruin without honour,
an object of scorn among the dead for ever,
because he will make them fall, dumb, head first,
and shake them from their foundations.
They will be completely destroyed,
they will find themselves in sorrow
and their memory will perish.
20 They will go away, trembling, at the report of their sins
and their iniquity will stand before them to accuse them.

Notes on the Text and Translation

v. 11. Some codices (cf. Ziegler) read πρίν instead of μή, perhaps a theological clarification to avoid expressing directly the intention behind Enoch's "translation" (as happens with μή) and so to offer a more neutral sense: "before wickedness corrupted his mind".

v. 12. With "whirl" we are translating *ῥεμβασμός which is probably a literary creation of our author, containing in itself the idea of agitation, continuous movement (cf. the Lat: *incostantia*); cf. Scarpat, *Sapienza*, 1:286.

The meaning of μεταλλεύω, here translated with "overwhelms", is disputed. It appears in Wis 16:25 with the sense of "change", but in Greek it indicates rather a "mining of minerals, extraction of metals". Cf. Larcher, *Études*, 182, who thinks of an imperfect knowledge of Greek on our author's part. Cf. also Winston, *Wisdom* 141-142; Reese, *Hellenistic Influence*, 29 (our author would be using the verb in a figurative sense of "undermine – undergoing a change"). It is, perhaps, possible to speculate on a confusion with the verb μεταλλοιοῦν.

Vv. 14-15. The verb σπεύδω (14b) could be understood in an intransitive sense, more in harmony with Greek usage ("the just hastened ..."; cf. Wis 18:21a). In this case, however, unusually, the just man would be the subject of his own liberation. Some (cf. Cornely, *Commentarius,* 163) prefer to understand the verb as transitive and so with God as subject (Lat: *properavit educere illum*, where *educere illum* is an explanatory addition to the Greek), thus understanding an object complement αὐτήν or αὐτόν.

The Syro-Hexaplaric version, together with the Armenian translation and the commentaries of Malachias and Cantacuzenus, however, interpret the text by thinking of the soul (ἡ ψυχή) as subject of σπεύδω: it "left in haste"; that is, the soul of the just man itself takes the initiative of escaping from a situation of wickedness, following the plans and call of God with joy. In this case, Wisdom would be taking up Greek concepts relating to the soul which aspires to its place of origin. Cf. Grimm, *Weisheit*, 106, Larcher, *Sagesse*, 2:338, Winston, *Wisdom*, 142.

In 14c, οἱ δὲ λαοί is read ἄλλοι by A* and other minuscules. This is a *lectio facilior.* The correction reveals a certain difficulty of the copyists in reading an unexpected mention of the "peoples" who do not understand the end of the just man. For this reason, Larcher chooses Kuhn's conjecture, οἱ δ' ἀλαοί ("but they, the blind ..."). However, the text can be well explained just as its stands without making recourse to this kind of conjecture, unsupported by any witnesses.

We note the use of the anacoluthon in 14cd where there is no main verb. The three participles in the nominative could stand for genitive absolutes (cf. Scarpat, *Sapienza*, 1:289). Also, the expression τὸ τοιοῦτο, which normally refers to what goes before, could be announcing proleptically the objective clause introduced by the ὅτι of v. 15.

Ziegler's edition puts v. 15 in brackets [ ], considering it as a doublet of 3:9 (cf. the textual note to 3:9). In v. 15, the first occurrence of the preposition ἐν is suspect. In fact the preposition is omitted by S and by other minuscules. We observe that, as in 3:9, codex A, together with other witnesses, reads with an inversion of the sequence ἐκλεκτοῖς ... ὁσίοις. Verse 15 is attested by all the textual witnesses, and the fact of repeating here the same text as 3:9 could come within the style of Wisdom. If it is a gloss, it must be really very early. Moreover, v. 15 appears fundamental in the overall scheme of the pericope: the "peoples" did not understand (14cd) the love of God in God's relations with the just (v. 15 thus refers to what was already said in v. 10).

v. 16. Verse 16 is considered a gloss by some (Gutberlet, Deane, Goodrick, and Winston, who puts it together with the γάρ which opens v. 17). If v. 16 constitutes a further anacoluthon, it could be considered as the conclusion of the whole argument relating to the just dying prematurely (cf. the *inclusio* with 4:7-8a: δίκαιος – γῆρας) and, at the same time, as the announcement of the second part (vv. 17-20) devoted to the judgement of the ungodly.

The verb κατακρινεῖ is a future with gnomic force. The reading θανών instead of καμών, as it appears in some codices (cf. Ziegler, apparatus), is a *lectio explicativa* which is to be rejected. The participle καμών is a euphemism for "dead" employed as far back as Homer (*Od.* 11.476) and has a nuance of "toiling" which is very suitable for the efforts of the just youth to reach perfection.

The verb τελέω is sometimes understood by "reached perfection", along the same lines as the τελειωθείς of v. 13. A thematic reprise does not seem impossible. However, the context leads us to think rather of the meaning of "ending (life)". In fact, the first stich plays on the opposition just/ungodly; living/dead. The second stich of v. 16, on the other hand, plays on an opposition of a temporal nature: youth terminated (early)/old age, bearer of years. Cf. Lat: *iuventute celerius consummata* (Luciani, "The meaning of the verb *teléô* in Wis 4,16"). The term *πολυετές ("the load of years"), *hapax* in the LXX, is also rare in classical Greek.

v. 19. We have translated πτῶμα in its usual sense of "ruin", following Scarpat, *Sapienza*, 1:292-293, and LXX usage (cf. Jdt 8:19; 13:10; Prov 16:18; Sir 31:6; Pss. Sol. 3:10). Modern translations often render it with "corpse" (cf. Jdg 14:8; Ps 109:6 LXX [110:6 MT]; Matt 14:12; 24:28; Mark 6:29; 15:45; Rev 11:8, 9). In this case, ἄτιμος could lead us to think of a body that was not buried or else deprived of funerary honours.

In 19c, ῥήξει could derive from ῥήγνυμι, "break, shatter", or from the later form ῥήσσω. The verb can be used in the military sense of "beat/shatter the enemy". Cf. the subsequent πρηνεῖς (for the more common πρανεῖς), "with face to the earth" (Lat has *inflatos*, cf. Eth, Arm; Syr reads probably πριστούς, "sawn", from πρίω or πρίζω). Along these lines, one could think of God who will cause the ungodly to fall to the earth on their faces and drop them into the pit, having reduced them to silence (ἀφώνους). Scarpat (*Sapienza*, 1:293-294), however, assumes the more classical construction ῥῆξαι φωνήν, "make the voice to be heard (lit.) to break" and thinks of the just as the subject of ῥήξει and the ungodly as the object (ἀφώνους), and translates thus: "they (the just) will beat them, silenced, to their knees".

Synchronic Analysis

Wis 4:7-16: The Premature Death of the Just

4:7-9 The subject of the premature death of the just opens with vv. 7-9 which are introduced by a statement of principle expressed in a condition: " even if a just person (δίκαιος, without the article) dies prematurely (ἐὰν φθάσῃ τελευτῆσαι), he will be at rest". Verse 7 is followed by two negative statements (v. 8) and a positive one (v. 9).

The first stage of the argument is clear: old age is not necessarily a sign of divine blessing and a reward for virtue because the old age which arouses respect is only that which is bound up with wisdom and integrity of life.

The premature death of a just person (v. 7) does not necessarily indicate the death of a youth. That what we have here is a young person is evident only from the context of the pericope as a whole. With the scandal of such a death, our sage contrasts faith in a future reality: he "will be at rest" (ἐν ἀναπαύσει). The use of the future (ἔσται) refers to the destiny of the just which has already been described in 3:1-9 and, in particular, precisely to that being in peace described in 3:3. However, the context here is different because this time there is no mention of the previous sufferings of the just person who has died prematurely.

Honoured (τίμιον; cf. 2:10) old age is not calculated by the number of years (cf. v. 8b), but by "discernment" and by a life "without stain" (v. 9). "Prudence/discernment" (for φρόνησις, cf. the comment on 3:15) is considered as a characteristic virtue of old age. Here, in a rather revolutionary way, it is also attributed to the young. The term *ἀκηλίδωτος, absent from the LXX (cf., however, Prov 25:18, where codices A e S^{corr} replace ἀκιδωτός, "sharp" [unique here in the LXX], with ἀκηλίδωτος), is an erudite word which returns in Wis 7:26 in connection with the description of wisdom and indicates being without stain. The adjective appears seven times in Philo (cf. *Virt.* 205, 222; *Spec.* 1.150, 167; *Cher.* 95; *Sacr.* 139; *Det.* 171). Thus, it must have been a term well-known to the Alexandrian world.

Verse 10 emphasises the consequences of the pure life mentioned in v. 9. The 4:10
asyndetic construction indicates the passage to a new stage in the argument. The just person becomes favoured, evidently by God (the participle γενόμενος is used; this "becoming" presupposes progress in virtue) and is loved by God (ἀγαπάω is employed here in the passive; cf. the comment on 1:1a). The verb εὐαρεστέω is applied to Noah in Gen 6:9 and to Abraham in Gen 17:1 with the same meaning, but it is found applied above all to Enoch in Gen 5:22, 24 (see below).

Allusion to Enoch?

The just person is then "translated": μετατίθημι, employed here too in the passive with reference to the action of God, recalls immediately the figure of Enoch (see below). In fact, the verb is used in the LXX only in our text, in Gen 5:24 and in Sir 44:16, precisely in connection with the antediluvian patriarch (cf. Heb 11:5). The allusion, therefore, must have been more than clear to the hearers of the book of Wisdom. The *translation* of the just person – evidently carried into the divine sphere – is explained by the fact that he lived "in the midst of sinners". The participle ζῶν has contemporaneous rather than causal value: "while he lived" and not "since he lived".

The passive form ἡρπάγη which opens v. 11 is a further allusion to the action of 4:11
God who "carried off" the just person from death. The verb ἁρπάζω reappears in the NT with a not dissimilar meaning (cf. 1 Thess 4:17; 2 Cor 12:2, 4; Rev 12:5). In the Greek world too, the verb is employed to emphasise a death that is sudden (cf. Plutarch, *Cons. Apoll.* 30 = 117c). The just person is "carried off" from this world so that his σύνεσις is not affected by evil. Here, σύνεσις indicates the faculty of understanding, discerning good from evil (cf. 1 Kgs 3:9 in connection with the gift Solomon requests from God (cf. Wis 9:5; 13:13). If κακία indicates evil in general, δόλος stands rather for that deceit or lying which can corrupt the soul (ψυχή) of the just. Here too, soul is again being understood not as an autonomous part but as the subject of the moral life. The verb ἀπατάω, "deceive/beguile", is probably taken from Gen 3:13 where it is employed in relation to the deceit of the serpent in its dealings with the woman.

Verse 12 provides the reasons that underlie the two previous verses. What is 4:12
noble (τὰ καλά) in people is obscured (ἀμαυρόω) by the attraction of vice. Βασ-

κανία (cf. 4 Macc 1:26; 2:15) is precisely an indication of seductive attraction with a clear allusion to magic, to enchantment. The term *φαυλότης is *hapax* in the LXX; φαῦλος, in the NT, is employed for the most part *in malam partem* and indicates what is despicable, base, or wicked (cf. Rom 9:11; 2 Cor 5:10). The whole expression could be translated with something like "the spell of vice", the fascination, the seduction of wickedness, of what is base.

The second stich of v. 12 tells us how a soul without guile (νοῦν ἄκακον) is overwhelmed by the whirl of desire. The νοῦς refers to the higher faculty of the soul. *Per se*, the term ἐπιθυμία does not have a negative sense (cf. Wis 6:17, 20), but it can assume it, as in this case (cf. Wis 16:2). Desire appears here as passion imagined metaphorically, like an overwhelming whirlwind which takes possession of a person and leads him or her to evil.

God, therefore,[45] knows that the just can be corrupted, living in the midst of sinners. Death thus becomes, paradoxically, an act of grace which keeps the just safe from a moral corruption. The text certainly wishes to allude to the situation of the Alexandrian Jews who also live "in the midst of sinners", but, with its gnomic flavour, the passage acquires a universal significance which makes it relevant to every period.

4:13 The first part of the diptych closes by recalling the surprising intention of God which is revealed to people precisely by the premature death of the just. Verse 13 sees the return of the idea with which the reflection opened (v. 7). If the children of the ungodly are "imperfect" (3:16; 4:5), the just young person, on the other hand, has attained "perfection" (cf. 4:13; 6:15). He "has fulfilled (ἐπλήρωσεν) a long life", that is, he has brought his own life to perfection as if he had really become very old.

4:14 The first two stichs of v. 14 make up a reprise of vv. 10-12. The soul of the just person, pleasing to God, hastened to leave this wicked world. The just thus seem to regard their own death with joy and not with resignation. For them, death is not ruin but the encounter with the Lord. Our author is here implying the whole message of 3:1-9.

Suddenly, in 14cd, with a clean break which strikes the reader (cf. the use of anacoluthon), the text goes on to consider the attitude of the "peoples", understood here in a pejorative sense. They did not understand "such a thing" (τὸ τοιοῦτο) (cf. 2:22), that is, the premature death of the just but also, proleptically, (cf. the textual notes) the divine mercy granted to the just themselves (v. 15).

The expression θέντες ἐπὶ διανοίᾳ has a Greek flavour. Διάνοια (present only here in Wisdom) is equivalent to mind or else to "conscience". In the LXX, it is almost a synonym of καρδία.

4:15 "Such a thing": in the light of v. 15, this is to be understood as the divine action in favour of the "elect" and the "holy ones". With ἐκλεκτοῖς, the emphasis is on the divine choice; with ὅσιοι, on the other hand, the reference is to the "pious", those who are faithful to the Lord (cf. Wis 6:10; 7:27; 10:15, 17; 18:1, 5, and 9). Divine activity towards the just is marked by "grace" and "mercy" (χάρις καὶ ἔλεος; cf. 3:9).

---

45 For the theological problems raised in the past by this text, cf. Larcher, *Sagesse*, 2:335-336.

The book of Wisdom adds the theme of "visitation" (ἐπισκοπή) which we have already encountered and which is a metaphor for the future salvation which the Lord will guarantee to his elect (cf. the comment on 2:20; 3:7, 13). In this case too, it is not possible to be specific as to the precise nature of God's intervention in favour of the just *post mortem*.

Verse 15 appears essential within the argument of our diptych because it serves to express the divine attitude in relation to the just, an attitude that is positive and salvific, rich in grace and mercy, and in faithfulness to the covenant. "The peoples" are not able to understand this because they are strangers to the logic of love of this God who guarantees to the elect a salvation beyond death.

With another stylistic leap (the peoples mentioned in 14c return as subject only in v. 17-18), v. 16 returns to speak of the just person who, in the same way as he had condemned the ungodly with his life (2:12-14), now condemns them with his death. 4:16

The text does not make clear what condemnation is being spoken of, although it is possible to think of the actual death of the ungodly, the definitive revelation of their wickedness. It is impossible for the ungoldy to destroy the existence of the just. Even if an unjust person dies, he or she becomes the tangible proof of the failure of their whole life. The idea is contained *in nuce* in the mention of the blood of Abel which cries to God from the ground (cf. Gen 4:9ff). The death of the just youth, which the ungodly had interpreted as a disaster (cf. 3:2), becomes instead, in an unexpected and paradoxical way, the sign of their own condemnation.

Despite the fact that they reached a more mature age and a much longer life (cf. 16b), the ungodly did not know how to attain what the just obtained with a youth that seemed to pass all too quickly. Our sage thus replies to the question behind the whole of the pericope: how is it possible for the ungodly to have a long life? Even if that were to happen, the ungodly have really lost the purpose of their lives which was attained instead by the just. Cf. the expression νεότης τελεσθεῖσα and what was already observed in connection with v. 13 (cf. the textual note).

Wis 4:17-20: The Sad Death of the Godless

In this last part of the diptych (4:17-20), the blessed destiny of the just person who dies prematurely (4:7-16) is contrasted with the definitive ruin of the ungodly, which, in v. 20, results in their final judgement, prelude to the majestic scene of the fifth chapter. 4:17

"For they will see the end of the wise person". The verb ὄψονται, a future with gnomic value like the subsequent οὐ νοήσουσιν, does not have a subject, but one could think *ad sensum* of the "peoples" mentioned in 14cd or more generically of the ungodly who see the just die but without understanding the meaning of such a death. "Seeing and not understanding" is a biblical expression (cf. Isa 57:1). The ungodly lack the ability to penetrate to the deeper meaning of events, to know how to discern in them the sign of God's will (cf. 17b). They do not know how to use their reason (οὐ νοήσουσιν) to penetrate beyond the superficial to recognise the deeper meaning of the things they see.

In the first stich, we note the mention of the "wise one" instead of the "just one" who has been protagonist of the whole text 4:7-16. That signifies that the just youth who dies prematurely is, at the same time, a sage whose virtue was not hidden from people although the ungodly, even if they saw it, did not understand it.

In the third stich, εἰς has final force and reveals the divine intentions for the sage which the ungodly have not understood (cf. also βουλεύω in 17b with the Lord as subject, understood). The use of ἀσφαλίζω refers to the idea of protection, defence (cf. Wis 10:12; 13:15). In causing the just sage to die, the Lord actually intended to make him safe from evil (cf. 4:10-12 and 14). Physical death appears yet again as an ambiguous reality – for the just, a passage to life with God. Significantly, the mention of the κύριος, the YHWH of Israel, closes the verse as a whole. Everything that happens to the just is nothing other than the fruit of the divine action.

4:18 Again, we have a reference to what the ungodly see (cf. 14cd). Not only do they not understand but they also scoff at the end of the just (ἐξουθενέω, cf. Wis 3:11). For this reason, their punishment will be terrible. The second stich is well constructed. The pronoun referring to the ungodly (αὐτούς) is placed in an emphatic position, and the subject of the action, which, again, is ὁ κύριος, is placed at the centre: "but it is at them that the Lord will laugh". The verb ἐκγελάω is used as elsewhere in the LXX (cf. Pss 2:4; 36:13 LXX [37:13 MT]; 58:9 LXX [59:9 MT]; etc.) with the sense of bursting into laughter, mostly in an ironic and sarcastic way. The reference to God's "laughing", a laugh of scorn with even tones of cruelty, seems rather crude, but undoubtedly effective, along the lines of an anthropomorphism used in Scripture (cf. the already mentioned text of Ps 2:4 which our sage could well have in mind). The Lord reveals himself to people in the way in which they imagine themselves. The ungodly do not accept the love and mercy of God (cf. v. 15) and so discover, not all that paradoxically, the terrible and fearful face of that God at whom they are laughing.

4:19 The basic problem here is to understand whether our sage is speaking of a collective punishment of the ungodly in this life or a punishment for them *post mortem*. The first stich should be read in the light of Isa 14:19 (see below). The ungodly will become a ruin without honour. The text could be alluding to the shameful fate of the ungodly in the hereafter. The second stich confirms this idea. They will be the object of scorn (εἰς ὕβριν) among the dead, precisely as happens to the king of Babylon in Isaiah's text. The mention of ὕβρις is certainly an indirect reference to that arrogance, that haughtiness of the ungodly mentioned in 2:19 which now, in the world of the dead, is punished by the dead themselves.

The third stich gives the reason for the two previous ones (cf. ὅτι). The ungodly are struck, beaten and reduced to silence. They can no longer reply or justify themselves (cf. the textual note). As opposed to the just (3:3b and 4:7), the ungodly will be in sorrow (19f) and not at rest. These are sorrows which originate in an encounter with the divine wrath, which derive from insults on the part of others (19b) and from the isolation caused by the discovery of their own unexpected barrenness.

At the end, their memory will disappear (cf. 19g). The term μνήμη refers in an *inclusio* to 4:1 and so has an analogous significance. In 4:1, our sage had placed a close link between memory and the personal immortality of the just. Human memory thus goes in step with that of God. The ungodly have lost both things: they are remembered neither by people nor by God, and with that, in the light of 4:1, they have also lost immortality.

In conclusion, the text of v. 19 seems to point to a collective punishment of the ungodly which happens after their death in an afterlife which is not clearly specified, along the lines of Isa 14:18-22, without it being possible to understand in detail what punishment our sage has in mind. This second part of the diptych shows us that physical death assumes quite different meanings for the just and for the ungodly. For the former, physical death is a passage to life with God, for the latter, the beginning of ruin which brings to an end a life without meaning. The life of the ungodly leaves behind nothing but ruin, barrenness, destruction and sorrow.

This verse serves simultaneously as a conclusion of the diptych but also as a 4:20
transition to the following section. Note the asyndetic construction. A new phase is beginning: that of the final judgement of the ungodly in which they become aware of their own errors.

Συλλογισμός indicates the final judgement, the rendering of accounts. We notice the indirect reference to the inquest (ἐξέτασις, ἐξετασμός) that was already mentioned in 1:9 and in 4:6. The first stich could be understood in relation to the ungodly who are now presented in judgement, full of fear (δειλοί; cf. Wis 9:14; 17:10), making account for their own sins on which they now must reflect. Cf. the Latin which reads *in cogitatione peccatorum suorum*, as if thinking of a sort of examination of conscience *post mortem*. On the basis of the use of συλλογισμός in Exod 30:12, it is possible to think also of the ungodly who will go away trembling at the assembly, that is, at the rendering of accounts for their sins.[46] In any case, what we have here is a real public judgement of the ungodly before the just who are now glorified (cf. 6:2) and not just an internal judgement.

The ungodly will be accused (ἐλέγξει αὐτούς) by their own sins (τὰ ἀνομήματα αὐτῶν) which will stand before them (ἐξ ἐναντίας). The expression ἐξ ἐναντίας is common in the LXX (53 occurrences) to indicate standing in front of an enemy, whether in a military or in a juridical sense. Here again, without saying so clearly, Wisdom is introducing the idea of an accusing moral conscience which will be explicit in Wis 17:11.

Diachronic Analysis

According to a way of thought typical of the Greek world "those whom the gods love die young": ὃν γὰρ θεοὶ φιλοῦσιν ἀποθνήσκει νέος (cf. Menander, frag. 425); *quem di diligunt adulescens moritur* (Plautus, *Bacch.* 4.7.18).[47] Armin Schmitt has shown that the author is making use here of something commonplace to the

46 Cf. Scarpat, *Sapienza*, 1:294-295.

47 "Non mehercule quemquam audivi adulescentulum aut puerum mortuum, qui mihi non a diis immortalibus raptus ex his miseriis atque ex iniquissima vitae conditione videretur [By Hercules, I have not heard of a young man or boy who has died who does not seem to have been seized by the immortal gods out of these miseries and highly unfair state of life]" (Cicero, *Fam.* 5.16).

Hellenistic-Roman literature of consolation. A premature death secures the one who is loved by the gods from all suffering and is therefore a sign of divine favour.[48]

From the biblical perspective, old age is one of the clearest signs of divine blessing. The patriarchs die "full of years" (Gen 25:8; 35:29; Job 42:17), and longevity constitutes the reward granted to the just (Ps 20:5 LXX [21:5 MT]; 22:6 LXX [23:6 MT]; 90:16 LXX [91:16 MT]; Prov 3:16; etc.). By contrast, an early death is considered a consequence of sin (cf. Prov 10:27; Ps 54:24 LXX [55:24 MT]). On many occasions, the psalmists seek to instil the faith that God will intervene to punish the wicked by depriving them of long life (Pss 36:5-7 LXX [37:5-7 MT]; 89:1-12 LXX [90:1-12 MT]; 101:24-29 LXX [102:24-29 MT]; 108:22-31 LXX [109:22-31 MT]). Yet, experience of life seems to wish to say the opposite: why do the wicked live? Indeed, why do they grow old? This is Job's question of God in the face of what he sees (cf. Job 21:7). The book of Wisdom tries to give a response to this pressing question, overturning the values held to be traditional.

4:7 The term ἀνάπαυσις ("rest"), referring here to the "rest" of the just person who has died prematurely, is applied in the LXX to the sabbath rest (cf. Exod 16:23), to that of death (cf. Job 21:13), or else to a generic state of peace and security (cf. Isa 32:17), of joy even (cf. Sir 6:28; 51:27). For an eschatological use of the term in the NT, one thinks of Heb 4:3-11. Here, the term is referring not so much to the rest of death (cf. the text of Isa 57:2, in connection with the death of the just, a text to which our author seems to be alluding [ἔσται ἐν εἰρήνῃ ἡ ταφὴ αὐτοῦ]) as, rather, to a state of tranquillity and peace lived in relation to God. Ἀνάπαυσις has also in itself the idea of "coolness". This is the understanding of the VL (*refrigerium*).[49]

4:8-9 In the light of the faith in the final destiny of the just, vv. 8-9 modify the biblical perspective relating to longevity according to a pattern that is already in some way present in texts like Dan 1:17; Sus 50 LXX + Θ, 63 LXX; Job 32:7-9; Ps 118:100 LXX [119:100 MT]. The author certainly does not mean to abolish the great veneration which the whole tradition of Israel had always attributed to old age (cf. Lev 19:32), but wishes, rather, to link the value of life not so much to the number of years as to the moral quality of a person. An idea like this is not foreign to Greek and Roman wisdom, from Plato to Seneca, and it will become a common theme in patristic tradition just as it was in the Judaism of the time. Thus, it is wisdom and not age which gives true value to life.[50]

---

48 Schmitt, "Der frühe Tod des Gerechten". Cf. also the texts cited by Engel, *Weisheit*, 98-101.

49 Cf. Scarpat, *Sapienza*, 2:450; Bauernfeind, Otto, ἀνάπαυσις, TDNT 1:350-351.

50 The *motif* is frequent in Philo (*Abr.* 271; *Fug.* 146; *Migr.* 201; *Her* 290; etc.) to the extent that it can be considered topical. Cf. Plutarch: τὸ γὰρ καλὸν οὐκ ἐν μήκει χρόνου θετέον ἀλλ' ἐν ἀρετῇ καὶ τῇ καιρίῳ συμμετρίᾳ· τοῦτο γὰρ εὔδαιμον καὶ θεοφιλὲς εἶναι νενόμισται (*Cons. Apoll.* 17 = 111AB). For the Latin literature, cf. Seneca: "sic vita non quam diu sed quam bene acta sit, refert" (*Ep.* 77.20). For the Fathers, cf. Jerome: "Noli, igitur, frater carissime, annorum aestimare nos numeros, nec sapientiam canos reputes, sed canos sapientiam, Salomone testante: "cani hominis prudentiam eius (Wis 4,8)" (*Epist. ad Paul.* 58.1, PL 22, 579). Cf. Cicero, *Tusc.* 1.45; *Sen.* 18. For other texts, cf. Larcher, *Etudes*, 174-175 and p. 174, n. 9; 2:329; Winston, *Wisdom*, 137-138.

In the use of the passive form μεμέτρηται (4:8b), we should see, perhaps, a polemic against astral determinism. This was the theory that each man's life is determined in advance by the stars. Whoever died prematurely was held to have to wander over the earth for all time, failing to complete the life that had been predetermined by the stars.[51]

The idea about old age in 4:9 finds a certain support in biblical texts, such as the aforementioned Dan 1:17; 13:50, 63; Job 32:7-9; Ps 118:100 LXX [119:100 MT]. However, the author is not thinking here so much of charismatic wisdom given to a youth (as in the case of the young Daniel or in that of Elihu), but rather of a spiritual maturity which a young man can possess in himself and which gives meaning to his life. Such a separation between physical and spiritual development is a typically Greek idea (cf. above).

In v. 10 too, it is possible to make out the presence of a *topos* common to the 4:10
Greco-Roman world. A long life can be an occasion of sin for a youth who has not been well educated or, conversely, for a particularly good youth who could therefore be corrupted over time. This is a consoling *motif* rather common in the case of premature deaths (cf. Seneca, *Marc.* 22.2; Plutarch, *Cons. Apoll.* 30 = 117D). The world is a sad and dangerous place and can easily corrupt the young. Better, therefore, a premature death than the risk of losing one's virtue. Such a basically very pessimistic view of humanity is here adopted by Wisdom, though within the profoundly biblical conviction relating to God's love for humanity. The just were, indeed, "loved" by God.

Wis 4:10-12 and the figure of Enoch

Allusions to Enoch

As background to vv. 10-12, our sage has in mind not so much the Greek myth of Ganymede[52] as rather the biblical case of Enoch. In fact, the use of the verbs "translate" (μετατίθημι) and "find favour" (εὐάρεστος) refer to Gen 5:21-24 LXX. It is necessary to note immediately, however, that while the biblical Enoch is "translated" while still alive, here the subject is a just person who has died prematurely. The figure of Enoch is evoked but not explicitly cited. The Enoch mentioned in Gen 5:21-24 is the antediluvian patriarch with the shortest life. He lives for only 365 years, that is, a "year of years", and is presented as a just man who "walked with God", carried off by God before his natural death, as will happen later to Elijah (2 Kgs 2:3, 9). Sir 44:16 makes of Enoch an example of conversion (cf. Philo, *Abr.* 19),[53] just as the Letter to the Hebrews (Heb 11:5) will later make him into a model of faith. As far as Ben Sirach is concerned, his opposition to the Enochic tradition seems rather clear.[54] The texts of Sir 44:16 and of Jude 14 seem to presuppose another tradition relating to the life of Enoch in the midst of a wicked generation, an idea which is also underlying 4:10b. Moreover, already in Gen 5, Enoch's shortened life lets him escape being a spectator of the catastrophe of the Flood before which he is carried off.

---

51 Cf. Cumont, *Lux Perpetua*, 307-311.

52 On the funerary use of the myth of Ganymede, the cupbearer of the gods, taken up on the eagle of Zeus, cf. Cumont, Franz V.M., *Recherches sur le symbolisme funéraire des Romains* (Paris: Geuthener 1942), 97-99.

53 Philo also makes him an allegorical example of the immortality of the soul; cf. *Mut.* 38.

54 Cf. Argall, Randall A., *I Enoch and Sirach: A Comparative Literary and Conceptual Analysis of the Themes of Revelation, Creation and Judgment*, Atlanta (GA): Scholars Press 1995; Wright III, Benjamin G, "Sirach and 1 Enoch: some further considerations", *Hen* 24 (2002): 179-187.

However, the figure of Enoch is to be understood not so much against the background of Genesis 5 as of the Enochic literature which was already widespread by the first cent. BCE. This tradition made the antediluvian patriarch into the privileged depositary of heavenly revelations regarding the origin of evil (the fallen angels) and the future salvation. The canonical Scriptures tend to minimise the figure of Enoch and make it fall within the canons of a Judaism which does not accept the theological perspective of the Enochians.[55] That happens also in our book which does not accept the apocalyptic speculations belonging to the Enochic tradition.[56] The youth who dies prematurely, described with a vocabulary recalling Enoch, is translated into the divine world, but his being carried off is to some degree preventative. He is carried off by the Lord so as not to be corrupted. Thus, he could have fallen into sin, like any other person; he was not an exemplary moral being like the patriarch Enoch.

We note again that Enoch makes no appearance in the list of the just presented in Wis 10. Even in the allusions to Enoch presented in Wis 4, the stress falls not so much on the faith of the patriarch and his right behaviour, and not even on his repentance, as happens in Ben Sirach. The attention falls rather on the action of God who makes the just youth the object of grace. The verbs, in fact, are all in the passive: was loved, was translated, was carried off. The premature end of the just can thus become a particular sign of divine grace, and of such an end, a celebrated figure like Enoch is only a distant sign. In this way, Wisdom makes use in part of a figure celebrated at that time but simultaneously shows its lack of acceptance of the apocalyptic speculations which the Enochians had created around him. Wisdom bases its own eschatology not on the claim to heavenly revelations but on the profoundly biblical faith in God's loving will for people.

4:13 As for the theme of the just person who "attained perfection", the use of τελειόω refers as we noted previously to the Greek idea of moral perfection, typical in Greek philosophy, whether in Plato or in Aristotle and in Stoicism, and widely taken up again by Philo in the Jewish-Hellenistic sphere.[57] The one who has lived in virtue is the τέλειος, "perfect" one. However, we must recall that later on the text of Wis 9:6 reminds us that, even if there were such a "perfect" person, such a person too would need the wisdom that comes from God. Our sage's ideal of "perfection", therefore, does not coincide with that of self-fulfilment, a life according to virtue, in harmony with nature and reason, typical of the Stoic world. Even being virtuous, "perfect", is seen as a gift from the Lord.

The idea that perfection can be attained in a short time, that is, even in the case of a premature death, is also not infrequently a *motif* of consolation.[58] Finally,

---

55 Cf. Bedenbender, Andreas, "Traces of Enochic Judaism within the Hebrew Bible", *Hen* 24 (2002): 39-48. The text of Gen 5:21-24 is reacting precisely in this way in its dealings with the Enochian set-up, and, *vice versa*, the Enochic tradition reshapes the "canonical" traditions relating to Enoch. On Enochic Judaism as the opponent of priestly Judaism (but also on the sapiential opposition to this kind of Judaism), cf. Boccaccini Gabriele, *I giudaismi del secondo Tempio*. Da Ezechiele a Daniele (Brescia: Paideia 2008), 91-134. See now: Mazzinghi, "Sap 4,10-14 e la figura di Enoch".

56 Cf. the introduction, p. 34, on the relationship between Wisdom and apocalyptic.

57 Delling, Gerhard, τέλειος, *TDNT* 8:69-72, 79-80. Cf. also the comment on 3:16, 19, and, later, below, on 9:6.

58 Cf. the texts of Seneca cited by Larcher, *Sagesse*, 2:337: "licet aetas eius imperfecta sit, vita perfecta est" (*Ep.* 93.7). Cf. also Philo, *Praem.* 112. For the patristic tradition, cf. Ambrose, *Ob. Theo.* 6: "est enim perfecta aetas ubi perfecta est virtus".

we cannot exclude a polemic against the mystery cults with their initiates who claimed to have attained perfection. On this point, however, the linguistic evidence is not decisive.[59]

In v. 14, the influence of the aforementioned text of Isa 57:1-2 LXX (cf. also Isa 44:18) is very probable. The verbal and thematic contacts between the text of Isaiah and v. 14 (but also with the whole context of vv. 7-16) are noteworthy: the death of the just man taken away from an environment of wickedness; his being in peace; and the lack of understanding of his death on the part of the people. The context in Isaiah is in fact slightly different. While the prophet laments that the just man perishes and no one takes it to heart, in Wisdom the emphasis is shifted on to the inability of the "peoples" to understand the divine plans relating to the salvation of the just. According to his style, the author of Wisdom makes free use of the biblical texts to which he refers and rereads them in a new context. 4:14

The use of διάνοια could thus be the way with which Wisdom replaces Isaiah's expression ἐκδέχεται τῇ καρδίᾳ (cf. above). Cf., in 14c, the replacement of Isaiah's κατανοεῖ with μὴ νοήσαντες. Echoes of Wis 4:14cd, or of its possible source, Isa 6:9-10, can be found in the New Testament, in Matt 13:14-15; Mark 4:12; John 12:40.

In the whole of v. 19, there is clear influence of Isa 14:18-22 LXX, a passage devoted to the description of the sad fate of the king of Babylon who wanted to rise up to heaven but was hurled into the abyss of Hades, condemned by God, and derided by all. Thus, the language of v. 19 imitates the prophetic style and makes use of strong and suggestive images. 4:19

Verse 19d contains a reminiscence of Ps 17[18 MT]:8 and Job 9:6. The ungodly, those who held themselves to be absolutely secure, have neither roots nor foundations. They are like a land that is dry and devastated (cf. 19e; there is a possible allusion to Jer 2:31), which recalls, by contrast, the "fruit" of the just mentioned in 3:13, 15.

The text of 4:19g is, again, a reprise of Isa 14:22; but the theme of the memory of the ungodly which disappears is common in Scripture. Cf. Job 18:17, 19; Pss 9:6; 33:17 LXX [34:17 MT]; 36:28 LXX [37:28 MT]; and Prov 10:7.

Summary of Wis 3-4

The tension produced by the discourse of the ungodly (2:1-20) is immediately resolved by the opening statement of 3:1: the life of the just is in the hands of God. Taking up what was anticipated in 1:13-15 and 2:21-24, our sage replies to possible objections of the ungodly with three examples: the suffering just man, the barren woman and the eunuch, and the just man who dies before his time. In all three cases, the author makes use of the scheme "appearance-reality" and employs the technique of inversion of images. This demonstrates that he is speaking not only to reason but also to the heart. What seems "reality" to the ungodly – the uselessness of the death of the just – is only appearance (cf. 3:2). The very

59 Delling, τέλειος, *TDNT* 8:69.

powerful images employed to describe the end of the ungodly serve, by contrast, to depict the blessed destiny of the just and to highlight the truth of our author's claims (cf., for example, 3:1, 3, 4, etc.).

In the first diptych (3:1-12), the image of the just man who suffers, which directly recalls the just man of 2:10-20, resolves the paradox of Job. Death is no longer a catastrophe but is eternal life with God. The author of the book of Wisdom shows himself to be really rather reticent about the details and, in particular, about the reality of the "visitation" and of the "judgement" which the Lord will carry out in the future. The emphasis falls, however, on the situation of peace and serenity which awaits the just beyond the present life.

In the two central diptychs, relating to the barren woman and the eunuch (3:13-4:6), attention is shifted to the moral aspect, suggested by rich botanical symbolism. It is virtue, and not material goods, that guarantees a person's happiness. The fruit of virtue (3:13, 15) is eternal life; the fruit of the ungodly is useless descendants. Here, an increasingly marked judicial vocabulary makes its appearance, heralding the judgement of the ungodly in chapter 5. The barren woman will have her fruit at the time of the "visitation of souls" (3:13); the ungodly will have no hope at the time of the "judgement" (3:18), and they will be accused at the time of the "inquest" (4:6). In the light of the intervention of God, the contrast between appearance and reality is thus loosened.

In the fourth diptych (4:7-20), the moral theme returns: a person's true maturity depends not on age, but on moral qualities. Life is to be understood as a continuous progression (4:13), and death is simply a "translation" (4:10-12), proof of the salvific love of God who preserves humanity from evil in the present. The chapter closes with another judicial image (4:17-20), described in language with an apocalyptic character. The ungodly regard suffering as useless, weakness a reality to be eliminated with violence, the death of the just to be the sign of their defeat (cf. 2:10-20). In overturning values well rooted in tradition, the four diptychs show the failure of such a perspective, a failure underlined dramatically by God's laughter (4:18).

Wis 5: Concluding Contrast of the Just and the Godless before the Background of the Cosmos

The Literary Structure of Wis 5

A brief introduction (vv. 1-3) evokes the final confrontation between the just and the ungodly. The verb στήσεται, "stand", which opens the entire section of Wis 5, is taken up again in v. 2b (ἐκστήσονται; "they will be amazed") and, in an *inclusio*, at the end of the chapter (v. 23, ἀντιστήσεται, "will rise"). Wis 5:1-3

Verses 4-13 contain a second discourse of the ungodly which is linked with that of chapter 2. The discourse is framed by the *inclusio* οὗτος ... ἔσχομεν / οὕτως ... ἔσχομεν (vv. 4 and 13). We can easily make out three sections. In vv. 4-5, the ungodly acknowledge the final success of the just (cf. the link between ἐλογισάμεθα and κατελογίσθη). In vv. 6-7, they recognise the errors of their life. There is a further *inclusio*, between v. 6a and v. 7c, "from the way of truth", ἀπὸ ὁδοῦ ἀληθείας, and "the way of the Lord", τὴν ὁδόν κυρίου. Finally, in vv. 8-13, the ungodly describe the feeble foundation of their project with a series of five comparisons each of which is opened by the repetition of the comparative particle "like, as" (ὡς). Cf. also the *inclusio* ἡμᾶς ... ἡμῖν (v. 8), ἡμεῖς ... ἡμῶν (v. 13). Wis 5:4-13

The discourse of the ungodly is followed by the judgement of the author (vv. 14-23) which is framed by the repetition of the highly rare word λαῖλαψ, "hurricane" (vv. 14 and 23), a passage which recalls the previous judgement of 2:21-24 at the conclusion of the first discourse of the ungodly. In v. 14, the ungodly are again described, this time with four comparisons introduced by ὡς. Finally, there follows the description of the just (δίκαιοι δέ, vv. 15-16) and, in conclusion, the description of the divine battle against the ungodly (vv. 17-23). In v. 23, the mention of the "earth" (γῆν) and of the θρόνους δυναστῶν prepares the link with the following chapter (cf. 6:1ab). Wis 5:14-23

Contacts between Wis 2 and Wis 5

From a literary point of view, this chapter is closely linked with the second and cannot be separated from it. The two chapters record direct discourse of the ungodly relating to both the just man and to the lifestyle of the ungodly themselves, discourse which is closed by the judgement of the author. The two chapters are connected by the repetition of key words. In relation to the just man, we find βίος αὐτοῦ, "his life" (2:15 and 5:4) and υἱός θεοῦ, "son of God" (2:18 and 5:5). Cf. also ὀνειδίζει (2:12c) and ὀνειδισμοῦ (5:4b). In relation to the ungodly, we find σκιά, "shadow" (2:5 and 5:9) and πλανάομαι, "err" (2:21 and 5:6) in addition to γενηθέντες (5:13) and ἐγενήθημεν (2:2); ἴχνος (2:4c; 5:10b). It is noteworthy that a rare lexeme like ἀλαζον- (cf. only otherwise in Wis 17:7) is used in Wis 2:16 in relation to the boast of the just whereas, in 5:8, it is employed in an opposite sense in relation to the boast of the ungodly. Again, it is noticeable that κακία appears in 2:21 at the beginning of the conclusion, and in 5:13, at the end of the discourse of the ungodly. δικαιοσύνη, on the other hand, appears in 2:11, at the beginning of the second part of the discourse of the ungodly, whereas, in

Wis 5, it appears in 5:6, at the centre of their discourse and, in 5:18, in the context of the judgement of the author.

Thus, we can conclude that Wis 5:4-5 corresponds to Wis 2:10-20 (life and destiny of the just); 5:6-8 corresponds to 2:6-9 (the error of the ungodly on the way of living one's life); 5:9-13, on the other hand, recalls the theme of the shortness of life which already appeared in 2:1-5. In this way, the discourse of the ungodly in 5:4-13 takes up, inversely, the themes already set out by the ungodly in Wis 2:1-20. However, it is the destiny of the just that is set on the highest level. Previously it was considered a disgrace; now, with surprise, the ungodly discover it to be a glorious destiny. In the second chapter, the ungodly man is depicted in contrast with the plans of God as well as being a persecutor of the just; in Wis 5, the ungodly are constrained instead to acknowledge the failure of their own plans and discover, despite themselves, that God is on the side of the just.

Finally, in the frame of the second chapter (1:13-15 and 2:23-24), the theme of creation and the cosmos appears. It is this that closes chapter five in vv. 17-20, and it is a theme which will be taken up again extensively in the third part of the book of Wisdom.

A Scene of Judgement

Wis 5 is also a text that is constructed with great dramatic ability. It has a judicial style which recalls at several points the lament of Isaiah on the fall of the tyrant (Isa 14).[1] Risen for a moment from the underworld where they had been hurled (cf. 4:19), the ungodly are called together for judgement, described with very suggestive images, and are forced to recognise, even if too late, the failure of their existence. We are before a real reversal of the situation. Only after their death, the ungodly acknowledge that their judgement on the life of the just man was totally wrong. He will now be seen to be numbered among the "holy ones" and the "sons of God".

The basic problem of the final section (5:15-23), one highlighted by the majority of commentators,[2] is to decide whether these verses should be linked with the previous material and so refer to the same eschatological stage presupposed by 5:1-14 (the ungodly described *post mortem* before their judgement), or if they refer to another occasion of the judgement of the just which is not specified more clearly. At first sight, in fact, it is not at all clear how one can speak of a future reward (5:16) for the just who have already been glorified (cf. 3:9) and who are being recompensed (5:15-16), while the ungodly, who have already been punished (cf. 4:19) are further destroyed (cf. 5:23). What, exactly, is our author thinking of? In the course of the commentary, we shall try to reply to these questions.

Wis 5:1-3: Introduction to the Second Discourse of the Ungodly

1 At that time, the just person will stand with great assurance
in the face of those who tormented him
and scorned his labours.

---

1 Cf. Alonso Schökel, *Sabiduría*, 107.

2 Larcher, *Sagesse*, 2:379-381; Gilbert, "Sg 3,7-9; 5,15-23", 315-316.

[2] When they see him, they will be shaken by a terrible fear
and will be amazed at his unexpected salvation.
[3] Changing their mind, they will speak to one another,
and, in anguish of spirit, they will groan:

Notes on the Text and Translation

v. 3. The verb μετανοέω is employed in the NT in the theological sense of repentance and conversion. Here, on the other hand, it simply means "change ideas", "change one's mind", and it is the only time that it appears in Wisdom.

In 3b, both Ziegler and Rahlfs adopt the reading στενάξονται which we retain here. In addition to the fact that it is better attested (A, B), it makes complete sense. Ziegler's apparatus also records the reading στενάζοντες, which is supported by the *gementes* of Lat and preferred by Larcher because better coordinated with the previous participle μετανοοῦντες, while S, *O*-V and other minuscules read, instead, στενάξουσιν.

Synchronic Analysis

The just man, ὁ δίκαιος, placed in emphatic position at the end of the stich, 5:1
represents here the ideal just man, persecuted by the ungodly (cf. 5:1bc, which refers to the just man of chap. 2). The singular has, therefore, a collective value, as in 2:10-20. The stich opens with an "at that time/then" (τότε) which indicates contemporaneity: we are at the very moment of the judgement of the ungodly which was described in the previous verse, in 4:20, which thus links Wis 3-4 to Wis 5. Here, there is a *post mortem* description in which the just and ungodly are living an existence which is quite different from what they could have imagined when they were alive.

The just man "will stand[3] with great / much assurance". "Assurance" is our translation of παρρησία which, in that period, was almost the slogan of the Cynic philosopher, the "freedom of speech", the courage of one who has no fear and no need of anyone (cf. below). Here, παρρησία should be seen in open contrast with the fear of the ungodly described in 4:20 (δειλοί) and repeated in 5:2 (φόβῳ δεινῷ). This παρρησία is thus a disposition of assurance, trust and interior freedom which arises from the clear conscience of the just man who is able to respond to the false accusations of the ungodly. The originality of Wisdom lies in transferring the παρρησία of the just man into a context that is clearly eschatological.

The just man will, therefore, stand with great assurance before the ungodly who have tormented him (θλιψάντων, an aorist participle which is to be contrasted with the following present participle, ἀθετούντων, which indicates instead a lasting action). Πολλαὶ αἱ θλίψεις τῶν δικαίων, Ps 33:20 LXX recites, but from them, the same psalm continues, the Lord delivers them. The idea is biblical, but our sage is rereading it in an eschatological context.

---

3 The verb στήσεται could be alluding to the Hebrew קום and lead to thought of the resurrection; cf. Puech, "The Book of Wisdom and the Dead Sea Scrolls", 130-131.

The "labours" (πόνοι) of the just man which the ungodly scorned (ἀθετέω, frequent in the LXX with this meaning; cf. Jer 15:15-16) should not be understood here as the concrete works of the just, but rather as strivings towards virtue (cf. Wis 3:15 and 8:7), strivings which are now obtaining the result which the just had resolved upon: eternal reward.

5:2-3 Verse 2 opens with an asyndetic construction. Subject of the participle ἰδόντες are the ungodly. They suddenly "see" the just person standing before them with παρρησία and are afraid. Ταράσσω returns in Wis 11:6 and 16:6 with the sense of "disturb, upset" or – more precisely – "torment".[4] Here, it has as a complement φόβος δεινός, "a tremendous fear" which refers to the fear described later in Wis 17:6, 12, 15. Both here and in Wis 17, the background of this fear is eschatological. In both cases, it relates to the final fate of the ungodly. Where and how can the ungodly "see" the just person who has been glorified? Once again, our sage remains vague.

Then the ungodly will be amazed (ἐκστήσονται, which recalls the στήσεται of v. 1a). What will leave the ungodly amazed is precisely "the unexpected salvation" obtained by the just man. The adjective παράδοξος is to be understood in the sense of something that is unbelievable. It is typical of educated circles and will return in Wis 16:17 and 19:5.[5]

Salvation of the Just "Salvation" (σωτηρία) acquires here an eschatological value and takes on a new significance compared with the normal usage of the LXX.[6] In the light of Wis 3-4, it is not only a matter of a physical liberation from suffering but of that state of peace and life with God which awaits the just after death. As happens in the gospel parable narrated in Luke 16:19-31, our sage is able to give a concrete description of a reality which would otherwise appear abstract. Final salvation is seen through the filter of the total amazement of the ungodly who, in fear and terror, become aware of something which they would never have imagined.

"They will speak to one another" (3a) recalls the beginning of the first discourse of the ungodly in 2:1. Ἐν ἑαυτοῖς refers to the ungodly who look at one another and speak among themselves in the face of the spectacle of the unexpected salvation of the just. Now the ungodly have had to change their mind (μετανοέω) in relation to the end of the just which they had imagined. They thus begin a tragic lament (cf. v. 3b) which wells up from inside them (διὰ στενοχωρίαν πνεύματος). Any prospect of conversion or repentance seems to be foreign to the ungodly. They simply regret their past life now that they themselves must undergo the divine judgement in all its gravity.

Diachronic Analysis

5:1 Verse 1 opens by emphasising the παρρησία of the just. The term appears already in classical Greek with a polemical force and a clear political significance. Παρρησία is that "freedom of speech" which distinguishes democracy from tyranny (Plato, *Gorg.*

---

4 Cf. Spicq, *Notes*, 2:881-886.

5 Cf. Reese, *Hellenistic Influence*, 97 n. 45.

6 Cf. Foerster, Werner, σῴζω κτλ, *TDNT* 7:965-1003.

461e). It is what distinguishes the Athenian citizen from slaves and foreigners.[7] Quite quickly, the term takes on a nuance of "frankness, candour, truth" and so, also, of "courage, self-confidence". In a negative sense, παρρησία can assume the meaning of "licence", excessive freedom of speech. Understood as a moral value, παρρησία is first and foremost that "frankness" which is also "trust", an indispensable virtue for all true friendship. A particular use of the term is that found in Cynic philosophy in which freedom of speech is known instinctively to be the greatest of goods together with freedom itself (cf. Philo, *Her.* 149).

The LXX uses παρρησία with the meaning that it has in classical Greek. The novelty is, rather, the inclusion of the term in a context characterised by faith in the God of Israel. Job 27:10 LXX speaks of παρρησία, that is, of the frankness which the ungodly *cannot* have in his relations with God on account of wickedness. The same thing is said in Prov 13:5 LXX, a passage which our sage could well have had in mind: "an ungodly man is shamed and will have no παρρησία". Here too, παρρησία is freedom of speech, the frankness which God allows the just to have in his presence. This is, therefore, the meaning to be given to παρρησία also in our text of Wis 5:1 (cf. in the NT 1 John 2:28; 4:17).

The description of the ungodly as "amazed", beside themselves, could have been 5:2
inspired by Isa 13:8 (καὶ ταραχθήσονται οἱ πρεσβεῖς ... καὶ ἐκστήσονται), but perhaps our sage is intending to allude to the beginning of the Fourth Servant Song, Isa 52:13-14 which lies behind the entire text of Wis 2-5. Isaiah's "servant" is exalted paradoxically before the eyes of those who despised him (ἐκστήσονται ἐπὶ σὲ πολλοί ...), just as happens now to the just who have been glorified. As for the "unexpected salvation", our author could have been again inspired by Isa 52:15: the nations will wonder (θαυμάσονται) when they see the "servant" who has been glorified.

Wis 5:4-13:
The Discourse of the Ungodly

4 "It was he whom once we covered with ridicule
and made an object of scorn. What fools we were!
We judged his life madness
and his end without honour.
5 Why on earth has he been reckoned among the sons of God[8]
and why is his lot now among the holy ones?

6 Thus we erred, far from the way of truth,
and the light of justice did not shine over us,

---

7 Scarpat, Giuseppe, *Parrhesia greca, parrhesia cristiana,* Brescia: Paideia 2001; Spicq, *Notes,* Supp. 526-534.

8 In keeping with the norms of the ancient text presented here, the translation of Wisdom reflects its patriarchal view. For example, υἱός in Greek is translated as "son" in English. The commentary sections observe a more inclusive vernacular, when possible.

nor did the sun rise upon us.
7 We filled ourselves with the ways of lawlessness and ruin
and we journeyed through impassable deserts,
but we did not know the way of the Lord.

8 What use to us has been our pride?
And what profit has our wealth brought us with all its show?
9 All these things have passed away like a shadow
and like a rumour that quickly vanishes;
10 like a ship which ploughs through the turbulent waves,
whose passage is left without a trace
and the track of its keel among the waves;
11 or like a bird which flies through the air
and no trace is left to reveal its passage;
the light air, struck by the force of the wing
and divided by power of the flight,
was crossed by those beating wings
and then no sign of its passing was found there;
12 or as, when an arrow is shot towards the target,
the divided air returns immediately to its place
so that no one knows its track;
13 so we too, only just born, have already disappeared
and we have not been able to show any sign of virtue.
We have consumed ourselves in our iniquity".

Notes on the Text and Translation

v. 6. With some authoritative codices (S, V, Origen's recension, and many minuscules; cf. Rahlfs), it is possible to read the verbal form ἐπέλαμψεν ("shine, sparkle above") instead of the simple form ἔλαμψεν ("shine") which is preferred by the majority of textual witnesses and also by Ziegler. However, it is probably the fruit of a scribal correction, perhaps due to the use of the verb λάμπω in the NT (never in the compound form) or to the influence of Isa 9:1 which uses the simple form (φῶς λάμψει ἐφ' ὑμᾶς). The reading ἐπέλαμψεν accords better with the idea of a light coming from on high.

v. 7. Ziegler (who takes up a conjecture of K.G. Bretschneider, 1805) proposes reading ἐνεπλέχθημεν (from ἐνπλέκομαι, cf. Prov 28:18; 2 Pet 2:20): "we are stuck among the thorns (τριβόλοις) of iniquity and perversion", but the reading of the Arab version, *in spinis*, is not a sufficient textual justification. Larcher (who, however, accepts the reading ἐνεπλέχθημεν; cf. *Sagesse*, 2:367-368: "we are set on the paths of iniquity ...") proposes reading ἐνεπλήσθημεν τρίβοις, "paths", with the majority of codices and versions where τρίβοις forms a good parallel with ὁδός (6a, 7c). The form ἐνεπλέχθημεν does not actually exist (the aorist of ἐνπλέκομαι is, in fact, ἐνεπλάκην). The verbal form ἐνεπλήσθημεν followed by the genitive is, therefore, to be retained with all the textual witnesses and to be understood in a metaphorical sense (cf. Sir 4:12; 32:15; Prov 28:19): "we filled ourselves – that is to say: we found our satisfaction – in paths of lawlessness ...".

Scarpat (*Sapienza*, 1:326) proposes a different solution: he retains both ἐνεπλήσθημεν and τρίβοις, but refers ἀνομίας to ἐνεπλήσθημεν, eliminates the following καί and links ἀπωλείας to τρίβοις, making this last term preceded by ἐν on the basis of minuscule 543, supposing its deletion through haplography. He therefore translates: "we filled ourselves with iniquity, hurrying through the pathways of perdition". However, the singular support of one minuscule constitutes too weak an attestation. For the Latin version, *lassati sumus*, "we tired ourselves out", cf. again Scarpat, *Sapienza*, 1:459-460.

The verbal form ἔγνωμεν is read by S and several other mss as ἔπεγνωμεν, "we applied ourselves", assuming an effort of application and reflection neglected by the ungodly. See also Rahlfs; cf. Scarpat, *Sapienza*, 1:327-328 who accepts this reading which, however, is poorly attested.

v. 8. In Greek usage, the term ὑπερηφανία indicates the scornful arrogance of one who despises others, approving only of himself (cf. Engel, *Weisheit*, 105). According to Plato (*Resp.* 391c), it could also have a religious value: ὑπερηφανία θεῶν τε καὶ ἀνθρώπων; cf. 1 Macc 1:21, 24 with regard to Alexander the Great. The LXX employs ὑπερηφανία mostly to translate the Hebrew גאוה or גאון in order to emphasise an attitude that was proud, presumptuous, insolent, and impious in relations with God or people. Cf., in the context of the sapiential literature, Prov 8:13 in connection with ὕβρις. Cf., again, Sir 10:7, 12, 13, 18; and 16:8. In Sir 15:8, ὑπερηφανία is opposed to wisdom. In the NT, ὑπερηφανία has a place within the catalogue of vices. Cf. Rom 1:30. Cf. Bertram, Georg, ὑπερήφανος, ὑπερηφανία, TDNT 8:525-529.

The term ἀλαζονεία (cf. Wis 17:7) is defined by Theophrastus as "pretence of specific goods which, in practice, do not exist" (*Char.* 23.1). In the LXX, it occurs only in 2-4 Macc outside Wisdom. In 4 Macc 8:19, ἀλαζονεία separates from God and leads to the ruin of the soul. In 4 Macc 2:15, it is linked with φιλαρχία and κενοδοξία among the more violent passions of the soul which reason is called to govern (cf. Scarpat, *Sapienza*, 1:328-329, and Mazzinghi, *Notte di paura e di luce*, 67-68).

v. 10. The rare term *τρόπιος indicates the ship's keel (cf. the Isis aretalogy of Andros, l. 153; Winston, *Wisdom*, 147). Note the paronomasia with ἀτραπός, "narrow path", "little-beaten way", just as, in 10c, the term κύμασιν ("waves") takes up κυμαινοίμενον in the first stich.

v. 11. The long and somewhat prolix description of the air struck by the force of the bird's wings (11c-e) contains various elegant terms and echoes the contemporary notions of physics. The entire construction of v. 11 is very careful. In addition to the fivefold repetition of ὡς, one can note also, again five times, the repetition of words beginning with δι-: διερχομένη (10a); διάβασης (10b); διιπτάντος (11a); διωδεύθη (11e); δίοδον (12c). The principal term of comparison (ὀρνέου διιπτάντος) is a genitive absolute and it is not found in the nominative as in the previous cases. In 11b, the subject changes to the air which, in 11a, was introduced with an accusative (ἀέρα). In 11c-f, "air" is associated, here as a synonym, with πνεῦμα, subject of the verbs of 11cde (μαστιζόμενον, σχιζόμενον, διωδεύθη). It is referred to by the final pronoun of v. 11, ἐν αὐτῷ. Thus, in fact, we have here a double comparison: the life of the ungodly passes away like a bird, but it is also like the air that leaves no trace, nothing of any substance.

In 11a, διιπτάντος is the reading chosen by Ziegler on the basis of B*, V and 443. Instead, the codices S, A, B^c and almost all the minuscules read διαπτάντος, a second aorist active from διαπέτομαι, "fly across". Cf. Larcher, *Sagesse*, 2:373, who chooses the latter reading. On the other hand, *διιπτάντος is a present of διίπτημι which is actually attested only in the middle, with the same meaning.

The term *τεκμήριον, typical of medical and poetic language, indicates a "certain proof".

v. 12. The passive form ἀνελύθη creates some difficulties. It indicates being loosed or dissolved. The author has in mind a certain physical theory about the air which expands and contracts for the passage of the arrow. After a long discussion (*Sapienza*, 1:332), Scarpat prefers to read, with codex V and Origen's recension, the form ἀνέλυσεν to which he attributes an intransitive value: "the divided air returns to itself at once".

v. 13. Ziegler chooses the reading γενηθέντες (B-V and other minuscules) instead of the better attested γεννηθέντες (Rahlfs); cf. 2:2. However, Scarpat holds that the two readings (2:2 and 5:13) should be brought into alignment, as with codices S and A (which read γενν-), but not so codex B (γενν- in 2:2 and γεν- in 5:13). In this case, the reading γεννηθέντες seems preferable, given that the context leads to the thought of birth ("we, only just born ...").

The verb *καταδαπανάομαι refers to a being consumed, a being completely destroyed. The sense is reflexive, not passive: "we have consumed ourselves". For this reason, ἐν τῇ κακίᾳ ἡμῶν is to be understood in a local sense, "in our iniquity" and not as a causal complement ("because of our iniquity").

The Latin version adds a supplementary stich: *talia dixerunt in inferno hi qui peccaverunt.* It is probably a translator's gloss which is not attested elsewhere but which makes explicit the place where the ungodly likely find themselves: hell.

Synchronic Analysis

5:4 Verse 4 opens with an emphatic pronoun: it was he (οὗτος ἦν; cf. Isa 14:16), that just person whom we previously despised (cf. 2:10-20) and covered with ridicule (ἔσχομεν εἰς γέλωτα; cf. Ps 27:6; Jer 3:3) whom we now see glorified and rewarded by God. The expression εἰς παραβολὴν ὀνειδισμοῦ can be understood as "a discourse / a saying of scorn", with παραβολή taken *in malam partem*.[9] If the first stich opens with an emphatic reference to the just, the second closes with a reference, equally emphatic, to the ungodly who have now – but too late – grasped their folly: οἱ ἄφρονες; cf. Wis 3:2, 12 (cf. also 1:3).

In 5:4c, ἐλογισάμεθα recalls the false reasonings of the ungodly (cf. 2:1, 22) who in 2:15 considered utterly singular the lifestyle (βίος) of the just, here described as madness (μανία). From the perspective of the ungodly, it is madness for the just to deprive oneself of the pleasures of life in the name of hope in a God who seems completely absent. Once again, the entire context of chapter 2 reappears. Overturning the previous judgement of the ungodly, our sage considers them as the true madmen (οἱ ἄφρονες also contains within itself this nuance of "madness").

Taking up again Wis 2:20, the ungodly then reflect on how they had considered the death of the just as "without honour" (ἄτιμον). Here, there is a further allusion to the "servant" of Isa 53:3: εἶδος αὐτοῦ ἄτιμον ... ἠτιμάσθη καὶ οὐκ ἐλογίσθη, "his appearance was dishonourable ... he was despised and held in no account". The end (τελευτή) of the just – we recall that the ungodly never employ the term θάνατος

---

9 Cf. Scarpat, *Sapienza*, 1:321-322. Cf. a similar expression in Tob 3:4^{BA}; Larcher, *Etudes*, 89. The text is perhaps taken up again in the *Letter of Barnabas* 7:9; cf. Jaubert, Annie, "Echo du livre de la Sagesse en Barnabé 7,9", *Recherches de Science Religieuse* 60 (1972) 193-198.

explicitly but have recourse to more neutral euphemisms – seemed ruin to them (cf. 3:2-3). Only now do they perceive their own tragic mistake. Too late.

The just person is now among the children of God and the saints, the assembly of the glorified just among whom the just person has been received. Κατελογίσθη is probably taken from Isa 14:10 LXX (ἐν ἡμῖν ... κατελογίσθης) and creates a play of words on the preceding ἐλογισάμεθα. The use of the aorist passive could lead us to think of a divine judgement *post mortem*, but the author is not at all clear on the details. Ones notes again that, in 5b, ἐστίν is in the present to underline the present state of the just. 5:5

Utilising the well-known biblical metaphor of the two ways together with that of light and darkness (cf. Prov 4:18), our author places in the mouth of the ungodly the recognition of their own errors. The verb "to err" (πλανάομαι) has already been used in 2:21 precisely to describe the erring behaviour of the ungodly: there, in the mouth of the author of the book; here, placed by him in the mouth of the ungodly. Cf., again, Wis 11:15; 12:24; 14:22; 15:4 and 17:1. The background of πλανάω in the mysteries, which we already observed in connection with 2:21, is not to be excluded. Those apostate Jews who believed that they had found the right way, truth and illumination by means of the mystery rites that they celebrated become aware, too late, of having erred and finding themselves plunged into darkness (cf. 17:1). The sun has not shined on them, and their life has been revealed, tragically, as a desert with no way out. 5:6

The "way of truth" is contrasted with the ὁδὸς ἀδικίας (Ps 118:29-30 LXX) and recalls, also, Tob 1:3^{SB} where the "ways of truth" indicates the sum of the ideals of the just Israelite who is faithful to the law; cf. the "way of justice" mentioned in Prov 21:16 LXX. In the light of Wis 3:9, "truth" seems to indicate knowledge of the ways of God and of God's plans, a knowledge that is more existential than theological, which also implies faith and fidelity on the part of the just. The "way of truth" is not so much the path that leads to truth as rather the right path, the life lived according to the will of God from which the ungodly only now realise that they have kept themselves aloof.

"The light of justice" (τὸ τῆς δικαιοσύνης φῶς) is an epexegetical genitive: the light which is justice. It is that "immortal justice" of God which was mentioned right at the beginning of the book (cf. 1:1, 15) from which the ungodly have distanced themselves, considering their strength as the norm of justice (2:11) and so becoming blind (2:21). Finally, the image of the sun refers again to 2:4e. The ungodly thought that life was only mist dissolved by the rays of the sun, but they have not allowed themselves to be illuminated by that sun which is now almost a symbol of God himself.

Verse 7 develops the metaphor of the path, thus taking up again the accusations which the ungodly had directed at the just. According to them, the just person avoided their ways (ὁδός), considering them impure (2:16). The ways (αἱ τρίβοι) of the just were very different from them (cf. 2:15). But now the ungodly must acknowledge that their way, that is, their lifestyle, was only the lawlessness (ἀνομία) that leads to ruin (ἀπωλεία; cf. Wis 1:13; 18:7). The metaphor of "being filled" refers to Wis 2:7: the ungodly, who had claimed to be filled with earthly goods, now perceive that they were filled only with injustice and death. 5:7

The metaphor of the impassable desert refers to Jer 12:10; ἄβατος is an adjective that is well suited to the desert. It connotes a place without streets or dwellings, a way which does not go anywhere, a contrast with the way of the Lord which leads instead to salvation. The "way of the Lord" is a frequent biblical expression: cf. Judg 2:22; 2 Kgs 21:22; Isa 26:8; Jer 4:4-5; Ezek 33:17. Together with the verb "know", this metaphor completes the previous image relating to the "way of truth" and refers to the knowledge of the plans of God for humanity (cf. again an allusion to Wis 2:21-24) which the ungodly have wittingly ignored.

According to an idea typical of our sage (cf. 14:22), therefore, the guilt of the ungodly consists in not having known God even before any morally illicit acts that they may have committed. The connection made by vv. 6-7 between light and knowledge is typical of Alexandrian theology. Cf., again, Wis 6:12 for the idea of a wisdom that is "radiant". Cf. the theme of the law as light in Wis 18:4.

5:8 A double rhetorical question introduces the final part of the discourse of the ungodly: what was the purpose of their arrogance, wealth and ostentation? The combination of the three terms reveals to us the author's intention. First of all, ὑπερηφανία, which is a good description of the pride and arrogance of the powerful (cf. the textual notes). Linking v. 8 with the previous v. 7, it emerges that ὑπερηφανία is closely bound up with not having known God and at the same time having carried out depraved actions, just as happens when the ungodly deal with the just in Wis 2:10-20.

Ostentation (ἀλαζονεία) is rather the insolent attitude of someone who does not recognise any authority above oneself, who does not respect any limits, and who boasts of what one ought not boast, as in this case of wealth (πλοῦτος), something on which the ungodly have based their way of life; ἀλαζονεία refers directly to the verb ἀλαζονεύω which was employed by the ungodly in 2:16. Then they accused the just of boasting of having God as their father. Now, they are forced to recognise the falsity of their own boast and the empty ostentatiousness of their wealth. In connection with wealth it should be observed that "Solomon" does not despise it, as long as it is wealth linked with wisdom (Wis 7:11-12; 8:5) and not with ἀλαζονεία. The problem, therefore, is not with wealth in itself (the author of the book is certainly from an affluent family) so much as in one's attitude towards it.

Finally, the three terms (ὑπερηφανία, ἀλαζονεία, πλοῦτος) add a "political" colour to the description of the ungodly. They form part of that class of rich and powerful people who, when set before the judgement of God, are forced to perceive, sooner or later, the uselessness of their power and possessions. Cf. Let. Aris. 211, 262-263: the king's conduct should exclude both ὑπερηφανία and wealthy ostentation (πλοῦτος).

5:9-12 With consummate rhetorical ability and notable poetic force, the five comparisons which follow in vv. 9-12 describe the insubstantial nature of the life of the ungodly (cf. the textual notes).

Our sage has taken examples drawn from the earth (5:9), the sea (5:10), and the air (5:11-12); from what is more substantial to what is less so. On the one hand, he has been inspired by biblical texts; on the other hand, he expresses himself with an educated and poetic vocabulary, at times in light of the physical theories of the day (cf. the theories about the air which underlie vv. 11-12). What our sage is offering is a short school exercise in rhetoric, not, however, as an end in itself. The literary effort is an indication of the intention to communicate the sense of the total fleetingness of life and the radical failure of the plans of the ungodly.

The basic theme is expressed right from the beginning: "all these things have passed away" (παρῆλθεν ἐκεῖνα πάντα; 9a). Ἐκεῖνα πάντα, that is, everything that was expressed in v. 8, but more generally all the plans of the life of the ungodly have now vanished. The ungodly opened their discourse precisely by lamenting the brief nature and emptiness of life (2:1-5), and in a certain sense they were right. For the ungodly, life is revealed to be just as they had feared: empty and too short. For the just, on the other hand, life is revealed to be full of meaning, even in the face of death. In Wis 5:9-12, the text of 2:1-5 is taken up again in an opposite sense. The Life of the Ungodly Vanishes

Like a shadow that passes; like a message handed on in a hurry and then forgotten; like the wake of the ship's hull among the waves of the sea that have been disturbed; like a bird that flies off beating the air with its wings; like the speedy passage of an arrow through the air: so the life of the ungodly does not leave any visible trace behind it and is immediately forgotten. Interestingly, it was the ungodly themselves who compared human life to a shadow (2:5). Now the ungodly are aware that what they took to be the lot of all is paradoxically true, but only for them! Moreover, the ungodly were those who wished to leave everywhere the "signs" of their own joy (2:9), but they perceive, too late, that only virtue can leave an enduring mark behind (v. 13; cf. 4:1). When the ungodly die, it is as though they had never existed.

We are at the end of the reasoning begun in v. 9 (the οὕτως which opens v. 13 5:13
constitutes the apodosis of the previous clauses introduced by ὡς). We were only just born, and now we are already dead! In v. 8, the term of comparison seems to be represented by pride and the ostentation of wealth. Here, it is the brevity of life that appears: just born, we cease to exist. It is as if the ungodly had never lived. They have already disappeared (ἐξελίπομεν, only occurrence of the verb in the book).

The ungodly perceive too late that it is in this sense that human life is short (cf. 2:1); or, better, they understand that they were not mistaken in judging it thus. Their error lies in not having known to draw the right consequence from this consideration. If life is short, in fact, it is necessary to leave a sign of virtue (ἀρετῆς σημεῖον) in it, that virtue which guarantees an eternal life with God. The ungodly, however, have thought only to leave signs of enjoyment (cf. 2:9), which leave no trace. In fact, it is only virtue that leaves an immortal memory (cf. 4:1). The ungodly, on the other hand, have destroyed themselves in their wickedness (13c; cf. the textual notes). The particles μέν ... δέ (13bc) reinforce the opposition between virtue and wickedness. In the context of the whole chapter, the dissipation of one's own life has also an eschatological value: missing the aim of their earthly life, the ungodly are precluded from a life beyond death.

Diachronic Analysis

G. Scarpat observes again that v. 4ab reflects the text of Ps 41:11 LXX where the 5:4
psalmist laments because, like our just person, he is suffering scorn and persecution from the ungoldy: "those who oppress me, taunt me (ὠνείδισάν με), saying to me every day: where is your God?" (cf. also Ps 43:14-15 LXX). In the psalm, as in Wisdom, the hope of the just lies in God: cf. Ps 41:12 LXX [42:12 MT]. Cf. the

experience of Jeremiah who was also an object of derision and scorn on the part of his enemies (Jer 20:7, εἰς γέλωτα; Jer 20:8; cf. 6:10, εἰς ὀνειδισμόν), but whose help was similarly in God. Wisdom takes up these themes but transfers them into the mouth of the ungodly and, once again, rereads them in an eschatological context.

5:5: The "Children of God"

The commentators discuss whether with "children of God" and with "holy ones" (ἅγιοι) our sage intends in Wis 5:5 to indicate the glorified just or the angels.[10] The external evidence does not appear decisive. In the Hebrew Bible, the "children of God" can sometimes indicate the angels (Job 1:6; Ps 28:1 LXX [29:1 MT]), who in some texts are also called "holy ones" (cf. Job 5:1; 15:15). This appellation is common in the book of Enoch and in the hymns of Qumran. Cf. 1QS XI, 5-8; 1QH XI, 22; XIX, 11; 1 En. 39:5; 104:6. In these texts, the just person appears in the company of the holy ones or the children of God. Cf. 1 En. 51:4 where the just are imagined becoming like angels of heaven. So too in the NT, in Mark 12:25; Luke 20:36.[11] We note that, in the context of Wisdom, angels are spoken of explicitly only in Wis 16:20, placed, however, in a certain relationship with the "children" (cf. 16:21). On the other hand, further texts exist in which the "children of God" and the "saints" are clearly the Israelites, or else the glorified just. Cf. Jub. 1:24-25; Pss. Sol. 17:27; Sib. Or. 3:702; T. Levi 18:8, 13. For the holy ones as distinct from the angels, cf. Tob 8:15^{BA}; for the holy ones understood as the just Israelites, cf. the texts of Ps 33:10 LXX [34:10 MT]; Isa 4:3.

Only examination of the context can help us settle the question. In Wisdom, the "children of God" are, on the one hand, the just, taken individually (2:8), on the other, the people of Israel as a whole, especially in the third part of the book (cf. Wis 9:7; 12:19, 21; 16:10, 26; 18:4, 13). The theme of the divine parentage of the people appears already in the texts of the OT/HB (Exod 4:22; Deut 14:1; Jer 31:9; Hos 11:1). It is a theme which will become more frequent in the postexilic period. In the panorama of the Judaism of its time, the book of Wisdom is, perhaps, the text where the theme of divine parentage occurs most frequently.[12] The use of the term "son/child" in relation to God in Wis 2:18 and 5:5 (even if in the mouth of the ungodly) makes it really difficult to think of different figures. In 2:18, it is the just person who is a child of God; in 5:5, the ungodly are forced to recognise them as such within the assembly of the glorified just. The "holy ones", in Wis 17:2 and 18:9, clearly refers to the Israelites, that is, to those who belong to the Lord, as is expressed in perfect parallelism in the second part of v. 5: those whose "lot" is with God (for κλῆρος cf. 2:9 and 3:14). In the light of the book as a whole, it is difficult to think of the "holy ones" as angelic beings different from those ὅσιοι of which Wis 3:9 and 4:15 speak, precisely in relation to the glorification of the just.

In fact, the text of v. 5 is not completely clear. There remains the problem of understanding from where the ungodly perceive that the just person is now to be found amidst the holy ones and children of God, understood as the glorified just. This is a reality in which the ungodly certainly did not believe. In fact, they are not surprised to see the holy ones and children of God so much as seeing the just man in their midst! This difficulty can be circumvented if one thinks that the ungodly – Jewish apostates – recognise in the glorified just the most famous figures of their own people

10 Cf. Giménez González, *"Si el justo es hijo de Dios"*, 200 n. 134 with an exhaustive list of the authors who defend one or the other opinion.

11 Larcher, *Sagesse*, 2:363-364; cf. Collins, "The Reinterpretation of Apocalyptic Traditions", 145-146.

12 Cf. Priotto, *La prima Pasqua*, 112-116; Mazzinghi, *Notte di paura e di luce*, 219-221.

(Moses, for example, is called ἅγιος in Wis 11:1), well known to them, and only then understand what has happened. One can go on to discuss whether the glorified just are being imagined as actual angelic beings, but Wisdom does not offer us any indication in this regard.

In Wis 5:6-7, the description of the conduct of the ungodly reveals the influence 5:6-7
of Isa 59:9-14, where the people of Israel confess their own sin: "righteousness is distant from us, justice has not reached us; we hoped for light and there was darkness; we looked for brightness and we walked in gloom" (cf. Isa 59:9 MT). If Isaiah's background relates to the people's repentance, Isaiah's words, placed by our sage in the mouth of the ungodly, take on rather the belated recognition of their own errors. Isaiah's influence can be detected already in the same use of πλανάω. Cf., again, Isa 53:6: πάντες ὡς πρόβατα ἐπλανήθημεν ἄνθρωπος τῇ ὁδῷ αὐτοῦ ἐπλανήθη. The metaphor of light in Wis 5:6c could also have been suggested by Mal 3:20.[13]

The inspiration of vv. 9-12 is mostly biblical. The theme of the shadow (9a) 5:9-12
could be recalling the comparison between the shadow and human life in Job 14:2, but the shadow is a frequent image in the Scriptures cf. Ps 143:4 LXX [144:4 MT]; Qoh 6:12; etc. The image of the rumour which passes quickly (9b) could have been freely inspired by Job 9:25 and evokes the transitory nature of life.

The image of the ship which leaves no trace (v. 10), which is highly developed in the span of a good three stichs, is inspired rather by the following verse, that is, Job 9:26 LXX. In the same text, the comparison continues with the image of the eagle which leaves no trace in the air, just as Wis 5:11ab introduces the image of the bird, developed over the span of a good six stichs (cf. the textual notes). However, bird and ship as images of something which leaves no trace could also have been suggested by Prov 30:19. Only the comparison of the arrow (v. 12) has no biblical parallels.

Wis 5:14-23: The Vain Hope of the Ungodly and the Blessed Destiny of the Just; the Cosmos, in Alliance with God

14 For the hope of the ungodly is like chaff borne by the wind
and like light foam driven by a hurricane
and like smoke scattered by the wind
and it vanishes like the memory of a passing guest.

15 But the just live forever
and their reward is with the Lord
and the Most High takes care of them.

13 Augustine cites together precisely Mal 3:20 and Wis 5:6; cf. La Bonnardière, *Biblia Augustiniana*, 191-193 and 276-277.

16 For this they will receive a glorious kingdom,
and a splendid diadem from the hands of the Lord,
because he will have protected them with his right arm
and shielded them with his left.

17 He will take his zeal for armour
and will make the creation a weapon to reverse his enemies.
18 He will put on justice as a breastplate
and wear irrevocable judgement as a helmet;
19 he will take invincible holiness as a shield
20 and sharpen inexorable wrath as a sword;
the whole world will thus fight with him against the foolish.
21 The well-aimed shafts of lightning will advance
and, like a bow well stretched, they will strike their target from the clouds;
22 and from a catapult of wrath great hailstones will be hurled.
The waters of the sea will rise against them
and the rivers will cover them without mercy.
23 A mighty wind will rise against them,
and destroy them like a hurricane.
Thus lawlessness will have rendered the whole earth a desert
and sin will overthrow the thrones of the mighty.

Notes on the Text and Translation

v. 14. With the Latin version and many other modern authors, we read "foam" (ἄχνη; cf. *Il.* 11.305-408) instead of the reading of the most ancient Greek codices, "frost" (πάχνη; cf. Wis 16:29), which does not offer an acceptable meaning, bound up as it is with the expression "driven by a hurricane". The recension of Origen reads instead ἀράχνη like the Armenian version (*aranea et pruina*; cf. Ziegler). See the long discussion in Scarpat, *Sapienza*, 1:334-336, who also prefers ἄχνη.

v. 16. The expression τὸ βασίλειον τῆς εὐπρεπείας is a Hebraism. Τὸ βασίλειον could indicate the "kingdom" (cf. Dan 7:18-22); cf. Scarpat, *Sapienza*, 1:337-338. The term εὐπρέπεια (literally: "majesty", "splendour"; in the LXX it mostly translates the Hebrew הדר) could have been suggested by Ps 103:1 LXX [104:1 MT] or else by Bar 5:1; cf. also Ps 92:1 LXX: ὁ κύριος ἐβασίλευσεν εὐπρέπειαν ἐνεδύσατο. The sense is that of a "splendid kingdom", or, if we wish to give force to the article, "the kingdom of (divine) magnificence".

v. 17. The majority of witnesses read τὸν ζῆλον as object of the verb λήμψεται. We thus have a double accusative: "he will take his zeal for amour". Only S* (cf. the Latin version: *zelus*) reads τὸ ζῆλος which, according to Larcher (*Sagesse*, 2:386-387), could be the original reading. In that case, personified zeal would become the subject of the sentence.
The verb *ὁπλοποιέω occurs here for the first time in Greek usage. It will return in Strabo (*Geogr.* 15.3.18) and is to be understood in the sense of "manufacture weapons". However, our sage uses it with the meaning of "transform into weapons". The variants ὅπλον ποιήσει and ὁδοποιήσει (Ziegler) are secondary.

The term *ἄμυνα has two possible meanings. It indicates repelling enemies (πρὸς ἐχθρῶν ἄμυναν; Philo, *Agr.* 147) or else taking revenge on them (cf. ἀμύναμαι in Josh 10:13; Esth 8:12-13). Translating with "reversing" is an attempt to preserve both nuances. After a long discussion, Scarpat privileges rather the sense of "revenge" (cf. *Sapienza*, 1:340-341).

v. 18. In 18b, our sage modifies the quotation of the text which he is following, namely, Isa 59:17 (see below). With regard to the helmet, instead of περικεφαλαία, he uses the more archaic *κόρυς.

In Wis 18:15, *ἀνυπόκριτος is being employed in the etymological sense of "not admitting reply". In connection with κρίσις understood in a negative sense, a good translation could be "an irrevocable judgement". In the NT, cf. Rom 13:9 and, in particular, Jas 3:17 in connection with wisdom where it is employed in the sense of "sincere, without hypocrisy or dissimulation", not "dishonest, without acceptation of persons". Cf. Spicq, *Notes*, 1:105-110. Along these lines, one could also think of a "sincere judgement", that is, an impartial judgement on the part of God.

v. 19. The adjective *ἀκαταμάχητος appears here perhaps for the first time in Greek usage (Larcher, *Sagesse*, 2:390) and has the sense of "invincible", "unbeatable".

v. 20. The verb ὀξύνω has as its complement divine "wrath". The sense of "arouse, provoke" could seem preferable, but in connection with the mention of the sword our sage could have used it precisely in the figurative sense of "sharpen".

The adjective *ἀπότομος has the sense of "inexorable, implacable". Dear to our author, it returns in Wis 6:5; 11:10; 12:9; 18:15, in this last passage in relation to the image of the punitive *logos* which is also described with the metaphor of the divine warrior. Cf. ἀποτόμως in 22c.

The term *παράφρων is rare and literary and normally indicates mad people who rave through fear or drinking too much, people to be pitied (cf. Scarpat, *Sapienza*, 1:309, 345). The term was perhaps suggested by a reminiscence of Plato (cf. *Leg.* 649d).

v. 21. The adjective εὔκυκλος, "well stretched", could have been suggested by a reminiscence of the text of *Il.* 4.124-125; cf. also the verb ἅλλομαι, it too is suggested by the same passage from the *Iliad.*

v. 22. The expression ἐκ πετροβόλου θυμοῦ creates some difficulties. It could be understood as "from a catapult of wrath" (understanding πετροβόλου as a substantive), or else "from a catapult which hurls stones" (understanding πετροβόλου as an adjective; cf. Lat: *a petrosa ira* and Scarpat's convincing analysis, *Sapienza*, 1:346-348). As for πλήρεις, it could be joined to θυμοῦ and read: "as from a catapult (ἐκ πετροβόλου) great hailstones (χάλαζαι) full of wrath will be hurled". If we accept πετροβόλου as a substantive ("catapult") and θυμοῦ in the genitive as an epexegetical genitive and read again the following πλήρεις in the sense of "really big", "heaped", one could also translate, partly following Scarpat, with: "from a catapult of wrath (that is, from the wrath of God transformed into a catapult) great hailstones will be hurled".

v. 23. The term *κακοπραγία is unknown to secular Greek with active force, but κακοπράγμων is used by Xenophon in a political context (*Hell.* 5.2.36; cf. Scarpat, *Sapienza*, 1:313-314) and could be alluding to misdeeds committed precisely in the political sphere.

Synchronic Analysis

Verse 14 draws the author's conclusions on the discourse of the ungodly, restating 5:14
their ephemeral state with four further poetic comparisons and thus opening a

new pericope (5:14-23). The hope of the ungodly (the singular here has a typical and collective value) is without substance (cf. Prov 10:28 LXX and Job 8:13a), by contrast with that of the just which is directed towards immortality. On ἐλπίς, cf. the comments on 3:4, 11, and 18. As people without hope, the ungodly are, therefore, people without a future. The author is confirming what he had stated already in 3:11 and anticipated in 2:22b (οὐδὲ μισθὸν ἤλπισαν ὁσιότητος).

The ungodly, who thought of life in categories of violence and abuse, are driven away like chaff, like foam, like smoke, like a passing guest. They are forced to undergo that violence which they practised when dealing with others.

5:15 "But the just live forever". δίκαιοι δέ recalls 3:1 and marks a new beginning, something which takes place in open contrast to the situation of the ungodly. It is noteworthy that, contrary to what happened in chapter 2, whereas in v. 14 the ungodly person is spoken of in the singular, the just are now no longer the singular just person, but a whole category of people who are saved. The use of the verb in the present (ζῶσιν) demonstrates the author's profound conviction: just as the ungodly, even if apparently alive, are as though dead – and this they will become in the not too distant future – so the just, even if persecuted and seemingly unhappy, are already "living" in the presence of the Lord who is taking care of them. In their earthly life, therefore, they are anticipating a life that will last forever.

In 15b, the expression "their reward is in the Lord" is not to be invested with the sense which the syntagma ἐν κυρίῳ will take on in the NT, especially in the Pauline writings. Our author is intending to indicate, more simply, the fact that the reward, the wages of the just are guaranteed to them by the Lord himself. They derive from him. To indicate "wages, reward", μισθός is used; cf. Isa 40:10; 62:11. In Wisdom, the term is to be understood in an eschatological sense as it is already in 2:22 (cf. 10:17). As the text of 15c goes on to put it, they are taken care of in the presence of God. Literally: "the care (φροντίς) relating to them (αὐτῶν)[14] (is) in the presence of the Most High".

It is difficult to clarify further what the author is thinking of when he states that the just "live forever" and that their reward is with the Lord who takes care of them. The use of the present, followed by the futures of v. 16, could lead to the thought of the earthly situation of the just in relation to a further final state. In light of v. 14, one could hold that the life of the just is full of hope by contrast with that of the ungodly who have none. However, within the perspective of 3:1-9, we could undoubtedly think that when our author refers to the reward of the just, he is referring to their eternal life with God. Actually, it is possible that in 5:14-15 our sage is thinking at one and the same time of the just who are still alive, considered in their earthly existence, and of the just who are already dead in the peace which they know after death.[15] However, v. 16 allows us to be more precise.

---

14 Thus, it is not a question of the care that the just have taken in following the Lord (αὐτῶν understood as a subjective genitive), but of the care that God had for them (objective genitive); despite the opinion of Hübner, *Die Weisheit*, 77. We note that in Wis 7:4 and 8:9 the term φροντίς is used *in malam partem*, in the sense of "preoccupations", burdensome thoughts.

15 Cf. Gilbert, "Sg 3,7-9; 5,15-23", 315.

Without any doubt, v. 16 marks a new stage in the life of the just: "therefore, they will receive". The first two stichs refer to the fulfilment of what was anticipated in 15b; 16cd, on the other hand, refers to the fulfilment of 15c. 5:16

The basic problem consists in the nature of the connection of διὰ τοῦτο ... ὅτι with v. 15. Some authors regard διὰ τοῦτο as a proleptic expression of the following ὅτι: this is why they will receive the crown: because the Lord will protect them.[16] However, it is more logical to read the futures of 16cd as future perfects: the Lord will crown them because he will have protected them.[17] In this way, it is possible to consider the just of 5:15 as the same as 3:1-9, already dead but, at the same time, living in God and in peace, and yet still, again, awaiting the final "visitation" (3:9) in which they will be crowned by God definitively (cf. 3:8). Thus, like 5:15, 5:16cd could be referring to the first stage of the glorified just, immediately after their deaths (3:1-3), with 5:16ab referring to the stage described in 3:7-9 and anticipated in 5:15ab, namely, the just at the time of the final visitation.

The last part of v. 16 (16cd) emphasises the divine protection accorded to the just by utilising biblical images once more. The association of "right" and "arm" with God is taken from Ps 43:4 LXX [44:4 MT]. This forms a close preparation for the image of the divine battle (vv. 17-23). The verb σκεπάζω is found, in analogous contexts, in Exod 33:22; Isa 51:6; Zeph 2:3; LXX-Pss 16:8; 26:5; and 60:5 in relation to divine protection.

The verb ὑπερασπίζω refers to the image of God who is described as the shield of Abraham in Gen 15:1 LXX, but cf. also Ps 39:18 LXX. In this case too, it is difficult to decide whether the divine protection concerns the just who are still on earth, protected from the perils of this life, or else whether it refers to the just who are already dead and who will be preserved from the eschatological punishments (or both these things). In the light of texts such as 1 En. 100:4-5 and Sib. Or. 3:705-706 (the just preserved by God at the time of judgement), it appears preferable to think of the just who have been glorified.

In the concluding verses of the chapter (5:17-23), our author returns to the theme of the cosmos which was already introduced in positive terms in the programmatic text of 1:13-15. There is an epic description of the Lord who arms himself for a battle that involves the whole universe. 5:17-23

Verse 17 opens with an asyndetic construction (employed also in vv. 18, 19, 21, 22b, 23) which underlines a new beginning. The first stich (17a) announces the idea which will be developed in vv. 18-20a (the armour of God); the second (17b), on the other hand, announces what is contained in vv. 21-23 (the punishment of the enemies). Thus, v. 20b emerges from the context as a statement of principle which acquires great weight.

The Lord puts on his zeal as armour (17a). This is the divine "zeal" (cf. Wis 1:10), or "jealousy" which intervenes to defend God's people and to punish the ungodly, or even to punish the idolatry of the people of Israel (2 Kgs 19:31; Zech 1:14; cf. Exod 20:5). 5:17

In 17b, our sage introduces an idea which he will develop extensively from chapter 11 onwards, and, above all, in the concluding chapters of his work (16-

---

16 Cf. Scarpat, *Sapienza*, 1:337; Sisti, *Il Libro della Sapienza*, 180.

17 Thus Larcher, *Sagesse*, 2:381, 385, and Gilbert, "Sg 3,7-9; 5,15-23", 316-317.

19). The creation (κτίσις) is as though personified and appears as a tool in God's hand which is transformed into a real weapon for the punishment of the enemies (cf. Wis 16:24).

5:18-20: The Divine Warrior

Here, there is a description of the elements of the divine panoply with the text of Isa 59:16-17 in the background (see below).

The breastplate which God puts on (18a) symbolises δικαιοσύνη (cf. 1:1, 15; 5:6) which, in this context, acquires the value of a punitive justice which does not allow itself to be harmed by the action of the ungodly, just as the breastplate of a warrior protects him from the blows of his enemies.

The helmet (18b) is related to judgement (κρίσις), to be understood as a sentence of condemnation, described as irrevocable (ἀνυπόκριτος), without appeal, but, perhaps also, sincere, impartial (cf. the textual notes), a judgement of condemnation which is bound to the head of the divine person precisely as a helmet which protects his head.

The holiness of God (ὁσιότης) is said to be invincible (ἀκαταμάχητον) and so compared to a shield battered by the blows of the enemy (v. 19). As already in 2:22 (cf. 14:30), holiness is a divine reality which is radically opposed to evil. It is a quality which is attributed directly to God only in this passage of Wisdom. Understood in this sense, the divine holiness does not contradict the punitive judgement already mentioned.

The δέ of v. 20 marks the passage from defensive weapons to offensive ones. First of all, there is the sword, a not infrequent symbol in Scripture. Cf., in particular, Isa 66:16, in an eschatological context, in addition to Ezek 21:8-22, 33-36. The sword is linked to the divine wrath (cf. Amos 4:10; Lam 2:21; Ezek 6:12; 23:25) In Wisdom, ὀργή appears on several occasions: Wis 11:9; 16:5; 18:20, 23, 25, always in relation to historical actions of God. In Wis 10:3, 10, ὀργή appears in relation to human beings. The divine wrath is here described as inexorable (ἀπότομος), of a clear eschatological stamp, something that leads to the thought that, in all the other five uses of the term in the book of Wisdom too, the eschatological nuance is not completely absent, even if the reference *per se* is to the concrete, historical actions of God.[18]

The term ἀπότομος, which characterises the divine wrath, always appears in a judicial context (cf. the textual notes) and sends us back to Wis 18:15, where the image of the divine *Logos* is also presented through the lens of a warrior and where the idea of the divine wrath appears three times (18:20, 23, 25), but in the battles of Israel. In the face of the ungodly's radical rejection of God, where they are concerned, the divine wrath also loses its possibility of being transformed into mercy and becomes the expression of a judgment without appeal. Yet, when in 11:15-12:27 our author reflects on the divine "philanthropy", he will describe God's action in leaving more room for mercy than for wrath.

5:20b

In 20b, the δέ marks the transition to a new subject. The stich appears exactly at the centre of the development of vv. 17-23 and announces anew the theme

---

18 For ὀργή in Wisdom, cf. Priotto, *La prima Pasqua*, 183-184. For the concept of wrath in the LXX and in the NT, cf. Fichtner, Johannes et al. ὀργή κτλ, TDNT 5:382-447. For a systematic treatment of the idea of the divine anger, cf. Kratz, Reihnard G. – Spieckermann, Hermann (edd.), *The Divine Wrath and Divine Mercy in the World of Antiquity*, FAT 33, Tübingen: Mohr Siebeck 2008.

already expressed in 5:17b which will be developed in the following verses (21-23). The image of the divine warrior is brought together with the idea of the created world which fights as an ally (συνεκπολημέω) in the service of God against the ungodly, here described instead as the mad, the fools (*παράφρων). Here we have the κόσμος, a term which takes up the κτίσις mentioned in 17b and also recalls 1:14 and 2:24.

The creation is as though personified and is placed at the service of God, in this case to give effect to God's work of punishment. This idea, which is not at all foreign to the biblical tradition (cf., for example, Josh 10:11 and Judg 5:20) will be taken up and developed in Wis 16:17 which we can consider almost a kind of *flashback* to our text.

In dramatic tones, vv. 21-23 describe the battle of God against the ungodly, 5:21-23
utilising a language inspired by prophetic texts. God intervenes against the ungodly with three different types of attack: a storm, with its accompaniment of lightning and hail, compared to arrows and missiles from a catapult (21ab, 22a); tempestuous waters and rivers in flood (22bc); and a hurricane (λαῖλαψ, 23ab).

In connection with the hail (22a), there appears a new reference to wrath, expressed by the term θυμός, which in Wisdom, here in 18:21 and in 19:1, refers to God; in 10:3, to the fratricide of Cain; while, in 7:20; 11:18; 16:5, it is reserved for the animals. In the usage of the LXX, it is difficult to distinguish θυμός from ὀργή (cf. 5:20a).[19] Our author too employs it as a synonym for the previous ὀργή. In 22c, we observe the presence of the adverb ἀποτόμως which takes up the preceding ἀπότομος (20a), thus reinforcing the idea of an inexorable wrath which has now broken out and been let loose on the ungodly.

The ungodly have abandoned God. This provokes their abandonment by the cosmos. Being good, the creation cannot remain outside the salvific plan of the Lord. Eschatology implies cosmology. This conclusion is important with regard to the final destiny of the just. The body too is involved in the process of eternal life which awaits them.

The reference to πνεῦμα δυνάμεως in 5:23a is debated.[20] Some authors (Larcher, Vílchez) think of a strong wind. The expression πνεῦμα δυνάμεως, absent from the LXX, could be understood as a Hebraism: a powerful breath, wind, in connection with the fire and water mentioned in vv. 21-22 as further elements of the divine judgement. Others (Scarpat) think of the Spirit of God, or, better, of a "powerful breath" connected with the activity of the divine spirit which has already been described at the beginning of the book in 1:7, a πνεῦμα which loves people, on the one hand (1:6), and, on the other, can also reveal itself to be capable of punishing them. It is by this "breath" that the mad ones will be completely destroyed (23b, as if by a hurricane, wiped out for good [cf. Isa 24:1]). Given the use of δύναμις in the book of Wisdom, which refers in three cases to God (1:3; 7:25; 12:15), this last interpretation appears preferable, if with some reservations. This makes us also appeal for this sense also in Wis 11:20, where the πνεῦμα δυνάμεώς σου appears in a context that is clearly punitive.

The drama is thus accomplished. The καί of 23c has consecutive force. In the face of the judicial action of God, the last two stichs of v. 23, assume a proverbial tone

19 Cf. Grether, Oskar – Fichtner, Johannes, ὀργή κτλ., *TDNT* 5:392-394.
20 Cf. a very brief *status quaestionis* in Hübner, *Weisheit*, 80.

to describe the result of lawlessness, ἀνομία (cf. 5:7), and of sin (κακοπραγία, the practice of evil, perhaps with a political nuance, cf. the textual notes). This result is a desert. Lawlessness ἐρημώσει πᾶσαν τὴν γῆν, will render the whole earth a desert (cf. Lev 26:43 for a connection between ἐρημόω and ἀνομία) while sin will overthrow the thrones of the mighty. Moreover, as already noted, the double mention of γῆ- and δυναστ- serves as a hook-word with the following chapter (cf. 6:1b, 3b).

The choice of terms and the reference to the overturning of the thrones of the mighty (cf. Hag 2:21-23; in the NT, Luke 1:52) connects us with what was seen in the previous verses: the ungodly are identified with those who hold power but exercise it to the detriment of others. The text thus prepares for the beginning of the following chapter, which will open precisely with a reference to "kings" (6:1). Although this is not explicit, the destruction of earthly kingship recalls the kingship of the just, as anticipated in vv. 15-16.

Diachronic Analysis

5:14 The comparisons contained in Wis 5:14 concerning the hope of the ungodly are a good example of our author's versatility. The first comparison, "like chaff borne by the wind", is probably drawn from Isa 29:5: the wealth of the ungodly is ὡς χνοῦς φερόμενος. The comparison of the foam driven by the hurricane arises, perhaps, from a reminiscence of the *Iliad* (11.305-308). The third comparison takes up an image that has already been heard in the mouth of the ungodly (2:2c). They thought that human life is only smoke; and for them it has really become so! The image of the smoke is biblical: Ps 101:4 LXX [102:4 MT]: ἐξέλιπον (cf. the same verb in Wis 5:13a) ὡσεὶ καπνὸς αἱ ἡμέραι μου; cf. Ps 36:20 LXX [37:20 MT]; 68:3 LXX [69:3 MT]. The fourth comparison, that of the passing guest, has no known biblical parallels.[21] The emphasis is on the rapidity with which one forgets somebody. The ungodly do not survive even in the memory of others.

5:16: The Kingdom of the Just

The image of the "glorious kingdom" or, perhaps better, the "kingdom of majesty" (Wis 5:16) is a common *topos* of Jewish apocalyptic in connection with the destiny of the elect. The mention of kingship leads our sage almost naturally to add that of the diadem (16b), not so much a crown as a canvas band adorned with precious stones worn inside the royal tiara by Oriental kings. Cf. a probable reference to Isa 62:3: Ἔσῃ στέφανος κάλλους ἐν χειρὶ κυρίου καὶ διάδημα βασιλείας ἐν χειρὶ θεοῦ σου (cf. 1QS IV, 6-8: the glorious crown which the just will receive at the time of their visitation). The relationship with Isa 62:3 is interesting because, precisely in the light of this text of Isaiah addressed to Jerusalem, our sage was able to think of the just as connected with the Jerusalem of the world to come.[22] In Wis 18:24, διάδημα appears in connection with Aaron. Our sage could thus have also had in mind the priestly צניף mentioned in Zech 3:5 and Sir 40:4. In this way, what characterises the glorified just would not only be their royal state but also their priesthood (cf. Exod 19:6).

5:17-20a Behind vv. 17-20a lies the description of the divine warrior in Isa 59:17. However, our sage uses this text with much freedom and recontextualises it within his

21 Winston, *Wisdom*, 148, notes some possible parallels in classical literature.
22 Cf. McGlynn, *Divine Judgement*, 86.

announcement of the final destiny of the ungodly and the just. All the verbs are in the future tense. In Isaiah's text, which arose in the context of the differences that animated the Jewish community immediately after the exile, the Lord is described as a warrior. Observing the presence of injustice among his people, he comes to the aid of those who feel themselves oppressed and destroys their enemies.[23] Isaiah's image of the divine warrior, which will also be developed in the NT (Eph 6:11-18; 1 Thess 5:8; Rom 13:12; 2 Cor 6:7),[24] is modified in Wisdom by the intervention of the cosmos.

Absent from the description in Isa 59:17 is the divine zeal mentioned in v. 17. It appears in prophetic texts in contexts of judgement (Zeph 1:18; 3:8; Isa 26:11; Ezek 36:6; 38:19). The divine zeal cannot remain indifferent in the face of evil and intervenes against the fools with its attributes of justice and judgement, holiness and wrath. Through the use of military language, the message is clear: the biblical God does not remain a passive spectator of injustice. God's holiness is incompatible with evil.

The theme expressed in 17b – the creation as a weapon in God's hand for punishing his enemies – constitutes an original development of an idea that is already contained in the Exodus account of the plagues (Exod 7-10 and 14) and not entirely absent from the sapiential tradition (cf. Sir 39:25-30). The novelty consists in placing the punishment of the ungodly by means of the intervention of the creation on a plane that is completely eschatological.

Mercy and Wrath in God

With regard to the "inexorable wrath" of God mentioned in 20a, we observe that in contemporary Judaism divine mercy did not necessarily contradict the existence of his wrath. Cf. Sir 16:11: ἔλεος γὰρ καὶ ὀργὴ παρ' αὐτῷ. By contrast with Philo, who shows a certain embarrassment over the theme of the divine wrath (cf. *Deo* 51.52), our sage, following the biblical models, has no difficulty in speaking of it. However, the subsequent uses of ὀργή will show us that God reserves his wrath for the ungodly whereas the wrath that falls on Israel is only brief (cf. Wis 11:9-10). From this point of view, one could rightly state that, for the author of Wisdom, God's wrath "is not antithetical to his mercy but serves to arouse it and reveal it".[25] In particular, the reference to the divine wrath in 11:9 and 16:5 sets it in a context of divine pedagogy. It is the wrath of the *paterfamilias* in his dealings with his rebellious sons.

5:21-23

The prophetic texts which could have inspired our sage in the concluding section of the chapter (5:21-23) are probably Hab 3:11 and Zech 9:14 (the lightning); Isa 28:2; 30:30 (the hail; but cf. also Exod 9:18-34 and Josh 10:11); and Isa 43:2 (the rivers; cf. Cant 8:7). However, in 22b, our author could have thought of the crossing of the Red Sea; in 22c, of the crossing of the Jordan or the defeat of Sisera (Judg 5:21). He could also have had still other texts in mind such as chapters 13 and 24 of Isaiah, both referring to a particular judicial intervention of God, the first (Isa 13) being directed against the king of Babylon. Wisdom shows itself able to rede-

---

23 Cf. Hanson, Paul D., *The Dawn of Apocalyptic. The Historical and Sociological Roots of Jewish Apocalyptic Eschatology*, Philadelphia: Fortress Press 1975, 113-134. We will not address here the differences between the MT and the LXX of Isa 59:16-17.

24 Cf. Miller, Patrick D., *The Divine Warrior in Early Israel*, Cambridge (MA): Harvard University Press 1973; Yoder Neufeld, Thomas R., *"Put on the Armor of God". The Divine Warrior from Isaiah to Ephesians*, JSNTSup 140 Sheffield: Sheffield Academic Press 1997.

25 Cf. Scarpat, *Sapienza*, 1:67.

velop a broad series of biblical references and create a new interpretative frame in which the judicial intervention of God against the ungodly appears to be reread decisively in light of the creation seen as the instrument and ally of God.

Making use of images analogous to those in our text, the book of Job hoped for the possibility in this world of a reversal of situation caused by God's intervention (Job 21:17-18). The book of Wisdom seems to contain an explicit recognition that such a reversal will never happen in the present but will have its inexorable fulfilment in the future. The ungodly will be swept away.

Summary of Wis 5

An Eschatological Judgement

The tone of the chapter is judicial, and the emphasis on the reversal of situation presupposes some form of survival for the just, whereas the ungodly seem doomed to destruction. Wis 5:17-23 is the description of a real eschatological battle. It is difficult to decide whether our sage envisages the just as participating in this battle or not.[26] Or again: when our author thinks of the glorified just, is he imagining them as already risen? In any case: at what moment in time should we locate the scene described here?

The Just and the Cosmos

Given our sage's reserve over the final destiny of the just, it is not easy to answer these questions. Taking up an opinion of C. Larcher, M. Gilbert holds that an answer can be obtained from the analysis of the overall literary structure of Wis 1-6.[27] In Wis 1-6, our sage is not following a precise chronological scheme in his presentation of facts about the future. In 6:1, 3, and 8, the book of Wisdom exhorts the "kings" not to draw down on themselves the divine punishment, which our text (5:17-23) has in fact already described in advance. Secondly, Wis 5:17-23 serves to deal with two problems which remain unresolved within the second discourse of the ungodly (5:4-13): first, their not having been punished for having fought the just; second, for having abused the creation through their way of life. This is exactly what happens in 5:17-23. The punishment of the ungodly will be their eternal ruin, which is set in the presence of the glorification of the just, and, at the same time, the creation which revolts against them. From a juridical point of view, Wis 5:17-23 constitutes the execution of the sentence as far as the ungodly are concerned.[28] The placing of 5:17-23 after the discourse of the ungodly (5:4-13) has, therefore, a certain logic. However, this does not entirely make clear to us whether the author of Wisdom thought that he had to place the battle against the ungodly before or after the rendering of accounts with them (something which is said precisely in Wis 4:20-5:13). As M. Gilbert concludes, it could simply be a question that the author had not posed to himself, thus revealing the imperfect coherence of his eschatological doctrine. What is certain is that, for our sage, eschatology implies a cosmology. Salvation comes through the cosmos.

---

26 Cf. also the comment on 3:7. Cf. Heinisch, Paul, "Das jüngste Gericht im Buche der Weisheit", *TGl* 2 (1910) 89-106. With regard to 5:17-23, Heinisch claims that our sage is referring to the just who have risen before the events recounted in 4:20-5:23.

27 Cf. Gilbert, "Sg 3,7-9; 5,15-23", 319-320; Larcher, *Sagesse*, 2:380-381; *Etudes*, 325.

28 Cf. Kolarcik, *The Ambiguity of Death*, 106-107.

Wis 6:1-21: A New Appeal to the Readers

The Literary Structure of Wis 6[1]

This chapter holds an important position in the book. The *incipit* of 6:1 seems to be almost a new beginning.[2] On the one hand, chapter 6 draws the conclusions which derive from the judgement of the ungodly described in Wis 5: if wickedness leads to death, the only way to follow is the path of justice. On the other hand, Wis 6:1-21 reconnects with the opening chapter (1:1-15) and extends the theme of kingship, addressing the young men who will be responsible in the future for the Jewish community of Alexandria and exhorting them to follow justice. Finally, above all in 6:12-21, we have the decisive appearance of the figure of Wisdom who, alongside God, will be the principal protagonist of the second part of the book. This is clear in the text of 6:22-25 which forms a bridge between the first and second part of the work (see below). In this way, Wis 6 constitutes a literary hinge between the first and second parts of the book.[3]

Wis 6:1 opens with an imperative (ἀκούσατε) which recalls the initial imperative of the book (ἀγαπήσατε; 1:1a). This is followed by a "then" (οὖν) which marks out the passage as a conclusion.[4] The term "earth" (γῆ, 6:1b) is a good example of a "hook-word" which immediately recalls the "earth" which was made into a desert by lawlessness, something just mentioned at the end of the previous chapter (5:23c).

Verse 21 constitutes a clear fixed point in the text. The term "(you) kings" (βασιλεῖς) in 6:1 is recalled here by the verb "reign" (βασιλεύσητε). Moreover, the mention of wisdom, also in v. 21 and taken up again at the beginning of the following verse, announces the theme of the second part of the book (Wis 7-9). Further internal links are represented by the fact that vv. 1-2, 11-12 and 21 have the same structure: imperative plural + οὖν + vocative.

The text of Wis 6:1-21 can easily be subdivided into two sections: vv. 1-11 and vv. 12-21. The latter are characterised by the *inclusio* of σοφία, introduced in 12a and repeated in 21b. With its asyndetic construction, v. 12 constitutes a rather clear literary and thematic break.

Within the first strophe (1-11), vv. 1-8 make up a literary unit centred on advice to the powerful concerning the divine judgement which awaits them and, at the same time, on the theme of the power that comes from God. The "rulers" (κρατοῦντες – κραταίοις) are mentioned in an *inclusio* in vv. 2 and 8 (cf. κράτησις in v. 3); cf. also διερευνήσει (3c) and ἔρευνα (8). Internally, vv. 1-8 can be divided

Wis 6:1-11

---

1 Cf. Wright, "Structure", 173; Bizzeti, *Il libro*, 63-67; Gilbert, "Sagesse", 68-69.

2 "It is as if the author's discourse were beginning here, and the five previous chapters were the preface", Alonso Schökel, *Sabiduría*, 115.

3 Cf. Engel, "Die Sapientia Salomonis als Buch", 137.

4 It is used in the concluding statement of a syllogism. Cf. Vílchez Líndez, *Sapienza*, 257.

into two further sections: 1-4 (invitation to listen addressed to the powerful) and 5-8 (the divine judgement).[5]

Verses 9-11 make up a further literary unit. As in 6:1-2, this is characterised by verbs in the imperative through which the powerful are exhorted to follow wisdom and the law. Note the repetition as an *inclusio* of the expression "my words" (οἱ λόγοι μου – τῶν λόγων μου, vv. 9 and 11) and the verb "learn" (μάθητε) of v. 9, which recalls the beginning of the chapter (μάθετε, 6:1b).

Wis 6:12-21

The second section (vv. 12-21) opens with vv. 12-16. These anticipate the *elogium* of wisdom which will follow in chapters 7 and 8. At the beginning and centre of the passage and creating a further *inclusio* (vv. 12 and 16), the verb ζητέω, "seek" appears. However, its meaning is not univocal (cf. the comment).

Finally, the closing section (vv. 17-21), draws the consequences for those who follow wisdom. It is structured according to the rhetorical form of the "sorites" (cf. the comment). It is opened and closed by the repetition of the term "desire" (ἐπιθυμία).

The Function of 6:22-25

The function of 6:22-25 within the scheme of the book is debated. According to many authors, this is the introduction to the second part of the book. However, there are good arguments for considering 6:22-25 the conclusion of the first part.[6]

The mention of the "kings" in v. 24 brings us back to the general theme of 6:1-21 just as does the reference to education (παιδεύεσθε, v. 25). This imperative (pres.), the last in the whole book, concludes the (aorist) imperatives of 6:1-2, 11, 21. "My words" (τοῖς ῥήμασίν μου) link up again with οἱ λόγοι μου in Wis 6:9 and 11.

On the other hand, v. 22 announces the themes that are going to be tackled (cf. the verbs in the future), that is, the nature, the origin, and the history of wisdom. The nature of wisdom will be especially the subject of Wis 7:22b-24; its divine origin is the basis of 7:25-26; and chapter 10 will follow its traces starting with Adam (cf. 10:1), though 7:27-8:1 already tackles this subject. In solemn tones, the sage states that he does not wish to hide the "secrets" (μυστήρια) of wisdom. On the contrary, he wants to expound them fully.

For all these reasons, 6:22-25 is to be considered the conclusion of the first part of the book but, at the same time, as the announcement of the *encomium* on wisdom (Wis 7-9).[7] An additional reason is the fact that Wis 6:22-25 can be linked to the conclusion of chap. 1 (cf. 6:24a with 1:14b) with which the whole of chap. 6 appears to be connected (cf. below). Further links appear between 6:22-25 and 2:21-24, thanks, principally, to the theme of μυστήρια. Cf. also the theme of envy in 6:23 and 2:24 (only here in the book by means of the term φθόνος). The link between 6:24 and 1:14 is particularly important on the thematic level. The generations of the world are bearers of salvation, and yet, thanks to the ungodly, death has entered the world. Thanks to the wise, on the other hand, salvation has entered it.[8]

---

5 For the reasons for the break between v. 4 and v. 5, cf. Gilbert, "Your Sovereignty", 124.

6 Cf. Gilbert, "La struttura letteraria", 37-41, correcting his previous position (cf. Bizzeti, *Il libro della Sapienza*, 65; Kolarcik, *The Ambiguity of Death*, 29-62 and Offerhaus, *Komposition und Intention*, 52-53).

7 Scarpat (*Sapienza*, 1:371-372) notes that in these verses we have a typical *parrhesia* discourse, close to texts like Eph 6:19 and John 16:29.

8 Bizzeti, *Il libro della Sapienza*, 64.

Thus, within the concentric structure which characterises the first part of the book, Wis 6:1-25 corresponds to Wis 1:1-15. It is an appeal to the addressees of the book but one which inverts its thematic order. In 1:1-5, there is a presentation of wisdom, which only reappears then after chapters 2-5 (cf. 6:9, 12, 20, 21, 22, 23). It remains conspicuous that the verbal pair in 1:1c, 2a "seek – be found" (ζητέω – εὑρίσκομαι), which there refers to the κύριος in 1b, returns in a key position in 6:12c, where it denotes wisdom (cf. also the ζητοῦσα said of wisdom in 6:16). The second part of the first chapter (1:6-10) introduces the theme of the judgement of the ungodly; this theme also opens chapter six. The reference, however is to the judgement of the powerful (6:1-11; the seldom attested lexeme εξετασ- appears in 1:9 and 6:3c, but appears otherwise in the book only in 4:6 and 11:10). cf. the two rare terms ἐξέτασις (1:9) and ἐξετάσει (6:3c). Moreover, the theme of the generations which bear salvation to the cosmos (cf. 1:14) is taken up in 6:24 and set in relation to the figure of the wise (σωτηρία κόσμου).

Wis 6:1-11: *Listen, O kings!*

1 Listen, then, O kings, and seek to understand!
Learn, you who are governors over all the earth!
2 Lend your ear, you who dominate multitudes,
who boast in the throng of your nations.
3 It was from the Lord that dominion was given to you
and supreme power from the Most High,
He who will examine your works and scrutinise your decisions.
4 Although servants of his kingdom, you have not governed rightly,
or observed the law,
or walked according to the will of God.

5 Terribly and swiftly, he will fall upon you
because inexorable judgement is carried out on tyrants.
6 For the lowly one is worthy of mercy,
while the mighty will be mightily punished,
7 because the Sovereign of all will not be afraid of anyone,
or have regard for greatness,
because it is he who has created the small and the great
and provides for all in the same way;
8 but a rigorous inquest looms up for rulers.

9 My words are for you, therefore, O sovereigns,
that you may learn wisdom and avoid falling.
10 For the one who will have kept the holy things in holiness will be acknowledged holy

and the one who has been taught in it will find a defence.
11 Long for my words, then,
desire them, and you will receive their instruction.

Notes on the Text and Translation

v. 1. At the beginning of v. 1, Lat adds, *melius est sapientia quam vires et vir prudens (magis) quam fortis*. Cf. Scarpat, *Sapienza*, 1:469. This is probably a scribal reflection, a kind of mosaic of biblical quotations (cf. Qoh 9:16; Prov 24:5 etc.). However, it fits the context well.

vv. 3-4. The two uses of ὅτι which open vv. 3 and 4 are usually considered causal and translated "since". However, I prefer to consider them declarative and so see in vv. 3 and 4 the realities which the powerful are called to understand. Cf. Scarpat, *Sapienza*, 1:379. For a different choice, cf. Gilbert, "Your Sovereignty", 123-124. He prefers to consider the ὅτι of v. 3 as causal and to see only in chapter 7 the content of what the "sovereigns" ought to hear.

v. 5. The adverb *φρικτῶς, "terribly", is a *hapax* of the LXX. As for the verbal form ἐφίστασθαι followed by the dative, cf. below on 6:8 and, again, 18:17 and 19:1 with the sense of "rise against", translated here with "fall upon". Cf. 1 Thess 5:3, a passage from which some codices (cf. Ziegler) take ὄλεθρος; cf. Scarpat, *Sapienza*, 1:380.

v. 6. The adjective *συγγνωστός (*hapax* of the LXX and the NT) signifies "forgivable", as in 13:8, and, when it governs the genitive, it indicates the reason for the pardon or the motive of the one pardoning. Following Grimm, Scarpat gives συγγνωστός the sense of "worthy", "deserving" (*Sapienza*, 1:381). Otherwise, the genitive ἐλέους would be quite difficult to explain.

v. 9. Here, the term τύραννος does not have the negative nuance which it sometimes assumes in the Hellenistic period. Cf. Philo, *Leg.* 3.79, who distinguishes between τύραννοι and βασιλεῖς; see Larcher, *Sagesse*, 2:412-413. The τύραννοι are no different from the βασιλεῖς mentioned in v. 1 and indicate simply rulers, even if the idea of a supreme and absolute authority is inherent in the term. Our sage could have had in mind Prov 8:16: τυράννοι δι' ἐμοῦ κρατοῦσι γῆς.

Synchronic Analysis

6:1-2 The beginning of the chapter takes up Ps 2:10 LXX almost to the letter. This is a text that was used already at the opening of the book (1:1a). By making use of biblical words this new pericope opens with a direct appeal to the powerful who are invited to draw the consequences of what has just been said (οὖν). Cf. an almost identical beginning in Mark 7:14.

Who is being addressed here? "Kings" (βασιλεῖς) are mentioned first and, immediately afterwards, δικασταὶ περάτων γῆς. The term "kings" also comes from Ps 2:2 and can indicate any kind of ruler in a generic sense. The term δικαστής, which comes from the context of Ps 2 (cf. οἱ κρίνοντες τὴν γῆν), recalls one of the qualities of the king, that of being "judge" (cf. Solomon's prayer in 1 Kgs 3:9-11 and 16-28). The expression περάτων γῆς is both classical and biblical (cf. Pss 2:8; 18:5 LXX [19:5 MT]; 20:28 LXX [21:28 MT]; 44:10 LXX [45:10 MT]; 47:11 LXX [48:11 MT]; etc.; for the Greek world, cf. *Il.* 8.478, *Od.* 4.563) and can indicate the entire inhabited world. If we take this reference literally, we could think that our author has in mind the Roman rulers who are exercising their authority over the whole earth.[9]

In v. 2, the mention of the rulers is tinged with negative aspects: the expression οἱ κρατοῦντες πλήθους, "you who dominate multitudes", prepares for the reflection of v. 3 on κράτησις, "dominion". The second stich describes the rulers as γεγαυρωμένοι ἐπὶ ὄχλοις ἐθνῶν, those who are proud of, who boast in their dominion over "throngs of nations". The use of the perfect indicates an habitual state, a lasting situation.[10]

To what should the "kings" listen? The content of what the previous imperatives are urging the addressees to attend to is expressed in 6:3 and 6:4 through object complements introduced by ὅτι (cf. the textual note). Verse 9 adds that the rulers are called to learn wisdom. 6:3-4

Power Is from God

The powerful have to understand first and foremost that their power comes from God. The first stich (3a) is constructed very carefully so as to put παρὰ κυρίου at the centre of the statement, as the true subject of the passive form ἐδόθη, and to cause the personal pronoun ὑμῖν to stand out at the end. Verse 3a is an explicit mention of the κύριος of Israel.

The term δυναστεία refers to power in a generic sense. However, a probable reminiscence of Exod 6:6 LXX could give this term a negative nuance: "despotic power". The term κράτησις (cf. Introduction, p. 29) is an unequivocal allusion to the Romans' seizing of Egypt.

The text of 3c has the Lord as subject (ὅς, with consecutive force: "he who, as a result ...") and, through the mention of the "inquest" (ἐξετάζω) recalls Wis 1:9 (cf. also 4:9). The verb *διερευνάω, which will return only in 13:17 but in a different context, has here the sense of "scrutinise". The powerful must betake themselves to the school of God because it will be he who will examine their actions and their decisions (βουλάς). Human power cannot be based on displays of force (the declarations of the ungodly in 2:11 are being recalled) because that would be a precise contradiction of the divine origin of power. It must be asked whether such advice could possibly be effective for the "rulers over all the earth". Perhaps it consists rather in a comforting piece of reassurance for the subjects of these rulers or even in an admonition which works for those who already believe in the κύριος of Israel and his presence in history.

Verse 4 gives further information about what the rulers must hear. This is linked to the previous statements on the sovereignty that comes from God. The expression ὑπηρέται ὄντες has concessive force: "although servants". The ruler is dependent on God. He is the "servant" "of his kingdom" (βασιλεία; cf. 6:20). Kingship is not only delegated by God to men but also subordinated to God himself. However, the rulers have not judged rightly (the formula οὐκ ἐκρίνατε ὀρθῶς is unusual for the LXX; the verb κρίνω links us back to Wis 1:1a). They have not observed the Law (see below) and they have not walked according to the will of God, here called θεός and no longer κύριος (4c).

---

9 However, the formulation of the text is unusual as already noted by Larcher, *Sagesse*, 2:401.

10 According to Scarpat, *Sapienza*, 1:378, the use of γαυροῦν is taken from Xenophon, *Hier.* 2.15, the only known case in secular Greek where the verb is constructed with ἐπί.

6:5-8 In vv. 5-8, there returns the idea of the judgement that awaits the "tyrants", those who have used their own power to practise oppression (v. 5), like the ungodly of chapter 2. Verse 5, which opens with an asyndetic construction, announces a sudden coming of God, the understood subject of the whole verse, to deal with the powerful. What awaits the powerful is precisely an inexorable judgement (κρίσις ἀπότομος; cf. 5:20a for the adjective). The use of the present form (γίνεται) after the future of 5a emphasises that our sage wishes to highlight a constant feature of God's action.

Verse 6 is built up on the play of contrasts between small and big, mercy and judgement. Note the play on words (*polyptoton*) which characterises v. 6b, "mighty" – "mightily" (δυνατοὶ – δυνατῶς). If "much will be required of those to whom much is given" (cf. Luke 12:47-48), the judgement that awaits the powerful will undoubtedly be more severe than that which awaits the "lowly man" (ἐλάχιστος; 6a), a figure which recalls the persecuted just person of chapter. 2. These "inferiors" have a particular claim to receive the mercy of God.

In a beautiful reflection, v. 7 provides the reason for this apparently unjust divine attitude: the only "Sovereign of all"[11] is the Lord (cf. Job 5:8 LXX and Wis 8:3).

In 7c αὐτός has emphatic value: "it is he". Just as in Prov 22:2, the reason for the divine judgement is expressed by recourse to an argument from creation. The use of ἐντρέπομαι (7b) could be a polemical reference to 2:10 where the ungodly boast of not having any respect for the weak. By contrast, God does, and he does not respect the right claimed by the strong.

The divine care for all does not exclude the ability to punish the wicked (cf. v. 8). In fact, divine providence does not exclude a rigorous judicial inquest (*ἔρευνα; cf Rev 2:23)[12] into the powerful (κραταιοί).

Verse 8 picks up on v. 5 and emphasises again that the power of the mighty cannot be arbitrary. It will be judged by the God who cares in the same way for every human creature that he has created (cf. 6:7c). Our sage seems to wish to respond to Qoheleth's complaint that, in this world, right always appears to be trampled on (cf. Qoh 3:16; 4:1; 5:7).

6:9 We find here a further invitation to listen, expressed again by two imperatives (v. 11) which take up the opening verses (6:1-2). This time, the double reference to "my words" in vv. 9 and 11 has the tone of a personal appeal, something which is not so common in our book.

Verses 9 and 11 frame the two sentences of sapiential character in v. 10. Right from the beginning of the book, the author has spoken to others and about others. Now, in 6:9 and 11, for the first time, he uses the first-person personal pronoun ("my" words), and, beginning from 7:1, starts to make use of the "I" which is increasingly recognisable as (the fictitious) "Solomon".

---

11 It is difficult to decide whether πάντων here has a neuter ("everything") or masculine ("everyone") value. The context of the book of Wisdom, with its attention to the cosmos, makes one prefer the first meaning, but the use of πάντων in 6:7d points decisively towards the masculine.

12 Cf. Passoni Dell'Acqua, Anna, "Indagine lessicale su ἐρευνάω e composti", *Anagennesis. A Papyrological Journal* (1985): 201-326.

Verse 9 opens in the same manner as v. 1 (cf. the repetition of the particle οὖν). Our sage addresses the "sovereigns" in a typically sapiential style, inviting them to listen to his words so that they may earn wisdom and be educated. The reference to σοφία and the use of the verb παιδεύω (cf. v. 11b) complete the invitation in 6:1 and explain that it relates not so much to the justice which the rulers ought to practise as rather to the wisdom which they are called on to live (cf. already in 1:4).

In Wisdom, ὅσιος refers not so much to a belonging to God (for which our sage prefers to employ ἅγιος) as to a moral holiness understood as faithfulness in dealings with the Lord.[13] However, the significance of ὁσιωθήσονται is not wholly clear. The only case in the LXX in which the verb is in the passive is Ps 17:26 LXX [18:26 MT]: μετὰ ὁσίου ὁσιωθήσῃ, a text which our author could have had in mind.[14] The passive form ὁσιωθήσονται can be understood as "will be made holy", that is, "will be sanctified". In the wake of Wis 5:5, where, *post mortem*, the ungodly recognise the glorification of the just, ὁσιωθήσονται could be understood, tentatively, as "they will be acknowledged holy", namely, God will recognise as holy, that is, faithful and just, all those who have observed God's law. The use of ὅσιοι in Wis 3:9; 4:15 points us in the direction of an eschatological sense of the term, something further confirmed by the last part of the verse. 6:10

Thus, whoever will have learned the law of God (οἱ διδαχθέντες αὐτά) will be considered part of the elect. In fact, they will find a "defence". Precisely in secular Greek, the term *ἀπολογία, implies a judgement which is here the divine judgement (cf. the theme of v. 8 taken up again through the play on words ἔρευνα – εὑρήσουσιν). The "holy ones" will find the words to defend themselves before God by contrast with the ungodly who are forced into a decisive and terrible silence (cf. 4:19).[15]

Verse 11 takes up the exhortation of v. 9 (οὖν), employing two verbs that are typical of amorous language, ἐπιθυμέω, "long" (cf. Sir 1:26) and ποθέω, "desire". The sage must be in love with wisdom. These two imperatives thus sweeten the harshness of the address to the powerful. 6:11

In this way, the educative path to which the "powerful" are called can be completed. The use of παιδεύω, employed here in the sense of "instruct", recalls the sapiential παιδεία introduced back in 1:5, but it does not exclude the way of the Greek παιδεία.

---

13 Cf. Mazzinghi, *Notte di paura e di luce*, 205-206. On the Platonic background of ὅσιος in the LXX, cf. G. Dafni, Evangelia, "ΟΣΙΟΣ und ΟΣΙΟΤΗΣ in der LXX und Platos Eutiphron. Lexicographisches, geistes- und kulturgeschichtliche Ueberlegungen", Bonney, Gillian – Vicent, Rafael, *Sophia - Paideia. Sapienza e educazione (Sir 1,27)*, FS. Mario Cimosa, LAS: Roma 2012, 55-87.

14 Without necessarily having to hypothesise a misunderstanding of the Greek text, as suggested by Scarpat, *Sapienza*, 1:359-360 and n. 19, p. 359.

15 *Contra* Larcher (*Sagesse*, 2:416), it does not seem that v. 10b has in mind different classes of people from 10a. The reference to learning "holy things" does not necessarily presuppose pagans. They could be precisely those very Jews who must be educated in God's holy law.

Diachronic Analysis

6:1-2: A Reflection on Kingship

It is difficult to deny that in 6:1-2 our sage has in mind the Romans, even if the allusions to the imperial power remain vague The plural βασιλεῖς cannot indicate Octavian Augustus: "while alluding to the latter, [he] did not allow himself to go any further; perhaps prudence was in order".[16] In any case, our sage intends to recall a teaching common in both the Greek and the biblical worlds: power has a divine origin and so the rulers are responsible for it. In the light of the neo-Pythagorean treatises on kingship (see below), the rulers are called to follow a law to which they are not superior. As already in Wis 1:1, the Stoic idea of kingship appears now here also: "the statements of our sage represent a very fine exposition of a Stoic theory in eminently biblical terms".[17] The sage is alone the true king. If the Romans seem to be the target, the addressees are in reality those young men who have to be educated to become the leaders of their own community. It is to them that our sage offers, in Wis 7-8, the positive example of a kingship different from that presented by the rulers of his time, the kingship of Solomon, a man like all the others (7:1-6), a "democratic kingship". Beginning from this chapter, and still more explicitly from 6:9, "Solomon", the fictitious author of the book, starts to speak here.[18]

Our sage addresses four imperatives of a clear sapiential stamp to these "rulers". The first two were certainly suggested by the biblical tradition: the verbs ἀκούω and συνίημι are found together in Isa 6:9; 52:15; Neh 8:2, and, above all, in the account of the dream at Gibeon in 1 Kgs 3:9. "Listen" and "understand" are typical attitudes of the sapiential tradition. For the invitation to listen, cf. also Deut 5:1; 6:4; Prov 4:1; 8:33. The third imperative, μάθετε, recalls the παιδεύθητε of Ps 2:10: listening and understanding in order to learn. So too ἐνωτίζομαι lies within the same sapiential orbit: "lend your ear" is a frequent expression in parallel with "listen" (Ps 48[49 MT]:2; Job 33:1, 31; Sir 33:19 and, above all, Jdg 5:3: ἀκούσατε βασιλεῖς καὶ ἐνωτίσασθη σατράπαι).

6:3-4

The idea expressed in v. 3a, that it is the Lord who gives power to people, is traditional: cf. 1 Chr 29:11; Dan 2:21, 37; 4:14; 5:18; Prov 8:15-16; Sir 10:4-5; for the NT, Rom 13:1 and 1 Pet 2:13-15. God alone (Dan 4:17, 25,32 LXX [4:14, 22, 29 MT]; Sir 10:4-5) is the true king of the universe. Even outside the Bible, the idea is frequent and well known as far back as ancient Greece (cf. *Il.* 2.197-198 and 205). In Alexandria, it was taken up in Stoic circles; cf. Let. Aris. 224: "no king is independent. All of them wish to share this glory, but they cannot – it is a gift of God". The idea recurs, in a particular way, in the neo-Pythagorean treatises on kingship.[19]

Rulers and Law

The use of νόμος without the article (Wis 6:4b) could lead one to think of the Mosaic *Torah*, something confirmed by the reference to the βουλὴ θεού which, as in 9:16-18, seems to refer to the will of God expressed in the Law. In this case, however – if our

---

16 Gilbert, "Your Sovereignty", 123.

17 Scarpat, *Sapienza*, 1:353-354.

18 Cf. Gilbert, "Your Sovereignty", 138-40; Newman, "The Democratization of Kingship".

19 Cf. Squilloni, Annamaria, "Il significato etico-politico dell'immagine Re-Legge animata. Il νόμος ἔμψυχος nei trattati neopitagorici Περὶ βασιλείας", *Civiltà Classica e Cristiana* 11/1 (1990): 75-94; Gilbert, "Your Sovereignty", 133-134.

author were referring to the Roman rulers – it would be necessary to think that when he speaks of the "law" he has in mind the *Torah* understood as an expression of the natural law, or even the Stoic idea of the law of nature.[20] Clarifying and improving the intuitions of Larcher, Gilbert shows that, in Wis 6:4, our sage is basing himself not so much on concepts that are directly Stoic as on the already mentioned neo-Pythagorean treatises on kingship, influenced in their turn by Stoicism.[21] In the "law" spoken of in Wis 6:4, therefore, we have to see the expression of positive laws understood as intermediate between the natural law – of divine origin – and the king. According to Gilbert, in Wis 6:4, νόμος refers directly to the Mosaic Law with some difficulty, given that the object of our sage's invective is clearly the pagan rulers.

However, it is necessary to make clear that the addressees of the book of Wisdom are nonetheless *Jews*. Texts like Wis 1:1 and 6:1 are not addressed *directly* to the Roman rulers, and our sage does not claim to be read or heard by them. The book is entirely an *internal* address to the Jewish community of Alexandria. Therefore, it cannot be totally precluded that Wis 6:4 is a possible allusion to the Mosaic Law *as well*. We thus must supplement Gilbert's argument. In accusing the pagan kings of not having observed the law, our sage could already have had in mind, from the very beginning of his work, some kind of association between the positive law, law of nature, and the Mosaic Law. This will happen later in Philo in a much more systematic way.[22]

The description of God as δεσπότης (6:7a) is not fortuitous. In fact, this term was a usual mode of address for the Roman Emperor (thus Philo, in *Leg.* 290 and 321). Polemically, our author wishes to claim that there is only one Sovereign, God, who actually has no regard for the greatness of the kings of this world. 6:7

The idea of divine impartiality (7b) is biblical (here, the text of inspiration is Deut 1:17; cf. Job 34:17-19), just like the reason expressed by the reference to the creation of both small and great (our sage is employing here the rhetorical figure of *merismus;* cf. Job 31:15; 34:19; Prov 22:2).

Although general, the reference to God's "providence" (7d) is new. The idea of a God who looks after all is also biblical but it is expressed here with προνοέω which recalls directly a typical idea of Stoic philosophy (cf. πρόνοια in Wis 14:3 and 17:2).

6:9: In the School of Wisdom

In the light of v. 9, wisdom is something which must be learned. This is an idea rooted in Israel's sapiential tradition, even if this is the only passage in the LXX in which σοφία appears as object of the verb μανθάνω. However, throughout the book of Proverbs, as indeed in Ben Sira, the addressees are pupils who have placed themselves in the school of the teacher of wisdom. As in Prov 8, wisdom has both ethical and practical dimensions. As well as being a way of life, it has a political dimension and concerns the art of good government. However, it is also that wisdom which comes from God and which will be the protagonist in Wis 7-10. If they join the school of wisdom, the "rulers" will avoid the possibility of falling (μὴ παραπήσητε). This verb evokes texts like that of Ezek 14:13: γῆ ἐὰν

20 Cf. Larcher, *Études*, 203, without further explanation. This identification is already present in Grimm, *Weisheit*, 124: "νόμος nicht das mosaische Gesetz, sondern die natürlichen Grundsätze des Rechts ...". Cf. Also Winston, *Wisdom of Solomon*, 153, who underlines, rather generally, that, in Hellenistic Judaism, the Mosaic Law was considered an expression of the natural law.

21 Cf. Gilbert, "Your Sovereignty", 132-135.

22 Cf. Mazzinghi, "Law of Nature", *passim.*

ἁμάρτῃ μοι τοῦ παραπεσεῖν παράπτωμα, and thus suggests a transgression of the law.

6:10 Verses 6:9 and 6:11 frame both of the wisdom pronouncements in 6:10. Verse 10a is not easy to interpret and has been much debated by various commentators. The initial γάρ is probably explicative. The powerful must place themselves in the school of the sages, "for", in doing so, they will be glorified. Here we have a play on words (*polyptoton*) centred on the repetition of the root ὅσιο-, "holy". The key to interpretation lies in τὰ ὅσια, "the holy things". This is a possible reminiscence of Isa 55:3 LXX (the only other occurrence of this expression in the LXX), where τὰ ὅσια refers to the promises and the covenant made with David. In our context, τὰ ὅσια should be understood as a reference to the "holy law", that is, what is held holy by the law of God. This is confirmed by the use of the verb φυλάσσω, "keep", which is often applied precisely to the law.[23] A text which could have inspired our sage is 1 Kgs 8:61 LXX: καὶ ὁσίως πορεύεσθαι ἐν τοῖς προστάγμασιν αὐτοῦ καὶ φυλάσσειν ἐντολὰς αὐτοῦ. Our sage would, therefore, be encouraging the "rulers" to keep the divine Law with holiness (ὁσίως), that is, with faithfulness and integrity. This exhortation makes more sense if the "rulers" are not so much pagan figures but rather Jews. Moreover, the probable allusion to 1 Kgs 8:61 LXX serves to create a biblical atmosphere.

6:11 Throughout Wis 6:9-11, our sage continues to employ ideas of Stoic origin but reads them against a clear biblical background (cf., also, below on the use of Ps 2:10). There is another return of the Stoic idea that only the sage is truly a king, and so only the sage is really able to be king (cf. *SVF* III, 81 frag. 332; III, 159 frag. 619; *SVF* III, 159 frag. 620; cf. Philo, *Mut.* 152). The idea that the wicked man can be educated and so become wise – and, therefore, king – is clearly of Stoic origin: cf. *SVF* I, 129 frag. 567, "virtue can be taught", and *SVF* III, 52 frag. 223, "from being wicked one can become good".

However, the verb παιδεύω has been suggested by the text of Ps 2:10. Our sage had alluded to the first part of this verse from v. 1 (cf. also 1:1): καὶ νῦν βασιλεῖς σύνετε παιδεύθητε πάντες οἱ κρίνοντες τὴν γῆν. It is as though he has split open the text of Ps 2:10 and inserted there a judicial scene aimed at recalling the reader to the severity with which the God of Israel will judge the powerful and, together with them, whoever behaves in the same way. By contrast, for the "small" (6:6) and for the "holy ones", those faithful to the Lord and his law, there will be a quite different kind of judgement. In this way, Stoic concepts familiar in the Alexandrian environment are bound up with a clear biblical background. This is confirmation that the addressees of these exhortations are primarily Jews.

Wis 6:12-21:
Wisdom Searches for the One Searching for Her

12 Radiant, wisdom does not fade.
She is easily understood by those who love her

23 For the use of this verb in Wisdom, cf. Mazzinghi, *Notte di paura e di luce*, 219.

and found by those who seek her.
13 She takes the initiative in making herself known to those who desire her.
14 The one who rises early on her behalf will not have to suffer toil,
for he will find her sitting at his gate.
15 For to reflect on her is the fulness of prudence,
and the one who keeps watch for her will soon be free from troubles.
16 For she goes in search of those who are worthy of her
and appears in their paths with kindness
and comes to meet them in every thought.

17 For her authentic foundation is the desire for instruction,
but the yearning for instruction produces love,
18 love is, then, the keeping of her laws
and respect for the laws is the guarantee of incorruptibility,
19 incorruptibility, then, makes one close to God.
20 The desire for wisdom, therefore, raises one to a kingdom.
21 If, then, you love thrones and sceptres, O rulers of peoples,
honour wisdom so that you may reign forever.

Notes on the Text and Translation

v. 13. The construction of v. 13 is complex. Φθάνω governs the accusative τοὺς ἐπιθυμοῦντας, "she takes the initiative with those who desire (her)" (αὐτήν has been added for clarity by various textual witnesses). The verb φθάνω, already employed in 4:7, has the sense of "pre-empt, anticipate" (cf. in 16:28 in relation to the manna). Here, it governs the infinitive προγνωσθῆναι. Προγινώσκω returns in Wis 8:8 and 18:6 with the same meaning: "know in advance". Thus, the entire phrase could be translated: "she takes the initiative so that she may be known early (in advance) by those who desire (her)".

v. 14. The verb ὀρθρίζω (cf. Scarpat, *Sapienza*, 1:386-387) has the meaning of "rising very early". In the LXX, it is usually constructed with πρός. Thus, the majority of textual witnesses read πρὸς αὐτήν. However, the reading of B-S, ἐπ' αὐτήν, should be retained as *lectio difficilior.* The preposition ἐπί indicates the purpose of "rising at dawn": "for her", to seek her.

v. 16. In 16c, codex B (cf. Ziegler) reads ὑπαντᾷ while all the other textual witnesses read ἀπαντᾷ. The verb ὑπαντάω occurs only in Tob 7:1^{B}; Sir 9:3; 12:17; 15:2; and Dan 10:14. Ὑπαντᾷ is thus *lectio difficilior.* The sense is that of "coming to meet". The verb could have been suggested by Sir 15:2 where wisdom is described as one who goes to meet a man like his mother.

Synchronic Analysis

We now come to the first part of the second strophe (6:12-21) which anticipates the *elogium* on wisdom. According to an attested tradition, she is seen as a lady who calls on people to follow her. More than a spouse, wisdom is a friend and mistress who goes in search of those who desire her (cf. the *inclusio* on ζητέω "seek": vv. 12 and 16). This movement of reciprocal searching recalls the divine disposition expressed by the prophets: "you will search for me and you will find me, because you are searching for me with all your heart, and I will let you find me" (Jer 29:13-14 MT; cf. Isa 65:24). Even before describing the nature of wisdom, our sage presents her as easily accessible to all.

6:12-13 The asyndetic construction underlines a new beginning. Introduced already in v. 9, wisdom now becomes the protagonist. Ἡ σοφία is in emphatic position at the conclusion of the stich. She is presented first of all as radiant, luminous (λαμπρά), a metaphor that will return later in Wis 7:29 (cf. the *flashback* of 17:20-21). The radiant nature of wisdom underlines how easy it is to get to know her but, above all, the fact that she belongs to the divine sphere. This is that light which, according to Wis 5:6, did not shine on the ungodly.

Wisdom is then said to be *ἀμάραντος (cf. 1 Pet 1:14 and ἀμαράντινον in 1 Pet 5:4), a term rarely used of wisdom previously. Wisdom is "unfading". She does not fail or wither like the crowns of flowers at the banquets of the ungodly (cf. μαραίνω in Wis 2:8). In the light of vv. 17-20, not only does wisdom not fail; she is the guarantee of incorruptibility for those who welcome her.

Seeking Wisdom

This wisdom is easily (εὐχερής, a term which secular Greek employs to express the availability of someone, understood (θεωρέω) by those who love her. The use of the form εὑρίσκεται takes us back again to the beginning of the book, in 1:2. Human life is described as a path of searching. The one who seeks wisdom finds her because she allows herself to be found. Although linked with God (cf. Wis 7-8), she is still within human reach.

Verse 13 demonstrates not only that wisdom comes to meet human searching but even anticipates it. The text is not very clear (see the textual notes). It is not easy to understand just how wisdom makes herself known in advance to those who desire her (cf. the repetition of the previous ἐπιθυμήσατε).

6:14 The sage takes up again the metaphor of searching but turns it around. The one who searches for wisdom finds her already waiting. Whoever rises early for her will not have to toil (for κοπιάω, cf. Wis 9:10). The search for wisdom is quite different from everyday work. In the latter case, people rise early in the morning and toil all day long whereas the one who searches for wisdom no longer has any need to toil. Wisdom is already sitting at the gate of the one searching for her.

6:15-16 Verse 15a forms a kind of parenthesis which is nonetheless not separated from its context (the γάρ has a force that is simultaneously explicative and causal). Thinking about wisdom (τὸ γὰρ ἐνθυμηθῆναι περὶ αὐτῆς; Lat: *cogitare de illa*) leads to the perfection of discernment (φρονήσεως τελειότης). For the notion of φρόνησις, cf. the comment on 3:15. Here, the term indicates discernment, the virtue of prudence, and is clearly distinguished from σοφία. This virtue will reach its perfection only through the exercise of wisdom.

Verse 15b returns to the metaphor of early rising in 14a. It is not only a question of rising early but also of keeping watch for wisdom. The verb ἀγρυπνέω was certainly suggested by Prov 8:34 LXX ("blessed is the one ... who watches [ἀγρυπνῶν] at my gates ..."). Those who thus watch for wisdom will be quickly (ταχέως) free from troubles (ἀμέριμνος). Despite his readiness for watching, the sage remains free from all cares. Wisdom helps him to live well.

Verse 16 prolongs the image of personified wisdom. Following the pattern of Prov 8:1-3, she is described as one who goes about (περιέρχεται) seeking those who are worthy of her (τοὺς ἀξίους αὐτῆς. In Wisdom, the term ἄξιος always has a theological nuance; cf. 1:16; etc.). If someone seeks wisdom (12c), she too goes in search for people. The path of searching is reciprocal.

To those who seek her, wisdom comes with kindness (16b). Ἐν ταῖς τρίβοις recalls Prov 8:2: ἀνὰ μέσον τῶν τρίβων ἕστηκεν. The paths of wisdom are a metaphor to indicate every aspect of human life in which wisdom makes herself present (cf. Wis 2:15; 5:7). The verb φαντάζομαι occurs in the LXX only in Sir 34:5 and normally serves to indicate a heavenly apparition or something in a dream.[24] Here we have an apparition, *εὐμενῶς, which is kind and amiable and which does not cause alarm.

Not only does wisdom come to meet people in the concrete acts of their lives (ἐν ταῖς τρίβοις) but also in what concerns their inmost being. Ἐπίνοιαι (cf. Wis 9:14; 14:12; 15:4, always *in malam partem*) indicates people's thoughts, intentions, and reasonings which risk being of no use if they are not enlightened by wisdom. Reason alone is not enough!

If we think that the wisdom spoken of here is none other than human wisdom seen as a gift of God,[25] these verses take on an important significance. Wisdom is born of human searching (12c) which encounters the gift of God (16a). In the very moment when someone is searching for the meaning of life (that is, for wisdom), he discovers that in this search God has already come out to meet him (with His wisdom).

6:17-20: An Example of Sorites

Verses 17-20 are an excellent testimony to the rhetorical technique of our author. Here, he is making use of the rhetorical figure of σωρείτης "sorites" (chain syllogism), known in Greek logic, even if not always highly regarded by authors more sensitive to the beauty of their discourse. Known already to Aristotle, sorites takes the form of a complex syllogism, i.e., a conclusion is drawn from a series of premises: A leads to or implies B; B implies C; C implies D; and so forth. The object or predicate of each individual step in the series appears as the subject of the next step. The ultimate conclusion reads: Therefore A leads to or implies F, whereby A presents the subject of the initial statement and F presents the predicate or object of the final statement. In Wis 6:17-20, the sorites has six members, expressed with a total of seven concepts.[26] The author's purpose in employing this rhetorical figure is to show, with the aid of Greek logic, that the desire for wisdom is none other than the beginning of a path that leads to God.

The stages of this path open with the mention of the origin (ἀρχή) of wisdom, an expression which recalls Prov 1:7; 9:10: ἀρχὴ σοφίας. Because of the article, the superlative ἀλεθεστάτη could refer precisely to ἀρχή.[27] It is possible, however, also to understand it with reference to ἐπιθυμία, desire, which has a positive value here by contrast with 4:12. In any case, it is from desire that the path of wisdom

---

24 A possible reminiscence of Euripides (*Phoen.* 93) is noted by Scarpat, *Sapienza*, 1:366 n. 29: ἐν τρίβῳ φαντάζεται.

25 So Heinisch, *Weisheit*, 118.

26 Cf. Larcher, *Sagesse*, 1:425-426, and Winston, 154-155, with examples drawn from rabbinical literature. An example of classical sorites is in Seneca, *Ep.* 85.2; but this is the same Seneca who distrusts such rhetorical games (cf. Scarpat, *Sapienza*, 1:367).

27 "Initium enim illius verissimum disciplinae concupiscentia est": Augustine, *Mor. eccl.* 1.17-32 (Scarpat, 1:368).

sets out. Desire returns later in the conclusion of the sorites, at the beginning of v. 20. The authentic origin of wisdom lies in the desire for παιδεία, that is, for education, the whole of human formation, even in its ethical and religious aspects (cf. the comment on 1:5; 2:12; and 3:11).

The second movement of the sorites sees the passage to love (ἀγάπη; only here in Wisdom. Cf. the comment on ἀγαπάω in 1:1). With a skilful variation of the terms, παιδείας ἐπιθυμία becomes φροντὶς δὲ παιδείας, the concern or aspiration for education (cf. 5:15; 7:4; 8:9; and 15:9). Sincere concern for education leads to love. Here, that is clearly love for wisdom.

Love leads to the observance of the laws of wisdom (τήρησις νόμων αὐτῆς). The connection between loving God and observing God's laws is deuteronomic (cf. Deut 5:10; 10:12-13; 11:1; 30:16; cf. John 14:15). "Loving" is not identical with observing the laws. It is a state of mind which needs to be objectivised in obedience. Here it seems that our sage does not have in mind the Mosaic Law (in this connection, the LXX uses ἐντολαί rather than νόμοι; cf., however, Jer 38:33; 2 Macc 4:17) so much as, more generally, the laws which everyone can observe.

In the fourth step, the observance (τήρησις) of the laws becomes προσοχή, a term which, in this context, indicates respect for the law (cf. προσέχειν ἐντολαῖς in Sir 23:27; 32:24; and 35:1). This respect is a guarantee (βεβαίωσις) of incorruptibility; for ἀφθαρσία, cf. the comment on 2:23. The use of ἀφθαρσία instead of ἀθανασία is significant. Our sage conceives eternal life as marked by the absence of that corruption which is characteristic of physical life. Without saying so explicitly, he is alluding to the resurrection which awaits the just.

The last link in this chain consists in being close to God. This is the nature of ἀφθαρσία, something which "renders one close to God" (ἐγγὺς εἶναι ποιεῖ θεοῦ, v. 19), a clearly original expression which is unique in Scripture. The author could have been inspired by the Oriental conception according to which kings permitted only their privileged subjects to stand close to them (cf. Esth 1:14). Standing close to God is even more important than obtaining incorruptibility.

The real conclusion, however, comes in v. 20 (ἄρα). Our sage transforms the "desire for instruction" which had opened the sorites in v. 17 into the "desire for wisdom". This leads all the way to the βασιλεία, to the kingdom. The use of ἀνάγω indicates a real "ascent", a progression which has been deliberately marked by the sorites. The connection with ἀφθαρσία leads us to think that this kingship is not only an earthly one but concerns rather the divine kingship (cf. 6:4), that is, the closeness to God in an eschatological dimension which transcends human kingship. We cannot exclude, however, that our author once again had in mind that kingship which, according to the Stoic view, belongs to every sage.

6:21 Once more, the author addresses the same sovereigns evoked in v. 9 (τύραννοι λαῶν), described here with a certain negative nuance as those who "love thrones and sceptres". These "rulers" are called on to "honour" (τιμήσατε) wisdom so as to be able to reign for ever. As in the previous verse, the kingdom which our author has in mind here is not of an earthly character but is the eschatological participation in the divine kingship, anticipated, for the just, in 3:8 and 5:16.[28]

Diachronic Analysis

The reciprocity between wisdom's allowing herself to be found in 6:12c and the human wish to love her arises probably from a reflection on Prov 8:17 LXX, ἐγὼ τοὺς ἐμὲ φιλοῦντας ἀγαπῶ; "I love those who love me". The idea of wisdom allowing herself to be found by the searcher is typical of the sapiential tradition; cf. Sir 6:27. 6:12

The image of Wis 6:14 is suggested by Prov 1:21 LXX or 8:3 LXX where, in both cases, wisdom is the subject of the verb παρεδρεύω. Πάρεδρος has here the sense of "sitting beside" by contrast with the more technical sense which it will assume in 9:4, in polemic with the Isiac cults. However, if wisdom is described in Prov 8:3 as sitting at the gates of the powerful (ἐπὶ δὲ πύλαις δυναστῶν παρεδρεύει), here, instead, she is described as a reality available to all. 6:14

For the image in 15b, cf. Ps 126:1-2 LXX in which κοπιάω, ἀγρυπνέω, ὀρθρίζω occur together. Without the help of God, people toil in vain, they watch in vain, they rise early in vain. Our author is replacing God's activity in Ps 126 LXX [127 MT] with that of wisdom. 6:15

The employment of φαντάζομαι (16b), particularly with πάρεδρος (cf. the comment on Wis 9:4) and λαμπρός recalls the terminology of the mystery cults.[29] In these cults, the divinity – for example, Isis, throne-companion of Sarapis, repectively of the sun god – manifests herself only to the initiate, often as light in the darkness. By contrast, the wisdom offered by the God of Israel shuns all secrecy. She offers herself spontaneously to all who desire her and becomes their guide. 6:16

Wis 6:22-25: I Will Explain the Nature of Wisdom to You

[22] I will tell you what wisdom is and how she was born,
I shall not keep her mysteries hidden from you,
I shall follow her traces from the origin of her existence
and set the knowledge of her in full light
and not distance myself from the truth,
[23] or walk with the envy that consumes,

28 According to Kloppenborg, we have here a deliberate reprise of an Isiac theme; cf. Isidorus' *Hymn* 3.7-11 ("Isis and Sophia", 75-76). "All who live of greatest bliss, the best of men / sceptre-bearing kings and those who are rulers, / if they depend on you, rule until old age, / leaving shining and splendid wealth in abundance / to their sons, and son's sons, and men who come after" (SEG 550; tr. Vanderlip).

29 Cf. Mazzinghi, *Notte di paura e di luce*, 45 n. 130.

because it has nothing in common with wisdom.
24 On the other hand, a multitude of wise men is the salvation of the world and a sensible king, stability for his people.
25 So let yourself be instructed by my words and draw profit from them.

Notes on the Text and Translation

v. 23. The verb συνοδεύω is refined and learned (cf. in the LXX only in Tob 5:17^{S}, cf. Act 9:7). It is sometimes used by astrologists as a technical term in connection with the stars in the sense of "being in conjunction". Here, συνοδεύω has its etymological sense of "walking with". Cf. the previous παροδεύω (6:22e) which has the sense of "distancing oneself".
When he speaks of the "envy that consumes", our author is using the figure of *hypallage* to indicate "one who is consumed with envy". Cf. Scarpat, *Sapienza*, 1:393, who prefers, however, to think of τετηκότι as a substantivised participle: "with one who is consumed with envy (φθόνῳ)". For a detailed analysis of τήκω (cf. Wis 1:16) used in the sense of "pine", cf., again, Scarpat, *Sapienza*, 1:394.
The verb κοινωνέω in 23b is rare in the LXX. In Sir 13:1, 2, it indicates camaraderie or, in Sir 13:17, the impossible commonality between two opposites. Here the verb is used in its normal sense without any particular theological nuance.

v. 24. Here, the term κόσμος has the meaning of the "inhabited world", as in Wis 2:24 and 14:6, in a sense which appears to be attested precisely about the time of the first cent. BCE. Cf. Larcher, *Sagesse*, 2:439.

v. 25. With εὐστάθεια, we have a technical term typical of Epicureanism (stability as the presupposition of happiness) and, in a political key, also proper to Stoicism (cf. Scarpat, *Sapienza*, 1:396-397). It is a term much used by Philo in the sense of stability of mind, interior calm (*Post.* 23, 27, *Cher.* 19, etc. Cf. Winston, *Wisdom*, 160).

Synchronic Analysis

6:22 The author intends to tell of (ἀπαγγελῶ) the nature (τί ἐστιν), the origin (πῶς ἐγένετο), and the history (the "traces") of wisdom. The first formula (τί δέ ἐστιν) serves to introduce a definition. The second (πῶς ἐγένετο) imitates the introduction to the sacred discourses which are meant to celebrate gods or heroes, especially in the mysteries. This is not just a matter of the wisdom of Solomon but of that wisdom which comes from God and is present in the world.

The "Mysteries" of Wisdom

The intention is that of not hiding the "mysteries" of wisdom. The entire context of chapter 6 allows us to think that our sage is intending to refer to the revelation of the "mysteries" of wisdom rather than the "mysteries of God" mentioned in Wis 2:22.[30] The entire chapter, in fact, is centred on the invitation to welcome wisdom. In particular, v. 22 is focused on wisdom. The text of 6:12-16 has emphasized the readiness and accessibility of wisdom who lets herself be found by the one who seeks her. Wisdom does not have any mysteries because she is present in the world and available to

30 Actually, in 6:22, two minuscules and the Latin version add "the mysteries *of God*", precisely to harmonise the reference to the "mysteries" with Wis 2:22. However, the Arabic version adds instead "*her* (i.e., wisdom's) secrets".

people (cf. Wis 6:12-16). Wisdom is, then, the means with which people can come to understand those "mysteries of God" which the ungodly of Wis 2 have not succeeded in grasping, precisely because they do not have her (cf. 2:21).

What is the content of these "mysteries of wisdom"? The text of 6:17-21 connects the desire for wisdom with the observance of the commandments, on the one hand, and with the gift of ἀφθαρσία on the other. The "mystery" has thus a value which is also eschatological and not detached from an ethical point of view. The novelty in 6:22, compared with 2:21, consists in the fact that the revelation of the mysteries of wisdom, which is offered to everyone who wishes to welcome it, is precisely the way to understand the mysteries of God, namely, the eschatological plan of God for the world and for people.

Finally, in 22de, "Solomon" states solemnly that he wishes to set in full light, to manifest (θήσω εἰς τὸ ἐμφανές) the γνῶσις of wisdom. We can leave the genitive αὐτῆς in all its ambiguity: Solomon's knowledge of Wisdom or else the knowledge which she possesses and communicates to Solomon.

In the last stich, "Solomon" concludes by not wishing to pass by or obscure the truth about wisdom. In the light of 3:9, the sense of ἀλήθεια is to be sought not in the intellectual sphere but in the theological-existential realm of the divine mercy, justice, and faithfulness (cf. also 5:6, the other occurrence of ἀλήθεια in our book).

To the programme traced by the author, verse 23 adds a clear ethical nuance. 6:23
Wisdom is accessible to all and has nothing in common with the envy that consumes (τετηκότι). The one who lets himself be governed by envy can give nothing to others out of fear of loss. The benefit of wisdom, on the other hand, increases at the same moment in which others are made sharers in it.

This brief section closes with two solemn statements proverbial in tone and 6:24-25
set in parallel (v. 24), and a concluding exhortation (v. 25).

Sages, Salvation of the World

Sages, the wise, are seen as the "salvation of the world". The δέ of v. 24 creates a neat opposition with the previous mention of envy. The term σωτηρία has a very broad significance and indicates, rather generally as elsewhere in the book (cf. 16:6; 18:7), liberation from evils. In this stich, however, our author's perspective does not seem to be eschatological (cf., on the other hand, 5:2). Taking up what he had already said in Wis 6:21, "Solomon" intends to emphasise that the liberation of the world from evil, its salvation from every peril, will come only from the presence of the wise.

The second part of v. 24, set in close parallel with the first, reinforces the idea that the text is referring polemically to the Romans but, at the same time is returning to the traditional relationship between kingship and wisdom: cf. Prov 29:4; Qoh 10:16; Sir 10:1, 3; *Let. Aris.* 124-125 and, with other emphases, already in Plato, *Resp.* 5.473d. What saves the world is not kingship in itself so much as the wisdom of the ruler. It is not the king as such who gives stability (εὐστάθεια) to the people, but his prudence (here, compared with σοφός, the adjective φρόνιμος places the stress more on practical wisdom). The book of Wisdom's vision of the world is very optimistic, with a hint of Utopia. Without wisdom, the world cannot be governed, but it is possible to hope for a "multitude of wise men".

The final reference to education (v. 25) reminds us that the wisdom being spoken of is that which has been described in 6:17-20, the wisdom that comes from God and leads to God. The verse opens with a consecutive ὥστε: "so". The use of παιδεύω brings us back to 6:11 and so connects us with the παιδεία mentioned at the very beginning (Wis 1:5). Israel's wisdom offers people an education, παιδεία which has no need to envy the Greek one, an education which constitutes a true benefit for the whole of humanity. In Wis 5:8, the ungodly asked what had been the use (τί ὠφέλησεν) of their foolish behaviour. Here, in the second and last occurrence of the verb παιδεύω in the book, that only wisdom is of any use.

Diachronic Analysis

6:22 The use of μυστήριον leads to thought of the book of Daniel (cf. Dan 2:18, 19, 28, 29, 30, and 47), but the significance of this term is certainly broader and makes one think immediately of the mystery cults.

Here we are on a plane that is antithetical to the mystery cults spread throughout the Hellenistic world. These were destined only for the initiates and covered by a rigorous secrecy which was their most evident external characteristic.[31] In Wis 6:22b, the use of ἀποκρύπτω should be read as a polemical allusion against the secrecy which characterised this type of cult. No secret and no initiation are required to understand the "mysteries" of wisdom. These are available to all who wish to welcome her.

Verse 22c presents the problem of deciding whether γένεσις should be referred to the creation of wisdom or the creation of the world. Opinions are equally divided.[32] We note that ἐξιχνιάζω is employed in connection with wisdom in Sir 1:3-4; 24:28; and Job 28:27, texts on which our author seems to depend. On the basis of Gen 1:1 (ἀρχή) and 2:4 (γένεσις), one could think that he is intending to retrace the origins of wisdom back to the beginning of creation. He would thus be operating within a well-established sapiential tradition, starting with Prov 8:22-30; cf. Job 28:21-23; Sir 1:4, 9; and 24:8. Nonetheless, in Wis 7-10, our author is not concerned to emphasis the precedence of wisdom over creation as in Prov 8:22-30, but simply wants to trace its origin. Then the text of Wis 7:5 must be considered. There the combination γενέσεως ἀρχήν appears with reference to human birth. So, one could hold that the same combination, in 22c, may indicate the origin, that is, the birth of wisdom which is the starting point for our sage's study.

Finally, in 6:22d, the term γνῶσις is deployed in a deliberately anti-gnostic sense: the knowledge bound up with wisdom is open to the light and at the disposition of all. It is not reserved, therefore, for the elect few. Philo too will be very hard on this aspect of the mystery cults. In fact, obscurity is not fitting for the divine (*Spec.* 1.319-325).

6:23 In 6:23, our author makes use of an idea that comes from Plato: φθόνος ἔξω θείου χοροῦ ἵσταται "envy is not a member of the divine choir" (*Phaedr.* 247a, quoted by Philo in *Spec.* 2.249 and *Prob.* 13; cf. Aristotle, *Metaph.* 983a 2-3). In Wisdom, envy is a quality of the devil (2:24). The closest parallels are in Philo: envy is incompatible with wisdom: "wisdom is the most divine and the most

31 Cf. Burkert, Walter, *Ancient Mystery Cults,* Cambridge (Mass.): Harvard University Press 1987, *passim.*

32 Cf. a detailed discussion in Larcher, *Sagesse*, 2:436-437, and Scarpat, *Sapienza*, 1:392. They both choose the first option.

generous (θειότατον καὶ κοινωνικώτατον) of things" (*Prob.* 13). In the Stoic conception, envy consists in feeling pain at the good of others (cf. *SVF* III, 100-101 frags. 413-415). The wise person has no relation (οὐ κοινωνήσει) with envy and is able to offer the wisdom he has received to all.

6:24a contains a polemical point against the Romans. Already, in the period 6:24-25
of Augustus, they had begun to call the emperor "saviour". This had happened for some time precisely in Egypt with the Ptolemaic monarchy.[33] However, despite the reference to the "king" in the following stich, our author has in mind primarily every type of sage. The book of Wisdom is thus taking up an idea dear to Philo also (cf. *QG* 3.44) and emphasising the social and political importance of the wise.

Summary

For our author, the wisdom presented in Wisdom is not comparable to a body of doctrine or to a collection of revealed truths. The personification of wisdom helps us to understand that she is being imagined as real presence which pre-exists human beings and so too their desires which she comes to meet.[34]

The first part (6:1-11) is linked to the initial exhortation of the book (especially to 1:6-10) However, the language and the judicial tone prolong the images of the judgement of the ungodly that was described in Wis 5. This exhortation is addressed to the "kings": primarily, the future leaders of the Jewish community of Alexandria. The search for wisdom guarantees a correct exercise of power. Here, there emerges an idea typical of Stoicism: only the sage is truly a king. In this way, the kingdom promised in 6:17-21 is to be understood as the rule of the sage over his own passions.

At the centre of the exhortation, in vv. 12-16, our author suddenly changes key. The language now becomes persuasive and attractive. Wisdom is described as a woman who comes to meet the man who is searching for her and, in turn, allows herself to be found by the one who desires her. This is a preparation for the subject of the second part of the book, the *elogium* on wisdom. However, there is still room to show how the desire for wisdom leads people to incorruptibility and to participation in God's own kingship (6:17-21). This has therefore to be understood in an eschatological key as participation in the eternal kingdom of God (cf. Wis 3:8).

Thus, the path marked out in Wis 6:17-21 is clear: the desire for wisdom leads to the true *paideia*, to the observance of the laws and, in the end, to incorruptibility. This, in its turn, leads people to stand close to God and makes them share in

---

33 Cf. Larcher, *Sagesse*, 2:439. There is more complete documentation with a more extended bibliography in Spicq, *Notes*, Supp. 629-643. For the Ptolemies, the use of σωτήρ in connection with the king is established from the time of Ptolemy I. For Augustus σωτήρ, cf. the famous inscription of the calendar of Priene in *OGIS* 458.

34 Larcher (*Sagesse*, 2:420) associates this idea with the Christian concept of *gratia praeveniens*. Cf., also, Hübner, *Weisheit*, 85-86.

God's eternal kingdom. Hence, everything begins from that movement of mutual searching between people and wisdom which our sage had described in the previous pericope (vv. 12-16).

As for Wis 6:22-25, the analysis of the literary structure has already shown that what we have here is a literary hinge which closes the first part and opens the second, the *elogium* on wisdom. This wisdom, still closely bound up with justice, is also linked to salvation. This thus anticipates a theme which characterises chapter 10 in a particular way (cf. Wis 9:18).

Introduction to the Second Part (Wis 7-9)

Wisdom is the protagonist of the second part of the book. She is presented in chapters 7-8. This is a unitary text placed in the mouth of a fictitious narrator who implies that he is King Solomon.[1] In chapter 9, at the heart of the book, this "Solomon" prays to obtain the gift of wisdom.

Wis 7-9: An "*Elogium*"

Wis 7-9 should be read within the context of the literary genre of the *encomium*, representing the eponymous praise properly (the "*elogium*", to use the language employed by Beauchamp, Gilbert, and Bizzeti).[2] To be more precise, Wis 6:22-25 should be regarded as the proemium of the *elogium* itself. There, at the end of the first part of the book, our sage announces what he intends to deal with next: the nature (cf. 7:22b-23), the origin (cf. 7:25-26), and the works of wisdom (cf. 7:27-8:1). All this happens in the centre of the *elogium*: in 7:22b-23 (nature), 7:25-26 (origin) and 7:27-8:1 (works).[3]

Chapter 7 opens with an unexpected development concerning the weakness of Solomon (7:1-6). This can be understood as the author's rhetorical reflection on his own inadequacy to speak about the object of the *elogium*, i.e., wisdom. It is a type of reflection which is not infrequent as a topic in the *elogium*. At the same time, 7:1-6 contains a repetition of the theme of chapter 6: thanks to wisdom, everyone can become a king. We are thus in the presence of a real democratisation of monarchy. This is a clear message for diaspora Israel, which no longer has a king.[4] It is noticeable in the conclusion of Wis 7-8, that is, 8:17-21, where the theme of wisdom as the gift of God is presented with greater clarity according to the concentric scheme of these two chapters (cf. below).

Moreover, the two sections of Wis 7:7-12 and 7:13-22a constitute an autobiographical movement. In fact, in both sections, and especially in 7:13-22a, there are elements relating to the nature, the properties, the characteristics, and the work of wisdom, the object of the *encomium*. The section 7:7-12 can be placed, then, in relation to the topic of the ἐπιτηδεύματα, the kind of life, that is, the "choice" of the value which is the object of the *elogium* and made by the person used as an example, in this case Solomon.

This unexpected autobiographical movement can be explained in two ways. First of all, our author wants to make his discourse on wisdom attractive to the young Jews to whom the book is addressed. He does this by presenting his own

1 "Speaking as the long-dead Solomon (cf. chs. 7-8), the rhetor addresses the 'judges of the earth' and kings (1:1; 6:1), likely only a rhetorical device, and yet it was possible for rhetors who represented constituencies to address public assemblies, gathered for open lectures, or to make a presentation in the prefect's court. In addition, the setting could have been a public forum in which a rhetor would have uttered his speech". Cf. Perdue, *The Sword and the Stylus*, 324, nn. 113 and 115.

2 Cf. Beauchamp, *De libro Sapientiae*, 1-40; Gilbert, "Sagesse de Salomon", 77-87; Bizzeti, "Il libro della Sapienza", 168-172. On the theme of the *topoi* of the *encomium* in Greek rhetoric and the differences in Wisdom, cf. Engel, *Das Buch Weisheit*, 120-123.

3 Cf. Leproux, *Un discours de sagesse*, 101-106.

4 Cf. Newman, "Democraticization of Kingship", especially p. 327; Hübner, *Weisheit*, 94.

character as a king and at the same time as a mortal like other folk (7:1-6). Furthermore, he takes up elements that belong not only to the *elogium* of a divinity or a virtue but even more to the *elogium* of a person. These correspond to the topic of the *elogium* such as is described for us in the works of Menander the Rhetorician.[5] In the two sections 8:2-9 and 8:10-16, our author returns again to this autobiographical theme. However, he does not forget wisdom, the object of his *elogium*. In 8:2-9, and in particular in 8:2-3, the topic of the ἐπιτηδεύματα, resurfaces while, in Wis 8:10-16, the theme of the actions and virtues of the person being praised appears.

Prominent in the scheme of the *elogium* is the prayer for obtaining wisdom (Wis 9). The theme of prayer is not totally absent from encomiastic literature, but, in this case, the aim of Wis 9 is not to sing the praises of wisdom, her origin, her nature or her works, although all of these are not absent. Without any doubt, Wis 9 is not a prayer to wisdom but a prayer to God to give wisdom. From this point of view, chapter 9 is undoubtedly original. Our sage is employing the epideictic literary genre, but, in the light of Wis 9, the content of his *elogium* is profoundly biblical.

5 In this connection, I refer to the detailed analysis of Leproux, *Un discours de sagesse*, 94-101.

Wis 7-8:
The Elogium of Wisdom

The Literary Structure of Wis 7-8[1]

Wis 7:1-6: Solomon, a Mortal Like Everyone

Wis 7:1-6 forms a first strophe. This is clear from the *inclusio* between ἴσος ἅπασιν (v. 1a) and πάντων ... ἴση (v. 6); cf. also πᾶσιν ἴσα in 7:3c. The μέν which opens v. 1 (εἰμὶ μὲν κἀγω) is matched by the δέ of v. 6. The strophe is concentric, at least on the thematic level: v. 1ab contains a statement about "Solomon", a mortal like everyone; 1c-2 describes what happened before his birth; at the centre, v. 3a describes his birth with the metaphor of breath; in parallel with vv. 1c-2, vv. 3b-4, describe the beginning of his earthly life; finally, vv. 5-6 return to the initial idea of "Solomon" as a mortal like everyone. Thus, seven elements appear that characterise the entire human experience: conception; (vv. 1-2); embryonic state; the moment of birth; the first breath; the first wail (v. 3); weaning (v. 4); and death (v. 6).

Wis 7:7-12: Wisdom, Mother of Every Good

A second strophe is identifiable in 7:7-12. Here, too, one can observe some examples of *inclusio.* Ἦλθέν μοι in 7:7b is matched by ἦλθεν δέ μοι in 11a; the term σοφία appears in 7:7b immediately after ἦλθέν μοι and reappears in 12a; to which must be added the double occurrence of πλοῦτος in 8b and11b.

After v. 7, which acts as an introduction, vv. 8-10b contain in seven stichs the description of the goods which Solomon has rejected in favour of wisdom, a description which closes in 10c. Verse 7 looks a little isolated and, with its mention of prayer, recalls the concluding passage of the *elogium* in 8:21. For this reason, it can be considered as the *propositio* of the *elogium* itself.[2] Verses 11-12 then close with the statement that wisdom is γενέτις of every good.

Wis 7:13-22a

A preliminary note: vv. 13-14 are difficult to place. We could consider the repetition of πλοῦτος in 13b as a hook-word with the previous occurrence in 11b. Verse 13 then recalls in a quite explicit way, the themes announced in 6:22b–23 (particularly that of envy), thus underlining a new beginning. Moreover, the double τε of v. 13a marks an asyndetic beginning which, in the style of the book, emphasises a separation from the preceding material.

Wisdom Communicated to Solomon

A third strophe is represented by 7:13-22a; an inclusion can be observed between ἀποκρύπτομαι in 13b and κρυπτά in 21. Verses 13-14 introduce the paragraph (see above). Verses 15-17a (v. 15a is parallel to 17a) form a first movement in seven stichs, relating Solomon's request to God for wisdom (whereby 7:15a and 7:17a are construed as an inclusion: ἐμοὶ δὲ δῴη ... γνώμην / μοι ἔδωκεν ... γνῶσιν). Verses. 17b-20 make up a second movement, it too in seven stichs. It concerns Solomon's knowledge. There is no true break between 17a and 17b. Verses 21-22 conclude the strophe, emphasising that wisdom is τεχνῖτις, crafts-

---

1 Cf. Wright, "The Structure", 173; Gilbert, "Sagesse de Salomon", 69-71; Bizzeti, *Il libro della Sapienza*, 69-72. For a different perspective, cf. Leproux, *Un discours de sagesse*, 34-38.38-72.

2 Cf. Leproux, *Un discours de sagesse*, 46.

man, of everything. The primary theme is thus the communication of divine knowledge to Solomon.

Wis 7:22b-8:1: The Description of Wisdom

At the centre of Wis 7-8, we find a fourth strophe: Wis 7:22b-8:1. Here is the description of the nature, the origin, and the action of wisdom.

The text of 7:22b-23 forms a first unit, which is a little isolated. It contains a series of twenty-one attributes of wisdom marked by a triple *inclusio*: πνεῦμα – νοερόν – λεπτόν (22bc) and πνευμάτων – νοερῶν – λεπτοτάτων (23de). There is a clear connection with the following section (7:24-8:1) by means of two clear hook-words: χωροῦν – καθαρῶν (23de) and χωρεῖ – καθαρειότητα (24b).

The text of 7:24-8:1 forms a second unit, marked by the *inclusio* πάσης – [διήκει] – πάντων (7:24) and [διοικεῖ] – πάντα (8:1b). Furthermore, 7:24 and 8:1 correspond with a certain parallelism. We can thus discern in 7:24-8:1 yet another concentric structure:[3] in 7:24, there is a description of the movement of wisdom (in fact, on the thematic level, v. 24 can be considered the conclusion of vv. 22-23); in 7:25-26, in six stichs, there are five metaphorical expressions concerning the nature of wisdom. In vv. 27-28, at the centre of the passage, there is a description of the omnipotence of wisdom and of God's love for those who dwell with her.

Verses 29-30, in five stichs, describe wisdom under the metaphor of light. In parallel with 7:24, 8:1 closes the strophe, emphasising the presence of wisdom in the universe.

Wis 8:2-9: Wisdom, Wife, Counsellor, Friend

A fifth strophe can be identified in 8:2-9: Solomon decides to take wisdom as his wife and also as his counsellor and friend. The *inclusio* is clear: ἀγαγέσθαι ... συμβίωσιν (2b, 3a) and ἀγαγέσθαι πρὸς συμβίωσιν (9a). The weight of this *inclusio* obliges us to consider v. 9 as the final passage of the strophe. Five substantives are used to indicate wisdom: μύστις (v. 4a), αἱρετίς (v. 5b), τεχνῖτις (v. 6b), σύμβουλος and παραίνεσις (v. 9), thus conferring further unity on the strophe.

Verses 2-4 make up an introduction concerning Solomon's search for wisdom (four aorists, v. 2) and wisdom seen in its relationship with God (vv. 3-4). Verse 5 is set in parallel with v. 6. In both cases, there are two stichs in the form of a question introduced by εἰ δὲ. Next, v. 7 is parallel to v. 8. Five stichs are introduced by καὶ εἰ ... τις. Thus, between 8:5 and 8:8, we have fourteen stichs in which the author expresses wisdom's superiority over created goods. This is because she is their τεχνῖτις (cf. 7:22a). Verse 9 then forms the conclusion of the strophe as a whole (τοίνυν).

In this strophe, we find the reprise of other terms already encountered in 7:13-22a: ἐπιστήμη (8:4a and 7:16b); πλοῦτος (8:5a; 7:13b); φρόνησις (8:6a; 7:13b). We note καιρῶν καὶ χρόνων (8:8e) and the same occurrence of the two terms, set in parallel at the end of the two stichs of 7:18. Finally, the verbs are in the present or the aorist and are to be distinguished from the futures of vv. 10-16.

These repetitions are at the service of theological emphases.[4] In both strophes, the fourth and fifth, wisdom is being presented as something which is superior to any other form of wealth (cf. 7:13-14; 8:5). It is from the wisdom that comes from God that φρόνησις and ἐπιστήμη (cf. 7:15-16 and 8:6; ἐπιστήμη in 8:4 has a

---

3 For the details, cf. Leproux, *Un discours de sagesse*, 53-56

4 Cf. Bizzeti, *Il libro della Sapienza*, 69-70.

different sense) originate. Everything can be known through wisdom (7:17-21 and 8:8: cf., especially, 8:8c).

Wis 8:10-16: Solomon's Expectations and Hopes

In the following strophe, 8:10-16, in a kind of monologue, Solomon describes his own expectations and hopes in connection with receiving wisdom. The term συμβίωσις (8:3, 9:16), which occurs only in Sir^{B} 34:22 as a variant of ἐμβίωσις, "means of subsistence", creates a strong link with the previous section and is a clue to the conclusion of the strophe. Cf. also ἀνδρεῖος in 15b which recalls ἀνδρεία in 8:7d. We note again that the verbs are all in the future. In the centre of the strophe, v. 13 is constructed in close parallel with the beginning of the passage. In this verse, the stress is moved on to what happens after death:

ἕξω δι' αὐτὴν δόξαν ... καὶ τιμήν (8:10)
ἕξω δι' αὐτὴν ἀθανασίαν ... καὶ μνήμην (8:13).

Verses 10-12, in seven stichs, describe the fame to be acquired through wisdom. Verses 14-16, again in seven stichs, describe Solomon's royal power which was obtained through wisdom. The repetition of ἐν ὄψει in 8:11b recalls the same expression from 7:9b (cf. also 3:4; 14:17; and 15:19). In 7:9, gold is as nothing in comparison with wisdom; in 8:11, the wise man is respected in the presence of the powerful. In both strophes (7:7-12 and 8:10-16), wisdom appears superior to the goods that usually belong to the king.

Wis 8:17-21: Prayer for Obtaining Wisdom

The final strophe of the *elogium* is in 8:17-21. 9:1 marks the clear beginning of a new pericope, the prayer for obtaining wisdom. The *inclusio* ἐν καρδίᾳ μου – τῆς καρδίας μου provides a very good demarcation for the strophe (cf. vv. 17b, 21d). Then, the term ἀθανασία links it with the preceding material (8:13 and 17). As in Wis 8:2-9 and by contrast with Wis 8:10-16, all the verbs are in the present or in the aorist (except for ἔσομαι which acts as a bridge with chapter 9).

Once again, as in 7:1-6, the underlying theme is the weakness of Solomon and, as in 8:2-9, the search for wisdom. However, the vocabulary takes up a series of themes that were scattered throughout Wis 7-8.[5] These verses thus take on the value of a real recapitulation. Taking up the orientation towards prayer already expressed in 7:7, they now direct the reader towards the prayer for obtaining wisdom which follows immediately in 9:1.

On the level of internal structure, the strophe permits the identification of a certain parallelism between 8:17-18 and 8:21. The aorist participles λογισάμενος und φροντίσας precede an object clause beginning with ὅτι (8:17a-18d), whereupon only then the verb with the rest of the main clause follows (8,18d). Similarly, in 8:21a an aorist participle and an object clause beginning with ὅτι (γνοὺς δὲ ὅτι) stand at the head of the phrase, and the verbs with the rest of the main clause (8:21c-d) appear only after the parenthetical (8:21b).[6] In this way, vv. 19-20 are at the centre of the literary process and with their reference back to the theme of Wis 7:1-6 form an *interjectory epiphonema* (cf. the comment).

5 Cf. the details in Wright, "The Structure", 194 and Bizzeti, *Il libro della Sapienza*, 70. Wis 8:17-21 takes up a series of words already present in 8:2-9: ζητέω (2b, 18e); πλοῦτος (5, 18b); φρόνησις (6, 7c, 18c, 21b); πόνος (7b, 18b); εἰδέναι (9b, 21b); φροντίς, φροντίζω (9c, 17b); εὐγένεια, συγγένεια (3, 17c). As for the reprise of elements belonging to 8:10-16, cf. ἀθανασία in 8:13, 17c and again ἀγαθός in 8:15b and 19b.

6 Cf. Leproux, *Un discours de sagesse*, 65 and 67.

A Concentric Structure

In sum, the two outer sections of 7-8 contain two strophes which emphasise Solomon's weakness (7:1-6 and 8:17-21) and so the need to turn to God for obtaining wisdom (8:17-21, which is taken up in 7:7). In the inner frame, two other strophes (7:7-12 and 8:10-16) underline the superiority of wisdom over all the goods which a king could desire. The third and the fifth strophes (7:13-22a and 8:2-9) correspond, placing the emphasis on wisdom's superiority to the benefits which come from culture and, in the fifth strophe, underlining the characteristics of wisdom herself as wife and friend. At the centre of the whole movement occurs the description of the nature, origin, and activity of wisdom (7:22b-8:1). The conclusions of the second and third strophes (7: 2, 22a) have already prepared the reflection on the active role of wisdom, γενέτις and τεχνῖτις (cf. 8:6). The wisdom which is with God (centre of the passage) becomes the wisdom that is communicated to Solomon.

Wis 7:1-6: Weakness of "Solomon"

1 I too am a mortal man, like everyone,
descendant of the first formed, born from the earth.
My flesh was fashioned in my mother's womb,
2 in the space of ten months curdled in blood
from the seed of a man and from the pleasure that accompanies sleep.
3 At birth, I too breathed the common air
and fell upon that earth which is the same for all.
Just as for all, my first sound was a cry.
4 I was nursed with swaddling clothes and surrounded with care
5 No king has had a different origin of his existence:
5 there is one entrance into life for all, and its exit is common.

Notes on the Text and Translation

vv. 1-2. Γηγενοῦς ἀπόγονος πρωτοπλάστου. The combination of these three words is particularly interesting. Ἀπόγονος, "born from, descending", is found in 2 Sam 21:11; 1 Chr 20:6; Jud 5:6, but it is rare and refined. The term *πρωτόπλαστος is absent in the LXX (cf. Wis 10:1) and in the NT. Larcher (*Sagesse*, 2:444; cf. Winston, *Wisdom*, 163) hypothesises that our sage believes in personal creation. The term appears in a fragment of Philo (*QE* 2.46). Πρωτόπλαστος indicates the "first formed" and is an allusion to Gen 2:7 LXX (ἔπλασεν ὁ θεὸς τὸν ἄνθρωπον χοῦν ἀπὸ τῆς γῆς). The term γηγενής, on the other hand, is known to Philo in contexts relating to the first created human being (cf. *Opif.* 169: ἐκεῖνος δ' ὁ πρῶτος ἄνθρωπος ὁ γηγενής; cf. also *Virt.* 199 and 203). In Greek usage, it recalls the myth of the first men who came out of the earth (cf. Herodotus, *Hist.* 8.55 and Plato, *Pol.* 269b). Both Philo and Wisdom could have used γηγενής to show that what is being narrated in Gen 2:7 (the man fashioned χοῦν ἀπὸ τῆς γῆς; cf. Ps 48:3 LXX) represents the true account of the origin of humanity.

In 2b, some mss (S, V and many minuscules; cf. Lat, Syr, Arab), read the genitive ὕπνου instead of the dative ὕπνῳ; cf. Blomqvist, "Interpretational Problems", 99-101; cf. also Gilbert, "La procreazione", 68 nn. 17 and 21, who supports the majority reading.

vv. 3-4. The adjective *ὁμοιοπαθής refers to people and not to things in every case in which it appears in the LXX or the NT (4 Macc 12:13; Acts 14:15; Jas 5:15). It means "who experiences the same sufferings" or "who suffers / feels in the same way". Fichtner (*Weisheit Salomos*, 28) translates 7:3b with: "and (I) fell upon the earth, which suffers in the same way". He accounts for his translation thus: "That the earth suffers in the same way can be justified literally, but is conceptually distant". Thus, one can follow the opinion of Scarpat (*Sapienza*, 2:94): here, the reference is not so much to the *people* who experience the same sufferings on earth as to the *earth* which experiences the same things on the part of all human beings, as something which "is the same for all".

Synchronic Analysis

Wis 7:1-2: Solomon, a Man Like Everyone

"I too (κἀγὼ) am a mortal man, like everyone". Solomon's presentation of himself is programmatic: no human being can boast of any superiority to the others. "Like everyone" is repeated as an *inclusio* at the beginning and end of the strophe, with reference to birth and death (7:1a, 6).

Verse 1 continues by recalling that everyone, Solomon included, is like the first human being, taken from the earth. 7:1b is thus alluding to Gen 2:7, introducing a reference to Scripture. To emphasise Solomon's complete equality with every other human being, Wisdom goes on to describe his birth in three stichs (1c-2). The formation of a person in his mother's womb is treated with general reference to the contemporary medico-scientific theories, especially those deriving from Aristotle. However, they are woven into a profound biblical pattern (see below).[7]

7:3-4: Birth and Death

Birth and death make everyone equal (cf. Qoh 2:14-15; Sir 40:1-2). To emphasise this radical equality, our sage makes use of literary *motifs* well known to the Greeks which give the text a pessimistic hue (see below). The earth on which Solomon "was thrown" (v. 3b) is the same for all, and the first sound of every human being is the cry of the new-born. By means of the figure of *zeugma*, v. 4 reminds us that, like every new-born baby, Solomon needed continual care ("swaddling clothes") and the concern of his parents (φροντίς).

7:5-6

The origin of life is the same for all, even for kings (v. 5). People come into (εἴσοδος) and go out of (ἔξοδος; cf. 3:2) life in the same way (v. 6). The syntagma γενέσεως ἀρχήν could be a further allusion to the time of creation (cf. Gen 1:1 LXX: ἀρχή; and 2:4 LXX: γένεσις), even if the reference here is clearly to birth (cf. 6:22c). The return of the royal theme and the link with the Genesis narrative serve to clarify the reason for the negative tone of the strophe. This is sharpened by the use of *topoi* common in the Hellenistic culture, a further sign of our author's way of proceeding by creating almost a Greek *midrash* on the creation account.[8]

7 Cf. Gilbert, "La procréation", 341-346; Bons, "Conception, grossesse, naissance", *passim*.

8 Cf. Leproux, *Un discours de sagesse*, 145.

Diachronic Analysis

7:1 Behind such a decisive statement ("I am a mortal man, like everyone"), it is not difficult to discern a polemic against the Hellenistic conception of monarchy. Both the Ptolemies and the Roman emperors, beginning with Augustus, tended to divinise themselves. The text of Wis 14:17-20 will be still more explicit in its refutation of this idea. The humanity of the king is a common feature in the Hellenistic treatises on kingship, but in these texts the king appears as the "superior" among human beings, just as God – of whom the king is an incarnation – is superior to all.[9] It should be observed that θνητός is a rare word in the LXX and without a true Semitic equivalent although it is very frequent in Greek usage. Our sage is thus presenting "Solomon" in a way which his Hellenised public will be better able to understand.[10]

However, there is another reason for such a clear statement on Solomon's mortality. We have seen that, in Wisdom, the metaphor of kingship was influenced by the Stoic concept of the wise man understood as the true king. "Solomon" is king because he is wise. This wisdom does not derive from any superiority of his on the human level; it is the gift of God which has been obtained through prayer. Verse 1 thus refers directly to v. 7: "therefore, I prayed to obtain wisdom". Like Solomon, therefore, everyone can obtain wisdom.

7:1-2: Solomon's Birth

The gestation of the embryo lasts for ten months (or, better, is completed in the tenth month; cf. 4 Macc 16:7), which constituted the optimal duration of a successful gestation according to the ancients.[11] The embryo is formed in the mother's womb (ἐν κοιλίᾳ μητρὸς) thanks to the coming together of three factors: the menstrual blood of the woman "clotted with blood" (by itself, πήγνυμι indicates the clotting or curdling of milk; cf. Aristotle, *Gen. an.* 729a 11), the seed of the man, and the pleasure experienced in the sexual act (2b: euphemistically, "sleep"). Thus, whereas 1b-2a refers to the passive role of the woman, 2b refers to the active part of the man.

Sexual pleasure is mentioned here completely naturally. There is no negative nuance to ἡδονή as will happen later in the NT. The mention of the male seed means that the reference is to the pleasure of the man and not that of the woman. Our author is basing himself on the medical theories current in the Greek sphere (cf. Hippocrates, *Genit.* 1.1; 4.1-2) according to which it is the man and not the woman who experiences pleasure in the act of generation. This pleasure generates that heat which allows the male seed to coagulate the female blood (cf. Aristotle, *Gen. an.* 739a 32-33). It is from this that the embryo originates.

Our author shows here that he is aware, at least in general terms, of the Aristotelian theory according to which the menstrual blood of the woman is the material cause of the embryo while the sperm is its efficient cause (cf. *Gen. an.*

---

9 Cf. Winston, *Wisdom*, 162-163; cf. also the texts cited in Scarpat, *Sapienza*, 2:18-22, who also mentions the figure of Caligula, to whose reign he attributes the composition of Wisdom. For the figure of the sovereign as superior to all, cf. Diogenes, 72.16-19 (ed. Hense). He is the θεὸς ἐν ἀνθρώποις (72.22-23).

10 Bons, "Conception, grossesse, naissance", 76.

11 Evidence in Gilbert, "La procréation", 343; Larcher, *Sagesse*, 2:446; Winston, *Wisdom*, 163-165, and especially in Scarpat, *Sapienza*, 2:23-28.

727a–728b). The heat generated by the male pleasure causes the female blood to "coagulate" within the male seed thus giving birth to the embryo. The latter is, therefore, to be considered already as a person since "Solomon" is speaking of himself. However, the book of Wisdom does not seem to have a particular theory of the development of the embryo and, in this case, avoids speaking of the soul, an idea which it will introduce in Wis 15:11. The use of σάρξ in 1c is, in this case, more biblical than Greek, and already indicates the "person" in his totality.

Finally, we should notice the poetic beauty of the images portrayed here. "Fashioning flesh" recalls the "weaving together" of Ps 139:13 and the "curdling" reminds us of Job 10:10 ("you made me curdling [ἐτύρωσας] as cheese"). They refer sensitively to the action of God who is at the origin of life. The verb γλύφω, "fashion", returns in Wis 13:13c where it is employed in connection with the idolater who carves an idol, but the image is unique in the Bible.

Verse 3a is an exact quotation from Menander (cited, in turn, in Plutarch, 7:3-4
Cons. Apoll. 103c-e) who, in relation to the baby who has just been born, recalls that he too breathed the common air (ἔσπασας τὸν ἀέρα τὸν κοινὸν). No one differs from the others. When they are born, all enter into the same world of sufferings. Menander makes clear that this way of speaking belongs to the language of the tragedians (καὶ τραγικώτερον λαλῶ). In addition, Plutarch comments: "not to be born is the greatest of all goods and to be dead is of more value than to live" (*Cons. Apoll.* 115c11). Wisdom is, therefore, evoking a tragic vision of life, frequent in the Greek world, but not entirely alien from Scripture (cf. Job 3:11; 10:18).[12]

Moreover, the theme of falling on the earth (3b) is another common *topos* in the ancient world. Cf. Lucretius, *Rer. Nat.* 5.222-227, who adds the theme of the person who has been flung down to earth like a castaway without knowing why.[13] The verb καταπίπτω returns in Wis 13:16 (about the standing idol, that it might now "fall down") and again in Wis 17:15 to express the sad condition of the Egyptians, but also to allude to their being cast into Hades.[14]

Finally, the idea in v. 4 – the baby needing care – could be echoing classical texts; cf. Aeschylus, *Cho.* 751-760.

By contrast with the Greek world, which emphasises death as the common human heritage, our sage prefers to put the stress on the moment of birth, as if it signified for people the beginning of their "being for death".

---

12 Cf. Leproux, *Un discours de sagesse,* 126-130. Leproux suggests that, in this context, κοινός acquires a negative nuance and takes on the sense of "profane" contrasted with the ἅγιος of the πνεῦμα in Wis 7:22, thus giving Menander's quotation a tone that is clearly more religious.

13 Cf. Scarpat, *Sapienza*, 2:95-96, who notes that the *proici* of Lucretius is a good illustration of the use of κατέπεσον by Wisdom (*tum porro puer ut saevis proiectus ab undis / navita, nudus humi iacet infans indigus omni / vitali auxilio ...*). For other citations, cf. Winston, *Wisdom*, 166.

14 Cf. Mazzinghi, *Notte di paura e di luce,* 27 n. 83.

Wis 7:7-12: Love Wisdom

[7] Therefore, I prayed, and prudence was given to me;
I called, and there came to me the spirit of wisdom.
[8] I preferred her to sceptres and thrones,
and wealth I held as nothing in comparison to her.
[9] I did not liken her to a precious stone, however priceless,
for, compared with her, all gold is a handful of sand,
and, in comparison to her, silver is reckoned as clay.
[10] I loved her more than health and beauty,
I chose to have her as light,
for the brightness which hails from her never sets.
[11] Together with her, there came to me all goods.
Incalculable wealth is in her hands.
[12] From all these goods I experienced joy, because wisdom guides them,
but I did not know that she was their mother.

Notes on the Text and Translation

v. 9. Ἀτίμητος, only in 3 Macc 3:23 in the LXX, has the sense of "priceless", "inestimable". This meaning is unknown to secular Greek where the word signifies, rather, "despised" (Scarpat, *Sapienza*, 2:99).
The idea of "sand" (Wisdom employs *ψάμμος) was suggested by 3 Kgdms 5:9 [1 Kgs 5:9 MT]: "and the Lord gave Solomon great prudence and wisdom in abundance (φρόνησιν ... καὶ σοφίαν πολλὴν σφόδρα) and largeness of heart like the sand (ἄμμος) which is by the sea".

v. 10. The expression προειλόμην ἀυτὴν ἀντὶ φωτὸς ἔχειν does not mean "I preferred her to the light", but "I chose to have her instead of light". Scarpat (*Sapienza*, 2:100-101) sees in προαιρέω an allusion to the Stoic idea of προαίρεσις the "pre-decision" understood as a value judgement on things.
In Aeschylus (*Prom.* 139), the adjective *ἀκοίμητος, "which does not rest, which does not sleep", refers to the Ocean which girds the earth with unceasing currents. Here, it is used of the light and could have eschatological resonance: to choose wisdom as light means choosing a life without end.

v. 12. The expression v. 12a, ὅτι αὐτῶν ἡγεῖται σοφία is understood by the Latin version as *quoniam antecedebat ista sapientia*; that is, wisdom bears within herself all the goods which she offers to Solomon. In itself, the verb ἡγεόμαι indicates "guiding" or "governing" whereas, in Wis 1:16; 7:8; 12:15; and 17:6, it always has the meaning of "considering". However, ἡγέομαι is employed by Plato in contexts relating to the value of goods with the sense of "guiding" (cf. *Euthyd.* 280B-281E and other examples in Larcher, *Sagesse*, 2:458). In this optic, it is possible to think of wisdom as "guide" of all the goods that she offers to people. They are legitimate to the degree in which wisdom is directing them.
Γενέτις is a form analogous to τεχνῖτις (7:22 [7:21b in Rahlfs]; 8:6) The term is attested only once in an author of the first century CE (the elegiac poet Aglaias; cf. Liddell-Scott, *sub voce*) and could be an authentic creation from our sage. This could

explain the correction with the more common γένεσις (B-S V and other miniscules plus some secondary variants; cf. Ziegler, *Sapientia*, 67).

Synchronic Analysis

7:7: Therefore I Prayed …

The initial διὰ τοῦτο of v. 7 is correlated with the μέν of v. 1. Thus, Solomon's prayer is motivated by the king's weakness and mortality, something shared by everyone.

The aorist εὐξάμην refers to 1 Kgs 3:11-12; 2 Chr 1:6-12. The verb ἐπεκαλεσάμην is in synonymous parallelism. In the LXX, it always has religious force and is to be referred to the calling on God in prayer.[15] The verb ἐδόθη, indicating the positive result of the prayer, is a divine passive. It is from God, in fact, that φρόνησις and the πνεῦμα σοφίας come to Solomon. Here, one could think that φρόνησις is meant to indicate the virtue of prudence within the Greek perspective whereas with πνεῦμα σοφίας our author is intending to recall that "spirit of wisdom" which he has already introduced at the beginning of the book (1:6) and which is a direct reference to the action of the God of Israel.

7:8-10: Wisdom, the Most Important of Goods

The indispensable condition for obtaining wisdom is to consider it the most important of goods (vv. 8-9) and to come to love it more than anything else (v. 10). In these seven stichs, Wisdom develops a *motif* already present in Israel's sapiential texts: cf. Prov 3:13-15; 8:13-21; and Job 28:15-19.

Verse 10bc introduces the comparison with light. Wisdom is superior to light because its brightness (φέγγος) never fades. On the contrary, it is the true light for people.[16]

7:11-12

Entering a debate that was lively in his time (see below), our author does not mean to despise earthly goods. However, for him they are the consequence rather than the cause of happiness. In fact, all possible goods (τὰ ἀγαθὰ πάντα) come to Solomon together with wisdom (cf. 11a). For the theme of incalculable wealth (11b), cf. 1 Kgs 3:13; 10:11-29; 2 Chr 1:12; etc. Now, in Wis 2:6 and 13:1, the ἀγαθά are without any doubt the goods of creation which the ungodly wish to enjoy (ἀπολαύσωμεν) as if they belonged to them (2:6). It is possible, therefore, to give v. 11 an additional nuance. In the logic of the *encomium*, the goods and wealth being spoken of are the description of the φύσις of Solomon, that is, his "natural" qualities, the goods with which wisdom has endowed him.[17]

Verse 12a adds the theme of enjoying the goods gifted by wisdom. Wisdom is then described as the "generatrix", or mother, of every good (12b). Employing a term very rare in Greek usage (γενέτις), our author is intending to show that the wisdom of Israel – and not Greek philosophy! – is the origin of every possible

---

15 Cf. Spicq, *Notes*, Supp., 286-292.

16 The term φέγγος is part of the mystery vocabulary utilised by Plato (*Phaedr.* 250b 3): "there is nothing of the splendour of justice and wisdom and all the other laudable things of the soul in the things here on earth ...". The use of φέγγος has, therefore, a probable polemical import. Cf. Mazzinghi, *Notte di paura e di luce*, 16.

17 Cf. Leproux, *Un discours de sagesse*, 158-163. Cf. also pp. 94-106 where he shows how in Wis 7-8 the rhetoric of an *encomium* on a reality such as wisdom intersects with that of the *encomium* on a person.

good and of the possibility of enjoying them (cf. Philo, *Sobr.* 56; *Virt.* 8). This is because "wisdom guides them", that is, because she leads people to a right use of these same goods and is herself their real good. With γενέτις our sage intends also to give wisdom an active role in creation. Cf. the comment on τεχνῖτις at Wis 7:22a.

Verse 12b is not to be understood in a simplistic way, namely, that at the time when he chose wisdom, Solomon did not know that with it there would also come to him all the other goods which he had rejected. Solomon's ignorance is bound up with his weakness (7:1-6). In Wis 14:18, 22; and 15:11, ignorance is then linked to the lack of knowledge of God and thus to idolatry. Solomon must pass from a state of ignorance to one of knowledge (cf. also v. 13). Wisdom is thus a gift of God on the one hand, and, on the other, the fruit of a searching and of a human path of education.

Diachronic Analysis

Contrary to Greek thought, wisdom is to be sought from God; cf. Jas 1:5. Making use of the good biblical *motif* in1 Kgs 3:4-15 and 2 Chr 1:2-12, this strophe offers an interesting rereading of Solomon's prayer at Gibeon to obtain wisdom as the art of good governance. Our author is thus elaborating another little midrash through which the experience of King Solomon becomes that of every person who searches for and obtains the gift of wisdom.[18]

7:7 As for φρόνησις and πνεῦμα σοφίας, these two expressions also seem to be in synonymous parallelism; cf. 3 Kgdms 3:12 [1 Kgs 3:12 MT] (δέδωκά σοι καρδίαν φρονίμην καὶ σοφήν) and, more clearly, 3 Kgdms 5:9 [1 Kgs 5:9 MT]: καὶ ἔδωκεν κύριος φρόνησιν τῷ Σαλωμων καὶ σοφίαν πολλήν; cf. also Prov 3:13 and 8:1. The term φρόνησις is common in the story of Solomon (cf. 3 Kgdms 10:4; 11:41 [1 Kgs 10:4; 11:41 MT]) and is well known in Greek philosophy (cf. the comment on Wis 3:15). In Wisdom, in this passage only, φρόνησις is associated directly with σοφία (cf., above, 3 Kgdms 5:9 [1 Kgs 5:9 MT]). In Wis 8:21, φρόνησις indicates the virtue of "prudence", that is, of practical wisdom in the sense of Philo and the Stoics.

The expression πνεῦμα [θεῖον] σοφίας appears in Exod 31:3 and 35:31, but above all in Isa 11:2, where it is used with reference to the qualities of the "root of Jesse". The "spirit of wisdom" is thus a reality that comes directly from God and is, at the same time, something internal to people (cf., in 7b, ἦλθέν μοι), an interior principle of knowledge, cf. ἀγνοέω in 12b: Without the gift of wisdom, Solomon "does not know". On the other hand, as has already been seen in Wis 1:4-7, the concept of πνεῦμα is not lacking in links with Stoic philosophy. The "spirit" has become a cosmic reality, albeit stripped of Stoic pantheism (cf. the comment on 9:17).

7:8-10 The list of goods opens with a clear value judgement. In the light of Platonic language (*Leg.* 870b; cf. Philo, *Leg.* 3.52), the verb προκρίνω indicates a choice. Solomon thus prefers wisdom to power ("sceptres and thrones"; cf. 9:7) and to wealth, a theme developed more extensively in v. 9 (cf. Prov 8:10-11). In 1 Kgs

18 Cf. Gilbert, "La figure de Salomon", 145-149, who gives a good sketch of the similarities and differences between the account of 1 Kgs / 2 Chr and the text of Wisdom.

3:13-14, among the goods offered to Solomon along with wisdom and in addition to wealth and glory, longevity also appears. In 1 Kgs 3:11, the death of enemies is not forgotten. The theme of longevity which was already allowed to fall out in the version of 2 Chr 1:11-12, is wholly absent from our text. For Wisdom, in fact, longevity is not something of value in itself (cf. Wis 4:8-16). The theme of the enemies' death is also passed over in silence.

Verse 10 introduces another three factors: Solomon loved wisdom more than health, beauty, and light. As in Wis 1:1, ἀγαπάω, indicates a preferential love, a love which chooses something in the place of something else.

The theme of health is not found as such in the Hebrew Bible; cf. only Sir 30:14-16. Εὐμορφία too causes a typically Greek theme, beauty, to emerge; cf. *Symp.* 218e, where, however, εὐμορφία is considered as external and deceptive beauty by contrast with the true kind (κάλλος). In Wis 8:2, in fact, κάλλος is applied to wisdom. With εὐμορφία, therefore, our sage is referring to an exterior beauty which, by contrast with wisdom, is not authentic beauty.

A Philosophical Debate over the Hierarchy of Goods

According to Winston, this strophe contains an echo of the philosophical debate over whether external goods are important. Wisdom's position would be like that of Philo. One must search for wisdom, and then all the other goods will follow because of divine providence.[19] In a *scholion* recorded by Plato (*Gorg.* 451e), the highest goods (πράγματα) considered classic by the Greek world are health, beauty, and honest wealth (ὑγιαίνειν μὲν ἄριστόν ἐστιν, τὸ δὲ δεύτερον καλὸν γενέσθαι, τρίτον δὲ τὸ πλουτεῖν ἀδόλως). However, they turn into evils if they are not accompanied by wisdom and prudence (cf. *Euthyd.* 281de). In *Leg.* 697b, Plato reserves the term ἀγαθά for the goods of soul and body, excluding wealth, a good which serves the body alone. Aristotle will return to a bipartite division of the goods: those of the soul and those of the body (nobility, friendship, wealth, honour; cf. *Eth. nic.* 1099b 9). Entering the debate between Platonic idealism and the Aristotelian distinction which distances itself from the dualism of Plato, the Stoics characterise external goods as indifferent. A hierarchy of goods is no longer necessary because the only true good is to live according to virtue: "quod si ita est, ut neque quisquam nisi bonus vir et omnes boni beati sint, quid philosophia magis colendum aut quid est virtute divinius?" ["If this be so, that only a good man, and all good men, are happy, what is more to be pursued than philosophy or what is more divine than goodness?"] (Cicero, *Fin.* 3.76).[20]

Our sage enters into this discussion. However, he takes his start from the biblical text of 1 Kgs 3:9-13 // 1 Chr 1:10-12 and from other sapiential texts mentioned above (Prov 3:13-18; 8:18-19; Job 28:15-17). The verbs employed (especially προκρίνω and ἀγαπάω) help us to understand that it is not a question of hierarchies of goods. Wisdom, in fact, surpasses them all. Power, wealth, health, and beauty are all desirable goods, but wisdom is the most desirable of them all. The metaphor of light and brightness orients us to considering wisdom herself as a reality connected with God (cf. 7:26). To the traditional triad (health, beauty, and honest wealth) Wisdom adds power which, for the Stoics, was among indifferent goods but which our sage takes up from his Solomonic context (cf. 1 Kgs 3:9).

19 Cf. Winston, *Wisdom*, 167-168.
20 Cf. a more detailed discussion in Leproux, *Un discours de sagesse*, 147-158.

There thus stands out the "political" dimension of a wisdom that is also a way to a stable and well governed society (cf. also Wis 9:7).

7:12 As for the theme introduced in 12a, the enjoyment of goods received, this is a sapiential theme which was already outlined by Qoheleth, although in a different context; cf. Qoh 5:18; 8:15 (εὐφραίνω). By contrast with Qoheleth, our sage here is perfectly able to enjoy the goods offered to him by wisdom. We note that in the LXX εὐφραίνω has a tone which is mostly positive and refers joy in relation to God; cf. Deut 12:7; 14:26; etc. These possible links with Job and Qoheleth confirm that, for our sage, the goods that are mentioned are not of the same order as the wealth mentioned in v. 8, which Solomon preferred to wisdom, but are, rather, the goods of creation.

Wis 7:13-22a: the gifts of wisdom

13 Without deceit, I have learned; without envy, I pass on;
I do not hide her riches.
14 For she is an inexhaustible treasure for people.
Those who use her contract friendship with God
and are commended by the gifts which come from her instruction.

15 May God grant me to speak according to my understanding
and to think in a way worthy of the gifts I have received,
because it is he who is the guide of wisdom
and makes straight the path of the wise.
16 For in his hand are we and our words,
every kind of understanding and technical skill.
17 For he has given me a true knowledge of the creation:
to know the structure of the world and the power of the elements,
18 the beginning, the end, and the middle of times,
the alternation of the solstices and the change of the seasons,
19 the cycle of the years and the position of the stars,
20 the nature of the animals and the instinct of the beasts,
the power of the winds and the reasonings of men,
the variety of plants and the property of roots.
21 What is hidden and what is open I have come to know:
22 because wisdom, the mistress of all disciplines, instructed me.

Notes on the Text and Translation

v. 13. The adjective *ἀνεκλιπής (cf. 8:18) is not attested elsewhere. The meaning seems to be that of "inexhaustible" or "unfailing"; cf. ἀνέκλειπτος in Luke 12:33. The term reappears in Clement of Alexandria, *Strom.* 5.4. Leproux (*Un discours de sagesse*, 175-176) prefers to give ἀνεκλιπής the sense of "immutable", or something which never decreases, which is not subject to the law of corruption.

v. 14 Some codices and versions (B-S*, O-V; cf. La, Sa, Arab, Arm) read χρησάμενοι, "who use her", while Ziegler prefers κτησάμενοι (cf. Sir 51:28). However, this is a reading that could have arisen as a corruption of a difficult text. With χρησάμενοι, in fact, a construction with the dative would be expected: ᾧ οἱ χρησάμενοι; χρησάμενοι is clearly to be considered a *lectio difficilior*; cf. Larcher, *Sagesse*, 2:461. Scarpat (*Sapienza*, 2:107) refers to the use of χράομαι in Wis 2:6: χρησώμεθα τῇ κτίσει. Larcher observes, moreover, that in the Greek world, the use of χρῆσθαι is frequent in connection with virtue. With regard to virtue (ἀρετή), Aristotle, and later ethics, distinguish between χρῆσις and κτῆσις, between "use" and "possession", or between ἕξις and ἐνέργεια, between "possession" and "realisation" (*Eth. nic.* 1098b). The reading ὅν οἱ χρησάμενοι respects the context better (Engel, "Weisheit", 2142): it is a question of learning wisdom (13a), communicating her (13b) and putting her into practice. Thus, ὅν οἱ χρησάμενοι refers to those who use wisdom or who appropriate her in a virtuous way.

v. 15. The verb ἐνθυμέομαι emphasises the intellectual activity of reflection; cf. Wis 3:14; 6:15; and 9:13. In 15b, beside the reading τῶν δεδωμένων attested by B, many minuscules, La, Sah and Eth, there appears τῶν λεγομένων. However, this must be considered a secondary reading for reasons well set out by Larcher (*Sagesse*, 2:464-465). The variant could have arisen from the difficulty caused by the order of reasoning in 15ab: speaking according to thinking and thinking according to the gifts received. First one thinks, then one speaks. Cf. the comment.

The term *διορθωτής indicates the "reviser", in the literary sense of the term and, more severely, the "censor". Larcher, *Sagesse*, 2:466, suggests the image of the *correctores romani* (in Greek διορθωτής or ἐπανορθωτής), but, as noted by Scarpat, *Sapienza*, 2:35-39, these are figures chronologically later than the book of Wisdom (Trajan's times). Here, the term is to be understood in a weak sense, not so much a God who is "censor", but rather "corrector", regulator or guide of the moral path of the wise, according to one of the possible senses of διορθόω; cf. Wis 9:18.

v. 16. The expression ἐργατειῶν ἐπιστήμη is not easy to translate. The term *ἐργατεία is very rare in Greek usage and indicates work in a very general sense; ἐπιστήμη indicates "knowledge" in a general sense (cf. Wis 8:4). There is a probable allusion to Exod 31:3 LXX. In this case, ἐργατειῶν ἐπιστήμη could indicate a technical competence in a particular sense. The reference to words (λόγοι) in 16a could serve to point the expression in the direction of "technical competence" relating to the art of speaking well, an appropriate rhetorical technique.

v. 17. The term σύστασις is employed by Plato with reference to the "foundation" of the world (cf. *Tim.* 32c: ἡ τοῦ κόσμου σύστασις) through the activity of the Demiurge (*Tim.* 29a); "our author is thus using a term legitimised by official secular science, less bound up with the Jewish tradition than κτίσις would have been..." (Scarpat, *Sapienza*, 2:45). Larcher (*Sagesse*, 2:468) prefers to think of a passive sense, the structure, the organisation of the world, just as it was conceived in the Stoic vocabulary (cf. *SVF* II, 555).

v. 19. Ziegler prefers the reading ἐνιαυτοῦ on the basis of several patristic witnesses. However, perhaps we should follow the reading of the majority of witnesses: ἐνιαυτῶν. In the first case, we have to think of the arrangement of time within the year, in the second, of the cycles of years which follow one another. An example would be the cycle of four years necessary for harmonising the civil with the astronomical calendar.

v. 20. The majority of modern translations prefer to understand "the power of the spirits" (πνευμάτων βίας), thinking of activities of an exorcistic nature. Jewish tradition in the Hellenistic-Roman period was well aware of the figure of Solomon as exorcist, something which had great currency in the *Greek Magical Papyri*. However, Wisdom is strongly hostile to magic and, except for Wis 2:24, makes no mention of the devil or the demoniac spirits believed in by the majority of Jews of the period. From the parallel with διαλογιμοὺς ἀνθρώπων, Larcher (*Sagesse*, 2:474-475), avoids this difficulty, thinking, with Grimm, of the knowledge of the human "spirit" understood in a psychological sense. Cf. Gilbert, "La figure de Salomon", 163-165. However, the context of 7:20 and of the book as a whole makes us prefer a meteorological interpretation (cf. the Latin *vim ventorum*). This is the opinion of Scarpat, *Sapienza*, 2:52-59, in a long discussion where he shows that we should understand πνευμάτων βίας as the power of the winds.

v. 21. The term *τεχνῖτις seems to be attested for the first time in two epigraphs of Delphi from the second century BCE with the sense of "craftsman". In a poem of Nicarchus (first cent. CE; cf. *Anth. Gr.* 11.73), it indicates the skill of the prostitute and, in a passage of Lucian (*Toxaris* 13; second century BCE), a "perfect courtesan".

Synchronic Analysis

7:13-14: "I Do Not Hide Her Riches ..."

The initial verses of this third strophe (13-14) emphasise our sage's intention not to hide the riches of wisdom but to make them available to all. Verse 13a seems to have a good rhetorical construction. Twice we have adverb + τε + verb. The verb ἀποκρύπτομαι makes up the conclusion of the argument. The two verbs of 13a lack an object which is supplied by πλοῦτος in 13b. In this way, the author creates a slight rhetorical tension which places the stress on the connection of μανθάνω and μεταδίδωμι rather than on the object itself: wisdom.

Wisdom is something that one learns without deceit. Ἀδόλως could be alluding to the fraudulent means employed in magic and in the mystery cults. In connection with μανθάνω, it could also be understood as a reference to an education without secondary goals. The verb μανθάνω (cf. Wis 6:1, 9) underlines the need for a personal effort in learning. Wisdom is thus a gift but also a task.

The verb μεταδίδωμι indicates making others share in what has been learnt. The theme of envy (ἀφθόνως) recalls Wis 6:22-23. The omission of the object of the two verbs of 13a renders them interchangeable: "I have learned in order to communicate" and "I have communicated because I have learned". The teaching that has been learned acquires its true meaning only when it is passed on to others.

The use of ἀποκρύπτω recalls Wis 6:22 once more. Here the verb is used in the present and in the middle voice: "I do not intend to hide" (in 6:22 in the active voice, future tense).

The theme of wisdom's wealth is an explicit echo of v. 11b. However, here we have a metaphorical sense of πλοῦτος: no longer the external riches, rejected by Solomon in favour of wisdom (7:8), but that true wealth that is wisdom herself. In 14a, this wealth becomes an inexhaustible treasure which is made available to people. Alternatively, if we give ἀνεκλιπής the meaning of "unchangeable", it is a treasure which does not vanish, which is not subject to the law of corruption as are earthly riches (cf. Luke 12:33).

Whoever possesses wisdom and makes use of her (χρησάμενοι), obtains a friendly relationship with God (7:14b). Scripture is not unaware of this theme: cf. Isa 41:8; 2 Chr 20:7 in connection with Abraham.[21] The reference to the commendation (συσταθέντες) of the "gifts which come from her instruction" could be considered a polemic in relation to offerings and sacrificial gifts which do not have the same value for God as the offering of a holy life. There is also a possible allusion to the Hellenistic practices of presenting oneself to the divinity with ritual offerings. However, chapters 7-8, taken as a whole, suggest that in παιδεία we need to see something more: the instruction, the education which arises from receiving the gift of wisdom and which also bears within itself all the values of contemporary Greek culture (cf. vv. 17-20). The topic of παιδεία thus becomes load-bearing for the whole strophe.[22]

Verses 15-16 express a desire, an indirect prayer to God, to help Solomon to 7:15-17a
give good expression what he is speaking. This makes clear that the author was aware of being inspired in some way by God (cf. Sir 24:30-34), considered as the fount of all human wisdom. God himself is the "guide" of wisdom and the one who "regulates" the wise, who corrects them and sets them back on the right path.

Verse 15 opens with a return to the first person singular. As in 6:22, Solomon expresses the intention of wishing to speak of wisdom but, as in 7:7, he returns to the necessity of prayer. Cf. *Tim.* 27b-d as an example of the Greek usage of invoking the divinity before every important piece of argument. Solomon asks God that his speech correspond to his thoughts (the probable sense of κατὰ γνώμην; cf. κατὰ ἐμὴν δόξαν in *Tim.* 27d) and that he may thus be able to reflect, that is, to think, in a way worthy of the gifts which he has received from God (15b), namely, all those goods that the Lord has already communicated to him (cf. the comment on 7:11-12).

The apparent difficulty caused by the inversion of the logical order in 15ab (one thinks first, then one speaks) could be resolved by observing that our sage wishes to highlight the existence of a very close connection between word and thought. The sage's word (εἰπεῖν) must correspond to his γνώμη, that is, his mode of thinking, while his thought (ἐνθυμηθῆναι) must correspond to the gifts received, that is, to wisdom and the qualities given to Solomon by God. Thus, prominence is given to all the importance which speaking, or the art of rhetoric, has for our sage, something normal within the framework of the Hellenistic world.[23]

In 15cd, Solomon accounts for his prayer by pointing out that God is the guide of wisdom. The term ὁδηγός returns in Wis 18:3; cf. ὁδηγέω in Wis 9:11; 10:10, and 17. This expression could be understood in the sense that wisdom is a reality with God at its source, which moves where God leads it. From the point of view of the wisdom that is present in people, one could think also that they need God in order to be wise because wisdom comes from God. It is thus clear that the

---

21 Cf. Ziener, *Die theologische Begriffssprache*, 88-94.

22 In this connection, Leproux (*Un discours de sagesse*, 167) speaks of "isotopia"; Larcher, *Etudes* 359 n. 4, thinks of the adaptation of a Stoic motif.

23 An interesting *excursus* in the value of the word in Wisdom in the light of Hellenistic culture is contained in Leproux, *Un discours de sagesse*, 180-195.

wisdom spoken of here is not the Greek variety; it is something that comes only from God.

Verse 16[24] expands the statements of v. 15: we all, including the wise, stand in need of God's help because we are all in God's hands. Not only are we in the hands of God, that is, we depend on God, but so too are our words, our knowledge (φρόνησις), and all our ability (ἐργατειῶν ἐπιστήμη), an expression which probably refers also to the art of speaking well and not just to technical competence.

Verse 17a is constructed as an *inclusio* with 15a (ἐμοί δὲ δῴη ... γνώμην / μοι ἔδωκεν ... γνῶσιν) and completes this first movement of seven stichs (15-17a). At the same time, however, it introduces the following movement which is also in seven stichs and which relates to the wisdom of Solomon (17b-20). Thus, "may God grant me to speak according to my understanding" (15a) is matched by "he has given me a true knowledge of the creation". In light of Plato's usage (*Theaet.* 152c; 160d), the term ἀψευδής indicates a knowledge that is not subject to error, so, certain and infallible. God has offered it to Solomon in relation to what exists, and that will be specified in the list that follows (vv. 17b-20).

7:17b-20: Solomon's Knowledge

This pericope is an interesting passage which has been rather passed over by commentators. Our sage's reflection takes its cue from the account in 1 Kgs 5:13-14 (cf. Prov 1:2-6) and from the Jewish traditions concerning Solomon's encyclopaedic knowledge. All human knowledge was given to Solomon by God (7:17a) and taught him by wisdom (7:22). The topics and disciplines which formed the base of secular studies in the Hellenistic world are not, in fact, rejected. At the same time, however, Israel's wisdom has no need to be jealous of that of the Greeks. Solomon is thus presented as an expert in cosmology (17b), astronomy (18-19), botany and zoology (20a), meteorology and psychology (20b), and medicine (20c).

7:21-22a: "Wisdom Instructed Me!"

The tone of v. 21 is hyperbolic. Solomon knows everything, both what is conspicuous and what is hidden. This pairing of opposed terms has the force of totality. Taken literally, v. 21 would lead us to think of Solomon as sharing in the divine knowledge. However, the allusion to hidden things (κρυπτά) is to be taken as a direct polemic against the mystery cults. Cf. 6:22, where Solomon articulates his programme. For our sage there are no hidden things that are reserved only for the elect.

Πάντων τεχνῖτις is referring to wisdom,[25] "mistress" of everything, that is, of all those disciplines (τέχναι) which have just been listed. Wisdom is the craftsman *par excellence*, as Philo writes: σοφία τέχνη τεχνῶν (*Ebr.* 88). We observe that, in 13:1, the term, employed in the masculine (τεχνίτης), is referring to God himself in a context of creation. The reference to a creator role for wisdom seems clear.

The context, as well as the presence of the verb διδάσκω, suggests giving τεχνῖτις a nuance that is also intellectual, referring to wisdom's ability as "teacher", mistress of the disciplines listed. Thus, our author is not devaluing the rational process of the sciences. If this verse contains polemic, it is not being directed so much at the Greek world and its scientific culture as against the idea

---

24 A verse dear to Augustine; cf. La Bonnardière, *Biblia Augustiniana*, 281-282.

25 We observe that a couple of mss and a few other witnesses (cf. Ziegler's apparatus and his preface, p. 67) modify the text by reading ὁ πάντων τεχνίτης, thus referring the term to God and circumventing the theological difficulty caused by the mention of a wisdom who is an "artisan".

that the knowledge of reality can be acquired through a hidden γνῶσις (cf. v. 21), such as that of the mysteries, or by means of a technique such as magic. Thus, with τεχνῖτις highlighted at the end of the strophe (cf. the literary structure), our sage is referring wisdom at one and the same time to the realm of creation (cf. below for the probable reference to Prov 8:30) and also to the realm of education (ἐδίδαξεν), that is, of παιδεία.

In conclusion, the apologetic element in Wis 7:17-22a should certainly be emphasised. The praise of Solomon's scientific knowledge is a reaction to the boasted superiority of the Greeks in that area. But there is much more: all human knowledge comes from God through God's wisdom. This is not a denial of the rational process typical of Greek science. On the contrary, it is being revalued as to its origin (God) and its purpose (God again). Furthermore, we should not undervalue the fact that, several times, this text sets itself in polemic with magic knowledge and, above all, with a mystery type of gnosis.

Diachronic Analysis

In the use of the verb μανθάνω, we should not exclude a reference to the deuteronomic use of this verb. In Deut 5:1, it is a matter of learning and putting into practice the laws and statutes of the Lord; elsewhere, of learning to fear him (Deut 4:10; 14:23; 17:19; 18:9; 31:12, and 13). On the other hand, a teaching passed on without envy could be another polemical allusion against the mystery cults which were a secret jealously guarded by their adepts.[26] The use of ἀποκρύπτω reinforces the idea of a polemic against the secrecy of the mystery cults. Moreover, the notion of a wisdom learned and passed on to others without envy marks the development of a universalistic tendency already present in Prov 1-9; cf. particularly Prov 8:4. Wisdom is addressed to everyone. However, the theme of the spiritual goods which are passed on to others and not hidden is a topic in both Judaism and Christianity.[27] The text is thus playing on two complementary levels: polemic against the mysteries and the logic of a teaching that is open to all, without envy and without deceit (13a). 7:13-14

The use of ὁδηγός (cf. Wis 7:15) also contains a polemical point against the mystery cults (cf. also ὁδηγέω: 9:11; 10:10, and 17). It is not Isis, in fact, who "guides" people to salvation but the God of Israel. It is God who also regulates and corrects (διορθωτής) the steps of the wise, who thus have a continual need to increase and be guided in the path of wisdom. From this perspective, v. 15cd is addressing a theological problem of great importance: it is only possible to speak of what comes from God thanks to the help of God himself. 7:15-17a

The text of v. 16, is taking up the idea that was already expressed in Qoh 9:1, although in a very different context and in a very different tone (cf. Acts 17:28). In the case of the reference to φρόνησις and to ἐργατειῶν ἐπιστήμη, one cannot

---

26 Thus Scarpat, *Sapienza*, 2:107.

27 Cf. van Unnik, Wilhelm C., ἀφθόνως μεταδίδωμι, Brussel: Paleis der Akademie 1971. For a Christian reprise of this motif, cf. Justin, *1 Apol.* 6.2: "to whoever wishes to learn, we pass on without envy (ἀφθόνως) what we have learned".

exclude a polemic against the Isis cults, for Isis is considered as the inspirer of skills and technology (cf. the comment on 7:21).

7:17b-20 In interpreting vv. 17b-20, it is necessary to give a brief analysis of the relationship which our sage shows himself to have with the Greek culture of the time.

Cosmology Verse 17b refers to the structure of the world (σύστασις κόσμου), understood as a well-ordered whole (κόσμος). The expression ἐνέργειαν στοιχείων refers to the power that binds the elements of the world together, probably the four traditional elements of Greek physics: earth, air, fire, and water. Solomon is the perfect expert in that science which the Greeks called cosmology.

Astronomy In 18a, "the beginning, the end, and the middle of times" is an allusion to astronomy. The "times" are probably those dictated by the movements of the stars (so Larcher, who cites a possible reminiscence of *Tim.* 37e-38e) or of the seasons (Scarpat). This formula, frequent in the Greek and Hellenistic world, especially in connection with Zeus, also recalls the rabbinic way of speaking of God who is without beginning, without present, and without end.[28] The second part of v. 18 continues to refer to astronomy: the τροπῶν ἀλλαγαί are the changes of the solstices, while μεταβολάς καιρῶν refers to the changes of the seasons, something to which the ancient world was very sensitive.[29]

Verse 19 is still concerned with astronomy. It is not entirely clear to what the "cycles of the years" (or of the "year") is referring, while the position of the stars is necessary for knowing the time of the year. Cf. Philo, *Spec.* 4.235 where the expressions τροπαὶ καὶ μεταβολαί and ἐνιαυτός occur. This Philonic text reveals the importance which the divisions of the year and the cycle of the seasons had in the world of Alexandrian Judaism.

Our sage carefully avoids using the term ἀστρονομία which, along with music, arithmetic, and geometry, made up part of the Pythagorean *quadrivium*. As in Philo, this is to avoid any confusion with astrology and astral fatalism: "Wisdom is well aware who guides human affairs and knows how to make use of astronomy without falling into idolatry".[30] In speaking of the "position of the stars", our author is alluding to the constellations. However, these do not serve to determine horoscopes, as happened in the particular branch of astronomy called *astrothesia*, but only to determine the seasons. Wisdom is not denying here the value of Greek discoveries in this field but is reducing them to what they really are, that is, scientific discoveries. We remember again how Isis is often described as patroness of the heavenly elements. She it is who regulates the movement of the stars: "elementorum omnium domina" (Apuleius, *Metam.* 11.5) and guarantees the alternation of the times and seasons. All this, however, is solely the fruit of wisdom.

Zoology Verse 20a refers to zoology which is concerned with the nature of the animals (φύσεις ζῴων) and of the instincts (θυμός) of the wild beasts (θηρίων). Our sage is developing the information contained in 1 Kgs 5:13. Solomon has not only a

---

28 Cf. Plato, *Leg.* 4.715e–716a, in connection with God and with a probable citation of an Orphic hymn (ὁ μὲν δὴ θεός ... ἀρχήν τε καὶ τελευτὴν καὶ μέσα τῶν ὄντων ἁπάντων ἔχων). For the rabbinic tradition, cf. y. Sanh. 1.1. Cf. Winston, *Wisdom*, 173-174; cf. also Larcher, *Sagesse*, 2:469-470.

29 For a careful study of the Egyptian context of this passage, cf. Larcher, *Sagesse*, 2:471-472.

30 Scarpat, *Sapienza*, 2:50.

deep knowledge of the animals useful to humans, but also of the wild beasts, the ones more inaccessible and dangerous, the ones most difficult to observe.

Meteorology and Pyschology

Verse 20b is debated (cf. the textual note). If we give πνευμάτων βίας a "meteorological" interpretation, we have to think that our sage is describing Solomon as a great expert on the power of the winds. The storms of nature are associated *ad sensum* with the διαλογισμοὺς ἀνθρώπων, that is, the "reasonings of men", where the term διαλογισμός is to be understood *in malam partem*, as happens in the LXX and in the NT (cf. Ps 93:11 LXX [94:11 MT] and Mark 7:21): the machinations or the plots of men. The allusion, therefore, is to the capacity for judgement displayed by the biblical Solomon (cf. 1 Kgs 3:16-28). On the one hand, Solomon knows the difficult occasions in nature, on the other, the difficult moments of the human spirit, the machinations of the mind. Meteorology and psychology, we would say today, are walking hand in hand.

Botany

Verse 20c refers to botany. Solomon knows of the different species of plants and the powers of their roots which were used in the medicine of the time. His interest, therefore, is not only in the theoretical but also in the experimental sciences. However, even these are closely linked to God by our sage. By contrast, one observes that, in 1 En. 8:3, such knowledge was revealed to humans by the rebel angels. This is a further example of Wisdom's anti-apocalyptic tone.

7:21-22a

Everything that Solomon knows was taught him by wisdom, the "mistress of all". The expression has a polemical tone which, again, could be directed against the idea that it was Isis who taught humans the sciences (cf. *Aretalogy of Cyrene* 12).

As for wisdom as τεχνῖτις, we should not exclude a rereading of the difficult Hebrew text of Prov 8:30 or perhaps even an original reading specially put forward by the author of Wisdom.[31] The disputed Hebrew term אמון would thus be being reinterpreted in the sense of "artisan", "artificer", thus giving personified wisdom an active role in creation (cf. Prov 3:19). In the light of Wis 9:1-2, the reference to a role of wisdom in creation cannot be excluded. Cf. also the comment on 8:6.

Wis 7:22b–8:1: The Nature of Wisdom

22b In her, there is a spirit that is intelligent and holy,
unique, manifold, subtle,
mobile, clear, undefiled,
pure, harmless, loving the good, sharp,
23 unhindered, beneficent, the friend of humanity,
secure, stable, free from troubles,
who can do all and survey all,
who penetrates through all the spirits
that are intelligent, pure, and very subtle.

---

31 Cf. Skehan, "The literary relationship", especially 172-191. Cf. already Grimm, *Weisheit*, 151; Larcher, *Etudes*, 98 and 389.

24 Wisdom is more mobile than any motion.
Through her pureness she pervades and penetrates everything.
25 She is a breath of the power of God,
a pure emanation of the glory of the Almighty
so that nothing defiled can enter her.
26 She is a reflection of eternal light
and a spotless mirror of the working of God,
an image of his goodness.
27 Since she is one, she can do everything.
Though remaining in herself, she renews everything
and across the generations, entering holy souls,
she prepares friends of God and prophets.
28 For God loves nothing more than the one who dwells with wisdom.
29 Indeed, she is more splendid than the sun
and superior to every constellation.
Compared with the light, she is found to be superior:
30 for it is succeeded by night,
but over wickedness, wisdom cannot prevail.
8:1 She extends mightily from one end to the other
and governs the universe with goodness.

Notes on the Text and Translation

v. 22. Codex Alexandrinus, along with other lesser witnesses (cf. Ziegler), reads ἔστιν γὰρ αὕτη instead of ἔστιν γὰρ ἐν αὐτῇ, which, in addition to being the majority reading, seems the better one as it avoids an explicit identification of wisdom with the spirit. For the theological use of this text in the Christian tradition, cf. Scarpat, *Sapienza*, 2:111-112.

v. 27. The expression μία δὲ οὖσα should have a causal not a concessive sense; "since she [wisdom] is one, she can do everything". In fact, the author is drawing the consequences of what he has just said about the nature of wisdom.
The verb καινίζω, which the majority of commentators translate in its proper sense of "renew", can also assume in classical Greek the meaning of "inaugurate" (cf. Aeschylus, *Ag.* 1071; 2 Macc 4:11). This meaning is defended by Leproux (*Un discours de sagesse*, 220-225) who sees in wisdom's action something inaugural rather than a renewal: wisdom shares in the creation of the world and of people. In this way, Leproux associates the following verb, κατασκευάζω, with the ἀκατασκεύατος earth of Gen 1:2.

v. 29. All the witnesses read προτέρα. On the basis of Ms 613 and with reference to Wis 6:12 (cf. Acts 26:13), Ziegler proposes reading λαμπροτέρα instead, but this is an unnecessary banalisation.
The manuscripts read κατισχύσει with exception of codex B (ἀντισχύει). Larcher prefers the latter (cf. *Sagesse*, 2:513-514), giving the verb the sense of "prevail over". Ziegler chooses the present κατισχύει on the sole basis of a quotation of John Damascene. The verb κατισχύω, attested by the majority, returns in 10:11 and 17:15 with the same meaning. It is more frequent in the LXX (cf., in the NT, Matt 16:18) and seems to be the reading to be preferred, read in the future with the majority of manuscripts.

8:1. The codices alternate the reading εἰς πέρας (B, V, etc.; cf. Ziegler) with that of ἐπὶ πέρας, attested by S, A and some miniscules (cf. Rahlfs). The latter seems preferable, linked to the preceding ἀπὸ πέρατος, wich indicates the point of departure, while ἐπὶ πέρας indicates the point of arrival.

Synchronic Analysis

7:22b-23: The Spirit of Wisdom

The strophe opens with a γάρ which links the statement of vv. 22b-23 with wisdom, the τεχνῖτις. Wisdom is a "artificer" because in her (ἐν αὐτῇ) there is the πνεῦμα. Here, once more, is the association of wisdom and spirit already seen as early as Wis 1:6. Wisdom is being presented as a personified reality which – like God himself – possesses the spirit. Wisdom and spirit are not actually identified (cf. Wis 1:6). Our sage tends to attribute to wisdom the qualities of the spirit so that wisdom and spirit come to assume the same activities.

The Attributes of the Spirit of Wisdom

The list of the twenty-one attributes of the spirit follows the literary genre of the *accumulatio*. The number is certainly not accidental (7 x 3) and underlines the importance of the number seven for our author.[32] We note immediately that almost every adjective presents difficulties of translation or interpretation which we can only hint at here (see below, diachronic analysis).[33] Moreover, the entire internal organisation of the series of adjectives is hard to read. The first ten adjectives are linked in pairs. The eleventh (φιλάγαθον) seems to be at the centre of the series and marks the passage from the description of the nature of the spirit of wisdom to the description of its activity relative to the world. The two concluding stichs 7:23d-e, the twenty-first attribute, mark a clear *inclusio* with the beginning of the series in 7:22b-c through the repetition of the lexemes πνεῦμ-, νοερ-, and λεπτ-.

7:24-8:1: The Nature of Wisdom

Verse 24 concludes the reflection of vv. 22-23 and, through the mention of the movement of wisdom, opens the following section of the strophe which, as already said, presents a concentric structure.

7:24: Wisdom, the Most Mobile of Movements

The text of v. 24 is an explicit taking up of the verb χωρέω and the notion of "purity" (καθαρός) from 23de. However, this time the subject is wisdom proper and no longer her spirit, which can, therefore, not be identified with wisdom herself *tout court.*

With the expression πάσης γὰρ κινήσεως κινητικώτερον σοφία, which alludes to the preceding attribute εὐκίνητος, our sage is intending to emphasise that wisdom is the most mobile of movements. Here our sage is thinking of the Stoic concept of the first cause as something essentially mobile which, although itself moving, does not vary and does not change but remains an active presence. This is far from the Aristotelian concept of the "unmoved mover".

On account of her "purity" (διὰ τὴν καθαρειότητα), wisdom pervades and penetrates the whole of reality. Purity is being understood here in a metaphysical not a moral sense. The intimate relation of wisdom with God renders her superior to every creature.

---

32 Cf. Scarpat, *Sapienza*, 2:113-114.

33 For a very detailed commentary on the individual attributes, cf. Larcher, *Sagesse*, 2:481-493; Scarpat, *Sapienza*, 2:114-128; Leproux, *Un discours de sagesse*, 201-209.

7:25-26: Five Metaphors

Through a series of five metaphors and the continuous use of philosophical vocabulary, the text describes the divine origin of wisdom. The use of these metaphors, however, shows that our author does not feel able to define wisdom but only to describe her in symbolic, if elevated, language.

Breath

The first metaphor describes wisdom as ἀτμίς, a term which in itself indicates "vapour", but which can also be translated as "breath" (cf. ἀτμίς with which Aquila translates Qoheleth's הבל). The "power of God" is an idea that was already introduced by our author back in 1:3 (cf. 12:15). In 5:23 and 11:20 there are mentions of the "spirit of power" in the sense of a divine intervention against the ungodly. This idea seems to be excluded here. Rather the thought is of wisdom understood as the "breath" of God himself, seen as the Almighty. Some authors see an allusion to Sir 24:3: "I came out of the mouth of the Most High, and like a mist I covered the earth".

If instead we understand ἀτμίς in its primary sense of "vapour", the image could have been taken from the pre-Socratics. It is in water vapour, in fact, that Animaxander sees the origin of life. Wisdom too has an origin but in God and God's power. It is consubstantial with God just like vapour and water. However, the five metaphors, taken in their totality, associate wisdom with God yet tend to distinguish the two. Wisdom is not God.[34]

Emanation

The term *ἀπόρροια is to be understood in the sense of "emanation", like the ray that issues from a source of light (cf. *Spec.* 1.40), like a reality which is separate from the substance emitting it. This metaphor refers to the idea of "emanation" which was part of Greek philosophy beginning with the theories attributed to Empedocles. Ἀπόρροια appears also in connection with astral influence.[35] This ἀπόρροια is called "limpid", *εἰλικρινής, that is, absolutely pure, transparent, completely transcendent.[36]

Wisdom is an emanation of the glory of the παντοκράτωρ. If δόξα is a typically biblical term, παντοκράτωρ belongs instead to the language of the LXX and refers to the idea of God as universal sovereign. The "glory" is the manifestation of the presence of God in the world, a reflection, but one which cannot be seen (cf. Ezek 1:28). In Wis 9:10, wisdom is said to come from the throne of the glory of God. The theme of glory is bound up with the idea of light and of the brightness which the glory of God recalls; cf. Isa 60:19-20 LXX and Bar 5:9, where glory and light go hand in hand (τῷ φωτὶ τῆς δόξης αὐτοῦ). Wisdom is, therefore, a ray from the luminous presence of God (cf. also 26a), although distinguished from God like the ray from its source.[37]

For this reason (25c), nothing defiled can enter her. *Παρεμπίπτω has a negative nuance: "attack suddenly, worm one's way into". Because of her purity, wisdom excludes all kind of contamination. With οὐδὲν μεμιαμμένον, our sage could be referring to a contamination that is both moral and physical. In the LXX,

---

34 Cf. Scarpat, *Sapienza*, 2:70-71; cf. also Larcher, *Sagesse*, 2:497-498 for ancient exegesis which interpreted ἀτμίς as "perfume", not infrequently in Christian exegesis with a Christological background.

35 Cf. Larcher, *Etudes*, 207 n. 6.

36 Winston notes (cf. *Wisdom*, 185) that this is the most ancient text where ἀπόρροια is used in connection with wisdom or the *Logos*.

37 Cf. Raurell, "The Religious Meaning", 371-373.

μιαίνω is very frequent in descriptions of ritual impurity. Because of her divine origin, wisdom does not risk being tainted with any form of impurity.

Reflection

The third metaphor describes wisdom as ἀπαύγασμα, "reflection" of "eternal light", that is, a quality possessed by God himself together with glory (cf. Isa 60:19-20 LXX, already quoted). The author avoids identifying God directly with light just as he avoided identifying God with glory. As throughout the OT/HB, the light is not God but rather a divine epiphany; cf., to the contrary, Philo in *Somn.* 1.75: ὁ θεὸς φῶς ἐστι; cf. 1 John 1:5.[38] The symbolism of light will have a notable dimension in Wis 17:1-18:4.

The term *ἀπαύγασμα seems to be attested here for the first time in Greek usage. It is used by Philo (*Opif.* 146; *Plant.* 50; *Spec.* 4.123). The sense could be active, as in *Spec.* 4.123, where Philo employs ἀπαύγασμα in a Stoicising sense in connection with the origin of the rational animal in God (cf. also 1 En. 1:3), and so to refer to wisdom as a "ray" or "radiation" of eternal light. The term ἀπαύγασμα could also have a passive significance, "reflection", as in the other two Philonic texts cited above. The context suggested by the following metaphors, that of the mirror and that of the image, favours the latter interpretation. God's eternal light has its perfect reflection in wisdom.

Mirror

In the metaphor of the mirror (ἔσοπτρον), the attention falls not so much, as in the other four metaphors, on the activity of wisdom which will be described from v. 27 as rather on its nature. Wisdom is a perfect, spotless mirror in which is reflected the divine ἐνέργεια, that is, that divine faculty which emphasises the ability of God to carry out effectively everything that God wills (cf., in the NT, Col 2:12). The translation with "activity" is thus imperfect. The mirror is described as *ἀκηλίδωτος, or spotless, clear, reflecting very well. The image of the mirror also recalls a well-known Platonic theme. Empirical reality is only a mirror of the world of ideas. It is, therefore, necessary to reject the mediated knowledge of God to arrive at knowing God directly. Wisdom, then, is the only reality which guarantees a direct knowledge of God and God's will.[39]

Image

The theme of the goodness of God (cf. Wis 1:1b; in the LXX, only in Sir 45:23), introduced in the fifth metaphor, is also typically Platonic (cf. the reprise of the *Timaeus* [92ce] in Philo, *Opif.* 21; *Cher.* 127), as also is that of the image (εἰκών) which implies likeness to a given model. Our sage is probably utilising the theme of the image in the sense in which Philo speaks of the *logos* as image of God (*Fug.* 101); cf. *Deo* 73 in connection with the perfect goodness which God employs towards all things. Our sage is superimposing on it the biblical concept of humanity as the "image" of God (cf. Gen 1:27; Wis 2:23). For our sage, not only wisdom but also people are images of God. For this reason, they can attain immortality by uniting themselves with wisdom (cf. Wis 8:17).

7:27-28: Wisdom in People

The unique nature of wisdom (μία δὲ οὖσα) is stated for two reasons. On the one hand, wisdom reflects the oneness of the God of Israel (Deut 6:5); on the other hand, her unicity excludes the intermediary powers which act as her assistants, as happens in Philo's philosophy.[40] In fact, Wisdom πάντα δύναται, "can do all".

---

38 Cf. Aalen, *Licht und Finsternis*, 577-579.

39 Larcher, *Etudes*, 382.

40 The expression μία δὲ οὖσα returns also in the Isiac aretalogy of Cyrene (l.6).

She possesses divine characteristics from the additional point of view of her activity.

7:27 "Remaining in herself": in relation to what was said about the movement of wisdom (v. 24), one could think that, although it is her activity that is being described, she is a reality which, remaining immanent in herself, does not change her own identity.[41] But this identity of wisdom with herself does not exclude her activity for "she can do all" as has just been said in the previous stich.

In the LXX, the verb καινίζω normally has the meaning of "improve, refurbish" (1 Macc 10:10), "introduce" (2 Macc 4:11), "renew, restore" (Zeph 3:17 LXX), "rebuild" (Isa 61:4), just as with the composite ἀνακαινίζω Pss 102:5 LXX [103:5 MT]; 103:30 LXX [104:30 MT]. The last passage, referring to the spirit of God which renews the earth (καὶ ἀνακαινιεῖς τὸ πρόσωπον τῆς γῆς), could have been in our sage's mind.[42] Thus, in light of the spirit described in Ps 103, wisdom is being described as the cause of the renewal of the universe (τὰ πάντα) and, so, of the continuation of life.

The second part of v. 27 makes us think also of a renewal of an interior character, a wisdom which descends continually into "holy souls" and creates new people. The idea is biblical. The text of 27b describes the activity of wisdom not in relation to the universe (τά πάντα), but in relation to people. The expression κατὰ γενεὰς refers to the succession of generations. Μεταβαίνω indicates passing from one place to another or from one subject to another. In the course of human history, wisdom addresses herself to "holy souls". Ψυχή (cf. 3:1) indicates the human person rather than a Platonically separate soul. Ὅσιος refers to a moral holiness. Holy souls are, therefore, "pious, faithful" souls. This is a general statement. It is difficult to say whether our sage has in mind here all the human generations, as would seem likely in the light of Wis 10:1-4, or only the Israelites; that is, whether wisdom is concerned with Israel or, in the wake of Prov 8, is seen as something available to all.

Friends of God and Prophets

The verb κατασκευάζω has transitive value and should be understood as "prepare, predispose". In Wis 9:1; 11:24; and 13:4, it is employed in relation to the work of God (cf. 13:11 and 14:2, however, in relation to the workman). Thus, by extending God's own work, wisdom prepares "friends of God and prophets".

7:28 Verse 28 is formulated in unusual Greek: "God loves nothing more than one who dwells with wisdom". For ἀγαπάω, cf. Wis 1:1a. The text of 11:24 makes it clear that this love of God extends to every creature. Our verse occurs at the end of a section in which our author places the stress on the need to obtain wisdom. In the LXX, the verb συνοικέω generally refers to conjugal cohabitation (cf. Deut 22:13; 24:1; and Sir 25:16). On the basis of this, many authors claim that our author is thinking of a symbolic spousal union between the sage and wisdom (cf. below).

7:29-30: Once More, Wisdom and Light

In parallel with vv. 25-26, the author returns to the metaphor of light in relation to the nature of wisdom. She is a friend and companion because of her beauty. In fact, wisdom is brighter (εὐπρεπεστέρα) than the sun. The comparison

---

41 According to Scarpat (*Sapienza*, 2:84-85) our author is polemicising against the Heraclitean concept that everything changes except for a permanent element which, for Heraclitus, is fire. Philo describes God as ἑστὼς ἐν ὁμοίῳ καὶ μένων (*Somn.* 2.221).

42 Cf. Skehan, "Borrowings from the Psalms", 389.

could have been suggested by Cant 6:10. Εὐπρεπής has more the nuance of "splendid". For εὐπρέπεια, cf. 5:16, where it refers to the divine majesty. By analogy, wisdom is magnificent, more splendid than the sun and every constellation (ἄστρων θέσιν; cf. 7:19). The reference to the constellations could also be understood as a polemical touch aimed against astrology.

The text of 29c adds that, compared (συγκρινομένη) to the light, wisdom is superior (or "brighter"; cf. the textual note). Thus, in reality, the metaphor of wisdom as light is not wholly exact. Wisdom is superior to light. We cannot exclude from προτέρα a temporal indication. Wisdom is "before" the light in the sense that she pre-exists light itself (cf. the strongly temporal aspect in Prov 8:22-25). From this point of view, Wis 7,:29-30 could be seen as a little midrash on Gen 1:3 Our sage is associating wisdom with the primordial light.[43]

Verse 30a gives the reason why wisdom is considered superior to light with reference to an empirical consideration. The light is succeeded by night. Verse 30b goes on to consider a more important point: wickedness does not prevail over wisdom. Wickedness (cf. 2:21; 4:11; 5:13) is being compared implicitly with darkness (cf. the whole of chap. 17). As already in Wis 1:12-14, all dualism is radically excluded.

8:1: The Presence of Wisdom

The text of 8:1 is to be seen in parallel with 7:24. Wisdom's movement is joined by its presence in the cosmos and its providential role. By means of the figure of wisdom, our sage is describing a kind of *creatio continua.*[44]

Diachronic Analysis

7:22b–23

For a better understanding of the meaning of the twenty-one attributes in Wis 7:22b-23, it is necessary to give a brief analysis of their background which is more Greek than biblical.

*Νοερός: This means "intelligent", capable of thought. In Stoic philosophy, it is attributed to the cosmic πνεῦμα or λόγος, that is, to God himself (cf. *SVF* I, 32, 110; II; 299 frag. 1009).

Ἅγιος: If νοερός is a term betraying Greek influence, ἅγιος, on the other hand, reveals a biblical background; cf. Ps 50:13 LXX [51:13 MT]; Isa 63:10, 11; LXX-Dan 5:12; 6:4; and Th-Dan 4:8, 9, and 18, where the expression πνεῦμα ἅγιον appears in connection with the spirit of God. Our sage has already used this adjective in 1:5 precisely in relation to the πνεῦμα, and he will use it again in 9:17. In Wisdom, ἅγιος indicates something that belongs to God, which is closely linked to God.[45] The spirit is "holy", therefore, precisely because it belongs to the divine sphere and is radically separate from the profane world.

Μονογενής: In itself, this term signifies "only-generated" and is employed in both the LXX and the NT in connection with an only son. If we place the stress on μονο-, the emphasis is on the spirit's "unique" mode of origin. If, instead, the emphasis is placed on the root -γέν-, the emphasis is on "unique in its generation", in relation to its essence and its qualities. In this case, it is not impossible

---

43 Cf. Leproux, *Un discours de sagesse*, 236-248.

44 Cf. Engel, *Das Buch Weisheit*, 138.

45 Mazzinghi, *Notte di paura e di luce*, 8.

that we have an anti-gnostic polemic: the spirit is not an emanation of God but his only-born[46].

*Πολυμερής: This adjective should be read in a pair with the preceding one with which it creates assonance. The fact that this spirit is "unique" does not involve a lessening of its properties. In fact, unique in its generation, the spirit is also "manifold" in its manifestations. This adjective, which was not adopted by Stoic philosophy, indicates something which is made up of different parts. However, it is preferable to understand it as an expression of the idea of multiplicity (cf. Aristotle, *Pol.* 1311a 33). The unique spirit performs a varied activity in the world, or else one can think of its interior richness, the multiplicity of energies contained in the unique spirit (cf. In the NT, 1 Cor 12:4).

Λεπτός: The term means "subtle". A careful analysis of the philosophical texts that use it leads us to reject the sense of "immaterial"[47]. In the *Cratylus* (412D), the idea of "subtle" is associated with that of movement, and so the ability to penetrate into the inmost parts of beings and to move everywhere with rapidity (τάχιστον καὶ λεπτότατον). The idea will be taken up again at the end of the following verse (7:23d-e). However, the subtle nature of the spirit does not cause it to be mingled with the creation from which it is distinguished. This avoids any falling into pantheism.

Εὐκίνητος: that is, "something that moves easily". In Stoicism, it is used of "reason" by contrast with Aristotle; cf. *SVF* II, 119 frag. 338. The first cause is a being in movement. In Stoic thought, therefore, movement is not, in fact, an imperfection but the characteristic of the cause *par excellence*. Thus, the spirit is characterised by mobility, another sign of its transcendent character, and, in its turn, establishes the same mobility of wisdom described in 7:24a. With this adjective, therefore, we are along the lines of the previous λεπτός.

Τρανός: In Greek usage, this adjective describes everything that is clear, sharp, and distinct. It is not certain that the term could have been used in a technical sense despite the use made of it by Philo. In Philo, τρανός, together with verbs of "seeing" and of "saying", indicates for the most part something that is "clear", especially in connection with representations of the mind.[48] This "clarity" can be understood in the sense of purity of spirit, but we should not overlook the idea of "eloquence" introduced by the Latin translation, *disertus*. From this point of view, the spirit would be enabling the person who received it to speak well (cf. Wis 10:21 with regard to the tongues of infants).

*Ἀμόλυντος: This is a rare and late term indicating something without stain or, better still, something which cannot be defiled. The term could thus be referring to purity of spirit uncontaminated by earthly realities and untouched by sin. It is difficult to set the adjective in relation to the previous one.

Σαφής, together with ἀπήμαντος, should be read in close parallel with τρανός. This adjective refers to what is clear, limpid, patent, with reference here to the nature of the spirit, to its absolute purity. In the field of oratory, σαφής indicates clear discourse without ambiguity.[49]

---

46 Cf. Scarpat, *Sapienza*, 2:116; cf. also Büchsel, Friedrich, μονογενής, *TDNT* 4:737-741.

47 Cf. Colombo, *Pneuma*, 117-120.

48 Cf. the texts cited in Scarpat, *Sapienza*, 2:118.

49 Cf. Leproux, *Un discours de sagesse*, 202-203.

Ἀπήμαντος indicates something that is not touched by evil and sometimes something which does nothing evil and is therefore "harmless", something which does not cause harm (perhaps an echo of Aeschylus, *Suppl.* 576).[50]

With φιλάγαθον, we find ourselves at the centre of the movement. This marks the opening of a new series of attributes culminating in φιλάνθρωπος. The term *φιλάγαθος, etymologically "friend of the good", indicates a disposition towards the good, connatural with the spirit of wisdom. For Philo, φιλαγαθία is one of the virtues required for the legislator, together with φιλανθρωπία (cf. *Mos.* 2.9; cf. Let. Aris. 124, in connection with the king, and in the NT, Tit 1:8, in connection with the ἐπίσκοπος).

The adjective ὀξύς means "sharp" (cf. Wis 18:16 [Rahlfs 18:15c], used of the sword). However, the exact sense of the adjective is disputed. Placed after φιλαγαθὸς, one could think of "swift, rapid" with reference to the speed of the action of the spirit in the world (cf. its use in Prov 22:29 LXX); cf. also the ὀξύτης praised by Plato in *Pol.* 306c–e.

The adjective *ἀκώλυτος indicates "something which is not hindered". Our author is probably using it in the same sense as the Stoics. It appears several times in Stoic texts in relation to human liberty or to the law of nature (cf., for example, *SVF* II, 269 frag. 937); and cf. Luke's use in Acts 28:28.[51] In this sense, ἀκώλυτος has some kind of connection with the previous ὀξύ.

The next two adjectives, *εὐεργετικός and φιλάνθρωπος are often associated in Greek usage. In Stoic language, one speaks of the gods who are εὐεργετικοὶ καὶ φιλάνθρωποι, beneficent and friends of men (*SVF* II, 323 frag. 1115). In the light of this usage, the spirit of wisdom is being firmly associated with God. At the same time, "philanthropy" is a human virtue, an ideal of the Hellenistic sage, which is also welcomed by the book of Wisdom (cf. the comment on 1:6).

Next, the spirit is βέβαιος, "secure". Again, it is ἀσφαλής, "stable", never cheating; "solid", as used in an oratorical context.[52] Together with the two previous adjectives, these can be understood in the sense that the spirit is firmly oriented in its love for people and in the search for good. In Stoic language, however, knowledge (ἐπιστήμη) is often described precisely as "secure and stable" (cf. *SVF* II, 30 frag. 95; it is a school definition), a kind of infallible knowledge possessed by the sage without doubts or disquiet, and here attributed instead to the spirit of wisdom. The two terms, therefore, can be understood in a moral sense (cf., for example, βέβαιος ascribed to virtue in *SVF* III, 111 frag. 459), as firmness and stability in one's decisions.

The adjective *ἀμέριμνος (cf. Wis 6:15) indicates something or someone without preoccupations or uneasiness, who does not know of surprises or upsets in

---

50 Cf. Scarpat, *Sapienza*, 2:119.

51 Other citations in Larcher, *Sagesse*, 2:488. The wise and virtuous man is free because he cannot be subject to constraint: *SVF* III, 88 frag. 363. For Fate described as ἀκώλυτον, cf. *SVF* II, 292 frag. 997.

52 Cf. Leproux, *Un discours de sagesse*, 204. Leproux seeks to reread the list of twenty-one attributes on the matrix of the word and instruction. This is possible for some of them, but the overall tone of the list stands within the cosmic rather than the rhetorical-educational matrix.

his activity, one of the characteristics of the philosopher who is detached from the disturbances of human life.

The adjective *παντοδύναμος is rare (perhaps a neologism of our author), but it features again in Wis 11:17 and 18:15. The Latin version translates here with *omnem habens virtutem*, cf. 7:27: πάντα δύνασθαι. The spirit possesses all power. The adjective refers to the spirit's omnipotence. It is thus closely bound up with a virtue that is typically divine.[53]

With *πανεπίσκοπος, our sage is referring to the spirit who "searches all"; cf. the sense of ἐπίσκοπος seen already in 1:6, though in reference to God. This ability to search the creation to its depths is now attributed to the spirit almost as if in an exchange of attributes. With these two terms composed with παν- (παντοδύναμος, πανεπίσκοπος), our sage reaches his conclusion.

The twenty-first attribute is particularly detailed: "who penetrates through all the spirits that are intelligent, pure, and very subtle". Χωρέω is used by the Stoics in a technical sense in connection with their theory of blending (κρᾶσις), according to which two or more moist bodies can penetrate one another without each of them losing its properties (*SVF* II, 153 frag. 471; followed by the example of water mixed with wine). The same verb was used to describe the corporeal nature of the divine πνεῦμα which penetrates the whole of the universe (*SVF* II, 307 frag. 1033). With the employment of this language, the spirit of wisdom is presented as superior to all other spirits and capable of penetrating them. It passes through all the spirits without blending them. Many ancient commentators saw here a reference to the angelic spirits. However, in the context of Wisdom, that seems to be excluded. Here, the text seems rather general. Thanks to its superiority, the spirit of wisdom exercises a particular influence over all the other spirits (our sage is probably thinking of human spirits), even the most intelligent, the purest, the most subtle, that is, those most separated from matter and close to God.[54]

The Theological Sense of Wis 7:22b-23 in Light of Its Sources

The Influence of Stoicism

The principal source of the list in vv. 22b-23 is certainly Stoic philosophy. Commentators agree in citing Cleanthes' *Hymn to Zeus*.[55] According to the particular Stoic viewpoint, the divinity is considered a "world soul", "reason" (λόγος), cosmic "spirit" (πνεῦμα), something shared by human souls. However, the Stoic λόγος is immanent in things and is a material reality just as the bodies which it penetrates are material. For the Stoics, the human soul is not a different reality from the λόγος and from the πνεῦμα of the world which it shares. However, thanks to its spirit, wisdom is foreign to matter and its sphere of action extends over souls,

53 According to Scarpat, *Sapienza*, 2:123-124, the adjective is alluding to the superiority of the spirit over the divine "powers" as conceived by Philo.

54 Cf. Larcher, *Sagesse*, 2:491-493; Scarpat, *Sapienza*, 2:126-128.

55 Cleanthes' *Hymn to Zeus* is recorded in a passage of Clement of Alexandria (*Protreptic*, 6.72.2; cf. *SVF* I, 126 frag. 557) and consists of a list of 29 epithets arranged in 9 verses. Cf. the complete text, with a brief comment, in Scarpat, *Sapienza*, 2:112-113, cf. Des Places, "Epithètes et attributes", *passim*. However, the similarity lies only in the style, not in the individual attributes.

that is, human spirits. Wisdom is thus distinct from people but at the same time is not identified with God. Without losing anything of the divine transcendence, our author has recourse once more to Stoic concepts, albeit with their pantheism removed, and affirms the immanence of wisdom, a moral and spiritual reality in human beings.

Many of the adjectives used here by Wisdom are found in connection with the human soul which was considered by these same Stoics as a microcosm in which the divinity is present.[56] Human beings, therefore, have God in them, or, better, they themselves are gods. In Stoic thought, a person can be perfect, τέλειος. The soul possesses the same characteristics as the divinity and can be invoked with the same attributes. For our author, that is possible only for wisdom, which is a gift to be sought from God, without which it is, in fact, impossible to be perfect (cf. Wis 9:4). According to the Aristotelian idea, people can attain immortal things because their intellect is divine: "it is not necessary to listen to those who advise man, given that he is man, to limit his thought to human things, and, given that he is mortal, to mortal things, but, as far as possible, man ought to concern himself with immortality (ἀθανατίζειν), and do everything to live according to the noblest part of his being" (*Nicomachean Ethics* 1177b 30). What is attainable by the human soul according to the Stoic-Aristotelian concept, is equally attainable for our author, but as the gift of wisdom.

However, the cultural background of these twenty-one attributes is undoubtedly much larger.[57] Reese thinks also of Isiac inspiration, at least for the four adjectives which are found precisely in some Isiac aretalogies. These are ἅγιος, σαφής, τρανός, εὐεργετικός.[58] In addition to individual lexical contacts like these, the Isiac aretalogies, intended to celebrate Isis "under many names", could have influenced our author's description of the spirit of wisdom.[59]

The first two attributes with which our text describes the spirit of wisdom are typical of our author's way of proceeding. The spirit is first of all "intelligent", according to the more pure Stoic terminology, but it is also the "holy spirit" of God spoken of in Israel's Bible. A careful scan of the list reveals that wisdom appears a reality foreign to matter and not identifiable with the creation, yet at the same time quite distinct from God. She is a reality with an activity that is also of the immaterial order. Wisdom acts in a beneficent way in her dealings with the world and with people.

In this way, wisdom, associated with the spirit under the influence of Stoicism, remains absolutely transcendent but can be described as present and active in the world and in people. At the same time, she does not fall into the typically pantheistic perspective of the Stoics. Moreover, all the qualities which Stoicism attributed to the spirit which animates the world and permits people to be themselves "gods" are attributed to wisdom by our text. The closeness to God which the Stoics held to be naturally attainable by every human soul is so, too, for our author but only as the gift of God which is obtained by means of wisdom. While

---

56 For the citations, cf. Scarpat, *Sapienza*, 2:67-68.

57 Cf. a broad overview in Winston, *Wisdom*, 178-180.

58 Cf. Reese, *Hellenistic Influence*, 46.

59 Cf. Engel, *Das Buch der Weisheit*, 132.

the influence of the biblical theology of the "spirit of God" leads our sage to highlight the activities of the spirit of wisdom, the influence of Stoicism leads him, perhaps more boldly, to see in that spirit a sign of the divine presence in all beings (cf. 23de).

7:24 In Wis 7:24, *διήκω is added here to the verb χωρέω (cf. 22d). It is also a technical term of Stoic philosophy: ἡνῶσθαι ... τὴν σύμπασαν οὐσίαν πνεύματός τινος διὰ πάσης αὐτῆς διήκοντος ὑφ' οὗ συνέχεται ... "the cosmic substance is unitary and is completely pervaded (διήκουντος) by a certain spirit that holds it together ..." (*SVF* II, 154 frag. 473). The sense of διήκω is that of "pervade, penetrate, pass through", and, again, in connection with the Stoic theory of blending (or *krasis*). Cf. again the texts of *SVF* II, 305 frag. 1021: τὸ μέρος αὐτοῦ τὸ διῆκον διά πάντων, in connection with God; *SVF* II, 306 frag. 1027: the spirit spreads through the entire world (πνεῦμα διῆκον δι' ὅλου τοῦ κόσμου); cf. *SVF* I, 111 frag. 495; II,112 frag. 310 (μεμῖχθαι τῇ ὕλῃ ... τὸν θεὸν διὰ πάσης αὐτῆς διήκοντα).

In Wis 7:24, the Stoic influence seems really very marked. Taken in isolation, this verse could make us think of an immanent wisdom not very different from the world soul known to the Stoics.

7:25-26: The Meaning, the Sources, and the Progression of the Five Metaphors

It is clear that God is always the term of comparison of the five metaphors:[60] God's power, the glory of the Almighty, eternal light, God's activity, and God's goodness. The nature of wisdom is dynamic, and her action involves the entire cosmos. That is possible because of her privileged relationship with God. Wisdom is the "breath, emanation, reflection, mirror, and image" of God himself. She is not identified with God although she comes from him and is almost consubstantial with him, like the vapour which comes from water or the ray which comes from a source of light.[61]

Wisdom seems to be nothing other than an aspect of the very nature and activity of God, image of his goodness, and so mediatrix between God and people. Our author is thus taking up an idea already present in Prov 8:22-30, and he is developing it in the light of the suggestions coming from Stoicism and Platonism. The philosophical background, especially the influence of Stoicism (but in v. 26, as we have seen, the influence of Platonism is not absent),[62] is the means our author uses to reformulate in a new way the biblical tradition about personified wisdom.

Alongside Stoicism, there is no absence of polemical references to the mystery cults. Osiris, spouse and brother of Isis, is described by Plutarch as the very sun, or, better, "they claim the sun to be the body of the power of good like the visible sign of an intelligible entity" (ἥλιον σῶμα τῆς τἀγαθοῦ δυνάμεως ὡς ὁρατὸν

60 Cf. Larcher, *Etudes*, 376-388.

61 Scarpat's interpretation, that wisdom, in essence, is God himself (cf. *Sapienza*, 2:74), does not take account of the overall value of the five metaphors which avoid such an identification, even though suggesting a very close relationship.

62 In this connection, Hübner asks if, in v. 26, one ought to take note of the "der Umbruch von stoisch beeinflußtem Denken in platonisch beeinflußtes Denken [the upheaval of Stoic-influenced thought on thought influenced by Platonism]", cf. "Die Sapientia Salomonis und die antike Philosophie", 72. In this way, according to Hübner, through the use of Platonism, our author would be able to neutralise Stoic materialism, thus showing a very intelligent use of Greek philosophy (*ibid.* 75).

οὐσίας νοητῆς ἡγούμενοι; *Is. Os.* 51). The world itself is an "image" and "ray" (εἰκών; ἀπόρροια) coming from Osiris. In *P. Oxy.* 11.1380.109, Isis is described as ἀμίαντος, undefiled, exactly like wisdom (7:25c). The Isiac litanies often associate Isis with the light of which she is the mistress.[63]

The text's allusions to the religious world of Alexandria do not end here. In the term ἀπόρροια, we should not overlook the influence of the world of astrology and magic. The 36 divinities which presided over the 36 constellations into which the year was divided by the Egyptian astrologers could have an influence (ἀπόρροια), negative or positive, on people. The magus is one who claims to share in the influence, the "ray" emanating from the divinity: δός μοι ἐκ τῆς σῆς ἀπορροίας.[64] In our text, but only through the gift of wisdom which can be obtained by prayer, it is possible to enter into a relationship with God. Magical practices are useless.

Finally, we notice how some of the terms employed in these verses will have a role also in the NT and in Christian theology: ἀπάγαυσμα and εἰκών are found, respectively, in Heb 1:3 and 2 Cor 3:18; 4:4; and Col 1:15, applied to the relationship between Christ and the Father. Also found is ἀπόρροια, a term which will be employed from the start of the early patristic tradition to indicate the divinity of the Holy Spirit. The Fathers made great use of these verses, often in a christological or pneumatological key.[65]

Speaking of "friends of God" is unusual for the OT/HB, although Isa 41:8 MT 7:27
(cf. also 2 Chr 22:7) speaks of Abraham as a friend of God. In the LXX, φίλος appears only in Exod 33:11 in connection with Moses. Only later do we find this theme in Philo in connection with the sage as a friend of God (*Her.* 21; *Prob.* 44; *Abr.* 129) and, in the NT, in Jas 2:23.[66] With regard to Solomon, the book of Wisdom could have taken its cue from texts such as 2 Sam 12:24 and Neh 13:26, which mention God's predilection for the king. In 27c-d, friendship with God does not appear as a human achievement but as a gift offered by wisdom (cf. the development of this theme in the NT, in John 15:14-15). In thinking of divine kingship, our sage could also have had in mind the figure of the φίλοι βασιλέως, the friends of the king who occupied the highest positions in the Ptolemaic court.[67]

Next, speaking of "prophets" introduces us into a biblical theme which, however, has to be clarified. The prophet is not being considered here as a charismatic, an exceptional figure whom the Lord raises at particular moments in the history of Israel. Every sage in fact is a prophet thanks to the gift of Wisdom. The association with "friend" makes us think first of all of the intimacy with God which characterises biblical prophets such as Moses. However, the prophet is primarily a person of the word. Thus, thanks to the gift of wisdom, every sage becomes the spokesperson of God himself. It is difficult to say whether, with the idea of "prophet", our sage sees also the knowledge of truth which escapes people, as is

---

63 Cf. Reese, *Hellenistic Influence*, 46-47.

64 Cf. Festugière, "L'idéal", 296s; Scarpat, *Sapienza*, 2:72-73.

65 Cf. Larcher, *Sagesse*, 2:501 and 505; Scarpat, *Sapienza*, 2:71-72; Harl, "A propos d'un passage"; Grant, "The Book of Wisdom at Alexandria", 70-82.

66 For the development of this theme in the ancient tradition, especially the Jewish, cf. Winston, *Wisdom*, 188-189.

67 Cf. Boffo, *Iscrizioni greche e latine*, 93-94.

the case in Philo (cf. *Mos.* 2.6; *Spec.* 4.192) where the prophet is also "interpreter" of the holy laws of God (cf. *Mut.* 126, where Moses receives from God the ἑρμηνείαν καὶ προφητείαν νόμων ἱερῶν). Thus, in every sage, as in the prophets, the divine voice continues to resound and, in some way, the work of revelation is extended in them.

7:29 The superiority of wisdom to light is still more comprehensible on the basis of a possible reference to Isis. In the Isiac litanies of the Oxyrhynchus Papyrus, she bears "the name of the sun" (11.1380.112). She is invoked as mistress of the light and of the flames: σὺ καὶ φωτὸς καὶ φλεγμάτων κυρία (*P. Oxy.* 11.1380.248). In the aretalogy of Chios (first cent. BCE), she is invoked as φῶς πᾶσι βροτοῖσι (*CIG* 3724, l. 8). Whatever Isis claims for herself, wisdom is to a far greater degree.

8:1 In 8:1, our sage is expressing biblical concepts in Stoic language.[68]

The verb διατείνει has the sense of "extend" and is typical of Stoic vocabulary. It is accompanied by the adverb εὐρώστως, "with power, mightily" (2 Macc 10:17; 12:27, 35) which underlines the idea of energy and activity. Thus, in the creation, wisdom extends from one end of the earth to the other (cf. Pss 18:5 LXX [19:5 MT]; 47:11 LXX [48:11 MT]). The verb διατείνει is found in connection with the theory of blending which we have already encountered: εἰς ὅλον, φησί, τὸν κόσμον διατενεῖν τῇ κράσει τὸν σταλαγμόν, "in the blending, a drop extends to the entire cosmos". Chrysippos says this in connection with a drop of wine thrown into the sea (*SVF* II, 158 frag. 480). It is used again in connection with the radiation of parts of the πνεῦμα (*SVF* II, 226 frag. 826). According to the Stoics, the πνεῦμα is able to "extend" through the entire cosmos, though remaining itself, on account of its extreme mobility. The cosmos is thus a great organism animated by God himself (cf. the Stoic concept of τόνος, the tension that pervades the entire cosmos). We find here an echo also of the Platonic theme of the world soul, according to the text of *Tim.* 34b: ψυχὴν δὲ εἰς τὸ μέσον αὐτοῦ θεὶς διὰ παντός τε ἔτεινεν "as for the soul, having set it in the centre of the body of the world, he spreads it (ἔτεινεν) through the entire body". Even if risking a degree of pantheism, our author is making use of such conceptions to emphasise the immanence of divine wisdom.

The verb διοικέω, which is used in its proper sense in 8:14a in connection with the administration of a city, is often used in relation to God's providential governing of the world, just as in Wis 12:18 and 15:1. Wisdom, therefore, is not only present in the world but also assumes a providential role. Once again, the language is Stoicising: "thus every reality in the world is completed (διοικεῖσθαι) in the best way, as in a well-governed city" (*SVF* I, 27 frag. 98). Wisdom assumes here the role performed by the πνεῦμα within the Stoic framework (cf. *SVF* II, 137 frag. 416: τὸ διῆκον διὰ πάντων πνεῦμα, ὑφ' οὗ τὰ πάντα συνέχεσθαι καὶ διοικεῖσθαι "the spirit that permeates everything, through whom everything coheres and is administered") or by the πρόνοια (cf. *SVF* II, 169 frag. 528 lines 30-31: οἷς ἀκολούθως νομιστέον προνοεῖν τῶν ἀνθρώπων τὸν τὰ ὅλα διοικοῦντα θεόν "through which one has to believe that the god who rules the universe provides for people"; cf. also *SVF* II, 264 frag. 913; II, 192 frag. 634).

---

68 Thus, the argument of 7:22-8:1 opens with a Stoic allusion, continues with Platonic allusions and concludes, once again, with Stoicism; cf. Hübner, *Weisheit*, 113.

This governing of the universe (τὰ πάντα) takes place χρηστῶς. In itself, this adverb indicates "appropriately". The Latin version has understood it as *suaviter.*[69] It should probably be understood, as elsewhere in the LXX, with the sense of "with goodness". Philo uses the formula χρηστὸς θεὸς to indicate the kindness and goodness of God (cf. *Leg.* 3.73; *Det.* 46), a significance which is really rare in Greek but quite common in the LXX, especially in the Psalms (LXX-Pss 24:8; 33:9 [MT-Pss 25:8; 34:9]; etc; cf. in the NT 1 Pet 2:3; cf. also Rom 2:4).[70] Thus, alongside a typically Stoic verb such as διοικέω, our sage joins a profoundly biblical concept relating to the goodness of God.[71]

Wis 8:2-9: Wisdom as Spouse, Friend, Counsellor

2 Her I have had as a friend and sought her from my youth,
and I sought her as my bride [as my Nymph]
and I became enamoured of her beauty.
3 Dwelling as the companion of God, she exalts her noble origin
because the Sovereign of the whole universe has loved her.
4 For she is truly an initiate in the knowledge of God
and understands his works.

5 If wealth is a desirable possession in life,
what wealth is greater than wisdom which performs all things?
6 And if it is prudence in acting,
who more than her, among the beings, is the one who fashions everything?
7 And if anyone loves justice,
her labours are the virtues:
for she teaches temperance and prudence,
justice and fortitude,
than which nothing is more useful in human life.
8 If anyone aspires to vast experience,
she knows the things that are past and foretells what is to come;
she understands the subtleties of speech and the solutions of riddles;
she is aware of signs and wonders before they happen,
the alternation of times and seasons.

---

69 In its Latin reinterpretation, this verse has become dear to the Catholic liturgy which every year, on 17 December, sings it as the "greater O antiphon": "O Sapientia, quae ex ore Altissimi prodisti, attingens a fine usque ad finem fortiter, suaviter disponensque omnia... [O Wisdom, which camest out of the mouth of the Most High and reachest from one end to the other, mightily and sweetly ordering all things...]".

70 Cf. Weiss, Konrad, χρηστός κτλ., *TDNT* 11, especially 485-486.

71 Cf. Scarpat, *Sapienza*, 2:183.

[9] I decided, therefore, to take her as my companion,
knowing that she would be a good counsellor to me
and encouragement in my cares and sadness.

Notes on the Text and Translation

v. 4. The term *αἱρετίς, an *hapax totius graecitatis*, has embarrassed scribes as is evident from the strange variants proposed by the versions (cf. Ziegler). Just like the preceding μύστις, it is a formation in –τις typical of the Hellenistic period: cf. Reese, *Hellenistic Influence,* 7; also, Scarpat, "Un *hapax* assoluto: αἱρετίς", who underlines that our author, perhaps coining this term himself, wished to recall his hearers' attention to something important.

v. 6. The expression εἰ δὲ φρόνησις ἐργάζεται is surprising because of the absence of the complement to ἐργάζεται. Some witnesses (O-V, Lat, Arm; cf. Ziegler) add τι (cf. the VL: *si autem sensus operatur aliquid*). Modern scholars have proposed many conjectures (cf. Larcher, *Sagesse*, 2:525-526; Scarpat, *Sapienza*, 2:145-146). Among these, the best seems to be Larcher, after Fichtner and following the Syriac: εἰ δὲ φρόνησιν εἰς ἔργα ζητεῖ τις; "and if man seeks the ability to act". Scarpat proposes instead to correct with: εἰ δὲ φρόνησιν ἐργάζεταί τις, the τις having fallen out through haplography: "if one works with skill". Without correcting the text, one could translate "if it is understanding that acts"; for φρόνησις, cf. 7:16. The second part of v. 6 should be constructed thus: τὶς ἐστιν τῶν ὄντων τεχνῖτις μᾶλλον αὐτῆς: "who more than her is craftsperson among the beings?"; cf. Scarpat, *Sapienza*, 2:147. The pronoun αὐτῆς refers *ad sensum* to the wisdom mentioned in 5b.

Synchronic Analysis

Wis 8:2-4: Wisdom, Friend and Counsellor

Thinking about his youthful experience, Solomon explains his choice to take wisdom as friend and counsellor (v. 2). She is noble in origin and loved by God (v. 3), and, again (v. 4), she has true knowledge of God himself and God's works (v. 4). As such, can put herself alongside people to guide them towards the Lord.

8:2 Ταύτην ἐφίλησα: "this/her", in emphatic position, refers to wisdom. The use of the aorist (ἐφίλησα, ἐξεζήτησα) has ingressive value: I began to be her friend, to search for wisdom from my youth, a time which one does not normally associate with wisdom. The author is alluding to the story of the young Solomon recounted in 1 Kgs 3 and viewed here retrospectively by "Solomon", the protagonist of Wis 7-8.

With the expression νύμφην ἀγαγέσθαι, the second stich of v. 2 is alluding to the practice of conducting the bride into the husband's house, sometimes by the groom himself (cf. *Od.* 14.211; Aristophanes, *Plut.* 529 etc.). At first sight, this image appears to be nuptial. Solomon sought (ἐζήτησα) to take wisdom as his bride. The pronoun ἐμαυτῷ, redundant in itself, reinforces the idea of belonging. The verb ζητέω strengthens the idea of searching contained already in the previous stich. Wisdom is a reality which has to be searched for with passion. The image of the wisdom-bride is already present in Sir 14:20-15:6 (cf. especially 15:2). In fact, νύμφη also refers to the Nymphs, daughters of Zeus, companions of the gods, personification of the forces of nature, often confused with the Muses, whose favours people seek to win. The temple of the Nymphs was near the Academy to remind the scholars that the source of their knowledge, of all their art, surpassed human powers. Here, wisdom, unique in the presence of the only God, is taking the role of the Nymphs in a polemical way, as initiator into the mysteries of God and counsellor of people.[72]

The third stich of v. 2 adds a new aspect: I became enamoured (ἐραστής) of her beauty.

Verse 3 provides the reasons why "Solomon" is enamoured of wisdom: a noble 8:3
origin is sought for his bride, εὐγένεια.

By contrast with the Greek world (see below), εὐγένεια represents a value because wisdom has her origin in God. For this reason, our sage can state that wisdom εὐγένειαν δοξάζει, glorifies, exalts her noble origin (presupposing a possessive). If, however, we understand εὐγένειαν in a more general sense, it is also possible to read "glorifies nobility".

The reason for such an unusual attitude on the part of wisdom is her intimacy with God: συμβίωσιν θεοῦ ἔχουσα. The term συμβίωσις (cf. also in vv. 9a and 16c) indicates "cohabitation", even in a conjugal sense. The term is used in the LXX only in these three passages. Wisdom is, therefore, being imagined as the "spouse" of God himself. However, the metaphors of vv. 25-26 avoid the danger of understanding wisdom as a sort of female divinity beside God. Nonetheless, we should note that συμβίωσις also indicates forms of cohabitation other than the conjugal. In *Flacc.* 158, συμβιωτής indicates someone who lives with a powerful person. Thus, wisdom appears not only as spouse but also as friend.[73]

Wisdom is intimately linked to God. The "Sovereign" of the whole universe (ὁ πάντων δεσπότης; cf. Wis 6:7; 13:3, 9) has loved her (for ἀγαπάω, cf. Wis 1:1a and above in 7:28). In this way, the universal activity of God comes to coincide with his love for wisdom, a love which, described with ἀγαπάω, is here undoubtedly more a spousal (or filial) love than friendship (cf., by contrast, φιλέω in 8:2a). If wisdom is people's friend and counsellor, she is, as such, loved by God himself.

The particle γάρ connects this verse with the previous one. Verse 4 thus gives 8:4
the reasons for wisdom's close intimacy with God. First of all, she is an initiate (μύστις)in the knowledge (ἐπιστήμη) of God.

Wisdom is an initiate in the "knowledge of God", another expression absent from the LXX. According to Greek usage, we should understand ἐπιστήμη as knowledge that is firm and secure, precisely as a "science". Here, the genitive θεοῦ cold be understood as subjective: the knowledge that God possesses, his knowledge of the whole of creation.[74] Therefore, in so far as she is an initiate in this divine knowledge, wisdom shares in it and can communicate it to people. It is also possible to read this as an objective genitive in light of the use that Philo

72 On all this, cf. Leproux's detailed analysis, *Un discours de sagesse*, 274-282.

73 Cf. Leproux, *Un discours de sagesse*, 266-268. The same Leproux (pp. 269-274) offers a summary view of the idea of friendship in the Hellenistic world. Of this friendship, the conjugal variety would be the highest. For this reason, a reading of wisdom as "spouse" does not deny but rather presupposes the idea of wisdom as "friend".

74 So, already, Grimm, *Weisheit*, 168-169; cf. also Gilbert, "La connaissance de Dieu", 318-319.

makes of the theme of the divine ἐπιστήμη in *Spec.* 1.345, that is, the knowledge which a person can have of God. Understood in this way, our text would then be affirming that wisdom alone permits the knowledge of God in a secure way. She is, therefore, theologically speaking, an instrument of revelation. In the translation, we have left both possibilities open.

Next, Wisdom is one who "chooses", or else "understands" (αἱρετίς) the works of God. This very term could refer to that wisdom described as counsellor of God in God's works,[75] or, in relation to people, as the one who guides them in their choices. It could be better to think of the Stoics' αἱρῶν λόγος, that is, of the "reason that chooses", a concept well known to Philo too.[76] The reference to the "works" of God will be taken up immediately, in v. 5, with ἐργάζεται, which refers, however, to the works of wisdom. Wisdom, therefore, is the one who is able to choose, understand, and value the divine works. She is thus able to counsel people as to what they ought to do in order to obey God and avoid evil. Once again, she is being presented as the counsellor of people, here on the plane of moral action. Thus, if 4a refers to the knowledge of God offered to people by wisdom, the "initiate" in this knowledge, 4b leads us on to the plane of moral action where wisdom is also the guide with her capacity for understanding (αἱρετίς).

Wis 8:5-8: Wisdom Is Superior to Every Good

In vv. 5-8, following his own style, our author heaps up a good four hypothetical statements for a total of fourteen stichs. He is thus able to emphasise that wisdom is superior to wealth, to understanding, to justice, and to every other kind of virtue, knowledge, and experience. At the same time, she gives all these things to the one who decides to choose her as a life companion (cf. v. 9 which takes up v. 2).

8:5 The first value with which wisdom is compared is wealth (πλοῦτος), a theme already introduced in 7:8-9 and 11. The first part of v. 5 contains an observation arising from experience: "if (εἰ δὲ) wealth is a desirable possession (ἐπιθυμητὸν κτῆμα) in life (ἐν βίῳ; that is, during concrete, earthly existence) ...". Wealth can also be a good, but only wisdom is an absolute good. There follows a rhetorical question: what is richer than wisdom?

Wisdom is described with the expression τῆς τὰ πάντα ἐργαζομένης. Τὰ πάντα should be understood as the whole of created reality (cf. 8:1b); ἐργάζομαι refers to some kind of activity of wisdom with regard to creation. However, this is not specified further but is to be seen along the lines of what was said in Wis 7:27 and 8:1. The contrast with wealth is illuminating. The rich believe that they can act in the world, but they do not realise that it is only wisdom that can work in everything (τὰ πάντα ἐργαζομένης) effectively. The following verse takes up this theme.

---

75 Winston's judgement is neat: "our author is saying in effect that wisdom is essentially synonymous with the Divine Mind, and this represents the creative agent of the Deity. The similarity of this conception with Philo's *logos* doctrine is unmistakable" (*Wisdom*, 196). Against Winston, we have to affirm that the author nonetheless keeps wisdom distinct from God.

76 Cf. Scarpat, *Sapienza*, 2:140-144.

The first part of v. 6 is not very clear (cf. the textual note); "if it is prudence in acting ...". Φρόνησις (cf. the comment on 7:16), a practical virtue relating to prudence and discernment, is able to act. It is possible to think that the one who possesses this virtue is able to imitate the ἔργα of wisdom referred to in 8:5b. However, the second part of v. 6 highlights the superiority of the action of wisdom herself. The text intends to suggest that the wisdom that comes from God always needs human wisdom as well. It is, therefore, a collaboration between God and people. 8:6

With τεχνῖτις, we find again here the same term that was already seen in 7:22. On that occasion, we gave it the sense of "artificer" without excluding that of "craftsperson". Here, the context, which relates to the activity of wisdom, causes us to go for this second meaning without any doubt; wisdom is the craftsperson of creation, responsible for the harmony in creation.

8:7: Wisdom and Virtue

The third hypothetical statement compares wisdom with the four "cardinal" virtues of later Christian theology: justice, temperance, prudence, and fortitude. It is the only time that these virtues appear together in Scripture.

The stress falls, first of all, on justice (δικαιοσύνη; v. 7a); if anyone loves her, he knows that her labours (πόνοι), that is, the works produced by wisdom, consist precisely in the virtues (ἀρεταί). Since justice is listed again in 7d together with the other three "cardinal" virtues, it must be that this first occurrence is not to be understood in the same sense, that is, justice as one of the four virtues listed immediately afterwards. Here, justice appears rather in the same sense as at the beginning of the book (1:1): ἀγαπήσατε δικαιοσύνην, human justice in dealings with one's fellows, but, also and above all, the justice of God, the justice that comes from God (cf. 1:15).

Wisdom, therefore, teaches (ἐκδιδάσκει) the virtues (ἀρεταί). If it might be clear what our author understands with φρόνησις (cf. above) and δικαιοσύνη, here certainly the human virtue of justice, it is not possible to be more specific about the other virtues which are cited only here in the book. Σωφροσύνη could be understood as in Philo (*Virt.* 13-14) as the virtue of temperance, which guarantees control over the passions (cf. also *Arist.* 237). Ἀνδρεία, on the other hand, is clearly the virtue of courage. It appears in the LXX only in late texts; cf. 4 Macc 1:6, in connection with σωφροσύνη and δικαιοσύνη.

8:8: A Vast Experience

The fourth conditional statement lists further qualities of wisdom. If anyone desires (ποθεῖ) vast experience (πολυπειρία), it is certainly to be found in wisdom; cf. Sir 25:6, the only other occurrence of πολυπειρία in the LXX. As attested in classical usage, the term refers to knowledge acquired through experience. That means that wisdom is able to communicate a knowledge that comes about not merely through study and teaching to those who possess her. We see that, here too, the image of wisdom as spouse is superseded by that of a wise counsellor (cf. 9b) and life-companion.

Such experience possessed by wisdom enables knowledge of both the past and the future. In fact, wisdom οἶδεν τὰ ἀρχαῖα. Our sage does not explain further. Wisdom is said to have a general knowledge of things of the past. Again, she τὰ μέλλοντα εἰκάζει. With τὰ μέλλοντα (cf. Wis 19:1), the reference is clearly to future things. The verb εἰκάζω, "conjecture" (cf. Jer 26:23 LXX [46:23 MT]) does not suppose a knowledge of lesser value than that acquired theoretically. The sense is rather that, if wisdom knows the things that are past, she can use such knowledge to be able to construct a conjectural knowledge of things in the future. It is not a matter here of knowledge gained by study or revelation but, precisely, by experience. Our sage could be leaning on Stoic ideas.[77]

Moreover, wisdom understands the subtleties of speech (στροφὰς λόγων; cf. Prov 1:3) and the solutions to riddles (λύσεις αἰνιγμάτων). This is certainly an allusion to Solomon's sapiential activity (cf. 2 Chr 9:1). Here we find an allusion to the field of the art of oratory and education. If wisdom is an "artificer" (τεχνῖτις), she is so by virtue of the fact that she knows the subtleties of speech and can solve every riddle. There is no need, therefore, to interpret λόγοι in the sense of "oracles" or mysterious words that need further revelation. As for the αἰνίγματα, they are a literary genre known to the sapiential tradition (the חידות); cf. 1 Kgs 10:1, 2 Chr 9:1, in both cases in connection with the figure of Solomon (the episode with the Queen of Sheba); cf. again Prov 1:6[78] and Sir 39:2-3. Our sage could also have had in mind some themes well known to the Greek world (the famous riddle of the Sphinx!).

The verb *προγινώσκω (cf. 6:13; 18:6) indicates knowing something in advance thanks to premonitory signs, whether the predictions of doctors or astrologers. Here, it has as its object σημεῖα καὶ τέρατα, "signs and wonders", an expression very frequent in Exodus contexts (cf. Exod 7:3, etc.; cf. Wis 10:16, but in a different context). Wisdom, therefore, which shares in the very knowledge of God, knows in advance the signs which God himself is performing in history. This interpretation seems to be supported by the final stich. Wisdom knows in advance the alternation, that is the "outcomes" of the times and seasons. In itself the term ἔκβασις indicates the "final result". The text of 8:8d-e could have been inspired by Dan 4:37 LXX where the lexemes καιρ- and χρον- appear precisely with σημεῖα καὶ τέρατα. Wisdom knows the rhythms of the cosmos and so knows the timely moment to act (cf. Qoh 3:1-8).

On rereading the whole of v. 8, the impression remains that wisdom is offering that knowledge of the times and of the creation which was often sought in revelations of an apocalyptic character (e.g., the Enochic tradition). However, because of her vast experience (8a), wisdom knows the things of the past and conjectures those of the future (8b), knows how to solve every type of riddle (8c), and knows how to read the signs of history (8d) and of the creation (8e). If the sage possesses wisdom, he does not need other forms of revelation; cf. what was already observed in connection with Wis 7:17-20.

8:9: This is the expression of Solomon's final resolution in relation to wisdom: "I decided, therefore" (ἔκρινα τοίνυν). The following expression, ταύτην ἀγαγέσθαι, refers us directly to 8:2. Here, however, the verb is followed by πρὸς συμβίωσιν, a term already present in 8:3 which refers to the shared, not necessarily the matrimonial, life. In fact, for Solomon, Wisdom will be a σύμβουλος ἀγαθῶν, a counsellor of good things. Frequent in the LXX (cf. 2 Chr 22:3; 2 Macc 7:25), the term σύμβουλος is followed here by an objective genitive: counsellor of good things, counsellor who advises the good (cf. Wis 16:6b).

---

77 Cf. A more extensive explanation in Larcher, *Sagesse*, 2:531.

78 Cf. Fox, *Proverbs 1-9*, 65-67. Perhaps חידות refers more to the act of interpretation of the text (which in this sens could be considered a "riddle") than to the text in itself.

Alongside this task, wisdom will also be *παραίνεσις, a term which indicates "encouragement, advice, counsel". Wisdom as Counsellor

Diachronic Analysis

The verb φιλέω (cf. φιλία in 7:14; 8:18 and φίλος in 7:27) is *hapax* in Wisdom and rare in the LXX, but our sage could have taken it from Prov 8:17 where the Greek translator uses for the Hebrew אהב first ἀγαπάω and then φιλέω in relation to ζητέω. Φιλέω seems to have been chosen intentionally instead of ἀγαπάω. The latter verb, beloved by the LXX and not infrequently applied to the God-people relationship (Deut 7:7, 8, 9, 13), indicates a gratuitous relation between two people of different standing (husband and wife, for example) whereas φιλέω refers to the love of friendship, denoting a pull towards the object of love itself.[79] This "friendly" dimension of φιλέω should make us more cautious in giving exclusive emphasis to the nuptial aspect of wisdom. 8:2

In the LXX, the verb ἐκζητέω is found in relation to wisdom, in Qoh 1:13; Sir 6:18; 24:34; 39:1; 51:14, 21, all texts which our author could have had in mind, especially Sir 51:14-15: ἐκζητήσω αὐτήν ... ἐκ νεότητός μου ἴχνευον αὐτήν ...; cf. also Sir 51:15: εὐφράνθη ἡ καρδία μου ἐν αὐτῇ, compared with Wis 7:12 (cf. the comment). Just as the wise instruct a young man on the need to choose a good wife (cf. Sir 25-26), so they instruct him on the importance of "marrying" wisdom.

As for 8:2c, the erotic dimension of love is not one of the more obvious characteristics of marriage either Jewish or Greek. The first consideration is children and the care of the family. Moreover, in the LXX, ἐραστής mostly has a pejorative sense; cf. Hos 2:9, 12, 14, 15; Ezek 16:33, 36, 37; 23:5, 9, 22; cf. Wis 15:6 which could be read as a kind of polemical *flashback* to 8:2.[80] Here, on the other hand, the sense is positive (cf., by contrast, Sir 9:8: "many have lost their way through a woman's beauty"), just as in Philo, who uses ἐραστής in connection with σοφία or φρόνησις (cf. *Migr.* 101; *Her.* 100; *Mut.* 37), following a usage which could betray reminiscences of Plato (cf. ἐπιστήμης ἐραστής in *Tim.* 46d). The idea of beauty (ἐραστὴς τοῦ κάλλους αὐτῆς) is a typically Greek touch, also of a Platonic flavour, even if an influence of the Song of Songs cannot be wholly excluded.[81]

As for εὐγένεια, the term occurs in the LXX only in 2 Macc 14:42 and 4 Macc 8:4, while the adjective εὐγενής is more frequent. Nobility of origins, together with beauty and wealth, is one of the things which the Stoics described as an ἀδιάφορον, something "indifferent" in comparison with the power represented by virtue (cf., for example, *SVF* III, 261 frag. 14). 8:3

In 8:4, the feminine *μύστις is a very rare variation of the more common μύστης, "initiate", typical of the mystery vocabulary (cf. the Isiac Aretalogy of Oxyrhyncus, P.Oxy. XI 1380.111, where μύστης is used of Isis). According to Philo, 8:4

79 Cf. Spicq, *Agapè*, 12-70.

80 Cf. Gilbert, *La critique des dieux*, 194.

81 Gilbert ("La figure de Salomon", 153-156) points out the lack of grounds for a reading of the Song of Songs in an allegorical sense which the book of Wisdom could be presupposing here. The relation to Song is limited to some echoes of the texts on the beauty of the beloved woman.

Moses is the true initiate in the mysteries of God; cf. *Gig.* 54 (μύστης ... καὶ ἱεροφάντης). Wisdom is the true "initiate" in those "mysteries" of God (cf. Wis 2:22) which are actually accessible to all (cf. Wis 6:22), precisely because they have been revealed to people by wisdom. Only wisdom – not even Moses, as Philo wishes – knows the secrets of God. There is, therefore, no mystery rite which is able to introduce people to the knowledge of God.

8:6 The mention of φρόνησις in 8:6 is a possible polemical reprise of Isiac themes. In fact, in the Isiac Litany of Oxyrhyncus (P.Oxy. XI 1380.34, 40, 60, 124), φρόνησις is invoked as a title of Isis.

As for the use of the term τεχνῖτις, it is possible that in this case too, and perhaps still more than in 7:22, our sage is offering us an interpretation of the mysterious אמון of Prov 8:30, interpreted in the sense of "workman, artificer". In that case, Wis 8:6 would be undoubtedly the most ancient witness to this type of interpretation.

8:7a–b Wis 8:7a contains a possible Platonic reminiscence. In fact, the text of *Resp.* 358a places justice among the goods which are to be loved. In this case, however, someone (τίς) is presupposed who loves that justice which comes from God, connected right from 1:1 with wisdom, and which, precisely because of this link with God, finds all the other virtues along with wisdom. The connection between justice and wisdom is made still more evident here by the use of the emphatic pronoun ταύτης instead of αὐτῆς. If someone loves justice, the labours produced by wisdom (ταύτης) are the virtues. The mention of the "labours" (πόνοι) of wisdom could be an allusion to the works performed by Lady Wisdom (cf. Prov 31:16, 31), a figure who could have been interpreted by our author as the image of wisdom or the sage.[82]

8:7c–e The four virtues listed in Wis 8:7cd are known from the time of Plato, were refined by Aristotle, and spread by Stoicism according to an order which became traditional and which was well known also to Philo (cf. *Mos.* 2.185 and 216): φρόνησις, σωφροσύνη, δικαιοσύνη, ἀνδρεία.[83] In our text, the order differs for no apparent reason.

It should be emphasised that, by integrating among wisdom's gifts a list of virtues well known to the Greek world, our sage is pointing to the strong ethical value of biblical wisdom. It is a value which not only does not deny but also includes the best aspects of contemporary Greek ethics.[84] Our sage embraces these four virtues almost as a given. There is nothing more useful (χρησιμώτερον) in human life than these virtues (7e). What we have here is not a utilitarian idea but the reprise of a Stoic theme. The true goods are actually those that are useful in relation to people's final end (cf. *SVF* III, 22 frag. 87).

8:8 In connection with Wis 8:8de, we observe that in Stoicism also "divination" is considered the science (ἐπιστήμη) that scrutinises and explains "the signs which the gods direct to men" (*SVF* II, 304 frag. 1018). In this case, the "signs and wonders" are to be understood, more simply, as the extraordinary natural phenomena

82 Cf. Gilbert, "La donna forte di Pr 31,10-31: ritratto o simbolo?".

83 Cf. Larcher, *Sagesse*, 2:528-529.

84 Contra Scarpat, *Sapienza*, 2:190, when he states that in this list "there is more polemic than agreement".

which wisdom is able to foresee without confusing events without significance with others which refer to the future. All in all, wisdom shares in that divine knowledge sung of by the psalmist: ἰδοὺ, κύριε, σὺ ἔγνως τὰ ἔσχατα καὶ τὰ ἀρχαῖα; Ps 138:5 LXX.

In connection with the rhetorical context of Wis 7-8, Scarpat sees in παραίνε- 8:9
σις a reference to the παραινετικὸς λόγος, the "paraenesis" which, in Greek philosophy, is that part which suggests the right forms of behaviour to people, freeing them from useless worries and sorrow (φροντίδων καὶ λύπης). In 9:15, the human νοῦς is described as "weighed down by many concerns" (πολυφροντίς) if it allows itself to be dragged down by the body without embracing wisdom.[85] We must, therefore, translate παραίνεσις with "encouragement", one who teaches and advises, who "counsels" people (cf. also the comment on 8:4b). We cannot wholly exclude an anti-Isiac polemic here: in the Third Hymn of Isidorus (line 6), Isis is one who offers people ὄλβον εὐτυχίην καὶ σωφροσύνην τε ἄλυπον „welfare, happiness, and prudence devoid of sorrow". Thus, she is the one who frees people from all sadness. Here, instead, the same role is attributed to wisdom.

Wis 8:10-16: On the Gifts of Wisdom Again

10 Through her I shall have glory in the assemblies
and honour among the aged, though I am young.
11 I shall be found sharp in judgement,
I shall be admired before the mighty.
12 When I am silent, they will wait in expectation;
when I speak, they will pay attention.
If I prolong my speech,
they will put their hands over their mouths.
13 Thanks to her, I shall have immortality,
and I shall leave an eternal memorial to those who come after me.
14 I shall govern peoples, and nations will be subject to me.
15 Fearful tyrants will be afraid at my words.
I will show myself gifted in the assembly and courageous in war.
16 When I enter my house, I shall rest with her,
for, in living with her, there is no bitterness,
and, in having her as companion, no pain,
but gladness and joy.

85 Cf. Scarpat, *Sapienza*, 2:154.

Synchronic Analysis

Wis 8:10-12: The Gifts Offered by Wisdom

8:10 The Solomon's interior discourse opens here. Attention is shifted again to the gifts offered by wisdom. The verbs in the future are accounted for by the reference to the biblical Solomon who thinks about the things that wisdom will be able to grant him, but also apply to all who intend to choose her. Verses 10-12, in seven stichs, make up the first part of a concentric strophe.

The theme of Solomon's glory is taken from 1 Kgs 3:13 and 2 Chr 1:11-12. It is not a question of purely human glory, rather of a reflection of the glory of God which is possessed by wisdom (cf. 7:25).[86] This glory will be granted by wisdom to the wise king ἐν ὄχλοις. In Wis 6:2, ὄχλος appears in parallel with ἔθνη and would seem to designate the pagan peoples. We would, therefore, have to think of a fame of Solomon going beyond the borders of Israel. However, the following reference to the "aged" could lead us to prefer the "assemblies" of Israel as the place where Solomon is being depicted.[87]

Alongside glory, the second stich introduces honour (τιμή), a term which privileges more the subjective aspect of Solomon's fame and renown. Solomon will have this honour among the "aged". Πρεσβύτεροι makes us think of the biblical context of the elders understood as the leaders of the people of Israel (cf. Exod 18:12; 19:7; Deut 31:28; 1 Kgs 8:1; 12:6, 8). These are contrasted, adversatively, with ὁ νέος, a term which, in Greek usage, does not necessarily indicate a boy but a young man under thirty years.

8:11 "I will be found sharp in judgement"; for ὀξύς, cf. the comment on 7:22e. Here, the term κρίσις does not allude simply to a context of judgement issued in the sphere of a tribunal according to the practice of Near Eastern monarchs (cf. a further, probable allusion to the episode of 1 Kgs 3:16-28) but more generally to the permanent activity of judgement and justice exercised by the king.

The second stich mentions the admiration (cf. θαυμάζομαι) which Solomon will obtain in the presence of the mighty (ἐν ὄψει δυναστῶν). As in Prov 8:3 and 15, δυνασταί should be understood in a general sense, for example – with reference to the biblical Solomon – those non-Israelites who came to listen to the wisdom of Solomon (1 Kgs 5:14; 10:1-13). There is no necessarily negative significance to δυνασταί as in Wis 5:23.

8:12 Once again, this verse shifts the attention to the oratorical abilities conferred by wisdom, a theme which takes up *motifs* dear to the Greek culture of the time but presented, significantly, by means of biblical images.

The first stich emphasis that when the sage is silent, the others will wait for him to speak while when he speaks, the others will remain silent. This is a free use of the text of Job 29:9-10, 21-24. On the silence of the sage, cf. also Sir 20:7.

The verb περιμένω, "wait patiently", is present in the LXX only in Gen 49:18 (cf. Acts 1:14); on the other hand, προσέχω, "pay attention" is much more fre-

---

86 Cf. Raurell, "The religious meaning", 378. Raurell also notes a possible Isiac background. In the Kyme aretalogy (l. 40) it says that "no one is glorified without my willing it".

87 For this interpretation, cf. Scarpat, *Sapienza*, 2:193.

quent, but could have been taken precisely from the passage of Job 29:21 just mentioned.

Then, if the sage speaks again (ἐπὶ πλεῖον), or prolongs his speech inordinately, his hearers will place their hands over their mouths because, even if he speaks for a long time, the sage never says anything useless.

Wis 8:13: The Gift of Immortality

This is the centre of the strophe. Repeating the formula that opened v. 10, the author introduces the idea of ἀθανασία as a further gift of wisdom to the king.[88] For this term, cf. the comment on 3:4. The immediately adjacent mention of the "eternal memorial" (μνήμη αἰώνιος) which the king leaves to those who come after him could lead to the thought that the sage has in mind immortality of the memory and not the eternal life evoked in 3:4. However, we have already observed that, in Wis 4:1-2 also, personal immortality is bound up with the memory. In 8:17, the reprise of ἀθανασία leads precisely to the thought of personal immortality. Immortality

Next, we note that, in introducing the two themes of immortality and eternal memory, v. 13 could be reread in connection with the double theme of glory and honour described in 8:10 (cf. the identical beginning of both verses). Finally, in v. 16 (cf. below), there is an emphasis on the "cohabitation" of the sage with wisdom. Thus, immortality is obtained through a close relationship with wisdom (cf. 8:17).

Wis 8:14-16: Wisdom, the Art of Good Governance

In vv. 14-16, attention is shifted to the art of good governance, another of wisdom's gifts. In v. 14, there is a reference to the political rule of Solomon with a verb (διοικέω) present in the LXX in Wis (4x) and in Dan 3:1 LXX, and typical of secular Greek. 8:14

At least at first sight, the two terms λαός and ἔθνη make us think of Solomon's rule over pagan peoples; cf. the ἔθνη and the λαοί of Wis 3:8. The two terms together should be understood as a general reference to the "peoples", just as in Ps 46:4 LXX [47:4 MT], in an analogous context.

The subject of 15a is represented by the τύραννοι, who have already been encountered in 6:9 and 21, that is, rulers who exercise their absolute and despotic power quite differently from legitimate kings. Here, they are described as φρικτοί, or terrible, harsh. On hearing Solomon's words (με ἀκούσαντες; cf. v. 12), or hearing of his fame, they will be afraid (φοβηθήσονται). In this case too, Solomon is being idealised. Our sage is projecting on to him Israel's messianic hope of being freed from fearful tyrants, perhaps from their actual Roman rulers. However, the text remains general, according to Wisdom's typical style. 8:15

The second stich contrasts ἐν πλήθει with ἐν πολέμῳ. The first term could refer generally to a multitude or a crowd (cf. Wis 14:20) or else, as in Exod 12:6, refer to the assembly of the people, as in Sir 7:14, 16 (cf., in the Greek world, Euripides, *Orest.* 944). The king is "capable" in the assembly in the sense that he

88 Immortality is also a gift often connected with the figure of Isis; σὺ τὸν μέγαν Ὄσιριν ἀθάνατον ἐποίησας "you made great Osiris to be immortal"; cf. P.Oxy. XI, 1380, 243.

is a good speaker and knows how to convince the people with his words. Thus, we return to the oratorical power typical of the sage who is being praised here. In war, on the other hand, the king shows himself courageous (ἀνδρεῖος) so that in this case too he appears as a victor; cf. the ἀνδρεία mentioned in 8:7.

8:16 As we have already noted, we must not overemphasise the idea that wisdom is being presented first and foremost as a spouse in this *elogium*. Verse 16 presents her as friend and counsellor. In any case, our sage avoids dwelling on the tradition of a Solomon distracted by his women (1 Kgs 11:1-8; Sir 47:19-20) and on the negative aspects of wives, so frequent in the sapiential literature of the Bible, but stresses only the positive aspect of conjugal life.

Wisdom as Friend

Verse 16 opens by recalling that each time Solomon enters his house, he rests with her, that is, with wisdom. The verb *προσαναπαύομαι can indicate both rest with one's own spouse and that with a friend (cf. Epictetus, *Diatr.* 3.13.2).[89] The term συναναστροφή returns only in 3 Macc 2:31, 33 where it indicates association, or frequentation, and in 3 Macc 3:5 where it indicates the social behaviour of a particular group. Here it refers to a form of association, to the company (Lat: *conversatio*) of wisdom (cf. Gen 30:8 LXX). The text again adds the term συμβίωσις (cf. 8:3) which refers, as already stated, to the idea of a common life, not necessarily one of a conjugal character.

Living with wisdom, having her as spouse and as friend and counsellor (or both of these things), frees people from suffering (πικρία) and sorrow (ὀδύνη). By contrast, those who live with wisdom will have εὐφροσύνη καὶ χαρά as a gift. The former, already used negatively in 2:9, makes one think of the joy of feasts and banquets. Here, however, the tone is positive.

Diachronic Analysis

8:10 In Wis 8:10b, our sage takes his cue from the biblical data on the youth of Solomon at the time of his accession to the throne (1 Kgs 3:7; 1 Chr 22:5; 29:1); 3 Kgdms 2:12 LXX speaks in fact of twelve years, but our author does not seem to be thinking of such a low age.

8:12 In 8:12d, the gesture of placing the hand over the mouth could signify an attitude of silence, as in Prov 30:32 and Sir 5:12,[90] or else – more probably – of wonder (cf., previously, the use of the verb θαυμάζω), as in Job 21:5 MT; 40:4. However, the passage which our author had in mind is, once again, Job 29:9, where this gesture, although expressed in different language, expresses precisely wonder and admiration on the part of the hearers.

8:13 The connection between the king and ἀθανασία appears important. It is an expression of the fact that ἀθανασία is actually a sharing by the sage in the divine

89 Cf. Larcher, *Sagesse*, 2:543-544.

90 Grimm, *sub loco*, thinks of an attitude of shame on the basis of the text of Ps 106:42 LXX. Cf. Couroyer, Bernard, "'Mettre sa main sur sa bouche' en Egypte et dans la Bible", *RB* 67 (1960) 197-209.

kingship, a way for the sage himself to reign over the whole of the universe analogously to the cosmic work of wisdom.[91]

The association of glory and immortality is a common feature of the Greek spirit, as appears as early as Plato (cf. *Symp.* 209b, a text that could have influenced Wis 8:18, cf. below).

The connection between the gift of wisdom and the art of good governance 8:14
is traditional (cf. Prov 8:15). The gift of good governance is also an Isiac theme[92]. Once again, it is noticeable how, by contrast with the Letter of Aristeas and Philo, Wisdom avoids describing rulers as living copies of the heavenly king, God, according to the typical notion of the neo-Pythagorean treatises on kingship. On the contrary, every virtue of the good ruler derives from the gift of wisdom which, in its turn, is the gift of God.[93]

In this verse, is our sage thinking of an extension of Solomon's dominion to all the peoples of the world or else an eschatological dominion in the wake of Wis 3:8 (cf. the comment)? Moreover, the idea presupposed here that the peoples will be subject (ὑποτάσσω) is a surprising one since the biblical Solomon did not in fact achieve this. This text could be explained by thinking of a midrashic idealisation (with special reference to the repetition of the military theme in v. 15) or, more probably, of a reprise of the biblical theme of the pagan nations subjected to God and God's Messiah (cf. LXX-Pss 17:48; 46:4 [18:48; 47:4 MT]). Here, Solomon would be acquiring a certain Messianic aura; cf. also the comment on v. 15.[94] If we think again of the Stoic background to the metaphor of kingship (cf. comment on 1:1 and 6:1), we could speculate on the possibility of a metaphorical reading. In this pericope (cf. v. 12), the king has characteristics typical of the sage, that sage who, in the Stoic philosophy, is precisely the true king. To this king-sage, everything will be subject.

The Greek virtue of courage – understood in 8:15 in a military sense – is 8:15
known already in Prov 10:4; 11:16; 13:4; 15:19; 28:3; and 31:10. As a further, possible source of inspiration, many commentators cite a famous verse of Homer about the ideal king: ἀμφότερον, βασιλεύς τ' ἀγαθός, κρατερὸς τ' αἰχμητής (*Il.* 3.179, on Agamennon, son of Atreus).

In 8:16b, our author could have had in mind Qoh 7:26 in which Solomon 8:16
records the traditional opinion relating to the woman who is considered more bitter than death (πικρότερον according to Qoh 7:26 LXX, which, however, is a translation of the beginnings of the second cent. BCE). By contrast, living with

91 A. Leproux devotes considerable attention to the fact that within what, for him, is the *elogium* of the sage (Wis 7-8), there is an absence of the classical *topos* of the description of the death of the sage himself. This would be a clue which would lead to confirmation of the eschatological significance of ἀθανασία. Instead of the death of the king-sage, the *elogium* of Wis 7-8 would be speaking of his immortality (*Un discours de sagesse*, 283-308). However, Leproux does not take into account that here we are actually within the *elogium* of *wisdom* and that it is the sage (Solomon) who is speaking in reality – and that he cannot describe his own death.

92 Cf. Reese, *Hellenistic influence*, 48.

93 Cf. Moore, "On Kingship in Philo and the Wisdom of Solomon", 416-417.

94 For Larcher (*Sagesse*, 2:542) "il s'agit d'une simple tendence à appliquer à Salomon un motif messianique".

wisdom causes neither bitterness nor sorrow. Another Homeric reminiscence is possible here: by marrying wisdom, Solomon will not become πικρόγαμος as happens to Penelope's suitors (*Od.* 1.266; 17.137).[95]

As for 8:16d, the text could depend on Prov 29:6 LXX where similar things are said of the just: δίκαιος δὲ ἐν χαρᾷ καὶ ἐν εὐφροσύνῃ ἔσται. Thus, εὐφροσύνη acquires the tone of a joy that is certainly interior, the joy which Sir 6:28 sets in relation to resting with wisdom.[96] The pair εὐφροσύνη and χαρά appear together in two important texts of Ben Sirach: Sir 1:12, where εὐφροσύνη and χαρά are seen as fruits of the fear of the Lord, and, again, Sir 30:16 (there is no better εὐφροσύνη than χαρά of the heart). The background created by these two texts leads to the thought of a joy that is interior in character, even if it is also revealed in an exterior form. It is a joy, therefore, that is different from that of the ungodly in Wis 2.

Joy and gladness, then, are the same results as those promised to the sage by Stoic philosophy; cf. *SVF* III, 106 frag. 434. These are "rational" pleasures, fruit of the one who dominates the passions. Χαρά is "an impulse (of the soul) governed by reason" (εὔλογος ἔπαρσις). As such, it is opposed to ἡδονή (cf. *SVF* III, 105 frag. 431), while εὐφροσύνη is none other than the χαρά which accompanies the sage's actions (*SVF* III, 105 frag. 432). In our case, εὐφροσύνη and χαρά do not appear as fruits of the sage's behaviour but, with a certain hint of polemic, as a pure gift of wisdom to the sage. Our author shares the Stoics' positive view of joy but emphasises that it should be seen in the perspective of gift, a viewpoint not that far from that of Qoheleth. We note, finally, that εὐφροσύνη is also used as a title of Isis in the aretalogy of P.Oxy. XI, 1380, 19 and 31.

Wis 8:17-21: A Prayer to Obtain Wisdom

17 Reflecting on these things within me
and meditating in my heart,
that in kinship with wisdom there is immortality
18 and in friendship with her sincere delight,
and in the labour of her hands inexhaustible wealth
and in her company prudence
and renown in taking part in her conversations,
I went about seeking how to be able to acquire her for myself.

19 So then, I was a boy endowed by nature,
I had received a good soul;
20 or, rather, being good, I had entered an undefiled body.

---

95 Cf. Scarpat, *Sapienza*, 2:198.

96 For Philo's use of these two terms, cf. Larcher, *Sagesse*, 2:545.

21 Knowing, however, that I would never have entered into possession [of wisdom] in any other way
if God had not granted it to me
– and it is a sign of understanding to know from whom the gift comes –
I addressed the Lord and prayed to him
and said from the depth of my heart:

Notes on the Text and Translation

v. 21. The term ἐγκρατής is read from the Latin version *non possum esse continens*: "knowing that I would never have been continent". Especially in the past, some commentators favoured such a reading (cf. Larcher, *Sagesse*, 2:557). In Sir 26:15, in fact, ἐγκρατής has the sense of "chaste". Already, Augustine (*Conf.* 6.11) follows this line. In Wis 7-8, therefore, our author would be defending a love of wisdom which, in some way, suggests the virtue of chastity. He would thus be a representative of that "encratistic" tendency which arose precisely in Egypt and which saw sexual continence as the foundation of every virtue. Cf. the discussion favourable to this in Scarpat, *Sapienza*, 2:167-172 and Beauchamp, "Epouser la Sagesse", 347-369.

In fact, in the light of Wis 7:1-2, it does not seem that our author had a negative view of sexuality. In the LXX, ἐγκρατής, with the genitive, normally indicates "to be in possession of"; cf. Tob 6:3^{S}; Sir 6:27; 15:1; 27:30; 2 Macc 8:30; 10:15, 17; and 13:13. Linking ἐγκρατής to the following expression, ἐὰν μὴ ὁ θεὸς δῷ, it is possible to translate thus: "knowing that I would never have entered into possession [of wisdom] if God had not granted [it] to me ...".

A. Leproux (*Un discours de sagesse*, 308-324) has proposed a different solution: in Greek use, ἐγκρατής also has the meaning of "strong" (cf. Sophocles, *Oed. tyr.* 941, in the sense of "able to reign"). In connection with the theme of "immortality" in v. 17 and linked to the development of vv. 19-20, the adjective would acquire here, according to Leproux, the nuance of "immortal", endowed, that is, with that strength which permits body and soul to remain in life.

Synchronic Analysis

In Wis 7-8, this strophe constitutes a recapitulation and also an introduction to the prayer of chapter 9. At the same time, it takes up the theme of 8:2-9: the search for Wisdom and Solomon's youth. However, that happens after the development of 8:10-16 with regard to what wisdom will offer to the king. There is then a return to the initial theme of Solomon's weakness (7:1-6). These literary contacts will be constantly borne in mind in the interpretation of the text. The basic theme is clear: "Solomon" discovers that, in his weakness, he is in need of that wisdom which God alone can offer him. Everything flows into his prayer (Wis 9).

8:17-18: Immortality Again

Verses 17-18 construct a clear rhetorical crescendo (*accumulatio*). In living with wisdom, people find immortality, honourable love (by contrast with illicit pleasures), inexhaustible wealth (cf. 7:14a), prudence (that is, discernment), the ability to do good, and fame.

The beginning of v. 17 refers to Solomon's decision: ταῦτα refers to everything previously listed from 7:1. Solomon has carefully reflected (λογισάμενος) and taken a decision (φροντίσας) "in his heart" (understood in the biblical sense of "conscience").

Verse 17c opens with an introductory ὅτι followed by a series of five reasons which have led Solomon to decide in favour of wisdom. The first is that in συγγένεια with wisdom there is immortality (ἀθανασία).

We need to ask if ἀθανασία is to be understood as immortality of the memory (cf. a similar problem in 8:13) or as personal immortality. The latter seems preferable. In v. 17, in fact, immortality is bound in kinship with wisdom who is, in her turn, a reality closely linked to God and shares in God's very life (cf. 8:3). Thus, the term ἀθανασία bears a deeper sense. Immortality is a gift of God which is obtained through familiarity with wisdom – and, therefore, participation through her in the very life of God.

The second reason leading Solomon to decide for wisdom is that, in friendship with her (ἐν φιλίᾳ αὐτῆς), there is a τέρψις ἀγαθή or a "sincere delight", an honest joy that is legitimate. One can think of friendship properly so-called or friendship in a conjugal key as in Prov 5:19 LXX.

The third reason is connected with the inexhaustible wealth which is offered to Solomon as the fruit of the labours which come from the hands of wisdom. The term πόνοι refers also to Wis 8:7b, while ἀνεκλιπής, "inexhaustible", refers to the description of wisdom in 7:14a. These two references help us to understand that the wealth spoken of here is not to be seen simply as wealth in a material sense (money, for example). It is to be understood in a broader sense as that richness of interior character which consists firstly of the moral virtues which wisdom teaches the sage, virtues which constitute a real treasure which can never be exhausted. Our sage is thus re-elaborating the traditional theme of the riches of Solomon in a highly original way.

The fourth reason is not very clear. The expression ἐν συγγυμνασίᾳ ὁμιλίας αὐτῆς is unusual. Ὁμιλία indicates some form of association or meeting, entertainment, gathering, or company. The first term (*συγγυμνασία) can indicate a common activity, a mutual relationship, even in a sexual sense.[97] It can be translated generally with "the practice of her company", or being together with wisdom whether as wife, if one wishes to maintain the nuptial metaphor, or as companion, friend, and counsellor. In this relationship with wisdom, in this activity with her (συγγυμνασία refers also to common sporting activity), the sage obtains the true φρόνησις, that is, the prudence already seen (cf. 8:6, 7), namely, the virtue which enables the sage to have discernment.

The fifth reason is that being with wisdom gains for the sage εὔκλεια, "renown" (cf. 2 Macc 6:19; 3 Macc 2:31). This renown is obtained ἐν κοινωνίᾳ λόγων αὐτῆς, that is, in taking part in her conversations. The connection is classical. It is a further return to the oratorical aspect of wisdom. Being with her and speaking with her, the sage acquires, in his turn, the ability to speak and so the renown to which the text of 8:12 and 15a alludes.

The argument which began with the participles of v. 17ab closes with the verb περιῄειν of v. 18e. *Περίειμι indicates a going here and there, "seeking" (ζητῶν).

---

97 As Scarpat clearly shows, *Sapienza*, 2:164-165, συγγυμνασία returns in the Stoic definition of the τέχνη and concerns the putting into practice of the principles regarding the customs.

The object of Solomon's search concerns how to be able to obtain wisdom. In LXX usage, the expression λάμβανω [εἰς] γυναῖκα indicates taking a wife. The expression ἔλαβον αὐτὴν ἐμαυτῷ εἰς γυναῖκα is found especially in Gen 12:19. Here, the marriage metaphor seems to be reappearing. Solomon is seeking how he can obtain wisdom as his bride. The response comes in v. 21: it is necessary to seek her directly from God. However, the relationship with Deut 30:12 ("who will go up to heaven for us and fetch her?": καὶ λήμψεται αὐτήν ἡμῖν, with regard to the commandment of God) and the absence of the term γυναῖκα lessens the weight of the conjugal metaphor. The text can also be understood as a wishing to take wisdom to oneself but not necessarily as a consort.[98]

8:19-20: Soul and Body

These two verses have always created problems for commentators on Wisdom.[99] From a rhetorical point of view, what we have here is an *epiphonema*, a brief reflection that is separate from the main theme but at the same time precedes it, accompanies it, or follows it, being set before, after, or, as in our case, between two phrases. According to the rules for the epilogue of a discourse, the *epiphonema* has the aim of arousing a particular sentiment, suggesting a thought.[100] It is not correct, therefore, to read into Wis 8:19-20 a systematic reflection on the soul and its nature, but, more simply, a reference to the mortal reality of people.

Verse 19 opens with a δέ which is both correlative and affirmative in force, "so then, I was a boy". Παῖς indicates a boy, an adolescent, no longer a child, and the verb in the past (ἤμην) refers to Solomon's youth as something which is now behind him at the time he is speaking.

"I was a boy εὐφυής", an adjective which, in Greek usage, indicates being well endowed by nature (cf. Plato, *Symp.* 209a; *Resp.* 410a); it otherwise appears in the LXX only in 1 Esd 8:3, "well-informed", and 2 Macc 4:32, "suitable, appropriate". The fact that it is only in the following stich that the idea of the soul is introduced explicitly makes us think that here εὐφυής indicates all of the natural human dispositions both intellectual and moral. To the Greek mind, there are people who are well endowed by nature and people who are not, εὐφυεῖς or κακοφυεῖς, both in body and soul (Plato, *Resp.* 410a). Solomon was indeed εὐφυής, and precisely for this reason receives the gift of wisdom. Being well endowed is certainly due to one's lot (cf. the following stich), but this lot is not comparable to the impersonal fate of the Greeks.

The second stich of v. 19 immediately creates different difficulties: I was well endowed by nature because I had received a good soul as my lot (λαγχάνω followed by the genitive; the aorist here is to be translated with a plusquamperfect[101]). In the light of Wis 15:11, one understands that our sage has in mind the idea of a soul that is created by God and breathed into the human being but not the notion of a pre-existing soul. In 19b, our sage is simply presupposing that there is a diversity of souls, and that God grants them to people in different ways. It seems as if our sage is accepting here an idea not unknown to Judaism, that is, the pre-existence of souls, but that at the same time he is adhering to the

98 Cf. Leproux, *Un discours de sagesse*, 281.
99 Cf. a list of commentators cited in Vílchez Líndez, *Sapienza*, 315 n. 125.
100 Cf. Leproux, *Un discours de sagesse*, 66.
101 Cf. Zerwick, Maximilian, *Graecitas Biblica* (Romae: Pontificium Institum Biblicum, 1966) n. 290.

anthropological view typical of the Hebrew scriptures according to which the body is the personal subject which receives the soul; cf. 3 Kgdms 17:21 LXX: "the ψυχή of the child returned to him".[102]

Verse 20 opens with μᾶλλον δέ which has the sense of "or rather, or better". It is an expression which serves to clarify something which has already been said without denying it and not to correct something said previously.[103] Now, in v. 19, our sage expressed himself as if the personal "I" were the destination of the soul. Here, he explains his thought and identifies the ψυχή with the personal "I". Although attributing importance to the body, our sage is attributing an even greater importance to the ψυχή.

Next, the text explains that "being good, I had entered an undefiled body". The reprise of ἀγαθός helps us to grasp the change of perspective. If, in v. 19, the goodness of the individual was attributed to the body, here, instead, it is being attributed to the soul. Moreover, after the mention of a good soul, the object of attention is now the undefiled body. Larcher assumes the idea of a body in embryonic state, similar to the use of σῶμα in the writings of Hippocrates.[104] The adjective ἀμίαντος, uncommon in connection with the body (cf. Philo, *Spec.* 1.250), indicates the absence of impurities whether physical or moral. The mention of an "undefiled" body helps us to understand that the language is only Platonic in appearance. In the Platonic conception, it is the soul, in fact, which is corrupted, dragged down by the body. Here, instead, Solomon receives an undefiled body, capable of obeying the soul. What we have here is a moral and psychological rather than a metaphysical perspective (cf. also 9:15).[105]

8:21: "I Addressed the Lord and Prayed to Him…"

People need God. The chapter closes with a return to the theme of human weakness already noted in 7:1-6. Everyone can be like Solomon if they seek the gift of wisdom from God. If we read ἐγκρατής in the sense of "strong" (cf. above, textual note), the author could be wishing to suggest that Solomon is a mortal like everyone (7:1-6) but discovers that in closeness to wisdom there is immortality (8:17). Thus the "strength" of wisdom itself is necessary which only God can give if soul and body are to remain in harmony. This would be a further indication that for our author human salvation also involves the body.

The text of 21b forms a kind of parenthesis. It is a particular characteristic of φρόνησις, here to be understood as the virtue of discernment, to know the origin of this gift (χάρις), that is, of wisdom (for χάρις cf. Wis 3:9, 14; 4:15). Wisdom is, therefore, to be sought from God in prayer. Suddenly, the κύριος of Israel appears. With three different phrases, "Solomon" now sets out his decision to pray. First

---

102 Cf. Gilbert, "La procréation", 349.

103 Cf. Porter, "The Pre-existence of the Soul", 65-70. One can define μᾶλλον δέ as an *epidiorthosis*, a rhetorical figure which reinforces and also clarifies something said previously. (Cf. 2 Macc 6:23; 3 Macc 6:31; 7:5; Rom 8:34; Gal 4:9; etc., texts already registered by Grimm, *Weisheit*, *sub loco*.) Cf. Adinolfi, "La dicotomia", 147-149. Cf. the long series of Greek texts cited by Gilbert, "La procréation", 349-350 and n. 32, which concludes that μᾶλλον δέ is a typically Greek expression and serves to go beyond – often, therefore, by explaining – what has been said before.

104 Cf. Larcher, *Etudes*, 273 and Gilbert, "La procréation", 351 and n. 34.

105 Cf. Larcher, *Sagesse*, 2:556. In the Isiac litany of Oxyrhyncus ἀμίαντος is a title applied to Isis (cf. P.Oxy. XI, 1380.109).

of all, he uses ἐντυγχάνω in a sense which we find again in the NT (Rom 8:27, 34; 11:2; Heb 7:25), namely that of "addressing" God in prayer. Then comes the verb δέομαι, frequent both in Greek usage and in the LXX in the sense of "pray". The final formula of v. 21, "said from the depth of my heart", recalls mainly a biblical style (cf. the deuteronomic style: Deut 4:29; 6:5; 10:12; 11:13). As has been seen, the mention of the "heart" forms a clear *inclusio* with 8:17b.

Diachronic Analysis

8:17c Friendship with Wisdom

In Wis 8:17c, συγγένεια indicates a general relationship of kindred or affinity. In the Hellenistic world, it is not uncommon to find the idea that people possess a natural kinship with God based on reason and that therefore this is such by nature. The theme is classical, present already in Plato (cf. *Tim.* 90a; *Leg.* 899d). The idea is taken up by Philo. He partly distances himself from the Greek concept and considers human kinship with God not so much as a human achievement but rather as a gift deriving from the presence in people of the reason which brings them close to God (cf. *Opif.* 145-146 and, especially, *Spec.* 4.14).[106]

In Hellenistic usage, συγγένεια also indicates a relationship of close friendship and solidarity (cf. Aristotle, *Rhet.* 1381b 34) to the point of assuming social and political meanings. The mention of friendship in the immediately following stich reinforces this line of meaning: the sage is able to secure a solid bond of friendship with that wisdom to which he is related. The kinship or, better, the friendship with wisdom which guarantees immortality is a gift of God (cf. χάρις in v. 21b) that is obtained only with prayer and is therefore not something acquired by nature.

8:18

The term τέρψις (8:18a) is rare in the LXX and could have been suggested by the text of 3 Kgdms 8:28 LXX in the context of Solomon's prayer. It could have been chosen in polemic with the Stoic concept for which τέρψις, delight, is a form of ἡδονή (cf. *SVF* III, 97 frag. 401) which, for the Stoics, is to be considered something negative, whereas, here, polemically, it would be being considered something positive[107].

More probably, τέρψις could have been suggested by the use made of it in the Isiac aretaolgies in a not dissimilar context; cf. the Isiac inscription at Philae (191 CE): Ἶσιν τὴν ἐν Φίλαις προσκυνήσας τις εὐτυχεῖ οὐχ ὅτι μόνον πλουτεῖ πολυζῳεῖ δ' ἅμα τούτῳ "whoever worshipped Isis on Philae experienced good fortune, not only because he became wealthy, but also thereby gained longevity".[108] Here, wealth is linked to the gift of life, which recalls the immortality of v. 17. However, the most interesting text is found within the Third Hymn of Isidorus (c. 85 BCE), where Isis is invoked thus (lines 2-6): "Isis pure, holy, great, Dēō [= Demeter], powerful in name, highly venerated benefactress (δώτειρ' ἀγαθῶν) for all mortals,

---

106 Cf. Des Places, Edouard, "La *syggeneia* chrétienne", *Bib* 44 (1963) 304-332; Michaelis, Wilhelm, συγγένεια, *TDNT* 7:736-742; Scarpat, *Sapienza*, 2:157-160; Spicq, *Notes*, Supp. 616-623.

107 Cf. Scarpat, *Sapienza, 2:*200.

108 Bernand, André, *Les inscriptions grecques et latines de Philae* (Paris: Centre National de la Recherche Scientifique 1969) 2:168.

you have given your worshippers great favours and wealth (πλοῦτον δέδωκας), and the possession of a sweet life and wonderful joy (τέρψιν ἀρίστην), advantage, good fortune and wisdom (σωφροσύνην τε ἄλυπον) without stress". We find again here many of the goods offered by Wisdom to Solomon: in particular, wealth, life, delight, wisdom, and the absence of stress. There is no longer any need, therefore, to follow Isis in the face of the wisdom of the God of Israel.

In 8:18b, the term πόνοι refers to an idea widespread in the Greek world; "all goods are sold to us by the gods at the price of labours" (Epicharmus, *ap. Xen, mem.* 2,1,20). Cf. again Philo in *Sacr.* 35: πόνος is at the root of every good and every virtue.

We note again that εὔκλεια (8:18d) is a secular term which, in Stoicism, constitutes one of the positive characteristics of the sage. According to Philo, the sage, like Abraham, enjoys not only respect, but, above all, a good reputation (οὐκ ἔνδοξος ἀλλ' εὐκλεής; *Sobr.* 57).

In 8:18e, many commentators observe a probable dependence on the Platonic text of *Symp.* 209b ("one goes in search of the beauty with which it will be possible to breed"). However, whereas the young lover of the Platonic *Symposium* is at the beginnings of his quest, Solomon has already decided to unite with wisdom. Larcher observes that, in making use of the *Symposium,* our sage wishes to show that the true beauty is divine and that true fertility is that of the soul.[109] We should note, however, that the theme of the search for wisdom could also have been inspired in our author by a small series of sapiential texts relating to the search for wisdom: cf. especially Prov 2:4-6; 8:35; Job 28:12-13; cf. also Qoh 8:16-17.[110] Wisdom is a gift but it is also a task which is entrusted to human searching.

8:19-20: Wisdom's Platonism?

Many authors have held that, in Wis 8:19-20, our sage is openly making use of Platonic concepts, even if he did not accept all the implications of the doctrine of the transmigration of souls, and is admitting *tout court* the pre-existence of souls, an idea also embraced by Philo, from some currents of ancient Judaism and, probably, also from Enoch (cf. 2 En. 23:4-5 [10:7-8]).[111] Some authors are concerned to interpret the text in a more orthodox (Christian!) key.[112] Because I was good, I attained an undefiled body, thus giving εἰσέρχεσθαι the unusual sense of "attain".

In fact, the text of v. 20 is stating in a different, more philosophical, way what had already been said in v. 19 in language that was more popular (but perhaps also more biblical): having said that "I" received the soul, our sage makes it clear,

---

109 Cf. Larcher, *Sagesse*, 2:550.

110 Cf. Mazzinghi, Luca, "The Verbs מצא 'to Find' and בקש 'to Search' in the Language of Qohelet. An Exegetical Study" in: Berlejung, Angelika –Van Hecke, Pierre, *The Language of Qohelet in its Context.* Fs A. Schoors (Leuven – Paris – Dudley (MA): Peeters 2007) 91-120.

111 "The verse is as clear as a statement of the concept of pre-existent souls as one could wish and there is no need to explain it away as many commentators have done (...). On the other hand, the more elaborate Greek doctrine of metempsychosis does not appear to be a part of our author's thinking" (Winston, *Wisdom*, 198; cf. also p. 26: "the author was plainly associating himself to some extent with Platonic doctrine..."); cf. also Hübner, *Weisheit*, 122.

112 Cf., for example, Reese, *Hellenistic Influence*, 84-85 and, even earlier, Grimm, *Weisheit*, 176-177.

in v. 20, that it is the soul which is united to the body.[113] Here, once again, is the function of the *epiphonema*, at the centre of the final strophe of the *elogium*: not that of offering some kind of complete teaching but of suggesting a reflection on what it is to be human: an incarnate soul, a being made of earth and the breath of life (cf. Gen 2:7) which can be truly "alive" only thanks to the Lord. The author is trying here to take a step forward in the direction of Greek thought, but he does not wish to betray his biblical faith.[114]

In any case, it is certain that the text is distinct from the more traditional biblical anthropology. For our author, the human being is more an incarnate soul than an animated body (cf. the comment on 1:4). In the light also of Wis 15:11, the author does not seem to want to state with the clarity which many commentators attribute to him the idea of a Platonic pre-existence of souls. At least he does not show that he shares Plato's dualistic anthropology. Nor is there in the book any trace of the Platonic disdain for the body. Perhaps our sage was thinking rather of a kind of "pre-creation" of the soul which God infuses into the human embryo at an undefined moment in its growth. However, the information to be more precise is lacking.

Finally, *à propos* of 8:21b, we note that, according to a Stoic conception, the virtue of εὐχαριστία "is the knowledge which teaches to whom to give gratitude (χάρις), when to give it and from whom it is due" (*SVF* III, 67 frag. 273). 8:21b

Summary of Wis 7-8

A New Model of Friendship

To the young Jews of Alexandria, future leaders of the Jewish community, our sage is offering in this strophe, as a good teacher, an ideal of friendship not that far from the one offered by Stoic philosophy by contrast with the false friendship of the Dionysian clubs put forward by the ungodly in Wis 2. This friendship is a strong, amicable relationship, based on common "nobility of origin" (cf. Wis 8:3), on "kinship" (8:17), on "living together" (8:3, 9, 16), on wise "conversation" (8:18), and on the sharing of those very same virtues which are the fruit of those who obtain wisdom, those virtues so typically Greek which are recorded explicitly in 8:7. Friendship with wisdom offers to those who embrace it all the characteristics which the contemporary world considered the property of the true friend.

It is legitimate, however to think that Wisdom's proposal could sound innovative to the Alexandrian Jews and even a little over the top. In any case, the mention of the friendly relation between Solomon and wisdom tells us that, for our sage, the traditional paradigm of the family which the Jews understood as the basic relational value (husband–wife / parents–children), is no longer the only paradigm possible.[115]

Through the figure of wisdom presented in Wis 7-8, our sage is trying to respond to a fundamental question: is God far or near? Emphasising the human

113 Cf. Engel, *Weisheit*, 145.

114 Cf. Clark, *The Wisdom of Solomon*, 61.

115 Cf. a more extended reflection in Mazzinghi, "I loved [Wisdom]".

aspect of wisdom, the sapiential tradition of Israel had reached with Job and Qoheleth the discovery of the impenetrable nature of the divine mystery. Precisely with wisdom, however, God makes himself present. Wisdom does not exclude the human values and is present in people, but, with her origin in God, she can be obtained only as his gift. It is not by chance that wisdom is presented with features which link her to the philosophy of the time and even to the mystery cults.[116] Moreover, wisdom has a cosmic role. She renews the world but she is identified neither with it nor with God. In this way, the book of Wisdom is seeking to save the transcendence and immanence of God, developing a theology of wisdom which is not too far from the Christian theology of grace. It is not by chance that the patristic tradition would draw on these chapters, which were probably already in the minds of some New Testament authors, in relation to Trinitarian theology.

116 For the Isiac background of Wis 7-8, cf. Kloppenborg's conclusions (relating to 8:2-9). "the mythic power which informed Egyptian royal ideology is captured and transformed for Judaism, enabling Jews to maintain themselves in an atmosphere of intense religious and political propaganda" ("Isis and Sophia", 78); "the use of mythic patterns from Isis served both aspirations: it helped revitalize Jewish tradition so that it could continue to provide religious identity and structure to a people under attack. But it also laid the basis for communication with the dominant group, to whose privileges and position Alexandrian Jews aspired" (*ibid.*, 84).

Wis 9:
The Prayer to Obtain Wisdom

Literary Structure of Wis 9

With “Solomon’s” prayer to obtain wisdom we are at the literary centre of the book.[1] There are clear indications revealing that Wis 9 is divided into three strophes.[2] We note first of all a *inclusio* between v. 1 and v. 18: τῇ σοφίᾳ ... ἄνθρωπον (v. 1); ἄνθρωποι ... τῇ σοφίᾳ. If wisdom is connected with creation in v. 1, in v. 18 it is connected with salvation. Thus 9:1-18 forms a very clear literary unit. Next, we observe that ἄνθρωπος returns at the beginning of v. 6 and v. 13 and is absent from vv. 7-12. That suggests a further inclusion (ανθρωπ-) between vv. 1 and 6, on the one hand, and between vv. 13 and 18, on the other, which leads us to hypothesise the existence of three strophes.

A first strophe can be discerned in 9:1-6. The term κύριε (v. 1) connects it as a hook-word with the previous passage (ἐνέτυχον τῷ κυρίῳ in 8:21c). At the centre of the strophe (v. 4), there is an imperative (δός μοι) relating to wisdom. Verses 1-3 describe the work of wisdom in her dealings with people. Verse v. 4 is a first prayer to obtain wisdom, vv. 5-6 a reflection on human weakness. Wis 9:1-6

The second strophe is marked out by the *inclusio* λαοῦ σου / λαός σου (vv. 7a. 12b). The strophe has a concentric profile. Verses 7-8 describe Solomon as king, judge, and builder. Verse 9 turns to wisdom’s presence beside God. Verse 10ab contains a second prayer to obtain wisdom with two imperatives, ἐξαπόστειλον αὐτήν and πέμψον αὐτήν. Verses 10c-11 return to the theme of v. 9: wisdom with God and also with people. We note the reprise of some words: εἰδυῖα (9a) and οἶδεν (11a); παροῦσα (9b) and συμπαροῦσα (10c); ἀρεστὸν (9c) and εὐαρεστὸν (10d). Finally, v. 12 returns to the idea of Solomon as builder, judge, and king (in the reverse order from vv. 7-8). Wis 9:7-12

The third strophe is also identified by the *inclusio* on the term ἄνθρωπος (13a. 18c); but we must add the reference to the will of God: τίς ... βουλήν (13a) and βουλὴν ... τίς (17a). We observe that βουλή appears in the book otherwise only in 6:4; it is impossible to know the will of God without the gift of wisdom.[3] If the first strophe opened with the mention of the “Lord”, this one opens with the Wis 9:13-18

---

1 Vignolo (“Sapienza, preghiera e modello regale”, 272 n. 5) speaks of Wis 9 as of a *mise en abîme* which gathers together the entire work: Wis 9:1-4 recalls the theme of Wis 1-6; Wis 9:5-12, the humanity and vocation of Solomon, recall Wis 7-8; and Wis 9:13-18 anticipates the third part of the book.

2 Cf. the fundamental study of Gilbert, “La structure de la prière”; on pp. 190-196, on the level of literary structure, Gilbert notes similarities and differences between Wis 9 and the model which inspired Wisdom: 1 Kgs 3 and 2 Chr 1. Of all the story of Solomon, it is precisely his wisdom which has most impressed our author; cf. also Gilbert, “La figure de Salomon”, especially 145-149.

3 Bizzeti (*Il libro della Sapienza*, 74) highlights other connections between Wis 9 and Wis 6, on the one hand, and 1:1-15, on the other. Wis 9 is thus taking up the initial exhortation to follow and love justice.

mention of humanity (13a), thus bringing together the anthropological and theological aspects.

The themes of the first strophe are recalled in the third strophe but in reverse order: vv. 13-17aα recall the theme of Solomon's weakness; two rhetorical questions each introduce (9:13ab) and conclude (9:16c, 17aα) the strophe.[4] Verse 17aα–b returns to the theme of the "giving" of wisdom and is the reply to Solomon's prayer, taking up the verbs δίδωμι from v. 4 and πέμπω from v. 10. The figure of the spirit is introduced alongside wisdom (cf. 1:5). Verse 18 closes the strophe and the entire prayer,[5] recalling the theme of 9:1-3. However, if creation was mentioned 9:1-2, here the talk is of salvation. This is the first occurrence of the verb σῴζω in the book of Wisdom.

Concentric Structure

The chapter presents a double concentric structure as follows:

1-6: first strophe		
1-3:	work of wisdom (creation)	A
4:	prayer to obtain wisdom	**B**
5-6:	human weakness	C
7-12: second strophe		
7-8:	Solomon, king, judge, and builder	D
9:	wisdom beside God	E
10ab:	prayer to obtain wisdom	**B'** (passage centre)
10c-11:	wisdom beside God and man.	E'
12:	Solomon, builder, judge, and king	D'
13-18: third strophe		
13-16:	human weakness	C'
17:	God gives wisdom and the spirit	**B''**
18:	the work of wisdom (salvation).	A'

All this shows that Wis 9 is primarily a prayer to obtain wisdom, a prayer which is found, in fact, at the centre of each strophe. Connected with the divine work of creation and salvation, wisdom is indispensable to people because of their weakness. She becomes counsellor of life and guide in action because she herself is in close relationship with God.

4 Gilbert identifies here a further concentric structure: 13ab / 16b, 17aα; 14ab / 16ab; and, in the centre, v. 15 (again with the *motif* of weakness); cf. "La structure de la prière", 176-178.

5 On v. 18's belonging to chap. 9 (and so not to be considered as the title of Wis 10), see the arguments of Bizzeti, *Il libro della Sapienza*, 72-73.

Wis 9:1-6:
The First Strophe – Wisdom, Creation, and Human Weakness

1 God of the fathers and Lord of mercy,
who have made everything with your word
2 and with your wisdom have created humanity
to rule over the creatures you have made
3 and govern the world with holiness and justice
and exercise justice with a fair mind:
4 give me the wisdom which sits beside your throne
and do not cast me away from your children.
5 For I am your servant and the son of your handmaid,
a man weak and short-lived,
too weak to understand judgement and laws.
6 For even if there were someone who was perfect among human beings,
if he lacked the wisdom that comes from you, he would be considered as nothing.

Notes on the Text and Translation

v. 1. In 1a, the majority of mss read τοῦ ἐλέους σου while only a few versions (Syr, Sah, Eth, Lat) read τοῦ ἐλέους. The formula κύριε τοῦ ἐλέους σου is *lectio difficilior*, but it is difficult to interpret. The second formula seems preferable, though less well attested than the first one, and it is the one chosen by the editors.

v. 2. Instead of the participle κατασκευάσας, some witnesses (B, C, Lat) read a finite verb, κατεσκεύασας (cf. v. 4. Scarpat, *Sapienza*, 2:254, accepts this reading). Κατασκευάζω appears with reference to the work of creation in texts such as Isa 40:28; 43:7; 45:9; 4 Macc 2:21; cf. Wis 11:24 and 13:4.

Synchronic Analysis

9:1-3: Wisdom, Word, Creation

Right from the first verse, there is an explicit address to God with the vocative θεέ, something rather rare in the LXX (cf. Judg^{B} 16:28; 21:3; 2 Sam 7:25; Ezek 4:14; Tob^{S} 3:11; 8:15; Sir 23:4; 3 Macc 6:2; 4 Macc 6:27). The addressee is the God of Israel's tradition, the "God of the fathers", that is, of the patriarchs (cf. Wis 12:21 and 18:22). He is a "You" very active in the history of Israel as "Lord of mercy". Ἔλεος recalls the Hebrew חסד, typical of the covenant vocabulary (cf. 1 Kgs 3:6), even if the expression κύριος τοῦ ἐλέους is not found elsewhere. Solomon too, in 1 Kgs 3:6-7 and 2 Chr 1:8-9 calls on God's faithfulness in his dealings with his father, David. The beginning of the prayer is an authentic profession of Jewish faith.

9:1b

In 1b, God is invoked as creator of the universe (ὁ ποιήσας τὰ πάντα), according to a usage not infrequent in the Psalms (cf. Pss 32:6-9 LXX [33:6-9 MT]; 103:5-

9 LXX [104:5-9 MT]; 135:5-9 LXX [136:5-9 MT]). On nine occasions, ποιέω is used in Wisdom in the sense of "create" (cf. 1:13; 2:23; 6:7; 9:1, 9; 11:24; 12:12; 15:61; and 16:24). As in Gen 1, creation takes place through the mediation of the word (ἐν λόγῳ σου, where ἐν has instrumental value: *with* your word). For the first time, we find in the book a mention of the word of God, a theme which will return in Wis 16:12, 26; and 18:15-16. Here (cf. 2a), the divine word is immediately associated with wisdom. In this way, the initial invocation gathers together three basic theological themes: the promise made to the fathers, the covenant (or salvation) and creation.

With clear reference to Gen 1:26-28, the creation of humanity is recalled in v. 2a as a divine work where God made use of wisdom. The dative τῇ σοφίᾳ has instrumental value.[6] The verb κατασκευάζω has the meaning of "create" in Wis 11:24 (in parallel with ποιέω) and 13:4, and it is used with reference to the creation of the human being. Our author has in mind Gen 1:1-2 where ποιέω refers to the work of the Creator while ἀκατασκεύαστος refers to a creation that is still without form – lacking the divine wisdom, one could say.

9:2b–3 In 9:2b-3, our sage extends the sense of the Genesis text. He reflects on the idea of "dominion" in Gen 1:26-28 (cf. also 8:7-9) and emphasises more broadly the task of people on the earth. Verse 2b expresses the purpose of God's action (ἵνα) in his dealings with people. The latter are called on to "rule" over the creatures. In Wis 12:16 and 18, δεσπόζειν is reserved rather for the activity of God. Immediately, it is added that this rule is over the creatures *you have made.* Κτίσμα is a late usage (Sir 36:14; 3 Macc 5:11; cf. Jas 1:18; Rev 8:9). Ὑπὸ σου γενομένων is to be understood as "those (creatures) who have come into being thanks to you". Human dominion over the world is linked solely to the awareness that the entire creation comes from God.

Human dominion over the cosmos is not absolute, therefore, but has to be exercised, as expressed in 3a, in holiness and justice. Our sage does not enter into details about the human role with regard to the created world, but limits himself to adding the *manner* of this dominion: ἐν ὁσιότητι καὶ δικαιοσύνῃ. Set in relationship with δικαιοσύνη, ὁσιότης refers to piety in relation to the divinity (cf. 2:22), while δικαιοσύνη represents a correct attitude towards other people, or, in a more general context, towards every other creature. A reference to Wis 2:11 is not to be excluded. In ruling the cosmos, people are called to reject the law of force which is invoked by the ungodly.

With the expression of v. 3b, our sage is employing a typically Hebrew style which could have been taken from texts like Gen 19:9; Deut 16:18; and Jer 5:8, where κρίσιν κρίνειν indicates the act of judgement, justice, often that of God. Moreover, this is the significance of κρίσις in Wisdom (6:5; 8:11; 9:5; 12:25, 26; 16:18; 17:1). In connection with the previous reference to justice, the expression is referring to the figure of Solomon as judge. Thus, there appears in the poem a political theme which will then be taken up in the second strophe.

---

6 Scarpat (*Sapienza*, 2:254-5) holds that τῇ σοφίᾳ indicates the modality of the creation: "wisely". Scarpat tends to minimise the action of wisdom which, however, in Wis 9 has a role that is quite other than passive, as already in Wis 7-8.

9:4: Give Me Wisdom!

The task entrusted by God to people in the world cannot be carried out without the gift of wisdom. People, in fact, are weak and fleeting. Without wisdom, they are good for nothing (7:1-6). For this reason, at the heart of the strophe (v. 4), we find the first request to obtain this gift from God: *Give me wisdom*!

The use of the term πάρεδρος could have a real polemical force (see below). For our author, only wisdom is close to God, and in wisdom, as we already know, there is also justice.

The second petition is formulated negatively. Solomon asks not to be cast away (μή με ἀποδοκιμάσῃς) from the number of your children. The expression ἐκ παίδων σου has partitive value and with παῖδες is to be understood here as children rather than as servants (cf. δοῦλος in v. 5). The Israelites are certainly the children of God (cf. Wis 18:4), but the text of 4b does not seem to intend to create an opposition between Israel and the other peoples. Simply, thanks to the gift of wisdom, it is possible to be numbered among the children of God, that is, to obtain a truly intimate relationship with him.

9:5-6: A Man Weak and Short-lived …

We find here the reason for Solomon's prayer: human weakness; cf. 7:1-6 and 8:17-21. Verse 5 opens with a literal quotation of Ps 115:7 LXX [116:16 MT], something rather rare in Wisdom. Solomon recognises his total dependence on God: he is God's servant and the son of his handmaid, that is, the inalienable property of God, according to the laws of Exod 21:4 and 23:12. As well as a profession of humility, 5a is also a trustful declaration of belonging to God.

Compared with the reasons expressed in the psalm texts (sin, illness, enemies ...), the one in 5b is more abstract, but more original: "I am a man weak (ἀσθενής) and short-lived". The theme of weakness may be taking up the text of Ps 6:3 (ἐλέησόν με κύριε ὅτι ἀσθενής εἰμι). The adjective has already been used in Wis 2:11 in the discourse of the ungodly. For them, what is weak shows itself to be useless. The only valid law is that of force.[7] Here, instead, consciousness of one's own weakness gives rise to prayer.

The theme of the shortness of life (ὀλιγοχρόνιος) has a meaning distinct from that in the mouth of the ungodly in Wis 2:1b and takes up themes present in Ps 39[38 LXX] or in 1 Chr 29:15 (David's prayer). However, the shortness of life is not a reason for despair but a source of prayer. Although being "of short time", people can attain the fullness of life thanks to the gift of wisdom.

The third reason refers to what the young Solomon expresses in 1 Kgs 3:7, 9, 11: I am too young to understand justice and laws and so to be king over this people. The expression ἐλάσσων ἐν συνέσει has the meaning of "too weak to understand". The term κρίσις, used here in the singular in connection with "laws", has a juridical value, as in 3b, and refers to the just judgement of the king in favour of the oppressed; cf. Ps 71:2 LXX [72:2 MT]. With the plural "laws", our sage does not seem to be referring to the Mosaic Law (always in the singular in this book; cf. 2:12; 16:6; 18:4, 9), but rather to the laws governing the life of every people.

Verse 6 is introduced by a conditional clause (κἄν = καὶ ἐάν) followed by a subjunctive with concessive value and also of possibility: κἄν γάρ τις ᾖ, "for even if there were someone ...". If then, among humans, there were someone, someone

7 The term ἀσθενής appears again in Wis 13:17 in connection with idols.

τέλειος, perfect, who had all the qualities which Solomon is aware of lacking, even that person too, without wisdom, "would be considered as nothing" (εἰς οὐδὲν λογισθήσεται). This is not an eschatological judgement, only the judgement of the author who makes use of a biblical formula to acknowledge the total nothingness of whoever is without the wisdom that only God can offer. At the same time, our sage is implicitly recognising that people are worth only how they stand in God's eyes.

Diachronic Analysis

9:1 The idea of a creation by means of wisdom was certainly suggested to our author by texts such as Ps 103:24 LXX [104:24 MT]; Prov 3:19; and Jer 10:12. However, in Prov 8 too, wisdom is set in relation both to the creation and to people, and so is a figure of mediation. Here, word and wisdom are not two hypostases, two intermediate beings used by God to create the world but rather two complementary aspects of the divine activity. As in Gen 1, the word indicates the creative power of God, wisdom the manner of God's acting, in particular in relation to the creation of humanity.[8]

9:3 The verb *διέπω returns in connection with God in 12:15 and has the sense of "govern", "administer", often in Greek usage with the sense of a delegated authority relating to the entire κόσμος, to the inhabited world (cf. 1:14 and the comment). The verb is absent from the LXX, but it is typical of religious language (cf. Philo, *Mos.* 2.187 *à propos* of Moses). In the Hellenistic treatises on kingship, the verb is used both for the rule of God and that of the king.[9] We note again that the distinction between δικαιοσύνη, and ὁσιότης is already found in Plato: cf. *Gorg* 507b; taken up also by Philo, *Abr.* 208. The expression ἐν εὐθύτητι ψυχῆς, on the other hand, is biblical and certainly comes from 1 Kgs 3:6 (καὶ ἐν δικαιοσύνῃ καὶ ἐν εὐθύτητι καρδίας), combined with 1 Kgs 9:4 (ἐν ὁσιότητι καρδίας καὶ ἐν εὐθύτητι) and refers to the rectitude of mind which is typical of the judge.

9:4 In the LXX, the term *πάρεδρος "who sits beside" is present only here and in Wis 6:14. Already Greek mythology knows of divinities who are πάρεδροι of Jove.[10] Philo attests the practice of calling Justice, Δίκη, πάρεδρος of God; cf. *Mos.* 2.53; *Mut.* 94; *Spec.* 4.201; *Ios.* 48; *Decal.* 177. The term πάρεδρος also evokes an image familiar to the Jews of Alexandria. This term was used, in fact, to describe the royal position of Isis, spouse of Osiris (Horus), companion (cf. πάρεδρος in the *Aretalogy of Andros* 139) of the sun, or of Serapis. Our author is continuing to describe wisdom as a real person, with the help of features of Isis without, however, making her a goddess. At the same time, he is seeking to reply in a positive

8 Wisdom joins up here with the tradition known to Tg. Neof. where the creation of the world takes place precisely through the mediation of word and wisdom; cf. Le Déaut, *Targum du Pentateuque*, 1:74.

9 Cf. Ecphantus, 274,11.6; 257,8 (ed. Hense; cf. Delatte, *Les traités de la royauté*, 107). Clement of Rome (*Cor.* 61,2) employs διέπω, revealing a clear knowledge of the book of Wisdom (Scarpat, *Sapienza*, 2:214).

10 Texts in Scarpat, *Sapienza*, 2:217-218.

way to the influences coming from the mysteries of Isis. Wisdom shares in the very dignity of God and is closely united to God.

Whereas the inspiration of v. 5 is profoundly biblical (see above), in 9:6, it is necessary to recognise a polemical point being made against the Stoics. In Stoicism, the sage is the perfect person who has acquired every kind of virtue. On the sage as τέλειος, cf. *SVF* III, 139 frag. 519; for Philo (*Leg.* 1.93), every act of the sage is perfect (cf. *SVF* III, 148 frag. 557). The Stoic sage knows everything. He is free from every evil and every wicked action, and he possesses every kind of virtue. Now, already for the Stoics, such a sage is rare, but, if such a sage were to exist, our author claims, he could be such only by virtue of a gift received from on high, that is, from God.[11] 9:6

Wis 9:7-12: The Second Strophe – Wisdom and God

7 You have chosen me as king over your people
and judge over your sons and daughters.
8 You have ordered the building of a temple on your holy mountain
and an altar in the city where you dwell,
an image of the holy tabernacle which you prepared from the beginning.
9 With you is wisdom who knows your works,
who was present when you created the world
and knows what is pleasing in your eyes
and right according to your commandments.
10 Send her from the holy heaven
and from the throne of your glory send her
that she may be with me and toil
and that I may know what is pleasing to you.
11 For she knows and understands all things
and will guide me in my actions with prudence
and guard me with her glory.
12 Then my works will be well pleasing
and I shall judge your people with justice
and be worthy of my father's throne.

Synchronic Analysis

9:7-8: Solomon, King, Judge, Builder

Verse 7 opens with an asyndetic construction which underlines a new beginning. The initial "you" is emphatic. The verb προαιρέω is to be understood as an allusion to the whole of Solomon's story (cf. 2 Sam 7:12-13; 1 Kgs 1:11-40; 1 Chr 28:5):

11 Many commentators see in this text one of the models used by Paul in 1 Cor 13:2.

Solomon becomes king following a particular divine choice. Προαιρέω is used in this sense in Deut 7:6, 7; and 10:15, precisely with regard to God's election of the people of Israel.

Solomon is chosen as king of a people which belongs to God. For λαός σου, cf. 1 Kgs 3:8, 9 and 2 Chr 1:10-11. Here it is God himself who acknowledges that the Israelites are God's people and also God's sons and daughters. Here, in fact is Wisdom's first mention of λαὸς with clear reference to the Israelites, something which will happen constantly later in the third part of the book.

The connection made by our sage here between "your people" (7a) and the theme of sonship (7b) serves, first of all, to link the people of God directly with the "son" who was the protagonist of the first part of the book, persecuted by the ungodly precisely because of his claim to have God as his father (cf. 2:12-20) and later recognised by the ungodly themselves as glorified by God and set among his sons (5:5). Thus, from the son of God who is the individual faithful Israelite, there begins a transition to the entire people of Israel, a people of sons (cf. Wis 12:19, 20, 21; 16:10, 26; 18:4, 13; 19:6).[12]

This people will have Solomon as their judge (δικαστής); cf. 1 Kgs 3:9; 2 Chr 1:10-11, one of the characteristics of the biblical kings. Moreover, in the LXX, δικαστής is applied to both kings and judges or to rulers in general (cf. Wis 6:1 in parallel with the kings and again Josh 9:2 LXX [8:33 MT]; 23:2; 24:1; 1 Sam 8:1-2 with reference to the judges).

The Temple

Verse 8 adds the memory of the temple built by Solomon (cf. 2 Sam 7:13 and 1 Kgs 5:15-9, 25), introduced by another asyndetical construction. The building is described as a divine command (εἶπας), left indeterminate because, according to 2 Sam 7:13; 1 Kgs 5:17-19; and 1 Chr 28:2, the order was given not to Solomon but rather to David. Thus, not "you have told me", but simply "you have ordered".

In the biblical texts speaking of Solomon's building of the temple (especially 1 Kgs 5:15-9:25 and 2 Chr 1:18-7:10), there is frequent use of the expression οἰκοδομεῖν τὸν οἶκον κυρίου. Instead of οἶκος, our sage employs ναός, according to a typical LXX usage.[13] The temple is to be constructed "on your holy mountain" (cf. Ps 14:1 LXX [15:1 MT]; 47:2 LXX [48:2 MT]). The mountain is considered "holy", even before the temple is raised there, probably on the basis of the information in 2 Chr 3:1. It was the site of the sacrifice of Isaac. However, one could also think of 2 Sam 24:18-25: the place was chosen by God beforehand for the construction of his temple.

The following stich places the temple alongside the θυσιαστήριον, a term proper to the LXX, indicating an "altar" (cf. 2 Sam 24:25; 2 Chr 21:26-22:1). This is probably the altar of the holocausts which Solomon ordered to be constructed according to 1 Kgs 8:64; 9:25; and 2 Chr 4:1. Here, the offerings were sacrificed (1 Kgs 8:22, 54, 62-64). In this way, the text of Wis 9 also refers directly to the worship performed in the temple.

The altar and temple are set ἐν πόλει κατασκηνώσεώς σου, "in the city where you dwell", more literally, "of your tent" or "of your encampment" (cf. 1 Chr 28:2, where, however, the term assumes the nuance of "building"). Jerusalem, which –

---

12 Cf. Mazzinghi, "L'idea di 'popolo' nel libro della Sapienza", 20-21.

13 Cf. Michel, Otto, ναός, *TDNT* 4:880-890.

following the style of Wisdom – is not called by name, is the city where God has decided to dwell; cf. Tob 1:4 (ο ναὸς τῆς κατασκηνώσεως). The term κατασκήνωσις is rare in the LXX. One could also recall Ezek 37:27 (καὶ ἔσται ἡ κατασκήνωσίς μου ἐν αὐτοῖς), in this case too in relation to the dwelling of God with men.

The temple is considered here as a model (μίμημα) of that "tabernacle" which God determined to pitch among people, coming down from the divine heavenly dwelling. The temple is the image of that "holy tabernacle". The expression is found only in Sir 24:10, precisely in connection with the temple. In the LXX, the "tabernacle" indicates the mobile tent that contains the Ark of the Covenant (cf. Exod 25:9), but here it refers to the heavenly dwelling of God of which the earthly temple is the symbol.

With the expression ἣν προητοίμασας ἀπ' ἀρχῆς, the text is suggesting a divine choice hailing from long ago. Προετοιμάζω is probably taken from Isa 28:24, the only passage in the LXX where the verb appears, but ἑτοιμάζω is often reserved for the action of God who "prepares" gifts and events for people. With reference to the temple, one could think readily of Exod 15:17.[14]

The connection of kingship, judgement, and temple is a good indication of what our sage expects from one who is called to build society: skill in governing, causing the laws to be observed with justice, and promoting the worship of the true God.

9:9: "With You Is Wisdom…"

Verse 9 marks a sudden transition to the figure of wisdom who is described as "one who knows your works", that is, the entire created reality (cf. 7:17a), or, better still, God's plan for creation since in the following stich it is stated that wisdom was present when God created the world; cf. also 8:4. Wisdom is thus seen as the source of revelation.[15]

This wisdom is described as "present" (παροῦσα) at the time of the creation of the world. The imperfect ἐποίεις refers to the creative act of God in its development over time, just as it is described by Gen 1. The verb πάρειμι is employed in Wisdom with its normal sense of "being present" (cf. Wis 4:2; 11:11; 14:17; 19:14).

Wisdom knows God's wishes (9cd). The participle ἐπισταμένη refers to that special ἐπιστήμη of wisdom which was described before in 7:16 and 8:4. The expression ἀρεστὸν ἐν τοῖς ὀφθαλμοῖς σου has the flavour more of Hebrew than of Greek (cf., for example, Isa 38:3) and appears as such only in Gen 3:6 (cf. Judg 12:14), in connection with the tree of the knowledge of good and evil. So to know what is pleasing in the eyes of God means to know God's will.

Wisdom knows not only the will of the Lord but also what is right (εὐθές) according to (ἐν) God's precepts, that is, the law of God, or the *Torah*. This is the preparation for an important development, that relation between wisdom and Law, understood as the revelation of the will of God, which will appear again in v. 17.

9:10a–b: "Send Her from the Holy Heaven…"

The prayer proper, at the centre of the strophe and of the poem as a whole, opens with an asyndetic construction which highlights the verb ἐξαποστέλλω. The

14 Scarpat, *Sapienza*, 2:261; Grundmann, Walter, ἕτοιμος κτλ., *TDNT* 2:704-706; cf. Prov 3:19; 8:27; and Jer 28:15, all in relation to God's action seen in connection with wisdom.

15 Cf. Tob 12:7 where τὰ ἔργα τοῦ θεοῦ is set in parallel with μυστήριον βασιλέως; cf. Scarpat, *Sapienza*, 2:226. With τὰ ἔργα, then, there is a reference to the purpose of God in creating the cosmos.

LXX uses it with God as subject in relation to the sending of an angel (Mal 3:1) or a prophet (Jer 7:25); Gen 3:23 in the context of the expulsion from Eden; cf. also LXX-Pss 17:17; 42:3; 56:4; 103:30; and 134:9 [MT-Pss 18:17; 43:3; 57:4; 104:30; and 135:9]. The verb, therefore, indicates a mission which God entrusts to someone or the divine act of sending people something. Wisdom is, thus, a reality which comes directly from God and is linked with God. It is to be seen as a gift received, not as a possession obtained. The expression "from the holy heaven", unusual for the LXX, but biblical in flavour, confirms wisdom's belonging to the heavenly sphere (heaven as the most noble part of the creation).

The following stich sees a return to the theme of God's throne (cf. in v. 4, in the plural). The expression θρόνον δόξης σου can be understood as "your glorious throne" or else as "the throne of your Glory"; cf. Wis 7:25. Our sage could have had in mind Sir 24:4: "my throne is in a pillar of cloud". The second imperative, πέμψον, "send her", repeats the sense of the previous sense verb, playing on the spatial symbolism of a wisdom which comes from heaven, from the place of the divine dwelling.

9:10c–11: Wisdom "Present"

According to the concentric structure which we have pointed out, vv. 10c-11 takes up what was already said in v. 9. In particular, 10c stands in a close relationship with 9b:

9b: καὶ παροῦσα ὅτε ἐποίεις τόν κόσμον
10c: ἵνα συμπαροῦσά μοι κοπιάσῃ

If 9b describes the presence of wisdom with God, 10c describes her presence with people. The final (ἵνα) clause stresses the purpose of the sending of wisdom herself: to be present with people (συμπαροῦσά μοι) and to work with them. Here, the pronoun μοι seems to have to refer to the verb συμπάρειμι (wisdom is present σύν μοι, "with me"), but at the same time it gives the verb κοπιάω a more precise nuance: "that she may toil with me". As in Wis 6:14a, κοπιάω refers to the idea of hard, exhausting toil.[16] Isa 40:28 LXX states that God is not weary (οὐδὲ κοπιάσει). Wisdom, wearies herself, however, toiling beside people and so assuming an active role. We must not limit wisdom's collaboration solely to the work of Solomon's building the temple; it applies to all his actions.

A further effect of the gift of wisdom is to know what is pleasing to God, παρὰ σοί (cf. "in your eyes" in 9c). The adjective *εὐάρεστον (which is taking up ἀρεστόν in 9c) is *hapax* in the LXX and the NT. Cf. 9:17: wisdom allows people to know the will of God. The text of 11a offers the reason for this: she "knows and understands all things" (for συνίημι, cf. 3:9 and 6:1). Our sage could be thinking of Ps 118:34-35 LXX [119:34-35 MT].[17] Through her closeness to God, wisdom is able to understand the whole of created reality, the meaning of things, perfectly; πάντα is to be understood in a very wide and general sense. Wisdom is being presented here as the interpreter of creation.

---

16 Cf. Hauck Friedrich, κόπος κοπιάω, *TDNT* 3:827-830; cf. also Scarpat, *Sapienza*, 2:1264-265.

17 "In the psalm there is expressed in the form of a prayer what in our text it is described as an action of Wisdom: she it is who knows and understands, who guides and keeps the just on the path of the commandments"; Scarpat, *Sapienza*, 2:235.

In the last two stichs of v. 11, our sage sets out two further actions of wisdom in her dealings with people. First, she guides people in their every action. The verb ὁδηγέω returns in Wis 10:17 (cf. 10:10) in connection with the pillar of cloud. Wisdom guides people in their actions (ἐν ταῖς πράξεσίν μου) with prudence (*σωφρόνως). The adverb indicates that prudence in action which is one of the characteristics of wisdom (cf. σωφροσύνη in 8:7). Wisdom as Guide

The second action is that "she will guard me (φυλάξει) with her glory". Wisdom's glory is a reflection of that of God from whom wisdom herself comes (cf. 9:10). The idea of guarding refers in its turn to the "glory" connected to the pillar of cloud in the desert to which the previous mention of "guiding" also alludes (cf. Exod 23:20. Wisdom is assuming here the role of the angel of the Lord in the exodus). In fact, guiding and guarding are the two roles of the cloud in the course of the exodus. Wisdom is the image of this cloud. Similar themes are found in Sir 14:27 and Ps 72:24 LXX [73:24 MT] (cf. also the comment on 18:3).

Verse 12 takes up the theme of vv. 7-8, but in reverse order and in more summary form: Solomon, builder – judge – king. All the works of Solomon (τὰ ἔργα μου here is of general import) will turn out to be well-pleasing to God (for this sense of προσδεκτός cf. Prov 11:20). He will be able to judge the people of God with justice (cf. 9:7b). Our author is taking up 1 Kgs 3:9 (καὶ διακρίνειν τὸν λαόν σου ἐν δικαιοσύνῃ); cf. also Prov 31:9. Διακρίνω occurs only here in the book and has a precise nuance: determining, deciding who is right in a legal dispute. Only with the gift of wisdom can Solomon be worthy of the throne[18] of his father (David). Ἄξιος (cf. 1:16) has a strong theological nuance: to be worthy in the sight of God. 9:12: Solomon, Builder, Judge, King

Diachronic Analysis

In this strophe, the royal fiction becomes explicit and we finally understand that Solomon is the one praying. However, the text has a deeper dimension: our sage addresses his public to make them understand that everyone who seeks wisdom from God can become a royal figure. Our author is making use of the Stoic idea of the sage as king (cf. 6:20), but the biblical background of Gen 1:26-28 is also important: God has reserved a royal destiny for people.[19]

We note that the mention of "daughters" alongside "sons" is unusual and could have been suggested by Isa 43:6. It is the sign of a certain attention to women on the part of our sage. The expression returns in the OT/HB only in these two texts, besides Deut 32:19 (cf. 2 Cor 6:18). 9:7

---

18 Here in the singular; cf. Scarpat, *Sapienza*, 2:266-267. Perhaps with the plural of v. 4, our author intended to emphasise the metaphorical significance of the term.

19 In Wisdom, the use of the metaphor of kingship shows itself very different from its use in Qoheleth; cf. Vignolo, "Sapienza, preghiera e modello regale", especially 286-300. If, in Qoh 1-2, we have an anthropological question and a kingship that has been relinquished, in Wis 7-9, we find a confession of anthropological finitude and at the same time a kingship that has been recovered, a kingship understood both politically and eschatologically as the true human vocation.

9:8 The exact significance of the reference to the Temple has been debated at length.[20] The possible connection with Sir 24:10 leads us to interpret the expression "holy tabernacle" and the allusion to the tent in 8b with reference to the Jerusalem Temple. However, our author also has the desert sanctuary in mind. The theme of the image, in fact, is taking up the divine order given to Moses and contained in Exod 25:40: ὅρα ποιήσεις κατὰ τὸν τύπον τὸν δεδειγμένον σοι ἐν τῷ ὄρει. The expression ἣν προητοίμασας ἀπ' ἀρχῆς suggests a divine choice which comes from the beginnings of things. God has chosen to dwell among people from the beginning of time. The earthly temple is a sign of God's presence just like the tent in the desert. Moreover, the idea is frequent in ancient Jewish tradition.[21]

We can conclude from this that our author is reinterpreting the Jerusalem Temple in light of themes relating to the tent in the desert. However, both realities are, in their turn, images (μίμημα) of a heavenly temple (cf. Heb 8:1-2; 9:11-14, 24 for a New Testament reprise of this theme) which constitutes the true dwelling of God of which the earthly temple is precisely a sign. Wisdom is striving to connect earthly realities with heavenly ones, seeking at the same time to go beyond the first and so begin to have some conception of the second. Finally, with regard to *μίμημα, we observe that the term is much used by Philo and refers to the model, the image of something.[22]

Isis and Wisdom[23]

9:9b, 10c One of the biblical texts behind Wis 9 is clearly Prov 8:22-31.[24] In Wis 9:9b, παροῦσα seems to have been suggested by Prov 8:30 LXX: ἤμεν παρ' αὐτῷ, while, in 9:10c, συμπαροῦσα undoubtedly comes from Prov 8:27 LXX: συμπαρήμην αὐτῷ. Outside these two texts, in fact, the verb συμπάρειμι appears in the LXX only in Tob 12:12^{B}, but in a different context. The dependence of παροῦσα on Prov 8:30 gives the verb the sense of "being present to help" (cf. the Latin *adesse*). However, it is necessary to observe that our author employs two expressions which, in Proverbs, both refer to the relationship of wisdom with God by linking the one (παροῦσα) to wisdom's relationship with the Lord, the other (συμπαροῦσα) to her relationship with Solomon.

There is another important difference from Prov 8:27, 30 LXX. In Prov 8:22-31 LXX, it appears clear that the Greek translator is seeking to emphasise wisdom's passivity more than in the Hebrew text. The choice of συμπαρήμην αὐτῷ (the pronoun is absent from the MT) is made precisely to subordinate wisdom to God.[25]

---

20 Cf. Larcher, *Sagesse*, 2:580-583; Sisti, *Sapienza*, 252-253.

21 Cf. the texts cited in Winston, *Wisdom*, 204-205.

22 Scarpat (*Sapienza* 2:223-224) observes that the use of μίμημα is not sufficient reason to think of a dependence on the Platonic notion of ideas (cf., on the contrary, Winston, *Wisdom*, 203 and Hübner, *Weisheit*, 125, especially n. 147). Wisdom is carefully avoiding πάραδειγμα which would have led directly to Plato.

23 Cf. Mazzinghi, "La sapienza presente accanto a Dio", *passim*.

24 Cf. Skehan, "The literary relationship", especially 174-175.

25 Cf. Cook, Johann, *The Septuagint of Proverbs. Jewish and/or Hellenistic Proverbs? Concerning the Hellenistic Colouring of LXX Proverbs* (Leiden - New York – Cologne: Brill 1997) 227-228.

In this way, the Greek translator did not wish to run the risk that wisdom could be seen as a divine figure, perhaps a Jewish Ma'at or perhaps even another Isis.[26] In Wisdom, concerns of this type are lacking. In fact, the *elogium* of wisdom (Wis 7-8) has reformulated her figure in Greek philosophical categories and presented an image of wisdom reread precisely in the light of the figure of Isis without our author's feeling any need to justify himself for this. Thus, the choice of συμπάρειμι in Wis 9:10c should not be read as an attempt to attenuate the active role of wisdom having the verb refer only to her presence alongside people. In fact, it is precisely the presence of wisdom, active alongside God, which causes her to be active also alongside people (κοπιάω).

The verb πάρειμι is typical of Greek religious language. Indeed, from the time of Homer πάρειμι is used to describe the presence of the gods. In particular, πάρειμι indicates the presence of a deity at the sacred ceremonies carried out in that deity's honour. The use of the term παρουσία in connection with the divine is well known.[27] As for συμπάρειμι, it is employed in the religious sphere by Josephus in relation to the presence and the help of God (τοῦ θεοῦ συμπαρόντος, *A.J.* 2.268; cf. *B.J.* 5.380; *A.J.* 1.260; 2.340; 3.316; 10.239). However, in this sense, the verb is very rare in Greek usage. In this context, the two verbs recall rather the figure of Isis; cf. the text of the first Isiac hymn of Isidorus (lines 29-34):

> The many who are prisoners of a fate that leads to death,
> the many who are tormented by long and sorrowful vigils,
> all those wandering through a strange and hostile land,
> the many who in winter venture into the vast ocean,
> when they are destroyed, their ships shattered,
> all those are saved when they pray to you to be present (παρεῖναι).

Here, πάρειμι has the sense of "being present to help" and the context offers a good clarification of what kind of help is brought by the presence of the goddess. The situations from which Isis saves people are *topoi*: danger of death, prison, sickness, and journeys by land and sea. All are found again in our book in relation to the works of wisdom. In Wis 10, the wisdom of Israel frees prisoners (10:13-15), rescues people (cf. already 9:18 and later 10:4), and frees them from the power of fate (cf. Wis 17:16-17). The same role of guide (ὁδηγός, ὁδηγέω cf. the Isiac litany of Oxyrhyncus = P.Oxy. XI, 1380, 122-123) is attributed to wisdom in Wis 9:11; cf. 10:10; 10:17 and, again, Wis 14:5 and 18:3. In Wis 14:1-10, the rescue of sailors in a storm is a typical Isiac feature.

The verb πάρειμι is found again in the second hymn of Isidorus (II, 5-8), in relation to the presence of Isis who guarantees wealth and recovery from sickness: "All who pray to you to assist (πάρειμι) their commerce / prosper in their piety forever; / all who are bound in mortal illnesses in the grip of death, / if they (but) pray to you, quickly attain your (renewal of) Life" (tr. Vanderlip). In the third hymn, the verb returns again (lines 26-28) in connection with the cosmic role of Isis and her justice, a theme which comes close to the role of wisdom alongside Solomon as art of good governance. Isis is, therefore, a benevolent and salutary presence: "En adsum tuis

26 Cf. Fox, Michael V., "World Order and Ma'at: A Crooked Parallel", *JANES* 23 (1995): 37-48.

27 Cf. Spicq, *Notes*, 673-675; Oepke, Albrecht, παρουσία, πάρειμι, *TDNT* 5:858-871.

commota, Luci, precibus (...). Adsum tuos miserata casus, adsum favens et propitia (...) iam tibi providentia mea inlucescit dies salutaris [Behold, I am here, Lucius, moved by your prayers (...) I am here, pitying your misfortunes, I am here as friend and helper (...) with my aid, your day of salvation is dawning]" (Apuleius, *Metam.* 11.5-6). Isis is *praesentissimum numen* [all-present divinity] (*Metam.* 11.12). In these texts there emerges the strong religious stamp and the profound personal relationship which binds the worshipper of Isis to this goddess.[28] This is also the tone which breathes through the prayer of Wis 9.

In 11b, we note again the presence of the verb ὁδηγέω. This verb is employed in exodus contexts in texts such as Exod 13:17; 15:13; 32:34; Deut 1:33; cf. Neh 9:12, and several times in the Psalter. One can think also of Ps 142:10 LXX [143:10 MT]: τὸ πνεῦμά σου τὸ ἀγαθὸν ὁδηγήσει με ἐν γῇ εὐθείᾳ. In Wis 9:17, in fact, wisdom, as the means which people use to know God's will, is associated with the spirit. However, the theme of the "guide" is also a characteristic element of the Isiac litanies (cf. 7:15). What Isis claims to be for people, that is, a guide, is much more the role of wisdom.

In conclusion, in his description of wisdom's presence with God and people, our author makes use, first and foremost, of biblical models (Prov 8:22-31 in first place) and does not intend to distance himself from the tradition of Israel; and yet the language and the choice of themes can be understood better in the light of the figure of Isis. In this way, we can speak of the *relecture* and *actualisation* of biblical themes in an Isiac key. One of the themes is certainly polemical and apologetic. Wisdom is intending to strengthen the Alexandrian Jews against the temptation to follow one of the more seductive figures available to them: Isis. We note in particular that if the use of πάρειμι is frequent for Isis, this is not the case for συμπάρειμι, which never seems to be attested for Isis. Much more than Isis, wisdom is placed beside people (σύν), in their company, and toils with them (κοπιάω). In this perspective, the link of Wis 9 with the themes of creation and of the history of Israel is an expression of a precise taking of position and a great clarity about personal identity within a hostile cultural context. It remains that the reprise of Isiac themes happens naturally. Wisdom is not Isis, yet the Jew, who could be seduced by Isis, can also find in wisdom much more of what was promised him by Isis. In this way, our author launches a bridge between his community and a culture which could seem too separate, and that without ever renouncing his own faith.

Wis 9:13-18: The Third Strophe – Wisdom, the Will of God, and Salvation

[13] For what person will be able to know the will of God?
Or who will be able to imagine what the Lord wills?
[14] The reasonings of mortals are hesitant,
and uncertain our reflections.

28 Cf. note 8. Cf. also Winston, "The Sage as Mystic in the Wisdom of Solomon".

[15] For a corruptible body weighs down the soul
and this tent made of earth oppresses a mind burdened with cares.
[16] Certainly, it is with difficulty that we imagine the things of the earth
and with labour that we find out what is close at hand.
Who could track down the things of heaven?
[17] Yet your will – who could know it,
if you had not granted wisdom
and sent your holy spirit from on high?
[18] Thus the paths of those who are on the earth were made straight
and people were instructed in what is pleasing to you
and through wisdom they were saved.

Notes on the Text and Translation

v. 16. The reading τὰ ἐν χερσίν alternates with the reading of S, V, and Arm: τὰ ἐν ποσίν, a circumlocution more frequent in Greek usage in the sense of "what is available". The first reading, less attested, has the sense of "to be within reach" and can therefore be retained here as *lectio difficilior.*
In 16c, the aorist ἐξιχνιάσεν alternates with the less attested ἐξιχνιάσει (cf. Ziegler). The aorist is preferable, in parallel with the other aorist ἔγνω in 9:17aα. The verb ἐξιχνιάζω is typical of the LXX and is used in Sir 1:3; 18:4, 6; 24:28; Job 9:10; and 11:7 in the sense of "explore, track", in all cases with some reference to wisdom.

Synchronic Analysis

9:13-17aα Wisdom, Guide to Know the Will of God

9:13

The third strophe opens with a double rhetorical question, in both cases introduced by an interrogative τίς. Both questions concern the impossibility of knowing the will of God.

The initial γάρ links up with the theme of the request in v. 10: give me wisdom. *In fact*, without her, it is impossible to know what the Lord wishes. From the particular case of Solomon in 9:1-6, there is a movement here to the universal case of everyone.

The expression γνώσεται βουλὴν θεοῦ is deliberately indeterminate. The verb in the future ("who will be able?") and the expression βουλὴν θεοῦ (without article) points us, as already in 6:4c, towards the divine "will" understood generically, that is, towards the demands and also the decisions of God in his dealings with people, a will which they are not able to know. The theme is biblical: cf. Isa 40:13; Rom 11:33-34 and, outside the biblical texts, 1 En. 93:11-14.

In the second question (13b), the verb ἐνθυμηθήσεται reinforces the previous γνώσεται and contributes to the rhetorical form of the *gradatio* or climax. Used already in 3:14; 6:15; and 7:15, ἐνθυμέομαι indicates here "developing an idea", conceiving, imagining, exactly as in Sir 16:20 (τὰς ὁδοὺς αὐτοῦ τίς ἐνθυμηθήσεται). In this case too, the question presupposes a negative answer. No one can imagine the will of the Lord.

9:14

In 9:14 our sage indicates the reasons why people cannot know the will of God. The term λογισμός has already been introduced right at the beginning of the book (1:3, 5) with a negative nuance. Here, λογισμοί recalls the λογισθήσεται which concludes the first strophe (9:6) and refers more generically to the reasonings of mortals (θνητῶν), a plural rare in the LXX, but frequent in Greek usage (cf. θνητός in 7:1). Human reasonings are described as δειλοὶ, (cf. 4:20 and 17:11a); cf. the Homeric expression δειλοὶ βρότοι, "wretched mortals" (*Il.* 22.31). If, in 17:11a, the sense is that of "vile", here, δειλός is, rather, "timid, reticent, weak".[29] Our sage is not denying *a priori* the value of human reasoning but rather showing its limits, precisely the "weakness", the provisional and never definitive nature of human thought.

In the stich which follows with αἱ ἐπίνοιαι (cf. 6:16; 14:12; 15:4), our sage is indicating the result of such reasoning, or the interior reflections produced by the reasoning itself. The term is relatively rare (cf. Acts 8:22). The adjective *ἐπισφαλής (cf. ἐπισφαλῶς in 4:4) indicates something unstable, precarious, even dangerous (cf. Acts 27:9 in connection with navigation). The reflections which people manage to make do not succeed in finding true certainty.

9:15 Now, towards the end of the prayer, our sage expresses the deepest reason for human weakness. The first stich has a clear Greek tone: "a corruptible (φθαρτός) body weighs down the soul (βαρύνει ψυχήν)".

In the second stich, with synonymous parallelism, our sage offers us a further reason for human weakness. The subject is τὸ γεῶδες σκῆνος, "this tent of earth", an expression that takes up the previous φθαρτὸν σῶμα and which, therefore, refers to the body. The use of the term "tent" as a metaphor for the body is a *topos* and refers to a transitory situation well known to Scripture (cf. Isa 38:12; Heb 11:9), just like the term "earthly", again with reference to the body.[30] The image of the tent for human life could have been suggested by texts such as Job 4:19 which recalls the clay houses in which people live. The reference to the person made of earth could be, in its turn, a reference to Gen 2:7 and 3:19 (cf. Wis 15:8).

The verb *βρίθω is rare and poetic, and still rarer is the meaning of "weigh down" which the verb assumes here. The object of βρίθει is "a mind with preoccupations", νοῦς πολύφροντις, an expression which takes up the previous reference to ψυχή, but in a more creative way. Νοῦς occurs only in Wis 4:12 and highlights that the problem is, rather, a psychological one (or, better, a gnoseological one: knowing the divine will). The term *πολυφροντίς is attested only once elsewhere (Anacreon, frag. 48,6 Bergk.; πολυφρόντιδές τε βουλαί) and, in this context, acquires the sense of "much preoccupied". According to our sage, the soul is constrained to be preoccupied with the things of the body, like food and clothing, things of daily life, and cannot manage, therefore, to think of the things of heaven.

9:16 Verse 16, above all in its final stich, takes up v. 13, returning to its basic question: how can one know the will of God? This question too has already been tackled by other biblical texts (Isa 40:12-14; Prov 30:2-5; Bar 3:29-30; Sir 1:3-6). It is a rhetorical question which expects an answer that is totally negative: no one can know the secrets of God unless God himself reveals them.

"With difficulty (μόλις), we imagine the things of the earth" (16a). The verb εἰκάζω, already employed in 8:8, has the sense of "conjecture, imagine". Human

---

29 Cf. Mazzinghi, *Notte di paura e di luce*, 77-78.

30 Texts in Larcher, *Sagesse*, 2:596.

knowledge is already relative and provisional in relation to earthly realities, even though they are available to people. The following stich completes this thought in chiasmic form: even the things which are at hand (τὰ ἐν χερσίν), which we are able to understand, we find out (εὑρίσκομεν) with labour (μετὰ πόνου).

The real question arrives in the third stich which opens with an adversative δέ. The answer to the question is clear: only through the gift of wisdom, which is evoked in the following verse (9:17), can people understand "the things of heaven", that is, the will of God (9:13).

After a fourth rhetorical question (17aα), which completes the series (13ab, 9:17
16c) and which, on the structural level, actually belongs to the previous pericope (13-17aα), v. 17aβb provides the answer, returning to the central theme of the chapter (9:4, 10ab): the gift of wisdom which here, however, is once again associated with the spirit.

In 17a, there is a new appearance of the reference to the will of God (βουλὴν δέ σου τίς ἔγνω) which had already appeared in 13a. As in that case, βουλὴν δέ σου should be seen as a reference to that will of God which is expressed especially in the law.[31] However, what remains inaccessible to human powers is not the law in itself as rather the knowledge, the deep understanding of the law. The gift of wisdom is, therefore, indispensable. Here there is added the gift of the spirit which is mentioned in the following stich in rigorous parallelism with wisdom. Only in Wis 1:5 has the spirit been called explicitly the πνεῦμα ἅγιον. In this way, the new use of this expression creates a kind of grand *inclusio* with the beginning of the book by recalling the *pneumatic* dimension of wisdom.

Verse 18 concludes the prayer by highlighting three effects of the gift of 9:18 Wisdom, the Saviour
wisdom. The three aorists refer to an action that has already happened in the past. Salvation is not only to be expected in the future but is already at work in history. The prophecies (cf. the references to Jeremiah and Ezekiel; see below) are being realised.

Verse 18 not only forms the conclusion of the prayer as a whole. By means of the mention of "salvation", it introduces chapter 10 and so the whole of the third part of the book. As in 9:2, the dative τῇ σοφίᾳ is to be understood as a complement of agency: people were saved *through wisdom*, which is, therefore, God's instrument, something that agrees closely with the activity described in chapters 7-8.[32] The active role of wisdom in chapter 10, from Adam to Moses, appears to confirm this interpretation.

The first action of wisdom is that of "straightening the paths", that is, of bringing people back to the right way. The verb διορθόω, *hapax* in Wisdom and found only six times in the LXX, has, in Jer 7:3, 5 and Prov 15:29 LXX [16:8 MT], the clear sense of "correct" with a moral nuance. As in this case, the "paths of those who (walk) on the earth" refers to moral conduct. What is being presupposed, therefore, is amendment of human conduct. As has been said, wisdom is also a moral power which renews people from within; cf. God who is called διορθωτής in Wis 7:15.

Moreover, "people were instructed in what is pleasing to you". Τὰ ἀρεστά σου – the expression seems to have been suggested by Bar 4:4, where it designates

31 Gilbert, "Volonté de Dieu", 213.

32 *Contra* Scarpat, *Sapienza*, 2:249.

the law – links up with the εὐαρεστόν of 10d, that is, the will of God which is precisely the basic issue of the whole text. Thanks to the gift of wisdom and the spirit people are enabled to learn what pleases God. The verb διδάσκω already appeared in Wis 6:10 and, in particular, in Wis 7:21 in connection with the teaching imparted by wisdom. It will return in 12:19 in connection with God.

How did wisdom instruct people? Our author is not more specific, although the association between wisdom and the spirit points towards an interior presence of wisdom which, ultimately, is the presence of God himself. There will be a more complete answer given in Wis 10-19: wisdom leads people and particularly the people of Israel to discover in the course of history the presence of a God who creates and saves.

This, then, is the first appearance in Wisdom of the verb "save" (σῴζω; cf. Wis 10:4; 14:4; 16:7; and 18:5). The use of the aorist passive, "they were saved", indicates something that has already happened through the action of another. Chapter 10, in fact, will present a gallery of men who were "saved" by wisdom in the course of the history of Israel.

Diachronic Analysis

9:13 In Septuagintal usage, the term βουλή in relation to God refers to the divine plan which God intends to put into action (cf. Isa 5:19; 14:26; Ps 32:11 LXX [33:11 MT]; etc.) and of which people are unaware. In only a few cases, as in Ps 106:11 LXX [107:11 MT], βουλή indicates what God wishes from people, that is, the demands in the law, a concept which, in Proverbs (cf. Prov 1:25, 30; 2:11; 3:21; 8:12, 14) evolves almost naturally into the idea of the demands of wisdom. However, the perhaps more convincing argument for interpreting βουλὴ θεοῦ as the will of God expressed in the *Torah* is the parallel which our sage makes in this same verse between the divine βουλή and "what the Lord wills". The distinction between βουλὴ θεοῦ and τί θέλει ὁ κύριος does not depend so much on a possible, different meaning of θέλω, which in Wisdom alternates with βούλομαι without too much difference,[33] as rather on the mention of the Lord, ὁ κύριος. Thus, the expression τί θέλει ὁ κύριος indicates "what the Lord wills", what is pleasing to him. Now, in the LXX, the will of the Lord, expressed with the term θέλημα, indicates precisely what God is seeking in the Law (cf. Pss 39:9 LXX [40:9 MT]; 102:7 LXX [103:7 MT]; 1 Esd 8:16). However, it is the entire context of chapter 9 which points us to discern in these references to the will of God in v. 13 the demands of the divine *Torah*, indispensable to Solomon if he is to be able to govern his people.[34]

9:15: A Platonic Text?

The language of v. 15 undoubtedly has a Platonic flavour. The verbs βρίθω and βαρύνω, for example, are found in the famous myth of the charioteers in *Phaedr.* 247b. This text, however, presupposes a tripartite anthropological division (σῶμα, ψυχή, and νοῦς) unknown to Wisdom. In the text of *Phaed.* 81b–c, Plato speaks of the soul which during its bodily existence has an inclination towards the body and is contaminated by it. Thus, the body becomes an obstacle. In the

---

33 For βούλομαι, cf. Wis 12:6; 14:19; 16:21; for θέλω, cf. 11:25; 12:18; 13:6; 14:5; cf. Larcher, *Sagesse*, 2:592.

34 Cf. Gilbert, "Volonté de Dieu", 210-212.

Platonic passage, in addition to the mention of soul and body, we find adjectives such as ἐμβριθές, βαρύ, and γεῶδες, as well as the verb βαρύνω, referencing τὸ σῶμα.[35]

In our text, the use of the term "tent" in connection with the body does not imply of itself a disdain for the body so much as the idea that the body is something transitory, a dwelling which presupposes a journey towards immortality or, in the language of Wisdom, towards ἀφθαρσία for which the corruptible body, φθαρτός, is destined. The vocabulary of v. 15 is thus Platonic in tone, but Wisdom is using it in a psychological and gnoseological sense rather than a metaphysical one. In any case, the presence of Platonic terminology does not actually imply the adoption of Platonism and of a consequent disdain for the body.[36]

However, the problem of the sources utilised by our sage in this verse remains a difficult one.[37] It seems simpler to clarify the overall thought. The body, made of earth according to the biblical conception and thus corruptible, draws people to material things, the things of the earth, and in this way weighs on the soul and the mind which is full of preoccupations (πολυφροντίς). However, the liberation from these preoccupations consists not in leaving the body but in embracing God's gift of wisdom, or, rather, soliciting this gift through prayer. Our sage hghlights how human weakness, the uncertainty and limitations of its reasoning, the many preoccupations filling its mind, prevent it from knowing the divine will unless God himself comes to help. This is far from conceptions that are directly Platonic. Our sage seems to be aware of these but intends to reproduce them within a profoundly biblical concept of the human being, one that is alien to any metaphysical dualism.

The question in v. 16 recalls the text of Ps 113:24 LXX [115:16 MT] which tells 9:16
us that God has given the earth to the children of mortals whereas "the heavens are the heavens of the Lord". Several times, Qoheleth states that he wishes to limit his own searching to what happens "under heaven" or "under the sun". The rhetorical question "who has been able to track down the things of heaven?" recalls passages such as Prov 30:4; Deut 30:12 (with reference to the law); Sir 1:2-3:6 (with reference to wisdom); and Bar 3:29 (wisdom and law). In all four cases, the rhetorical questions are being formulated within a context of revelation, with particular reference to the *Torah*.[38] In the light of these texts, therefore, the "will of God" mentioned in 9:13 seems to be what is expressed in the law.

9:17: Wisdom and Spirit

The text of v. 17 reflects a typical problem of the Jewish world in the Hellenistic period. In fact, Ben Sirach had already associated "wisdom" and "law" (cf. Sir 1 and 24), without actually identifying them. Neither does Wisdom identify them. On the contrary, despite placing them in relation to each other, our sage distinguishes the two realities more clearly. He highlights that wisdom is necessary so

35 "A widespread Platonic motif", Winston, *Wisdom*, 207, who stresses Wisdom's dependence on Plato. The text was much used by Augustine; cf. La Bonnardière, *Biblia Augustiniana*, 206-221 and 289-292.

36 Cf. Reese, *Hellenistic Influence*, 86-87. Cf., already, Grimm, *Weisheit*, 188-189.

37 Cf. Larcher, *Sagesse*, 2:598-599; Heinisch, *Weisheit*, 188-189, hypothesises an indirect knowledge of Plato on the part of Wisdom.

38 Cf. Gilbert, "Volonté de Dieu", 205-210. The motif expressed in v. 16 is a *topos*; cf. the texts mentioned by Winston, *Wisdom*, 208.

that people "may be instructed in what is pleasing to you", or so that they may be able to understand the demands of the law. Wisdom is, therefore, more important than the law.

The second and more original association between wisdom and the spirit serves to explain this relationship still better. Already, the prophetic tradition, above all in the texts of Jer 38:33-34 LXX [31:33-34 MT] and Ezek 36:26-29 (cf. Joel 2:28-29 LXX [3:1-2 MT]), spoke of the necessity of internalising the law. That cannot happen, however, unless God intervenes with his spirit into people's hearts, enabling them to understand the will of God as it is expressed in the law. According to Ezekiel, the interiorisation of the law announced by Jeremiah is fulfilled precisely thanks to the gift of the spirit. In our text, the spirit mentioned by Ezekiel is associated with wisdom which, in the light of Wis 7-8, takes on the force of a special and interior moral power which God grants to people so that they may understand God's law. Thus, the message of Jeremiah and Ezekiel is not to be lost and is fulfilled in the gift of wisdom invoked by Solomon.[39]

Wis 9: Between Biblical and Greek Prayer

The main sources of Wis 9 are the two accounts of Solomon's dream at Gibeon (1 Kgs 3 and 2 Chr 1). Wis 9 chiefly adopts the account of Chronicles where there is more emphasis on wisdom than on a right heart. However, the account of 1 Kgs 3 is not absent (cf. 9:3 in relation to 1 Kgs 3:6 and 9:12 to 1 Kgs 3:9). The text of 1 Kgs 3:7-9 has a close relationship with the whole of chapter 9. In fact, in 1 Kgs 3:7 there appears the theme of weakness, in v. 8, the theme of "your people", and, in v. 9, Solomon's request. This biblical text could have been the starting point which suggested to our author the literary structure of Wis 9. However, the role of wisdom alongside God and consequently with people (creation and salvation), as well as the multiple references to the theme of prayer, are innovations of our sage within the Hellenistic world.

The ancient world is well aware of prayer addressed to the divinity. In Greek culture, both classical and Hellenistic, prayer from that of the private citizen to that of the philosophers to obtain wisdom is formulated in a stereotyped language which we find partly in our text also. This is the case with the initial vocative, θεέ, and with the imperative, δός μοι.[40] However, already in v. 1, the mention of the "fathers" and the reference to mercy underline the typically Jewish character of this prayer.

In the Stoic view, prayer is for no other purpose than to ask the divinity for one to be able to submit to the will of fate: "*fata aliter ius suum peragunt, nec ulla commoventur prece; non misericordia flecti, non gratia sciunt; cursum irrevocabilem ingressa ex destinato fluunt* [fate fulfils its law in another way: it is moved by no prayer, not swayed by mercy or favour; when it has set out on its unalterable path, it flows on its appointed way]" (Seneca, *Nat.* 2.35.2). More generally, in the Greek world, there are ideas unfavourable to prayer: "*Aiunt pagani fato omnia fieri et nihil preces, nihil orationes valere* [The pagans say that everything happens through fate and neither prayers nor supplications avail anything]" (Maximus of Turin, *Oratio contra paganos*),[41] We recall the information of Suetonius (*Tib.* 69)

39 Gilbert, "Volonté de Dieu", 228-229.

40 Cf. Scarpat, *Sapienza*, 2:207-213.

41 PL 57, 782A; cf. Nock, Arthur D., *Conversion. The Old and New in Religion from Alexander the Great to Augustine of Hippo* (Oxford: Clarendon Press 1961) 288.

according to which the emperor Tiberius neglected the cult as something useless: *Circa deos ac religiones neglegentior, quippe addictus mathematicae plenusque persuasionis cuncta fato agi* (*Tib.* 69). The book of Wisdom counterposes trust in the efficacy of prayer which, in Wis 9:15-17, serves precisely as a means to know the will of God which is expressed in the law. Without prayer (cf. Wis 8:21; 9:6), wisdom is not accessible.

The world of the mysteries is familiar with the use of prayer. To limit ourselves to the Isiac mysteries, the prayers addressed to the goddess by the initiate arise from a desire for real contact with the divine. Prayer is simultaneously the instrument of praise and supplication.[42] Compared with classical religiosity, the Isiac mysteries bring the certainty that Isis, the goddess who is superior to fate, listens to the prayers of her devotees: "I am coming to you, Lucius, moved by your prayers (*ecce adsum ... tuis commota precibus*)" (Apuleius, *Metam.* 11.5). In the hymns of Isidorus, the worshipper prays to Isis thus: "hear my prayer, be favourable to me, free me from all suffering" (1.35-36). The Greek-Egyptian papyri often attest invocations to Isis and Serapis at the end of private letters. The prayers to Isis attest a profound sense of the divine bound up with very personal concerns: *Regina caeli ... tu meis iam nunc extremis aerumnis subsiste, tu fortunam collapsam adfirma, tu saevis exanclatis casibus pausam pacemque tribue; sit satis laborum, sit satis periculorum.* "Queen of heaven ... help me in my overwhelming misfortune! Strengthen my uncertain fate! After such cruel vicissitudes, grant me rest and peace! Let the hardship cease! Let the danger cease!" (Apuleius, *Metam.* 11.2).[43] The prayer of the initiate is never a means of forcing the gods to act. Power and destiny remain in the hands of Isis. She, however, can be moved by prayer to come to the aid of the worshipper. Prayer is discovered to be submission to a benevolent deity from whom people seek and ask favour (cf. Wis 8:21c). Just as in the Isiac mysteries so too in Wisdom prayer presupposes a close and personal link with the divinity. Wis 9 contains features borrowed precisely from the world of Isis. However, it is no longer a goddess, Isis, that Solomon addresses but rather the God of Israel who is able to grant that wisdom which guarantees to the one demanding it much more than Isis guaranteed.

To the magus too, prayer is not unknown.[44] The *Papyri Gracae Magicae* have preserved various prayers for us (cf. *PGM* 4:2785-2879; 8:1-26; 17; etc.), structured according to a classical scheme: invocation of the god, his celebration, and the prayer proper. Expressions like ἐλθέ μοι, δός μοι, ἐπικαλοῦμαί σε, δέομαι (cf. Wis 8:21) are very frequent. By contrast with the mystery prayers, those of the magus always have an immediate purpose: obtaining material salvation. The prayer can also be useful, but for exclusively practical ends. Solomon's prayer, on the other hand, is not aiming at material goods but at the gift of wisdom.

---

42 Cf. Malaise, Michel, "La piété personnelle dans la religion isiaque", in: Limet, Henri – Ries, Julien (edd.), *L'expérience de la prière dans les grandes religions* (Louvain la-Neuve: Centre d'Histoire des Religions 1980) 83-117.

43 Cf. Nock, *Conversion*, 138-155.

44 Cf. Graf, Fritz, "Prayer in Magic and Religious Ritual", in Faraone, Christopher A. – Obbink, Dirk (edd.), *Magica Hiera. Ancient Greek Magic and Religion* (New York – Oxford: Oxford University Press 1981) 188-213.

Summary of Wis 9

What then, finally, is this "wisdom" for which Solomon is praying to God? It is first a gift of God which is to be sought from God, a reality analogous to God's creative word (v. 1) and spirit (v. 17). It can, therefore, be described as God's "presence" in the world and in people, an interior moral power which renders the one who embraces it able to understand the will of God as expressed in the Mosaic law.

In this chapter, then, the interior dimension of wisdom, both theological and moral, is combined very well with the practical-political value of wisdom, the art of good governance and of civil living. Our sage is in harmony with the sapiential and prophetic tradition of Israel, a tradition which, however, is deepened and renewed through a courageous confrontation with the perspectives opened from a profound dialogue with the Hellenistic world.

In making Solomon the protagonist of Wis 7-9, our sage is not following the model of the Jewish apologists of his time (Artapanus, Eupolemus, Aristobulus) where Moses is presented as a *Kulturbringer*, an example of Jewish superiority over the Greek world.[45] Solomon is a man like all, the model for every human being who wishes to become wise by embracing a wisdom which, in principle, God grants to everyone. Thus, particularism is welded with universalism. Within the Hellenistic world, authors like Maneto and Berossus or like the Jewish apologists attest a clear attempt to strengthen their own tradition, making it accessible and significant for the Greek world too, or even in the face of the Greek world, an attempt which Philo too will make in Alexandria a little later. The author of Wisdom too takes up the biblical figure of Solomon and reproduces it within Hellenistic cultural categories in order to show the perennial validity of Judaism.

The studies of Mark Turner and Gilles Fauconnier offer us the category of "conceptual integration" ("conceptual blending") which they define as "a basic cognitive operation for creating new meanings out of old".[46] From this point of view, Wisdom manages to create a new text in which the old texts are not simply recalled to memory, summarised, or mixed together with skill. In fact, in the light of the Hellenistic culture, the book of Wisdom offers something completely new, but at the same time authoritative and sacred.

Finally, wisdom brings about salvation, a salvation which, according to Wis 9:18c, is already in operation when a person embraces the gift of wisdom and allows himself or herself to be guided by it in order to attain one's own vocation according to the will of God. The link between v. 1 and v. 18 puts the theme of creation which opened the prayer in close connection with that of salvation, a

---

45 Cf. Sterling, Gregory E, *Historiography and Self-definition. Josephus, Luke-Acts and Apologetic Historiography*, NT Supp. 64, New York – Leiden – Cologne: Brill 1992. On all this, cf. Mazzinghi, "Testi autorevoli".

46 Turner, Mark – Fauconnier, Gilles, "A Mechanism of Creativity", *Poetics Today* 20 (1999), 397; Lacoste, "Solomon, the Exemplary Sage".

constant dimension of the author's theology.[47] Thus, there is no fracture in God's plan. God creates people in view of salvation, and wisdom is the point of contact between these two poles of the divine action. If the first part of the book put the basic problems concerning the problem of salvation, the third will offer the responses. In this perspective, Wis 9, at the heart of the literary structure, assumes a fundamental importance. Wisdom is the central actor of the salvation offered by God, and this salvation is in the closest relationship with the creation as was evident as far back as Wis 1:14 (the generations of the world are the bearers of salvation).

"Salvation" here is not to be understood as "redemption" in a Christian sense, i.e., as salvation from sin and death. As is seen in Wis 10, it is, first of all, salvation from *physical* death but also, as the third strophe has shown, it is to live in harmony with the will of God.[48] However, the fact that "Solomon" prays to obtain wisdom reveals, on the other hand, that this "salvation" has to be realised continually. We thus understand why the prayer to obtain wisdom occurs only after the first part of the book which was devoted to the people's future destiny (Wis 1-6), chapters in which our author never makes use of the verb "save". Thus, the gift of wisdom also guarantees to people salvation from *eternal* death, that is, the incorruptibility for which God has destined them (cf. Wis 6:17-21).

In conclusion, the prayer of Wis 9 could have some echoes in the New Testament. We note in particular that ἐξαποστέλλω is used by Paul in Gal 4:4 in connection with the sending of the Son and in Gal 4:6 in connection with that of the Spirit. A dependence on the text of Wisdom does not seem impossible.

---

47 The reference to the beginnings, that is, to creation and, at the same time, to the beginnings of Solomon's experience, the dream at Gibeon, is particularly important: the readers are being recalled continually to their own past but with a view to the future. Solomon's experience leads him to discover the value of the wisdom that is already present in creation, but also to desire to possess her through living a right and happy life in the present, and to possess, in the future, life without end. Cf. Gilbert, "The Origins", 396.

48 Noël, "Quelle sotériologie dans le livre de la Sagesse?", especially p. 193; cf. also Kolarcik, "Creation and Salvation", *passim.*

Introduction to the Third Part (Wis 10–19)

In Wis 9:18, Solomon's prayer to obtain wisdom closes with the reference to the salvation performed by wisdom itself. The book's first mention of the verb σῴζω opens the series of the salvific acts of wisdom presented in Wis 10. At the conclusion of this chapter, the text of Wis 10:20 forms a sweeping inclusion with Wis 19:9 (the only occurrences of the verb αἰνέω in the book), an inclusion noted long ago by M. Gilbert and one which makes the entire text of Wis 11-19 into a real "hymnic anamnesis" of the exodus.[1] Moreover, Wis 10:1-21 and Wis 19:10-22 are the only texts of the book which use the literary form of the series; Wis 10:6-8 and 19:15-17 are also the only passages that refer to the people of Sodom.

These factors permit the conclusion that Wis 10:1 is the opening of a new section of the book. At the centre of the entire book, after the *elogium* of wisdom (Wis 7-8) closing with the prayer to obtain wisdom itself (Wis 9), our sage follows the style of the *encomium* (see below) by introducing a series of examples from history, both positive and negative. These are chosen to illustrate his basic thesis. This is the meaning of the list in Wis 10, a chapter which makes a bridge between the *elogium* of wisdom properly so called (Wis 7-9) and the seven antitheses of Wis 11-19.

Wis 10:15, then, is the beginning of a rereading of the events of the Exodus which, after the introduction in 11:1-4, finds its main explanation in 11:5 (repeated in 11:16) and its first antithetical example in 11:6-14. There is a reprise of these antitheses in 16:1 in six further pictures which are elaborated up to 19:5.[2]

Starting from 11:15, following the style of the encomium, our sage includes two extensive digressions: the theme of the first (Wis 11:15-12:27) is the "philanthropy" of God. In fact, reflection on the plagues of Egypt leads the author to an extensive theological treatment of the divine moderation towards people. The second, much more structured, digression (Wis 13-15), is concerned with idolatry, understood as the most radical human opposition to God's project of salvation. Here is a very general picture of the third part of the book:

Wis 10: wisdom in action in history
Wis 11:1-5: introduction to the seven diptychs
Wis 11:6-14: *first diptych*: water of the Nile / water from the rock
Wis 11:15: presentation of the next two diptychs
- 11:15-12:27: first digression; the divine philanthropy
- 13-15: second digression: idolatry

Wis 16:1-4: *second diptych*: frogs / quail
Wis 16:5-14: *third diptych*: gnats and locusts / bronze serpent
Wis 16:15-29: *fourth diptych*: rain and hail / manna
Wis 17:1-18:4: *fifth diptych*: darkness / light

---

1 Gilbert, "The Literary Structure", 20-25; "L'adresse à Dieu", *passim.*

2 Cf. Gilbert, "Sagesse", 73-74, also for the discussion of the number of the diptychs (five or seven); see below for the problem of the seventh diptych (19:1-5 rather than 19:1-9).

Wis 18:5-25: *sixth diptych*: death of the firstborn / salvation of Israel
Wis 19:1-5: *seventh diptych*: destruction in the Red Sea / crossing in the sea
Wis 19:6-21: the book's epilogue
Wis 19:22: the book's conclusion.[3]

The Israelites are contrasted with the Egyptians thus: the former are presented as historical models of the persecuted just and the latter of the ungodly who oppress them, so reprising the figures of the just and the ungodly from Wis 1-6. By means of numerous flashbacks (cf. Introduction, p. 19-20), Wis 10-19 returns constantly to what was said in the first part: reflection on Israel's past becomes a model for the future that awaits the just and the ungodly. What was at the beginning thus becomes the basis of what will happen in the future.

However, a third party intervenes in the clash between the just and the ungodly: this is the cosmos, allied with God to punish the ungodly and to reward the just (cf. 16:24) It is a constant element of the seven diptychs. Our author thus wishes to show that salvation occurs not only by means of history but also through a renewed creation (cf. 19:6-12, 18-21). The rereading of the events of the exodus often happens, and not by chance, in the light of the texts of Gen 1–11.

Midrashic Style

Our author's method in putting forward the seven antitheses from the Exodus is characterised by a double movement: on the one hand, he rereads the biblical texts, seeking to show their contemporary relevance and thus employing a style that is undoubtedly *midrashic* (cf. Introduction, p. 26-27).[4] If the principal characteristics of *midrash* are, as been said, the constant reference to Scripture and the ability to actualise it, this is what is found in the third part of Wisdom. In fact, the starting point of the seven diptychs is the biblical account of the exodus which our author treats with great freedom, re-presenting it not only as an example of a glorious past but unveiling its profound significance for the Israel of his time, that is, for the Jewish community of Alexandria. Our sage leaves out anything that does not suit his aim – for example, he minimizes the allusions to the sin of Israel such as the example of the fear of the people at the Red Sea, and their murmurings disappear entirely in Wis 19:1-5. Moreover, our sage summarises and harmonises various biblical texts. He is thus rereading the religious history of his people in a new historical and cultural context. The absence of proper names makes the account more general and applicable to every generation.

Wis 10-19 as *Synkrisis*

On the other hand, our sage employs a literary genre that is typically Greek: the encomium (cf. Introduction, p. 25-26) and, within it, the σύγκρισις, that is, the "comparison".[5] Within the epideictic genre, the σύγκρισις it to be considered a prolonged and systematic comparison between two realities in order to emphasise

3 The subdivision of chapter 19 is undoubtedly the most complex; cf. below.

4 Cf. Bizzeti, *Sapienza*, 176-181 and, for a more extended discussion, Vílchez Líndez, *Sapienza*, 40-47. Cf. also Busto Saiz, "La intención del midrash"; Camps, "Midraš sobre la historia de las plagas".

5 Cf. a comprehensive presentation in Vílchez Líndez, *Sapienza*, 47-51; cf. Priotto, *La Prima Pasqua*, 19-28. The first author to speak of σύγκρισις in connection with Wis 11-19 was Focke (*Die Entstehung*, 12-15; "Synkrisis", *Hermes* 58 [1923] 330), followed by Beauchamp, *De libro Sapientiae Salomonis*, and, in more detail, by Heinemann, "*Synkrisis*", 241-251; cf. Reese, *Hellenistic Influence*, 98 (on various positions); Bizzeti, *Sapienza*, 172-174; Maneschg, *Die Erzählung*, 105-108; Gilbert, "Sagesse", 85 and 87.

which of them is preferable. Often understood as recourse to events in the past, the comparison is a fundamental feature of the *elogium*; cf. Aristotle, *Rhet.* 1.9,38; Cicero, *De or.* 2.84,348-349; in the Jewish sphere, cf. Philo, *De virtutibus* (negative examples: *Virt.* 201-210; positive examples: *Virt.* 211-225) and *Prob.* 62-136 (a long section of the work in which Philo give examples of wise men and wisdom, both of groups [73-91] and of individuals [92-130] and even of animals [131-136]). Within the σύγκρισις, it is not unusual to find digressions (cf. Philo, *Prob.* 147-151, and Cicero, *Amic.* 40-42), as happens here with the two digressions on God's philanthropy and idolatry.

Although following classical models, the comparison in Wisdom nonetheless takes on aspects of striking originality. In fact, the elements being compared are not two, as in the classical comparisons known to us from the Greek world, but three: Egyptians and Hebrews are placed in relation to each other through the cosmos, a *tertium quid* which does not constitute a passive background but is itself also an actor in the story which unfolds (cf. the principles set out in 11:5, 15 and repeated in 16:24). The constant presence of the cosmos gives the whole σύγκρισις a powerful theological texture, demonstrating that the future salvation announced in the first chapters takes place through history and leads to a world renewed.

We thus have a σύγκρισις which has, first and foremost a pedagogic and didactic value (11:16: "so that they might learn"; cf. also 16:6, 11). The events of the exodus teach the faithful that God is present in history to save them and to warn them not to fall into the same error as the Egyptians. Negatively, the comparison is a denunciation of religious infidelity and, positively, a call to Israel to take on the task to which God has summoned it. Both aspects highlight a further element of originality in Wisdom, namely the heavy attention paid to the historical context of the addressees of the work.

Wis 10: Wisdom's Work in History from Adam to Moses

The Structure and Literary Genre of Wis 10[1]

In 10:1, the pronoun αὕτη is the clear opening of a new section, the subject of which is σοφία. The action of wisdom which is now described is almost naturally prepared for by the conclusion of the prayer of Solomon in Wis 9:18.[2] The same pronoun αὕτη returns in vv. 3, 5, 6, 10, 13, and 15, following the style of the *anaphora* which is typical of the aretalogies;[3] only in v. 4 does the subject explicitly become σοφία, recalled later in 10:8, 9, and 21.

The terms αὕτη and σοφία are associated with the repetition of δίκαιος (vv. 4, 5, 6, 10, 13, 15) along with the repetition of verbs related to saving and giving; this gives rise to the framework that follows which is subdivided into eight units, four short (the first ones) and four long, analogous to the eight steps of the four diptychs of Wis 3-4:

vv. 1-2 (Adam)	αὕτη		διεφύλαξεν	ἔδωκεν
v. 3 (Cain)	ἀπ' αὐτῆς	ἄδικος		
v. 4 (Noah)	σοφία	δίκαιος	ἔσωσεν	
v. 5 (Abraham)	αὕτη	δίκαιος	ἐφύλαξεν	
vv. 6-9 (Lot)	αὕτη	δίκαιος	ἐρρύσατο	
	σοφία		ἐρρύσατο	
vv. 10-12 (Jacob)	αὕτη	δίκαιος	διεφύλαξεν	ἔδωκεν
vv. 13-14 (Joseph)	αὕτη	δίκαιος	ἐρρύσατο	ἔδωκεν
vv. 15-21 (Moses)	αὕτη σοφία	δίκαιοι	ἐρρύσατο	ἀπέδωκεν

The use of the *anaphora* has a powerful theological value: it serves to show the constant features of God's salvific action in history on behalf of the "just". The four texts with the reference to "giving" have an analogous construction (vv. 2, 10d, 14f, 17), so as to stress further the gift offered to people by wisdom. The latter's action is described comprehensively by the use of 35 verbs (7 x 5).

---

1 Cf. Wright, "Structure", 175-177; Gilbert, "Sagesse", 71; Bizzeti, *Sapienza*, 75-79; cf. especially 76-77 for a detailed analysis of the correspondences internal to the chapter.

2 Schmitt ("Struktur", 2-4) considers 9:18 as belonging to chapter 10. His position is neatly refuted by Gilbert, "Literary Structure", 20-22.

3 Winston, *Wisdom*, 212-213. Schmitt, "Struktur", speaks of an "anaphorischen Prädikationen im ‚Er-Stil'" (6).

The use of σύγκρισις appears already in Wis 10 (cf. above): Abel and Cain are contrasted; the generation of Cain and Noah; Abraham and the sin of Babel; Lot and the people of Sodom; Jacob and Esau; Joseph and his brothers; the Israelites in the time of Moses and the Egyptians.

Wis 10 displays links with other parts of the book: 10:6-7 recalls 4:4-6 (five terms in common).[4] In both cases, there is a reflection on the "fruits" of people and their actions (children, in the case of 4:4-6). Furthermore, through the reference to μισθός, reward, 10:17 recalls 2:22 and, therefore, the theme of eternal life, a reward denied to the ungodly and promised to the just (5:15) which sinks its roots into the exodus (10:17). Μισθός appears only in these three places.

The conclusion of chapter 10 recalls both the beginning and the end of the book. 10:20 creates the aforementioned inclusion with 19:9 (αἰνέω) while the text of 10:21 creates a link with 1:6, 11, the only passages in the book where γλῶσσα and στόμα appear together. The tongue and the mouth are no longer sinners, as at the beginning of the book, but open in praise.

Finally, we note that 11:1 is to be considered the title of what follows and not as the conclusion of chapter 10. It is undoubtedly true that in 11:1 wisdom is still implicitly the subject of the action and that it then disappears entirely from the book (except for Wis 14:2, 5). However, the text of 11:1-4 is well constructed (see below), forming the introduction to the first diptych (11:5-14). The text of 11:1 can best be seen as a transitional text which serves to link the series of Wis 10 with the texts that follow, relating to the *synkrisis*.

As for the literary genre, Wis 10 has no real parallels in Israel's Bible; only the so-called historical psalms (Pss 77[78 MT]; 104[105 MT]; 105[106 MT]) come close to it. Sir 44-50 shares with Wis 10-19 the same interest in history and a common apologetic viewpoint. In Wis 10, however, (and also in the seven antitheses which follow in 11-19) our sage does not confine himself to presenting a gallery of "fathers" considered just; he contrasts each figure with the unjust. In Wis 10, the life of each just man is entirely in the shadow of wisdom's activity. Peculiar to our sage, then, is the continual search for an actualisation of the biblical account.[5]

The Beispielreihen

Wis 10 can primarily be compared with the sub-genre of *Beispielreihen,* within the genre of the encomium which characterises the book as a whole.[6] This nomenclature is generally applied to a title, which expresses the purpose of the list, then the list proper, which only mentions the most relevant factor about each person with respect to the aim of the list. Often there is repetition of one or more terms

---

4 We have ἀτελέστοι (4:5) and ἀτελέσιν (10:7c); καρπός (4:5b) and καρποφοροῦντα (10:7); μάρτυρες (4:6b) and μαρτύριον (10:7); πονηρίας (4:6b and 10:7) ἄωρος (4:5b) und ὥραις (10:7).

5 Cf. Gilbert, "The Review of History".

6 Glicksman, *Wisdom of Solomon 10*, 95-99. Although not recognized by all as such, biblical *Beispielreihen* are 1 Macc 2:50-61; 4 Macc 16:16-23; 18:9-19; Sir 44-50; Heb 11; cf., again, CD 2.17-3.12; in Philo, *Praem.* 13-78; *Virt.* 199-227; Cf. Thyen, Hartwig, *Der Stil der Jüdisch-Hellenistischen Homilie* (Göttingen: Vandenhoeck & Ruprecht 1955), 112-115. Accepting the idea of J. Reese, Glicksman considers the book of Wisdom as a whole as a protreptic rather than an *encomium* (cf. Glicksman, *Wisdom of Solomon 10*, 64-101). On this question, cf. the Introduction, p. 24-26.

in order to connect the various parts of the list. Wisdom 10 weaves together the πράξεις of wisdom and the examples of famous men who were guided by it.[7]

Glicksmann has analysed this aspect carefully, showing in more detail the likenesses and differences of Wis 10 with the *Beispielreihen* known to us. In particular, we must note that in Wis 10 the protagonists are not so much the eight figures presented but rather wisdom itself (cf. above). Moreover, following the typical style of our book, no character is named explicitly. It is possible to envisage a precise strategy of the author, constrained by the wish to universalise these figures within a Hellenistic context, according to a style not wholly unknown to the Greeks (cf. the *Characters* of Theophrastus). Our author presupposes a public very familiar with the biblical texts, able to understand the allusions in his text without difficulty. In fact, like the rest of the book, the chapter is addressed to an exclusively Jewish public. A Greek reader would have understood really much less.

The Aretalogies

Wisdom 10 presents notable points of contact with the Isiac aretalogies.[8] This is revealed by the use of anaphora (cf. above), as well as the attention given to the "works" performed by wisdom, two elements typical of the Isiac aretalogies. Absent from Wis 10 is the description of the nature (φύσις) and the powers (δυνάμεις) of wisdom – present, however, in Wisdom 7-8 – and wholly lacking is the self-celebratory style typical of the aretalogies where Isis speaks in the first person.[9] This is a style absent from the entire book of Wisdom where wisdom never speaks – by contrast with what happens in Prov 8 and in Sir 24. It is the narrator who speaks of it, in relation to God. Wisdom 10 thus shows some clear aretalogical features while not being itself an aretalogy.

In conclusion, in Wisdom 10, our sage's originality stands out: he is able to make an intelligent use of Greek models (*Beispielreihen* and aretalogies), while remaining with profoundly biblical content.

Wis 10:1-4: Adam, Cain and Abel, Noah

1 It was she who protected the father of the world, the first formed,
who had been created alone
and snatched him from his fall
2 and gave him the power to rule over all things.
3 But an unjust man, distancing himself from her in his anger,
perished in his fratricidal fury.
4 When the earth was submerged because of him, wisdom saved it again,
piloting the just man on a fragile craft.

---

7 Schmitt, "Struktur", *passim*; Bizzeti, *Il libro della Sapienza*, 172.

8 Glicksman, *Wisdom of Solomon 10*, 89-95; McGwlynn, *Mercy Dialogue*, 123-130.

9 Cf. the Isiac aretaolgy of Kymé.

Synchronic Analysis

10:1-2: Adam The text opens with the stress on the pronoun αὕτη. The first work of wisdom is the protection of the first man formed by God, "created alone". To understand the import of this expression, we need to compare it with the sources drawn on by our sage (see below).

The "fall" (1c) is clearly that described in Genesis 3. παράπτωμα has the sense of "sin, transgression" as in 3:13b (cf. Rom 5:15-20). This sin is called ἴδιος (here in emphatic position), to be understood in its normal sense of "own", the sin which was precisely that committed by the first man. The author intends to remove all responsibility from God – or perhaps he wishes to challenge the view which thought to attribute the Genesis sin only to the woman.

The verb ἐξαιρέω, has the sense of "snatch away", but here it assumes the nuance of "save", as in 1 Chr 16:35, precisely in parallel with σῴζω. Many commentators think of the work of wisdom in showing the first man the way of conversion and procuring pardon for him, a theme known to the *Greek Life of Adam and Eve* (1-11), and not unknown to the Fathers of the Church.[10] However, in Wis 1:12, 16; and 2:23-24, sin has as its consequence the eternal death of the ungodly. By snatching the first man from sin, wisdom would have removed him from the dominion of death (our sage would thus be expanding the theme contained in Gen 3:17-19) and headed him towards immortality. Therefore, for Wisdom, there is no original sin which passes from Adam to his descendants. Sin is personal (ἴδιος), and, thanks to wisdom, the first man already obtained the possibility of being "snatched" out of this situation.

The first man thus retains (v. 2) the dominion God gave him over the world (cf. Wis 9:2). For ἰσχύς, "power" or, better, "ability", cf. 2:11; for κρατέω, "rule", cf. 6:8; 6:2; 14:19. The role entrusted by God to man in Gen 1:26-28 is realised thanks to the gift of wisdom (cf. Wis 9:2-3).

10:3: Cain From the first man, the text passes naturally to Cain and his fratricide "with verses worthy of a great poet".[11] Cain is not named, but, for everyone with a knowledge of Scripture, it is obviously he that is being spoken of. The attention falls on him and not on Abel. Cain is presented as unjust, ἄδικος. His example thus illustrates the truth of the first part of the book, that the unjust are destined to death (cf. 3:19; 4:16). Cain is unjust because he distanced himself from wisdom (ἀποστὰς δὲ ἀπ' αὐτῆς; cf. 3:10 in connection with distancing oneself from God) on account of his anger (ὀργή). That is why wisdom did not help him, as it had done Adam. If the latter sinned through weakness, Cain sinned through obstinacy, and wisdom did not enter into him, as our author noted right at the beginning of his work (1:4-5).

Cain "perished in his fratricidal fury". Θυμός is "fury", anger; as in Philo (*Fug.* 60; *Cher.* 52), the adjective *ἀδελφοκτόνος indicates "fratricide"; συναπόλλυμαι can be understood as "perish together with".

10:4: Noah and the Flood Through the initial δι' ὅν, v. 4 links the flood to the sin of Cain: because of him, the earth was submerged. Κατακλύζειν refers to the κατακλυσμός of Gen

---

10 Cf. Niccacci, "Wisdom as Woman", 372 n. 14.

11 Scarpat, *Sapienza*, 2:283.

6:17; 7:6, 17; 9:11, and 15. Wisdom saved the submerged earth "again". The πάλιν can be explained only by thinking of the "earth" as the whole of humanity which wisdom saved again having done it once with Adam. The absence of Enoch here is surprising and a further sign of the anti-apocalyptic character of our text.

The concrete way in which wisdom saved the earth is expressed in the second stich: it piloted (κυβερνάω) "the just man" (cf. Gen 6:9) by means of a fragile piece of wood. The adjective εὐτελής has a negative nuance and indicates, as in 9:15; 13:14; and 15:10, something worthless, small, and, in this case, fragile. The ark will be indicated with the term "wood" in 14:7, while, in 14:5, "wood" is a pejorative term indicating the smallness of the ships to which sailors entrust their lives. Thus, wisdom is being imagined here as "pilot" of the ark; in 14:3, the "pilot" will be, rather, divine providence.

Diachronic Analysis

For *πρωτόπλαστος, cf. 7:1. The term refers to Gen 2:7 (καὶ ἔπλασεν ὁ θεὸς τὸν 10:1
ἄνθρωπον...). The expression "father of the world" can be understood in two ways: first of all, in the sense that Adam is the father of the whole of humanity since all descend from him. As in 6:24 and 14:6, κόσμος indicates the human world. Secondly, by understanding "father" in the sense of "*padrone*", the text is reinterpreting the theme of dominion expressed in Gen 1:26-28.

The expression μόνον κτισθήντα has always created difficulties for commentators.[12] Μόνον could be referring to the absence of Eve (cf. Gen 2:18 LXX: οὐ καλὸν εἶναι τὸν ἄνθρωπον μόνον), who is not mentioned because she is replaced here by wisdom with a nuptial value. A second possibility is to read μόνον in the light of Esth $4:17^{l+t}$ [Esth C,14 and 25 LXX]: the man is alone in the sense that he needs divine help.[13] The best interpretation, however, seems to be that suggested by the Tg. Ps.-J. on Gen 3:22: "behold, Adam is alone on the earth as I am alone in the highest heavens";[14] thus Philo in *Opif.* 151 (Adam "through his uniqueness [κατὰ τὴν μόνωσιν] was like the world and God"); Adam's solitude makes him like God. There is also a certain link between Adam's solitude and that of wisdom, created before all things (Prov 8:22-26) and unique of its kind (Sir 24:5; Wis 7:27). From this point of view, Adam symbolizes humanity as a whole, viewed in its relationship with wisdom. If Proverbs and Ben Sirach draw a close parallelism between marrying and loving wisdom, in the book of Wisdom there is no wife of flesh and bone beside the sage but only wisdom with whom the sage can have a really exclusive relationship.[15]

---

12 A wide survey of opinions in Larcher, *Sagesse*, 2:609-611; cf. Beauchamp, "Epouser la sagesse", 360-369; Gilbert, "La relecture de *Gen 1-3*", 314-315; Glicksman, *Wisdom of Solomon 10*, 107-108 who also thinks of the "uniqueness" of Adam, the only one created whereas the other human beings were "generated" (cf. Philo, *Opif.* 140).

13 Cf. Niccacci, "Wisdom as Woman", 371.

14 Cf. Beauchamp, "Epouser la sagesse", 367-368.

15 Cf. Beauchamp, "Epouser la sagesse", 363. "Il est remarquable que ce livre puisse à la fois faire désirer la solitude avec la Sagesse et préserver d'identifier la chasteté avec le marriage"; *ibid.* 369; cf. Niccacci, "Wisdom as Woman", 384-385.

Why then is it said that wisdom protected (διεφύλαξεν) Adam if he was so close to his creator? Unless διαφυλάσσω is understood in a general sense, wisdom guaranteed Adam its protection, guarded him in his unique being. However, perhaps the text wishes to say that wisdom was close to the man right from the beginning of his creation.

10:2 In the light of v. 2, it should be stressed that the dominion granted by God to the man appears here *subsequent* to the sin, and not prior to it, as in Gen 1:26-28. There is no sin which can annul God's plan of salvation for humanity. At the same time as he is basing himself on the Genesis texts, our sage is reinterpreting them in the light of his own theological conception.

10:3 Emphasising Cain's anger is a new element with regard to the account in Genesis. The sapiential tradition is very clear in relation to the danger of anger; cf. Prov 15:18; 22:24 (about an ἀνὴρ θυμώδης), but, above all, Prov 15:1 LXX: ὀργὴ ἀπόλλυσιν καὶ φρονίμους, "anger also ruins the level-headed"; but Stoicism considers wrath (ὀργή) a negative passion together with θυμός (cf. *SVF* III, 96, frag. 395-397); cf. the *De ira* of Seneca. Wrath is not worthy of the sage. By underlining Cain's anger (cf. Symmachus and Aquila in Gen 4:5), our sage is aligning himself with the sapiential biblical tradition but also with Stoic philosophy.

The reference to Cain's death is also new. In fact, Cain does not die, at least according to Genesis, even if this happens in some Jewish traditions.[16] However, the text can be understood in a very linear way: because of his action, Cain died together with all his anger. He thus becomes a symbol of that *eternal* death which, according to our author, affects the ungodly (Wis 1:16; 2:21-24). We can also recall Philo's reading of the killing of Abel (*Det.* 47-48): the biblical text which states that "Cain killed him" (καὶ ἀπέκτεινεν αὐτόν) is not to be understood of Abel, according to Philo, but of Cain who, in murdering Abel, actually killed himself.

10:4 In what way does our sage claim Cain as the origin of the flood (cf. v. 4a)? In Wisdom, the idea that the descendants of the ungodly are cursed is a frequent one (3:12, 16-19; 4:3-6). Thus, the humanity which provoked the flood is conceived as those descendants for whose wickedness Cain is held responsible. In 14:6, our sage will offer a second explanation for the flood: the proud giants, an allusion to Gen 6:1-4. Here, the initial δι' ὅν has also another function: our sage is interpreting all the generations which in Genesis 5 separate Cain from the flood as further propagations of that violence which arose precisely with Cain.

The idea of God as the pilot of the ark is also absent from the biblical account. In 14:1-10, we shall see how our author is taking his cue from the background of the figure of Isis described as the true pilot of ships because she is the pilot of destiny.[17]

---

16 Cf. Ginzberg, *The Legends*, 5:146-14, for some traditions about Cain's immortality.

17 Cf. the comment on 14:1-10 and Mazzinghi, "La barca della Provvidenza", *passim*.

Wis 10:5-9: Abraham, Lot and His wife

5 It was she again, when the nations had been confounded
in their agreement in wickedness,
who knew the just man and kept him without stain before God
and kept him strong, despite his tenderness for his son.

6 While the wicked were perishing, she rescued a just man
impelling him to flight from the fire which fell upon the Five Cities.
7 As a witness to their wickedness,
there exists to this day a land that is desolate and smoking,
fruit trees which do not ripen in their seasons,
and, as monument to an unbelieving soul, there stands a pillar of salt.
8 For, by neglecting wisdom,
not only were they harmed so as not to know the good,
but also they left the living a memorial of their folly
so that in the things in which they were mistaken they could not remain hidden.
9 But wisdom freed from their sufferings those who serve her.

Notes on the Text and Translation

v. 6. The adjective *καταβάσιος is unknown to classical Greek which uses καταιβάσιος instead in connection with Zeus' lightning and καταιβάτης, again in connection with Zeus (cf. Liddell-Scott, *sub voce*; Aeschylus, *Prom.* 359: καταιβάτης κεραυνός).

v. 7. Ziegler's apparatus records that some versions (La, Syh, Sy, Sa, Arab) suggest reading a καὶ at the beginning of 7d to avoid the asyndeton. This seems to be original, however, underlining a new point of view.

Synchronic Analysis

In a few words, v. 5 binds together a huge series of biblical texts. The "nations" 10:5
are those listed in Genesis 10 who decide to build the Tower of Babel (Gen 11:1-9). The aorist passive participle of συγχεῖν recalls the presence of the same verb in Gen 11:7, 9 LXX. Abraham is called simply "the just man" (cf. Gen 15:6). In two words, our sage summarises the call of Abraham in Gen 12:1-3: wisdom "knew the just man"; that means first of all that Abraham's call is seen as an initiative of the divine wisdom presented in Wis 7-9. At the same time, it is presupposed that Abraham is already just and that wisdom does not make him this but "knows" it in the sense that she discerns it, chooses him for a specific mission and takes care of him (cf., in the NT, 1 Cor 8:3; John 10:14; 2 Tim 2:19).

Not only did wisdom "know" Abraham but kept him without stain before God. The adjective ἄμεμπτος comes from Gen 17:1 (cf. Wis 10:15; 18:21). Thus, being faithful to God, without stain before God is not an act of Abraham but a gift of wisdom.

The last part of v. 5 alludes to the sacrifice of Isaac (Genesis 22) cryptically and in unusual language which would be incomprehensible to someone who does not know Scripture. Abraham was kept (ἐφύλαξεν) strong by wisdom. Ἰσχυρός refers to strength and courage with a meaning unusual in the LXX.[18] Abraham's blamelessness before God is put to the test by the sacrifice of Isaac, but it is wisdom that gives the patriarch the strength to overcome.

10:6-9 Abraham gives way to his nephew, Lot. Here he is considered a "just man". In v. 6, wisdom's action is described with the verb ῥύομαι (10:9, 13, 15; cf. 2:18; 16:8; 19:9), which refers to liberation from mortal danger. The rescue of Lot is set against the background of the ungodly who perish (ἐξαπολλυμένων ἀσεβῶν), that is, the people of Sodom who were destroyed by the divine punishment evoked in 6b with the image of Lot fleeing from the fire which fell (cf. Gen 19:24) on the "Five Cities" (*πεντάπολις; Gen 14:2, 8; Josephus, *B.J.* 4.484). This is the only case in the book (together with v. 18, the Read Sea) in which a geographical name is mentioned explicitly.

The arid region to the south of the Dead Sea is a "witness" (μαρτύριον) (v. 7) both of the severity of the punishment that fell on Sodom and of the salvation offered to the "just man", Lot. Μαρτύριον is a term used widely in the LXX but it appears only here in Wisdom. The divine action has rendered the land a καπνιζομένη χέρσος, a region that is desolate and smoking (cf. Gen 19:28), with trees that do not give fruit or, better, give fruit that does not ripen (cf. Tacitus, *Hist.* 5.7). The adjective ἀτελής (which does not attain completion, which is not able to do anything) recalls ἀτέλεστος of Wis 3:16 and 4:5 which is said of the incompleteness of the life of the ungodly. Like many ancient authors, Wisdom too considers the extraordinary phenomena described by Genesis as still existing, with clear allusion to the particular geographical situation of the Dead Sea; cf. the descriptions in Josephus, *B.J.* 4.483, and Philo, *Abr.* 140-141.

Lot's wife, turned into a pillar of salt (Gen 19:26), becomes the sign not of the wickedness of the people of Sodom but rather of her own lack of faith (cf. also Gen 19:17). For ἀπιστέω, cf. Wis 1:2. The pillar of salt is described as a funeral monument (μνημεῖον) which still exists. However, the text does not go into geographical details.[19]

The reason for the space given to the episode of Sodom and Lot's wife is expressed in vv. 8-9, a real theological commentary on the biblical episode. The beginning of v. 8 has a proverbial character and refers, generically, to all the wicked mentioned up to this point, the people of Sodom and Lot's wife, those who neglected wisdom (for παροδεύω cf. 1:8; 2:7, 5:14 and 6:22), something which reflects a lack of faith in God. The first effect of this is being rendered incapable (ἐβλάβησαν) of knowing the good, described here with a typically Greek expression, τὰ καλά, noble, virtuous things.

---

18 For the possible Isiac echoes of the theme of Abraham's strength, cf. Glicksman, *Wisdom of Solomon 10,* 117.

19 On the various ancient testimonies about the pillar of salt representing Lot's wife, cf. Winston, *Wisdom* 216.

A further effect of having neglected wisdom is having left humanity (ἀπέλιπον τῷ βίῳ) a memorial (μνημόσυνον) of their own foolish behaviour.

Verse 8 closes with a final clause: all this happened so that the ungodly could not remain hidden ἐν οἷς ἐσφάλησαν, in the things in which they were mistaken (cf. 2:4 and, above all, 17:3). God does not allow it. The ungodly leave behind them a terrible memory, very different from that left by the just (cf. 4:1). On the contrary, wisdom frees those who serve her (v. 9). Θεραπεύω is being used here in a sense rare in the LXX but common in Greek usage.

Diachronic Analysis

The section on Abraham is an interesting *relecture* of the Genesis account combined with suggestions from the Greek world. In the expression ἐν ὁμονίᾳ πονηρίας, we should see an ironic allusion to that ὁμονοία ("harmony") which constituted the Hellenistic ideal of living together. Harmony, in fact, is "the knowledge of the common good", a virtue which characterizes the Stoic sage and leads him to live in peace with others (*SVF* III, 160 frag. 625 and 630). The "confounding" spoken of is not so much that of the "languages", but rather the failure of the wicked project of humanity from which, however, Abraham is preserved. We are not far from Philo's interpretation: in the *De confusione linguarum*, he reads the σύγκυσις as the name given to Babel (cf. Gen 11:5 LXX), not as a confusion of languages but as the destruction of that wicked agreement which set men against God.[20] 10:5

Moreover, our sage places Abraham's call against the immediate background of the confusion of peoples caused by the Babel rebellion, thus reading a close link between Gen 11:1-9 and Gen 12:1-3.[21] On the one hand, there is human sin; on the other, the grace of God is at work and meets people who welcome it and who set in motion the history of salvation.

The use of σπλάγχνα ("bowels, innards") in a translated sense (v. 5c) is redolent more of classical Greek than of that of the LXX. However, our author has in mind rather the Hebrew רחמים. Like a Stoic sage, Abraham too is in some ways imperturbable (cf. Cicero, *Tusc.* 3.18 = *SVF* I, 95 frag. 434; *SVF* III, 162 frag. 640). Tenderness for his son does not deflect him from obeying God.

Lot, introduced in v. 6, is described positively (a "just man") by contrast with the Jewish tradition which generally judges him rather severely (cf., in the NT, 2 Pet 2:7).[22] In this verse, wisdom assumes the function of the angels in Gen 19:12-22 (cf. Wis 19:13-17). 10:6-9

As for Lot's wife, changed into a pillar of salt (v. 7d), we should note that this salty monument is the memorial of an "unbelieving soul"; as if the pillar were

20 Cf. Scarpat, *Sapienza*, 2:295-302. For this verse, cf. Mazzinghi, "La figura di Abramo in Sap 10,5".

21 The tradition which connects Abraham with Babel is rather ancient; cf. Jub. 11:12-16; 12:1-14. According to Vermes, it is to be dated between 150 BCE and 50 CE; cf. Vermes, Geza, "The Life of Abraham (1)", in: Id., *Scripture and Tradition in Judaism* (Leiden: Brill 1973) 67-126, especially 85-90.

22 Cf. Ginzberg, *The Legends*, 1:223; 5:223, 240, and 243.

being identified with the body of Lot's wife. The episode is thus being reread in a key that is especially religious (cf., in the NT, Luke 17:31-32). We note, in passing, that, like everything else that happens in this chapter, this episode of the pillar of salt is not interpreted by our sage in an allegorical key, unlike Philo's typical practice (cf. *Fug.* 122; *Somn.* 1.247).

The episode of Sodom reminds our author of the theme of folly (v. 8c). Already, Wis 1:3; 3:2, 12; and 5:4 had employed ἄφρων to indicate the ungodly. In the LXX, the term ἀφροσύνη (relatively frequent in Proverbs, Qoheleth, and Sirach) indicates behaviour that is not only foolish but also wicked and contrary to the divine will. In the Greek world too, ἀφροσύνη is the greatest of evils. It is defined in Stoicism as ignorance of good and evil (*SVF* II, 50 frag. 174), and such ignorance is the only true evil (*SVF* III, 19 frag. 79).

Wis 10:10-12: Jacob

10 A just man flying from the wrath of his brother
she guided on right paths.
She showed him the majesty of God
and gave him the knowledge of holy things.
She made him prosper in his hard labours
and made his toil fruitful.
11 She stood by him against the greed of his oppressors
and made him rich.
12 She guarded him from his enemies
and protected him from the one who laid snares for him.
She judged in his favour in a difficult struggle
so that he might learn that piety is the most powerful thing of all.

Notes on the Text and Translation

v. 10. Some witnesses read τοὺς κόπους instead of τοὺς πόνους (S A O-V and some minuscules), perhaps to distinguish them from the ἀγαθοὶ πόνοι of 3:15, so accentuating Jacob's difficulties, or adapting the text of Gen 31:42 LXX (τὸν κόπον τῶν χειρῶν μου εἶδεν ὁ θεός). On the basis of this variant, Larcher (*Sagesse*, 2:632) imagines a corrupt text and suggests some possible conjectures which, however, are without textual support. Among these are τοὺς ἐκ κόπου αὐτοῦ, namely "his descendants", the sons of Jacob whom wisdom would thus have multiplied.

v. 12. The verb *βραβεύω (cf., in the NT, Col 3:15) means "acting as judge", "arbitrating". Since the Syriac and Armenian versions translate it with "render him victor", it is often translated thus in modern times, given also the sense of βραβεῖον, "reward". Bearing in mind the dative αὐτῷ, one could understand ἐβράβευσεν in the sense of "judged in his favour".

Synchronic Analysis

Our sage introduces one "flying from the wrath of his brother", that is, Jacob (cf. 10:3);[23] cf. Gen 27:41-45. However, the subject of the verse is, once again, wisdom (αὕτη). She "guided" Jacob "on straight paths"; ὁδηγέω refers explicitly to the action of wisdom already described in 9:11b (cf. the comment). 10:10

The following two stichs make an interesting rereading of the nocturnal vision at Bethel (Gen 28:10-22; cf. below).

Wisdom "made him prosper in his labours (εὐπόρησεν αὐτὸν ἐν μόχθοις)" and "made his toil fruitful (ἐπλήθυνεν τοὺς πόνους αὐτοῦ)": πληθύνω is to be understood as "increase, multiply". These two stichs are an extreme summary of the episodes narrated in Genesis 29-31 and relating to Jacob who enriched himself during his sojourn with Laban, overcoming every type of difficulty.[24]

Verse 11 is an original summary of Jacob's last years with Laban (Gen 30:25- 10:11
31:16) in the course of which Jacob enriched Laban (Gen 30:43). We should underline the presence of the verb παρίσταμαι ("assist, help") which will return only in Wis 19:22, precisely at the conclusion of the book, with God as subject. In the story of Jacob recounted in Genesis, it is God himself who helps him (cf. Gen 31:42 and, for a similar use of the verb, cf. Ps 108:31 LXX [109:31 MT]). The divine presence is here replaced by that of wisdom. It is she who enriches the man, a theme already encountered in the *elogium* of wisdom (cf. 7:11 and comment; cf. Prov 8:14-21).

The initial asyndeton emphasizes a new point of view. Verse 12 opens with a 10:12
reference to the enemies of Jacob in general and to the adversaries who lay snares (for ἐνεδρεύω cf. Wis 2:12). One could think of Jacob's meeting with Esau (cf. Gen 32:4-22); in this case too, it was wisdom who guarded him and protected him.[25] For διαφυλάσσω, cf. the comment on 10:1 (cf. also 17:4), for ἀσφαλίζομαι ("make secure") cf. Wis 4:17, in relation to the final destiny of the just.

The last two stichs of v. 12 constitute an interesting rereading of the famous episode of Jacob's struggle with God (Gen 32:23-32; see below).

Diachronic Analysis

Here, our sage seems to be excusing Jacob from all fault, describing him as a "just 10:10
man". His mother, Rebecca, is not even mentioned. The "straight paths" could certainly be alluding to Jacob's journey to Haran (Gen 28:10). However, the metaphorical use of the term term τρίβος, which we have already seen in Wis 2:15 and 5:7, leads us to think of an analogous use that is attested in the LXX. As in Isa 40:3 (εὐθείας ποιεῖτε τὰς τρίβους τοῦ θεοῦ ἡμῶν); Prov 2:19, 20; and 3:17, the

23 "Like Cain and Esau, the apostate Jews have turned against Wisdom and out of hate and anger persecute their brothers (cf. Wis 2:12-20; 4:17-19)"; Glicksman, *Wisdom of Solomon 10*, 124.

24 Larcher, *Sagesse*, 2:632, claims that, with πληθύνω, Wisdom is also alluding to the sons Jacob had in the course of his sojourn with Laban.

25 Deane (*The Book of Wisdom*, 101) thinks of Jewish traditions about Joseph's enemies reflected in Jub. 34:1-9; T. Jud. 3-7.

"paths" are a metaphor for human conduct; cf. Ps 26:11 LXX [27:11 MT]: ὁδήγησόν με ἐν τρίβῳ εὐθείᾳ; cf., again, Ps 22:3 LXX [23:13 MT]. Seen in this light, Wisdom's action on behalf of Jacob is also and above all an action of interior guidance. Jacob becomes the model of that just man whom wisdom guides along the right path.

The nocturnal vision at Bethel (Gen 28:10-22) is covered in two stichs as an interior revelation (ἔδειξεν αὐτῷ) and as a communication of knowledge (ἔδωκεν αὐτῷ γνῶσιν). The object of the vision is described with the expression βασιλεία θεοῦ (*hapax* in the LXX) which is not readily understood.[26] The use of βασιλεία in Wis 6:4, 20 points us in the direction of "majesty" and so towards a reference to the exercise of God's royal power in the world which Jacob understands precisely by means of the vision of the ladder, reread here as the fruit of the action of wisdom. We cannot entirely exclude a second meaning of βασιλεία, that is, the metaphorical use of the theme of kingship according to the well-known Stoic concept. The only true king is the sage or philosopher, and the kingship shown to Jacob would be precisely that connected with the exercise of justice and the other virtues which come from wisdom itself.[27]

The second expression, object of ἔδωκεν αὐτῷ γνῶσιν ἁγίων, is also debated.[28] If we take ἁγίων as neuter, the text could be referring to Jacob as one who obtained the knowledge of "holy things", that is, of the sanctuary which, according to Gen 28:21-22, he founded at Bethel after the vision of the ladder. Moreover, τὰ ἅγια often refers to the Temple in LXX usage (cf. τὸ ἅγιον τῶν ἁγίων the "Holy of Holies").

The rabbinic traditions tend to link the construction of the sanctuary at Bethel with the Jerusalem Temple (cf. Gen. Rab. on Gen 28:27; Pirqe R. El. 35). We must not forget that, in Wis 9:8, the Jerusalem Temple is an image of the heavenly temple. In that case, the vision of the ladder connected with the construction of the sanctuary at Bethel could also be intended as an image of the heavenly temple. These are, therefore, probably the "holy things" which wisdom made known to Jacob: the vision of the Temple which, in any case, does not exclude a dimension of knowledge of God (cf. Gen 28:16).

G. Scarpat's proposal could make a good complement to this interpretation. The genitive ἁγίων is taken as a neuter, and, together with γνῶσις, is understood as the knowledge of holy things, that is, as one of the two purposes of σοφία according to an idea widespread in Greek culture and especially in Stoicism; cf. *SVF* II, 15 frag. 35, where wisdom is defined precisely as knowledge of things divine and human: θείων τε καὶ

---

26 See some old interpretations in E. Burrows, "Wisdom X 10," *Bib* 20 (1939): 405; cf. Larcher, *Sagesse*, 2:629-630.

27 Cf. Scarpat, *Sapienza*, 2:311-313, and the texts cited by him; Engel, *Weisheit*, 173-174.

28 The genitive ἁγίων could be understood in the light of Wis 5:5b as referring to the angels whom Jacob saw ascending and descending on the ladder according to the Genesis account. It could also be a periphrasis to indicate God in the light of Prov 30:3 LXX: what was revealed to Jacob was not God in himself but what God is for him; cf. Gilbert, "La connaissance de Dieu", 321-322. Winston (*Wisdom*, 217) thinks instead of a link with T. Levi 9:3 which attributes to Jacob a vision about the future priesthood of Levi. For the vision of the heavenly sanctuary, cf. Burrows, "Wisdom X,10", who cites Jub. 32; T. Levi 9,3, and recalls Wis 9:8.

ἀνθρωπίνων ἐπιστήμην.[29] In that case, the wisdom that comes from God is of the same order as that wisdom searched for by the Greek philosophers, the possibility of knowing the things of God, a knowledge which is not the fruit of human efforts but is rather in the order of a gift.

Verse 11 mentions Laban's πλεονεξία, a term which, in Greek usage, indicates greed, or, more generally, the attempt to possess oneself of more than is appropriate. The term is not very frequent in the LXX where it is always used in negative contexts (cf. 2 Macc 4:50); it returns thus in the NT (cf. Col 3:5). Philo contrasts πλεονεξία with δικαιοσύνη (*Prob.* 159) and the other virtues (*Praem.* 15). For Philo, πλεονεξία is also something more than simple greed: it becomes a pushing of oneself beyond the limits set for humans.[30] Laban is described as an exemplary case of greed, and, at the same time, he becomes an image of all those who oppress the just: κατισχυόντων αὐτόν. For κατισχύω used in the sense of "oppress", cf. Wis 7:30; 17:5. The plural can be explained as a generalisation in the case of Laban, unless our sage is associating Laban with his sons or with his entire family (cf. Gen 31:1, 23). 10:11

The orientation of the whole story of Jacob in Wis 10:10-12 is didactic. The text closes with the highest of the teachings which the patriarch learned in the school of wisdom: "so that he might learn that piety is the most powerful thing of all". Here again we have a *midrashic relecture* of the biblical texts. In only three verses, our sage condenses the whole teaching which he has obtained from the long text of Genesis 28-36 and reproduced it for his contemporaries.[31] 10:12

The episode of Jacob's wrestling with God (Gen 32:23-32), which is recalled in the final two stichs of v. 12, embarrassed the ancient commentators. Our sage summarises it magisterially in a few, well-chosen words. The expression of 12c is not easy to understand (cf. the textual notes). If we give to βραβεύω the sense of "judge in favour", one could think of wisdom helping Jacob in his struggle against God, turning the combat in his favour. Already in 4:2, the term ἀγών was used in a metaphorical sense.

In fact, Wisdom does not mention God openly but speaks only of a "difficult contest" from which Jacob emerged as victor thanks to the mediation of wisdom. The Jewish tradition oscillates between seeing Jacob's adversary as a "man", following the text of Gen 32:25; an angel (cf. Hos 12:5); or even God himself (Gen 32:29). In our text, the presence of εὐσέβεια, *hapax* in the book, is to be understood as *pietas* towards God (cf. below). This points us in the direction of seeing in 12c an allusion to the struggle with God himself from which Jacob emerged victorious precisely on account of his piety, which is a fruit of wisdom's help. Wisdom thus appears as that which leads people to a right relationship with God, overcoming every difficulty that can be experienced in such a relationship.

In Hellenistic usage, the term εὐσέβεια indicates piety towards God; cf. Prov 1:7 (εὐσέβεια εἰς θεόν) and Isa 33:6 (εὐσέβεια πρὸς τὸν κύριον). The term is frequent in 4 Macc and is used by Philo in the sense of "religiousness", understood as one of the highest virtues (cf. *Decal.* 52); cf., in the NT, 1 Tim 3:16. The Letter of Aristeas defines εὐσέβεια as "the "Piety"

---

29 Cf. also the other texts cited in Scarpat, *Sapienza*, 2:313-314.
30 Cf. Delling, Gerhard, πλεονέκτης κτλ., *TDNT* 6:266-274.
31 Cf. Leproux, Alexis, "La 'pieté' du patriarche Jacob".

understanding that God acts absolutely in everything and knows everything, and that man cannot hide if he commits injustice or does evil" (Let. Aris. 20).[32] Thanks to piety, humanity is able to understand the divine realities (cf. Wis 10:10cd) and to overcome every difficulty. In fact, piety is more powerful than everything (10:12d).

Wis 10:13-14: Joseph

13 She did not abandon the just man who had been sold,
but delivered him from sin.
14 She went down with him into the prison
and did not abandon him when he was in chains,
until she obtained for him a royal sceptre
and authority over those who ruled him.
She showed that his accusers were liars
and gave him eternal glory.

Notes on the Text and Translation

v. 14. For λάκκος, to be understood as "prison", with reference to Joseph's imprisonment in Egypt, cf. Larcher, *Sagesse*, 2:636. The term is taken from Gen 40:15, although, in Gen 37:24, it refers instead to the cistern where Joseph is put by his brothers.

Synchronic Analysis

Verse 13 opens with a further reference to wisdom (αὕτη). She did not abandon (οὐκ ἐγκατέλιπεν) a just man who had been sold (πραθέντα δίκαιον). The reference is to Joseph, sold into Egypt by his brothers (Gen 38:26-28, 36; cf. Ps 104:17 LXX [105:17 MT]). The verb πιπράσκω is present in the account of T. Jos. 1:5; 10:6. The verb ἐγκαταλείπω, *hapax* in Wisdom, is frequent in the LXX to indicate divine assistance; for Abraham (cf. Gen 24:27); cf. Pss 9:11, 26:9 LXX [27:9 MT]; 36:25 LXX [37:25 MT]; etc.

The divine assistance for Joseph consists in having delivered him from sin (for ῥύομαι, cf. 10:6.9). Wisdom is referring to the episode of Potiphar's wife (Gen 39:7-12). Sin is here described as ἁμαρτία (cf. Wis 1:4 and comment), in this case, temptation with a sexual background (cf. Gen 39:9 LXX: πῶς ἁμαρτήσομαι ἐναντίον τοῦ θεοῦ;). The term does not yet bear the weight which it will later have in Paul.

The text of 14ab is equally clear: wisdom is imagined as a person who goes down with Joseph into prison (συγκατέβη is probably taken from Dan 3:49) and

32 Cf. Scarpat, *Sapienza*, 2:316-317, and Id., *Quarto Libro dei Maccabei*, 76-77; cf. also Wieger, Madeleine, "Εὐσέβεια et 'crainte de Dieu' dans la Septante": Joosten, Jan / Bons, Eberhard (edd.), Septuagint Vocabulary. Pre-History, Usage, Reception (SBLS 48), Atlanta (GA): SBL 2011, 132-137.

does not leave him alone (οὐκ ἀφῆκεν) when in chains. Our sage is referring here to the episode of Joseph's imprisonment recounted in Gen 39:20 and to the fact that God made him find favour with his gaoler (Gen 39:21-23).[33]

In 14cd, our sage also attributes to wisdom the rise of Joseph, freed from prison and appointed minister of Pharaoh over the whole land of Egypt (Gen 41:40-44). All that is described with the image of the royal sceptre offered to Joseph by Pharaoh, although Genesis does not speak of a sceptre. However, there exists a tradition which makes Joseph into a real king (cf. Jos. Asen. 5:5; 29:11; Philo, *Ios.* 119).

In second place, Joseph is granted ἐξουσία, that is, power over all those who oppressed him (τυραννούντων αὐτοῦ). The only other occurrence of ἐξουσία in the book of Wisdom is in 16:13, in connection with divine power. Here, the term refers to human power, that is, authority, the exercise of political power, according to a usage that is not rare in the later writings of the LXX (Dan and Macc).[34]

The last two effects of Wisdom's action on behalf of Joseph are described in 14ef: wisdom showed that Joseph's accusers (τοὺς μωμησαμένους αὐτόν) were liars (ψευδεῖς). Μωμάομαι occurs only in Prov 9:7 and Sir 34:18 with the sense of "accuse", "slander".[35] According to a common opinion, the reference here is to those who with their slanders (Gen 39:14-18) had had him thrown into prison.

Diachronic Analysis

Verses 13-14 summarise the whole of Joseph's story (Genesis 37-50) in a few lines. However, this story assumes a certain additional importance in the eyes of our sage because it deals with an episode located in Egypt which allows some reference to the historical situation of the Alexandrian Jews. Our sage follows a scheme typical of the biblical accounts: humiliation and glorification (cf. the servant of Isaiah, Job, old Tobit...). In this case, however, the whole life of Joseph is viewed as under the direct protection of wisdom.

An Attempt at Actualisation

The use of τυραννέω in 14d makes us think of a despotic power (cf. the τύραννοι mentioned in Wis 6:9, 21; 8:15). Here, this cannot be Joseph's brothers, given that the verb is in the present and the episode of the brothers who sold him belongs to his past. Moreover, according to the account of Gen 50:19-21, Joseph does not intend to lord it over his own brothers. The text could thus refer to those who intended to oppress Joseph such as Potiphar and his wife. However, the use of ἐξουσία together with τυραννέω (cf. also 16:4) could lead to the thought of an attempt at actualisation. Wisdom grants the just man – image of the faithful Israelite – a real power over those who oppress him, that is, all those who denied the Alexandrian Jews those rights which they claimed (cf. Wis 19:13-17).

---

33 The presence of wisdom in prison, alongside Joseph, is a unique case in Jewish tradition. Our sage probably has in mind one of the attributes of Isis who is, in fact, one who frees prisoners (cf. Isidorus' *Hymn* 1.29, 34; *Aretalogy of Andros* 144-145; *Aretalogy of Kymé*, 48); Glicksman, *Wisdom of Solomon 10*, 132.

34 Cf. Foerster, Werner, ἐξουσία, *TDNT* 2:562-574.

35 Cf. the long digression in Scarpat, *Sapienza*, 2:355-356.

In connection with stich 14e, we note that to speak of "liars" seems too strong to refer to the accusations of being a false dreamer made by Joseph's brothers previously. Scarpat suggests seeing in these figures all those who slandered Joseph in Egypt after his rise to power; he is thinking of well-known traditions, both the *Testamentum Iosephi* and the *Liber Iosephi et Aseneth*. In this perspective, the text of Wisdom clearly acquires a more solid logic with regard to the life of the Jews of Alexandria.[36]

The final stich is inspired by the information contained in Gen 45:13 when Joseph invites his brothers to tell their father, Jacob, of "all his glory" (πᾶσαν τὴν δόξαν μου); but here, it is "eternal glory" that is being spoken of. It is that glory which wisdom offers to those she protects, such as Solomon (8:10), a glory which wisdom possesses as reflection of the divine glory (7:25; cf. 9:10, 11). The fact that this glory is "eternal" links us to the first part of the book. Thus, it is not a case of the memory which the just man, Joseph, leaves behind him, as an example of life for future generations.

With its reversal in his situation, the story of Joseph becomes the model and example of that life without end which awaits the just man after his death: cf. Wis 3:7-9 and 5:15-16. The use of αἰών and αἰώνιος in Wisdom confirms this interpretation; cf. 3:8; 4:2, 19; 5:15 where this vocabulary is applied to the final destiny of people.[37]

Wis 10:15-21: Moses

15 A holy people and a race without stain
she freed from a nation that afflicted them:
16 she entered into the soul of a servant of the Lord
and he resisted fearful kings with wonders and signs.
17 She recompensed the holy ones for their labours,
she guided them along an astonishing way
and was like a shelter for them during the day
and like a flame of stars in the night.
18 She made them pass through the Red Sea
and led them through great waters.
19 But she drowned their enemies
and threw them up from the deep.
20 Thus, the just plundered the ungodly
and sang hymns, O Lord, to your holy name,
and celebrated with one voice your hand, which had been joined with them:

36 Cf. Scarpat, *Sapienza*, 2:355-356. In *Ios.* 51, Philo seems to assume a tradition relating to the accusations which the whole house of Potiphar – not just his wife – are supposed to have made against Joseph.

37 Cf. Raurell, "The Religious Meaning", 378-381.

[21] for wisdom opened the mouth of the dumb
and made firm the tongues of infants.

Notes on the Text and Translation

v. 19. The verb κατέκλυσεν is read κατέπαυσεν ("made to cease, destroyed" ?) by S* and by codex 46 (an error of reading? ΚΛ = ΠΑ?). Scarpat (*Sapienza*, 2:359) thinks instead of an original κατέπαυσεν dumbed down into κατέκλυσεν to deny the allegorical aspect of the text (which, however, does not seem to be allegorical). For κατακλύζω, cf. Wis 10:4 and, in an exodus context, Ps 77:20 LXX [78:20 MT]. According to Scarpat (*Sapienza*, 2:359-360), the scribes did not grasp the allegorical character of the text which originally had κατέπαυσεν. However, the reading κατέκλυσεν has almost unanimous attestation. *Contra* Scarpat, Wisdom 10 does not present any trace of allegory. Codex S* also reads instead of ἐκ βάθους ἀβύσσου ("from the deep of the abyss") the term ἐκ βάθους θάμβους, "from the deep of amazement".

Synchronic Analysis

After the story of Joseph, our sage concludes his presentation of the works of wisdom with the figure of Moses and with a reflection on the liberation of the people of Israel from Egypt. In a few verses, he summarises the first fifteen chapters of Exodus: the oppression in Egypt (15b); Moses's mission to Pharaoh (16b); the spoiling of the Egyptians (17a); the guiding of the pillar of cloud (17bc); the passage through the Sea (18-19); and the song of victory in Exod 15 (20-21).

10:15-16: A Holy People, a Servant of the Lord

Wisdom (αὕτη) is described as the author of the liberation from Egypt, here summarized by the verb ῥύομαι (cf. 10:6, 9, 13) which has as its object "a holy people and a race without stain". This people was freed "from a nation which afflicted them". The idea is biblical (cf. Ps 33:7 LXX [34:7 MT]). The use of θλίβω also recalls Exodus texts and so alludes to the oppression described in Exod 1:8-14; cf Exod 3:9; 4: 31 LXX.

The expression "holy people" is also biblical and, as such, is mostly found in deuteronomic contexts.[38] The use of ὅσιος makes us think here of the people's fidelity to God, but also of the people understood as subject of the divine faithfulness.[39] The reference to the people's blamelessness (σπέρμα ἄμεμπτον) is also reprised from biblical models[40] and, in particular, from the text of Gen 17:1; cf. ἄμεμπτος used in Wis 10:5 precisely in relation to Abraham.

Verse 16 begins to describe the way in which wisdom liberated Israel. In a single stich, our author rereads in a sapiential key the call of Moses who is described as a "servant of the Lord". Wisdom is following here the use of the LXX which frequently applies the term θεράπων to Moses (cf. Exod 4:10; 14:31; Josh 1:2; 9:2 LXX; 1 Chr 16:40).

---

38 Cf. especially Deut 7:6; 15:2, 21; and 26:16.

39 On ὅσιος, cf. Mazzinghi, *Notte di paura e di luce*, 205-206.

40 The adjective ἄμεμπτος is frequent in Job LXX (11x) where it translates a wide range of Hebrew words.

Taking up an idea already seen in 1:4 and 7:27c-28, our author then describes wisdom as a "spiritual" reality, an interior principle of strength and of particular divine assistance which penetrates the soul of the elect: εἰσῆλθεν εἰς ψυχήν. It is thus associated indirectly with the spirit once again, in this case the spirit that filled Moses (Num 11:17, 25).

Verse 16b summarises in a single stich Moses' mission to Pharaoh (Exod 5:1-6:1). The verb ἀνθίστημι very probably refers to Moses himself and not to wisdom, the subject of the previous verb. We must, therefore, assume a change of subject: "he (Moses) resisted fearful kings". The plural βασιλεῦσιν is undoubtedly strange, seeing that there is only a single Pharaoh in the biblical account (but cf. Ps 104:30 LXX [105:30 MT] and Sir 45:3 gr. where the use of the plural returns). It could be understood as a rhetorical amplification (cf. 10:11a) or as a plural which embraces Pharaoh and all his court.[41] Could the plural not also be looking ahead beyond Egypt to the other kings defeated on the way to the land (cf. Exod 17 and Num 20-21)?

Moses opposes Pharaoh "with wonders and signs". In reverse, this expression is frequent in the Pentateuch in connection with the plagues of Egypt (cf. Exod 7:3, 9; 11:9, 10; Deut 4:34; 6:22; 7:19 etc.), and it is to these that our sage is referring.[42]

10:17: An Astonishing Way

Here, our author begins to describe Israel's departure from Egypt. Wisdom "recompensed (ἀπέδωκεν ... μισθόν) the holy ones for their labours". The "holy ones" (ὅσιοι) are the Israelites already mentioned in 10:15a; their "labours" are the forced works to which the Egyptians had subjected them (Exod 1:8-14).

Wisdom as Guide

In 17b, we have now reached the moment of Israel's departure from Egypt, and wisdom is presented as the people's guide. For ὁδηγέω, cf. Wis 9:11b and 10:10b. The verb is found in the LXX in analogous contexts (Num 24:8; Deut 1:33; Ps 77:14 LXX [78:14 MT]). Here, wisdom is their guide on an "astonishing way" (for θαυμαστός cf. Exod 34:10) because of the miracles God did for his people but especially because of the information in Exod 13:17: God did not guide Israel (οὐχ ὡδήγησεν) by the way of the Philistines lest the people should want to return to Egypt. In this sense, in 18:3b, the author will speak of an "unknown journey", again with reference to the theme of "guiding". For this reason, θαυμαστός is to be understood more in the sense of "surprising" than of "wonderful" (cf. Wis 19:8).

The two following stichs (10:17cd) leads us to understand (cf. 18:3 and 19:7) that wisdom's guiding is associated with that of the pillar of cloud which accompanied Israel on the way of the Exodus (Exod 13:21-22; cf. below).

10:18-19: The Red Sea

From the way to the sea, following the thread of Exod 14, our sage goes on to describe the episode of the crossing of the sea, salvation for Israel and death for the Egyptians. The asyndetic construction of 18a underlines a new beginning.

The Crossing of the Sea

The verb διαβιβάζω, only here in the book but present sometimes in the LXX, is to be understood as "transport beyond", and so "made them pass through". The expression "Red Sea" is the LXX's usual translation for the Hebrew "Sea of Reeds", but is surprising here given that our sage carefully avoids proper names (cf. the reference to the Pentapolis in 10:5). The second stich expands the image of the

---

41 On the whole question, cf. Enns, *Exodus Retold*, 45-52.

42 Cf. Mazzinghi, "The figure of Moses", 184-186.

crossing with the use of διάγω, taken, perhaps, from Ps 77:13 LXX [78;13 MT]. Wisdom led the people through great waters. This theme is taken up again and developed at the end of the book in 19:7-8.

If v. 18 describes the salvation of the Israelites, v. 19, in antithesis, describes the ruin of the Egyptians. The verse opens with the emphasis on the object of the action: τοὺς δὲ ἐχθροὺς αὐτῶν, "their enemies" the sea drowned. In the second stich, ἀναβράσσω is rare and poetic (cf. Nah 3:2; Ezek 21:26; cf. Philo, *Mos.* 2.255) and indicates a hurling up from below by foaming. It can be understood as "she threw them up from the deep". The deep is the Red Sea, called תהום in Exod 15:5, 8 (cf. the use of ἄβυσσος in Isa 63:13 and Ps 105:9 LXX [106:9 MT] in an analogous context). The text is referring to the information in Exod 14:30 about the Egyptians dead on the seashore and so as if thrown back by the sea which had drowned them.

10:20-21: They Sang Hymns to You, O Lord

With the presence of αἰνέω, v. 20 is particularly important as it creates an *inclusio* with 19:9 (cf. the same use of the vocative κύριε), where the same episode of the crossing of the Red Sea reappears. The verse opens by recording that "the just plundered the ungodly". The collective use of the term δίκαιοι is a sign of the clear idealisation of the people of Israel which, as has been said, characterises the whole chapter. The initial διὰ τοῦτο links this action directly to the previous verse. Thus, it is something that the Israelites did to the dead Egyptians who had been returned from the depths of the sea.

In 20bc, the combined use of the verbs ὑμνέω and αἰνέω refers to the canticle in Exodus 15. In LXX usage, ὑμνεῖν τὸ ὄνομα occurs in Isa 12:5; 25:1; Tob 12:6^{S}. Here, the construction τὸ ὄνομα τὸ ἅγιόν σου highlights precisely the "name" of God which is at the heart of Exodus 15 (Exod 15:3 κύριος ὄνομα αὐτῷ). This is also why there appears in 20b the vocative κύριε (cf. Wis 12:2; 16:2-26; 19:9, 22) which gives the text a clear tone of prayer, something that characterizes the entire third part of the book. It is not an historical retelling of the events of the exodus but precisely a prayer addressed to YHWH.

The verb αἰνέω, "celebrate", is linked with the celebration of God's hand, that "right hand" (ἡ δεξιά σου [χείρ]) expressly cited in Exod 15:6, which represents the divine power at work (cf. Wis 11:17; 14:6; 16:15). This divine "hand" is described here as ὑπέρμαχος, a term of military character which, in Wis 16:17 indicates the universe "allied" to God. In an identical context, cf.Philo, *Somn.* 2.280: μεγάλη γε ἡ ὑπέρμαχος χείρ.

The celebration of the divine presence takes place ὁμοθυμαδόν, with one voice, in harmony (cf. 18:5, 12).

At first sight, v. 21 could appear unusual: what does it actually mean to say that wisdom opened the mouth of the dumb and firm the tongues of infants? A diachronic analysis is necessary (cf. below). Meanwhile, we note that wisdom appears explicitly once again, registered precisely at the end of the chapter and that the ὅτι which opens the verse makes us read it as an explanation of the previous one: the Israelites were able to praise the Lord because wisdom had allowed them.

The reflection on wisdom's action in the history of Israel closes with a very beautiful image: infants celebrate the praise of God (cf. Ps 8:3 MT; Matt 11:5; 21:18). The reflection on the events of the exodus acquires a strong theological depth. The exodus becomes, on the one hand, a lesson for Israel and, on the other a motive of praise.

Diachronic Analysis

10:15-16: An Idealised People

Verses 15-16 see the beginning of a special characteristic of the third part of Wisdom: emphasis on the faithfulness and holiness of a people (cf. 10:17, 20) which the biblical account describes instead as obstinate and sinful. To the point of hiding everything, Wisdom minimises the sins committed by the people during the journey through the desert, sins which the biblical texts highlight to the full. Thus, with the sole exception of the third diptych (Wis 16:5-14), Israel appears for the most part as a people absolutely faithful to God and almost completely without sin. Quite different is the description of the Egyptians who are always judged with extreme severity.

A first reason for this is undoubtedly of an apologetic character. The children of Israel are not ἀνόσιοι, "ungodly", as intended by the anti-Jewish propaganda of the time;[43] rather, they are holy, just, and faithful to God. In this way, Wisdom intends to reinforce Jewish identity against a world that was often openly hostile to the Jews. Moreover, according to the *midrashic* style typical of the book, the exodus events are reread and actualised in the light of the situation of the Jewish community of Alexandria. In avoiding any emphasis on Israel's sin, our author makes the exodus journey into a paradigmatic and exemplary event, the history of an ideal Israel, valid for all time.

However, there is a deeper reason: in the exodus journey, Israel is the recipient of divine favours and, through this experience, has to discover its own vocation as "child", called to bring to the world the light of the law (cf. 18:4). The emphasis on the holiness of Israel, therefore, has within itself a clear theological intention: the ideal Israel described by Wisdom must become aware of its own vocation. Its holiness and its justice constitute more a goal to be reached than a path already realised, and the holiness of the people is primarily something which has to be bound up with God's faithfulness towards "his" people. In this way, the emphasis on the "positive" nature of the behaviour of Israel highlights how the holiness and justice of the people depend first and foremost on the action of God.[44]

In 16a, our sage is also thinking of the text of Isa 63:11-14 which recalls the action of the spirit in Moses at the time of the exodus. Isaiah's text offers notable points of contact with our pericope (cf. the use of ὁδηγέω, the reference to the "name" and "hand" of God, to the "deep"...) to the extent that one can conclude that, in Wis 10:15-21, our sage is attributing to wisdom what Isaiah's text describes as the work of the spirit of God.[45]

10:17 In v. 17, we find an attempt at exegesis of the texts of Exod 3:21-22; 11:2; 12:35-36 relating to the spoiling of the Egyptians, reread here as the pay due for hard labour by slaves. In this way, our sage is responding to an apologetic concern that was clearly popular in his time: to remove from the Hebrews any possible

43 For this accusation, cf. *C. Ap.* 1.248-249; *CPJ*, 1:89-80; 2:157, col. 31, 43; 158 col. 21, 13 and 41, 14; these are texts from the time of Trajan and Hadrian; cf. Tacitus, *Hist.* 5.4: "profana illic omnia quae apud nos sacra".

44 Mazzinghi, "L'idea di 'popolo'", 28-29.

45 Cf. van Imschoot, "Sagesse et Esprit", 42. The text of Acts 7:22, which mentions Moses' wisdom, could have been inspired precisely by this passage of Wisdom; cf. Mazzinghi, "Aspetti della tradizione sapienziale", 100-101.

accusation of theft at the expense of the Egyptians. The objects taken at the time of the exodus are only the pay due to the Hebrews from the Egyptians. There is a similar idea in Philo (cf. *Mos.* 1.141-142; cf. also the tradition in Jub. 48:18; Ezek. Trag. 162-166).

Wisdom and the Pillar of Cloud

Associated then with the pillar of cloud, wisdom acts at the same time both as shelter (σκέπη; cf. Isa 4:6 and σκεπάζομαι in 19:8) and as illumination (17cd). These are the two roles which the pillar of cloud has already in the biblical text; Exod 13:21-22 and Deut 1:33 underline its role as guide, while Num 10:34 and 14:14 (cf. εἰς σκέπην in Ps 104:39 LXX [105:39 MT] in relation to the pillar of cloud) underline rather that of protection, a role which is taken up again by Isa 4:5-6 in an eschatological key. In 10,17c-d it is wisdom that clearly takes the place of the pillar of cloud, as already this place was taken in the targumic traditions by the Word or Glory of God.[46]

The expression in 10:17d requires a certain care. Wisdom "became" (ἐγένετο is understood from the previous stich) "like a flame of stars (εἰς φλόγα ἄστρων) in the night". The luminous aspect of the pillar of cloud is noted by the difficult text of Exod 14:19-20. The MT reads: "and it [the pillar of cloud] came between the camp of the Egyptians and the camp of Israel and there was the cloud and the darkness and it lit up the night, so that the one did not approach the other during the whole night", while the LXX reads instead: καὶ ἐγένετο σκότος καὶ γνόφος καὶ διῆλθεν ἡ νύξ, without any reference to the light. However, Exod 13:21-22; Deut 1:33; Pss 77:14 LXX [78:14 MT]; 104:39 LXX [105:39 MT] speak of the luminous aspect of the pillar of fire which illuminates the night.[47] What is surprising is the association with the stars, undoubtedly a novelty on the part of our sage. This expression recalls themes in Wis 17:1-18:4. For the use of φλόξ, cf. 17:5 in connection with the stars which are not able to illuminate the night in which the Egyptians find themselves while, on the other hand, wisdom is able to do so for the Hebrews; cf., also, the description of the pillar of cloud in 18:3 as πυριφλεγῆ στῦλον. In addition to possible polemical references to the mystery cults (cf. 17:5 and 18:3), our sage had already indicated the superiority of wisdom over the stars (7:29). Wisdom, associated here with the pillar of cloud in its illuminatory function, is superior to every earthly light and in particular to that of the stars.

In referring to the crossing of the sea, our sage avoids the miraculous description found in Exodus 14 concerning the parting of the waters. The probably deliberate use of a creational type of language (ἄβυσσος "abyss, deep") becomes significant if read in the light of Wis 19:6-9 where the passage through the sea appears as the biblical prototype of a creation renewed. 10:18-19

Verse 10:20 begins with a tradition not found in the biblical text: "the just plundered the ungodly". The verb σκυλεύω with the meaning "to despoil the fallen of their armaments and goods" is used in the LXX version Exodus to for the undertakings described in Exod 3:22 and 12:36. The Israelites would have gathered up the weapons and precious objects owned by the Egyptians who had been 10:20-21

46 Cf. the comment on 18:3 and Mazzinghi, *Notte di paura e di luce*, 235-239.

47 Our sage could be basing himself on a type of exegesis of this text in the light also of Exod 10:22-23 and 14:24; cf. Engel, *Weisheit*, 179. In Wis 17:1-18:4 also, our author will play again on the idea of a night simultaneously dark and light.

drowned in the sea and vomited back on the beach. This is a tradition known to Mekilta (*Besh.* 7.94-108) and to Josephus (*A.J.* 2.349).[48]

In 20c, our sage draws on the information in Exod 15:1 which states that the song was sung both by Moses and the sons of Israel; Exod 15:20 adds the women. Rabbinic tradition expands this idea by supposing an antiphonal song between Moses and the people. Our sage is probably trying to explaining how, in Exod 15:1, the subject is in the plural ("Moses and the sons of Israel") but the verb "sang" (ישיר) is in the singular followed then by a "they said" (ויאמרו) in the plural.[49]

As for the images in v. 21, "opening the mouth" can be understood in a real sense, as in Num 22:28 and Ezek 3:27, where a genuine state of dumbness is presupposed, or as relating to a metaphorical dumbness such as that of Moses in Exod 4:11, 12, and 15. However, the episode of Moses being incapable of speech has no sense in the context of the crossing of the sea. Here, both aspects are probably present. Wisdom opens the mouth of the Israelites who were dumb because incapable of praising the Lord, but it also opens the mouth of those who were physically dumb (κωφοί), enabling them to speak. This interpretation can be reinforced by thinking of a reading which seeks to explain Exod 14:14: "the Lord will fight for you, and you תחרישון", a verb which can also be understood as "stand in silence" (in fact, the LXX translates with σιγήσετε). Now, through the operation of wisdom, those Hebrews who were dumb and terrified become able to praise the Lord.[50]

The final stich points us in the direction of this interpretation. It mentions the νήπιοι, that is, the babies, still unable to speak, the infants whose tongue becomes loosed, firm (for τρανός in relation to "speaking", cf. Wis 7:22). Our sage could have had in mind the texts of Isa 35:6 or of Ps 8:2-3, but what exactly does he intend to say? P. Grelot has shown that Wis 10:21 is the most ancient witness of a tradition attested in the targumic and midrashic spheres; cf. Frg. Tg. (long recension) which says: "from the womb of their mothers the infants make a sign to their fathers with their finger and say ..."; cf. *Midr. Exod. R.* on Exod 15:1, taking up Ezek 16:4-6 and Deut 32:6, 13 understood in a realistic sense. It is probably the same operation as that carried out by our author.[51]

Summary of Wis 10

Taken as a whole, Wisdom 10 represents a fine document of Greek-speaking Judaism in which the author rereads Scripture in a *midrashic* way, seeking to clarify some internal difficulties (cf. the comment on 10:17-21) and, at the same time

---

48 The plundering of the Egyptians' corpses is one of the reasons why the Lord caused them to be vomited dead on the shore; cf. Enns, *Exodus Retold*, 66-70, and the texts cited in Ginzberg, *The Legends*, 3:30-31; 6:10-11.

49 Cf. Enns, *Exodus Retold*, 75-81 and Ginzberg, *The Legends*, 3:33-34; 6:12-13.

50 For this solution, cf. Enns, *Exodus Retold*, 82-88.

51 Cf. Grelot, "Sagesse 10,21 et le Targum". Cf. also the texts cited by Winston, *Wisdom*, 222-223, and by Ginzberg, *The Legends*, 3:34; 6:6.

showing its relevance for the Jews of Alexandria who were immersed in the Hellenistic culture (cf., for example, the Isiac allusions in 10:4).[52]

A comparison with Sir 44:16-23 (the praise of the fathers; but cf. also Sir 45) reveals some important differences: our sage is silent about every proper name (cf. above), thus rendering his figures universal; he contrasts each positive figure with a negative one, while, at the same time, idealising his characters; and he leaves the wisdom of God as the only salvific agent – in the same way in which Heb 11, in a not dissimilar list, emphasises the role of faith.

We find ourselves here with a real reinterpretation of the history of salvation. Our sage avoids describing in detail or emphasising too much God's direct interventions in history, as, for example, with the parting of the waters of the sea. He prefers rather to highlight the mediation of wisdom. He then succeeds in bringing together, in a few stichs, different biblical episodes, thus offering a unitary vision of the biblical account (cf., for example, in Wis 10:5, the whole story of Abraham seen against the background of the Tower of Babel and the Flood).

By contrast with the rereading of the exodus events in Psalm 77 LXX [78 MT], our sage does not emphasise the people's sin but rather their justice (cf. the view of Lot as a "just man" in Wis 10:6; cf. also Wis 10:15) and so the salvation obtained by the people right from the story of Adam presented in Wis 10:1-2. In this way, Israel's past, linked in a literary way with the first part of the book, becomes, at the same time, an explanation of the present situation of the people together with a foundation for the future. This twofold temporal hook constitutes perhaps the most important theological characteristic of the third part of the book; future salvation is founded on the history of the past.

52 Enns describes this as "talking about the Bible"; cf. *Exodus Retold*, 35. However, Enns neglects the influence of the Hellenistic world on the text of Wisdom.

Wis 11:1-14: The First Antithesis

Literary Structure of Wis 11:1-14

The literary structure of this section has not been studied very much. A first point of discussion relates to v. 1. It has, once again, as subject the wisdom of chapter 10, a figure which will not appear any more in the book with the exception of a passing mention in 14:5. From here on, God himself will become the protagonist. Many authors link v. 1 with chapter 10 as its natural conclusion, but there exist good arguments for making it the beginning of a new section.[1] We have already seen that 10:20 should be considered as a clear *inclusio* with 19:9, thus connecting chapter 10 with the conclusion of the book as a whole. The mention of Moses in 11:1 corresponds very well with the mention of the same Moses in 11:14, at the end of the first antithesis, thus creating a certain unity between 11:1 and 11:14.

The asyndetical beginning of 11:1 already points to a new section. The play on words εὐόδωσεν – διώδευσαν links v. 1 to v. 2a. The fact that the implicit subject of v. 1 is still wisdom makes 11:1 a bridge with chapter 10 and serves almost as a useful title to introduce the final part of the book in which wisdom will give way directly to God. God is directly evoked with the "you" in v. 4, and to this divine "you" the author will address himself again right at the end of the book.

The object of vv. 2-4, which are also constructed asyndetically (cf. 11:2a, 3, 4a), is the journey of Israel in the desert, but Wis 11:2-4 also serves to introduce v. 5 which is constructed chiastically over two stichs that begin in a similar way (δι' ὧν ... διὰ τούτων). Verse 5 recalls a construction similar to v. 16, thus being linked to the principle repeated in 11:15-16 which, together with this same v. 5, governs the seven exodic antitheses: everyone is punished through the sins with which they have sinned. We can, therefore, consider vv. 1-5 as the introduction to the whole of the final part of the book.

The section that follows is clearly identified by the presence of the double formula ἀντὶ μέν (11:6) – ἀντὶ δέ (11:15). The first introduces the first diptych and responds to the principle expounded in v. 5; the second, on the other hand, introduces the new principle laid down in vv. 15-16 and serves to introduce the digression on divine philanthropy (11:15-12:27). In themselves, the two formulas have a relationship between them that is more formal than real since, in 11:6, ἀντὶ μέν has the sense of "instead of" while, in 11:15, ἀντὶ δέ has the meaning of "in return

---

1 Cf. Winston, *Wisdom*, 226-227; Reese, "Plan and Structure", 391-399; Offerhaus, *Komposition*, 125-129; Vílchez Líndez, *Sapienza*, 355; Engel, *Weisheit*, 165; Glicksman, *Wisdom of Solomon*, 10, 43-47; cf. also Wright, "The Structure", 177-179. For 11:1 belonging to what follows, cf., instead, Gilbert, "Sagesse", 73-74.89; Bizzeti, *Il libro della Sapienza*, 79-80. For an overview of the question and a different proposal (10:1-11:4 as an ode to wisdom) cf. Zsengellér, "The Taste of Paradise", 199-202.

for". However, for our sage, the formal correspondence was probably more than sufficient.

Thus, the first diptych opens in v. 6 and ends in v. 14. Particularly noticeable is the inclusion διψήσαντες (14c) and δίψους (8a). However, the theme of thirst and water also makes a hook with vv. 1-4; cf., again, δίψης in 4c and ἐδόθη ... ὕδωρ (4b) – ἔδωκας ὕδωρ (7b). The diptych is inspired, therefore, by the account in Exod 7:17-25, the first of the ten plagues of Egypt, the water of the Nile changed into blood and, at the same time, by the episode commented on previously (v. 4), the water gushing from the rock.

The diptych hinges around v. 10 which takes up the principle of v. 5, inverting its subjects and justifying it through the historical experience of Israel. Verse 10 is preceded by vv. 6-9, a total of eight stichs and followed by vv. 11-14, another eight stichs. The diptych thus enjoys a well-balanced construction. The theme of punishment links the two parts of the diptych (cf. ἐκόλασας in 11:8b and κολάσεων in 11:13a).[2]

Wis 11:1-5:
The Introduction to the Seven Antitheses

1 She [wisdom] made their works successful by the hand of a holy prophet.
2 They crossed uninhabitable deserts
and in inaccessible places pitched their tents.
3 They resisted their adversaries and repelled their enemies.
4 They were thirsty and called upon you.
Water was given them from an impenetrable rock
and a remedy for their thirst from a hard stone.
5 For the very thing that served to punish their enemies
was a benefit for them in their difficulties.

Notes on the Text and Translation

v. 5. The Vg adds two stichs: "a defectione potus sui / et in eis cum abundarent filii Israel laetati sunt" (cf. Ziegler). According to Larcher (*Sagesse*, 2:675), this is a gloss of obscure origin (an explicative gloss according to Grimm, *sub loco*); cf. Scarpat, *Sapienza*, 2:534.

---

2 The unity of the text calls into question the proposal of E. Haag who claims to discover in 11-12 an original layer, two subsequent elaborations and a final redaction, with different theological emphases: cf. "Die Weisheit ist nur eine", *passim*.

Synchronic Analysis

11:1: Wisdom as Guide

The subject is still the same as in the previous chapter, namely, wisdom. As has been said, from now on, the Lord himself will become the protagonist. How is it that wisdom gives way to God? The question does not seem to have been studied very much by commentators. A possible answer is that wisdom, the very image of the divine activity (7:25-26), has now completed its *literary* role: it has led Israel – and the readers – right to the beginning of the journey through the desert where Israel now discovers the actual presence of God, no longer mediated by God's wisdom.[3]

Wisdom is the subject of εὐοδόω ("guide on a good path"), a typical verb of the LXX which here has the transitive-causative meaning of "make succeed" and has as its object τὰ ἔργα, "the works" of the Israelites recalled in 10:18-21 at the moment of the crossing of the sea. However, the verb does not lose here its connotation of "ensuring a good journey" (cf. Tob 7:13^{S}, where the subject is God) and appears well chosen to summarise the entire journey of Israel in the desert.

Wisdom makes use of a "holy prophet", clearly Moses (cf. ἐν χειρὶ Μωυσῆ: Lev 26:46), called a "prophet" as in Deut 34:10 (cf. Num 12:6-8; Deut 18:15, 18; and Hos 12:14). As we have already said, "holy" (ἅγιος) does not indicate a moral quality of Moses but rather his special belonging to the Lord.

11:2-3: The Journey in the Desert

Verses 2-3 compress into a very small space the long journey of Israel in the desert (Exod 15:22-17:16). Διοδεύω recalls the previous εὐοδόω, underlining again the idea of the "path" (ὁδός). The two adjectives ἀοίκητος and ἄβατος refer to a notion of inaccessibility, an unusual way, as happened to the Israelites in Sinai. The "enemies" mentioned in v. 3 (note the refined chiastic structure) could be the Amalekites of Exod 17:8-16.

Verse 2 contains a flashback to the first part of the book. With an almost identical vocabulary, the wicked of Wis 5:7 lamented at "having journeyed through impassable deserts" (ἐρήμους ἀβάτους), that is, at having lost their way through their own wickedness. It is only by receiving the interior guidance of wisdom that these "deserts" of human wickedness can be passed through, as already happened to Israel on its desert journey. Only in this way is it possible to defeat the enemies. Verse 3b is a further reference to the first part: in 5:17, in fact, the creation itself rises up εἰς ἄμυναν ἐχθρῶν. What happened to Israel in the desert is what will happen in the end to the just and the ungodly.

11:4: The Water from the Rock

Verse 4 alludes to the episode of the waters at Meribah (Exod 17:1-7 and Num 20:2-13; cf. Wis 1:2-3). The "impenetrable rock" from which the water gushed is an image taken from Deut 8:15 (cf. Ps 113:8 LXX [114:18 MT]) The passive form ἐδόθη refers to God's action which is not explicitly mentioned here.[4] In 4b, the

---

3 Cf. Hübner, *Weisheit* 146: "*Es geht in der Sap um Gott!* Die Sap ist ein höchst theologisches Buch!".

4 The "hard stone" (described with the same, rare adjective, ἀκρότομος) is, in Philo, the same "wisdom of God" (*Leg.* 2.86), and will later be identified by Paul with Christ (1 Cor 10:4). In our text, there is no explicit allegory of the exodus theme (contra Scarpat, *Sapienza*, 2:363: "it seems to us that this chapter has been carefully thought out to be read in an allegorical key"). Rather, the events of the exodus are being reread in a *midrashic* key to show all its relevance for the Alexandrian Jews. Although becoming symbolic and paradigmatic, the events of the exodus set out in Wisdom 11-19 never lose their connection with the present time in which the author of Wisdom lives.

water is described as a "healing" for the people's thirst. For the term ἴαμα, cf. the comment on 16:9, the only other occurrence of this word in Wisdom. The theme of God who cures belongs also to the exodus: cf. Exod 15:26 LXX: ἐγὼ γάρ εἰμι κύριος ὁ ἰώμενός σε.

At the conclusion of this introductory reflection (cf. the γάρ), v. 5 contains, a first, important, principle which will animate the whole of the first part of the book. One and the same created reality (δι' ὧν ... διὰ τούτων) serves to punish the Egyptians and to favour the Israelites. The verb κολάζω is very frequent in Wisdom (cf. the comment on 3:4). The participle ἀποροῦντες is to be understood in relation to the difficulty in which the Israelites find themselves, struck by thirst in the middle of the desert. 11:5: God Favours and Punishes

If the Egyptians were punished, then, the Israelites were favoured (cf. the passive form εὐεργετήθησαν which refers to the divine action; cf. the comment on 16:2). The book of Wisdom, as already the Psalter (cf. LXX-Pss 12:6; 56:2; 114:7 [MT-Pss 13:6; 57:2; 115:7]), reserves to God the verb εὐεργετέω, since God is the only true benefactor. This theme (punish / favour) appeared for the first time in Wis 3:4-5 and will reappear in 11:13; 16:1-2; 16:24, thus constituting an important motif for our author. If the God of Israel is a God who punishes the sins of the ungodly, still more is God presented as a benefactor of God's people. The exodus is the best proof of this.[5]

Diachronic Analysis

An interesting detail concerning the mention of Moses in v. 1 is the fact that our sage does not even record in passing the role which Moses had at Sinai in relation to the covenant and the gift of the law (cf. Sir 45:1-5), a theme which does not appear particularly significant for the book of Wisdom (but cf. Wis 16:6).[6] 11:1

In taking up the episode of the waters of Massah and Meribah (cf. above), the author omits mentioning the continual "murmuring" of the people which is actually described as calling on the Lord. This is a device already seen in Wisdom 10. According to a usage well attested by Jewish tradition, our author tends to minimise the faults of the Israelites while underlining those of the Egyptians. 11:4

In this verse, the exodus motifs are completed by the introduction of the theme of the cosmos. Verse 5 thus suggests that God's judicial action together with God's work of salvation takes place through the cosmos which is thus not a simple, neutral spectator in the drama of history. The "creatures of the world" are really "bearers of salvation" (cf. Wis 1:14) and intervene actively at the side of the Lord to save or to punish. The following verses offer the first proof of this. 11:5

5 Cf. Mazzinghi, "The antithetical pair 'to punish' and 'to benefit'", *passim.*

6 Cf. Mazzinghi, "The figure of Moses", 184-191.

Wis 11:6-14:
The First Antithesis. The Water Changed into Blood; the Water from the Rock

6 Instead of the perpetual flowing of a river,
muddied by putrid blood,
7 as punishment for the decree of infanticide,
against all hope, you gave them abundant water,
8 showing by their thirst at that time,
how you had punished their adversaries;
9 for when they were put to the test, although they were disciplined in your mercy,
they knew how the wicked were tormented when judged by your wrath.
10 For you put them to the test like a father who gives a warning.
On the others, however, you opened an inquest, like a severe king who condemns.
11 All were equally tormented:
12 for a double grief seized them,
and a groaning at the memory of the past.
13 For when they heard that through the same punishment
the others had been favoured, they became aware of the Lord.
14 The man, who, at one time, they had exposed, thrown [into the river], rejected and spurned,
at the end of events they had to respect,
having had a thirst very different from that of the just.

Notes on the Text and Translation

v. 6. The term *λυθρώδης ("putrid, corrupt") is attested only in Anth. Pal. 11.258,3, towards the end of the first cent. CE. It refers to the mixture of blood and dust which results from the killing of sacred victims (cf. Scarpat, *Sapienza*, 2:401).
Together with other witnesses of the text, codex B reads ταραχθέντες, "distressed" (instead of ταραχθέντος), the nom. pl. of the aorist pass. ptc., with reference to the Egyptians. However, the reading of S, A, and many other witnesses, ταραχθέντος "muddied" (gen. sg. aorist pass. ptc.), with reference to the Nile muddied by the blood (Exod 7:14-25), appears better.

v. 9. Codices B and A read ἐν ὀργῇ (cf. Ziegler); it is preferable to read with Rahlfs μετ' ὀργῆς (S and other codices; cf. Lat: *cum ira*; Scarpat, *Sapienza*, 2:404-405). In this way, there is a still better contrast between the educative action of God which takes place ἐν ἐλέει, "in / with mercy", and the judgement of the ungodly in which the divine wrath becomes the instrument with which God judges them.

v. 11. Καὶ ἀπόντες δὲ καὶ παρόντες, literally "whether absent or present". However, it is not clear to what the text is referring (to the Egyptians who are at the Red Sea and those still in their houses in Egypt?); We follow Scarpat's proposal (*Sapienza*, 2:404) which is based on solid philological arguments: the phrase would simply be indicating all the Egyptians without exception who were equally tormented (*τρύχω "rub wrong, torment, enervate, plague"; cf. 14:15).

v. 12. For the discussion of the problems relating to 12b, cf. Larcher, *Sagesse*, 3:667. He chooses to read στεναγμὸς μνήμῃ τῶν παρελθόντων instead of στεναγμὸς μνημῶν and translates "with a groan, at the memory of the past". Scarpat, after a long discussion (*Sapienza*, 2:405-406), underlines the strong dependences of v. 12b on the vocabulary of the tragedians and chooses instead to read στεναγμὸς μνήμων, with the same meaning.

v. 13. "They had been favoured". We are translating with the pluperfect the perfect participle εὐεργτημένους, which is attested by S, A, C, and other minuscules, preferred by Rahlfs, and well correlated with the previous aorist, against the reading of B, which reads the present participle εὐεργετουμένους and is preferred by Ziegler.

v. 14. The initial article, τὸν, is read as a relative, ὅν, by codex A, and some minuscules and versions (cf. Ziegler). This reading, chosen by Rahlfs (cf. Larcher and Scarpat) to avoid the anacoluthon, seems preferable (cf. Engel, "Weisheit", 2146).

Synchronic Analysis

11:6-9: The Waters of the Nile Changed into Blood

The waters of the Nile are changed into blood (v. 6) as retaliation (cf. εἰς ἔλεγχον, "as punishment" [7a]; cf. 1:9; 2:14) for the decree (διάταγμα; cf. Heb 11:23) of Pharaoh in Exod 1:22: every new-born male Hebrew is to be thrown into the Nile. *Νηπιοκτόνος, "infanticide" [v. 7a], is perhaps a neologism coined by our author. The whole of v. 6, however, is constructed with rare and poetic terms. There is an anticipation here of the principle expressed in 11:15-16; everyone is punished with that with which they have sinned.

The punishment of the Egyptians is contrasted with the water given in abundance to Israel, a people who seemed to have lost hope. The adverb ἀνελπίστως, "against all hope" seems to be a discrete allusion to this theme. The subject here is precisely the water gushing from the rock mentioned in v. 4; cf. the connection ἐδόθη (...) ὕδωρ (4b) – ἔδωκας (...) ὕδωρ (7b). This is something which transcends human hopes.

In v. 8, what happened in the past becomes, once again, instruction for the present. The thirst experienced by Israel in the desert (cf. Exod 17:1-3; Num 20:2-5) is not to be seen as a punishment but as a salutary divine warning so that Israel could have a better understanding of the punishment awaiting the wicked together with the mercy of God for his people (v. 9). As already in 10:20, the enemies are called ἀσεβεῖς, thus recalling the "ungodly" of Wisdom 2.

Verse 9 is an interesting window on our sage's theological conceptions. The divine "wrath" mentioned in 9b is not directly contrasted with "mercy" (ἔλεος in 9a); cf. also 12:15-18. The vocabulary employed recalls explicitly that of 3:1-9: cf. πειράζω, παιδεύω, and εὐεργετέω in 3:5; βάσανος in 3:1; κρίνω in 3:8; ἔλεος in 3:9; cf. also the theme of the divine wrath (ὀργή in Wis 5:20) on the ἀσεβεῖς (cf. 3:10). Βασανίζω (cf. 12:23; 16:1, 4) – as already βάσανος in 2:19; 3:1; and, later, in 17:13 and 19:4 – has a clear eschatological tone. Here the theme does not concern the final destiny of the just and the ungodly, as in 3:1-9, 10-12, but rather the historical experience of Israel in the desert, which thus becomes a lesson for the present and, at the same time, a prefiguring of the future, to be precise, of how God will punish the ungodly and save the just.

11:10: Experience of God as Father

Here we are at the centre of the diptych: the experience of thirst serves above all to give Israel experience of the fatherhood of God (cf. the comment on 2:16). The theme will return later (cf. 11:22 – 12:2) and is inspired by texts like Deut 8:2-5 (cf. also Prov 3:12). The journey through the desert is a test for Israel but also a sign of the divine care. For our sage, therefore, the plagues have an eminently didactic value.

To the just, God shows himself as a father who corrects his own children and educates them by testing them (cf. the connection with δοκιμάζω). This is the sense of νουθετέω (cf. 12:2, 26). To the ungodly, on the other hand, God shows a different side, that of a severe king who judges. The vocabulary employed here (ἀπότομος, καταδικάζω, ἐξετάζω) leads to the thought that, after the earthly judgement of the Egyptians, our sage is already imagining the eschatological judgement of the ungodly described in the first part of the book: cf. ἀπότομος in 5:20; 6:5; ἐξετάζω in 6:3; ἐξέτασις in 1:9; ἐξετασμός in 4:6, but also δοκιμάζω in 3:6, there in connection with the just.

11:11-14: The Thirst in the Desert

From the Israelites, the attention shifts to the Egyptians: to the thirst suffered by the changing of the waters of the Nile into blood (cf. v. 14c) is added the suffering of seeing the Israelites in the desert saved precisely by water. On this point too, our author is expanding the exodus account.

The rather obscure text of vv. 11-12 is probably to be understood in the sense that all the Egyptians were equally tormented (cf. the textual notes above), and that this torment was doubled when they saw the Israelites being favoured although they too had suffered thirst. The Egyptians experience a suffering (λύπη) which is not only physical but moral. The "double grief" probably refers to the memory of the plagues and, at the same time, to the knowledge that the Israelites were favoured in the desert. However, it is possible, as in Isa 40:2, to take "double" in a sense that is simply intensive.

The elements of the cosmos (here, water) and, at the same time, the events of history also lead the ungodly to recognize God. The same thing happened to Israel: cf. ἔγνωσαν in 11:9b.

Moses

Verse 14 refers, retrospectively, to the events relating to Moses' birth (Exod 2:1-10; cf. Acts 7:21). As already they had to do in the case of the glorified just in 5:4, the ungodly are forced to respect (14b) those whom they had previously rejected. In fact, the thirst experienced by the Egyptians (14c) was quite different (οὐχ ὅμοια, a *litotes*) from that experienced by the just, that is, the Israelites.

Diachronic Analysis

11:6-9

The connection in v. 6 between the water changed into blood (cf. Exod 7:17-25) and Pharaoh's decree of infanticide is absent from the account in Exodus and also unknown to the ancient Jewish tradition.

Verse 8 too goes beyond the biblical account, presupposing that whereas the Egyptians experienced thirst, the Israelites did not. The idea is present both in Philo (*Mos.* 1.144) and in Josephus (*A.J.* 2.14.1). Both think that, although the water of the Nile was changed into blood, it remained drinkable for the Israelites.

In Wis 11:12a, the expression διπλῆ λύπη seems to have been inspired by Plato.[7] 11:11-14
In *Phileb.* 36ab, a suffering without hope is a double suffering as seems to be that of the Egyptians here.

Continuing to go beyond the biblical data, our author is presupposing here that the Egyptians were somehow aware of what happened to Israel (cf. also v. 13). The Egyptians must then "be aware" of the Lord in the moment when they hear of the favours granted to Israel (ἤκουσαν ... εὐεργετημένους αὐτούς). Verse 13 takes up the same theme as v. 5: the plagues are a sign of the punishment of the ungodly and of the favours granted to the just.

The expression ᾔσθοντο τὸν κύριον (13b) is unique in the LXX. There is a similar expression in Isa 49:26 LXX (καὶ αἰσθανθήσεται πᾶσα σὰρξ ὅτι ἐγὼ κύριος ὁ ῥυσάμενός σε); cf. Xenophon, *Mem.* 1.4.13 where αἰσθάνομαι is employed in relation to knowledge of the gods. "Awareness of the Lord" can happen also to the ungodly both in their own punishment and in reflection on the salvation of the just.[8] In the case of the Egyptians, it is not a question of coming to the faith but of having experienced that their punishment is of a divine nature: a probable response to the objections of Pharaoh who, in Exod 5:2, claims not to know the Lord. Thus, our author is thinking here of the refrain which in the book of Exodus pulses through the account of the plagues and constitutes one of its theological rationales: "from this they will know that I am the Lord" (Exod 7:5, 17 etc.).

In v. 14, the mention of spurning, which is based on texts such as Exod 11:1 (cf. 10:11, 28) which describe how Moses is driven out of the presence of Pharaoh and from the land of Egypt, is a thinly veiled allusion to the way in which the Jews of Alexandria felt themselves treated (cf. 4 Macc 5:22 with the same verb, χλευάζω, and, above all, Philo, *Legat.* 211).

---

7 Cf. Larcher, *Sagesse*, 3:666.

8 Cf. Gilbert, "La connaissance de Dieu", 323.

Wis 11:15–12:27: The Divine "Philanthropy"

Literary Structure of Wis 11:15–12:27[1]

This long digression seems as if a break in our author's thought: after having described the first plague (11:6-14), he now reflects on the divine action with regard to the Egyptians: why did God not destroy them but instead punished them gradually with numerous plagues? The answer comes in the realisation of the mercy and clemency of God towards the wicked. In this case too, our sage employs scriptural texts as a starting point, then rereads them and actualises them in the light of the culture and historical situation in which he lives.

In 11:15, the formula ἀντὶ δέ seems intended to echo the ἀντὶ μέν in v. 6, marking the beginning of a new pericope. The conclusion of the digression is found in 12:23-27. Here our sage takes up the themes already presented in 11:15-16 which concern the criticism of the worship of animals by the Egyptians (cf. πλανάομαι, τὰ ζῷα, in 11:15 and repeated in 12:24). This criticism will return at the close of the subsequent digression (15:14-19) and will constitute the theme of the second antithesis, in 16:1-4. In this way, 12:23-27 concludes the reflection on divine philanthropy and, at the same time, anticipates the criticism of zoolatry.

Wis 11:15-12:2

The digression presents a careful internal structure. A first section goes from 11:15 to 12:2, as demonstrated by the *inclusio* ἁμαρταν- in 11:16 and 12:2b. The excursus consists of 33 stichs centred on the theme of the divine moderation towards Egypt. These revolve around the principle expressed in 11:20d, which is preceded and followed by 16 stichs. In more detail, we shall discover a subdivision of a concentric nature which highlights clearly the unity of the passage which has as its basic theme the love of God for all God's creatures, a love founded on the divine omnipotence which is the foundation of God's tolerance towards sinners. Here is the theme of the first section:

a. 11:15-16: introduction to and general principle of the digression: punishment is along the lines of the sin committed (cf. the reference already noted in 12:23-27).

b. 11:17-20c (cf. the quasi-*inclusio* παντοδύναμος, 17a – δυνάμεως, 20c). The initial γὰρ governs the entire pericope where there is a description of the more terrible punishments which God could have sent upon the Egyptians but did not do so. The text outlines six possibilities, all introduced by ἤ (ἤτοι in 18b).

x. 11:20d: centre of the section; the divine moderation.

b'. 11:21-12:1: the reason for this divine moderation, God's mercy on God's creatures (*inclusio* πάντοτε, "everywhere", 11:21a and ἐν πᾶσιν, "in everything", 12:1).

This small section is powerfully constructed: in the centre, v. 24a, preceded and followed by six stichs (43 words in both cases); in 21b and 25b, two rhetorical questions;

1 Reese, "Plan and Structure", 393 n. 3; Wright, "The Structure", 177-179; Bizzeti, *Il libro della Sapienza*, 79-92; Gilbert, "Sagesse", 73.

the construction of 23a (ἐλεεῖς δὲ πάντας ὅτι) is identical to that of v. 26 (φείδῃ δὲ πάντων ὅτι) and takes up an important theme: the mercy of God towards every creature. The expression τὸ γάρ opens both 11:21 and 12:1; cf. also ὁ κόσμος in 11:22a which takes up the same term as 11:17b; cf. also πνεῦμα in 11:20ac and 12:1.

a'. 12:2: conclusion and summary (again ἁμαρτάνω, in 12:2b); the therapeutic purpose of God's punitive action.

The second section comprises Wis 12:3-21 and has as its theme the divine moderation towards the Canaanites.[2] In this case too, we can detect a well-ordered structure with its centre in v. 12: Wis 12:3-21

– 12:3-11 (nine verses with 21 stichs): the divine moderation towards the Canaanites. At the centre is the declaration of principle in v. 8a. Verses 3-7 are characterised by the *inclusio* γῆς–γῇ (3, 7b; cf. also the pronouns σου in 3 and παρὰ σοί in 7b) and describe the divine hatred of the Canaanites in a single, long sentence. In this long sentence the object stands at the head in 12:3, the participial construction beginning with μισήσας (12:4-6a) serves as the basis for the decision pronounced in the main clause (6b). The subordinate final statement (v. 7) describes the intention bound up with this decision.

Verses 8b-11 revolve around a new principle which is expressed in 10a and which takes up the theme of μετάνοια expressed in 11:23c. The expression κατὰ βραχύ is directly linked with 8c, while ἐδίδους is taken up again at the close of the pericope, in 11b. The theme of vv. 8b-11 is God's therapeutic punishment.

– 12:12a-d represents the centre of this whole section and formulates a new fundamental principle through four rhetorical questions (τίς – ἢ τίς – τίς – ἢ τίς): no one can judge God's action. Upon this follow another 22 stichs in nine verses (vv. 13-21).

– 12:13-18: the reasons for the divine moderation. At the centre of this little pericope, in 16a, there is a further declaration of principle. The power (ἰσχύς) and justice (δικαιοσύνη) of God are recalled. In 13-15, the basic theme is that of God's justice (cf. 15a) whereas, in 16b-18, the theme is, rather, God's power (ἰσχύν; ἰσχύος: 17a, 18b); cf. the repetition of δεσποζ- and of φειδ-, followed by an explicative γάρ (16b, 18ab). The introduction of the pronoun ἡμᾶς in 18b, referring to the Israelites, constitutes a hook with the following section which moves from the consideration of the divine action on the Canaanites to the consequences of this action for Israel.

– 12:19-21: the lessons of this moderation; summaries of preceding themes; cf. πατράσιν in 21b which takes up πατέρων in 6b and παίδων in 7a and 20a. The form ἔκρινας in 13b connects us directly with 21a, creating a real inclusion and making of v. 21 the true end of the pericope which opened in v. 13.

The text of 12:19-21 is structured according to a characteristic scheme: AB A'B' CD E D'C'.[3] This thus causes 20a (C) and particularly 20c (E) to stand out, so underlining how the principle of divine mercy works both for God's children and for God's enemies.

---

2 Cf. Bizzeti, *Il libro della Sapienza*, 90-91, for the list of expressions which 12:13-21 takes up again from the previous section (11:21-12:2).

3 Cf. Bizzeti, *Il libro della Sapienza*, 86-87 for the details, and for the justification of v. 21 as the end of the pericope, contrary to Gilbert, who claims that 12:22 is the conclusion of 12:19-21.

We note the repetition in this section of the terms of the declaration of principle in 12:10a: μετάνοιαν (19d); δούς ... τόπον (20c).

Wis 12:22-27 The digression closes with a third, shorter, section: 12:22-27 which has the double function of recapitulation and announcement of a new theme. The author returns to his central theme of God's mercy and, at the same time, introduces the theme of idolatry which anticipates and prepares for the digression that follows (Wisdom 13–15).

Verse 22, in particular, forms a bridge with the preceding material: the first stich takes up the theme of Israel (ἡμᾶς ... ἡμῶν), as well as that of the enemies (τοὺς ἐχθρούς), together with the theme of "correction" or "instruction" (παιδεύων); the second and the third stichs take up, instead, the double theme of the judgement (κρίνοντες, κρινόμενοι) and mercy (ἀγαθότητα, ἔλεος) of God.

In their turn, verses 23-27 can be subdivided into two parts. In vv. 23-25, there is a description of the sin of the Egyptians – zoolatry – and their consequent punishment. Verse 24 expands and explains verse 23 (καὶ γάρ), and verse 25 draws the conclusions (διὰ τοῦτο). Verse 26 returns to the theme of the Egyptians' sin, adding the theme of their obstinacy in this sin. Verse 27 specifies it (cf. γάρ in 27a) while 27d draws the definitive conclusion (διό), the ruin of the Egyptians. In these final verses, our sage returns to the theme of zoolatry announced in 11:15 and prepares for the subsequent development of 15:18-19. This pericope thus acts as a conclusion to the first digression and, at the same time, as a preparation for the second.

Wis 11:15–12:2: Divine Moderation towards Egypt

15 Instead of the foolish reasonings produced by their wickedness,
in which they wandered in error, offering worship
to irrational reptiles and contemptible creatures,
you sent against them as punishment,
a multitude of irrational animals,
16 so that they might know that punishment comes by means of the thing with which one sins.
17 Certainly, your almighty hand,
which had created the world from unformed matter,
was not unable to send against them a horde of bears or ferocious lions,
18 or astonishing beasts, full of fresh fury,
who exhaled fiery breath,
or poured forth crackling smoke,
or flashed fearful sparks from their eyes,
19 (beasts) who could not only attack and exterminate them,
but even whose terrifying appearance could annihilate them.
20 And though, without all this, they could fall at a single breath,

pursued by justice
and scattered by your powerful breath;

yet you have ordered everything by measure, number, and weight.

21 For it is always possible for you to deploy a mighty force;
and who could resist the sovereign power of your arm?
22 The whole world before you is like a speck of dust on the scales
and like a drop of morning dew fallen on the earth.
23 Be merciful to all, for you can do everything,
and close your eyes to the sins of humanity, in view of their repentance.
24 For you love everything that exists
and despise nothing that you have made:
if you had hated something you would not have created it.
25 How could something have been able to exist unless it were pleasing to you?
How could anything have been preserved if it had not been called by you?
26 You spare all things, for all are yours, O Sovereign, friend of life.
12:1 For your incorruptible spirit is in all things.
2 Therefore, you gradually correct those who err,
and warn them, reminding them of how they have sinned,
so that, forsaking evil, they may believe in you, O Lord.

Notes on the Text and Translation

v. 15. Θρησκεύω (15b) is an important term for the dating of Wisdom. In the sense of "offering worship", it disappears from the classical period to reappear in the Augustan age; cf. Robert, Louis, *Etudes épigraphiques et philologiques* (Paris: Bibliothèque de l'Ecole des Hautes Etudes 1938) 226-235; Scarpat, "Ancora sull'autore", 178.

v. 17. οὐ γὰρ ἠπόρει: note the use of *litotes* with an intensive value: "certainly, he was not unable ..."; cf. an exhaustive discussion in Scarpat, *Sapienza*, 2:412.
The term *παντοδύναμος seems unknown before Wisdom. In addition to this passage, cf. 7:23 (in connection with πνεῦμα; see the comment) and 18:15 (in connection with the λόγος).

v. 18. The adjective νεόκτιστος, "of new creation", is a very refined term which the majority of commentators refer to the beasts. The reading νεοκτίστους (acc. pl.), chosen by Ziegler, comes from PsChr 8.662, while A, C* and other textual witnesses read the genitive νεοκτίστου, referring it to "fury" (θυμοῦ). Our sage is thinking of already existing beasts full of a different fury, stronger than usual: "a new fury" (Engel, "Weisheit", 2146).
The term *πυρπνόος (to be corrected with Rahlfs; Ziegler has πύρπνοος instead; cf. Walters, Peter, *The Text of Septuagint.* Its corruption and their emendation [Cambridge: Cambridge University Press 1973] 126) is refined and poetic (taken from the tragedians; cf. Euripides, *Med.* 478, said of bulls): "who breathe fire".
In 18c, some prefer to read: "who exhaled an infected (βρῶμον) breath", according to some minuscules. Larcher (*Sagesse*, 3:682) prefers to read βρῶμον λιχμωμένου, with some codices (cf. Ziegler, *Sapientia*, 71): "who fire infected smoke (namely,

breath)". However, the majority of the codices read βρόμον λικμωμένους, "hissing from smouldering embers". One can think of the "rumble" emitted from the monsters' throat alongside their scorching breath.

v. 19. The verb *συνεκτρίβω is *hapax totius graecitatis*. It has the sense of "crush together" (cf. ἐκτρίβω in Exod 9:15). The latter verb is chosen by some codices; cf. Ziegler.

v. 20. Larcher's emendation, ἑνί νεύματι, "at a single sign", based solely on the Arabic version (cf. 2 Macc 8:18), appears to have little foundation in the text despite the support of Scarpat, *Sapienza*, 2:420-421 (cf. also Engel, "Weisheit", 2416) who refers also to Eusebius, *Praep. ev.* 7.8,17. If we read ἑνί πνεύματι with the entirety of the Greek mss we have to think of the "breath" of the divine anger as in Job 4:9 and, above all, in Exod 15:7.

v. 23. Other than in Wis 11:23; 12:10, 19, the term μετάνοια appears in the LXX only in Prov 14:15, Sir 44:16, Odes 12:8. In Greek usage, it mostly has the sense of "change one's mind, alter one's opinion". It indicates a change of life rarely, and only in later texts. In the LXX, only in Jer 8:6, 38:19; Isa 48:8; and Sir 48:15, the verb μετανοέω is used with reference to the conversion of a person to God. In this sense, μετάνοια becomes increasingly frequent in the writings of Greek-speaking Judaism. In Wis 12:10, the term is used in the more classical sense (change of ideas). In 5:3 too, it is not too far from this meaning (more precisely, "remorse"). Here, instead, μετάνοια indicates, rather, conversion in a religious sense according to a usage that is approaching that of the New Testament; cf. A. Tosato, "Per una revisione degli studi sulla 'metanoia' neotestamentaria", *RivB* 23 (1975) 3-45.

v. 25. Codices B and A read ἔμεινεν instead of διέμεινεν (S); but the latter seems to be the original reading; cf. Scarpat, *Sapienza*, 2:425-426. The verb has the meaning of "remain, last" and refers here to the creation which remains in existence thanks to the action of God; cf. Philo, *Spec.* 1.96 in relation to people, but the verb could have been suggested also by Ps 118:90-91 LXX.

v. 26. The term *φιλόψυχος, in the sense of "friend of life", is not attested in Greek usage before Wisdom. In classical Greek, it has the sense of "attached to one's own life" and so "cowardly, craven" (cf., for example, Euripides, *Hec.* 348). Here, Wisdom overturns its meaning and transforms it into a term of positive value. There is no need to speculate with Larcher, *Etudes*, 182, that the author of Wisdom knew little Greek; cf. also Reese, *Hellenistic Influence*, 29.

12:2. The verb πιστεύω, which is already in Wis 1:2, returns later in Wis 14:5; 16:26; and 18:6, but cf. the theme of πίστις in 3:14 and of ἀπιστία in 1:2. In the form πιστεύω ἐπί + acc., unusual for the LXX, it is found more frequently in the NT. Only here and in Wis 16:26 does the verb refer to believing in God.

Synchronic Analysis

11:15-16: Egyptian Zoolatry

The error of the Egyptians is introduced in v. 15, at the beginning of this first section (11:15-12:2) by means of the expression λογισμῶν ἀσυνέτων ἀδικίας αὐτῶν in which occur together three terms, two of which (ἀσύνετος, ἀδικία) are not found in our book except in 1:5, where ἀδικία also appears. The foolish reasonings of their wickedness (that is: produced by their wickedness) are, therefore, those λογισμοὶ ἀσύνετοι found in Wis 1:3 and directed against God.

Here we discover that these reasonings are bound up with what for our author is the worst form of idolatry, namely, zoolatry. It is a cult which is immediately branded with irrationality (note the repetition of ἄλογος; cf. Rom 1:21-23). The text of 11:15b introduces the condemnation of zoolatry with the use of πλανάω, "err", or, better still, "wander in error", a verb already encountered in Wis 2:21 (cf. the comment) and dear to our author (Wis 12:24; 13:6; 14:22; 15:4; 17:1). It always has a distinct religious nuance and is not without polemical reference to the mystery cults.

The Egyptian zoolatry is described with the verb θρησκεύω which, in classical usage, indicates simply worship but which, in Wis 14:27 (cf. 14:16-28) is employed *in malam partem* in connection with this idolatrous worship. This is the cult of animals typical of Egypt, worship offered to reptiles without reason and contemptible creatures (*κνώδαλα; one could think of the insects which played a leading role in the plagues of Egypt: flies, gnats). The pair ἑρπετά καὶ κνώδαλα appears already in Let. Aris. 138; 169 (cf. Alcman, frag. 67)[4] and reappears later in Wis 17:9 (κνώδαλα again in 16:1).[5] In addition to being described as "irrational" the creatures are *εὐτελῆ, "contemptible" (for εὐτελής, cf. Wis 10:4; 13:14; and 15:10), so as to highlight, the sordidness of the Egyptian worship of animals in the eyes of a Jew.

For this reason, the punishment of the idolaters (ἐκδίκησις; a term taken directly from the Exodus account of the plagues; cf. Exod 7:4; 12:12) consists in the sending to these same Egyptians precisely such animals. Taken up in an analogous context in Wis 16:3, ἐπαποστέλλω comes again from the Exodus account (Exod 8:17) where it is used precisely in connection with the plague of gnats. Note also τὸ πλῆθος which, in its turn, recalls Exod 8:20, and returns later in Wis 11:17; 16:1; and 19:10, always in not dissimilar contexts.

Punishment with What One Sins

Verse 16 indicates the purpose of the divine action: ἵνα γνῶσιν, "so that they might know". The historical events become revelatory signs of the divine action for the ungodly also. This is a principle which our sage found already in the book of Exodus. The Lord sends the plagues in order to be recognized by the Egyptians (cf. Exod 7:5, 17; 8:6, 18; 9:14, 29; 11:7). The passive κωλάζεται refers to the divine action. But why is the punishment actually less serious than the ungodly deserve? Is this, perhaps, a sign of divine weakness? These are the questions to which our sage is preparing to reply.

11:17a–b: Your Almighty Hand

According to our sage, God can do everything, even what could seem impossible, because it is God who created the world (ἡ παντοδύναμός σου χεὶρ καὶ κτίσασα τὸν κόσμον) "from unformed matter" (v. 17b). The reference to the creation as the work of God's hand is biblical (cf. Ps 8:7; Isa 45:11-12; 48:13). The use of the rare term παντοδύναμος seems, instead, to be an allusion to the divine "powers" in the work of creation (the *Logos*, in particular, but cf. Wis 9:1), according to a conception typical of Philo (cf. *Abr.* 121; *Plant.* 50) which, however, is not developed here by our sage. We note again that τὸν κόσμον as object of the verb κτίζω is late and rather rare: cf. 2 Macc 7:23 and Rom 1:20; for κτίζω, cf. Wis 1:14.

11:17c–19: The Monsters which God Could Have Created

In a poetic and refined language which echoes that of the Greek tragedians, our author now describes the fearful monsters (θῆρας) which the Lord could have sent (ἐπιπέμπω, a verb which in Greek usage is often employed with reference to the action of the gods) against the Egyptians, if only God had wished. Here, the adjective ἄγνωστος does not have the sense of "unknown" but of "astonishing".

4 Cf. D.L. Page, *Poetae Melici Graeci*, Oxford: Clarendon 1962.
5 Cf. Mazzinghi, *Notte di paura e di luce*, 73-74.

These are absurd, unimaginable beasts. The ferocious animals are among those listed in Lev 26:22-26; cf. Ezek 14:12-23 and Sir 39:28-31. Verse 18 concerns, rather, monsters which, as it says in v. 19, can already kill just by their presence.

11:20a–c: Breath of God and Justice

This text explicitly recalls Wis 5:23. In this case too, there is a divine battle. If in 5:2, however, the battle is an eschatological one, here the reference is rather to an historical event (the exodus) and, at the same time, to something which God could have done but did not do.

The text plays on the double reference to the divine πνεῦμα (cf. the textual notes) which is to be understood here, as in Isa 11:4 and, above all, Job 4:9 and Exod 15:7, as the breath of the divine anger with which the wicked are punished. God could have punished the Egyptians directly without any intermediary (χωρίς τούτων).

There then appears the personified justice of God, the Δίκη, set in chiastic parallel with "your power". It is a typical Greek personification, well known to the tragedians, which has already appeared in 1:8 and which will reappear in 14:31b. This is the punitive justice of God, well known to the LXX: cf. Exod 21:20; Lev 26:25; Deut 32:41-43; Philo often uses this image (cf. *Conf.* 118; *Mut.* 194; *Ios.* 48).

11:20d: Measure, Number, Weight

The principle drawn from the reflection in these verses is set out in v. 20d: "yet you have ordered everything by measure, number, and weight". This stich acquires a special importance, placed, as it is, in the centre of a precise literary structure (11:15-12:2).[6]

In our text, particular importance is acquired by the verb διέταξας which has πάντα as its object. The aorist, along with a formula of proverbial character, has a gnomic value and refers not so much to the divine punishment by means of the animals decreed by God and described in the previous verses as rather to the action of God considered in its entirety, to an orderly and precise arrangement by God. This is actually the value of διατάσσω.

The text of 11:20d intends to say that there is no need for God to destroy God's creatures to punish them, even if they are guilty. There is not even any need for a new creation and even less for a destruction of an apocalyptic character. Nor is there any need for God to do violence to God's creation. In fact, the creation itself has already been ordered by God with "measure, number, and weight". No divine action, therefore, can be considered arbitrary. Punishment is sent by God through the creation according to the principle already set out in 11:15-16. This is a basic idea which governs the whole of the third part of Wisdom, an idea expressed here by a formula that is typically Greek (see below).

11:21-23: God between Power and Mercy

Verse 21 introduces a new argument of a positive nature. It is always (πάντοτε) possible for God to prevail with force, and no one can resist God, the sovereign of all things. The text recalls what was already said in 11:17a. The initial γάρ accounts for the entire argument of 11:17-20 and governs everything that follows up to 12:1:[7] the Lord punished the animal-worshippers with a punishment that was actually less than they deserved because God acts "with measure, number, and weight". God is indeed almighty (vv. 21-22), but God is also merciful (v. 23).

---

6 Cf. Genzmer, "Pondere, numero, mensura"; des Places, "Un emprunt de la Sagesse"; Pesce, "Numero, peso e misura"; Nielsen, "La Misura divina". For the use of the formula in Augustine, cf. La Bonnardière, *Le livre de la Sagesse*, 90-98.

7 Cf. Cornely, *Commentarius*, 422-423; Heinisch, *Weisheit*, 230.

The thought in v. 21 is biblical; cf. Isa 40:12-14 and Esth LXX C 2:30 (4:17b, z); in the NT, Rom 9:19. The verb ἰσχύω, with God as subject and referring to the salvation of the people, is used in Isa 10:21; 50:2; 59:1; Jer 20:11; Esth LXX C 30 (4:17z). Here, ἰσχύω, together with the adverb μεγάλως, acquires the sense of "having the power to act with force", a force which, in the light of the texts mentioned, acquires a physical, almost military value.

The formula κράτει βραχίονός σου is not found as such in the LXX (cf. Jer 21:5 ἐν βραχίονι κραταιῷ). We recall, however, that the terms in Wisdom which use the root κρατ- always refer to sovereignty.[8] Here, therefore, God is being imagined as a very powerful king. The rhetorical question τίς ἀντιστήσεται with reference to God is relatively frequent in the LXX: it is found in Ps 75:8 LXX [76:8 MT] and Nah 1:6, in both cases in relation to the divine wrath which no one can resist; cf. also Job 41:3; Jer 27:44 LXX [50:44 MT] = 30:13 LXX [49:13 MT]. Here the response is implicit: no one can oppose the power of the Lord.[9]

The poetic comparison of v. 22, which recalls what was said in 11:17b concerning the creation, is referring to Isa 40:15 which, in the MT, presents various textual problems. Wisdom is perhaps reading it in a version different from that of the LXX. However, it is this whole section of Wisdom which is inspired by Isa 40:12-15.[10] Before the divine omnipotence, the whole world is only a speck of dust on the scales, a drop of morning dew which vanishes at sunrise. However, our sage is not intending to undervalue the creation. Rather, he is emphasizing the gap between God and creatures while, at the same time, the text highlights the extraordinary care of the Lord for creation. God could destroy it with astonishing ease, but God does not wish to do so. Paradoxically, that goes too for the very enemies of God. In fact, God's historic action with regard to Israel's enemies has demonstrated this (cf. 11:17-20).

God's power is not destructive. Precisely because God is omnipotent, God is merciful to all and pardons, giving time for μετάνοια, for conversion (v. 23; cf. Philo, *Spec.* 1.308). Here, the sense is clear: if God deployed God's omnipotence (v. 21), the world would be destroyed (v. 22); but, even in the face of sin, God causes mercy to prevail. God's omnipotence lies in this: man does not encounter in God an implacable sovereign but a God who loves (11:24c, 26).

We note again that ἐλεέω returns only in Wis 15:1, once again in the context of the forgiveness of sins. Object of the divine mercy are not only the Israelites but all people (πάντας). The idea of a mercy of God for all people is not unknown to the Bible (cf. Sir 18:13). The γάρ of v. 24, placed at the centre of this section (see above), offers a more solid basis for it: love.

11:24a: You Love Everything!

Verses 24-25 go deeper into the description of the divine mercy: God loves τὰ ὄντα πάντα, "everything that exists", that is, the entire creation which he has called into existence (cf. καλέω in v. 25b). In fact, the immediate context (cf. 11:17b, 24bc) refers to the creation and revolves around the notion of totality (cf. the comment on 12:1).

---

8 Cf. Gilbert, *La critique des dieux*, 182.

9 Clement of Rome (1 Clem. 27:5; 28:2) cites this verse, the most ancient patristic citation of Wisdom known to us.

10 Cf. Gilbert, "Les raisons de la modération divine", 245-247. Scarpat (*Sapienza*, 2:424) observes that the highly rare πλάστιγξ could be a Platonic reminiscence (*Tim.* 63b). For the connection ῥανὶς δρόσου, it too a *hapax* of the LXX, cf. Euripides, *Andr.* 228.

The initial γάρ accounts for the statements of the previous verses. It is noticeable how, in the three stichs that make up v. 24, God's disposition is expressed with three verbs in the present (two indicatives and a participle: ἀγαπᾷς, οὐδὲν βδελύσσῃ, οὐδὲ μισῶν τι) which express the lasting nature of this divine disposition. Verse 24bc follows with two verbs in the aorist which, instead, underline God's creative work (ἐποίησας, κατεσκεύασας).

11:24b–12:1: Still on the Universal Love of God

The text of 24bc, two stichs in synonymous parallelism, completes the idea expressed in 24a: God does not despise his creatures (βδελύσσω, a term typical of the LXX, present only here in the book), nor, still less, can God hate them.[11] For the combined use of ποιέω and κατασκευάζω, cf. Wis 9:1-2 and Isa 43:7; 45:7.

11:25

Verse 25 passes from the idea of creation to that of the preservation of what has been created, given that it too is the act of the divine will (cf. the use of θέλω). In v. 25b, the use of διατηρέω stands out: in its sense of "preserve", it is foreign to classical Greek (cf. Wis 16:26). The idea here is that God is acting continually in creation to keep it in the existence for which God created it (Wis 1:14).

11:26: God, a Sovereign Friend of Life

The Lord appears here as a δέσποτα φιλόψυχος, that is, a "sovereign friend of life" (v. 26) who, precisely for this reason, "spares" (φείδει) everything (πάντων, to be taken as a neuter; cf. the subsequent σά). The text is recalling v. 23a with which it is in close parallelism. However, whereas, in v. 23, God's love is motivated by God's omnipotence, here, instead, it is motivated by the fact that everything belongs to God: "all are yours" (cf. a similar idea in 1 Chr 29:11, 14, 16).

The verb φείδομαι appears in the story of Jonah (Jonah 4:11: God spares Nineveh), but here things go further: God spares everything that exists. As for the substantive δεσπότης, which in itself indicates the master of the house and, more generally, the absolute sovereign, it is used for God in Wis 6:7; 8:3; 13:3, and 9. Philo's text of *Mut.* 18-19 is interesting: the reference to God as δεσπότης (instead of θεός) is reserved for the foolish. Within this perspective, one can say that, for our sage too, God is certainly an absolute sovereign but does not behave as a tyrant, rather as a "friend of life", a "master" who has the greatest respect for the life of those who are under him.

12:1: The Spirit of God Is in All Things

The γάρ of 12:1 offers a further reason for the divine mercy. The divine πνεῦμα is called ἄφθαρτος, a clear reference to the ἀφθαρσία of Wis 2:24. Being incorruptible, the spirit of God is the guarantee of incorruptibility and so is opposed to the destructive spirit evoked in 11:20. The divine spirit is ἐν πᾶσιν, "in all things". The neuter sense is suggested by the use of the particle τι in v. 24b (cf. also 25a) which prevents restricting ἐν πᾶσιν to human beings alone.

12:2: The Pedagogic Activity of God

Verse 12:2 which opens with διό constitutes a conclusion to the whole section. The text of 2a refers in retrospect to the Egyptians whom God corrects κατ' ὀλίγον, "in steps". Our sage is certainly thinking here of the ten plagues of the exodus. The text of 12:2b forms an application of the principle expressed in 11:15-16 and illustrated further in 11:17-20: the Egyptians are warned (νουθετέω; cf. 11:10; 12:26) in order to remind them of their sins or – better – remind them of what it is with which they have sinned. For the theme of memory in the book of Wisdom, cf. further in connection with 16:6, 11.

---

11 Augustine comments: "naturarum enim, non vitiorum conditor, mala quae odit ipse non fecit" (*Tract. Ev. Jo.* 110.6; PL 35, 1924).

At the same time, by introducing the theme of faith (12:2c), our sage is preparing a new development. In fact, the text of 12:2c returns to the theme of conversion, but with something new: the Egyptians too can have the possibility of repentance. "Forsaking evil" (12c) is thus the first objective of the divine correction. Arousing faith even in the one who rejects it is the peak of the divine activity described at the end of this first section of the digression on the "philanthropy" of God. This is also the first occurrence of πιστέυω in the book (cf. textual notes). Faith thus means forsaking evil but also recognising in history the presence of that "Lord" who is being invoked in the second person and with the use of the vocative κύριε at the close of the first part of the digression.

Diachronic Analysis

The mention of the ἑρπετὰ καὶ κνώδαλα (cf. above) makes it clear that here we have a common subject of the direct polemic against Egyptian zoolatry which was not confined to Jewish literature but also involved the Greek philosophers (cf. in connection with Wis 15:14-19). 11:15-16

As for the observation in v. 16, the text of Exod 7:4-5 LXX is certainly one of the passages which inspired it: καὶ ἐπιβαλῶ τὴν χεῖρά μου ἐπ' Αἴγυπτον ... σὺν ἐκδικήσει μεγάλῃ καὶ γνώσονται πάντες. In Wis 11:16, it is not a matter of the recognition of the powerful presence of God but of the acknowledgement that "punishment comes from the thing by means of which one sins". Here lies the originality of our author at the very moment when he shows himself faithful to the biblical text. For our sage, in fact, God does not seek revenge or punishment as such but the acknowledgement by sinners of their sin.

The principle expressed in v. 16 is not, as could seem at first sight, the so-called *lex talionis* (cf. Exod 21:23-25; Lev 24:19-20; Deut 19:21). It is not to do with punishing sins committed against other people but against God, even if, according to our sage, the punishment of the guilty takes place in this world. It is not even a question of applying the principle of retribution well known to the wisdom of Israel: "whoever digs a ditch will fall into it" (Prov 26,27 LXX; Qoh 10:8), even if this aspect is not wholly absent from the horizon of our text. There is no proportion here between sin and penalty. In fact, the sin committed is much greater than the punishment undergone. It is not even a matter of applying the rabbinic principle of "measure for measure" (cf. Matt 7:2) or of invoking a kind of earthly retribution: the punishment is actually much less severe than the sin would require (cf. Wis 12:25). The reason is explained in the following verses and lies in God's mercy. The sole relationship is that between the means employed with which to sin and the means which God uses for punishment, that is, the elements of the cosmos, here, the more contemptible animals, reptiles and insects. It is precisely on this aspect – the elements of the cosmos – that the attention of our sage is focused.[12]

---

12 Cf. Gilbert, *La filantropia di Dio*, 7-11, and, above all, "On est puni par où l'on pêche", *passim*. Gilbert recalls the text of T. Gad 5:10, as a possible parallel to Wis 11:16 (cf. already Larcher, *Etudes*, 131-132), even if T. Gad lacks the similarity between sin and punishment. The same thing can be seen in Philo, *Mos.* 1.98.

11:17b: Unformed Matter The expression ἐξ ἀμόρφου ὕλης (11:17b) is of a clear philosophical stamp and is found, as such, for the first time, in a commentary on the *Timaeus* by Posidonius of Apameia: "Posidonius states instead that the substance of the universe is also undetermined and unformed matter (ὕλην ἄποιον καὶ ἄμορφον)".[13] Only the doxographs attribute this idea to Plato. In the quotation from Posidonius, ἄμορφον does not indicate so much an eternal matter as rather the undetermined substratum belonging to every being. In the Stoic conception, the world comes about when the divinity gives "form" to matter which is considered to be eternal and uncreated. This idea is taken up by Philo who utilizes the combination ἄμορφος ὕλη in *Spec.* 1.328, but within a Jewish conception which allows for a creator quite distinct from his creature and in clear reference to Genesis 1.

However, these philosophical conceptions seem foreign to our author,[14] who is thinking, rather, of the primordial chaos described in Gen 1:2, seeking to paraphrase the Genesis text through the use of terms borrowed from Platonic philosophy, though without adopting its premises.[15] If ἄμορφον is being used by Wisdom in Posidonius' sense, our sage was probably intending to make his public understand that God is able at pleasure to exercise God's own creative activity by making use of the common substratum, that is, the nature underlying beings, which already contains in itself, potentially, the four elements of the cosmos. On the basis of Wis 1:14, it could be said that the ἄμορφος ὕλη is the unformed matter – it too created by God – which is brought into being (εἰς τὸ εἶναι) by God's "hand". As has been said, this divine hand is, παντοδύναμος, it includes within itself all the divine powers. Contrary to Philo's conception, therefore, God is directly the creator of everything and nothing escapes God's omnipotence, not even the primordial chaos.[16]

11:17c–19 In the description of the monsters in 11:17c-19, our sage has in mind perhaps mythological monsters such as the chimera, vomiting flames, the basilisk, with its mortal gaze, or the gorgon with its petrifying stare,[17] or even the biblical Leviathan (Job 40:25–41:26). However, God does not make use of such mythological creatures, if they were really to exist. Philo has a similar idea (cf. *Mos.* 1.109-110): God could have destroyed Egypt by making recourse to the ferocious beasts there. As in Wisdom, among these are listed bears and lions.

---

13 Cf. Edelstein, Louis – Kidd, I.G., *Posidonius*, 1. *The Fragments* (Cambridge: University Press 1972) 99, frag. 92; cf. Larcher, *Etudes*, 117.

14 Cf. a discussion on the positions of the most ancient commentators in Grimm, *Weisheit*, 212.

15 Cf. a long discussion in Larcher, *Sagesse*, 3:677-680; Gilbert, "La relecture de la Genèse", 416-418; Scarpat, *Sapienza*, 2:375-381. Scarpat concludes that "the author of *Wis.* perhaps did not think that Plato had compromised himself to the point of some commentators suspecting him of believing in eternal matter!" (p. 379). The proof of these statements lies already in the fact that the Church Fathers did not experience any embarrassment with the text of Wis 11:17.

16 "By contrast with Philo, our author never shows himself involved in philosophical speculations or in violent harmonisations between Greek philosophy and the doctrine of the fathers. He is interested only in the doctrine of the fathers which he was able to expound with terms drawn from Greek poetry and philosophy"; Scarpat, *Sapienza*, 2:381.

17 For the details, cf. Gilbert, *La filantropia di Dio*, 15-16.

The expression "measure, number, and weight" is juridical in character and of clear Greek provenance, a school-phrase known from the time of Plato (cf. *Leg.* 6.757b 3-4; cf. *Phileb.* 55 and *Resp.* 10.602d; Xenophon, *Mem.* 1.1.9) and present also in the tragedians (cf. Sophocles, frag. 432 Pearson; Euripides, *Phoen.* 541-542). Only Plato gives the three terms in the order offered by Wisdom and, in the *Leges*, in the same case also (the dative). However, the Platonic context is rather different. In the *Leges*, Plato is referring to equality in the state, and not to God. It is difficult to think, therefore, of direct dependence on Plato. In our case, it would be possible to hold that Wisdom is taking over the Platonic triad in the light of Isa 40:12 LXX, which refers to God the creator with no dissimilar vocabulary (cf. εμέτρησεν, σταθμῷ). 11:20d

Jewish literature makes use of this formula to express the moderation, harmony and order of the divine action even towards the wicked (cf. 4 Ezra 4:36-37; T. Naph. 2:3): God's measure is precisely mercy, sometimes even under the appearance of severity. Philo makes an interesting use of the triad in *Somn.* 2:192-194 against Protagoras who considers humanity the measure of all things whereas only God is.[18]

In vv. 21-23, as has been seen, our sage's argument is basically biblical. In v. 22, in particular, in describing the divine figure, he takes his basis and inspiration in texts of Scripture (see above). That appears still more significant after the references to "unformed matter" and to "measure, number, and weight" which were inspired, rather, by Greek culture. Yet, the link expressed here between divine omnipotence and mercy is a theme that is not very frequent in the OT/HB (cf. Num 14:17-20; Ps 61:12-13 LXX [62:12-13 MT]), but which begins to be used more in more recent texts such as Sir 2:18 and Sir 18:1-14, though here the emphasis is on human weakness more than on divine mercy. Also, the expression παρορᾷς ἁμαρτήματα (23b) is unique in Scripture (cf. a similar idea in Acts 17:30). The "closing of his eyes to the sins of people" is an action which God performs εἰς μετάνοιαν, in view of their repentance. The idea is close to the thesis of the book of Jonah. 11:21-23

11:24a: God Loves His Creatures

This is the only case in the LXX where ἀγαπάω is employed with reference to God's universal love for his creatures; it is also the only OT text where it is stated that love is the reason why God created the world, thus emphasizing God's personal involvement with the creation (cf. also the comment on 12:24b-c). In the Greek world too, there are no texts comparable to this. Plato affirms the goodness of the Demiurge, described as ἀγαθὸς, but not as lover of the creation even if it shares his goodness (cf. *Tim.* 29de; Philo, *Opif.* 21). Even without the verb "love", the theme had already been announced in Wis 1:13; for the NT, see John 3:16. Here we have a love that excludes disdain, which arises from the power of the Sovereign of the universe, from God's will (cf. ἠθέλησας, v. 25a) from God's compassion towards God's own creatures ("all things are yours", cf. 1 Chr 29:11, 14, 16). It is a love which seeks conversion (cf. 11:23b) and which manifests itself as the desire to educate people, even through trials, so that they may be converted and believe "in you, O Lord" (cf. 12:2c); it is a love founded on the will of God (11:25a) which excludes every form of hatred or disdain (11:24bc). Again, one

18 Cf. a summary of Philo's thought in Nielsen, "La misura divina", 11-16.

observes the universal dimension typical of Alexandrian Judaism. The mercy and patience which characterise the God of Israel (Exod 34:6-7) are extended to all people, indeed, to the whole of creation (cf., in the NT, Acts 17:30; Rom 2:4-6; 2 Pet 3:9).[19]

11:24bc–25 In 11:24bc, our sage is distancing himself from the use which the biblical texts make of μισέω. According to a widespread biblical conception, God can hate and does in fact do so, even if God's "hate" is one which is actually expressing the divine rejection of evil. The passages are very numerous.[20] Even in Wis 12:4, the only other occurrence of μισέω in the book, it is affirmed that God hates someone. Wis 11:24 is thus the only passage in the OT which explicitly excludes God's hatred towards any of God's creatures. This highlights the difference between our author's thought and the language of Qumran; cf. 1QS I, 4 ["...to hate everything which he (God) abhors..."]; I, 10 ["to hate all the sons of darkness, each according to his guilt..."]; cf. also CD II, 15.

The reference to the creation as the result of God's call is already known partly to the OT/HB (Isa 41:4; 48:13), more clearly to Philo (especially *Spec.* 4.187) and the NT (cf. Rom 4:17). The chiastic structure of v. 25 combines the will of God who wishes to preserve creation (25aβ) with the divine call into existence (25bα), which guarantees this preservation. In dense and concise language, v. 25 expresses an idea which is only hinted at in the Hebrew Bible (cf. Ps 103:29 LXX [104:29 MT]).

12:1 The idea that the spirit of God is in all things could have been influenced by a text such as Ps 103:28-30 LXX [104:28-30 MT] (cf. Job 34:14 and Isa 63:11-14), but is certainly to be seen against a Stoic background. Though without ever falling into the pantheistic viewpoint typical of the Stoics, our author affirms here the presence of God in the world through God's spirit which is, as it were, personified (cf. Wis 1:7) and becomes the source of life for every being since it dwells in them. The πνεῦμα, therefore, cannot be limited to the concept of the soul which God breathes into everyone (cf. 15:11).[21]

From this point of view, it also appears clear that the theme of totality, which runs through the whole pericope (cf. the terms with the root παν- in 11:20d and then 11:21, 23, 24, 26; and 12:2) also arises from the influence of Stoicism and thus reinforces that universalist vision which characterises diaspora Judaism.

---

19 For an "ecological" reading of Wis 11:24, cf. Zenger, "Du liebst alles was ist". For the patristic rereadings of this verse, v., cf. Larcher, *Sagesse*, 2:694; De Carlo, "Ami, infatti, gli esistenti tutti", 423-432.

20 Cf. Michel, Otto, μισέω, *TDNT* 4:683-694.

21 *Contra* Scarpat (*Sapienza*, 2:430-431) who reads "in all" as masculine, claiming that otherwise the phrase acquires an openly Stoic sense which would be unacceptable for an Alexandrian Jew. Cf. van Imschoot, "Sagesse et Esprit"; Gilbert, "L'Esprit Saint". Verbeke's study, *L'évolution de la doctrine du pneuma*, 223-236, shows similarities and differences with the Stoic concept of the *pneuma*; Verbeke notes that Wisdom lacks an explicit philosophical elaboration of this concept.

Wis 12:3-21:
Divine Moderation towards the Canaanites and Its Lessons

3 The ancient inhabitants of your holy land
4 you hated because of the hateful practices which they committed
– [practices] of magic and sacrilegious rites of initiation,
5 slayers, that is, of their sons without mercy,
feasts of human flesh and blood where entrails are consumed,
initiates amidst an orgy,
6 murderous parents of defenceless life –,
you wished to destroy at the hand of our fathers,
7 that they might receive a colony worthy of the children of God,
that land which, for you, is the most precious of all.
8 But even these you spared, because they were humans,
sending wasps against them as vanguard of your army,
to destroy them little by little.
9 It was not impossible for you to deliver the wicked into the hands of the just in battle,
or to annihilate them at one stroke with fearful beasts or with your relentless word.
10 By judging gradually, however, you gave time for conversion,
although not unaware that their race is wicked,
innate their iniquity,
and that their way of reasoning would never be changed.
11 For they are a race cursed from the beginning,
and it was not through fear of anyone that you allowed their offences to go unpunished.

12 Who, then, will dare to say to you: what have you done?
Or who can resist your sentence?
Or who can accuse you of the destruction of nations which you yourself have created?
Or who can appoint himself as defender of unjust people in order to placate you?
13 For there is no other God beside you who cares for all,
to whom you have to show that you have not acted unjustly;
14 nor is there a king or ruler who can stand up to you
on behalf of those you have punished.
15 Being just, you govern the universe with justice.
To condemn one who does not deserve punishment
you consider unworthy of your power.
16 For your might is the foundation of justice
and your dominion over everyone causes you to spare everyone.

17 You show your might to those who do not believe in the fullness of your power
and you punish the arrogance of those who experience it.
18 But you, the master of might, judge with clemency,
and govern us with great leniency:
for when you wish, power is at your disposal.

19 With such works you have taught your people
that the just must be friend of humanity,
and you have given your sons the good hope
that you grant them (the possibility) of repenting for their sins.
20 For if the nation hostile to your children, those destined to death,
you have punished with such care and leniency,
giving them time and opportunity to abandon their wickedness,
21 with how much more care have you judged your sons,
with whose fathers you concluded pacts and covenants of good promises?

Notes on the Text and Translation

v. 4. With Scarpat (*Sapienza*, 2:456), we read ἔργα in 4b as attribute to ἔχθιστα, removing the comma after πράσσειν and understanding the subject αὐτούς. The "erstwhile inhabitants" are the object of μισήσας in 12:3.

v. 5. In 5b, *σπλαγχνοφάγον, joined to the accusative with θοῖναν, is read in this form by some minuscules (cf. Ziegler) and is to be translated with: "a feast which eats entrails", by hypallage: "a feast where entrails are eaten". Outside Wisdom, σπλαγχνοφάγος is attested only by Ps. Plutarch, *De fluv.* 5.3 = 282b in relation to the eagle devouring Prometheus' liver. All the other textual witnesses, and especially the greater codices, read σπλαγχνοφάγων, joining it thus with the following ἀνθρωπίνων σαρκῶν, which seems, however, to be a *lectio facilior*: "feasts of those who devour human entrails and blood"; cf. Scarpat, *Sapienza*, 2:460; cf. the reading of Lat: *comestores viscerum* which refers, rather, to the σπλαγχνοφάγους, a reading preferred by Cornely, Goodrick, and Gilbert. If we accept Ziegler's text (σπλαγχνοφάγον), the plural genitive σαρκῶν is to be connected instead with the following καὶ αἵματος: "a feast of human flesh and blood where entrails are eaten". However, the construction of the whole stich appears difficult.
5c also offers many variants, attesting the embarrassment of the versions. If we read Ziegler's text, ἐκ μέσου μύστας θιάσου, the passage is to be understood with reference to the initiates (μύσται) seen right in the middle of their rites (ἐκ μέσου θιάσου). θίασος is present in the LXX only in Jer 16:5 and is a term which, in itself, refers in the first place to Dionysian orgies or feasts. A different solution is suggested by Fichtner, followed by Reese and Winston, who read καὶ αἵματος ἐκ μέσου μύστας θιάσου as a double hyperbaton: "and initiates on the occasion of a bloody feast".

v. 10. The term ἔμφυτος is to be understood in the sense of "connatural", "congenital". In Greek usage, it is found in philosophical language, in the discussions relating to innate or acquired virtue (cf. Philo's distinction in *Spec.* 3.138).
In 10d, the expression ὅτι οὐ μὴ ἀλλαγῇ depends on οὐκ ἀγνοῶν. The double negative is intensive. The aorist of ἀλλάσσω is to be understood intransitively: "(not

unaware) that their way of reasoning (λογισμός; cf. comment on 1:3, 5) would never be changed".

v. 12. In 12d, the term κατάστασις has a juridical sense. *Hapax* in Wisdom, it indicates the "re-establishment" of order that has been disturbed. The expression εἰς κατάστασίν σοι is to be understood in the sense of "in order to re-establish something that concerns you", that is, in order to "please you" (cf. Scarpat, *Sapienza*, 2:435-437).
The term ἔδικος (in the LXX only in 4 Macc 15:29 and Sir 30:6) oscillates between the meanings of "defender" and "avenger". The first meaning seems better adapted to the context: before God, no one can think of appointing himself as defender of the unjust. With good arguments, Scarpat considers ἔδικος a reference to a class of officials known in the Roman world as *defensores civitatis*, magistrates who looked after the interests of a city in international disputes (cf. *Sapienza*, 2:433-434).

v. 15. The Latin translation of 15b ("ipsum quoque qui non debet puniri condemnas") created theological problems for the Fathers, appearing almost blasphemous; cf. Larcher, *Sagesse*, 2:725.

v. 17. Ziegler's text reads ἰσχὺν γὰρ ἐνδείκνυσαι: "you show (deploy) your might"; but there are different variants to ἐνδείκνυσαι, a sign of the difficulties which it already created for the scribes (cf. Ziegler; cf. Kuhn who reads ἐκδείκνυται with ms 755). This is followed by the participle ἀπιστούμενος, "the unbelieving". In many codices, it is preceded by the article (ὁ) which is missing, however, in B, *O*, S^{c}, V and some minuscules. A introduces with ὅτι. If the article were original, it would be possible to follow Larcher's reading: "show (ἐκδείκνυται) the might of the one who does not believe in the fullness of your power". In this case, the expression would be referring to someone powerful on earth who shows his might in the very moment when he is not believed to be really powerful. Our sage would actually be thinking of Pharaoh. In fact, it is sufficient to take ἀπιστούμενος as passive (cf. Scarpat, *Sapienza*, 2:473) and to understand it with reference to God: "you, being made the object of doubt". The stich can then be read thus: "you show (your) might to the unbelieving in the fullness of your power (namely, in your perfect power)".
The second part of the verse is equally difficult: ἐξελέγχεις is recorded by almost all the witnesses (cf. S* which corrects to ἐξελέγχεται) and has the sense of "convict" (in the punitive sense) or "confound" (the composite ἐξελέγχω appears otherwise in the LXX only in 4 Macc 2:13 and Mal 4:3, always in the active voice). The object is τὸ θράσος which indicates insolence, arrogance or audacity (in the LXX, mostly in 1-3 Macc). The verb ἐξελέγχω normally governs the accusative (ἐξελέγχω τινά τι) or the participle; the construction ἐξελέγχω τι ἔν τινι seems peculiar to Wisdom. Here, the verb is referring to ἐν τοῖς εἴδοσιν: "those who know / who recognise" (but also in this case there are different variants: cf. Ziegler) or, better still, as in Wis 15:2: "those who attempt". So we have: "those who have experienced (understood: your power), you convict (hold culpable) of audacity". That is: God condemns the audacity of those who, like the Egyptians of the exodus, have experienced the first signs of his power but have not known how to react to it.

v. 19. For the term εὔελπις (cf. Prov 19:18; 3 Macc 2:33), cf. the discussion in Scarpat, *Sapienza*, 2:438-440, and, by the same author, "La 'buona speranza' in Sap 12:19". He notes how our sage chose this word to avoid the combination ἀγαθὴ ἐλπίς, typical of the mystery cults, and to emphasise that hope is not the achievement of the initiate after a cathartic process but a free gift of God. Philo portrays the εὔελπις man in *Abr.* 8-9, 11, 14, and 16; only the εὔελπις is a true man (cf. *Det.* 139 [on Gen 4:8]), because he believes in God.
The expression ὅτι διδοῖς ἐπὶ ἁμαρτήμασιν μετάνοιαν can be understood in an objective sense, with ἐπί having local value in a transferred sense: you have rendered

your children full of good hopes; these consist in the fact "that you give for sins [the possibility of] conversion"; cf. Scarpat, *Sapienza*, 2:442-443.

v. 20. The middle form ἐτιμωρήσω (second per. sg. aorist), more usual in the LXX with the sense of "take revenge, inflict a punishment", is attested by A and chosen by the editors (in Wis 18:8a *all* manuscripts read this form); the other codices (B, S, V, and many minuscules) have the active form ἐτιμωρήσας.
The rare term *δίεσις, literally "letting go", here to be understood as "tolerance" or "gentleness", is recorded only by codex S; the other codices (B, O, Sy, Arab) have instead (μετὰ ...) δεήσεως "(with ...) prayer, supplication", which is perhaps a *lectio facilior* (Grimm refers to Isa 65:2: God would pray the pagans also to convert just as he had done Israel). Scarpat (*Sapienza*, 2:476-78) proposes reading, along with some minor codices and with Lat (*tu liberasti*), διέσωσας, "you have saved" (Engel, "Weisheit", 2147). The text would thus be alluding to a salvific action of God for the enemies of the people of Israel also.

v. 21. The term ἀκρίβεια (Sir 16:25; 42:4; Dan 7:16) has the sense of "care", "precision", with a tone that, in this context, is certainly positive: "care, concern", while it can also indicate the "severity" of the judge (Philo, *Decal.* 71; *Post.* 133).

Synchronic Analysis

12:3-7: The Sins of the Canaanites

From his reflection on the divine moderation with regard to the Egyptians, our author passes on to reflect on the divine moderation towards the Canaanites against whom Israel had to fight over and over again and whose story seems at first sight to be far from the benevolent disposition of God, which will not be recalled until v. 8. Moreover, our sage feels he must justify Israel's possession of the land although the Canaanites had not done them any wrong. This is a not infrequent theme in Jewish apologetic.[22]

In v. 3, the Canaanites are introduced with a periphrasis as "the ancient inhabitants of your holy land". This expression refers to the belonging of the land to God and is already present (but without the "your") in Zech 2:16; 2 Macc 1:7; but Jer 2:7; Ezek 38:16; and Joel 1:6 speak of "my" land. Wis 9:8 has already mentioned the holiness of Jerusalem.

Verses 4-6 describe the abominable practices attributed to the Canaanites preceded by "you hate" (μισήσας) (v. 4a). The idea that God hates someone is biblical; cf. Hos 9:15; Mal 1:3; and especially Ps 5:6. This is another example of how our sage returns to traditional language just after he has described the mercy of God who does not hate any of God's creatures (cf. 11:24c). However, this mercy does not exclude God's ability to "hate", that is, to reject thoroughly, human sin "the hateful practices" committed by people (ἐπὶ τῷ ἔχθιστα πράσσειν indicates the reason for the divine hatred).

Magic and Mysteries

In v. 4b, the first Canaanite practice to be condemned is magic (ἔργα φαρμακειῶν), condemned already in Deut 18:10-11; cf. the magicians mentioned in Exod 7:11 (συνεκάλεσεν ... τοὺς φαρμακούς); for φαρμακεῖαι understood as magical and idolatrous works, cf. Gal 5:20; Rev 21:8; 22:15. As we shall see in connection with Wis 17:7-10, our sage has more in mind the magicians of his own time. With the expression τελεταὶ ἀνόσιοι, the book of Wisdom is taking aim at mystery rites (cf.

---

22 Cf. Winston, *Wisdom*, 238.

14:15, 23), even if in 1 Kgs 15:12 τελεταί (cf. Hos 4:14; Deut 23:18) indicates, rather, sacred prostitution. However, in Philo, the pair τελετὰς καὶ μυστήρια are understood precisely as mystery rites (cf. *Spec.* 1.319). For our sage, these are sacrilegious (ἀνόσιοι) practices. Thus, the charges directed at the Canaanites are really aiming at the two aspects which constitute the worst characteristics of Hellenised Egypt for our sage: the practice of magic and the mystery cults.

Verse 5, joined to the previous one by the construction τε ... καί, recalls the practice of infanticide, an accusation made by various biblical texts: Deut 12:31; Jer 19:5; Ezek 16:20-21; cf., again, Jer 7:31-32; Isa 57:5; 2 Kgs 17:31.

Verse 6a completes the charges, alluding to those parents who themselves (αὐθέντας) became murderers of defenceless lives.

Verse 6b expresses the divine decision to destroy the Canaanites which our sage keeps back to the end of the seventh colon after 4a. This divine will, which here is carried out by the hand of "our fathers", namely, the Israelites who arrived in Canaan from Egypt (cf. Exod 23:31), is expressed in many biblical texts: cf. Exod 23:23 and, with the same verb ἀπόλλυμι, in Num 33:52; Deut 2:12; 7:23-24; etc.; our sage is taking his inspiration from deuteronomistic theology (cf. Josh 6:17-21).

Verse 7 expresses the purpose of the divine action with regard to the Canaanites: the land of Israel ("the land which, for you, is the most precious of all") can thus receive "a colony worthy of the children of God". In Wisdom, ἄξιος has always a theological value (cf. 1:16; 3:5; 6:16; 9:12 etc.). For the theme of the Israelites as "sons" or "children", cf. Exod 4:22-23; Hos 11:1; and the comment on Wis 9:4.

12:8-11: God Punishes, but with Moderation

In this second part of the section, 12:3-11, our sage returns to the basic principle animating the whole digression: despite human behaviour, God punishes the guilty with moderation, "little by little " (8c and 10a: cf. Exod 23:29-33), inasmuch as the Canaanites too are human beings. Thus, there is a resumption of the principle set out in v. 2 concerning a gradual, because therapeutic, punishment (κατ' ὀλίγον).

The punishment which the Canaanites receive "little by little" is accounted for in 8b with the memory of the sending of the wasps which the LXX mentions in Exod 23:28 and Deut 7:20 (with the plural σφηκίαι); cf. Josh 24:12 (in the singular: σφηκία). The form σφῆκες, from the singular *σφῆξ, is *hapax* of the LXX. The verb ἐξολεθρεύω ("destroy completely") is, on the other hand, typical of the LXX (cf. Deut 7:17) and is probably an elaboration of the text of Exod 23:30, with reference to the progressive expulsion of the Canaanites from the land.

Verse 9, which opens with a litotes ("it was not impossible for you"), is a response to whomever considers such an intervention by God pathetic. The expression which closes the verse, ὑφ' ἓν ἐκτρῖψαι, is to be understood as "annihilate at one stroke". God could have done it, that is, destroyed all the Canaanites altogether in one single blow, whether by delivering the ungodly into the hands of the just in the course of a battle, or by giving them over as prey to fearful beasts (cf. 11:18), or by God's relentless word (cf. 18:15; for ἀπότομος cf. 5:22c).

A second principle stated in 10a returns to what was said in 11:23 and 12:2: God wishes to give the guilty the possibility (τόπος) of converting, changing their life. We find μετάνοια again, a term which already appeared in 11:23 and which will return later in 12:9 (cf. the notes to 11:23), one of the key themes of this digression.

The text of 10b opens with another litotes (οὐκ ἀγνοῶν) with concessive ("although not unaware") or causative ("since not unaware") value. God knows that the Canaanites' origin (γένεσις) is wicked, that is, that the parents transmit to their children all their inclination to evil (10b); God is not unaware that their iniquity is innate (10c) and that their way of reasoning (10d) will never change.

With a probable reference to the cursing of Ham/Canaan in Gen 9:25, v. 11 considers this curse not as the cause of the divine hatred but as a further proof of the wickedness of the Canaanites. Yet, despite knowing all this, God has not denied them the possibility of repentance; that is the sense of v. 11b. The imperfect ἐδίδους refers to the past when God granted the Canaanites, too, the possibility of conversion. That is not to be considered an expression of weakness in God; cf. the use of εὐλάβεσθαι [τινα] in the sense of "having fear of someone".

12:12: The Problem of God's Freedom

Placed at the centre of the section, 12:3-18 (see above), v. 12 is constructed on four rhetorical questions introduced by a fourfold interrogative τίς (τίς γὰρ ... ἐποίησας; ἢ τίς ... τίς δέ ... ἢ τίς). The response is negative: no one can resist God or judge God's actions (τί ἐποίησας;). The first stich takes up Job 9:12b LXX almost to the letter (cf. Isa 45:9 and Dan 4:35 MT + Th). The second stich, on the other hand, takes up Job 9:19b.[23] This is the only use of κρίμα ("decree, sentence") in Wisdom. The term, however, is frequent in the LXX where it generally translates the Hebrew מִשְׁפט. The divine sentence leaves no room for any possible opposition of a juridical character (cf. Job 9:32).

The third stich states that no one can judge God for the destruction of the nations which he himself has created. There is, however, a certain tension with what was affirmed at the beginning of the book: that God does not wish the destruction (ἀπώλεια) of the living (1:13). In the light of the textual notes, the fourth stich is to be understood thus: who can appoint himself as defending advocate (ἔδκικος) to placate your wrath (εἰς κατάστασίν σοι) in the face of wicked people? God, therefore, is supreme justice, and whoever is accused by God has no need of a defender.

12:13-15: The Justice of God

In this first part of the section represented by Wis 12:13-18, which revolves around the principle expressed in 16a, our sage begins to respond to the questions of v. 12. There is no other God beside God (cf. Isa 44:6, 8) – the text addresses itself to God with "you" – who cares for (μέλει)[24] all, or, better for "everyone", if one thinks of the context which is referring to human beings. The second part of v. 13 is clearer: God has no need to offer proofs for God's actions nor does there exist another God, superior to God, with whom God has to compare himself. No monarch or ruler of this world (v. 14) can stand up to God (ἀντοφθαλμέω: literally "look in the eyes", a rare and refined verb, not attested before Polybius, 200–120 BCE), accusing God of having judged unjustly the people God has punished.

Verse 15 completes the author's thought by elaborating on another theme well known to Scripture, the universal justice of God (15a), which excludes being able to condemn one who does not deserve it (15bc). The author is thus respond-

---

23 Opinions diverge on whether Wis 12:12 depends or not on the LXX text of Job: Larcher is favourable (*Etudes*, 96-97), Skehan against, "Studies in Israelite Poetry and Wisdom", 200-203.

24 Μέλω referring to the divinity is frequent in Greek usage but also in the LXX; cf. Scarpat, *Sapienza*, 2:471.

ing to a possible objection: could not God's omnipotence result in arbitrary behaviour? The text of 15c refers to the divine power (δύναμις; cf. 1:3; 7:25) understood as the foundation of God's justice.

12:16-18: Justice and the Exercise of the Divine Power

Verse 16a expresses a new principle: God's power, better here, God's might (ἰσχύς), is the principle, that is, the foundation (ἀρχή) of God's justice. This is in contrast with the monarchs of the earth just mentioned (v. 14) because God possesses power in all its fullness and so can exercise justice in a perfectly objective way without any need to affirm God's own power. This is the antithesis of the declaration of the ungodly: "let our might be the law of justice" (2:11). For them, justice consists in the law of the strongest and in disdain for the weak (2:11b); for God, instead, justice is carried out in clemency towards the guilty. This completes the response to the objection implied by v. 15. It is what is being said in 16b, returning to an idea already expressed in 11:23 and 26, and, through the repetition of πάντων, underlining the totality of God's acting. In the first case, πάντων δεσπόζειν could refer to the universe over which God exercises power; in the second case, πάντων φείδεσθαι refers to the people whom God spares (cf. the same idea expressed in 11:26 and 12:8). Therefore, God's omnipotence is not only source of justice but a power which God uses on behalf of people, a power that is joined with divine clemency (cf. Sir 16:11). Indirectly, our sage is offering a lesson to the powerful of this world: real power has to be closely bound up with justice.[25]

Verse 17 is problematic. Following our proposal in the textual notes, v. 17a would be tackling the problem of unbelief and affirming that God shows his might to those who do not believe in his perfect power. This is exactly the case with Pharaoh (cf. Exod 9:13-16). Verse 17b also refers to the Egyptians rather than the Canaanites and highlights their obstinacy. Although they experienced God's power, they persevered in their θράσος, in that arrogance typical of the pagans (cf. 1 Macc 4:32). It is obstinacy like this which causes ever heavier plagues and punishments.

Verse 18 completes (σὺ δέ) the argument of v. 17 (γάρ): God is not only omnipotent, God is the master of might. The verse is constructed in a thematic inclusion on this idea: "you, the master of might / judge us with clemency // and govern us with great leniency (clemency) / because you are the master of might". Furthermore, the expression διοικεῖς ἡμᾶς is a thematic reprise of τὰ πάντα διέπεις (v. 15a).

The emphasis in v. 18a falls on the expression ἐν ἐπιεικείᾳ κρίνεις. For ἐπιείκεια, cf. Wis 2:19; the term indicates a virtue belonging to the just and scorned by the ungodly who act in the name of brute force.

The second stich adds the theme of the leniency (φειδώ only here, in Esth B 6 [3:13^{f}] and Pss. Sol. 5:13; but cf. φείδομαι in Wis 11:26; 12:8, 16) with which God governs "us" (note the use of the first-person plural, ἡμᾶς). For διοικέω, cf. 8:1 where we pointed out a possible Stoic background. Here, however, it is not a matter of the idea of a lenient, clement, providential dominion of God over the world but of the conviction that this rule of God is *for us*, that is, for the Israelites. From consideration of what happened to the Canaanites (and the Egyptians), our sage draws a lesson for Israel: God's clemency towards the pagans demonstrates *a fortiori* God's clemency towards God's people.

---

25 Cf. the reflections of Vílchez Líndez, *Sapienza*, 391-393.

The third stich (18c) returns to the initial idea expressed in this verse. God can use his power when he wishes. Already in 11:25, our sage had referred, again with the verb, θέλω, to the will of God. Even if expressed in anthropomorphic form, the idea is really profound: God is omnipotent; God can use his power at his pleasure but makes use of it only in the name of God's goodness.

12:19-21: God's Action as a Lesson for God's People

Verses 19-21 draw a first conclusion from the reflection of God's way of acting towards the Egyptians and the Canaanites: the just person must be φιλάνθρωπος, a friend of humanity. The author is thus replying to a question that has remained in suspense: why did God leave time for the repentance of the Canaanites even knowing that they would not repent (cf. v. 20)? It all happened for the instruction of the Israelites (v. 22)! Here we touch on one of the aspects of midrashic literature that is typical of Wisdom: what is said in Scripture always has a pedagogic aspect for Israel. The Canaanites were indeed destroyed by God, but, for our sage, even this does not contrast with God's mercy. In fact, the destruction of the Canaanites was the result of a precise choice: not to accept the possibility of conversion; and this is also a lesson for Israel. Even in the case of the Canaanites, God does not deny the absolute value of the free moral choice to which everyone is called. This is why our sage chooses not to mention an exodus theme which for him perhaps would have been problematic: the hardening of Pharaoh's heart.

12:19: The Just Must Be a Friend of People

The great works of God (διὰ τῶν τοιούτων ἔργων) become a lesson for the present. The verb διδάσκω (cf. 7:22) points in this direction. We observe how, in 19b, the mention of "your people" passes almost naturally into that of the "just person" (cf. 10:15a) who is such if he or she possesses the same dispositions as God (cf. Lev 11:45; 19:2; Matt 5:48). Thus, the just person must show to people the same φιλανθρωπία which God shows to us (cf. 1:6; 7:23). The attitude of love and compassion which God shows towards creation (11:24-12:1) now becomes that of people in their relations with their neighbours.

Not only that: "your people", a just people, are also a people of "children". This takes up here a theme anticipated in 2:18a and expressed in 9:7b. It will then be taken up again in this pericope, in 12:21a, and, later, in 16:10, 26; 18:4, 13 (cf. the comment on 9:7). Being children means having experienced the favours of a God who offers his pardon and so urges God's people to conversion. We then notice that, in relation to the people considered children of God, there begins to appear in the following verse (Wis 12:20) a set of themes which we shall find again in the subsequent chapters: on the one hand, there are children, the Israelites, on the other, the enemies who oppress them. The same themes appear once again in Wis 15:14 where there is the only recurrence of the expression "your people" within the second digression (Wis 13-15).

These "children" are made εὐέλπιδες (cf. Prov 19:18; 3Macc 2:33), that is, full of good hope, hope bound up both with faith in God (cf. above), according to an idea known also to Philo, as well as with the possibility of conversion after sins which is then the object of "good hope". Here again, we find the theme of μετάνοια already present in 12:10 in connection with the Canaanites. Even if discreetly, Wisdom is alluding also to the sins of the Israelites and underlining that, *a fortiori* for them, there is time for conversion, a conversion which arises from the benevolent attitude of God and which, here significantly, is linked to the kindness to their neighbour to which, in their turn, people are called to live. Conversion is, therefore, not a human work but one of God (cf. Jer 38:18b LXX [31:18b MT] for a similar idea).

Verse 20 is the protasis of a conditional clause with comparative value. The verb is in the aorist (ἐτιμωρήσω) since the reference is to the past. The apodosis is in v. 21. The argument is of the type *a minore ad maius*. God punished (ἐτιμωρήσω) the enemies of the children mentioned in v. 20a, who deserved death,[26] both the Canaanites and the Egyptians, but with care and leniency, God gave them "time and opportunity" to abandon their evil. The term προσοχή is rare (cf. 6:18c) and can be understood as "care, concern"; for δίεσις, cf. the textual notes. 12:20-21: Divine Leniency

The apodosis of v. 21 contains the consequences for the people of Israel of God's acting in this way. If God has treated our enemies so leniently, then all the more us! The attitude is thinking of God's attitude to Israel in the course of the whole of their journey through the desert. The verb κρίνω alludes discreetly to the sins committed by Israel who, however, were not judged severely by God on account of the promises made to the ancestors (21b): ὅρκους καὶ συνθήκας; ὅρκος ("oath") is frequent in the LXX; συνθήκη ("contract, agreement"), on the other hand, is employed only in a secular sense; the LXX prefers διαθήκη (cf. Wis 18:22). The theme of the oath linked to the covenant with the fathers is Deuteronomic; cf. Deut 4:31; 7:12; 8:18; 9:5; 31:20; Judg 2:1; Ps 88:4 LXX [89:4 MT]. The Israelites become the recipients of "good promises". Here, our sage uses another *hapax* of the LXX (*ὑπόσχεσις) which in itself has a secular meaning but is frequent in Philo in a religious sense (cf. *Leg.* 3.203).

Diachronic Analysis

In connection with God's hatred for the Canaanites (v. 4a), our sage cannot deny the fact that in the biblical texts the Canaanites are presented as destroyed by God himself. However, the aorist participle μισήσας does not indicate a constant divine attitude but a punctual action by God directed against specific cultic and moral practices (cf. Deut 12:31: τὰ βδελύγματα ἃ κύριος ἐμίσησεν). Nevertheless, a certain tension remains between mercy and hate, a sign that the idea of a God who wishes the salvation of all and who loves all his creatures has not yet eliminated that of judgement. However, as we shall see in connection with 12:8-11, it is necessary to keep in mind also the theme of the freedom of God as against that of people. 12:3-7

The charge in 5b, relating to the feasts where entrails and human flesh are consumed, is not found in Scripture and is very probably borrowed from Greek tragedy and certainly a little exaggerated.[27] In addition to the references to the texts of the tragedies, there is almost certainly an allusion here to the practice of omophagy, which is attested in the Dionysiac rites but a practice no longer in use in Hellenised Egypt where the Dionysiac rites enjoyed widespread support at this time. Verse 5 returns still more clearly to participation in the mystery cults (cf. the textual notes). The term μύστης refers to the initiates in these cults (cf. 8:4a)

---

26 Larcher, *Sagesse*, 3:732, observes that here there could be a possible reference to Simonides (*Anth. Pal.* 10.105). For the Greek poet, however, all are destined for death whereas, for our sage, the enemies, who are also so destined, can also be saved.

27 Cf. Gill, "The Greek Sources"; Winston, *Wisdom*, 239-240.

while θίασος suggests that they are Dionysiac cults.[28] Our author raises the tone of the polemic by creating accusations without real foundation. It seems clear that he is concerned with the seductive potential of the Dionysiac cults for young Alexandrian Jews.[29]

The charge that they consumed the flesh of their own children calls to mind the story narrated by Herodotus, *Hist.* 1.119, which recalls the feast (θοίνα) where the King of the Medes, Astyages, allows Harpagus to eat the flesh of his son without knowing it. In the Bible, one remembers the sacrifice of the King of Moab's son in 2 Kgs 3:27.

The idea of ἀποικία, "colony", introduced in v. 7, is employed by Philo both in connection with the departure from Egypt (*Mos.* 1.71) and with the settlement of the Hebrews in Canaan (*Mos.* 1.163, 222, 236; 2.246), but also in connection with death understood as an escape to a better land (*Praem.* 16, 80; *Fug.* 36). Like Philo, the book of Wisdom uses ἀποικία in the sense of a "settlement" in the land and not in the sense of place of "exile" as in the LXX. Here, in Wisdom, ἀποικία serves to claim the legitimacy of the possession of the holy land, given by God to Israel as a "colony", taken away from inhabitants that were wicked and devoted to idolatry. The whole passage has a strong apologetic tone if read in the context of Alexandrian Judaism.

12:8-11 The statement of principle contained in 12:8a ("you spared them because they were humans") betrays a typical Stoic reflection on the dignity of people and their connatural link with God.[30] According to the Stoics, God takes care of people and exists for human benefit (cf. *SVF* II, 323 frag. 1116; II, 325 frag. 1118). Between the divine world and people there exists an ἀγαθὴν καὶ φιλάνθρωπον κοινωνίαν δαιμόνων καὶ ἀνθρώπων (a good and philanthropic relationship between gods and humans) (*SVF* II, 327 frag. 1129). There is no similar motivation in the Bible. Our sage is thinking not so much of innate human weakness as of human nature as such. God loves people precisely as people.

Verse 6 mentioned the divine decision to destroy the Canaanites "at the hand of our fathers", a possibility which is excluded here in v. 8. We are simultaneously faced with a reading of a midrashic character in which our sage intends to exonerate Israel from the charge of having destroyed the Canaanites: there was no battle.

Verses 10-11 have a very harsh tone, not rare in the book. Our author seems almost to wish to set aside his reflections on the universal love of God to emphasise God's severity towards a people considered radically and irremediably wicked.[31] We should not be surprised at our sage's harshness: the condemnation of the Canaanites is the fruit not of the action of a God who has forgotten his mercy but of people who, in their freedom, have rejected it.

12:12 Leaning on the authority of the book of Job, this text highlights a theological problem: that of God's freedom. In the face of the evil that seems to triumph, the

---

28 Cf. Liddell Scott, *sub voce.*

29 "We are far from authentic Dionysianism here"; Baslez, "The Author of Wisdom", 44.

30 Thus Grimm, *Weisheit,* 223, but without citing any text; Reese, *Hellenistic Influence*, 76, thinks rather of the Hellenistic ideal of kingship.

31 Grimm, *Weisheit*, 224, already observes that we cannot speak of predestination so much as of divine foresight ("Nicht eine Vorher*bestimmung* zum Bösen, sondern ein Vorher*wissen*...").

text urges us not to be scandalized nor to minimize the mercy of God, considering it as impunity (ἄδεια; cf. 11b) for sinners. Not only is God's action not subject to human judgement, but even God's severity (cf. the last two stichs) does not contradict divine mercy. After the repeated warnings offered by God, the destruction of the ungodly is to be understood as the fruit of their own obstinacy.

The ideas in vv. 13-14 are biblical. However, our sage emphasizes the theme of the divine omnipotence (which is, nevertheless, a benevolent omnipotence; cf. 13a) and underlines that God cannot be subjected to any human judgment. 12:13-15

In v. 15, the novelty of Wisdom lies in the connecting of the justice of God with the divine governing of the world (τὰ πάντα) and, at the same time, with God's omnipotence (cf. also 16b). On διέπω and on its possible Greek echoes, cf. Wis 9:3, the only other occurrence of the verb in the LXX. The verb is used in this sense in the pseudo-Aristotelian treatise *De mundo* (399a 18) which is influenced by Stoicism.

The term ἐπιείκεια, which appears in 18a and was often used for earthly rulers, refers to God himself in texts like 2 Macc 2:22; 10:4; Bar 2:27; Dan 3:42 and acquires a tone of moderation, clemency and gentleness which tempers the use of authority and naked justice. In Let. Aris. 207-208, it appears in connection with the φιλανθρωπία required of people (cf. Let. Aris. 192). God does not punish in proportion to sins or according to God's greatness and power but acts with clemency, and with this ἐπιεικεία guides everyone. God is absolute master of might and so can allow himself to temper the use of power with moderation and clemency. 12:16-18

The text of Wis 12:19 is an excellent example of fusion between a typically Hellenistic idea (φιλανθρωπία) and the biblical faith in a God ready to offer the possibility of conversion. Being "your people" does not only create a situation of privilege but opens Israel to the responsibility of becoming friend to the whole of humanity. This statement is not free from a polemical reference to those accusations of μισανθρωπία directed against the Jews which circulated in the environment of Alexandria which was not entirely exempt from a certain anti-Semitism.[32] Our sage wishes to underline that being people of God does not mean being enemies of the human race but rather being the champions of that φιλανθρωπία which the Hellenistic world considered one of the highest "political" virtues.[33] 12:19

Wis 12:22-27: God's Mercy and Zoolatry

22 While you correct us, you punish our enemies in a thousand ways,
so that we may reflect upon your goodness when we judge,
and, when we are judged, may obtain (your) mercy.

---

32 We recall the well-known phrase of Tacitus, that the Jews have *adversus omnes hostile odium* (*Hist.* 5.5.1); Philo too tackles this theme: cf. *Spec.* 2.167, where he defends Israel from the accusation of ἀπανθρωπία. Cf. Schürer, *History*, 3:150-176; Feldman, *Jew and Gentile*, 125-131.

33 Cf. Let. Aris. *208*: the king must become φιλάνθρωπος, as God is (Philo, *Abr.* 137).

23 This is also why those who lived unjustly
with foolish behaviour
you began to torment with their own abominations.
24 For they strayed a long way along the path of error
holding as gods the most vile among repellent animals,
deceived like senseless youths.
25 Therefore, as though to children without reason,
you sent a chastisement to make fools of them.
26 But those whom trivial rebukes did not cause to reflect
will experience a chastisement worthy of God.
27 For they who in their suffering complained against those beings
whom they held as gods, with which they were being punished,
seeing the one whom they had earlier refused to see,
acknowledged him as the true God.
Therefore, there fell upon them the supreme condemnation.

Notes on the Text and Translation

v. 22. In 22a, the *textus receptus* reads ἐν μυριότητι, which Kuhn (1931), Vanhoye, and Gilbert propose emending to ἐν μετριότητι; *μυριότης is *hapax totius graecitatis* and contradicts 22bc (but also 11:9). Moreover, the whole context of this first digression speaks of the moderation of God towards the wicked and not of the punishments that God hands out. Gilbert adds the existence of parallelism between 12:19 and 12:22 which would confirm the soundness of this conjecture. However, the reading ἐν μυριότητι could be referring to Prov 3:11-12, where παιδεύω occurs in parallel with μαστιγόω, though with reference to the "child" loved by God. By contrast with this passage, Wisdom would be emphasising that the enemies are punished in much heavier ways than the "child". Also, the probable reference to Ps 31:10 LXX [32:10 MT] suggests reading ἐν μυριότητι with the *textus receptus*; the Psalm speaks of μάστιγες τοῦ ἁμαρτωλοῦ, as opposed to the ἔλεος, that surrounds those hoping for the Lord. Thus, a contrast is created between the educative attitude of God towards Israel and the "lash" which falls on their enemies in a thousand different ways. This does not at all contradict what our sage affirmed earlier, that God knows how to use clemency with the wicked as well.

v. 23. Codices B-S* and 543 prefer the reading ἀδίκους, which would thus introduce another category, "the unjust". It is preferable to read with the majority of witnesses the adverb ἀδίκως which modifies the verb βιώσαντας (note the aorist which refers to past facts; ἀδίκους, on the other hand, would require a present participle). For the difference which Wisdom makes between ζωή and βίος cf. Larcher, *Etudes*, 294-295. In 23b, the aorist ἐβασάνισας has an inchoative value: "you began to torment them".

v. 24. In 24b, the majority of the codices read τὰ καὶ ἐν ζῴοις τῶν ἐχθρῶν ἄτιμα: "those animals that are abhorred by the enemies", but the text is not clear. Who are these enemies? Those of the Israelites or those of the Egyptians? The construction can be better understood as "the most abhorred among the hateful animals", thus taking τῶν ἐχθρῶν in an adjectival sense. Ἐχθρός has its normal sense of "hateful". On the basis of some minuscules, Ziegler and Rahlfs read ἐν ζῴοις τῶν αἰσχρῶν ἄτιμα, which offers a slightly more linear text: "the viler among the repugnant animals". In both cases, the text remains uncertain.

Synchronic Analysis

12:22: Divine Correction

In v. 22, our author draws a second conclusion from his reflection on divine moderation while preparing at the same time for the digression which follows (13-15). Although Israel are the chosen people, they must not make themselves implacable judges of the pagans, even if there is a difference in the way God judges each of them (the case if we read μυριότητι in v. 22a). For Israel, the divine correction is that of a parent whereas for the pagans it is that of a strict judge (see the same theme in Wis 11:10). The covenant between God and Israel does not exempt the Israelites nor does it place them in a situation where they can look down on the pagans from on high with a claim to superiority; cf. the "philanthropy" mentioned in v. 19b. For the idea of imitating God in judging, cf., in the NT, Matt 7:1-2; 18:33; Jas 2:13.

If, on the other hand, we accept the conjecture ἐν μετριότητι, the text would be saying, along the lines of 11:9, that where God's enemies too are concerned, God corrects them "with measure". In this way, God's clemency becomes an invitation to reflect on divine goodness towards sinners when we have to judge others (22b) and, at the same time, a source of hope when it is our turn to be judged (22c). This would be a reprise of the ideas expressed in v. 19 with which v. 22 seems to be constructed in parallel (cf. above).

12:23-25: The Obstinacy of the Egyptians

The Egyptians' answer to this divine moderation was one of obstinacy. Verses 23-27, in particular, return to the subject of the worship of animals which was condemned in 11:15-16. This theme will be taken up again in 15:14-19 at the end of the second digression. The plagues sent on the Egyptians, who were guilty of worshipping created beings, were trivial punishments in comparison with the decisive punishment, the "supreme condemnation" which awaited them, death. God's justice is exercised in its harshest form only in the face of the tenacious and systematic rejection of divine mercy.

Verse 23 introduces the Egyptians with a periphrasis: "those who lived unjustly with foolish behaviour". For the notion of ἀφροσύνη, cf. 10:8c. According to the principle laid down in 11:5 and 11:15-16, they were tormented with what they had used to sin, in this case, the βδελύγματα, the "abominations". The term βδέλυγμα appears in Exod 8:22 in relation to the animal sacrifices of the Israelites, which were an abomination to the Egyptians, and in the sapiential literature with the ethico-religious nuance of what is an abomination to the Lord (cf. Prov 10:20; 11:22; 15:8, 9; etc.). Here it more probably indicates the animals considered such by Lev 11:41-43 which the Egyptians worshipped (cf. βδέλυγμα in Lev 11:41.42).

In v. 24, there is a hyperbolic statement that the Egyptians strayed a long way (again, πλανάω; cf. 2:21; 5:6). In fact, they held as gods (cf. 13:3) vile and repugnant animals and were taken in like little children. This is why (v. 25), God's judgement is εἰς ἐμπαιγμόν, a judgement which makes fools of them (25b). For ἐμπαιγμός in the sense of "derision", cf. Sir 27:28; Ezek 22:4; and especially Isa 66:4, on which our author seems to depend, and, again, in the Exodus context, Exod 10:2 LXX (ὅσα ἐμπέπαιχα τοῖς Αἰγυπτίοις). Note also, in a polemical context against magicians, the presence of ἐμπαίγματα in Wis 17:7.

12:26-27: The Supreme Punishment

Verse 26 marks the passage to a new and more serious type of sin: obstinacy. From God's point of view, the wonders wrought in Egypt are παίγνια ἐπιτιμήσεως, "trivial rebukes" (cf. the wordplay on παι- "child": ὡς παισίν "like children" – εἰς ἐμπαιγμόν "a (childish) chastisement"; παιγνίοις ἐπιτιμήσεως "trivial rebukes"). Since these corrections did not prove to be sufficient, the Egyptians will experience "a chastisement worthy of God": death. Our sage is alluding to the death of the firstborn and the drowning of the Egyptians in the Red Sea. However, the general import of the verse causes the reader to think more generally of that eternal punishment of the ungodly which was already anticipated in Wisdom 5.

Verse 27 is difficult in construction. In the light of 12:17, one could detect the description of a twofold progression in the Egyptians' sin: first, the zoolatry, then, the obstinacy in this sin despite their having experienced the divine action.

The condemnation (*καταδίκη) thus "falls" (for ἐπερχόμαι used in this sense, cf. 16:4-5; 17:5; 19:13) on the guilty. The use of the aorist alludes to the events of the exodus (cf. above). With this harshest of statements, our sage is preparing for the digression which follows and which will serve to explain the gravity of the sin of idolatry while at the same time alluding to the eternal death of the idolaters.

Diachronic Analysis

12:25 The Egyptians are compared in 12:24c and 25a to children (νηπίων δίκην ἀφρόνων – ὡς παισὶν ἀλογίστοις), as in Wis 15:14, a comparison known also to Philo (*Mos.* 1.102; *Decal.* 69). It is possible that this comparison with the νήπια is borrowed from a Greek proverb known since Homer (ῥεχθὲν δέ τε νήπιος ἔγνω; cf. *Il.* 17.32; 20.198) and Hesiod (*Op.* 218).

12:27 The text of v. 27 alludes to those passages in Exodus where Pharaoh, following the plagues, is forced to acknowledge the presence of God (cf. Exod 8:24; 9:27-28; 10:16, 24), and yet each time, his heart is hardened. Thus, the recognition of the "true God" does not go hand in hand with a path of conversion and abandoning of idols. The two verbs employed here (ὁράω and ἐπιγινώσκω) are technical. With θεός as object, ὁράω does not seem to be attested before the Hellenistic period.[34]

Summary of Wis 11:15–12:27

In conclusion, we can affirm with Schmitt that "letzlich erklärt sich aber die breite Behandlung dieser Thematik aus der hellenistischen Welt in der der Vf. lebt: Philanthrope Ideale, irenische Tendenzen und eine humanisierte Rechtsauffassung des ptolemaischen Diadochenstaates, die vor allem in einer verbesserten und aufgeklärten Strafjustiz zum Ausdruck kommt, lieferten die Anstöße zu einer eingehenden Auseinandersetzung mit diesem heiklen Gegenstand [Finally, however, the broad treatment of this topic is to be explained from the Hellenistic world in which the author lived: philanthropic ideals, irenic tendencies and a

34 Cf. Winston, *Wisdom*, 246.

humanised view of the Ptolemaic State of the Diadochi, which comes to expression especially in an improved and enlightened criminal justice system, provided the stimulus for a detailed debate with this awkward subject]".[35]

This digression intends to highlight the value of the divine pedagogy both for the wicked (11:16) and for the Israelites (12:22a). In fact, God punishes in order to educate both of them, to teach everyone the value of conversion (11:23b; 12:10a, 19d, 20c) and faith in God (12:2, 27c). The aim of this pedagogy is that people recognize their deepest motivations: in particular, God's love for all his creatures (cf. 12:8). It is precisely this reflection on the power and omnipotence of God (11:17-20; 12:16-18) that leads our sage to see in this same divine power the root of God's mercy rather than of God's severity. People will draw the lesson from this divine moderation (12:19) by becoming "philanthropists" in their turn.

Thus, the Jews of Alexandria are being presented with the face of a God who cares for everyone, who is clement even towards the wicked, very different from the despotic image offered by contemporary sovereigns. At the same time, the superiority of Israel, the people of God, is revealed by an equal mercy shown to all, even to their most obstinate enemies. The harsh tone of the digression's conclusion should not surprise us: on the one hand, in reading the biblical account, our author can do no less than see there its conclusion with the death of the Egyptians and the Canaanites, something highlighted by many texts of Scripture. On the other hand, the digression oscillates between the desire to defend God's absolute freedom (12:12) and that of not denying human freedom which, draws down ruin with its own hands (cf. 1:13-16). Moreover, Egyptians and Canaanites become (see especially 12:3-7) images of those Jews who – at the time of writing – were allowing themselves to be seduced by idolatry, magic and mystery cults, thus drawing down on themselves that eternal death of which the ruin of the ancient Egyptians and Canaanites is a first and distant symbol.

35 Schmitt, *Weisheit*, 55.

Wis 13–15: The Criticism of Idolatry

The previous digression, on philanthropy and divine moderation towards human sins, closed nevertheless with a very harsh treatment of the sins of the Egyptians (12:23-27). This consisted in the worship of idols and, particularly, the cult of animals. At this point, our sage introduces a more extensive reflection on the activities of the idolaters considered in antithesis to the goodness of God towards all God's creatures. In the same way, in the first part of the book, the description of the plans of the wicked (Wisdom 2) was set in antithesis to the divine plan of eternal salvation for the just (Wisdom 3-4). The ample space given to this criticism reveals the importance for Wisdom of the condemnation of idolatry within the religious context of Alexandria. As well as an antithesis to the reflection on divine moderation, chapters 13-15 are placed as a kind of antithesis to chapters 7-10 which were devoted to wisdom.[1]

Wisdom 13-15 criticises idolatry by means of an interesting thematic progression: in the initial section (13:1-9), the attention is focused on a form of piety of a philosophical character. From 13:10 to 15:13, we have a long section devoted to the criticism of idolatrous cults properly so called. The final section (15:14-19) is devoted to the unreserved condemnation of the worst form of idolatry, Egyptian zoolatry. In this way, our sage is able to justify the reason for the harshness of the plagues that fell upon the Egyptians described in the subsequent chapters (16-19). It is no coincidence that in the second antithesis, in 16:1-4, the midrash on the exodus will resume with a reference to the plagues caused by the vilest of animals.

This tripartite plan is known to Philo (cf. *Decal.* 52-54) and, at the same time, seems to be a common pattern which Hellenistic Jewish apologetic created on Stoic models. Although taking his cue from well-known biblical themes relating to idolatry, our sage follows, rather, both Hellenistic and Hellenistic-Jewish models, thus displaying all his originality.[2]

The purpose of the digression is clear: this full-scale attack against idolatry points out the reason for the punishment of the Egyptians which is one of the big themes of the seven antitheses of Wisdom 11-19. At the same time, this attack constitutes an attempt at encouraging those Alexandrian Jews who were daily tempted precisely by the worship of these idols and so also has an apologetic purpose. Our author had in mind many biblical texts which condemn idolatry: the Decalogue, in Exod 20:3-5 (Deut 5:7-9) and also Deut 4:16-19, but, above all, Isa 44:9-20; Jer 7:16-8:3; Bel; and Ps 113:12-16 LXX [115:4-8 MT]. In these three chapters, the book of Wisdom undoubtedly offers us the most extensive and structured biblical reflection on this subject, combining, according to the book's typical style, biblical and Jewish themes with elements belonging to Hellenistic culture.

---

1 Alonso Schökel, *Sabiduría*, 164.

2 For the details, cf. Winston, *Wisdom* 248-249.

Literary Structure of Wis 13-15

The literary structure of Wisdom 13-15 has been dealt with in detail by M. Gilbert in his volume *La critique des dieux* so it is not necessary for us to discuss it again. However, we shall present its main points with a few variations.[3] Wis 13:1-9

These three chapters can easily be subdivided into three large literary units. The first comprises Wis 13:1-9 (μάταιοι μέν: v. 1a) where our sage is thinking of the religion of the philosophers. This receives lighter criticism.

The inclusion ἴσχυσαν εἰδέναι (1b, 9a) guarantees the unity of the section. At the same time, the verb εἰδέναι, together with ἐπέγνωσαν in 1c, forms a clear link with the previous section (cf. the same two verbs in 12:27c). The γάρ of v. 1 links 13:1-9 with the preceding material; the μέν, on the other hand, links up with a δέ which is reached only in v. 10.

Verses 1-2 form a first, small section with six stichs. In v. 1, God is evoked in three different ways (θεόν, τὸν ὄντα, τὸν τεχνίτην). Verse 2 provides a contrast (ἀλλά), with a false way of knowing him. Introducing the themes of beauty and power, vv. 3-5 are linked with one another by the repetition of καλλονῇ – καλλονῆς (3a and 5a) and by the play on γενεσιάρχης (3b) and γενεσιουργός (5b). In verses 6-9, on the other hand, ἀλλ' ὅμως introduces the author's judgment on the piety of the philosphers (cf. a quasi-*inclusio*: τάχα in 6b and τάχιον in 9c).

A much larger unit, 13:10-15:13 (ταλαίπωροι δέ: 13:10) criticises the idolatrous cults proper with greater severity. A series of indications of a literary character permits further subdivisions of the pericope, highlighting a precise internal structure of a concentric character. Wis 13:10-15:13

A. Wis 13:10-19: the making of idols of gold, silver, stone, and wood. We note the *inclusio* among νεκροῖς (13:10a), ἔργα χειρῶν (13:10b), χειρὸς ἔργον (13:10e), ἐργασίας in 13:12a, which are recalled by ἐργασίας ... χειρῶν (13:19a) and χερσὶν (13:19b); cf. τὸ νεκρόν in v. 18; cf. also ζῴων ... ἄχρηστον (v. 10) and ζωῆς ... χρῆσθαι (v. 18). 13:10-19

Within this section, v. 10 constitutes the introduction to the new theme; cf. the contrast between μάταιοι μέν in 13:1 and ταλαίπωροι δέ in 13:10. The concern here is with idols made by human hands. Actually, v. 10 serves to introduce the entire section of 13:10-15:13. In 14:8-10, we find the same theme again, expounded in similar words: on the one hand, the idolaters ἐκάλεσαν θεοὺς ἔργα χειρῶν ἀνθρώπων, on the other τὸ χειροποίητον ... θεὸς ὠνομάσθη (14:8ab).

In their turn, vv. 11-15 make up a small literary unit while a third unit seems to be identifiable in 13:16-19.

B. Wis 14:1-10: invocation of God, reference to the history of salvation, and transition to the following section. The term πορισμός forms a hook-word with the previous section (13:19a; 14:2a). Verse 1, in particular, opens with the expression τις πάλιν which, as in 13:11 (εἰ δὲ καί τις), marks the beginning of an example. Verse 1 forms a redactional link with the previous text through repetition of the theme of prayer (cf. 13:17-19). At the same time, vv. 1-3a introduce a new theme: the sailor who calls on an idol to obtain a safe journey, not understanding that it 14:1-10

---

3 Cf. Gilbert, *La critique des dieux*, especially 245-257; cf., also, Wright, "The Structure", 180-182.

is Providence that is guiding him. These verses are constructed by means of a fine thematic progression.

In vv. 3b-7, we find the exposition proper of the theme: a new reflection on navigation (3bc), followed by a general theological statement (4a) and by a further argument relating to navigation (4b); a second general theological statement (5a), followed by another reference to navigation (5bc) and by a clear reference to the history of salvation (6); the text closes with a third theological statement (7).

Verses 8-10 constitute a general conclusion concerning the idols which takes up the initial theme of 14:1 and anticipates the theme of the section that follows.

The whole pericope contains some significant repetitions: the theme of "wood" (ξύλον) in 1b, 5b, and 7 to which is added the double mention of σχεδία (5b, 6b); the theme of "saving" (σῴζειν in 4a; διεσώθησαν in 5c); human skill (τέχνη) (4b) contrasted with wisdom, the "craftsman" (τεχνῖτις; 2b), a "working" "wisdom" which appears again in v. 5a. One also observes the theme of "piloting" or "steering": the divine providence which pilots the ship (διακυβερνᾷ; 3a) and the hand of God which pilots the ark (τῇ σῇ κυβερνηθεῖσα χειρί; 6c). Finally, the text of 14:8 recalls the beginning of the entire section in 13:10; cf. χειροποίητον → ἔργα χειρῶν; ἠργάζετο → χειρὸς ἔργον; θεὸς ὠνομάσθη → ἐκάλεσαν θεούς; the idol is a human artefact which claims to take the place of God!

14:11-31 C. Wis 14:11-31. The section opens with a διὰ τοῦτο which connects it to the preceding material but which, at the same time, opens a new development on the "idols of the pagans": "it is for the reason that follows that there will be a visitation on the idols because...". Εἴδωλα is a term that governs the whole section (cf. 14:11a, 12a, 27a, 29a, and 30b). This word always appears otherwise, six times, in the plural in Wisdom in contradistinction to the object of the idolatry / of worship in 13:11-19 and 14:1-10, which appears in the singular. Verses 11-14 constitute a first part of this section, with a concentric structure which places v. 12 at the heart of the pericope[4]: the punishment announced in 14:10 becomes the "visitation" proclaimed in 14:11a. A second διὰ τοῦτο closes this introductory section (14:11-14) which announces the judgement on the idols (11) and wishes to examine their origin (ἀρχή; 14:12-14).

A second pericope comprises vv. 15-21. Here, our sage offers two examples of the origin of idolatry: the family cult (vv. 15-16a) and, more extensively, the imperial cult (16b-21). We can see internal repetition: εἰκόνα ποιήσας (15b), ἄνθρωπον (15c) and εἰκόνα ... ἐποίησαν (17c), ἄνθρωπον (20b). It is clear that the theological statement of 21c constitutes the literary centre of the whole digression, 13-15. We note in particular that v. 21 (which alludes to the "unutterable name") occurs at the centre of the literary structure of 14:11-31 and of the whole digression of Wisdom 13-15.[5]

The εἶτα of 22a (cf. 16a) introduces a new pericope (22-31) devoted to the consequences of idolatry (cf. the inverted reprise of μυστήρια καὶ τελετάς 15d in 23a: τελετὰς ἢ ... μυστήρια). In vv. 23-26, there is a list of twenty-two vices, the number of letters in the Hebrew alphabet. The first vice in the list begins with the letter τ (τεκνοφόνους τελετάς), the last with α, ἀσέλγεια, a kind of alphabet

4 For the details, cf. Bizzeti, *Libro della Sapienza*, 92-93.

5 Cf. Gilbert, *La critique*, 254-255 and 257.

in reverse which perhaps is intended to indicate a total overturning of values. The twelfth vice, at the centre of the section, is φθορά, the complete ruin of every moral value. Verses 27-31 take up the theme of θρησκεία ("worship"; 27a), already introduced previously (14:16b, 18a.); cf. παντὸς ... κακοῦ (27b) which takes up in a quasi-*inclusio* τὰ τοσαῦτα κακά of 14:22c; cf. also ἀρχή in 12a and 27b.

Verse 31 is clearly separate from the new beginning in 15:1 (σὺ δέ, ὁ θεὸς ἡμῶν) in which the tone of prayer recurs, as in 14:1-10 (ἡ δὲ σή, πάτερ, πρόνοια 14,3a). The term τῶν ἁμαρτανόντων (31b) can be considered as a hook-word with the following pericope (ἁμαρτῶμεν; 15:2a).

B'. Wis 15:1-6.[6] 15:1 is the opening of a new section (σὺ δέ...) in which the 15:1-6
author once again addresses the divine "you" (1a, 2ab, 3ab) together with the "we" of Israel. The "we" remains in v. 4 but the mention of God disappears. In this way, the pericope can be subdivided into two sections: 15:1-3, which highlights the faithfulness of God but also that of Israel, against the background of the Sinai covenant; 15:4-6, where the "we" of Israel is contrasted with the idolaters. Both at the literary and thematic levels, Wis 15:1-6 manifests a link with 8:1-4 (cf. 8:1b and 15:1a; 8:2c and 15:6a; 8:4a and 15:3a). If the sage is in love with the wisdom that governs the universe, the idolater is in love with a statue!

This pericope also reveals strong connections with the previous text of 14:1-10: cf. the return of the divine "you"; the mention of human δικαιοσύνη (14:7; 15:3); and the repetition of ὄρεξις (14:2; 15:5) and of δράω (14:10; 15:6). The reference to salvation-history and the theme of divine providence brings these two pericopes still closer.

The conclusion of v. 6 (οἱ σεβόμενοι) will find an echo in the conclusion to the whole digression on idolatry, in 15:18a (σέβονται).

A': Wis 15:7-13. In these verses, the author illustrates the statement of v. 6. 15:7-13
The section is characterised by a series of inclusions. First of all, there is σκεύη (7d) which returns at the end of v. 13. Added to this is the mention of the lexeme γη- at the beginning (γῆν in 7a) and the end (γεώδους in 13b). Then there is the verb typical of idolatry, πλάσσω, which unifies vv. 7-9 (7b, 8a, 9e). Again we note ἐπίμοχθον (7a) which recalls κακόμοχθος in 8a. Verses 7-9 thus form a small unit concerning the role of the potter (κεραμεύς in v. 7) who is not aware of the futility of his own activity.

Constructed asyndetically, v. 10 opens a new step in the argument (vv. 10-13): the potter does not know the God who formed him. Also, he wishes to profit from evil (v. 13). Verse 10 is constructed with three nominal phrases while v. 11 contains three participles in succession. The final term of v. 11, ζωτικόν, forms a hook-word with v. 12 (ζωήν). Finally, the παρὰ πάντας of 13a forms a hook with πάντες δέ which opens the following section (vv. 14-19).

This whole section appears in close relationship with the opening section, 13:10-19. The quotation of Isa 44:20 LXX in 15:10 recalls Isa 44:9-20 which was utilised in 13:10-19. Noticeable also is the use of ὑπηρεσία in the LXX, only in Wis 13:11; 15:7 (with the meaning of "use"); and Job 1:3 (with the meaning of "service, servitude"); cf., again, the lexeme πορι- in 15:12c (πορίζειν; "to do business, make money") on the one hand and in 13:19 and 14:2a (πορισμός; "profits") on the other hand; σκεύη in 15:7d and

6 Gilbert, *La critique*, 193-196.

13:11d; χρυσουργοῖς καὶ ἀργυροχόοις in 15:9c and χρυσὸν καὶ ἄργυρον in 13:10c. However, while 13:10-19 describes craftsmen who appear to believe in their idols, this is not the case with the potter of 15:7-13, even if both are acting for financial gain.

A Concentric Structure

The text of this second and extensive literary unit (Wis 13:10-15:13) is so arranged as to call into prominence, at the very centre of the unit (C), the theme of the origin and perversion of idolatry while, at the same time, announcing the punishment of idolaters. In the inner frame (B-B'), the worship of idols is contrasted with the salvific presence of God for God's people with examples drawn from Scripture and salvation-history. The author also tries a reflection of a more rational character on the nature of idolatry and the reasons for its perversion, passing here too from the less serious (A) to the more serious case (A').

Wis 15:14-19

Finally, the third and final unit of this long digression, namely Wis 15:14-19 (πάντες δὲ ἀφρονεστάτοι; cf. 13:1 and 13:10; the superlative marks a progression in our author's thought) is devoted to the unreserved condemnation of the worst form of idolatry, zoolatry, that is, the worship of animals that was commonly practised in Egypt. In this way, the crescendo is complete: from the partial condemnation of the philosophers (13:1-9) through the decisive condemnation of idolaters (13:10-15:13) to the total and radical condemnation of Egyptian zoolatry.

In v. 18a, the verb σέβονται takes up the same verb that was in 15:6 (σεβόμενοι), at the end of the pericope recalling the history of salvation (15:1-6); cf. also σεβασμάτων in 15:17b. The expression ἐλογίσαντο θεούς (15a) connects us directly to similar expressions contained in 12:27; 13:2, 3, and 10, thus confirming the subdivision of Wisdom 13-15 in three parts. This final pericope, relating to the worship of animals is also taking up what was anticipated on a good two occasions in the first digression: see the connections between 15:14-19; 11:15; and 12:23-27; cf. 15:18a (τὰ ζῷα τὰ ἔχθιστα) and 12:24b (τὰ καὶ ἐν ζῴοις τῶν ἐχθρῶν ἄτιμα); cf. also 11:15bc.

After the introductory material in v. 14, two reasons are given for the condemnation of zoolatry, the first in v. 15 and the second in v. 18; the two καί of 15a and 18a are set in parallel. Verse 15 displays a certain internal unity. After the initial statement of 15a, the following five stichs adopt the text of Ps 113:13-15 LXX [115:5-7 MT] from which they take their inspiration, breaking down the parallelisms in the psalm into a different series (eyes – nose – ears – fingers – feet). Verses 16-17 form a definite unit and respond to the statement about the incapacity of the idols in the previous verse. Verses 18-19 conclude the whole section with a very harsh judgement on idolatry.

Wis 13:1-9: The Religion of the Philosophers

13:1 For naturally foolish were all those
by whom ignorance of God was present
and who, beginning with goods that are seen,
were not capable of knowing the One who is,

or, by examining his works, did not recognise the Craftsman,
2 but the fire or the wind or the nimble air
or the orbit of the stars or the turbulent water
or the torches of heaven, princes of the world,
they considered as gods.
3 If, enchanted by their beauty, they took them for gods,
let them recognize how much more excellent than these is their Sovereign
because it is the very author of beauty who created them.
4 And, if they were amazed at their power and operation,
let them reflect from those elements how much more powerful is their Maker.
5 For from the greatness and beauty of his creatures,
one can contemplate by analogy the Author of their existence.
6 However, the blame for them is slight
because they deceive themselves, perhaps seeking God and wishing to find him.
7 For, applying themselves assiduously to his works, they scrutinise
and are seduced by appearance because the things that are seen are so beautiful.
8 Yet not even they can be excused
9 for if they were able to know so much
as to be able to speculate on [the principle] of the cosmos,
why did they not find the Master of all things more quickly?

Notes on the Text and Translation

v. 1. The dative φύσει is not easy to interpret. If we translate "foolish through nature", that could make us think of a philosophical view of humanity which was very pessimistic by contrast with the biblical vision put forward by our sage. It is also possible to think of "foolish about nature"; that is: people should believe in God through nature but do not do so. It is simpler to take φύσει in an adverbial sense: "naturally foolish". However, it does not seem correct to link it with ἄνθρωποι as Larcher does (*Sagesse*, 3:750-751) and read it in the sense of: "being by nature human...". Gilbert (*La critique*, 47-50) proposes reading φύσει in a weak adverbial sense: people are naturally foolish" ("d'un naturel vain"), that is, "folly" is closely connected with the reality of being human. This is a general statement which does not intend to say anything about the possible "natural" depravity of humanity. Scarpat seems to be of a similar opinion (*Sapienza*, 3:24 and 74, although, I think, misunderstanding Gilbert's thought) and proposes to translate φύσει with "in reality". Gilbert suggests a reminiscence of the famous Aristotelian sentence πάντες ἄνθρωποι εἰδέναι ὀρέγονται φύσει (*Metaph.* 980a 21). Our sage would thus be highlighting the negative aspect of human study which is impossible in reality without the gift of the wisdom that comes from God (cf. also Engel, *Das Buch der Weisheit*, 215).
The verb πάρειμι, "to be present", is certainly being used in an ironic sense: just as wisdom is present with God and people (cf. Wis 9:9-10), so ignorance of God is present in people.

v. 2. The expression κύκλον ἄστρων is unique and difficult to interpret. Perhaps the author is thinking of the circular movement of the stars in the sky and so of concepts of an astrological character; cf. Gilbert, *La critique*, 15n55. As for the strange expression *πρυτάνεις κόσμου, it should certainly be referred to φωστῆρας οὐρανοῦ, that is, to the sun and moon considered as "princes" who rule the world (the reference to Gen 1:14-16 seems deliberate), or else to the stars who were held to influence people and things (cf. Gilbert, *La critique*, 17-19, who cites Plutarch, *Mor.* 601A); similar criticisms are also found in Philo: *Opif.* 58-60 and *Abr.*78.

v. 5. The adverb ἀναλόγως occurs only twice in texts prior to Wisdom; cf. Gilbert, *La critique*, 25-26.

v. 6. The adverb τάχα means "perhaps", but also "easily". On this basis, Scarpat (*Sapienza*, 3:59-61) considers vv. 6-7 as the intervention of a fictitious interlocutor who seeks to excuse the pagans who are actually (vv. 8-9) being condemned by the author. According to Scarpat, in 13:6-9 we encounter a typically diatribal style: according to our sage, who is responding to the objection raised in vv. 6-7, the pagan philosophers are actually without excuse. In this case, the tone of the whole pericope would change and become much more severe. If, on the other hand, we understand τάχα in its more usual sense of "perhaps", the emphasis falls on the v. 6 as a whole and so on the participle of the third stich (cf. Gilbert, *La critique*, 5 n. 7), and the author's tone undoubtedly appears more positive.

v. 9. In the expression στοχάσασθαι τὸν αἰῶνα, the verb στοχάζομαι, "aim at" and so "observe, investigate, search", but also "conjecture, infer", is probably used in the same sense as Plato uses it in texts where it acquires the meaning of "conjecture" (*Gorg.* 464c, by contrast with γινώσκω). In the LXX, cf. Deut 19:3 (in the sense of "observe"); Sir 9:14 ("to judge"); 2 Macc 14:8 ("to take care of"). Philo uses it in *Praem.* 43: through reasoning, some people conjecture, infer the existence of the demiurge from his works (ἀπὸ τῶν ἔργων εἰκότι λογισμῷ στοχασάμενοι τὸν δημιουργόν).

In LXX but also in Hellenistic usage, the term αἰών indicates the "world" generally (VL: *aestimare seculum*), as in Wis 14:6 (with a temporal nuance, however) and 18:4 (cf. the comment). Αἰών can also refer to the cosmos in its temporal development (cf. Larcher's translation: "conjecturer le cours éternel des choses"; *Sagesse*, 3:768-772). However, αἰών is a term of elevated use which can indicate the cosmic god, a kind of soul or principle of the world which keeps all things together. Its veneration is attested at Alexandria (cf. Gilbert, *Critique*, 34-35 and n. 164; Winston, *Wisdom* 256-257; Reese, *Hellenistic Influence*, 58: "in contrast to this personification of the eternal vital cosmic forces, the Sage holds out as the only proper goal of all human religious striving the personal Master of all things ..."; *ibid.*, 60). Therefore, we understand the phrase στοχάσασθαι τὸν αἰῶνα as "investigate the [principle] of the cosmos".

Synchronic Analysis

13:1-2 Recognising the "One Who Is" from the Visible Goods

The beginning of the pericope is certainly negative. In the LXX, the term μάταιος very often translates the Hebrew הבל and is not infrequently used to indicate idols (Jer 2:5; 8:19; 10:15; Hos 5:11; Isa 2:20; Ezek 8:10; cf. 3 Kgdms 16:13, 26; 4 Kgdms 17:15; and Lev 17:7). Here, our author could be being inspired more directly by Isa 44:9. We must not forget that ματαιότης, from the same root as μάταιος, is the word chosen by the LXX, to translate Qoheleth's הבל. A clear moral tone is thus given to it by the Greek translators.[7] However, to this very typically biblical ex-

7 Cf. Mazzinghi, Luca, *Ho cercato e ho esplorato*. Studi sul Qohelet (Bologna: EDB 2009²) 366.

pression our sage immediately adds a second one which is not found in the LXX: θεοῦ ἀγνωσία, the culpable ignorance of God which recalls, by antithesis, the γνῶσις θεοῦ, a central concept in Hellenistic culture.[8] In this context, the idea of "ignorance" does not refer to the existence of God pure and simple, something which was certainly not denied by the Greek philosophers, but to the lack of a knowledge of God's real being: the Greek philosophers do not understand the *identity* of the true God.

The expression which opens v. 10, ταλαίπωροι δέ, makes us think that μάταιοι μέν indicates here only those who are referred to in this first pericope (13:1-9), that is, the philosophers. At the same time, the expression that follows, πάντες ἄνθρωποι, gives μάταιοι a more general significance.

Although in the negative, under the accusation brought against the ignorance of the idolaters, v. 1b contains a statement of capital importance: our sage is really convinced that starting from (ἐκ) the good things that are seen, it is possible to know God: yet these men were not able to know the "One who is". The aorist οὐκ ἴσχυσαν refers to something that has already happened. God is described here with a double appellative: the "One who is" (ὁ ὤν), clearly drawn from Exod 3:14 LXX, and the Craftsman (τεχνίτης). The expression of Exod 3:14, ὁ ὤν, juxtaposed with τῶν ὁρωμένων ἀγαθῶν, is to be understood of a God who exists in himself (cf. the same idea in Philo, *Abr.* 125), understood as the principle of existence, of created, visible things. This biblical reference invests with great dignity the description of the biblical God which Wisdom is seeking to offer his Jewish readers. At the same time, the mention of the "One who is" marks the distance between our author's thought and that of Plato: for the former, there is no room for an intermediate God, a "demiurge" between the world and the divine being.

Verse 1c continues by recalling that, in examining the works (of God: understood), people were not able to recognize their τεχνίτης (wisdom was already called τεχνῖτις in 7:22a and 8:6; cf. the comment). Employed in connection with God, the term is known to Philo (*Leg.* 3.32, 97-99, etc.), but the idea is already present in Aristotle (cf. below) and is not foreign to Stoicism (τεχνικὴν εἶναι τὴν φύσιν; *SVF* II, 135 frag. 411). The use of the verb ἐπέγνωσαν recalls the theme of ἐπίγνωσις, to be understood as the recognition of the true God (cf. Heb 10:26; 2 Pet 1:2).

Divinising Nature

In v. 2, our author lists a series of elements of the cosmos which "they" considered as gods: fire, wind, air, the stars, the power of water (for the Egyptians, the River Nile was certainly divinised: ὁ μέγας θεὸς Νεῖλος; cf. *OGIS* 168.6), and the stars, divinized in Egypt as also in the Greco-Roman world. In part, this language recalls the polemic of other parts of Scripture against similar mythological concepts (cf. Deut 4:19; Jer 8:2; 19:13; Ezek 8:16; Job 31:26-27), polemic well known to Philo also (cf. *Decal.* 52-53).

But who are the "they" who are the real object of this criticism? Many of the elements listed here recall different philosophical schools of the time.[9] At least

8 Cf. Norden, Eduard, *Agnostos Theos*. Untersuchungen zur Formengeschichte Religiöser Rede, Leipzig u.a.: Teubner 1913 (= Darmstadt: WBG 1956), 96; Scarpat, *Sapienza*, 3:26-28.

9 For the details, cf. Larcher, *Sagesse*, 3:756-760, who excludes a reference to the doctrine of the divinisation of the four cosmic elements; cf. Scarpat, *Sapienza*, 3:29-59.

some of them, however, seem to refer to pantheism of a Stoic character in which there is no place for the transcendence of God in relation to the world.[10] In fact, according to the Stoics, the "spirit" (πνεῦμα), the divine and universal principle of cohesion, pervades everything and is identified with the divinity: θεός ἐστι πνεῦμα νοερὸν διῆκον διὰ ἁπάσης οὐσίας.[11] Thus, every element of nature – particularly fire, wind, and air[12] – serves to express the presence of a unique, divine reality, impersonal and immanent. Everything is, therefore, in God, and the divinity penetrates everything.

It would seem, then, that our author is thinking of a form of "educated" piety, which was precisely that of the philosophical currents of the period. In fact, it is difficult to be clear if he was actually taking aim at a precise philosophical current of the time, even if a deliberate reference to Stoicism seems very probable, as also a certain trace of astrological (but also magical) concepts still present in Hellenised Egypt and widespread at the popular level, as Philo attests. In particular here, we recall the reference to the fire, the air, and the cycle of the stars.[13] However, the whole passage has a good grasp of the Stoic idea of the world as a dynamic whole, made up of powerful internal relationships and animated by a divine spirit.

13:3-5: Knowing God "by Analogy"

In these verses, the polemic opened in 13:1-2 continues, but, surprisingly, it is conducted with the aid of dialectic tools proper to Greek philosophy. The reflection starts out from a further argument which the Stoic philosophers used to prove the existence of God: beauty and the contemplation of creation, a theme not entirely absent from Scripture: cf. Jer 38:36-37 LXX [31:35-36 MT]; 33:20-21 MT; Ps 92:4 LXX [93:4 MT]; Isa 55:8-9; Job 11:8-9; and, in particular, the hymn of Sir 42:21-43:33. The contemplation of the beauty of creation seems to have deceived the philosophers, leading them to consider these created elements as gods (13:3a); but the Sovereign (δεσπότης; cf. Wis 6:7; 8:3; 11:26) of these elements (God) is greater than they. God is the very author of beauty, the Sovereign of all things. Here, although employing a Platonic verb (τέρπω: cf. *Hipp. Maj.* 298a), the author avoids speaking of the "beautiful" as understood by Plato, and, instead of τὸ καλόν, makes use of the rare καλλονή (but cf. *Symp.* 206D).

---

10 Cf. Verbeke, *L'évolution de la doctrine du Pneuma,* especially p. 38.

11 Posidonius, frag. 100 Edelstein-Kidd; but this is a very widespread idea in Stoicism: cf. *SVF* II, 112 frag. 310; II, 306 frag. 1027; II, 307 frag. 1035.

12 For the *pneuma*, cf. *SVF* II, frag. 310.442.786; for the fire, *SVF* I, frag. 124.157; II, frag. 423. 1026-1027. 1031. 1045. 1047; for the air, *SVF* I, frag. 85. 154. 169; II, frag. 1075. 1100.

13 Cf. some Stoic texts cited in Vílchez Líndez, *Sapienza,* 408-409, in addition to the many references provided by Gilbert, *La critique*, 14-20. Scarpat (*Sapienza*, 3:33-35) does not accept this possible polemical reference to Stoic concepts but prefers to think of a direct reference against ideas of a Gnostic character. Among others, the term ἀγνωσία would be referring to the Gnostics. According to Scarpat, the cosmic elements listed in v. 2 can be understood only in the frame of a condemnation of the astrology practised in Egypt by the Gnostic currents of the time, of Chaldean origin (cf. the clear judgement on p. 47 and the references to a similar polemic conducted by Philo in *Abr.* 69). However, it does not seem that Scarpat's theory necessarily removes the reference to Greek philosophy and, especially, to Stoicism. For a study of the cultural background of astrology, cf. Cumont, Franz, *L'Egypte des Astrologues*, Bruxelles: Culture et Civilization 1937; Festugière, Andé Jean, *La révélation d'Hermès Trismégiste*, I. L'astrologie et le sciences occultes, Paris: Gabalda 1950[3].

The term γενεσιάρχης, which is introduced in 3c, is a neologism, probably coined by our sage, to be understood in the sense of "generating principle", here, of "beauty". As we have said, the argument from the beauty of creation was known to the Stoics. However, our sage seems to wish to say that they did not arrive at the conclusion that behind visible realities there is a creator. The author also distances himself from the Platonic concept of the beautiful. The verb κτίζω, in fact, together with the reference to γένεσις contained in γενεσιάρχης introduces a clear reference to creation.

Verse 4 adds a further argument, of the *a minori ad maius* type. Impressed by the power and energy in the creation, the philosophers should have understood how much more powerful the creator is. God is described here with the participle of the verb κατασκευάζω (cf. 9:2a; 11:24c). A similar reflection is found in Philo, *Praem.* 42, but, in this case too, it is not entirely foreign to Stoicism (cf. Cicero, *Nat. d.* 2.90).

The verb νοησάτωσαν refers to an act of reflection and understanding of an intellectual character; referring to God, νοέω appears in Rom 1:20; cf. Philo, *Leg.* 1.38: the human intellect is drawn by God to himself and so is able to grasp him.

In this connection, for the first time in the history of philosophy, our sage is applying to the knowledge of God the logical tool of the analogy of proportion (v. 5; see below),[14] thus showing great courage as well as a discreet familiarity with Hellenistic culture. Verse 5 takes up in reverse order the double theme of the greatness (cf. v. 4) and the beauty of things (v. 3).

13:6-9: The Philosophers, Seekers of God Despite Everything

How then are we to rate the attitude of the philosophers? These verses keep another surprise in store for us: "the blame for them is slight", because they nevertheless sought God and wanted to find him. Verse 7 adds that these men applied themselves to knowing and scrutinising the works of God but were seduced by appearances, that is, they halted at the external beauty of things without going back to their creator. The typically Greek aspect of sight and beauty returns here. The verb διερευνάω is found in the LXX only here and in Wis 6:13, but it is used by Philo in relation to the study of natural phenomena (*Abr.* 69; *Spec.* 2.45; *Plant.* 79).

In the Greek philosophers, Wisdom discovers a real wish to seek God (cf. a not dissimilar idea in Acts 17:27; Philo, *Decal.* 66). That is why the judgement on them cannot be wholly negative. Secondly, the path they trod was correct in itself. As v. 9 affirms, the Greek philosophers succeeded in discovering the "principle of the cosmos". That is, they grasped the existence of God by starting from the contemplation of visible things. The book of Wisdom thus recognizes the basic validity of Greek philosophical logic of which the book itself, through the use of the analogy of proportion (*analogia proportionalitatis*), has shown the unexplored potential. Our sage has, therefore, taken the search of the philosophers very seriously.

Why, then, "cannot even they be excused" (v. 8)? The Greek philosophers were able to conjecture the existence of a unifying principle of the cosmos (αἰών), but, attracted by the seduction of what can be perceived by the senses (cf. v. 7), they did not recognize in this principle the Master of all things, the creator spoken of by the Scriptures. Thus, they ended up by divinising the cosmos itself.

---

14 Cf. Vílchez Líndez, *Sapienza*, 415 n. 62, cf. also Winston, *Wisdom*, 252-253.

The concluding question, which strikes a note of great astonishment, leads us to think that the philosophers could actually have known God. Why then did they not succeed? There is no explicit statement of what they lacked but it is clearly that wisdom which is obtained only as a gift of God through prayer (cf. Wisdom 9). Our sage does not consider human study as flawed in itself; on the contrary, it is seen as necessary and can lead to true results. Faith in the possibility of reason is the soul of our author's arguments. It has to be completed, however, by revelation which leads to the discovery that the God searched for by the philosophers cannot be a different God from the one revealed in Scripture.

Diachronic Analysis

Here we have one of the most powerful and significant passages in the book where our author's biblical faith is carefully combined with the Hellenistic world. The Alexandrian sage takes the risk of setting out in poetic form arguments which are of a markedly philosophical character. The aesthetic experience attached to poetry can also be a step leading people to God.[15]

Scripture is undoubtedly the principal source of inspiration. Verse 1 refers immediately to the God of Israel who reveals himself to Moses in the burning bush in the famous passage of Exod 3:14, here cited in the LXX version (see below). The two neologisms employed in vv. 3 and 5 (γενεσιάρχης, γενεσιουργός) recall the creator God of Genesis. However, if this inspiration is biblical, the starting point for our sage's reflection here is typically Greek, as is the vocabulary used which is, in good part, foreign to the LXX. Indeed, the language is rich with *hapax,* with refined words and neologisms, like the two just mentioned.[16] Moreover, for the first time, we find in Scripture a reflection on the rational search for God, conducted with arguments drawn from the typical logic of Greek philosophy. Furthermore, the plethora of references to the beauty of the creation betray a sensibility that is typically Greek.

Wis 13:1-9 should not be understood as an attempt to demonstrate the existence of God; neither the Jews of Alexandria nor the Greek philosophers were actually atheists! The biblical background leads our author to take for granted that the God of whom he is speaking is the God of the faith of Israel. The problem is, rather, the relationship with the philosophical vision of the contemporary Greek world and, therefore, a deep discussion on the *nature* of God: of what God are we speaking? As happens frequently in Scripture, the problem is not a supposed *atheism* but, rather, *idolatry.*

13:1: Between Aristotelianism and Stoicism

As the basis of v. 1, Wisdom places a well-known Stoic-Aristotelian proof of the existence of God. The first to affirm that it is possible to know God from visible things was, in fact, Aristotle, in a treatise that has been lost (περὶ φιλοσοφίας) but which is known through the use made of it by the Stoics. Philo seems to be referring to these Stoic-Aristotelian ideas when he writes that, starting from the world, it is possible to obtain an idea of its cause just as when seeing a house, one postulates

---

15 Gilbert, *La critique*, 35-38.

16 Gilbert, *La critique*, 5-8.

> the existence of the architect (τεχνίτης). Thus, seeing the elements of nature and seeing the cosmos as a well-ordered construction, one postulates the existence of a craftsman of the universe (δημιουργός; cf. *Leg.* 3:97-99). The same argument is found in other texts of Stoic inspiration.[17] An example from Cicero: "tantum ergo ornatum mundi, tantam varietatem pulchritudinemque rerum coelestium, tantam vim et magnitudinem maris atque terrarum, si tuum ac non deorum immortalium domicilium putes, nonne plane desipere videare?" (*Nat. d.* 2.6,16-17). The Craftsman of whom the Greeks speak is thus identified with the biblical God of Exod 3:14. For our sage, the philosophical argument used by the Greeks to arrive at postulating the existence of God is basically correct. What they lacked is the discovery that this God, Craftsman of the world, is the same God who revealed himself to Moses. This is the God the pagans have not known.

As Cicero had already done, our author too distinguishes in v. 2 between the existence and essence of God, or, better, he seems to presuppose such a distinction. For him, in fact, the problem is not so much the existence of God, which the ancients took as given, but God's essence, God's nature. In these verses, our author's aim is to demonstrate not so much that God exists as *who* God really is. The Greek philosophers had come to postulate the existence of a Craftsman,[18] but they had not grasped his essence; rather, they had fallen into panentheism. The Greeks' philosophical argument was correct, and our sage recalls it. Yet they did not succeed in grasping that the God of whom they spoke is the creator of the world who revealed himself to Moses. Here is an important step forward which will be largely preserved by the Christian tradition: the God reached by philosophy is not, and cannot be, a different God from the one received by faith; and, for our sage, the God of faith is the one who reveals himself in Scripture: the God of the exodus and the creator God; the one who creates and the one who saves. 13:2

The procedure of analogy mentioned in v. 5 was employed for the first time by Plato and is described thus by the Stoics: ἀναλογισμὸς δ' ἐστὶ λόγος ἐκ τοῦ φαινομένου ὁρμώμενος καὶ τοῦ ἀδήλου κατάληψιν ποιούμενος, "a reasoning which starts out from what is seen and goes on to master what is not seen".[19] It is a rational procedure which begins from experience of what can be sensed to reach understanding of realities which transcend experience itself. To do this, analogy makes use of the so-called "relationship of proportion", enlarging or decreasing the properties of the objects of experience (for example: the earth is to be thought of as an infinitely large circle). When applied to the beauty of visible things, precisely the use of this logical instrument should have led the Greek philosophers to a correct reasoning on the nature of God. According to our sage, through the use of analogy, it is possible to get back to the creator from the things created, but God is infinitely greater than they are and so cannot be identified 13:5: Analogy

17 Cf. *SVF* II, 301-305 frags. 1011-1020; the argument of the beauty of the cosmos as proof of the existence of God was known already to Chrysippus (*SVF* II, 301 frag. 1011).

18 Our author carefully avoids using the term "demiurge", which, in the Platonic view, is a kind of intermediate divinity who "fashions" the world from the pre-existing Ideas. Our sage wishes to remove every doubt: the God of whom he is writing is the personal God of the exodus, the creator and saviour God of Israel's tradition.

19 Cf. *SVF* II, 89 frag. 269; extensive discussion in Gilbert, *La critique*, 25-30.

with material reality as the Stoic philosophers postulated. A similar argument is used by Paul in Rom 1:19-20.[20]

According to our author, it is precisely the use of the logical tools at the disposal of the Greek philosophers which should have led them to correct reasoning concerning the nature of God. In particular, the principle of analogy should have led them to the creator, here described with a further neologism: γενεσιουργός, "the author of their existence", a term which will return later only in the Hermetic writings. With great genius, Wisdom thus makes use of the Greek idea of the analogy of proportion to break out of the Stoics' closed circle of immanence. It is true that one can go back from the creatures to their author, but it is precisely the analogy between the two realities which logically places the Craftsman of things well above them; and the Craftsman is the God of the Bible: of the exodus and of creation.

Importance of Reason

In this connection, the importance which Wisdom gives to reason stands out (cf. also the description of fear in Wis 17:11-12). In v. 4, our author calls on the pagan philosophers to reflect (νοησάτωσαν) precisely by beginning with the analogy of proportionality. However, the end of the path described in v. 5 is expressed with the verb θεωρέω, that is, "contemplating"; analogy, or the rational process, is only the first step towards this. Perhaps Wisdom is taking up a passage from Ps-Aristotle's *De mundo* (or the ideas contained therein) in which there is the same opposition between the impossibility of seeing God directly and the possibility of being able to contemplate God through God's works: "here is what we must say about God, who is the most powerful with regard to strength, the most noble with regard to beauty, immortal with regard to life, and the most excellent with regard to virtue: though remaining invisible to every mortal nature, he nonetheless allows himself to be seen (θεωρεῖται) from his works" (6.399b 19ff). We note that, at the beginning of v. 5, the preposition ἐκ, which refers to the θεωρεῖται that closes the verse, adds to the Greek flavour of the text. God is contemplated not within the creation, present in it, but "starting out from creation". The application of reasoning to the creation leads to contemplation.

13:6-9: Polemic or Dialogue?

Retaining vv. 6 and 7 as the objection of a hypothetical interlocutor, who would then be being contradicted by the author in vv. 8 and 9, appears extreme (cf. the textual notes). The text of Wis 13:1-9 certainly has a polemical tone, but, along with the rest of the book, is undoubtedly more open to the Greek world than some have sometimes wanted to admit: "thus the author implicitly recognises the value of the pagans' effort to prove the existence of God but claims that they have not come to know the nature of this God".[21]

G. Scarpat's position appears compromised by a basic prejudice: that the book of Wisdom shows "uncompromisingly a path learned in the school of the Fathers, totally different from that indicated by the Greek philosophers".[22] Without doubt, the relationship with the Greek world should be set out in a less drastic way. As M. Gilbert writes: "with this example [13:1-9] we have wanted to show that our

---

20 For the patristic echoes of this text, cf. Larcher, *Sagesse*, 3:763.

21 Gilbert, *La critique*, 38.

22 Scarpat, *Sapienza*, 3:8.

author has taken seriously the study of the philosophers of his time: he responds to them by using their own methods and so purifies their results".[23]

Wis 13:10–15:13: Criticism of Idolatry

After his explication of the religion of the philosophers and of those who deify elements of nature and the stars, the lengthy middle portion 13:10–15:13 addresses honouring divine statues and images. The five subsections will be discussed individually in the following.

Wis 13:10-19: The Birth of an Idol

10 Wretched, then, are those whose hopes are placed in dead things,
those who have called gods the works made by human hands,
gold and silver fashioned with skill,
figures of animals,
or a stone without value, fashioned by an ancient hand.
11 Take a carpenter: having sawn through a tree that is easy to handle,
he peels off all the bark around it with skill
and, having fashioned it with care,
has prepared from it a vessel useful for the needs of life.
12 Then, the discarded remnant from his work
he has burned to prepare his food and eaten his fill.
13 Taking the remnant, which is of no use for anything,
a twisted and knotty piece of wood,
he has carved it in order to occupy his moments of leisure
and has chiselled it with skill to distract himself.
Thus he has given it the image of a man
14 or has made it like a contemptible animal.
He gives it a coat of paint, covers its surface with red,
conceals every crack,
15 He prepares a suitable niche for it
and sets it in the wall, fixing it with a nail.
16 So that it may not fall, he watches over it,
knowing that it cannot help itself:

---

23 Gilbert, "Inculturazione", 18.

it is only an image and has need of help!
17 Yet, when he prays to it for benefits, for marriage and children,
he is not ashamed to address a lifeless object.
For health, he calls on weakness itself,
18 for life, he prays to a dead thing,
to obtain help, he pleads to one who is incapable,
to have a good journey to one who cannot even walk;
19 for profit, work and the success of his business,
he seeks strength from one who has feeble hands.

Notes on the Text and Translation

v. 10. The term *ἐμμελέτημα is found only once in the Greek literature known to us (*Ant. Gr.* 6.83.4: ἁρμονίης ἐμμελέτημα); the sense is that of "care", a practical attention paid to some activity; the expression τέχνης ἐμμελέτημα can be translated as "fashioned with skill".

Also *ἀπείκασμα is *hapax* of the LXX, but appears in Plato (*Crat.* 402d, 420c) with the sense of "copy", "representation".

v. 11. The text is overloaded, and rich in rare and refined words: *ὑλοτόμος is a Homeric term (*Il.* 23.123); *εὐκίνητος ("easy to handle") and *ἐκπρίω (perhaps to be understood as "split" or "chisel") are *hapax* of the LXX; so too the rare *περιξύειν ("scrape / scour all around") and, again, *φλοιός ("bark"), *εὐμαθῶς, "easily", and *τεχνάομαι, "fashion" (perhaps taken from Xenophon; cf. Scarpat, *Sapienza*, 3:87).

vv. 12-13. The very rare and unusual *ἀπόβλημα has given rise to great uncertainty in the mss (cf. Ziegler). Perhaps it was coined by our author from ἀποβάλλω, "reject" and so to be understood as the "remnants" (cf. the purist correction of codex A and many minuscules: ὑπολείμματα, the "remains").

The expression of 13b, *ὄζοις *συμπεφυκός, "twisted and knotted", referring to the carpenter's piece of wood, is made up of two other LXX *hapax*: *ὄζος, "branch, knot" and the ptc. act./intrans. of *συμφύω, "grow together".

In 13c, some codices and versions (A, S^c, 766, Sa, Sy, Arab, Arm) read ἐν ἐπιμελείᾳ ἐργασίας αὐτοῦ, "in the course of his work" thus losing the irony in the better attested expression, ἐν ἐπιμελείᾳ ἀργίας, "in his moments of leisure". The idol is created by the carpenter in his moments of leisure! Scarpat (*Sapienza*, 3:89 and 118) suggests a possible ironic reference to the sabbath rest.

In 13d, the verb ἐτύπωσεν, "moulded" (in the LXX only in Sir 38:30, but τυπόω is Platonic), marks a progression in the argument. The complement of the verb has two textual forms: S^c, 248–249–254–411–754, La, Sa, Arm read ἐν ἐμπειρίᾳ συνέσεως; *ἐμπειρία signifies "skill, ability"; but the expression "with the skill of art" (cf. La: *per scientiam artis*) is to be rejected in favour of the majority reading: ἐμπειρίᾳ ἀνέσεως, or "with the skill of free time". Thus, there is the continuation of the ironic reflection on the birth of the idol from the *otium* of the carpenter who constructs the idol in his spare time.

Together with 14a, 13a seems to be the main clause of a very long period that began in v. 11 with εἰ δὲ καί τις ὑλοτόμος. After the verb ἀπείκασεν, Codex A and other lesser witnesses introduce the conjunction τε, thus eliminating the asyndetic construction which seems, however, to be original.

v. 14. For the details of these expressions relating to the painting of the idol, cf. Scarpat, *Sapienza*, 3:90-91. *τὸ φῦκος ("rouge, ferrous") and *ἐρυθαίνω ("to colour red") are *hapax* of the LXX; ἡ μίλτος, "red chalk, ruddle" only in Jer 22:14.

v. 18. The term *ἐπικουρία signifies "help, protection". The object of ἱκετεύω, "plead", rare in the LXX (cf. 2 Macc 11:6; 3 Macc 5:51 in a religious context) is the difficult ἀπειρότατον which is illuminated by a passage from Xenophon (*Mem.* 4.7.1) where it has the sense of "not trained, unable" (from the substantive πεῖρα), which is well suited to the context (cf. Scarpat, *Sapienza*, 3:93-94).

v. 19. The term *εὐδράνεια is *hapax totius graecitatis* and is coined from the previous *ἀδρανής, "powerless, feeble"; it could be translated with "efficiency" (but cf. εὐδρανίης attested in a Phrygian inscription of the third cent. BCE; cf. LS Supp., *sub voce*). In Greek usage, the term *ἐπιτυχία indicates "success".

Synchronic Analysis

13:10: The Dead Idols

The idolaters are "wretched" (ταλαίπωροι; cf. 3:11). The term underlines an increasing negativity in relation to the μάταιοι which opened the section on the philosophers in 13:1. "Wretched" are they, first of all, because they worship "dead things" (v. 10a). The idea returns at the end of the section (cf. v. 18a). The biblical texts that speak of idols as "dead things" are few. One can think of Ep Jer [Bar 6:]26, 70 and Ps 105:28 LXX [106:28 MT], but, in neither of these texts is the idea of the idol as a dead thing contrasted with the living God. The parallel with 13:17b, which contains ἄψυχος, that is, without ψυχή, i.e., life, leads to the thought that, with "dead idols", our sage understands beings which, unlike the human being, are, precisely, without life.[24]

Verse 10 closes with the mention of the idols of stone[25] which have become such on account of their antiquity. The text is playing on the ironic value of "ancient" understood as "antiquated".

13:11-15: The Carpenter

Verse 11 introduces the figure of the carpenter, taking its inspiration freely from Isa 44:13-17. His work makes sense if it is aimed at fashioning an object of some use for human life. Here, Wisdom is probably inspired by Ep Jer [Bar 6:]58.

With great irony, vv. 12-13 describe how the idol arises from the "remnants" or "chippings" of the carpenter's work, or, better, with the remnant of the remnants (cf. the deliberate repetition of ἀπόβλημα in 13a), utilized in the spare moments of the carpenter who has nothing better to do (13d; see the textual notes). The use of the verb γλύφω, "carve", in 13c refers to a background in Isaiah (cf. Isa 44:10 LXX), but, in the Greek world too, the verb is used in connection with idols (Herodotus, *Hist.* 2.46.2).

The carpenter finishes his work (13e). He gives the idol the image (εἰκών) of a man (*ἀπεικάζω: "copy, represent"). The text is alluding to Isa 44:13 (ἐποίησεν αὐτὸ ὡς μορφὴν ἀνδρός), but the use of εἰκών could be a deliberate polemical recalling of a term from Genesis (cf. Gen 1:26): the human being, image of God (κατ' εἰκονά), is replaced by an idol, made by a human being who creates a god in his own image. Idolatry thus appears as a kind of anti-creation, a conscious negation (εἰδώς; 16b) of God's plan for the world. Verse 14a adds the possibility that the idol may be the image of a contemptible animal, thus anticipating the criticism of Egyptian zoolatry. The verb ὡμοίωσεν reinforces the idea that there

24 Cf. Gilbert, *La critique des dieux*, 75-81.

25 On sacred stones in Middle Eastern worship, cf. Winston, *Wisdom*, 259-260.

is a deliberate ironic reference here to a context in Genesis (cf. καθ' ὁμοίωσιν; Gen 1:26, cf. also Isa 40:18 and Deut 4:15-17).

Verses 14b-15b portray the effort of the craftsman (who cannot be described as an artist) who tries to give an impression of life to the idol that he has constructed. The niche built into the wall to fix it and prevent it falling (cf. Isa 40:20; 41:7; 46:7) leads to the thought of domestic idols.

13:16-19: Trusting in Idols?

After the description of the birth of the idol, a second-class product constructed by the carpenter in his spare time, vv. 16-19 constitute the culmination of this section (13:10-19): people are not ashamed to entrust their life and their needs to a being which they themselves have constructed. Ironically, it is the craftsman himself who has to look after his work so that the idol does not fall (v. 16a). Here, our sage uses the verb προνοέω (cf. 6:7) which recalls πρόνοια, divine providence (cf. Wis 14:3). The idol, in fact, is incapable of helping itself (16b). The idea comes from Ep Jer [Bar 6:]57, but is frequent in anti-idolatry criticism: cf. Isa 46:1-2; Jer 10:4b-5; Ps 113:13-14 LXX [115:5-6 MT]). The idol is only an image; the term εἰκών, which was introduced in 13e is taken up again. Here, as often in the LXX, εἰκών is employed precisely to indicate the idol (Deut 4:6; 2 Kgs 11:18; Isa 40:19, 20; etc.) and is in polemical contrast to the Greek conception in which the image is, rather, an idealisation of reality. On the contrary, the idol is only a pale copy of it. This is why it is in need of help (16cβ). The use of βοήθεια is certainly ironic: people seek help from God (LXX-Pss 59:13; 69:2; 70:12 [MT-Pss 60:13; 70:2; 71:12]; etc.) whereas the idol is unable to help itself.

Despite this, the one who has made the idol is not ashamed to pray to it for his needs; those mentioned are benefits or goods, marriage, and children (17a). However, the idol to whom the idolater addresses himself is only a lifeless (ἄψυχος) being. From 17b on, the use of anaphora (five times, the preposition περί) increases the sensation of absurdity around praying to an idol. There is no biblical text on idols comparable with this one, even if the text of Ps 113:15 LXX [115:7 MT] could have inspired it. The idolater invokes the idol for health, without taking account of the fact that the idol is weak; he prays (ἀξιόω, according to the linguistic usage of the LXX) for life, although the idol is dead (17c-18a). The idol is invoked as an aid and companion on journeys, although it is without experience and cannot walk (18bc). Also for the success of his work and the relevant gain, the maker of the idol seeks help from one unable to offer it (13:19).

Diachronic Analysis

The criticism of idolatry opens with this section, ironic in tone, which describes the "birth" of the idol produced by human means and so unable to bring help of any kind to people. Similar criticism is also found in the Greco-Roman world, for example in the famous satire of Horace against the *inutile lignum* (*Sat.* 1.8.1-3) where the idol is described polemically and ironically as the work of a craftsman who does not know how to spend his time better. However, the background in Wisdom is chiefly biblical and is represented by the criticism of the idols in Isa 44:9-20 where the prophet describes the work of the idolaters as a counterfeit of the actions which God has performed for God's people. Our sage makes broad use of the Isaiah text, but with a certain freedom and showing all his creative ability.[26] The prohibition of the Decalogue concerning making images (Exod 20:3-4 = Deut 5:7-8) is also behind this reflection, the tone of which is clearly more severe than that of 13:1-9.

The presentation of the idol as the "work of human hands" is a traditional cliché of the anti-idolatrous polemic frequent in Scripture (cf. Deut 4:28; 2 Kgs 19:18 = Isa 37:19; 2 Chr 32:19; Ps 113:12 LXX [115:4 MT]; Ps 134:15 LXX [135:15 MT]; Ep Jer [Bar 6:]50). The gold and silver appear in Pss 113:12 LXX [115:4 MT]; and 134:15 LXX [135:15 MT]; the wood and stone in Deut 4:28 and 2 Kgs 19:18; in Hab 2:19, the wood, the stone, the gold, and the silver: here, gold, silver and stone, and, from v. 11, wood. However, the text of Wisdom does not seem to have been inspired by a particular biblical passage. The reference to the images of the animals place us in a context that is more typically Egyptian. 13:10

In the description of the idol in these verses, Wisdom often heightens the polemic by highlighting aspects connected more to its Hellenistic cultural context than to the biblical world. 13:11-19

The mention of the painting of the idols in 14b is an example of a Greek touch which is not found in the biblical world.[27]

The term ἄψυχος (v. 17b; cf. 14:29) has a Greek flavour and is found in *Syb.* 5.84; 8.47 in connection with idols, as also in Philo (*Leg.* 2.22; 3. 160; *Decal.* 76; *Virt.* 219). Here our sage sharpens the polemic, presupposing that the idolaters identify their divinity with the object they have constructed. In fact, Egyptian ritual was notably complex, as was the Egyptian conception of the divine. An accurate knowledge of the thought of the other gives way here to irony.[28]

Wis 14:1-10: The Ship of Providence

[14:1] Another, moreover, preparing to set sail and on the point of tackling the wild waves,
calls upon a piece of wood that is more rotten than the ship carrying him.
[2] For it was the desire for profit that planned that (ship),
artisan wisdom that equipped it;
[3] but it is your providence, o Father, which steers it,
for you have marked out a path in the sea
and a safe way between the waves,
[4] showing that you are able to save from every peril,
so that everyone without skill can embark.
[5] For you wish that the works of your wisdom are not in vain.

---

26 Cf. the very careful comparison of Gilbert, *La critique des dieux*, 64-75.
27 Cf. Gilbert, *La critique des dieux*, 88-90.
28 Cf. Winston, *Wisdom*, 262-263.

Therefore, people trust their lives to an insignificant piece of wood,
and, having passed through the billows on a raft, they were saved.
6 For, in the beginning, when the proud giants were dying,
the hope of the world, taking refuge on a raft,
left to future centuries a seed of life, guided by your hand.
7 Blessed is the wood through which justice comes!
8 But what is fashioned from human hands is cursed, both it and the one who made it,
the one, because he constructed it,
the other because, though corruptible, it was held to be a god.
9 For, in the same way, God hates the ungodly and their ungodliness;
10 the work will thus be punished along with its author.

Notes on the Text and Translation

v. 1. The combination *πλοῦν στελλόμενος is classical; cf. Sophocles, *Aj.* 1045. Here, the present participle has final value and is used instead of the future (Blass/Debrunner/Rehkopf, *Grammatik*, 418.4). The whole verse is constructed with refined terminology and great rhetorical ability. Cf. ἄγρια κύματα, the only use of ἄγριος in Wisdom in a metaphorical sense: "the wild waves" (cf. Jude 13). The term σαθρός, "rotten", is present in the LXX only here and in Job 41:19, again in connection with ξύλος. Also, the verb ἐπιβοάω, "cry, call upon", is present in the LXX only in 4 Macc 6:4, but it is a Homeric verb: cf. *Od.* 1.378 with reference to the gods.

v. 2. In 2b, the majority of witnesses read τεχνῖτις δὲ σοφία, while some minuscules (cf. Lat: *et artifex sapientia fabricavit sua*) read τεχνίτης δὲ σοφίᾳ, a reading chosen by various modern scholars who prefer to think of a reference to the wisdom of the builder of the ship; the reading τεχνῖτις would have been formed on the basis of Wis 7:22a and 8:6c. However, cf. Ziegler, 67, for the alternation of η / ι in Wisdom. If we allow the majority reading, τεχνῖτις σοφία is to be understood as the "artisan / craftsman wisdom", that is, the ability of the builder of the ship.

v. 6. In Wisdom, the term αἰών has a spatial value (cf. 13:9), but also an anthropological one (humanity; cf. 18:4), but it is also not without a temporal nuance. Here, it could be understood as "world", but perhaps better as "future centuries", the "generations" which follow. The association with the theme of descendants (σπέρμα) confirms this interpretation.

Synchronic Analysis

14:1–3a: Your Providence Steers the Ship!

Our sage's attention is suddenly pointed to the sea and sailing which appears as something dangerous according to an idea common in the ancient world. In the Hellenistic period, naval symbolism is very rich: sailing is seen as a mortal danger, a challenge to fate but also a brave human act. "Ancient literature is, as it were, woven through with naval symbolism".[29]

---

29 H. Rahner, *Symbole der Kirche: die Ekklesiologie der Väter* (Salzburg: Müller 1964) 434; cf. 432-472, for the range of naval symbolism in classical and patristic literature.

At the time of departure, someone undertaking a voyage calls on the idol which was often set on the ship's prow (cf. Acts 28:11).[30] With remarkable irony, this becomes a "rotten piece of wood", which is in a worse state than the ship itself (πλοῖον, term which indicates a merchant ship) which has to be protected. A possible biblical background is in the text of Jonah 1:5. As we shall see, our sage does not criticize the idea that it is necessary to entrust oneself to God on a voyage but rather that sailors call upon an idol made with human hands and incapable of saving them.

Verse 2a refers to the reason for which men go to sea: the ship was planned (ἐπενόησεν) with the desire for profit (ὄρεξις πορισμῶν). The term ὄρεξις is not used here in a philosophical sense, as happens in Stoicism, where it indicates the appetite, the natural inclination (a form of the impulse [ὁρμή]; cf. *SVF* III, 40 frag. 169), but in the negative sense of "desire", as in 4 Macc 1:33, 35; cf. Sir 18:30; 23:6; and Rom 1:27. People embark, therefore, for reasons bound up with trade and the wealth which follows (cf. Horace, *Ep.* 1.45-48; Juvenal, *Sat.* 14.277).[31]

The text of 2b refers to the "artisan wisdom" which built the ship, that is, the technical wisdom of the builder. Here, σοφία is alluding to a form of human wisdom, not the divine wisdom mentioned in v. 5a. In fact, v. 3a, contains a neat contrast: the ship is built by technical human wisdom but is steered by providence.

The invocation to the idol is contrasted with the prayer addressed to the God of Israel, here called on in the second person as πάτερ. The passage to dialogic form is not only stylistic in purpose (a transition from the didactic style to that of prayer) but underlines the clear opposition between the God of Israel and the dumb idols. This thus completes the image of God in Wisdom 13-15: that God who, in 13:1-9, is the God "who is" of Exod 3:14 and the creator God, is now also a caring Father. The influence of Stoic philosophy is not absent here.

Such a God conceived as Father (cf., already, Wis 2:16) is behind the term πρόνοια, of clear Greek flavour, rare in the LXX (apart from 2-4 Macc, only in Dan 6:18 MT [6:19 LXX]) but frequent in classical literature; cf. Xenophon, *Mem.* 1.4.18; Plato, *Tim.* 30c (πρόνοια θεοῦ) and 44c. In Wisdom, the idea of divine providence reappears in 17:2 in a punitive context; but remember also προνοέω in Wis 6:7 and 13:16.[32]

14:3b–5: A Fragile Piece of Wood

These verses make up a further reflection on sailing, which is described in a language with tones of the Exodus. The text of 3bc recalls in particular Ps 76:20 LXX [77:20 MT], but also Ps 105:7-9 LXX [106:7-9 MT] and Isa 43:16. The "path in the sea" and "a way between the waves" do not seem to be alluding directly to the crossing of the Red Sea (cf. Wis 10:18 and 19:7); otherwise the ἵνα of v. 4b ("so that even one who is without skill embark") would be difficult

30 Cf. Vílchez Líndez, *Sapienza*, 428 n. 3; Winston, *Wisdom*, 263. At Alexandria, the goddess Isis was particularly invoked as the patron of navigation: cf. Mazzinghi, "La barca della Provvidenza", 78-82. However, in Egypt, the practice of carrying individual cultic objects is also attested: cf. Dunand, Françoise, *Dieux et hommes en Egypte. 3000 av. J.-C. - 395 apr. J.-C.: anthropologie religieuse* (Paris: Colin 1997), 267-268.

31 Cf. Larcher, *Sagesse*, 3:789-790; Winston, *Wisdom* 263-264.

32 Gilbert, *La critique des dieux*, 103-104 n. 27; Mazzinghi, *Notte di paura e di luce*, 11-13.

to understand.[33] Only God can save from the perils of the sea (3bc), as from every other danger (4a). This is a statement of theological character on which our sage puts his emphasis. In this way, one can understand that even the inexperienced person who puts to sea can be saved if only he trusts in Providence. It is clear that for our sage the sailors' skill has to give way to faith in the divinity. The problem is: *which* divinity? The idol made with human hands, or the caring Father, the God of Israel?

Verse 5 opens with a second general theological statement: "you wish that the works of your wisdom are not in vain" (note the rhetorical figure of *oxymoron*: ἀργὰ / ἔργα; cf. Jas 2:20, in a different context). By contrast with the human wisdom mentioned in 2b, here, σοφία is clearly that wisdom praised in Wisdom 7-9 and seen at work in Wisdom 10. This is the last mention of wisdom in the book. This statement suggests that the wisdom that comes from God requires the collaboration of people whose action God himself guarantees. According to our sage, the example of sailing is a very good illustration of this collaboration between divine wisdom and human action.

The Raft

Trusting in the wisdom given by God, men trust themselves (here ψυχάς clearly has the biblical sense of "lives") to an "insignificant piece of wood" – a synecdoche to indicate a boat – a raft, in fact (σχεδίον; see below), but they are saved all the same (διεσώθησαν; 5bc).

14:6-7: Noah, the Hope of the World

Our author enriches his reflection on sailing with the aid of an example drawn from Scripture. The text of 6a is probably referring to the episode narrated in Gen 6:1-4, but the biblical text is being reread through the filter of a midrashic process that is already traceable in Sir 16:7-8 and 3 Macc 2:4. Behind Gen 6:1-4, there are complex traditions many of which lie behind the Enochic literature. Here, our sage limits himself to mentioning the "proud giants" who "perished".

Against this background, the text of 14:6bc recalls the episode of the flood, in a very singular way. Noah, whose name is not mentioned according to our author's practice, is called "the hope of the world", and his ark becomes a "raft" (σχεδία), so as to highlight the disproportion between the danger and the salvation obtained from God. In connection with the ark, therefore, our sage is prolonging his reflection on the "insignificant piece of wood", which was already introduced in 10:4, and returning to the theme of the fragility of the boat from the previous verse (14:5). Noah can leave the world a seed (6c; this is the only text in which the idea of σπέρμα is associated with Noah; cf., on the theme of the "remnant on the earth", κατάλειμμα τῇ γῇ, Sir 44:17). That is because the ark-raft is steered by the very hand of God (τῇ σῇ κυβερνηθεῖσα χειρί).

The biblical episode of the flood concludes with a third statement of theological importance (after those of vv. 4a and 5a): "blessed is the wood through which justice comes!". The use of εὐλογέω, a unique instance in Wisdom but frequent in the LXX, refers to the action of God. The perfect recalls action in the past with effects that last also into the present: it was and remains blessed. The "wood" is Noah's ark which was mentioned in v. 6, and the divine blessing contrasts with

---

33 *Contra* Gilbert, *La critique des dieux*, 104-109; cf. Beentjies, "You Have Given a Road" and Mazzinghi, "La barca della Provvidenza", 65-66; along these lines, cf. Larcher, *Sagesse* 3:793.

the curse (8a) which falls on the idol. Here, "salvation" is replaced by "justice". This is certainly a reference to the "just" man, Noah (Gen 6:9; cf. Wis 10:7), and so to the justice performed by people who use aright the wisdom offered by God, in this case by building a "piece of wood" with a purpose not linked to idolatry. However, the "justice" is certainly that of God (cf., especially, 1:15). Thus the "wood", an element of creation, is blessed because, contrary to the idol (cf. the ξύλον mentioned in v. 1), its use is in harmony with the will of God, that is, with God's "justice".[34]

14:8-10: Cursed is the Idolater!

This last section is a very harsh judgement on idolatry formulated in terms well known to Scripture. For the idol described as χειροποίητον, cf. Lev 26:1; Dan 6:27 MT [6:28 LXX]. Frequent too is the idea that God hates evil and the wicked (cf. the comment on Wis 12:4a). One of idolatry's greatest errors is to give a "corruptible" idol (cf. 13:10, 17, 18) the name of God (cf. 14:21). However, the idea of the "cursed" idol appears new, even in relation to the biblical texts which lie at the base of Wisdom 13-15. As in Gen 3:14, 17, the curse follows the divine blessing on the creation (Gen 1:22, 28) and constitutes its antithesis. In fact, from our sage's perspective, the idol is the very negation of the creative plan of God. The text closes with the mention of a vague divine punishment, expressed here with the verb κολάζω, which is dear to our author (cf. 3:4; 11:5; etc.).

Diachronic Analysis

14:3: Providence of God

Πρόνοια indicates God's concern for people. Plato (cf. above) combines the idea of "providence" with that of a God who "steers" the world: God is τοῦ παντός ... ὁ κυβερνήτης (*Pol.* 272e). In our text, there is possibly also a reminiscence of *Tim.* 42e (κάλλιστα καὶ ἄριστα τὸ θνητὸν διακυβερνᾶν ζῷον); but the image of the helmsman applied to divine providence is well known to Philo also: *Conf.* 98 (ὁ κυβερνήτης θεός); *Decal.* 53, 155; *Ebr.* 199 (God is pilot and helmsman).

Denied by Aristotle and Epicurus but defended by the Stoics,[35] the concept of God's providence was widespread in the environment of Greek-speaking Judaism; cf. 3 Macc 4:21; 5:30; 4 Macc 9:24; 13:19; 17:22. The Letter of Aristeas speaks of providence under the clear influence of Stoicism (προνοίᾳ γὰρ τῶν ὅλων διοικουμένων; Let. Aris. 201). Philo devoted an entire work to providence (περὶ προνοίας), unfortunately lost in its Greek original. In *Prov.* 1.25,[36] the image of divine providence is linked, among other examples, to that of commanding a ship (cf. above, and again, *Opif.* 9; *Deo* 29; *Decal.* 58). Josephus too mentions divine πρόνοια a good 160 times.

The text of Wis 14:3 acquires a clearer polemical tone if set against the background of the Isiac mysteries. Isis is not only the patron of sailing (see below),

---

34 M. Gilbert has studied in detail the history of the exegesis of v. 7, which the Fathers often understood as a reference to the cross of Christ, but this is a reading unsupported by the text (cf. *La critique des dieux*, 114-124); Larcher is more open to the idea writing in *Sagesse*, 3:800: "le texte reste ouvert à une plénitude de sens que devait lui apporter la Croix du Christ".

35 Cf. *SVF* II, 306 frag. 1029; II, 924 frag. 1118.

36 *SVF* II, 322 frag. 1111.

but it was also she who invented ships (*Aretalogy of Kyme,* 15; *Aretalogy of Andros,* 152-154).

God as Father As for "Father!", it is a rare invocation both in Greek and in biblical usage. In relation to God, it appears here, for the first time in the LXX, with decidedly universalistic features (for God invoked as "father", cf. also Sir 23:1; 3 Macc 6:3). It is known to Stoicism: Cleanthes makes use of it (Hymn to Zeus, 30).[37] In presenting a universal fatherhood of God, of all people, our text betrays Hellenistic rather than biblical influence, as is the case in Philo (*Opif.* 56, 72, 74, and 135).

Together with the invocation "Father!" and the symbol of the ship's helmsman, the mention of providence is easily understood against the philosophical and cultural background marked out above. The reflection on sailing serves our sage as the occasion to recall that, behind human affairs, there stands not an impersonal fate but the providence of a God who guides the world as a father (cf. 3 Macc 6:2, where διακυβερνάω is employed in precisely this sense), who is concerned for people (cf. 6:7d). The example of Noah's ark, introduced in v. 6, sets against a biblical background a Hellenistic-flavoured notion of God.

14:5 The theme of the "insignificant piece of wood" to which the sailors entrust their lives is topical: "i nunc et ventis animam committe dolato / confisus ligno, digitis a morte remotus / quattuor aut septem, si sit latissima, taedae" ["Go, and entrust your life to the winds, entrusted to a piece of rough-hewn wood, separated from death by three or four fingers, if the side [of the ship] is larger"] (cf. Juvenal, *Sat.* 12.57-59). But why call the ship a "raft" (σχεδία) exactly? This happens also in v. 6, in relation to Noah's ark which could certainly not be described as a "raft" (cf. below). The term σχεδία, already known to Homer (*Od.* 5.33: ἐπὶ σχεδίης: the means with which Ulysses continues his voyage), is found in the LXX only in 1 Kgs 5:23 = 2 Chr 2:15 and 1 Esd 5:53 (in 3 Macc 4:11, Σχεδία is the name of a city in Egypt). On the one hand, our sage intends to refer to another topical subject: for Greek literature, the raft is the first means used by people to sail.[38] However, the text of Wis 14:5, 6 acquires greater depth if read in the light of a probable Platonic reminiscence: in *Phaed.* 85d, in the words of Simmia, the "raft" is the expression of the human *doxa* which seeks tirelessly to cross the sea of life. In the absence of a sturdier ship, namely a divine revelation, it is necessary "to take up the best and least refutable of human discourses and, embarking on it as on a raft (ὀχούμενον ὥσπερ ἐπὶ σχεδίας), to take the risk of making the crossing of life". However, such a fragile raft requires superior reasoning, as Socrates later replies (*Phaed.* 99d). It is not improbable that the Alexandrian reader would think of these texts of the *Phaedon* which could help him to reflect on the need for the guidance of a Providence superior to the fragile raft of human reasoning. In this way, the naval symbolism employed by our sage is laden with a more directly philosophical sense.[39]

14:6-7: Isis at the Ship's Rudder Verse 6c sees the return of the theme of "steering" which takes up what was already seen in v. 3, in connection with providence, and explicitly recalls 10:4. These three texts (Wis 10:4; 14:3, 6) are united among themselves by the presence of (δια) κυβερνάω

---

37 Cf. *SVF* I, 122 frag. 537.

38 Cf. Larcher, *Sagesse*, 3:796-797; Winston, *Wisdom*, 266-267.

39 For greater details, cf. Mazzinghi, "La barca della Provvidenza", 73-75.

which has its subject wisdom (10:4), providence (14:3), and the hand of God (14:6). In all three cases there is an explicit allusion to salvation: ἔσωσεν (10:4); σῴζειν (14:4a); διεσώθησαν (14:6). The idea of wisdom as "pilot" is not wholly foreign to biblical wisdom (cf. Prov 8:15), nor is it possible to rule out a possible philosophical background entirely (cf. above). However, the reason for this emphasis on the divine activity of "piloting" and so procuring salvation is really to be sought in the area of the Isiac mysteries. One of the best-known portrayals of Isis at Alexandria is that of the *Isis pelagia*, Isis, the patron of sailing who, in the Isiac aretalogy of Oxyrhyncus, is invoked as κυβερνῆτις, "pilot" (P.Oxy. XI, 1380, 69), but also as πρόνοια (P.Oxy. XI, 1380, 43; cf. Apuleius, *Metam.* 11.5, 12, 15, 18, 21) within a *reinterpretatio* of the ancient Egyptian Isis in a Stoic key.[40] There are statues of Isis-Tyche which represent the goddess with a ship's wheel in her hand.[41] The first Isiac hymn of Isidorus (32-34) describes Isis as the "present" one (πάρειμι; cf. Wis 9:9-10) who saves people from the perils of the sea. At the same time, Isis is not only "pilot" and "providence" but also "saviour", as we have already noted in connection with Wisdom 10 (cf. *Isid.* 1.26; P.Oxy. XI, 1380, 20, 91, 203).

In 10:4 and 14:3-4 + 6, to describe the action of God and his wisdom, our sage makes use not only of examples drawn from the world of sailing but also images which closely recall the facts about Isis. Like Isis, the wisdom, the providence, and the hand of God are described by the metaphor of "pilot" and are bearers of human salvation, in the first instance by saving people from the perils of the sea. In this way, the biblical tradition (here, the account of the flood) is being read in a key that is more relevant and comprehensible for the Jews of the time, that is, through the seductive figure of Isis. What we have here is a bold remythologisation of the wisdom of Israel which, by assuming characteristics of Isis, is presented to the faithful in this new garb. The danger of idolatry, represented in this case precisely by the seduction of the Isiac mysteries, is thus combatted from within; the wisdom of the God of Israel is capable of performing the same works as Isis, and much greater ones. Wis 14:1-10 is placed simultaneously with the need to defend Israel's faith in the face of the attraction of the Isiac mysteries and the urgency of dialogue with that world which was so foreign to Judaism. In that case, we could risk, albeit with caution, describing the task performed by our author as a real work of "inculturation".

Wis 14:11-31: Origins and Consequences of Idolatry

11 Therefore, there will also be a visitation on the idols of the pagans
because, among the creatures of God, they have become something of an abomination,
an obstacle for the souls of humans
and a snare for the feet of the foolish.

---

40 On all this, cf. Mazzinghi, "La barca della Provvidenza", 80-87.

41 Merkelbach Reinhold, *Isis Regina - Zeus Sarapis. Die griechisch-ägyptische Religion nach den Quellen dargestellt* (Stuttgart-Leipzig: Teubner 1995), tables 67, 95, 96, 98, 99, and 230.

[12] For the beginning of unfaithfulness was the idea of fabricating idols,
their discovery was a corruption of life.
[13] For they did not exist from the beginning, nor will they exist for ever:
[14] because of the shallow opinions of people they entered the world,
and, therefore, a sudden end has been decreed for them.

[15] A father, consumed by premature grief,
made an image of the son who had been suddenly taken away,
and now worships as a god one who, before, was only a dead man;
later, he handed on to his family mysteries and rites of initiation.
[16] Then, in time, when this ungodly tradition had been strengthened,
it was observed as a law.

Also, by order of rulers, statues became the object of worship.
[17] Some, who lived far away, not being able to honour them in person,
represented their likeness at a distance
and made a visible image of the king they venerated,
so as to flatter with such zeal the absent one as though he were present.
[18] Then, to magnify the cult among those who did not know it,
the ambition of the artist made a contribution.
[19] For he, wishing perhaps to please the powerful one,
skilfully forced his image to make it more beautiful,
[20] but the people, seduced by the charm of his work,
now considered as an object of worship
the one who, before, they honoured as a man.
[21] This became a snare for life:
that is, that humans, slaves to misfortune or power,
attributed to stones or wood the unutterable name.

[22] Then, it was not enough for them to err in their knowledge of God,
but also, though living in a great war of ignorance,
they hailed such great evils with the name of "peace"!
[23] And while they practise rites of infanticide, or secret mysteries,
or feverish orgies from strange rituals,
[24] they keep pure neither their life nor their marriage:
the one does away with the other though treachery or afflicts him with adultery.
[25] Everything is dominated by a chaos of blood and murder, theft and fraud,
corruption, disloyalty, anarchy, perjury,
[26] perversion of values, forgetfulness of benefits received,
impurity of souls, sexual perversions,
marital disorders, adultery and lack of self-control.
[27] The worship of idols which cannot be named
is the origin, cause and culmination of every evil.

28 For whether it is those who frolic in their pleasures or prophesy false things,
or live in injustice or perjure themselves with ease,
29 trusting themselves to lifeless idols,
they do not expect to be punished, although they have sworn wicked oaths.
30 For two reasons, a just judgement will overtake them:
because they conceived a false idea of God by having recourse to idols,
and because they perjure themselves in deceit, despising holiness.
31 For it is not the power of the things on which one swears
but the justice reserved for sinners
that always overtakes the transgression of the unjust.

Notes on the Text and Translation

v. 14. The subject of εἰσῆλθεν in 14a is the term εἴδολον of 12b. Not understanding this, some witnesses (S*, A, and many minuscules; cf. Ziegler) have inserted θάνατος on the basis of 2:24. In itself, the term *κενοδοξία signifies "vain glory", but, in this context, it is preferable to understand it as "shallow opinions" (cf. Lat: *supervacuitas*). This term, of Epicurean provenance, was not chosen by chance. It refers to something wholly devoid of logic and consistency (Winston, *Wisdom*, 273).
In 14b, the expression σύντομον αὐτῶν τὸ τέλος could be understood as a "sudden end". The adjective σύντομος appears in the LXX only in 2 Macc 2:31 and 4 Macc 14:10 and is usually used in connection with a speech.

v. 15. With codices B, S, V and many other witnesses, we read τόν τοτε instead of τόν ποτε; cf. Scarpat, *Sapienza*, 3:126-127.

v. 17. The verb *ἀνατυπόω is a technical term attested only later than Wisdom. It means "reproduce, represent" or also "give form" to an idea, or, in the middle, "have an idea of something". The expression of 17b can be understood as "having represented the likeness [of the rulers] at a distance...", or, as Scarpat prefers (*Sapienza*, 3:128), "the distant figure".
In 17d, the present subjunctive κολακεύωσιν is to be preferred to the aorist subjunctive found in some witnesses (cf. Ziegler); cf. Larcher, *Sagesse*, 3:818. The verb κολακεύω has a negative nuance: "flatter".

v. 18. The term θρησκεία, in the LXX only in 4 Macc 5:7, 13, always has a religious nuance in Greek usage. Here, it indicates the "cult" generically; cf. the reprise of this term in v. 27. It seems to have been little used in the Hellenistic period only to reappear in the Augustan age: cf. Winston, *Wisdom*, 278.

v. 23. The term *ἐμμανεῖς is probably an accusative referring to κώμους. Ἐμμανής indicates "crazed, raging", like the Bacchants in the Bacchic ecstasies (Euripides, *Bacch.* 1094). With the term κῶμος, our sage is referring to the orgies (cf. 2 Macc 6:4; Rom 13:13) which accompanied the Bacchic rites. Larcher (cf. the texts cited there: *Sagesse*, 3:828-829; Festugière, André Jean, *Le monde graeco-romain aux tempx de Nôtre Seigneur*, II, Bloud & Gay: Paris 1935, 167-181) thinks of real Dionysiac processions which were celebrated solemnly at Alexandria; cf. the description of Callixeinos cited by Athenaeus, *Deipn.* 5.25-35, as well as the votive inscription of 150 CE (*AJA* 37, 1933, 232-262). These orgies of the crazed are characterised by "strange rituals". Ἔξαλλος, a term rare both in the LXX (4x) and in secular Greek, indicates something "different" from what has been established. Here, θεσμοί is used of the religious "rituals" which were held to have been fixed by the divinity.

v. 25. The expression which opens v. 25, πάντα δὲ ἐπιμίξ ἔχει, can be understood as "everything is in a confused state, dominated by blood and killing...". The adverb *ἐπιμίξ is *hapax* of the LXX (it is a Homeric term: *Od.* 11.537) but could have been suggested by the text of Hos 4:2 LXX, which lists the same vices as Wis 14:24c-25a (... ψεῦδος καὶ φόνος καὶ κλοπὴ καὶ μοιχεία) and which also speaks of blood: καὶ αἵματα ἐφ' αἵμασιν μίσγουσιν (the verb μίσγω has the same root as ἐπιμίξ).

v. 26. The expression θόρυβος ἀγαθῶν is not easy to interpret. If we take ἀγαθῶν as masculine, we can think with Scarpat (*Sapienza*, 3:136) of "disturbance of good people", that is, that confusion, that fear which overtakes even someone who is good. If, instead, we take ἀγαθῶν as neuter, we can think of the "confusion of goods", that is, the perversion of values; cf. the explanation added by Arm.: "the forgetfulness of the goods that deserve recognition". In fact, in the second part of the stich there follows the χάριτος ἀμνηστία, or the forgetfulness of goods or benefits (understood: received). For the unusual Latin version, *immemoratio Dei*, cf. Scarpat, *Sapienza*, 3:359.

v. 30. With τὰ δίκαια, Philo often intends "the just laws" (cf. *Ebr.* 81). In classical usage, τὰ δίκαια indicates what is owed, for good or evil (Scarpat, *Sapienza*, 3:139-140). Here, the expression suggests the "just judgement" which personified justice (cf. 31c) will see comes to the idolaters. For μετέρχομαι in the sense of "overtake" cf. 4 Macc 10:21; 18:22.

Synchronic Analysis

Wis 14:11-14: The Insubstantial Nature of the Idols

At the centre of the digression on idolatry, after a brief introduction (14:11-14), this long section (14:11-31) is taken up with describing the origins of the worship of idols (14:15-21) and, above all, of demonstrating its disastrous moral consequences (14:22-31).

14:11 The polemical beginning of the whole section (v. 11) is conducted along the lines of a quotation from Jer 10:15, but the theme of the divine judgement on idols is common in Scripture (cf. Zech 13:2; Isa 2:18 LXX; Jer 10:14-15). It is difficult to say what kind of "visitation" (ἐπισκοπή) our sage has in mind: whether an eschatological "visitation" of God or one within history. However, the use of ἐπισκοπή in Wis 2:20; 3:7, 9, 13; 4:15 (always in a positive sense) makes us think of a visitation in the future.

The reason for this "visitation" lies in the fact that the idols have become an abomination (εἰς βδέλυγμα, a frequent expression in the LXX; cf. βδέλυγμα used as a synonym for "idol" in Deut 7:25-26; 27:15; 29:16; 32:16; etc.) within the creation (ἐν κτίσματι θεοῦ). The reference to the creation is important: it does not cease to be "good", and, if it becomes an "abomination", that is only because of the distorted use of it made by people. Not only that: the idols have also become a cause of immorality: an "obstacle" for people, and a "snare" for the foolish. For the parallelism between σκάνδαλον and παγίς, two terms found only here in Wisdom, cf. Josh 23:13; 1 Macc 5:4; Pss 68:23 LXX [69:23 MT]; 139:6 LXX [140:6 MT]; 140:9 LXX [141:9 MT]. "Obstacle" indicates an impediment on the way of God (Judg 2:3), "snare", every trap found on the path of the upright person (cf. Ps 56:7 LXX [57:7 MT], a text which probably inspired our author).

Right from these initial verses, the text establishes a direct link between idolatry and immorality, as Paul does in Rom 1:18-23, a text which probably betrays the influence of these passages of Wisdom.

Idolatry is then described in 14:12 as the beginning of "unfaithfulness" (πορνεία). With this term, the LXX indicates both "prostitution" proper[42] and in a translated sense, that is, Israel's unfaithfulness towards God (Hos 4:12; 5:4; 6:10; Jer 2:20; 3:2, 9; etc.). The significance of πορνεία is illuminated by the chiastic structure of v. 12, at the literary centre of the pericope (14:11-14): 14:12

ἀρχὴ γὰρ πορνείας	ἐπίνοια εἰδώλων
εὕρεσις δὲ αὐτῶν	φθορὰ ζωῆς

Πορνεία is matched by φθορὰ ζωῆς, the "corruption of life". Thus, πορνεία must have a theologico-moral sense and can be suitably translated with "unfaithfulness" towards God on the basis of the biblico-prophetic background noticed above. The "corruption of life" is concerned more with human morality in general. Both the religious and the moral life are corrupted on account of idolatry. The two following sections (14:15-16a, 16b-21) will be devoted to the ἐπίνοια εἰδώλων ... εὕρεσις δὲ αὐτῶν (cf. 14:12), namely, the story of the birth of the idol. Ἐπίνοια is to do with having thought of or imagined idols; εὕρεσις, with having concretely found them, brought them into being. From v. 21, there is a return to immorality as the consequence of idolatry (cf. the repetition of ἀρχή in v. 27).

In v. 13, which is also composed in chiastic form, it is stated that idolatry did not exist at the beginning and that, thus, it will not be able to survive. Our sage limits himself to setting a time limit to idolatry: it is posterior to creation and will come to an end before human history story finishes. 14:13

Verse 14 completes this introductory sketch and responds to the real question which our sage has in mind: not "when" was idolatry created but "who" created it; and the answer is clear: idolatry is born from shallow human opinions.[43] Once again, as often happens in our book, the stress is placed on reason.[44] Thus, the principal aim of our sage is to highlight how the responsibility for idolatry falls exclusively on humanity. 14:14

The mention of the rapid, sudden end for the idols brings us back to the "visitation" of 11a and leads us to understand that the eschatological perspective is not absent from our text: the presence of idolatry is somehow a sign that anticipates the divine judgement in history. One could easily observe that our author's position towards idolatry is undoubtedly very harsh, and contrasts with the divine moderation seen in the previous digression. Divine moderation ceases at the point when people refuse it by constructing an idol.

42 Thus, Winston, *Wisdom*, 271-272 who underlines the dimension of sexual corruption in idol worship.

43 For the history of the interpretations of vv. 13-14, cf. Gilbert, *La critique des dieux*, 140-146.

44 "Der nichtige Mensch denkt den nichtigen Gott. Und zugleich: Wer den nichtigen Gott denkt, wird zum nichtigen Menschen..."; Hübner, *Weisheit*, 178.

Wis 14:15-21: Premature Grief, Worship of Rulers, Birth of Idols

14:15 In this section, our author does not actually intend to show the *when* of the origin of idolatry but, rather, the *how*. Verse 15 seeks to explain the origin of the family cult of idols as the consequence of worship offered to the dead. In its turn, this arose from a very human need, the grief experienced by the death of a relative and, in particular, premature death.

The theme of "premature grief" (ἀώρῳ πένθει) is topical in the ancient world (cf. also the comment on 4:7-20) and is frequent also in Jewish funerary inscriptions.[45] Verse 15 intensifies the drama of such grief by linking it to the pain of a father who is consumed (τρυχόμενος) with the premature and unexpected loss (cf. 15b) of his son. A corpse (νεκρός ἄνθρωπος) thus becomes nothing less than a god!

The mention of the "mysteries and rites of initiation" (μυστήρια καὶ τελετάς; cf. Wis 12:4) handed down by the father to his family (τοῖς ὑποχειρίοις) highlights the topicality of the text for Alexandrian Jews who were tempted precisely by cults like this. The mention of mysteries and initiations makes it plausible that v. 15 is referring to the Dionysian mysteries in fashion in Alexandria (cf. below) and already targeted by our author. Verse 16a acts as a conclusion: with the passage of time, the ungodly practice established by the father for the death of his son acquires the force of a tradition (νόμος).

Worship of Rulers

Verses 16b-20 are devoted to idolatry seen as an effect of the worship offered to rulers: honour given to the king ends up, inevitably, in idolatrous worship. Starting with 16b, there is a clear beginning to a new development (cf. the point placed by the editors at the end of 16a), devoted to the public worship of rulers. The change of theme accounts for the separation between 16a and 16b. Whereas the cult of the dead son is spread through family customs, the worship of rulers is disseminated by a decree issued by the ruler himself.

14:17 Verse 17 describes in detail the origin of the statue of the ruler: people need the most faithful possible image of their sovereign "so as to flatter the absent one as though present".

14:18-20 The artist's ambition makes a notable contribution to the worship of the ruler (v. 18). Verses 19-20 compare the activity of the artist, who is forced to please the ruler, called ὁ κρατῶν in v. 19, a term which recalls the Roman κράτησις over Egypt (cf. also 6:2) with the attitude of the crowd who are seduced by the beauty of the work (20a). A similar concept appears in Philo, *Spec.* 1.29. Thus, a man – namely, the ruler – is venerated as if he were a divinity.

In this way, the passage to idolatry takes place thanks to the concurrence of various factors: the ability and ambition of the artist, the beauty of the statue, and the seduction practised on an ignorant crowd (cf. 18a: τοὺς ἀγνοοῦντας).

14:21 Verse 21 summarises the observations made in vv. 15-20: human misfortune, a premature death (v. 15; cf. the mention of συμφορά) and the power of rulers

---

45 Cf. Griessmair, Ewald, *Das Motiv der Mors Immatura in den griechischen Grabinschriften*, Innsbruck: Wagner, 1966. For the Jewish inscriptions, cf. Horbury – Noy, *Jewish Inscriptions*, who record at least 37 funerary inscriptions from Roman Egypt with the motif of premature (ἄωρος) death. Cf. also Blischke, *Die Eschatologie in der Sapientia Salomonis*, 223-263.

(vv. 16-20; τυραννίς) have created idolatry, a real slavery to which people are subjected (21b).

In a rhetorical crescendo, idolatry consists in applying to created realities the "unutterable name". Here, as we have seen, we are at the centre of the whole literary structure of Wisdom 13-15. Here, our author is making use of an expression that is unique in the whole of the Bible, even if he could be thinking of the text of Isa 42:8. The "unutterable name" is that which God reveals to Moses in Exod 3:14 (cf. Wis 13:1-3), that κύριος constantly invoked in the book of Wisdom, especially in the third part (cf. 9:1; 10:20; 12:2; 16:12, 26; 19:22) which is actually (although expressed in Greek) the *qᵉrē perpetuum* of the tetragrammaton YHWH. It is noticeable, however, that κύριος is significantly absent from Wisdom 13-15 in the context of anti-idolatrous polemic. Our sage seems to be forcing this polemic here: it is not really the idolaters' intention to attribute to their idols the name of the God of Israel. From this point of view, the text of 21c shows a certain lack of consistency with the two previous examples (the divinisation of the son and the imperial cult). However, our sage knows well that, in the Greek world, the title of κύριος was widely employed in connection with very many divinities. Yet, for a Jew, this is a profanation of the divine name. For Wisdom, κύριος is an "unutterable name" precisely because of the ambiguous use of it made in this period.[46]

Wis 14:22-31: The Birth of Immorality

The verses from 22 to 31 conclude this long section which opened at v. 11, developing what was already anticipated there in the introduction (14:11-14). At the beginning (v. 22) and the centre (v. 27) of the passage are two important statements of principle: immorality arises from ignorance of God and, also, from the worship of idols. The ἄγνοια, or ignorance spoken of in v. 22 is actually through antonomasia, that ignorance of God which already in the Stoic view was considered the source of immorality (cf. below). Accepting this widespread motif of his time, our sage engages in a battle which is not so much for the defence of moral values as for the faith. It is from faith in the God of the Bible that the ethical criteria for a new society arise.

Verse 22, well constructed on a double contrast (knowledge/ignorance; war/ 14:22
peace), opens with an εἶτα which underlines a transition and the passage to a new subject: the idolaters not only err in relation to their knowledge of God but their error is also of an ethical nature. We have already encountered the verb πλανάω in Wis 2:21; 5:6; 11:15; and 12:24, applied, in the last two cases, to the error of idolaters; we shall find it again in 15:4 and in 17:1. We have already underlined its echoes of the mystery rites, particularly significant here (cf. 14:23a and comment on 2:21). In this case, the error of the idolaters is related to γνῶσις θεοῦ, to the "knowledge of God". In fact, the whole of the first half of the digression on idolatry (from 13:1 as far as the centre, 14:21) has shown us that their error lies precisely in misunderstanding the true nature of the one and transcendent God, the biblical God whom our author has clearly presented from 13:1-9, and to whom people must be subject.

46 Cf. Bogaert, "Kurios, le nom incommunicable".

Verse 22bc introduces the list of vices with an ironic statement: ignorance of God renders people as enemies who fight a cruel war which, however, they hail with the name of "peace", thus forgetting that true peace is that which God grants to the just after their earthly life (cf. Wis 3:3, the only other use of εἰρήνη in the book). In this way, our sage is connecting faith with ethics: the knowledge of the true God leads to a life lived in justice.

14:23-26 The catalogue of vices in vv. 23-26 does not follow a specific order and reflects a usage very widespread in the period both in the Greek and in the biblical and Jewish worlds (cf. Hos 4:2; Jer 7:9; T. Reu. 3:3-6; Sib. Or. 3:36-45; Philo, *Cher.* 92; in the NT, Gal 5:19-21 and Rom 1:29-31; Eph 4:17-19; Col 3:5-9).[47] However, our sage certainly has in mind the text of Hos 4:1-2 which, in its turn, seems to presuppose the text of the Decalogue.

The vices listed in the book of Wisdom number 22, like the letters of the Hebrew alphabet (even if our text is written in Greek, but by a Jew!). The first vice mentioned, "rites of infanticide", τεκνοφόνους τελετάς, begins with the Greek letter *tau;* the last, "lack of self-control", ἀσέλγεια, begins with the letter *alpha,* which, in Hebrew, would correspond precisely to the last and first letter of the alphabet (*aleph - taw*). We thus have a compendium of immorality, a kind of alphabet in reverse. At the centre, in twelfth place, the term φθορά, "corruption", indicates the total overturning of values.[48] Undoubtedly a grim picture, it reveals the overall impression of a pious Alexandrian Jew of the pagan society of his time. Yet, despite this, our sage tirelessly seeks to express himself in categories comprehensible to a public versed in Hellenistic culture.

14:23 In v. 23, the first vice mentioned is the "rites of infanticide" (note the alliteration: τεκνοφόνους τελετάς). It is difficult to establish what our sage is referring to here: *τεκνοφόνος is *hapax totius graecitatis.* If we think of a biblical context, it could refer to the child sacrifices repeatedly condemned by Scripture (Deut 12:32; 18:10; Lev 18:21; 2 Kgs 16:3; etc.) but not unknown in Israel (1 Kgs 16:34; 2 Kgs 3:27). In the context of the mysteries, one could think of similar accusations that were brought against Dionysiac cults. It could be argued that similar rumours had reached the ears of the Alexandrian Jews.[49]

The second vice also brings us to the atmosphere of the mystery cults to which the text explicitly refers: the κρύφια μυστήρια underline "secrecy" as the best-known and basic characteristic of these rites (cf. Diodorus Siculus in connection with the Dionysiac mysteries: IV, 4,1).[50] For our sage, however, this "secrecy" is viewed in a very negative sense (cf. in connection with Wis 17:3a): if these mystery celebrations take place in secret, that is all the more reason to condemn

---

47 The classic work of Vögtle Anton, *Tugend- und Lasterkataloge im Neuen Testament,* Münster i.W.: Aschendorff 1936 and, again, Deissman, Adolf, *Licht vom Osten* (Tübingen: J.C.B. Mohr 1923[4]) 267-270.

48 Gilbert, *La critique*, 133-134.

49 Schwenn, Friedrich, "Menschenopfer", PW 15, 1:956. For the Dionysiac cults, cf. Cumont, Franz, *Les religions orientales dans le paganisme romain* (Paris: Paul Geuthner 1929) 195-202 and 303-312. The case of the Bacchanalia mentioned by Livy, 39.8-19, is well known.

50 Burkert, *Ancient Mystery Cults*, 7-9.

them. We note that the two vices, τελεταί and μυστήρια, are mentioned together also by Philo, *Spec.* 1:319.

The third vice lists the "feverish orgies from strange rituals", a probable allusion to the Dionysiac processions held at Alexandria (cf. the textual notes).[51]

In v. 24, the catalogue of vices continues with a main clause (cf. 24a: φυλάσσουσιν) which draws the first consequences of the mystery-cult celebrations just mentioned. Those who frequent them do not keep either their life or their marriage pure. Keeping one's life (βίος) pure signifies having a morally upright way of life. The second stich of v. 24 provides an example of conduct that is not upright, the extreme case of treacherous murder. The connection with the mystery rites is not accidental since it could happen that precisely in these rites the occasion was grasped for a settling of accounts.[52] The reference to the purity of marriage prepares for the following mention of adultery and also for a second series of vices later on that are connected with sex. Adultery is described here with the rare term *νοθεύω (cf. Philo, *Ios.* 45; Josephus, *A.J.* 4.244; cf. νόθος in Wis 4:3). 14:24

Verse 25 opens with a clear reference to the Decalogue. "Blood" refers to violence and, in fact, is coupled with murder (φόνος). They are followed by the pair of theft and fraud. The life of the idolaters becomes a chaos (ἐπιμίξ; cf. the textual notes) of senseless behaviour. This new series highlights some vices that concern destructive behaviour towards others. 14:25

The list continues with φθορά, corruption, that is, the perversion of all values, a vice that is certainly generic but which is placed, significantly, at the centre of the literary development (see above). For φθορά understood in a moral sense, cf. 2 Pet 1:4; 1 Cor 15:33. This is followed by the mention of ἀπιστία which is to be understood in a secular sense as disloyalty, lack of faithfulness to one's word (cf. Philo, *Decal.* 172, in connection with false witness). With τάραχος, our sage is referring to the chaos which the behaviour of the wicked causes in society (cf. Sir 28:9). If we try to be more specific, we could think of the denouncing of a particular kind of political "anarchy", a state of affairs not rare in the Hellenistic cities, including Alexandria (cf. ταραχή in Philo, *Leg.* 68, 113). Next to be mentioned is "perjury". *Ἐπιορκία is *hapax* of both the LXX and the NT; but ἐπίορκος is found in Zech 5:3 and 1 Tim 1:10; cf. Plato, *Gorg.* 525a. We refer to the comment on vv. 28-31 which returns to the theme of oaths understood as a means of social stability, oaths which the idolaters evidently do not keep.

Our author varies his style with skill so as not to weary the reader. After two pairs of vices (25a) and four single vices (25b), each one recorded with one word, the text of 26ab presents another four vices, each described by a pair of words. The first, θόρυβος ἀγαθῶν, probably indicates the "confusion", that is, the perversion of goods, that is, of values (cf. the textual notes). This is followed by forgetfulness of benefits received (χάριτος ἀμνηστία) which appears to be a very concrete sign of this radical perversion. Everything appears to be owed, and what is free is no longer acknowledged. 14:26

---

51 For the Bacchic Theasi (θίασοι), cf. Vogliano, Emanuele, "La grande iscrizione bacchica del Metropolitan Museum", *AJA* 37 (1933) 214-231; Cumont, Franz, "La grande inscription bachique du Metropolitan Museum", *ibid.* 232-262.

52 Lenormant François, "Bacchanalia", *Dictionnaire des antiquités grecques et romaines* I, 590.

The third pair, ψυχῶν μιασμός, makes us think of the "impurity of souls". The metaphor of the corrupted soul is classical (Plato, *Phaed.* 81b; *Resp.* 10.621c) However, the term μιασμός is present in the LXX only here and in 1 Macc 4:43 and can have a very broad sense: corruption or perversion that is ritual, moral, or spiritual.[53] The ψυχή has a central role in our sage's anthropology. His ideal is a soul "without fault" (cf. 2:22). The "corruption" is, therefore, a result of human sin which leaves its traces on the soul. Our sage is probably thinking of corruption of a sexual nature (cf. the woman who is "barren but undefiled" mentioned in Wis 3:13). In fact, the following terms refer to disorders of a sexual nature. However, the "corruption/impurity" here seems, in the context of the other vices cited, to be an action that is committed rather than suffered: in this case, the text is referring to the idolaters who, with their sexually perverse behaviour, corrupt the souls of others, perhaps in the sense that, by their example, they incite them to similar behaviour.

With the syntagma γενέσεως ἐναλλαγή, our sage is indicating "exchange" (ἐναλλαγή is in itself a term used in the grammatical field, here employed *in malam partem*) of "generation". The text is certainly taking aim at practices of a homosexual nature, whether masculine or feminine, which were often condemned in contemporary Judaism: cf. Sib. Or. 3:596; T. Naph. 3:4; Ps.-Phoc. 177; one recalls the Pauline polemic in Rom 1:26-27.

All three of the vices which conclude the entire series are of a sexual nature. With γάμων *ἀταξία, the author intends "marital disorders" of an unspecific nature: perhaps the frequency of divorce? The contemporary widespread marital infidelity? Or else, is the allusion to marriages lived in a disordered way, namely, without the procreative intention inherent in marriage itself? The text remains vague. Clearer is the following reference to μοιχεία, adultery (cf. 3:16), although this seems to be a repetition of what was already condemned in 24b. The list is definitively closed by ἀσέλγεια (cf. in the LXX only in 3 Macc 2:26) which, in the NT, indicates that unbridled sex which was the most negative characteristic of Sodom and Gomorrah according to the text of 2 Pet 2:7.

The Punishment of the Idolaters

At the conclusion of this passage, vv. 27-31 describe the divine punishment awaiting the idolaters in the strongest terms. The word "idols" (εἴδωλα) occurs three times in a few verses (27a, 29a, 30b).

14:27

Verse 27 reiterates the principle already stated in 14:22: idolatry is the origin (ἀρχή), cause (αἰτία) and culmination (πέρας) of every evil. The statement is constructed in a very solemn way and gives a good idea of what our sage wishes to communicate: idolatry is the true cause of all wickedness. The idols are described with the adjective *ἀνώνυμος, "nameless", firstly, because they cannot be invoked (Exod 23:13; Ps 15:4 LXX [16:4 MT]), then, because, by contrast with the God of Israel, whose name is "unutterable" (cf. 14:21c), they do not have a name, that is, they do not have any substance. In Philo (*Sobr.* 52), the term ἀνώνυμος has also the sense of "unable to be named", with reference to the evil which, by contrast with the good, is not worthy to be named. Understood in this sense, ἀνώνυμος could refer to those idols that are exactly "unable to be named", unworthy of being recorded.

---

53 Cf. Larcher, *Sagesse*, 3:832-833.

Verse 28 introduces a plural subject which refers, *ad sensum*, to idolaters in gen- 14:28
eral. The verse goes on to specify a further four illicit activities of the idolaters which place the stress on the problem of swearing oaths (cf. the ἐπιορκία mentioned in 25b) and complete the previous list of twenty-two vices.

The idolaters' life is described as an unjust life which thus fails with regard to one of our sage's basic values which is, indeed, "justice". This small, additional series of four vices closes with the mention of "perjury with ease". Here, ἐπιορκέω does not mean false oaths but broken ones that have not been kept.

Verse 29 focuses again on oaths and connects them directly with "lifeless" 14:29
(ἀψύχοις) idols. Those who trust in the latter do not even expect to be punished. To broken oaths are added those made in order to cover wicked actions; that is the sense of the expression κακῶς ὀμόσαντες. Our author has a particular situation in mind; people who swear many oaths before lifeless idols, and the fact of having done this before these idols, leads them to consider their oaths as invalid.[54] As a good Jew, in fact, our sage does not mean to take away from the religious value of the oath; on the contrary, he presupposes it.

In verses 30-31, our sage contrasts the presumption of escaping punishment 14:30
on the part of the ungodly with the mention of the divine justice which will certainly punish them. The two reasons given for this punishment summarise what has been said so far. The first is having had perverse ideas about God through having recourse to idols. The first part of the stich (30b) recalls the beginning of the book almost to the letter (1:1b), thus returning to one of the major concerns of our sage: the knowledge of God.

The second reason for the punishment is once again connected with oaths, here linked to the mention of unjust (ἀδίκως) and deceitful (ἐν δόλῳ; the idea is biblical: Ps 23:4 LXX [24:4 MT] ἐπὶ δόλῳ) behaviour towards one's neighbour.[55] Once again, there is a return to the emphasis placed on the "social" aspect of sins. Still more, however, this way of swearing constitutes a "despising of holiness". In Wisdom, ὁσιότης is employed both with reference to God (5:19) and people (2:22; 9:3). In our sage's view, therefore, perjury consists of an act of despising the divine holiness which is made to witness to falsehood, but also of despising all that complex of moral values which goes to make a person's life "holy" (cf. the reference to justice and deceit).

Verse 31 makes clear that the punishment cannot come from any presumed 14:31
power of the idols over what is sworn but from the justice of God, the δίκη, which here is as though personified, as already at the beginning of the book (1:8). The idea that divine justice always overtakes the transgressions of the ungodly (31c) has a clear Greek tone.[56] The mention of a justice which always (ἀεί) "overtakes" (ἐπεξέρχομαι; in the LXX, only here and in Jdt 13:20) the unjust acquires a certain eschatological flavour and so recalls the punishment of the ungodly described in the first part of the book.

---

54 Larcher, *Sagesse*, 3:842.

55 Cf. the alliteration εἰδώλοις – ἐν δόλῳ.

56 Scarpat (*Sapienza*, 3:141-142) recalls the principle expressed by Sophocles, *El.* 528, 529: Justice is the divine punisher whom no one can escape; in the biblical world, cf. 4 Macc 4:21; Acts 28:4.

This pericope closes with the theme of the punishment of the unjust (ἀδίκων). Injustice and idolatry go hand in hand. The following pericope (15:1-6) contrasts the attitude of the God of Israel towards God's people and the quite different style of life of the people themselves, far from the behaviour of the idolaters.

Diachronic Analysis

14:11-14 The leading lines of our sage's anti-idolatrous polemic in 14:11-31 are basically two: in the light of the faith of Israel, idolatry is criticised in relation to the Decalogue but also as a result of a wholly positive vision of creation which the cult of the idols turns on its head. In the light of the cultural and religious context of Alexandria, the criticism focuses particularly on the attack on the mystery cults and, more specifically, on those of Dionysius.[57]

In v. 13, the statement that idolatry did not exist from the beginning and that it will, therefore, not continue to exist, has a Greek tone and recalls the euhemeristic theories which at that time were circulating also in Alexandria.[58] However, the text is vague. In fact, the Genesis accounts do not give much importance to a possible rise of idolatry at the beginnings of humanity nor does our sage seem to be alluding here to the texts of Genesis 1-3. Rather, he is alluding to the book of Jubilees (Jub. 11:3-6).

14:15-21 It is very difficult to grasp whether, in Wis 14:15-16a, our author is alluding to a particular episode (perhaps the divinisation of the young Dionysius killed by the Titans, or else that of Berenice II by her husband Ptolemy III, attested by the Decree of Canopus of 237 BCE, or, again, of Antinous, the favourite of Hadrian) or rather to be laying down an exemplary fact, read against the background of the Greek heroisation of the dead and, in particular, the apotheosis of a dead baby, the whole read against the background of euhemeristic theories.[59] It is more probable that our sage is taking his cue from the typical practices of the gymnasium and museum attested at Alexandria. Young men cut off in the flower of their youth were associated with the muses and became tutelary divinities responsible for the care of the family to which they belonged. This explains our sage's mention

57 Gilbert, *La critique,* 173.

58 In about 300 BCE, the philosopher, Euhemerus, expounded his theory, subsequently very famous, according to which the gods were originally great figures who, only later, after their death, were divinised. The Letter of Aristeas shows knowledge of these theories in the passage where he attacks idolatry (Let. Aris. 134-137). Our author is making use of euhemeristic sources no longer available to us (especially in relation to v. 15), but within a perspective that is more clearly Jewish than that of Aristeas; cf. Winston, *Wisdom,* 270-271; cf. also pp. 272-273 on the positions of ancient authors on the origin of idolatry.

59 Cf. a very detailed summary of various interpretations discussed Gilbert, *La critique,* 146-157; Larcher, *Sagesse*, 3:812-815 and Winston, *Wisdom,* 273-277, with numerous citations of ancient texts relating to the fate of babies who died prematurely. Scarpat, on the other hand, thinks of an exemplary fact of a general character, *Sapienza*, 3:101-102. Cf. Larcher's conclusion, *Sagesse*, 3:823: "les sources possibles de Sg. XIV, 16a-20 apparaissent complexes et se combinent d'une façon qui reste originale et porte la marque d'une réflexion personnelle de l'auteur".

of the "father" and the "family". The case of Epictetus at Thera, in about 200, is well known (*IG* 12:3.330). The statues of his two sons who died prematurely were placed in a sanctuary of the muses whose cult was looked after by the family. No new divinities arose, but dead youths were associated with the existing gods. As v. 15c expresses it, a dead man was now venerated as a god.[60] The environment referred to by our sage is not, therefore a popular one but an educated one made up of people who frequented the gymnasia.

The use of σέβασμα in 14:20b is striking. It is a late term, not attested before the first cent. BCE, which refers to the divine object to be venerated. Σέβασμα appears in this sense and once only (in the plural), precisely towards the end of the first cent. BCE, in Dionysius of Halicarnassus (*Ant. rom.* 1.30.3). In the LXX, it occurs only in Wis 14:20; 15:17 and BelTh 14:27; in the NT, cf. Acts 17:23 and 2 Thess 2:4. The use of σέβασμα recalls the epithet of Caesar Octavianus *Augustus*, σεβαστός in Greek, referring to the divinisation of the Emperor Octavian which took place from 27 BCE onwards[61]. Σεβαστός appears in this sense already in Strabo around 20 BCE (*Geogr.* 3.3.8; 12.3.14, 35: ὁ Σεβαστὸς Καῖσαρ; τοῦ Καίσαρος τοῦ Σεβαστοῦ). In 60 BCE Diodorus Siculus used the substantive σεβασμός "honour, worship" (*Bibl.* I, 22.83), in both cases in the context of Egypt and combined with the theme of worshipping divine images; σεβασμός then appears multiple times in the writings of Dionysius von Halicarnassus and Plutarch.

The overall negative conception of the arts in this section seems to be Platonic in inspiration. The theme of the seduction exercised by art on the masses is not infrequent in Greek literature.[62] In fact, our sage is well aware of the practices of his time. The image of the sovereign does not aim at the likeness but at the idealisation of the sovereign who makes up for the distance from his subjects precisely by the use of an image that is able to seduce the masses. The statue of the emperor is a ἐμφανὴς εἰκών (14,17c), a visualisation (ὄψις, twice in 14:17ab) which attracts the masses (cf. v. 20).[63] Our sage pays careful attention to the attraction of the visual (cf. already in 13:1-9), an attraction which is especially typical of the Dionyisiac cults, here being singled out once again.

Egypt knew the practice of attributing divine honours to the Ptolemaic monarchy, but the text is vague. There is no mention of a direct claim by the rulers to be worshipped as gods (apart from the mention of the "order" in 16b). Our sage is probably thinking of the cult of the Roman Emperor, begun by Octavian Augustus. However, although polemical, the tone does not appear dramatic. Our sage's aim is to describe the birth of idolatry; the polemic against it is not his principal objective, as perhaps would have been the case were the context that of the time of Caligula.[64]

---

60 Cf. Baslez, "The Author of Wisdom and the Cultured Environment", 37-40.

61 Cf. Foerster, Σεβαστός, *TDNT* 7:174.

62 Gilbert, *La critique*, 191.

63 Cf. Smith, R.R.R. *Hellenistic Royal Portraits*, Oxford: Clarendon Press 1988; Elsner Jas, "The Origin of the Icon: Pilgrimage, Religion and Visual Culture in the Roman East as "Resistance" to the Centre", in Alcock, Susan E. (ed.), *The Early Roman Empire in the East*, Oxford: Oxbow 1997, 513-533. For all this, cf., above all, Baslez, "The Author of Wisdom and the Cultured Environment", 45-49.

64 Cf. Larcher, *Sagesse*, 3:822.

14:22-31: Ignorance of God and *Pax Romana*

In 14:22b, the knowledge of God (14:22a) is contrasted with the "great war of ignorance" in which the idolaters find themselves living. The term ἄγνοια, little used by the LXX (cf. Wis 17:12), is employed already in Plato with reference to the ignorance of God as the generator of all evils (*Theae.* 176C). In the Stoic view, ignorance is connected with ethics according to an idea taken up again by Philo (*Ebr.* 157-161); cf. Epictetus, *Diatr.* 1.26.6; *SVF* III, 23 frag. 95; III, 60 frag. 256.[65] The idea of ἄγνοια thus seems to be taken up by the Cynic-Stoic diatribe, but also the distinction between ignorance of God and immorality. The first is the result of the second. However, although the formula γνῶσις θεοῦ is not in the LXX (apart from Wis 2:13; 14:22; cf. Philo, *Deo* 143), "knowing God" is a profoundly biblical idea (Hos 13:4; Isa 45:4); cf., in particular, the ἐπίγνωσις θεοῦ spoken of in Hos 6:6 and, above all, Hos 4:1-2, a passage which seems to be the main biblical source in this section. Where there is no knowledge of God, there is only immorality. Indeed, this is the situation of the nations (cf. Ps 78:6 LXX [79:6 MT]). Thus, the inspiration of v. 22 is biblical at the same time as our sage is leaning on Hellenistic concepts. The theme will be taken up again in v. 30 which, in its turn, recalls the beginning of the book (1:1b). The knowledge of God is a subject dear to the author's heart. However, the idolaters do not realise that they are living in this state of ignorance (of God), and that is why, to their lack of knowledge of God, they add a further error, immorality, although they do not recognize it as such and actually call it by the name of "peace".

In the mention of "peace" (14:22c), which, in reality hides a "great war of ignorance", an allusion to Jer 6:14 is plausible, but the context is different. Rather, it should probably be seen as a polemical reference to the *pax romana*, symbolically celebrated by Octavian Augustus in January 29 BCE with symbolic closing of the doors of the Janus Temple in the Roman Forum and with the dedication of the *Ara Pacis* in 9 BCE. "Robbing and murdering and assaulting they call by the false name of empire, and the sowing of desolation they call peace (*auferre trucidare rapere falsis nominibus imperium, atque, ubi solitudinem faciunt, pacem appellant*)"; thus, a famous passage of Tacitus, *Agr.* 30. This is not only an interior war, as some texts of Philo suggest (*Conf.* 46-49; *Gig.* 51), influenced by the Cynic-Stoic diatribe (cf. Ps. Heraclitus, *Ep.* 7).[66] Corruption and violence dominate the world, and people have the audacity – says our author – to call all this "peace". It is possible also to think of a polemic against the mysteries. The initiate reaches "peace" after celebrating his initiation ("*ad portum quietis et aram misericordiae tandem, Luci, venisti*"; Apuleius, *Metam.* 11.15).

As we have seen, in the list of vices in vv. 23-26, there emerge some connected with the celebration of the mystery cults (v. 23), in particular, the Dionysiac rites. In our view, it is these polemical references that account for the originality of the series of vices put forward by Wisdom. They are followed by the vices connected with family life and social life (cf., especially, v. 24, but also vv. 25 and 26a) and, immediately afterwards, the vices linked to corruption of a sexual nature, especially those bound up with the distortion of marriage.

---

65 Cf. Gilbert, *La critique*, 157-161. In the mention of ignorance, Scarpat, *Sapienza*, 3:103-107, sees, rather, a reference to anti-Gnostic polemics.

66 Cf. R. Hercher, *Epistolographi Graeci*, Paris: Didot 1873, 284.

Comparison with similar lists coming from Jewish spheres, especially those contained in Sib. Or. 3:36-43; 763-765; 4:31-34; cf. 1QS IV, 9-12, but also Rom 1:26-31,[67] shows, as has already been observed, that our author does not intend to offer an exhaustive list of vices but an exemplary catalogue, choosing examples of vice that were very relevant for his hearers who lived in a highly Hellenised environment,[68] without ever forgetting the Decalogue as his principal starting point. This type of choice also reveals his originality. The emphasis on "anti-social" vices, closely linked with idolatry and the mystery cults as triggers of these vices, reveals the power of his polemic. He sees that the ethical foundations of the society of his time have been demolished, and, for him, the cause of all this (cf. v. 27) is to be sought in the lack of knowledge of the true God which is the basis of all ethically upright behaviour.

It should be observed again that, in using the verb εὐφραίνω in v. 28, our sage probably intends to recall manifestations of joy which, together with the verb μαίνω (cf. ἐμμανεῖς in 23b), bring to mind, here too, the excesses typical of the Dionysiac banquets. The false prophecies (echoing texts like Jer 14:14-15; 23:26; 34:10, 15) display a polemic against a type of enthusiastic manticism bound up with ecstatic manifestations, exactly like those that were typical of some mystery cults (cf. Euripides, *Bacch.* 298-301). However, the use of oracles is typical of contemporary piety: diviners, oracles, and prophets were consulted both within celebrations and in places reserved for them.[69]

False Oaths

The emphasis on the serious nature of perjury, the theme around which the whole pericope of 14:28-31 revolves, is a further sign of the dependence of all this section on the Decalogue (14:22-31; cf. Exod 20:7; Deut 5:11). Swearing on idols of gods which do not exist is an act which only promotes injustice. The idea is not absent from Scripture (Josh 23:7; Jer 5:2, 7). In the Decalogue, the prohibition of false witness goes hand in hand with the prohibition of images and so of idols, contrasted with the God of Israel.

However, this emphasis on false oaths is also to be read in the light of the context in which our sage lived. In Alexandria, in fact, the oath had a very important role and became the instrument of political and social equilibrium, often losing its religious dimension. Many educated people took oaths without believing in the idols on whom they were swearing. The spectacle of people who swear for whatever reason and do so before idols has certainly attracted the attention of our sage, and this is clearly the main reason for his polemic.[70]

---

67 For a comparison between Paul's list and that of Wisdom, cf. J.M. Lagrange, "Le catalogue des vices dans l'Epître aux Romains (I-28-31)", *RB* 8 (1911): 546, who holds that Paul was directly inspired by Wisdom.

68 Reese observes that many of these vices, little mentioned in or even unknown to the LXX, are found instead in the texts of the Epicurean, Philodemus (cf. ἀπιστία, ἐπιορκία, ἀμνηστία χάριτος, γενέσεως ἐναλλαγή, ἀταξία γάμων, ἀσέλγεια); "the author of Wis, then, was familiar with the technical terminology found in hellenistic literature and used it to describe moral dispositions" (*Hellenistic Influence*, 21).

69 Humbert, Gustave, "Divination", *Dictionnaire des antiquités grecques et romaines* II, 292-319; Monceaux, Paul, "Oraculum", *Dictionnaire des antiquités grecques et romaines* IV, 214-223.

70 Cf. Larcher, *Sagesse*, 3:841; Alonso Schökel, *Sabiduría*, 177.

Wis 15:1-6:
Faithfulness of God; Fidelity of the People

15:1 But you, our God, are good and faithful,
you are patient and have mercy while you govern all things.
2 Even if we sin, we are yours, acknowledging your dominion,
and we will sin no more, because we know we belong to you.
3 To know you is perfect justice,
to acknowledge your dominion is the root of immortality.

4 For neither has the invention of a wicked art deceived us,
nor the sterile work of those who draw shadows,
an image smeared with different colours,
5 the sight of which arouses the passions of the foolish.
Someone desires the breathless form of a mortal image.
6 Enamoured of evil and deserving to have such hopes
are those who make them, desire them, worship them.

Notes on the Text and Translation

v. 1. The term ἀληθής could have here, as in Wis 12:27, the sense of "true", in opposition to the idols who are false. These are the only two passages in the LXX in which the adjective refers to θεός. In Exod 34:6, we have, instead, ἀληθινός, "faithful", a nuance that cannot be wholly ruled out (it is the reading of authors like Grimm, Cornely, and Heinisch), given the clear reference to Exodus and to the context of the covenant (the LXX of Exod 34:6 translates the Hebrew רב חסד ואמת with πολυέλεος καὶ ἀληθινός).

v. 4. The term *σκιάγραφος is rare and refined, unknown before Wisdom. The term σκιαγραφία is employed by Plato (*Phaed.* 69b; *Resp.* 602d) in a negative sense, a "stage set" which deceives the spectator. Larcher (*Sagesse*, 3:855-856) thinks that our sage is referring to the "shadow painting", that is, that type of picture which makes the perspective stand out. However, Plato's use points more to the pejorative idea of a "painter of shadows", that is, an artist who deceives his public with a fictitious representation.

In 4c *σπιλωθέν is *hapax* of the LXX. The verb σπιλόω has the sense of "stain, smear": thus the text refers to "an image smeared with different colours". Our sage is very probably thinking of murals of idols, here judged very severely. Perhaps there is also a reference to the paintings which could be employed in the mystery cults (cf. Turcan, *Les cultes orientaux*, 295).

v. 5. Authoritative witnesses (S*, A*, and others; cf. Ziegler) correct the plural ἄφροσι into the singular ἄφρονι because of the following singular ποθεῖ. Scarpat suggests a case of haplography: from an original ποθεῖ τίς τε to the present ποθεῖ τε (*Sapienza*, 3:155); this could explain the presence of ἄφροσι.

Synchronic Analysis

In stark contrast with the previous list of vices, this invocation addressed in the second person to God stands out (cf. "Father!" in 14:3): "But you, our God!...". The use of δέ creates a neat antithesis with the previous long section on the origin of idolatry and introduces a warm and personal tone of prayer similar to that in 14:1-10. The invocation "you, our God" appears in Scripture in contexts in which Israel recognizes its sin and calls on the divine mercy (cf. Ezra 9:10; Ps 98:8 LXX [99:8 MT]; Dan 9:15 LXX; Bar 2:12, 15, 19, 27); but notice also Isa 26:12-13; Jer 3:19, 22; Bar 3:5-6, which imply a new role for Israel in relation to the covenant and its relationship with God, and so a rejection of sin.

15:1: "But You, Our God…!"

The God of Israel is invoked here with the most classical biblical attributes, starting from Exod 34:6, as one who is good, or χρηστός, a term which also adds the idea of gentleness; cf. the Latin *suavis* (cf. Pss 85:5 LXX [86:5 MT]; 99:5 LXX [100:5 MT]; 144:8 LXX [145:8 MT]); true (or faithful: ἀληθής); patient (μακρόθυμος; *hapax* in Wisdom, but frequently applied to God in the LXX; cf. Exod 34:6; Num 14:18, but in Proverbs and Qoheleth referring to people), and, finally, merciful, and, therefore, with a reworking of the adjectives ἐλεήμων and πολυέλεος of Exod 34:6, described as one who has mercy, governing all things (ἐλέει διοικῶν τὰ πάντα); for ἔλεος, cf. Wis 9:1; 11:9; and 12:22. This pericope expands the image of God offered in Wisdom 13-15: the God "who is", the creator God (13:1-9), the God who is a parent and caring (14:3-5) is now the God of the covenant, a God who works in history contrasted with idols incapable of any action whatever.

Verse 2 opens with the expression of a possibility: "even if we sin...". The exodus background turns our minds immediately to the episode of the golden calf. However, even if it is serious, sin does not destroy the belonging of the people to God. "We are yours" is another echo of Exod 34:9 LXX: καὶ ἐσόμεθα σοί; cf. also Jer 3:22. Our sage could be thinking of the biblical formula of the covenant, "you shall be my people, and I will be your God" (Jer 7:23; cf. Jer 11:4; 24:7; 38:33 LXX [31:33 MT]; 39:38 LXX [32:38 MT]; Lev 26:12). The people's belonging to God, ratified by the covenant, is bound up with the divine "dominion" (κράτος). The people acknowledge (εἰδότες) it and become aware of belonging to God, regardless of every possible sin.

15:2: "We are yours…"

This awareness leads to the will not to sin any more, expressed with a future middle (οὐχ ἁμαρτησόμεθα) which takes on both a volitive and exhortative tone: "we will sin no more". We note that, in 15:2a, εἰδότες indicates "recognise, admit", whereas, in 15:2b, the same participle stands for a knowledge which arises from a direct experience of the divine actions in history. The author is not referring here to Israel's sin in general but to idolatry, the golden calf. Israel knows it belongs to God and so does not intend to choose other gods any more. To God's "dominion", which recalls God's action in history, is added here the awareness of the divine election. The perfect λελογίσμεθα ("we know that we belong to you") underlines the permanent effects of the election in the people's present.[71] In the rather dark picture which our sage paints of humanity within Wisdom 13-15, this text marks a moment of hope.

---

71 On Augustine's reading of this verse, cf. Gilbert, *La critique*, 186-187.

15:3: "To Know You Is Perfect Justice"

With a decisive theological statement, this verse closes the reflection opened in v. 1. The mention of sin in v. 2 disappears here and is transformed into a positive statement: "to know you is perfect justice". Faithful Israel possesses knowledge of God, a knowledge similar to that possessed by wisdom (8:4a), and this knowledge is identified with "perfect justice". This is human justice, that perfection of virtue which it is possible to obtain from a personal relationship with God ("to know *you*"). Once again, for our sage, ethics is the product of faith. In vv. 2-3, the repeated use of verbs connected with knowledge (ἐπίσταμαι, οἶδα) can also be linked to our sage's polemic against a certain type of intellectual "knowledge" pursued by the more Hellenised Jews. The only true knowledge is that of the God of Israel.

In parallel with "know you" appears "acknowledging your dominion" (κράτος; cf. 2a). The recognition of the great acts of God in history and, therefore, of God's universal dominion is the "root of immortality". The idea of "root" (ῥίζα; cf. Sir 1:6, 20) indicates one reality which is simultaneously an anticipation and foundation of another. Faith in God, therefore, gives rise to justice (3a), that is the upright moral life, but also gives birth to ἀθανασία, eternal life, which, in the light of the previous verse, is described as "being with him" (cf. 3:1-9). This is the final occurrence of ἀθανασία in our book. Immortality, therefore, appears not only as a gift but also as a task which lies before people: fruit of faith in God and of a life led according to justice. Thus, according to our sage, this earthly life holds the seed of eternal life with God. Knowledge of God, therefore, does not concern only the present but, also and above all, the future (cf. a possible New Testament echo in John 17:3). Thus, we note that the connection between God's power and God's power over death is biblical (cf. Pss 48:16 LXX [49:16 MT]; 138:8 LXX [139:8 MT]), but is reworked here by our sage and laden with perspectives that are new and much richer.

15:4-5: Israel and the Idols

Verses 4-6 contrast the attitude of the Israelites with that of the idolaters. In fact, the γάρ of 4a marks a new development. In vv. 4-5, our sage returns to condemning idolatry anew, with a very negative judgement, relating to skill being employed for idolatrous ends (cf. also 14:18-20). Here, our sage is thinking of images (cf. the textual notes).

In v. 4, despite the previous reference to Israel's sin (15:2a), our sage expresses with a certain pride the position of a people which has not allowed itself to be led astray by idolatry (again, the verb πλανάω). This is a surprising statement, and the aorist (ἐπλάνησεν) cannot be referring to a specific event since our sage knows well that Israel yielded to idolatry as in the case of the golden calf just evoked. Rather, our sage is thinking of an ideal Israel which, like the just person of chapter two, never fell into the error of forgetting its own God. For Wisdom, clearly, such a faithful Israel has never ceased to exist. Unless our sage is thinking of contemporary Israel, which had already for a long time abandoned idolatrous practices, and so could make this bold statement (cf. Jdt 8:18).

Verse 5 introduces the theme of desire linked to the work of art described in 4bc. The term ὄρεξις was already present in 14:2 and will return later in 16:2 and 3. As in Rom 1:27, ὄρεξις acquires a sexual connotation: the sight of these pictures (ὧν) arouses the passion of the foolish.

Verse 5b adds some biblical borrowings. In connection with Wis 12:24; 13:10, 18, we have already seen that the theme of the idol understood as a "dead thing" (νεκρός) is bound up with ideas well established in Scripture. Biblical too is the theme of the "breathless idol" (ἄπνουν): cf. Jer 10:14; 28:17 LXX [51:17 MT]; Ep Jer [Bar 6:]24; Hab 2:19; Ps 134:17 LXX [135:17 MT]. This is the "desire" (ποθεῖ) of the idolaters: the search for something dead, which cannot give any help to people, unlike the personal and caring God invoked at the beginning of the pericope.

This verse has a solemn tone and, at one and the same time, constitutes an excellent conclusion to the pericope and a transition to the one that follows. The use of ἐραστής and the return of the verb ποθέω (6b) confirm the erotic background of this criticism of idolatry which affects every category of idolatry: those who make idols, those who desire them and those who worship them. Just as the sage is "enamoured of (the beauty of) wisdom" (cf. 8:2), here, the idolater is "enamoured of evil". Thus, the latter deserves (ἄξιος) to have only empty hopes (cf. 5:14), as opposed to the Israelites who, instead, are εὐέλπιδες (12:19), who hope in immortality, as was seen in v. 3. 15:6: "Enamoured of Evil..."

Diachronic Analysis

Even in calling on the God of Israel, our sage does not hesitate to make use of the Greek world. The expression employed in 15:1b, διοικῶν τὰ πάντα, "while you govern all things", is actually of Stoic derivation (cf. the same verb διοικέω used in Wis 8:1 in connection with wisdom) and recalls the idea of a God who is caring and kind to everything and everyone. A similar formula is employed by the Stoics in connection with the πνεῦμα (*SVF* II, 137 frag. 416) or fate (*SVF* I, 24 frag. 87; 50 frag. 98; II, 169 frag. 528; 264 frag. 913). However, the formula is more ancient and is taken up again in Greek-speaking Judaism by Aristeas (Let. Aris. 201, 234, 254: θεός τὸν πάντα κόσμον διοκεῖ μετ' εὐμενείας) and Philo (*Conf.* 170).[72] The connection of this formula with the theme of providence is typically Stoic: "...one must believe that the god who governs the universe (διοικοῦντα) cares for people in that he is kind, good (χρηστός), a lover of humanity (φιλάνθρωπος), just, and rich in every virtue" and for this reason is identified with πρόνοια, providence (cf. *SVF* II, 169 frag. 528; Josephus, *A.J.* 4.47). 15:1

Despite the borrowing from Stoicism, however, the background of the invocation in Wis 15:1 is even more biblical than Greek. Our author is thinking primarily of Exod 34:6-9, within the famous account of the golden calf. "Our God" is thus the God of the covenant who does not reject the people of God even in the face of their sin. In fact, God's universal dominion is closely bound up with God's disposition of mercy towards all things.

In vv. 4-5, our author, like Philo (*Leg.* 3.22; *Decal.* 7, 66, 156, etc.), does not go to the point of criticising art in general (cf., instead, Josephus in *C. Ap.* 2.74-75). The art is described here as "wicked" (κακότεχνος; cf. 1:4) because employed for perverse purposes. The idea is found in Posidonius and not unknown to classical culture. Not the popular arts, nor those that have arisen to entertain or even to educate, but only the *artes liberales* (ἐγκύκλιοι) can have virtue as their object (cf. Seneca, *Ep.* 88.21-23). 15:4-5

---

72 Gilbert, *La critique*, 175-177.

In v. 5, the text could be alluding to the story of Pygmalion, well known to the ancient world,[73] but, more particularly, leads to the thought of cases famous in the ancient world of a real erotic attitude held by devotees towards an idol, whether a statue or a painting.[74] Verse 6 (cf. the use of ἐραστής) confirms this interpretation.

Wis 15:7-13: The Folly of Idolatry

[7] Consider the potter, who, moulding the soft clay with toil,
creates for our use every type of object,
but with the same clay fashions
vessels that serve for pure uses
or for opposite uses, all in the same way:
what has to be the use of each of these
is what the potter decides.
[8] With wicked labour, he fashions with the same clay a vain god,
he, the man who, born a little earlier, from the earth,
will return in a short time to the place from which he was taken,
when the life lent to him will be required of him.
[9] But he is not concerned that he is going to die,
or that he possesses a life of short duration;
rather, he competes with goldsmiths and silversmiths,
imitates workers in bronze
and boasts of making false things.
[10] Ash is his heart, and his hope is more contemptible than earth,
his life worth less than clay,
[11] because he did not acknowledge the one who formed him,
who infused him with an active soul
and breathed in him a living breath.
[12] But he considered life as a game,
and existence as a fair, an opportunity for gain:
"one must – he tells himself – from everything, even from evil, draw a profit".
[13] And more than anyone else he knows that he is sinning,
the one who fashions fragile vessels and statues with earthy material.

---

73 Gilbert, *La critique*, 192-193. Ovid speaks of it, *Metam.* 10.243-297; Clement of Alexandria, *Protr.* 4.57.1-5; Arnobius, *Adv. Gent.* 6.22.

74 Cf. the texts cited in Scarpat, *Sapienza*, 3:155.

Notes on the Text and Translation

v. 7. In 7c, ἀνεπλάσατο is an aorist with narrative value, alternating with the present πλάσσει.
In 7f, Ziegler, proposes reading τούτων δὲ ἑκατέρου; authoritative codices (B, S^{c}, V) read ἑτέρου instead. With some minuscules, we prefer (cf. Heinisch, Fichtner, Larcher, Gilbert) the reading τούτων δὲ ἑκατέρων; Scarpat (*Sapienza*, 3:159) holds, however, that ἑκατέρου is a purist gloss which ought to be expunged.
The term that closes v. 7, *πηλουργός, "one who works with clay, i.e., a potter", is rare and refined, attested here for the first time (Winston, *Wisdom*, 286).

v. 8. The adjective *κακόμοχθος seems to be a creation of our sage, following a usage frequent in the Hellenistic period, and has the etymological sense of "one who devotes himself to a wicked task"; cf. the explicit recalling of *ἐπίμοχθος in 7a, it too *hapax* of the LXX. The expression θεὸς μάταιος as such is also absent from the LXX; for μάταιος, cf. 13:1.

v. 9. The text of 9c is composed of three LXX *hapax*. The verb *ἀντερείδομαι has the sense of "face up to, resist", but the majority of commentators hold that it assumes here the sense of "compete"; cf. the old conjecture of Grabe who suggests reading ἀντερίζεται. Scarpat proposes translating it in its normal sense of "resist", in the sense that the potter "resists" the competition of craftsmen more able than he, imitates the lowly smelters of bronze and works the clay to produce idols at a good price for the superstitious populace (*Sapienza*, 3:162).
The verb ἀντερείδομαι has as complements χρυσουργοῖς καὶ ἀργυροχόοις, those who work with gold and silver, two terms rare also in Greek usage; *χρυσουργός is *hapax* of the LXX; *ἀργυροχόος is *hapax totius graecitatis,* as is also the following *χαλκοπλάστης. All these refined terms give the text a tone of ironic solemnity.

v. 11. The verb ἐμπνέω has an active sense and is more acceptable to Greek ears that the ἐνέφυσεν of Gen 2:7; cf. Philo, *Leg.* 1.36, and the discussion in Scarpat, *Sapienza*, 3:164.

v. 12. Codex B, together with S^{c} and several minuscules, reads the singular ἐλογίσατο, chosen by Ziegler. All the other witnesses have ἐλογίσαντο. Taking up a proposal of W. Smits, Gilbert (*La critique*, 200-201) proposes reading the much better attested ἐλογίσαντο with an impersonal form: "life is considered a game"; so too the following φησίν can be well understood as impersonal, "it is said", following a use not unknown to the diatribe.

v. 13. The major codices (S, A, C, V) read an impossible εὔθραστα which is usually corrected to *εὔθραυστα, *hapax* of the LXX, a rare term which can be translated with "fragile". Scarpat (*Sapienza*, 3:166-167) prefers to read the slightly attested but more usual εὔθλαστα, with the same meaning.

Synchronic Analysis

The unity of the section is provided by the theme of the potter who makes idols of clay. While vv. 7-9 have a more descriptive style, vv. 10-13 are devoted to a more profound reflection. We are at the end of the section devoted to idolatry in which, as has been said, our sage has followed an order of decreasing quality: the potter who creates clay idols is the worst of all the idolaters, one degree higher than the animal worshippers for which the final pericope is reserved.

15:7-9: The Potter

Verses 7-9 describe the commonest activity of the potter (cf. Sir 38:29-30), who ends up making idols, something well known in Alexandria.[75]

Verse 7 describes in detail the construction of a clay vessel which is utilized for the most common uses. It is for the potter to decide the fate of his vessels. This idea is used in a theological key in Jer 18:2-4, in relation to the free action of God which is compared precisely with that of a potter (cf. Isa 29:16; 45:9-10; 64:7). As for the idea of the potter who makes vessels for noble and less noble uses, it is found again only in Rom 9:21, but in a different context.[76] However, the potter decides to use his skill for the construction of an idol as well, as v. 8 explains.

In v. 8, the moral judgement on the potter is clear: with the *hapax* *κακόμοχθος, our sage judges the whole of his work to be wicked, aimed at creating a "vain god" out of clay. However, the potter's most serious fault is that of misunderstanding his state as a creature. Verse 8bc recalls that, like everyone else, the potter is born from the earth and must return there.

Our sage seems to be employing ψυχή here in the biblical sense of "life", vital principle, and so shows himself closer to the Hebrew than the Greek anthropology. However, the ψυχή appears also as a personal subject here, following a use already seen in our book (cf. 8:19-20). In fact, it is the ψυχή which God requires from a person. The idea expressed here is complex, therefore. The potter becomes the model of everyone who shows himself or herself incapable of communicating life to others, but who, in the end, will see that his or her own life is required by God (cf., in the NT, Luke 12:20, with the same verb, ἀπαιτέω).

Verse 9 introduces a new idea: instead of thinking of his own mortality, the idolatrous potter deceives himself into thinking he can escape it by creating an idol. Wishing to imitate more sophisticated artists (9c-d), the potter considers it an object of boasting (9e) to achieve something false (κίβδηλα; cf. 2:16), namely, the idols he is fashioning. He is motivated by the search for a purely human δόξα but also, as we shall see in vv. 10-13, by the desire for gain. The text has an ironic and even sarcastic tone which pillories the potter's ridiculous claim.

15:10-13: Condemnation of the Potter

In vv. 10-13, our author goes on to consider the condemnation of the idolatrous potter, employing a tone that is extremely severe.

Verse 10a opens with a quotation from Isa 44:20 LXX; in the light of this text, idolatry is seen as the negation of God's activity on behalf of God's people. The idolater's "heart", that is, all his will and rationality, becomes only ash (cf. 2:2d). He loses all hope (cf. the false hope of the ungodly in 3:18 and 5:14), bound as he is to the earth, since his life, that is, his style of life (βίος), is worth less than the clay that he works (10b).

Verse 11, which again takes up Gen 2:7 (τὸν πλάσαντα αὐτόν), is interesting for analysing our author's anthropological conceptions. The potter "did not acknowledge the one who formed him", does not understand, that is, that he was fashioned by God, as described in the Genesis account. For the sin of "ignorance", cf. 13:1a. The subsequent reference to the soul and the spirit leads to the thought

---

75 Fraser, *Ptolemaic Alexandria*, 1:140.

76 For a possible but problematic relationship of Rom 9:21 with Wis 15:7, cf. Larcher, *Sagesse*, 3:862; Gilbert, *La critique*, 204 n. 38.

that αὐτόν/αὐτῷ in 15:11a.b refers to the body, but all dualism of a Platonic stamp seems to be excluded.

The charge against the idolatrous potter is completed in v. 12 which expresses three ideas each of which are frequent *topoi* in classical literature (see below).

Life a Fair and Occasion for Profit

The idolatrous potter, who plays at the little demiurge (v. 13), becomes here a symbol of people without God for whom looking after their own interest is the most important thing. However, he does not succeed in "fashioning" (cf. Wis 15:7, 8, 9, 11, 16: πλάσσω) "earthy material" (ὕλη γεώδης, cf. Wis 11:17) and putting into it that vital soul (15:11b-c) which God has given to people. The verb δημιουργέω, which occurs only here in the whole book, is deliberately placed at the end of the pericope. It is this impotent imitation of divinity that constitutes the true tragedy of idolatry for our author. The irony concerning the Platonic concept of the "demiurge" is sharpened by the reference to matter (ὕλη γεώδης) which opens the stich. By contrast with God, who creates the world ἐξ ἀμόρφου ὕλη (11:17), the potter, who uses "earthy material", is not able to give it life.

Implicitly, our sage is assuming that, beginning from the careful consideration of their own fragility and mortality, everyone has the possibility of getting back to the creator, ideas already underlying 13:1-9. Thus, the idolater's ignorance is to be held culpable ignorance which places him on an even lower level than the idols which he himself has made. In the case of the potter, the sin is still more serious since he does not show that he believes in the idols which he has made solely to satisfy his personal interest and thinking of possible gain.

Diachronic Analysis

15:7-9

In v. 7, in addition to the background of the biblical image of God as potter, our sage is making use here, even if in a rather generic way, of a *topos* common in the ancient world. E.g., the story of Pharaoh Amasis, recounted by Herodotus, which reveals how a statue worshipped by the Egyptians was originally a bowl for washing feet (Herodotus, *Hist.* 2.172).[77] However, the theme of the craftsman who fashions an idol out of common materials is a commonplace of anti-idolatrous polemic. Almost all the commentators mention Horace's celebrated satire on the fig tree (*Sat.* 1.8.1-4 : *Olim truncus eram ficulnus, inutile lignum ...*). Yet again, our sage is combining biblical motifs with ideas from the Greek world.

In v. 8, the expression ἐξ ἧς ἐλήμφθη recalls Gen 3:19 to the letter, a quotation easily recognisable by the Jewish readership of Wisdom. The idea was already implicit in the discourse of the ungodly (2:1-2) and was taken up again in the mouth of Solomon (7:1-2). However, the idea that people come from the earth and return to it is not only typically Jewish (Job 34:15; Qoh 3:20; Sir 41:10), but also at home in the Greek world.[78]

The expression "when the ψυχή that has been lent to him is required of him" is, in its turn, a rereading of Gen 2:7 (but cf. Qoh 12:7). A person has received his or her vital breath from God; therefore, life is something that comes to humans from an external source. Hence the idea of a debt to be repaid. Moreover, in the

77 Cf., for the details, Gilbert, *La critique*, 205-207.

78 Cf. the texts mentioned by Larcher, *Sagesse*, 3:864.

classical world, the idea of life granted as a loan is a common consolatory motif: "vitaque mancipio nulli datur, omnibus usu" (Lucretius, *Rer. Nat.* 3.971); a motif of Platonic origin (*Tim.* 42E), frequent in Stoicism (cf. Cicero, *Tusc.* 1.39, 93) and well known in Hellenistic Judaism: cf. Philo, *Cher.* 118; *Her.* 104-108.[79]

In v. 9, the theme of "concern" (φροντίς) introduced in 9a, again recalls Platonic themes. In fact, the true philosopher thinks continually of death (*Phaed.* 67D-69E, 80E, 81A); life is something that people receive for a short time (*βραχυτελής; *hapax* of the LXX and of classical Greek). Thus, there is a return to the theme of death, which has already been seen with regard to the ungodly in Wisdom 2, that thought which they would have liked to eliminate by enjoying life without restraint.

Thus, the charge brought here against the idolaters is taking up themes frequent in the Hellenistic world, but the background and the thought remain profoundly biblical. People are considered responsible for the life given them by God.

15:10-13: Soul and Spirit

The expression of v. 11bc, "who infused him with an active soul (ψυχὴν ἐνεργοῦσαν) and breathed in him living breath (πνεῦμα ζωτικόν)", seems more distant from the biblical account and is following Greek models, at least in part. The two terms, "soul" and "spirit", are probably synonyms here and refer to two different activities of the soul: the "active" soul, the soul understood as source of life but, above all, source of people's moral activity, according to a conception already encountered in the book (cf. the comment on 1:4; 8:19-20 and, above, in 15:8). The "vital spirit" refers to the soul considered as source of that life which comes from God. The mention of the πνεῦμα probably arises from the wish to clarify the nature of the ψυχή better. On the one hand, the πνεῦμα recalls Gen 2:7 more directly. Philo too tends to replace the biblical πνοή with the more Greek πνεῦμα (*Leg.* 3.161; *Det.* 80). On the other hand, πνεῦμα recalls that "spirit" associated with wisdom (cf. 7:22-23) which makes of wisdom itself something of the divine and which, in people, is what renders them close to God. In this way, our sage is rereading Gen 2:7 from a Greek perspective and applying to everyone what the Genesis text says of the first human created.[80] Thus, all forms of pre-existence of souls is to be excluded: the soul is like a breath of life coming from God himself, breathed into the body to make it live, the source of the moral life.

As has been said, v. 12 contains three *topoi* of classical literature. First of all, for our potter, life is a παίγνιον (cf. 12:26), a child's game, a farce, as seems to have been the expression of the dying Augustus as reported by Suetonius, *Aug.* 99.1: "if the farce (τὸ παίγνιον) please you, applaud!".

Furthermore, the whole course of human life (βίος) is only an occasion of profit, a fair or market (*πανηγυρισμός). Our potter lives his life like those traders who take part in fairs only to conclude business deals. "Life is a farce (παίγνιον), a trick (πλάνη), and a fair (πανηγύρις)", so says the Greek-speaking astrologer

---

79 Cf. Gilbert, *La critique*, 208-210: "Sg 15,8d et 16b reflètent un thème d'origine grecque que les auteurs latins et juifs hellénisés ont assimilé" (210); Larcher, *Sagesse*, 3:865-866. For the Greco-Roman world, see also the observations of Vílchez Líndez, *Sapienza*, 464 and the texts mentioned by him in note 81; cf., again, Scarpat, *Sapienza*, 3:160-161, and Winston, *Wisdom*, 286-287.

80 For these conclusions, cf. Gilbert, "La procréation", 353-355.

Vettius Valens around the second cent. CE.[81] The idea that life is a "fair" seems to go back to Pythagoras and is mentioned several times by ancient authors (cf. Cicero, *Tusc.* 5, 3.9) Only the more noble souls raise themselves to contemplation above those who follow material goods.

Finally, from everything one must draw gain, even from evil.[82] Thus, behind idolatry too sprouts the delusion of money and of search after self-interest. Believing or not in the idols produced is negligible in the face of the thought of profit, as in the case of the goldsmiths of Ephesus (Acts 19:24-25). Quite different is the case of Israel which searches for the true God (cf. 15:3).

Wis 15:14-19: Criticism of Egyptian Zoolatry

14 But they are all totally without sense
and unfortunate, less intelligent than a child,
those enemies of your people who have oppressed them,
15 for they consider as gods all the idols of the nations,
which do not have eyes that can see,
or nostrils to breathe the air,
or ears to hear,
or fingers of the hand to touch,
and their feet are no use for walking.

16 For it is a man who has fashioned them,
they were modelled by one of borrowed breath.
For no man can form a god which is like him.
17 Being a mortal, with his wicked hands he produces a dead thing.
For he is worth more than the objects that he worships
because, compared with them, he possesses life,
while they will never have it.
18 They also worship the most hateful animals
which, for stupidity, are worse than all the others;
19 and, insofar as one can find an animal attractive,
they are not even beautiful
but have escaped God's approval and his blessing.

---

81 *Vettii Valentis Anthologiarum libri*, Kroll, Wilhelm (ed.) (Berolini: Weidmann 1908) 246,1-2.

82 For other interesting examples, cf. Gilbert, *La critique*, 214-216; Winston, *Wisdom*, 288. Cf. *Anth. Pal.* 10.72: "all of life is a play and a game: either learn to play, casting care aside, or endure the sufferings". Suetonius also mentions, in connection with the levies on the "Vespasiani" (urinals), that "pecunia non olet [gold does not stink]"! (*Vesp.* 23.5); cf. Juvenal, *Sat.* 14.204-205: "lucri bonus est odor ex re qualibet [profit smells good wherever it comes from]".

Notes on the Text and Translation

v. 14. In 14a, codices A, C, and other witnesses read πάντων δὲ ἀφρονέστατοι [C, with S and several minuscules, reads ἀφρονέστεροι]. However, this is *lectio facilior* to which is preferable the more difficult but better attested πάντες, which is, therefore, the subject of the phrase while οἱ ἐχθροί is in apposition. The initial δέ is to be understood in an adversative sense and the better attested ἀφρονέστατοι read as a superlative: "but (they are) all totally without sense...".

In the same stich, the expression τάλανες ὑπὲρ ψυχὴν νηπίου is to be understood literally "more wretched in soul than a child". Τάλας, exceptional in the LXX (Isa 6:5; 4 Macc 8:17; 12:4), is frequent in the tragedians in the sense of "wretched" or "miserable". The reference to the child (νήπιος) is topical and refers to the lack of intelligence which was held to be the case with children (*Il.* 17.32; Plato, *Symp.* 222b, where he cites Hesiod, *Op.* 218 [παθὼν δέ τε νήπιος ἔγνω]; Euripides, *Med.* 885ff. associates νήπιος precisely with ἄφρων); cf. Wis 12:24 and the related comment.

v. 15. In making use of the text of Ps 113:12-15 LXX [115:5-7 MT], our sage introduces some modifications. He eliminates the mouth that does not speak (cf. Gilbert, *La critique*, 235-237). The term *συνολκή seems to be a creation of our author and returns in T. Reu. 2:5, in a possible interpolation which takes the term precisely from Wisdom. It is a technical term employed in the medical writings of the second cent. CE where it underlines the vital role of respiration (Gilbert, *La critique*, 237-238). Another technical term of the medical literature is *ψηλάφησις, "to feel, touch" (Hippocrates, *Steril.* 213).

v. 16. The text of 16c is corrupt; cf. an extensive discussion in Larcher, *Sagesse*, 3:881-882. Accepting Ziegler's text (with B, S, C, O, Lat, Sah, Syr), we translate: "for no man can form a god which is like him" (Lat: *nemo enim sibi similem homo poterit deum fingere*).

v. 18. The verb σέβονται is a middle form (Gilbert, *La critique*, 225 n. 1). The subject is the same as v. 15, that is, the "enemies". Scarpat (*Sapienza*, 3:174) considers it to be a deponent form with active sense.

In 18b, ἀνοίᾳ creates some difficulties; cf. Ziegler, apparatus, and Larcher, *Sagesse*, 3:884; Grimm (*Weisheit*, 262) proposes reading with some mss, ἀνία ("Plage, Unheil" [plague, disaster]). Ἀνοίᾳ is to be understood as a dative of relation which could refer to the animals: "for stupidity they are worse than all the others". Although animals are without νοῦς, there exist different degrees of intelligence among them, and the Egyptians worship the worst ones.

Synchronic Analysis

15:14: Folly of the Animal Worshippers

Already in 11:15-16, at the beginning of the digression on philanthropy, our sage had introduced the theme of animal worship which now reappears at the conclusion of the long attack on idolatry. This short pericope opens with a very harsh judgement on the enemies of "your people", clearly the Egyptians who have oppressed "your people" (v. 14). They are totally without sense (ἄφρων; cf. Wis 1:3; 3:2, 12; 5:4;12:24; 14:11; 15:5), less intelligent than a child (cf. Philo, *Mos.* 1.102; *Decal.* 69). With the exception of Wis 12:20, 22, the term ἐχθρός is always used for the Egyptians. The verbs καταδυναστεύω is employed for the ungodly in Wis 2:10 and for the Egyptians in 17:2. The use of the aorist participle is a reminder of the events of the exodus rather than an indication of current hostility.

In 15a, after an explicative ὅτι, the καί introduces a first series of observations which correspond to those introduced by the καί of v. 18a. Verses 15-17 continue the reflection on idols, inspired once again by biblical texts. The charge is now brought against religious syncretism of which the Egyptians offered a good example. The "enemies" have held as gods (ἐλογίσαντο θεούς) all the idols of the nations. The description of the idols in 15b–f is inspired by Ps 113:12-15 LXX [115:5-7 MT], a psalm with an exodus background (cf. Ps 135:15-17 LXX [136:15-17 MT]), quoted with some learned modifications (see the textual notes). 15:15: Religious Syncretism

In v. 16, there returns a theme already seen (cf. 15:8d, 11): people play at creator, modelling a god in their image, people who themselves are images of God. Thus, the verse is taking up in an ironic key the texts of Gen 1:27 and 2:7 which have already been used extensively. See also the comment on 15:8. There, ψυχή was used; here, instead, πνεῦμα. The terms are used as synonyms and refer in both cases to the "soul", understood in the Bible as the life God lends to people (δεδανεισμένος). 15:16-17: People Play at Creator

Verse 17 gives further reasons for the condemnation of the idolater. A mortal can only produce dead things; and this action is already something wicked (17a). Paradoxically, mortals are superior to the things that they themselves worship (17b) because mortals at least have life (ἔζησεν, inchoative aorist), whereas the idols will never have it (17c).

Verses 18-19 refer explicitly to the Egyptian cult of animals. The animals targeted seem to be the reptiles and other repugnant creatures worshipped by the Egyptians (ἑρπετὰ καὶ κνώδαλα: Wis 11:15; 17:9). The text is alluding to the curse in Gen 3:14. There are beings, therefore, that escape the divine approval (Gen 1:21, 25); this explains the difficult text of 19b.[83] A further possible explanation lies in the fact that the blessing and divine approval is not withheld from these animals as such but only insofar as they have become objects of worship and so reduced to being idols. 15:18-19: Egyptian Zoolatry

Diachronic Analysis

The phenomenon of religious syncretism characterises the Hellenistic period. The religion of classical Greece was open to contacts with the oriental religions. If, in Egypt, the indigenous population was more bound to the local divinities, the Ptolemaic dynasty favoured a broader encounter between the Greek and Egyptian religions. In the Roman period, syncretism is undoubtedly one of the most characteristic elements of beliefs and religious practices. Often the syncretism takes on a more philosophical garb: the various divinities are considered as manifestations of the one god (in this case, one speaks of "henotheism"). The accusation brought by Wisdom in 15:15 is directed more against the educated" part of the population than against the more widespread attitudes on the popular level. After all, Egypt knew the custom of προσκύνημα, leaving an inscription in the temple so as to be remembered by all the gods.[84] 15:15

83 For Winston "this is not a Jewish teaching" (*Wisdom*, 290) but of Zoroastrian origin.

84 Cf. Dunand, Françoise, Lévèque, Pierre, (edd.), *Syncrétisme dans les religions de l'Antiquité*, *EPR* 46, Brill: Leiden 1975; Geraci, Giovanni, "Ricerche sul *proskynema*", *Aegyptus* 51 (1971) 3-211.

15:18-19 In vv. 18-19, the accusation brought against the zoolatrous cults combines the biblical prohibition of animal worship with a *motif* that was widespread also in classical culture. Strabo (*Geogr.* 16.2.35) praises Moses for having rejected Egyptian zoolatry. Precisely in Alexandria, in a text very close to ours (*Decal.* 76), Philo takes up the theme of the stupidity and lack of beauty of the animals worshipped by the Egyptians. Already, the Letter of Aristeas had attacked Egyptian zoolatry (Let. Aris. 138). Josephus records that in the anti-Jewish version of the exodus by Manetho (*C. Ap.* 1.239), one of the accusations against the Israelites was that of having offered in sacrifice animals sacred to the Egyptians: "our religion is as different from that in vogue among them as the nature of God is from that of irrational beasts" (*C. Ap.* 1.224). The attacks on Egyptian zoolatry in Greek-speaking Judaism have primarily an apologetic purpose: that of strengthening the faith of the Jews to whom these texts are addressed.[85] Our sage belongs to this chorus of reprobation of Egyptian zoolatry. Finally, the mention of the "beauty" of the animals is a Greek touch that we have already come across in Wis 13:1-9; cf. the Greek translation of the טוב of Genesis 1 with καλός.

Already in Lev 11:41-45, the list of impure animals was based on the fact that many of them were objects of worship among the other peoples. Our author's originality lies in giving the Leviticus list a strong theological grounding in the light of a typically Hellenistic sensitivity. Thus, the polemic against zoolatry combines, very closely, clear biblical themes, influenced by the rationalist Greek mentality, with a powerful polemic against the cults of contemporary Egypt, all in such a way as to strengthen the identity and faith of the Jewish people.

Summary of Wis 13-15

In the whole of the OT, there is no passage on idolatry as long and as detailed as Wisdom 13-15. However, Scripture is, once again, our author's starting point. At the base of the polemic against the idols lie, first and foremost, the texts of the Decalogue (Exod 20:3-5; cf., also, Deut 4:16-19) and many other texts which we have been able to note in the course of the commentary. At the same time, all this biblical material has been reread and re-presented in the light of the Hellenistic culture and so made relevant for the Alexandrian Jews, especially those tempted by cults such as those of the mysteries. If, on the one hand, therefore, there is polemic against idolatry – and very harsh polemic in the case of Egyptian zoolatry (15:14-19) – on the other hand, as Wis 13:1-9 demonstrates, the rejection of the pagans is not total and unreserved.

A further theme which emerges in these chapters is the conviction that the creation is good (but also beautiful: cf. 13:7; 14:3, 7). Idolatry thus consists in the overturning of the meaning of creation. In fact, idols are a way of dishonouring creation (14:11). In fashioning an idol, the creature takes the place of the creator

---

85 Bickerman, *The Jews*, 253 and 256; Smelik, Klaas A.D. – Hemelrijk E.A. "Who Knows Not What Monsters Demented Egypt Worships? Opinions on Egyptian Animal Worship in Antiquity as Part of the Ancient Conception of Egypt", in: *ANRW* 17/4 (1984) 1885-2000.

(cf. 15:7-13), and the idolater plays at substituting himself or herself for God (cf. 15:16). The consequences of idolatry are immorality and injustice (14:11-31). In this way, our author is going back to the first part of his work where he had already highlighted the theme of the goodness of the creation (1:13-15) and the injustice of the ungodly who do not understand it (Wisdom 2 and 5). Thus, his criticism of idolatry is founded more on religious than on philosophical or rational bases, as is also the case in similar texts of Philo. At any rate, Wisdom 13-15 opens up a rather gloomy picture of humanity. In a particular way, the extended section of 14:11-31 links the overturning of the image of God with the growth of widespread immorality.

On several occasions, idolatry is contrasted with the revelation of the God of Israel, the creator and saviour, on whom our sage reflected in the previous digression (cf. 11:15-12:27): God is the God of Genesis (cf. 13:3, 5; 14:5; 15:8, 11, 16, 18-19) but, at the same time, of the exodus and the covenant (cf. 13:1 and 15:1-3). This is a God who is a caring Parent (cf. 14:1-10), whom the Greek philosophers were searching for but never found. To recognize this God, rich in pardon, who acts in the history of God's people, and, at the same time, in the creation, is the root of immortality (15:1-3). The criticism of idolatry, therefore, is conducted in the name of a vision of history understood as a history of salvation. Here too, we are on solidly biblical foundations.

Wis 16: Three Antitheses: God Punishes and Favours; God's Word Is Nourishment

The Literary Structure of Wis 16

The division of the chapter into three diptychs (the second, third, and fourth antitheses) is generally accepted: 16:1-4; 16:5-14 and 16:15-29. However, the commentaries show little awareness of the connections between these three diptychs, connections which make chapter 16 into a thoroughly compact unit. First of all, the theme of *nourishment* (τροφή) appears which is introduced in 16:1-4 and developed in the diptych on the manna (16:15-29); cf. v. 2c, with reference to the Israelites; v. 3a with reference to the Egyptians; and v. 20a with reference to the Israelites again. In 16:2c and 20a, the nourishment is provided by God in an extraordinary way (2c: ξένη γεῦσις) or directly given from heaven (20b). Towards the end of the fourth antithesis, vv. 24-25 draw the theological consequences of this reflection, which links 16:1-4 directly with 16:15-29. Thus, the theme of nourishment develops the much wider theme of the cosmos which animates the whole of the third part of Wisdom and becomes an existential "cipher" to describe the human attitude towards life and death.

The third diptych (16:5-14) introduces the theme of the *word that saves*, which the antithesis on the manna again takes up; cf. the relationship between 16:12 and 16:26 both of which have an invocation, κύριε.[1] In this way, the fourth antithesis is found to be linked simultaneously to the second, through the theme of nourishment, and to the third, through the theme of the word of God. Moreover, in 16:7, 12, and 26b-c, there is an identical mode of expression: a negation followed by a contrast, the warning not to dwell on the material nature of the exodus events but to grasp their salvific aspect. The one who saves is God himself, "Saviour of all" (17:6), and his word (16:12).

Furthermore, a third theme is found in all three diptychs, that of the *favours* of God for God's people. The verb εὐεργετέω, which appears in Wis 16:2a, is taken from the substantive εὐεργεσία which appears in connection with the divine favours in the third (16:11d) and fourth (16:24c) diptychs, further proof of the profound unity of this chapter. Through antithesis, the theme of punishment connects the first two diptychs: the verb ἐπέρχομαι acts as hook-word in 4a and 5a, with reference to the divine anger; so too κολάζω in 16:1a and 9c (ἐκολάσθησαν ἀξίως... ἄξιοι ἦσαν κολασθῆναι).

1 Cf., for the details, Passaro, "Il serpente e la manna", 196.

Wis 16:1-4: The Second Diptych – The Plague of the Beasts and the Quails

The Literary Structure of Wis 16:1-4[2]

Somewhat neglected in the commentaries, this little passage can serve as a useful exercise for understanding our author's compositional techniques. Note that some key terms are repeated twice, following a technique dear to our sage:

Israel	Egypt
v. 2b: εἰς ἐπιθυμίαν ὀρέξεως ξένην γεῦσιν τροφὴν ἡτοίμασας	v. 3abc: ἐπιθυμοῦντες τροφήν... καὶ τὴν ἀναγκαίαν ὄρεξιν
v. 3de: ἐνδεεῖς γενόμενοι	v. 4: ἀπαραίτητον ἔνδειαν

Note also the repetition of ἐκολάσθησαν – κολάσεως (1a - 2a); ξένην – ξένης (2b - 3e); γεῦσιν – γεύσεως (2b - 3e). Other repetitions are taken up in the third diptych (16:15-29): ἐκολάσθησαν (cf. 16:24b, εἰς κόλασιν) and εὐεγρετήσας (cf. 16:24c, εἰς εὐεργεσίαν). Thus emerge the *motifs* of food and desire, punishment and favours, or, rather, the great theme of divine action.

This pericope is to be read in close continuity with the previous one (15:14-19). The punishment of the Egyptians through animals is to be seen as a direct consequence of their zoolatry. Thus, the digression of 13-15 appears to be closely linked with what follows, precisely by means of Wis 16:1-4, which, although introducing a second antithesis after that of Wis 11:6-14, is a strong continuation of the previous chapters.

Finally, we note the apparent obscurity of the construction of this passage: it is difficult to identify the subjects of the verbs. Only attentive readers, capable of recognizing the biblical background could recognise the allusions here to the Egyptians and the Israelites at the time of the exodus.

The inclusio on βασανίζω (vv. 1 and 4) frames the pericope, which can be subdivided thus:

- v. 1 (*two stichs*): the subject is the Egyptians; statement of the basic principle governing the antitheses (cf. 11:5, 15-16): punishment comes with that with which one has sinned.
- v. 2 (*three stichs*): "your people", contrasted with the Egyptians (ἀνθ' ἧς); God is the subject.
- v. 3abc (*three stichs*): ἐκεῖνοι; the Egyptians again; repetition of the vocabulary of v. 2.
- v. 3de (*two stichs*): οὗτοι δέ; the Israelites again; repetition of the vocabulary of v. 2.
- v. 4 (*two stichs*): ἐκείνοις; τούτοις δέ; the Egyptians and the Israelites; summary and repetition of the vocabulary of v. 3; inclusio with v. 1.

2 Cf. Reese, "Plan and Structure", 398; Wright, "The Structure", 182; Gilbert, "Sagesse", 75; Bizzeti, *Sapienza*, 101-103.

Thus we have a harmonious composition, laden with meaning, in twelve stichs: Egypt (two stichs) – Israel (three stichs) – Egypt (three stichs) – Israel (two stichs) – concluding summary (two stichs). The author is seeking to contrast Egyptians and Israelites to obtain a theological conclusion: he points out the antithetical actions of God who gives nourishment to God's people and strikes the Egyptians with hunger.

Text

1 Therefore they were justly punished by means of similar beings
and were tormented by a multitude of beasts.
2 Instead of this punishment, you favoured your people:
when their appetite desired a taste that was out of the ordinary,
you provided them with quails as food,
3 so that the ones [the Egyptians] who desired food,
because of the repulsive appearance [of the beasts] sent against them,
lost even their most basic appetite
so that the others [the Israelites], by contrast, finding themselves in need for but a short time,
experienced a taste out of the ordinary.
4 For it was necessary that on those [the Egyptians]
fell inexorable hardship because they were oppressors,
but only to these [the Israelites]
was it shown how their enemies were being tormented.

Notes on the Text and Translation

v. 2. Verse 2b appears a little overloaded. The expression εἰς ἐπιθυμίαν ὀρέξεως is to be understood with reference to the desire (ἐπιθυμία) aroused by the appetite (ὄρεξις); cf. in 16:3 the mention of the ἀναγκαίαν ὄρεξιν, the "necessary", that is, natural, ordinary appetite. Still in 2b, ξένην γεῦσιν is an accusative of relation depending on ἐπιθυμία: cf. the reading of *Arab*: "because of their desire to taste a strange flavour".

v. 3. Scarpat (*Sapienza*, 3:191) chooses to read τροφῆς following S, V, and many minuscules and not the accusative τροφήν with Ziegler and Rahlfs, although the accusative with ἐπιθυμέω is typical of Alexandrian Greek and the LXX. But the sense remains the same. Reversing the argument, one could think of τροφῆς as a stylistic variation.
The substantive *εἰδέχθεια is *hapax* of the LXX. Not so the adjective εἰδεχθής, more common in the sense of "putrid, fetid", perhaps a school term. Some codices read δειχθεῖσαν (the food "offered"), but this is a *lectio facilior*; cf. Risberg, "Textkritische Anmerkungen", 217.

v. 4. The term *ἀπαραίτητος (cf. Wis 16:16) has the sense of "inexorable, inevitable"; cf. Scarpat, "Ancora sull'autore", 179.

Synchronic Analysis

16:1: Tormented by Beasts

The initial διὰ τοῦτο does not only refer to the digression on zoolatry (15:14-19) but anticipates the ἵνα of v. 3. The plague of the beasts is a worthy punishment for those who worshipped them. It is referred to both by the adjective ὅμοιος (to be understood not in the sense of "equal" but of "similar, analogous") and the adverb ἀξίως, the latter derived from an adjective dear to Wisdom,[3] almost always used in a theological sense. Ἀξίως is to be understood as "justly", according to what the Egyptians deserved for their actions. Κολάζω also has a strongly theological sense in Wisdom and is always used in connection with the punishment of the ungodly.[4] That applies also to βασανίζω, which always refers to the punishment of the Egyptians (cf. 11:9; 12:23; 16:4). In Greek usage, this verb evokes the tortures inflicted on the guilty to make them confess.[5] According to Reese, Wis 16:1-4 is a *flashback* to 3:4-5, something that reinforces the eschatological dimension underlying this diptych.[6]

For the mention of the "beasts" (κνώδαλα), cf. Wis 11:15 and 17:9.[7] The reference is to those animals who were the instrument of some of the plagues (cf. Exod 7:25-8:11, the frogs, but also Exod 8:16-19, the gnats, and 8:20-24, the flies). It is difficult to specify exactly which animals our author is thinking of here. We are translating generically with "beasts" (cf. VL: *bestiae*). This connects us directly with 11:5 and 11:15-16, the animating principles of the diptychs; cf. also the repetition of κολάζω. Here, however, the principle is not being applied rigorously. In fact, the Egyptians are not punished with the *same* animals with which they sinned but with *similar* ones (δι' ὁμοίων).

16:2: The Quails and Desire

The particle ἀντί introduces the antithesis proper: ἀνθ' ἧς κολάσεως „instead of this punishment". The substantive κόλασις indicates a means of correction or punishment; cf. κολάζω in the previous verse. The plague which struck Egypt is contrasted with the favour which the Lord did for the people of God. Here, the author addresses the Lord directly. For εὐεργετέω, cf. Wis 3:5; 11:5, 13, always with the same positive tone. The favour in this case is the gift of quails recounted in Exod 16:13[8]; Num 11:31; Ps 104:40 LXX [105:40 MT]. The slightly overladen mention (see the textual notes) of the desire and the appetite is probably drawn from Num 11:4 and Ps 105:14 LXX [106:14 MT] (καὶ ἐπεθύμησαν ἐπιθυμίαν). The presence of the genitive ὀρέξεως specifies the "desire" as "desire of appetite", namely, that deriving from the normal need to eat (cf. 16:3c) which, therefore, is not to be considered as negative.[9] The mention of "desire" (ἐπιθυμία), however, points in a

---

3 Cf. the comment on 1:16. For the sense of the adverb, cf. Wis 7:15.

4 Cf. Wis 3:4; 11:5, 8, 16; 12:14, 15, 27; 16:9; and 18:11.

5 Cf. Schneider, Johannes, βάσανος κτλ., *TDNT* 1:561-563.

6 Cf. Reese, *Hellenistic Influence*, 135.

7 Cf. Mazzinghi, *Notte di paura e di luce*, 73; see the comment on 11:15.

8 Wisdom follows the text of the LXX by speaking of ὀρτυγομήτρα, which means not "mother quails", but quails bigger than normal (Scarpat, *Sapienza*, 3:191). The LXX would thus be intending to underline the greatness of God's gift. Josephus (*A.J.* 3.299) speaks simply of "quails" (ὄρτυγες). Philo employs the plural of ὀρτυγομήτρα (cf. *Mos.* I, 209; *Spec.* IV, 128).

9 In connection with food, ἐπιθυμία does not have a negative connotation *per se*; cf. Thucydides 2.52; 7.84; cf. Larcher, *Sagesse*, 3:891.

negative direction, as in Num 11:4 LXX and in Wis 4:12. The desire for a "taste that was out of the ordinary" (ξένος; in this sense, cf. Wis 16:16; 19:5, 14) allows our sage to highlight, on the one hand, the object of the people's desire during their journey through the desert and, on the other hand, the power of the divine response which is capable of satisfying every taste (cf. Wis 16:20).

16:3: A Taste out of the Ordinary

Verse 3ab is probably referring to the frogs of Exod 8:9-10 (but cf. Exod 10:6) which rendered food disgusting to the Egyptians (cf. Exod 7:28 LXX). The Egyptians lost even (καί) their natural appetite (τὴν ἀναγκαίαν ὄρεξιν).

Verse 3d-e, on the other hand, stresses the less serious nature (ἐπ' ὀλίγον, understood: χρόνον) of the test undergone by Israel which was immediately aided by God with a "taste out of the ordinary", represented by the gift of the quails. As for Israel, so for Egypt: the starting point is the "desire" (vv. 2 and 3), an elementary human need which is, at the same time, a temptation. In the case of Israel, this need was filled beyond expectations; in the case of Egypt, the need to eat was drastically eliminated by the disgust experienced by the Egyptians on account of the beasts sent to them.

16:4: A Providential Lesson

In Wisdom, the verb ἐπέρχομαι is always encountered in negative contexts; cf. 2:5; 12:27; 16:5; 17:14; and 19:13. Here, two ideas converge: one of hostility (ὁ ἐπελθὼν is the oppressor) and the other relating to something unexpected which happens. In the LXX, ἐπέρχομαι appears in contexts which refer to God's anger (cf. Isa 13:13), sometimes with eschatological tones (Isa 41:22; cf. in the NT Luke 21:26).[10] The participle τυραννοῦσιν should be understood as "oppressors, tyrants"; cf. Wis 10:14d, in a pejorative sense. The present seems to be alluding to a current situation, probably a reference to the struggle of the Alexandrian Jews for their civil rights (cf. 18:4 and 19:13-16).

Verse 4a leads to the supposition that the Egyptians' hunger lasted well beyond the plagues even to the time of the miracle of the quails; cf. the imperfect ἐβασανίζοντο which refers to a punishment that lasts over time and which assumes a clear pedagogic value. The "it was necessary" (ἔδει) which opens v. 4 confirms the theological orientation of the diptych: what happened on this occasion was in harmony with God's plan, with the emphasis on its antithetical aspects of a God who reveals both his pedagogy towards the enemies of Israel and his favour towards his people. The absence of meat is no longer understood as a punishment but rather as a way of understanding the chastising of the enemy. This is the sense of v. 4b. It must not be forgotten that the diptych is not in the form of a reflection of the author but in that of an appeal addressed to God, a hymn to his providential actions and his goodness; an appeal addressed to the sinners too so that they may learn their lesson and be converted (one realizes the importance of the particle ἵνα which opens v. 3).

Later (cf. Wis 16:20), our sage will affirm that the manna could assume every sort of taste for the people. Why, then, are the quails necessary? From v. 3, we learn that everything happened to show the difference between a delicate pleasure, given as a response to a temporary need (the desire for meat; cf. 2b), and the tormenting hunger that resulted from the disgust for every food.

10 Cf. Mazzinghi, *Notte di paura e di luce*, 129-130.

Diachronic Analysis

ὄρεξις

Starting with Aristotle, the term ὄρεξις becomes usual to indicate "the spiritual tension, as far as it is dependent on a conscious decision of the will, which, therefore, stands within human power and is accessible to reason", or, rather, "the spontaneous inclination which precedes the intervention of reason", a positive "appetite" of the soul.[11] Only when the ὄρεξις does not follow reason it becomes a "desire" (ἐπιθυμία; cf. Stobaeus, *Flor.* 2.90.7-8, ed. C. Wachsmut). Wisdom employs the term in the transferred sense of "appetite" (or of "tension" towards something; cf. 14:2; 15:5), for which the Stoics prefer προθυμία. Thus, in Wisdom, ὄρεξις and ἐπιθυμία become synonyms; cf. analogous cases in Philo, *Leg.* 3.115 (ἐπιθυμία = ὄρεξις ἄλογος) and Plutarch, *Cupid. divit.* 2 (*Mor.* 523C), in connection with the passion for wealth (φιλοπλουτία).

A Midrash on Exod 16 / Num 11

In 16:1-4, our sage presents a real midrash on exodus themes, with a free combination of the two accounts relating to the quails in Exodus 16 and Numbers 11, according to a procedure known also to Philo (cf. *Mos.* 1.209); the two accounts are also harmonised in the rabbinic traditions.[12] In *Spec.* 4.126-130, the episode of the quails becomes for Philo a way of condemning the unbridled desire which loses sight of the law of God. However, this type of allegorical interpretation is totally absent from our text.

According to Num 11:4, the people desired meat. God's response appeared to be more a punishment than an act of favour (cf. Num 11:18-19, 33). In the Exodus account, on the other hand, although the people's murmuring is underlined on several occasions (Exod 16:2-3, 7-9, 12), the tone appears more positive. The gift of the quails, connected with that of the manna, is not linked to any divine punishment. The theme of the quails reappears in Ps 104:40 LXX [105:40 MT]: here, the negative aspect is passed over in silence as in Wisdom. The quails and the manna are presented as a positive response to a request from the people.

According to his pattern, our sage records the events of the exodus without their unpleasant aspects. He eliminates the mention of Israel's murmurings (cf. Exod 16:2-8 and Num 11:33-34), aiming to highlight the "just" Israel, and minimising, though not wholly excluding, its faults. Our sage does not deny the human motivation at the base of the miracle, namely, the desire for food, but he prefers to display the greatness of God's kindness, resulting in the harmonisation of the two biblical traditions (Exodus and Numbers) which, at least in appearance, are not in perfect agreement with each other.

---

11 Cf. Heidland, Hans Wolfgang, ὀρέγομαι κτλ., *TDNT* 5:447-448; Spicq, *Notes*, 2:626-628. The Stoics knew the treatises περὶ ὀρέξεως (cf. Epictetus, *Diatr.* 4.4.16). In the NT, the term appears only in Rom 1:27 in the sense of sexual passion.

12 Cf. Ginzberg, *The Legends of Jews*, 6:20 n.116. However, Wisdom does not have the miraculous expansions typical of the rabbinic accounts.

Wis 16:5-14: The Third Diptych – The Serpent in the Desert

The Literary Structure of Wis 16:5-14

The literary unity of the diptych is guaranteed by the presence of two quasi-inclusions: ἐπῆλθεν (v. 5a) and ἐξελθόν (v. 14b); ἔχοντες (v. 6b) and ἔχεις (v. 13a). The progression of the third diptych presents a phenomenon analogous to that seen in the previous diptych apart from the inverting of the order of the actors, Egypt and Israel:

vv. 5-7:	αὐτοῖς	Israel (*7 stichs*)
v. 8:	τοὺς ἐχθροὺς ἡμῶν	Egypt (*2 stichs*)
v. 9:	οὓς μέν	Egypt (*3 stichs*)
vv. 10-12:	τοὺς δὲ υἱούς σου	Israel (*8 stichs*)
vv. 13-14:	σὺ... ἄνθρωπος δε;	conclusion; God and humanity (*5 stichs*).

We note the repetition of some key terms which set the tone for the entire diptych which is centred on the theme of salvation and on the healing performed by God through the word of God's law:
- σωτηρίας (6b), ἐσῴζετο (7a), σωτῆρα (7b), διεσῴζοντο (11a);
- ἴαμα (9b), ἰάσατο (10b), ἰώμενος (12b); all in the central part of the diptych.
- εἰς ἀνάμνησιν ἐντολῆς νόμου σου (6b); εἰς ὑπόμνησιν τῶν λογίων σου (11a). The two stichs have the same construction; ἀνάμνησις and ὑπόμνησις are synonyms; similarly, ἐντολῆς νόμου σου recalls τῶν λογίων σου.

The parallelism between 7b and 12b reinforces the link between vv. 5-7 and 10-12:

ἀλλὰ διὰ σέ	τὸν πάντων σωτῆρα
ἀλλὰ ὁ σός κύριε λόγος	ὁ πάντας ἰώμενος

This means that 16:5-7 and 16:10-12 are closely related and that, beside the theme of healing and salvation, there appears that of the remembrance of the law and the word of God. In particular, vv. 11-12 form an expansion and explanation of vv. 6-7. Significantly, the same construction as 7b and 12b is found again in 16:26c, still with reference to the theme of the saving word of God. The literary structure serves a precise theological emphasis: a superficial reading of the events could dwell simply on the miracle without grasping its symbolic aspect. The true protagonist is the Lord and his word, and it is towards this revelation that the text is directed.

Text

5 Even when there struck them the terrible fury of poisonous beasts
and they were being destroyed by the bites of writhing serpents,

your wrath did not last to the end.
6 As a warning, for a short time, they were troubled,
having a sign [or: a counsellor] of salvation,
so that they might remember the commandment of your law.
7 For whoever turned [to it] was not saved
by what he was looking at,
but by you, the saviour of all.
8 And in such a way you persuaded even our enemies
that you are the one who frees from every evil.
9 They [the Egyptians] were killed by the bites of locusts and flies,
and no cure was found for their life,
because they deserved to be punished by such means.
10 Your children, however, not even the teeth of poisonous reptiles could overcome,
because your mercy rushed [to their help] and healed them.
11 That they might remember your words, they were bitten [goaded]
– but they were immediately saved –
lest, falling into deep forgetfulness,
they might be excluded from your favours.
12 For it was not a plant or a poultice that cured them,
but your word, o Lord, which cures everything [or: everyone].
13 For you have power over life and death,
you bring to the gates of Hades and cause to rise up again.
14 People, however, can kill in their wickedness,
but not restore a spirit that has been breathed out
or free an imprisoned soul.

Notes on the Text and Translation

v. 5. For ἐπέρχομαι, to be understood in the negative sense of "fall on top of", cf. the comment on 16:4. Cf. Exod 10:1 LXX: ἵνα ἐπέλθῃ τὰ σημεῖα ταῦτα ἐπ' αὐτούς.
With regard to ἔμεινεν, we note, as in 18:20, the use of the aorist instead of the imperfect with a verb that normally expresses duration. This is a "complexive" aorist (BDF § 332; Zerwick, *Graecitas Biblica* § 253) which, if used without temporal reference, refers to an act in itself, regardless of its duration. God's anger is, therefore, limited in time.

v. 6. For many commentators (cf. Grimm, Goodrick, Farrar, Deane, Heinisch, Feldmann, Reider), the final clause of 6b (εἰς ἀνάμνησιν...) refers to the whole of v. 6. Ἔχοντες is to be considered a *participium coniunctum* (BDF § 418) which indicates how an action is carried out, what precedes it and what accompanies it, a circumstance to be understood here as having final value. The meaning of the verse is, therefore: "for a short time, they were troubled, since they had a sign of salvation, so that they might remember...".
Instead of σύμβολον, the text of S and A (cf. also V 149-260-471-485-606 68 249-754 359* 542 613 and some ancient versions), reads the term σύμβουλον, "counsellor". This reading was accepted by K. von Tischendorf (*Vetus Testamentum graece iuxta*

LXX interpretes, Leipzig, 1887, 1:165). We should note the reading *consiliarium salutis* in two glosses (94-95) to the *Vetus Latina*; cf. Thiele, *Sapientia Salomonis*, 526. It is a reading which could refer to the bronze serpent personified (but the idea of the bronze serpent as "counsellor of salvation" is rather strange), or to the figure of Moses. In this case, Moses would be being mentioned not so much as lawgiver but simply as "counsellor", that is, responsible for making the Israelites remember the divine law. The reading σύμβουλον is rejected by the more ancient commentators and almost ignored by contemporary ones.[13] However, the textual witnesses which support σύμβουλον deserve greater consideration.

A. Leproux ("Moïse – conseiller de salut") observes that σύμβουλος appears in Wis 8:9 referring to wisdom, which is taken by "Solomon" as spouse, friend and counsellor. Moreover, σύμβουλος appears 27 times in the LXX (cf. 2 Macc 7:25: σύμβουλον ἐπὶ σωτηρίᾳ and 4 Macc 9:2, συμβούλῳ Μωυσεῖ). Σύμβουλος corresponds to the Hebrew יועץ which mostly designates a royal "counsellor" (Leproux, 172). The correction of σύμβουλον to σύμβολον could have happened at the time when the text of Wisdom was being interpreted along the lines of a Philonian allegory (perhaps under Christian influence?). In fact, in rereading the episode of the bronze serpent, our sage interprets it in a midrashic and not a symbolico-allegorical sense. The reading σύμβουλον could certainly be more consistent with the thought of our author and with his allusive style. However, the opposite to what Leproux thinks could also have happened: the variant σύμβουλον could have arisen from the experience of a certain tension between the statement of the efficacious and present possession of the sign (σύμβολον ἔχοντες σωτηρίας) and the uselessness of the visible object in relation to salvation (οὐ διὰ τὸ θεωρούμενον ἐσῴζετο). This would have led a scribe to introduce a term (σύμβουλον instead of σύμβολον) which could refer to Moses more easily.

v. 7. In translating 7a, it is necessary to take account of the observations of Scarpat (*Sapienza*, 3:195): the modern translations do not give sufficient emphasis to the passive form of the participle τὸ θεωρούμενον. What is being underlined is the absolute passivity of the object looked at (τὸ θεωρούμενον), that is, the bronze serpent which, moreover, is not even named as such.

The expression of 7b, τὸν πάντων σωτῆρα, presents a problem that is exegetical rather than textual. In 12b, ὁ πάντα ἰώμενος is to be understood as "[your word] which heals *everything*", that is, which heals from every evil. In 14:4a, it is God who saves "from every danger", just as, in our diptych, God "frees from every evil" (cf. 8b). The context of the entire diptych, however, is referring to the salvation of the *Israelites*, and this suggests, rather, translating τὸν πάντων σωτῆρα as "saviour of *everyone*", that is, all those who know to turn to God.

v. 11. The term ἀπερίσπαστοι is to be understood in the sense of "be free" (cf. Sir 41:1), here, in the negative sense of "be excluded" (cf. Maneschg, *Die Erzählung*, 147: "[damit sie nicht] von deinem Wohltun abgezogen würden"). This is an objective state resulting from forgetting the divine words: if the trial of the serpents had lasted longer and the divine mercy had not intervened to save them, then, forget-

13 Cornely, *Commentarius in librum Sapientiae*, 531: "parum verisimile est". However, Cornely does not understand that "counsellor" could be referring to Moses and not to the bronze serpent. Larcher, *Sagesse*, 3:898, confines himself to saying that this variant "ne mérite pas de retenir l'attention". Maneschg (*Die Erzählung*, 109) also dismisses the possibility as "hoch unwahrscheinlich", but even he does not consider that "counsellor" could refer to Moses.

ting the words of God, the Israelites could have been separated from God and excluded from God's favours.

v. 12. In 12b, some codices (A, C, and others; cf. Rahlfs) read ὁ πάντας ἰώμενος; Ziegler chooses to read πάντα with B-S, La, and others. Scarpat (*Sapienza*, 3:200) chooses the first reading on the basis of the arguments already adopted in connection with 7b, the use of ἰάομαι in the LXX and the parallel with ἐθεράπευσεν αὐτούς in 12a. He notes, moreover, that, with reference to the creation, πάντα ought to have the article, τὰ πάντα, as in codex V. Thus, the text would be referring to God who heals *everyone* (along these lines, Hübner, *Weisheit*, 193). A good biblical parallel would be Ps 106:20 LXX [107:20 MT]: ἀπέστειλεν τὸν λόγον αὐτοῦ καὶ ἰάσατο αὐτοὺς. The second reading however enjoys better attestation; cf. the discussion on 7b and also the text of 8b: God saves *everyone* (7b), from *every* evil (8b). In this case, the text would be referring to the word of God which "heals everything", that is, to the Lord who is able to restore and save the whole of creation.

Synchronic Analysis

16:5: The Serpents in the Desert

The previous diptych closed with the "pedagogic" memory of the torment of the Egyptians (16:4b). Thinking now of the episode in Num 21:4-9, our sage seems to be wishing to reply to an objection: in the desert, even the Israelites were tormented by the serpents' bites; even they were punished by the Lord for their faults. However, this punishment acquires a wholly new sense when compared with the plague which struck Egypt. Thus, the initial καὶ γὰρ ὅτε assumes a sense of gradation and is to be translated with "and even"[14]. On the Israelites fell (ἐπῆλθεν) the terrible (δεινός)[15] fury of the poisonous beasts (θηρίον); cf. Acts 28:4, where θηρίον indicates a viper (ἔχιδνα); one could think of Deut 32:24 LXX (ὀδόντας θηρίων ἀποστελῶ εἰς αὐτούς μετὰ θυμοῦ συρόντων ἐπὶ γῆς; cf. v. 33: θυμὸς δρακόντων ὁ οἶνος αὐτῶν; we note that δράκοντες appears later in Wis 16:10 in relation to the θηρία of 16:5).

The serpents "destroyed" the Israelites with their bites (the imperfect underlines the duration of the action). Διαφθείρω acquires a theological importance; it is always employed in Wisdom in connection with divine punishment, here, of the Israelites (cf. the use of the divine passive), in Wis 16:19 (cf. also 16:27 in Codex S and many minuscules) and 18:12, of the Egyptians. The punishment is the result of unfaithfulness to the law and has as its aim a return to the observance of the law and of the word of God, as in 16:19, 27. Here, the reference to the law appears in v. 6. In 18:4, the light of the law is called ἄφθαρτος, "incorruptible". The Egyptians perish because they lack that law which is the source of life.

The serpents are said to be "winding, writhing" (σκολιοί), like the human reasonings in Wis 1:3a. Perhaps these are those huge constrictor snakes which wrap themselves around their victims to kill them and then eat them, a reminis-

---

14 Cf. BDF § 442.8a.

15 The adjective is present in Wis 5:2; 11:18; 12:9; 18:17; and 19:16. It can mean "extraordinary, marvellous" (cf. Sophocles, *Ant.* 334). In Wisdom, it is more frequent in the sense of "terrible, fearful": cf. 5:2 and 18:17. Apart from 19:16, the context is always of a judicial character and refers to the action of God. Cf. Mazzinghi, *Notte di paura e di luce*, 19-20.

cence of the Egyptian environment in which our author is writing; more probably, he is combining Num 21:6 LXX ("deadly serpents" ὄφεις θανατοῦντες) with Isa 27:1 LXX (ἐπὶ τὸν δράκοντα ὄφιν σκολιόν).

The serpents are the sign of the divine wrath which, however, did not last "to the end". In Numbers, the divine wrath is not mentioned explicitly, but the theme of ὀργή is common in Wisdom. In Wis 10:3, 10, in connection with people as agents; in the remaining six cases, always with reference to God. Wis 5:20 and 11:9 speak of the divine wrath against the ungodly; Wis 16:5; 18:20, 23, 25 of the divine wrath against the chosen people which, however, has the characteristic of being of limited duration (cf. Isa 57:16). Even in its sin, Israel is always under the sign of the divine mercy. It is noticeable how Wisdom avoids presenting the causes of the divine anger and so every direct mention of the sin of Israel which provoked it; cf., by contrast, Ps 77:21, 31 LXX [78:21, 31 MT] and the account in the book of Numbers (see below).

16:6: Memory of the Law

Verse 6 contains a new application of the principle of Wis 11:10. In dealing with God's people, God's punitive action has a double purpose, well expressed by the double use of the preposition εἰς: first of all, the serpents' bites are presented as a "warning" (νουθεσία)[16] rather than as a punishment. They were a warning which only for a short time (cf. Isa 54:7-8) "troubled" (ταράσσω) the Israelites, which reinforces the idea, contained in the previous stich, relating to the brief duration of God's anger. Wisdom avoids emphasising the death of the Israelites as a result of the serpents' bites. Thus, ταράσσω is to be understood in the sense of an interior troubling, as in 5:2 and 14:25. The use of the passive presupposes the action of God. Secondly, the serpents' bites urge the remembrance (εἰς ἀνάμνησιν) of the law of God.

The "memory of your law" is linked to the disputed expression σύμβολον [σύμβουλον] ἔχοντες σωτηρίας. If we accept the reading σύμβολον (cf. the textual notes), our sage is alluding here to the bronze serpent which, in the text of Num 21:8–9 LXX, is connected with the term σημεῖον. In fact, the LXX translates with ἐπὶ σημείου the Hebrew expression עַל־נֵס: Moses was ordered to place the serpent "on a sign", on a pole. By contrast with the use made of it by Philo, σύμβολον is to be understood in its normal sense of "sign, demonstration", as in Wis 2:9. Σημεῖον appears in Wis 5:13 with a similar meaning.[17]

The text does not say that this "sign" is the bronze serpent. That can be understood only by someone who has a good knowledge of the biblical account. The use of the present participle ἔχοντες could be surprising.[18] Our sage is perhaps intending to emphasise the shortness of the trial and the speed of the divine aid. We recall that in Wisdom "salvation" is to be understood as preservation from every danger, a physical salvation from death.[19]

---

16 Cf. νουθετέω in 11:10; 12:2, 26. The verb expresses the pedagogic attitude of God towards Israel. Cf. the use made of it by Paul precisely in an exodus context in 1 Cor 10:11; cf. Maneschg, *Die Erzählung*, 122 n. 63.

17 A good explanation of this meaning is in Maneschg, *Die Erzählung*, 124-128.

18 Cf. Larcher, *Sagesse*, 3:899.

19 Cf. σωτηρία in 5:2; 6:24; 16:6; and 18:7; for σῴζω, cf. 9:18; 10:4; 14:4; 16:7; 18:5; cf. σωτήρ in 16:7; σωτήριος in 1:14 and διασῴζω in 10:4 (codex B); cf. 14:6; 16:11. Cf. Noël, "Quelle sotériologie dans le livre de la Sagesse?".

> Whoever transmitted the reading σύμβουλον (see the note to the text) probably wanted to indicate that what the Israelites possess (ἔχοντες) is not a visible sign (τὸ θεωρούμενον, the bronze serpent[20]), and it is not the serpent that saves, but, rather, a "voice", that of Moses, "counsellor of salvation", who reminds the people to listen to the word of the law (cf. v. 11, in close connection with v. 6). In the end, it is the Lord himself (16:7b) who saves, and God's word (12b), of which Moses is the spokesman. The correction of σύμβολον to σύμβουλον (if the first reading is original) could thus be evidence of a kind of sapientialisation of the figure of Moses, set in relation to the Torah, but without being considered as a legislator, as in the texts of contemporary Judaism and especially in Philo (cf. *Mos.* 2.1-7, 292), but rather as a sage.[21]

The bronze serpent is necessary εἰς ἀνάμνησιν ἐντολῆς νόμου σου. The term ἀνάμνησις cannot be endowed here with the force that it has in Philo;[22] it indicates, more simply, the recalling to memory of something that has been forgotten. With νόμος is intended here the Mosaic Torah, as in 2:12 and 18:4. Only in 2:12 (and, what is more, in the mouth of the ungodly) does Wisdom insist on the normative character of the law. The parallel of 16:6 with 16:11 reveals that in this case, as later in 18:4, the text is pointing more to the revelatory aspect of the law.

16:7: God, Saviour of All

The aorist participle ἐπιστραφεὶς preserves the proper shade of the middle voice. Ἐπιστρέφομαι is used here in the sense of "turn to", but very often, in the LXX, it has the sense of "repent, be converted",[23] which perhaps is not totally excluded by our author. He could be thinking of Isa 6:10 LXX: καὶ ἐπιστρέψωσιν καὶ ἰάσομαι αὐτούς, where the "turning towards God" has the sense of "being converted", a conversion which leads to healing (cf. also Isa 45:21-22; 46:8).

What saves is not the serpent but God, invoked in the second person as "Saviour" (σωτήρ) for the only time in the book. The expression "Saviour of all" is unique in the OT (cf. 1 Macc 4:30; 3 Macc 7:16: "Saviour of Israel"; cf. also T. Gad 8:1). It is found in 1 Tim 4:10 (σωτὴρ πάντων ἀνθρώπων). God is saviour because God is the preserver of life, as already announced in the programmatic text of Wis 1:13-14, but also because God acts concretely in the history of his people.

16:8: God Frees from Every Evil

Verse 8 returns to the didactic aspect of the divine actions. If the "enemies"[24] remained such and were not converted, at the very least they had to experience that the Lord acts in such a way as to persuade (ἔπεισας) people that only God "frees" from every evil.

The verb employed here to indicate salvation is ῥύομαι (cf. Wis 2:18; 10:6, 9, 13, 15), which has the almost exclusive meaning of "save" both in the LXX and the NT. The texts of Isa LXX 44:6; 47:4; 48:17; 49:7; and 54:8 (cf. 3 Macc 6:10)

---

20 Cf. Scarpat, *Sapienza*, 3:195.

21 For Moses in Wisdom, cf., again, 10:16; 11:1, 14 and 18:5. Cf. Mazzinghi, "The Figure of Moses", *passim.*

22 Cf. Boccaccini, *Middle Judaism*, 191-204.

23 Cf. the interpretations of many ancient commentators in the sense of "conversion"; Maneschg, *Die Erzählung*, 129 n. 85.

24 Cf. Wis 10:12, 19; 11:3, 5; 12:20, 22; 16:8. 4, 22; 18:5[S*], 7, 10. Wis 15:14 clarifies that these "enemies" are the Egyptians who oppress Israel (with the exception of 12:20, 22, where the enemies are the Canaanites). The harshness of the judgement on the Egyptians is motivated by the historical circumstances in which our author was writing and certainly contrasts with the proclamation of a God who is "Saviour of all".

employ the aorist participle, ῥυσάμενος, with reference to God. Only in Isa 59:20 LXX do we find the present participle, as in our case. That perhaps serves to underline that the reflection on history is being shifted on to the present of the actions of God. Taking up the language of Isaiah 40-66 LXX, however, our sage avoids an over-nationalistic tone. Isa 44:6 speaks of ὁ θεὸς ὁ βασιλεύς τοῦ Ισραηλ ὁ ῥυσάμενος αὐτόν; here God saves "from every evil" the faithful Israelites. However, they are not explicitly mentioned.

16:9. Plagues without a Cure

This verse opens a new part of the diptych. The Egyptians (οὓς μέν) were killed by the bites of small beasts that are not usually lethal while the Israelites were saved from the bites of animals that are normally mortally venomous, the serpents (v. 10).

The mention of the locusts refers to the eighth plague (Exod 10:1-20), while the flies[25] seem to be alluding to the fourth (Exod 8:16-28 [8:20-32 in English translations]) or even to the plague of gnats (σκνῖφες; 8:12-15 [8:16-19 in English translations]). Both species are associated in Ps 104:31 LXX [105:31 MT] (κυνόμυια καὶ σκνῖπες). Our sage is extending the significance of these plagues by speaking of the bites of animals which kill (ἀπέκτεινεν δήγματα). He is taking his cue from expressions like those of Exod 10:17 LXX where, in connection with the plague of locusts, there is mention of τὸν θάνατον τοῦτον. In this case, too, we are presented with a midrashic expansion (cf. Josephus, *A.J.* 2.14.3-4 [ed. Niese II § 296-303]).

For this plague, "no cure was found". Ἴαμα retains here its normal meaning of "medicine, cure". The terms ἴαμα, ἰάομαι occur three times in our diptych (vv. 9, 10, 12); cf. Wis 11:4 and 2:1c. The expression οὐκ ἔστιν ἴασις is employed metaphorically in texts like Prov 29:1 LXX, Jer 14:19 LXX[26] with reference to salvation from sin or death.[27] The ungodly of Wisdom 2 claim that the scriptural phrases relating to a God who saves from death are not true (Wis 2:1c). There is no remedy for death; there is no point in them praying to the Lord as does the prophet in Jer 17:14 (ἴασαί με κύριε καὶ ἰαθήσομαι, σῶσόν με καὶ σωθήσομαι). Thus, the third diptych is intended to give a response to the objections of the ungodly, above all by means of vv. 13-14: on the contrary, God can save people from death.

For v. 9c, cf. the comment on 16:1a. The connection of κολάζω and ἄξιος refers to the reflection on the antithetical actions of God and on the justice of the punishment of the Egyptians.

16:10: The Discovery of the Divine Mercy

"*Our* enemies" are contrasted with "*your* children". After οὓς μέν (v. 9), one would expect οὓς δέ. However, our author varies the construction: τοὺς δὲ υἱούς σου. For the theme of divine childship, cf. Wis 9:7 and 18:4.

The children were not "overcome" (οὐδέ ... ἐνίκησαν) either by the venom (*ἰόβολος) or by the serpents' teeth, a reprise of v. 5b. Δράκων indicates a particularly huge and fearful serpent, another expansion.

---

25 Our author speaks simply of "flies" (μυῖαι) and not of "dog flies" (κυνόμυιαι), as in Exod 8:16-28 LXX; cf. Philo, *Mos.* 1.130, perhaps to heighten the contrast between the venomous serpents which do not kill the Israelites and the very ordinary flies which, instead, destroy the Egyptians.

26 Cf. also Ps 37:4, 8 LXX [38:4, 8 MT]; Sir 3:28; 21:3; Nah 3:19; Zech 10:2.

27 With reference to the plagues of Egypt, cf. Jdt 5:12: καὶ ἐπάταξεν πᾶσαν τὴν γῆν Αἰγύπτου πληγαῖς ἐν αἷς οὐκ ἦν ἴασις.

It is God's mercy (ἔλεος), which now replaces God's anger (cf. Ps 77:38 LXX [78:38 MT]; Isa 54:8 LXX; cf. Wis 9:1 and also 3:9; 4:15), that prevents the serpents from overcoming. The verb ἀντιπαρέρχομαι* has the etymological meaning of "passing by someone coming in the opposite direction".[28] Here, it could be being employed in the sense of "come to meet". While in Numbers 21:4-9, the divine help seems to have to be waited for, the two aorists of v. 10b describe an aid from God that is immediate and punctual. God did not leave his children as prey for the serpent but came to meet them and immediately saved them.

16:11: God's Favours

The theme of v. 11 takes up, even verbally, what was expressed in 6b. Εἰς ὑπόμνησιν takes up the previous εἰς ἀνάμνησιν. Our author expands the reference to the "commandment of the law", linking it to the "words" (λόγια), that is, to the whole of the divine revelation. Israel has never forgotten them, our author seems to be saying, but they have to be recalled to the memory continually.

The verb ἐγκεντρίζω* (cf. Rom 11:17, 19, 23, 24 in the sense of "insert") has here the meaning of "bite", or, better, "goad".[29] Thus, the bites of the serpents in the desert were not lethal. The punishment, as the parenthesis in 11b clarifies ("but [καί] soon they were saved"), was meant to save the people, to stimulate them to conversion, not to destroy them. Once again, there is emphasis on the speed of the divine action.

The second part of v. 11, introduced by a form with final value (ἵνα μή), wishes to show once more (cf. v. 6) what God's intentions were in sending the serpents. The participial parenthesis (εἰς βαθεῖαν ἐμπεσόντες λήθην) is clear. The salvation from the serpents served to avoid Israel's falling into forgetfulness of the actions of God (cf. Ps 77:11 LXX [78:11 MT]: ἐπελάθοντο τῶν εὐεργεσιῶν). That could result in exclusion from the favours (cf. 16:2a) which God grants to God's people. Such forgetfulness would be more serious than the possible sin committed (but not described here) by Israel. What is being asked of Israel, therefore, is the "recalling", the memory, of the divine words.

16:12: The Word of God Heals

Israel's fidelity to the divine "words" results in the intervention of the saving "word" described in v. 12b. Neither nature (a medicinal plant: βοτάνη) nor science (a poultice, an ointment: μάλαγμα) can provide people with healing. It is the word of God, the central theme of the diptych, which heals "everything" (or "everyone", cf. the textual notes). Like God's mercy, the word of God is the sign of God's salvific activity for the world.

16:13: You Bring down to Hades and You Bring up

Σὺ γάρ: our sage addresses God directly, explaining why he is able to heal everything with his word (v. 12). God holds absolute power (ἐξουσία; cf. 10:14) over life and death. The structure of the verse is chiastic: "life" and "death" in 13a are matched by the verbs κατάγω and ἀνάγω in 13b.

The dependence of 13a on 1 Sam 2:6b and Deut 32:39 is clear. The most important difference lies in the fact that, whereas the two texts cited stress the passage death/life, our passage puts the dominion of God over life before the mention of death. Deut 32:39, which expresses the power of the one God, is taken up by

28 The verb appears for the first time in the Stoic Chrysippus (cf. *SVF* II, 248 frag. 901) and is employed in the sense of "penetrate". Reese (*Hellenistic Influence*, 16 n. 82) claims that Wisdom uses it with a similar significance with reference to the hidden but efficacious action of God.

29 Cf. Caird, "Toward a Lexicon", 469.

Wisdom as a hermeneutical key to understand the meaning of God's action on behalf of God's people. In other words, Scripture serves our sage as an interpretative principle of Scripture itself.

God's power over life and death is expressed by means of an image already known to the LXX: going down to and coming up from the underworld or Hades. In addition to 1 Sam 2:6, our author seems to have been thinking of Tob 13:2 (BA), the last stich of which is echoed, in fact, later, in Wis 16:15: ὅτι αὐτὸς μαστιγοῖ καὶ ἐλεᾷ κατάγει εἰς ᾅδην καὶ ἀνάγει καὶ οὐκ ἔστιν ὃς ἐκφεύξεται τὴν χεῖρα αὐτοῦ.[30]

16:14: The Imprisoned Soul

Verse 14 is not just an addition to v. 13.[31] By contrast with the favours offered by God, who can give life (16:11d), people for their part are capable only of giving death in their wickedness (κακία). The two verbs ἀναστρέφω and ἀναλύω could be understood in an intransitive sense, but the presence in parallel of the two accusatives, πνεῦμα and ψυχήν, removes any ambiguity: the subject is still people, unable to "restore a spirit that has been breathed out" or "free an imprisoned soul" from death (see below).[32] The chiastic construction of 14bc again highlights the contrast between the impotence of human actions and the omnipotent action of God.

Diachronic Analysis

16:6 The "commandment of your law" in Wis 16:6 is expressed in the singular whereas the LXX mostly uses the plural, ἐντολαί. Some think of the divine command in Gen 2:17 and see in the serpents some kind of allusion to the serpent of Genesis 3,[33] as happens in the targumic tradition (cf. Tg. Neof. and Tg. Ps.-J. on Num 21:9). In fact, the serpent of Genesis 3 has no importance in the book of Wisdom, except in the allusion to the devil in Wis 2:24. Perhaps precisely for this reason, Wis 16:7 avoids speaking explicitly of the bronze serpent, limiting itself to a neutral "what he was looking at" (τὸ θεωρούμενον). In the references to the "serpents" in v. 5, it is easier to discern a polemical point against cults and rituals typical of the Hellenistic world, such as those of Asclepius, Serapis, or Isis-Thermouthis, represented by the form of a serpent, and the Dionysiac rites.[34]

---

30 Here the Greek texts of Tobit (I-II-III) and 4Q 200,6 substantially agree. In any case, in Tobit, the idea that the Lord causes to die and to live does not result in the proclamation of any form of resurrection but revolves around images that are rather generic.

31 Cf. Gregg, *Wisdom*, 155 ("only an appendix").

32 For further arguments on the need to understand the two verbs as transitive, cf. Maneschg, *Die Erzählung*, 162; for ἀναλύω, cf. Wis 2:1. Humanity, the subject of 14a, is also that of 14b. Human actions are being compared with those of God. That would not make sense if the two verbs were being employed intransitively. The verb ἀναστρέφω, in particular, returns in a transitive sense with reference to death both in the LXX (cf. Jdt 1:11, 13) and in classical texts (cf. Sophocles, *Phil.* 446ff.).

33 Cf. Larcher, *Sagesse*, 3:900.

34 Cf. Maneschg, *Die Erzählung*, 183-187; Mazzinghi, *Notte di paura e di luce*, 94-95, 97-98; Isis-Termouthis is often represented under the form of a serpent. In the Dionysiac cults, Dionysius could appear in the form of a serpent. For Asclepius, cf. Pausanias 2.10.3; 4.14.7; 2.26.1-27,6. Cf. Walton, Alice, *Asklepios. The Cult of the Greek God of Medicine* (Ares: Chicago 1894), 91.

A similar construction (ἐντολὴ νόμου) is found in Prov 6:23 LXX, where ἐντολή is to be understood in the sense of "instruction, pedagogic prescription", and refers to the *law as a whole*, considered as "instruction" for the life of the people rather than as law understood as a body of individual precepts to be observed.[35] Thus, what the Israelites have to call to memory is not so much a precept (or a series of precepts) to be observed as the βουλὴ θεοῦ, the will of God expressed in the law (Wis 9:17), impossible to know without the gift of wisdom. The Tg. Ps.-J. to Num 21:8 similarly links the episode of the serpents to the word of God: "and it will happen that whoever is bitten by the serpent and turns towards it, will keep his life, *if he directs his heart towards the name of the word of the Lord*".

The verb θεωρέω does not appear to have been chosen by chance. As in Wis 16:7
6:12; 13:5; 17:6; and 19:7–8, it indicates a "seeing" which is, at the same time, a "contemplating" and an "understanding". In Num 21:8-9, in connection with the bronze serpent, the LXX employs the more common ἰδὼν and ἐπέβλεψεν. Our sage removes these active forms and replaces them with the middle-passive θεωρούμενον which, by referring to an insistent and almost contemplative gaze, takes away all importance from the reality of the object contemplated (the serpent) and underlines the attraction which the image could have for those who looked at it. The criticism of the Alexandrian view of religion, which put great emphasis on the value of the image is, therefore, clear.

The text of v. 8 goes beyond the account in Numbers which lies behind 16:8
this diptych by assuming that the Egyptians could have known what happened to Israel in the desert and were, therefore, convinced by what they saw that the Lord alone is able to free from every evil. Perhaps our author has in mind texts like Exod 32:12 and Num 14:13-16, but this is the tendency to expand which is typical of midrash. The emphasis on "our" enemies gives this verse a note of strong relevance. Our author seems to be intending to say that the Egyptians who live with us in Alexandria have to be aware of the favours granted by God to Israel, precisely those people on whose rights they are always trampling.

The association of the themes of God as saviour and as benefactor can un- 16:11
doubtedly be considered as a polemical reference to the royal titles of the Ptolemaic monarchy and, subsequently, of the Roman Emperor, σωτὴρ καὶ εὐεργέτης.[36] Especially in the treatise on kingship attributed to Diotogenes, the Stoic-Platonic idea of a "benefactor" is translated into that of a monarch who, incarnating on earth the universal law and action of God, becomes – in his turn – a "benefactor", doing only good for his subjects. Among the recommendations addressed to the king in this treatise, the one relating to guarding oneself from greed advises that "the king must possess the wealth necessary to benefit (εὐεργετεῖν) his friends".[37] A little later, εὐεργεσία is recorded by Diotogenes as one of the principal qualities

---

35 Cf. Spicq, *Notes*, 1:250-253.

36 Thus Augustus in the year 13/12 BCE; cf. Dittenberger, Wilhelm (ed.), *Orientis Graeci Inscriptiones selectae*, Hirzel: Leipzig 1903-1905, 2:657.1; Cf. Maneschg, *Die Erzählung*, 186-187.

37 Cf. Diotogenes, 265, 20-21: ed. Hense, in: Delatte, *Les Traités de la Royauté*, 39-40; cf. Mazzinghi, "The antithetical pair 'to punish' and 'to benefit'", *passim.*

of the king, together with the swiftness he must show in knowing how to punish the wicked (κολάσιος). In thus knowing how to combine closely the ability to punish with that, above all, of benefiting his subjects, the king reveals himself to be θεόμιμος, imitator of the divinity; cf. similar ideas in Let. Aris. 190, 208.[38] Wisdom reveals the effort to adapt the Stoic-Platonic idea of the divinity capable of doing only good, and, by extension, the concept of the earthly sovereign who incarnates that action, to the biblical faith in a God who is good and generous towards all God's creation but able to punish the wicked, as is shown in the exodus narrative which lies behind Wisdom 11-19.

In the Alexandrian environment, the vocabulary of salvation is very frequent with reference to Isis. On several occasions, she is called σώτειρα because she saves her devotees from situations of danger or death. Only later is this idea extended to *post mortem* salvation, and, especially from the time of the Roman period, Isis becomes the goddess who guarantees immortality (cf. the comment on 9:18; 14:1-10). Moreover, the idea of "saving" connected with the theme of the serpents recalls the cult of Asclepius (cf. the textual notes to v. 6). Furthermore, there is a clear polemic against the world of magic where, on several occasions, the vocabulary of saving returns in connection with the healing of illnesses. No magic rite can give healing; only the word of God[39].

16:12 The theme of the word of God which heals could have been inspired by the text of Ps 106:20 LXX [107:20 MT]: ἀπέστειλεν τὸν λόγον αὐτοῦ καὶ ἰάσατο αὐτοὺς καὶ ἐρρύσατο αὐτοὺς ἐκ τῶν διαφθορῶν αὐτῶν. Our author shows here that he is aware of a type of midrashic exegesis reflected in two marginal readings of Tg. Neof. on Exod 15:26[40].

In connection with v. 12, we note again that, not infrequently, the book of Wisdom utilises a medical vocabulary. Philo (*Sacr.* 70) compares God's action in relation to the world to that of a doctor.[41] The distinction between a "medicinal plant" and a "poultice" is classical and taken up already by the ancient commentators.[42] The use of

38 Diotogenes, 267.8ff. Ed. Hense, in: Delatte, *Les Traités*, 42; cf. also pp. 214-216.

39 Cf. *PGM* 1:195-222 (prayer for liberation addressed to the divinity; fourth cent. CE), 4:1167-1225 (prayer addressed to Aion as sun god; time of Diocletian; especially lines 1211ff.); incantation against a serpent, *PGM* 13:262ff.; in all three texts, the theme of "saving" occurs in connection with the healing of illnesses obtained by means of a magical rite; cf. Vermaseren, Maarten J. "La sotériologie dans les *papyri graecae magicae*", in: Bianchi, Ugo, – Vermaseren, Maarten J,. (edd.), *La soteriologia dei culti orientali nell'Impero Romano*, Atti del Colloquio internazionale su "La soteriologia dei culti orientali nell'Impero Romano" (EPRO 92; Leiden: Brill 1982), 17-32.

40 Exod 15:26 LXX reads, with a precise translation from the MT, ἐγὼ γάρ εἰμι κύριος ὁ ἰώμενός σε; Tg. Neof. : "I am, YHWH, who heals you with his word" (marg1); "with the word of YHWH" (marg2); Priotto, *La Prima Pasqua*, 124-132. Wis 16:11 seems to be the most ancient witness to the theme of the healing word of God. Cf. Hayward, Robert, *Divine Name and Presence: The Memra* (Allanheld: Totowa, NJ 1981), 121; cf. pp. 39-56 for the targumic association word/mercy. Cf. also Muñoz Leon, Domingo, *Dios-Palabra, Memra en los Targum del Pentateuco* (Santa Rita: Granada 1974) 355-356.

41 Cf. Larcher, *Etudes*, 179-201. Beauchamp, "Sagesse de Salomon: de l'argumentation médicale à la résurrection".

42 Cf. the citations in Maneschg, *Die Erzählung*, 149-150.

medicinal plants is frequent in magical circles.[43] Our author makes a powerful contrast between it and the saving efficacy of the word of God.

The expression of Wis 16:13b "the gates of Hades" takes up similar biblical expressions (cf. Isa 38:10; 3 Macc 5:51; "the gates of death": Job 38:17 LXX; Pss 9:14 LXX; 106:18 LXX [107:18 MT]. Being at the gates of Hades means being close to death. Some commentators have thought that v. 13b refers only to God's power to free people from the danger of physical death; others have gone so far as to speculate on a possible resurrection of the dead: "Hic de resuscitatione mortuorum agi tenemus".[44] According to Vílchez Líndez, the "content of v. 13 (...) does not seem to go beyond the Old Testament teaching. In fact, it does not allude to the resurrection of the dead, but underlines strongly the life-giving power of God who gives life and frees from dangers that threaten it, including the greatest of them all, death".[45] Taking up the comment of Goodrick, Larcher proposes four arguments to demonstrate a different theory:[46] the use of εἰς which suggests a real descent into death; then, the fact that the OT already knows of the possibility of returning from death in exceptional cases (cf. 1 Kgs 17:21-22; etc.); again, v. 13 constitutes a progression in relation to the previous development which is limited to speaking of physical healing; finally, v. 14 emphasises that, whereas people are incapable of giving back life, God can do just that. Thus, without saying so explicitly, the text seems to be alluding to the real possibility that God has of bringing back people from death to life, and so goes beyond the content of the biblical texts utilised. Although retaining the biblical idea of *she'ôl* understood as place of the dead, our author considers it as incapable of detaining the just. We are on the path that will lead us to see in *she'ôl*/Hades what we think of as hell, the place for the punishment of the ungodly[47]. 16:13

In Wisdom, the terms "soul" and "spirit" tend to be assimilated.[48] The "spirit that has been breathed out" is an idea which leans heavily on the biblical image of the "breath of life" which God infused into Adam; cf. Gen 2:7; Qoh 12:7; cf. Ps 145:4 LXX [146:4 MT] (ἐξελεύσεται τὸ πνεῦμα αὐτοῦ). The soul is described as παραλημφθεῖσαν, the aorist passive participle of παραλαμβάνω, normally understood as "be received"; cf. Lat, *quae recepta est*: "anima quae jam a Deo recepta, in aliam vitam, suo quoque loco pro meritis in aeternum assignata est" (Cornelius a Lapide, *sub loco*). However, it is possible to understand the passive of παραλαμβάνω in the sense of "receive" the soul as a prisoner of Hades, according to an idea frequent in the classical world about Hades imagined as a prison (cf. also Wis 17:16) or, in any case, a place from which there is no escape (for the Bible, cf. Job 16:14

43 Cf. Scarborough, John, "The Pharmacology of Sacred Plants, Herbs and Roots", in: Faraone, Christopher A. – Obbink, Dirk (edd.), *Magica Hiera. Ancient Greek Magic and Religion* (New York – Oxford Univ. Press: Oxford 1981) 138-174.

44 Cornelius a Lapide, *Commentaria in Scripturam Sacram*, 8:354; Maneschg, *Die Erzählung*, 155.

45 Vílchez Líndez, *Sapienza*, 487.

46 Larcher, *Sagesse*, 3:911-912.

47 Cf. Wis 1:14; 17:14; Mazzinghi, "Non c'è regno dell'Ade sulla terra", *passim*.

48 Cf. Larcher, *Etudes*, 262-279; Gilbert, "La procréation: ce qu'en sait le livre de la Sagesse"; our sage makes use of "spirit" to describe "soul", describing it as something that has been "breathed" into people by God; cf. 15:11.

7:9; 10:21; etc.).[49] The context seems to support such an interpretation. People cannot free their souls from death, whereas God has this power. We can see in this verse a reply to the scepticism of the ungodly who, in 2:1d put in doubt that anyone is able to save from death (οὐκ ἐγνώσθη ὁ ἀναλύσας ἐξ ᾅδου).[50]

Summary of Wis 16:5-14

The theme of salvation, attained through the word of God and the observance of the law, reaches its culmination in vv. 13-14. Here, salvation is no longer a physical peril; the Lord is the God who can really save from death by contrast with people, who can only inflict it. The prospect created by vv. 13-14 sheds light *a posteriori* on the whole of the second diptych. Linking up with both Wis 1:13-14 and 2:1, the text of 16:13-14 by contrasting the action of God with that of people extends the eschatological perspective typical of the first part of the book. Thus, the salvation offered by God to God's people on their journey in the desert becomes the sign and foundation of the future salvation that attends the just.

In conclusion, Wis 16:5-14 can be described as a real *midrash* on the episode of the bronze serpent (Numbers 21), composed in the light of other biblical texts and continually actualised in the context of the Alexandrian culture. Such a procedure is not foreign to Greek-speaking Jews.[51] Characteristics of this *midrash* are, firstly, the idealisation of Israel's past, seen as paradigmatic for the Israel of every age; then, the tendency to expand and go beyond the biblical account. A third characteristic is the importance given to the Torah, even if it is being filtered in a sapiential key and replaced by the theme of the "word" which clearly has a greater importance. Finally, Wisdom's midrash offers a generalisation of the figures of the just and the ungodly which, together with a certain sapiential reduction of the figure of Moses,[52] removes the over-apologetic character typical of the Exodus account of the plagues, concentrating on a more universalistic, and certainly more sober and irenic, tone.

From a theological point of view, there emerges the motif of the antithetical actions of God already present in the previous diptych. Just as God corrects the just to save them, so God punishes the ungodly with an appropriate punishment which, in the final two diptychs, will be transformed into the definitive punishment of death because they refuse to be converted. In fact, God's antithetical actions illustrate the just/ungodly antithesis which characterises the whole of the first part of Wisdom, rooting it in the historical context of the exodus. Our commentary has highlighted the links between Wis 16:5-14 and the figure of the

49 Cf. Mazzinghi, *Notte di paura e di luce*, 44-45. 183. For the idea of the soul as "prisoner", cf. Maneschg, *Die Erzählung*, 160; Larcher, *Sagesse*, 3:913. For the Greek world, cf. Polybius, *Hist.* 3.69.2 where παραλαμβάνω is used in the sense of "receive", but in reference to prisoners.

50 "Hierin könnte man einen Hinweis auf den Auferstehungsglauben des Verfassers erblicken", Maneschg, *Die Erzählung*, 164.

51 Cf. Maneschg, *Die Erzählung*, 164-167, who speaks of "wiedererzählenden Midrash".

52 Cf. Mazzinghi, "La memoria della Legge nel libro della Sapienza"; Id., "The figure of Moses".

ungodly in Wisdom 2. Egyptians and Israelites represent the ungodly and the just of Wisdom 1-6 or, better, give an historical foundation to the eschatological destiny of humanity announced in the first part of the book.

This relationship is of fundamental importance. The salvation that awaits the just, as also the punishment which strikes the ungodly, are not an exclusively eschatological reality. In fact, this diptych inserts salvation and punishment within the history of salvation. The future salvation of the just is not something unexpected and detached from history but is precisely a salvation that is deeply rooted in the history of the people. In this way, by means of the literary links between the first and final parts of the book, our author is expressing the bond between eschatology and history, through the role of the cosmos.[53]

An interesting New Testament perspective can be opened up by comparing the text of Wisdom 16:5-14 with that of John 3:14-15, an association which seems to have been ignored in the patristic literature. In both cases, the point of reference is the account of Numbers 21, reread for its theological significance. The commentators of the past are explicit: for Cornelius a Lapide "allegorice, hic serpens quoad figuram similis serpentibus veris et vivis, sed carens illorum veneno, significabat Christum innocentem, aestimatum tamen noxium et sceleratum, pro nobis crucifixum... [allegorically, the form of this snake is like that of a real, living snake, but it does not have their poison; it signifies the innocent Christ who was crucified for us and yet was taken for a guilty criminal]" and he notes that "certum verum est, aheneum serpentem typum esse Christi in crucem acti [it is certain that the bronze serpent is a type of Christ crucified on the cross]".[54] Both Wisdom and John, with respect to their text of reference in Numbers, emphasise the universal, salvific will of God. That is, they emphasise God's precise plan for the life of every human being. In both cases, Wisdom and John, the negative aspect of the bronze serpent is eliminated. A further point of contact is the common emphasis on the saving word of God. In Wisdom, this is along the lines of the Targum; in John, the bronze serpent refers directly to Jesus, the *logos* made flesh.[55]

Wis 16:15-29: Fourth Antithesis – The Hail and the Manna

The Literary Structure of Wis 16:15-29

The fourth antithesis is another excellent example of midrashic style. Wis 16:15-29 is a comment on the episode of the manna narrated in Exodus 16 and in Num 11:6-9 (cf. Pss 78:25 LXX [79:25 MT] and 105:40 LXX [106:40 MT]), contrasted here with the plague of hail that fell on the Egyptians according to the account in Exod 9:13-35.

The superscription, the monostich in v. 15, creates a direct link with the previous diptych, especially with 16:13-14, but, at the same time, introduces the

---

53 Cf. M. Kolarcik, "Creation and Salvation in the Book of Wisdom".

54 Cornelius a Lapide, *Commentaria in Scripturam Sacram*, 8:591, 531.

55 Cf. M. Pérez Fernandez, *Tradicciones mésianica en el Targum palestinense*, San Jerónimo: Valencia – Jerusalen 1981, 61 n. 89.

entire diptych.[56] The first part of the diptych (16:16-23) perfectly divides into two strophes of twelve stichs each: 16:16-19 and 16:20-23. The first strophe concerns the ungodly, the second, introduced by ἀνθ' ὧν, the just (n.b. the *inclusio* τρεφ- in 16:20a and 16:23a). Seven lexemes from the first section are repeated in the second: ὑετ- (16:16c, 22d); χαλαζ- (16:16c, 22c; another *inclusio*); πῦρ- (16:16d, 22ac); φλεγ- (16:19a, 22c; the verb φλέγω, "to flare up", appears nowhere else in the book); δυναμ- (16:19a, 22c); δικαι- (16:17c, 23a); ἰσχυ- (16:16b, 20c). "Fire" (16:16d, 17b, 19a, 22ac, 27a) and "water" (16:17a, 19a, 29b) are the two leading terms of the entire diptych. The same elements have different effects depending on whether they are acting in relation to the just or the ungodly; cf. the principle stated in 16:17. In each strophe, the aim of God's action is formulated twice (ἵνα: 18b, 19b, 22b, 23a).

The second part of the diptych comprises vv. 24-29: six stichs on creation (24-25); three central stichs on the lesson to be learned (v. 26; cf. with τρέφουσιν the lexeme τρεφ- in vv. 20a and 23a); and six stichs on the manna (27-29), which take up vv. 20-23.

Part One of the Diptych: Wis 16:15, 16-19, and 20-23

15 But it is impossible to escape your hand!

16 The ungodly who refused to know you
were punished by the might of your arm,
pursued by strange rain, by hail and by relentless storms,
and consumed by fire.
17 What is most surprising: in the water which extinguishes everything,
the fire took on even more force;
for the universe is the ally of the just.
18 At one time, the flame was weakened,
so as not to consume the animals sent against the ungodly,
but so that the latter might acknowledge, at this sight,
that they were being pursued by the judgement of God;
19 but, at another time, even in the midst of water,
the flame burned more powerfully than fire
to destroy the crops of an unjust land.

20 Instead, you satisfied your people with the food of angels,
and, without toil, you offered them fresh bread from heaven,
able (to provide) every flavour and adapt itself to every taste.
21 This sustenance of yours manifested your sweetness towards (your) children,
adapted itself to the taste of the one who ate,

---

56 Cf. Bizzeti, *Il libro della Sapienza*, 93-95.

and transformed itself into what each one wished.
22 Snow and ice withstood the fire and did not melt,
so that it might be known that the fire, burning in the hail
and flashing in the rain,
was destroying the crops of the enemies.
23 However, it too, that the just might be fed,
forgot its own strength.

Notes on the Text and Translation

v. 20. "Without toil" translates ἀκοπιάτως*, a very rare adverb (Philodemus, *de pietate*: ἀπολαύων ἀκοπιάτως: cf. T. Gomperz, *Philodem über Frommigkeit*, Leipzig; Teubner 1866, col. 8, lines 12-13 [p. 82]) which could refer to the people who did not have to toil to obtain the manna (cf. Dumoulin, *Entre la Manne et l'Eucharistie*, 72 n. 58), or to God who did not strain himself to provide it; cf. Ias 40:28 LXX (οὐδὲ κοπιάσει). For the Stoic, Cleanthes, Providence is ἀκάματος καὶ ἀκοπίατος, it feels neither suffering nor fatigue (*SVF* I, 125 frag. 549). After a long discussion, Scarpat (*Sapienza,* 3:206-207) refers it to the verb παρέσχες, and so to God as subject.

In 20c, instead of ἰσχύοντα, Lat reads *omnem delectamentum in se habentem* (cf. ms. 534: ἔχοντα; V and other minuscules read ἰσχύουσαν), but this seems to be a free translation. The participle ἰσχύοντα corresponds to an adjective, accompanied by an accusative of relation. As elsewhere in Wisdom (11:21; 13:1, 9; 15:16; 19:20; cf. Scarpat, *Sapienza*, 3:207), ἰσχύω has transitive value: the manna is "able (to provide) every flavour".

The term ἡδονή comes from Num 11:8 LXX and has here the sense of "flavour", rather than that of "pleasure". For the very rare *ἁρμόνιος, Codex S and some minuscules have substituted the more common ἁρμονία.

v. 21. The term ὑπόστασις has created difficulties of interpretation. In Stoic usage, ὑπόστασις indicates the substance, nature, belonging to a particular thing (cf. *SVF* II, 163 frag. 503); in *SVF* III, 267 frag. 8 serves to oppose real substances to imaginary ones. (At 16:21, Cornelius a Lapide writes that "manna non erat phantasma, sed substantia ac res vere subsistens"; *Commentarius in Libro Sapientiae*, [Paris 1910], 542). If our author is thinking of this philosophical usage, perhaps he is intending to say that, although possessing its own substance, the manna is able to change for whomever receives it. Otherwise, ὑπόστασις can be used in the simpler sense of "means of subsistence" (cf. in the LXX Deut 11:6; Judg 6:4; Ps 38:8) with reference to the manna which allows the Israelites to live. Or else ὑπόστασις could be being used in a sense that is deliberately generic and unspecific (cf. Dumoulin, *Entre la Manne et l'Eucharistie*, 74-76). It is interesting to note that in the NT the sole employment of ὑπόστασις with a possessive pronominal adjective relating to God is in Heb 1:3 and refers to the Son of God.

The form μετεκιρνᾶτο comes from *μετακιρνάω, a verb present only here in Greek usage. The simple verb, κιρνάω, is employed in connection with the Stoic theory of *krasis* (cf. the comment on 7:23, 24; Larcher, *Sagesse*, 3:930) and indicates the "mixing" of the elements (*SVF* II, 155 frag. 473 line 1.38). Here, the compound verb could be indicating "changing the mixture", namely the transformation into something else (La: *convertebatur*).

Synchronic Analysis

16:15-16: "It Is Impossible to Escape Your Hand!"

In these verses, attention is focused on the punishment reserved for the Egyptians. Taking its inspiration again from the texts of Deut 32:39 and, especially, Tob 13:2, in a similar context (cf. the two previous verses), v. 15 states a general principle: the power of the Lord has no limits (cf. Job 26:6; Ps 138:8 LXX [139:8 MT], in relation to God's power over the afterlife).

Verse 16 recalls the seventh of the Exodus plagues (Exod 9:13-35). The ungodly (ἀσεβεῖς) are described as people who refuse to know God (cf. 12:27c; cf. Exod 9:34-35), who is evoked here in the second person. For this they are punished (cf. 12:22a and the same verb in Exod 5:14; cf. 2 Macc 9:11) by the "might of your arm", an expression used in an unusual sense (cf. Isa 51:9 LXX; 62:8 where it is employed, instead, in a salvific context). From the Exodus account, our sage takes up the theme of Pharaoh's refusal to know God, expanding it and attributing it to the whole group of the "ungodly". Thus, the sending of the plagues is being seen as an attempt by God to get himself recognised as such.

In 16c, the plague described in Exod 9:13-35 is expanded. There is special emphasis on the rain and the relentless storms (ὄμβρος can also mean "flood"; *ἀπαραίτητος is *hapax* of the LXX; cf. Philo, *Deo* 48: ἀπαραίτητος δίκη). Verse 16d adds the destructive action of the fire, here too expanding the biblical account; but cf. Exod 9:24: καὶ τὸ πῦρ φλογίζων ἐν τῇ χαλάζῃ; for the verb καταναλίσκω, cf. Deut 4:24, in connection with God, described as a devouring fire. Philo (*Mos.* 1.118-119) presents a similar expansion of this plague, perhaps pointing to the existence of similar midrashic exegesis.

16:17: The Cosmos, Ally of the Just

Verse 17 begins a theological reflection on what happened. 17c constitutes the centre of this small section (vv. 16-19). The text of 17ab introduces an extraordinary fact (παραδοξότατος; cf. 5:2b; 14:5a): in the water which extinguishes everything, the fire takes on even more force.[57] On the basis of Exod 9:24, our sage is struck by the simultaneous presence of fire and hail (water). The conclusion of 17c persuades us that he was thinking of the fire as an "element" of the cosmos that bows to the will of the creator. The plague of hail becomes a miracle in which the deep meaning of the cosmos is revealed: to be at God's side the ally (ὑπέρμαχος; cf. 10:20c) of the just (v. 17c; cf. 5:17-20). We are at the heart of our sage's theological perspective: the salvific value of creation which was announced right from the programmatic text of 1:13-15.

16:18-19: Acknowledging the Action of God

It is very difficult to say what details of the Exodus account our author was thinking of in writing vv. 18-19. According to Larcher, what we have here is an example of "cumulative exegesis".[58] In fact, vv. 18-19 meld the Exodus account of the hail with that of the plague of locusts, as already appears in Ps 77:46-48 LXX [78:46-48 MT]. Thus, the same fire is able to be weakened in order to avoid destroying the locusts (ποτὲ μέν; 18a) and able to resume its strength in order to burn the crops of the Egyptians (ποτὲ δέ; 19a; cf. Exod 9:25). This is so that the latter can understand that they are being judged by God (18c) and acknowledge the punishment that God has sent them.

---

57 On the theological value of ἐνεργέω, cf. Scarpat, *Sapienza*, 3:203-204.

58 *Sagesse*, 3:921-922.

16:20: Bread of Angels

Again with the particle ἀντὶ, v. 20 (ἀνθ' [ὧν]), introduces the antithesis proper. From heaven, for "your people", there rained neither lightning nor hail but rather the "bread of angels", the manna (which, however, is never called by name), a food with which God nourishes Israel, as a parent nourishes his or her own child (for ψωμίζω used in connection with the manna, cf. Deut 8:3 and 16).

The expression "food of angels" is taken from Ps 77:25 LXX (Ps 78:25 MT has, instead, "the bread of the strong"). The manna is, therefore, a food that does not belong to the earthly sphere. According to Tob 12:19, the angels do not eat, but cf. the addition of Lat: *sed ego cibo invisibili et potu qui ab hominibus videri non potest, utor* [But I use food that is invisible and drink which cannot be seen by men].[59] The angels are mentioned here for the only time in Wisdom, just as the "devil" is only mentioned in 2:24. The manna is the "bread of angels" because it comes from heaven (cf. Ps 104:40 LXX [105:40 MT]), but, already in Exod 16:4, God causes bread to rain from heaven (ὕω ὑμῖν ἄρτους ἐκ τοῦ οὐρανοῦ), that is, from God himself who offers it tirelessly. However, the manna is not called ἄρτον, as in Psalm 77:25 LXX [78:25 MT], but "food" (τροφή), referring thus to the general theme of chapter 16 and preparing for the eschatological development of 19:21 (cf. the comment). It is a food that is already prepared: ἕτοιμον ἄρτον παρέσχες (cf. Ps 77:19–20 LXX [78:19–20 MT]: ἑτοιμάσαι τράπεζαν). Our sage does not take into account the preparation of the manna made by the Israelites on the eve of the Sabbath (cf. Exod 16:5 and 23).

The presence of the adverb ἀκοπιάτως reminds us of Wis 6:14, where it is recalled that people will not have to toil (οὐ κοπιάσει) to find wisdom. Thus, a clue is revealed which will lead us to discover some kind of relationship between the manna and the figure of wisdom. In 7:27, wisdom, a single reality, although remaining the same in itself, is capable of every activity, just as the manna, in 16:20c, is capable of providing every flavour.

16:21-23: The Manna and the Creation

Verses 21-23 deepen the reflection on the relationship between the manna and the creation, a theme which is present only implicitly in the biblical texts (in Exodus 16 and Numbers 1, the manna follows a seven-day rhythm, respecting the Sabbath). In the most ancient Jewish traditions, the manna is seen as a reality existing right from the beginning of creation (as in Tg. Yer. I on Exod 16:15; Tg. Ps.-J. on Num 22:28). For this reason, the manna is an extraordinary food.

In Wis 16:21, the term ὑπόστασις does not refer to God, as the majority of ancient authors thought, seeing there an indicator to the Trinity,[60] but to the manna itself. The sense of ὑπόστασις is rather difficult to clarify (cf. the textual notes): one could think of "substance" or "means of sustenance" (cf. Judg 6:4 and Ps 38:8 LXX [Ps 39:8 MT], passages which our sage could have had in mind). It is a term which allows our author to remain vague concerning the precise nature of the manna, which is able to change at will and which reveals something extraordinary to people: it allows them to "taste" God and God's sweetness (γλυκύτης). This theme is suggested by the texts of Exod 16:31 and Num 11:8.

---

59 Cf. also Nicklas, "Food of Angels"; Zsengellér, "Interpretation of Exodus and Manna".

60 Cf. Dumoulin, *Entre la Manne et l'Eucharistie,* 169-170; for a brief summary of the history of the exegesis, cf. Larcher, *Sagesse*, 3:927; Grimm (*Weisheit*, 270) sees there a reference to the very essence of God ("kann nur seyn Gottes Wesen...").

However, for our sage, the sweet taste of the manna becomes a tangible sign of the sweetness of God himself towards God's children, an idea that is certainly original in Scripture (but cf. Pss 33:9 [34:9 MT]; 118:103 [119:103 MT] and, in the NT, 1 Pet 2:3).[61]

The theme of "desire" is an explicit recalling of the second diptych (cf. the comment on 16:2). Here, however, the desire is considered a positive element to which God himself responds. The exchange of the elements (21c) witnesses to God's sovereignty over the cosmos, in this case on behalf of the just.

Like vv. 18-19, vv. 22-23 are difficult to interpret. The manna is associated boldly with the snow and ice. Our sage is probably leaning on Exod 16:14 LXX (ὡσεὶ πάγος) and on Num 11:7 (εἶδος κρυστάλλου);[62] cf. Philo who, in *Mos.* 1.20, compares the manna with snow. In any case, our sage considers the manna similar to snow and ice, and this allows him to emphasise, in 22a, that they did not melt because of the fire but remained intact (ὑπέμεινεν). As for the "fire", it is not clear whether it is the heat of the sun or the fire kindled to cook the manna (cf. Exod 16:23; Num 11:8).

Verse 22cd has as its implicit subject the Israelites. What happens to the manna, which is not melted in the fire, makes the opposite phenomenon stand out even more: the fire which burns in the hail (cf. Exod 9:24 LXX) and flashes (διαστράπτω*) in the rain (namely, the lightning) is able to destroy the crops of the enemy, that is, of the Egyptians (cf. 16:19b).

Verse 23 is a further explanation of v. 22a. The fire forgets its properties so that the just might be fed. Thus, if the first section of the diptych (15-19) closed with the "unjust" (19b), this second section closes with the favours granted by God to the "just", namely, the Israelites.

Diachronic Analysis

16:16-19 The analysis of the text has shown us how, in describing the plague of Exod 9:13-35, our sage carries out an interesting operation; he not only expands the biblical account but gives it greater theological richness. The book of Exodus actually tends to describe the plagues as natural phenomena. Their extraordinary nature lies in the accumulation and intensity of these phenomena, which indicate their divine origin. Here, instead, what is "paradoxical" (17a) is, rather, the alteration, or, better, the exchange among themselves of the properties of the elements. Our sage makes use of the physical theories of his time to show that the cosmos is truly an "ally" of God on behalf of the just (cf. 17c and, further, v. 24).

---

61 For the possible reminiscences of Xenophon in 21ab, cf. Scarpat, *Sapienza*, 3:208. It is not appropriate to refer the "sweetness" to the manna, as does Ziegler, Joseph, "Dulcedo Dei: Ein Beitrag zur Theologie der griechischen und lateinischen Bibel", *ATA* 13.2 (Münster 1937): 15.

62 Skehan, "Borrowings from the Psalms", 397, sees rather a dependence on the elements mentioned in Ps 148:8 and associated with the word of God – here, with the manna.

As will happen only in some much later rabbinic traditions (cf. Mekilta on Exod 16:23 but, above all, b. Yoma 75a),[63] our author imagines the manna as miraculous food, able to adapt to every taste (cf. v. 21bc). Thus, he goes beyond the exodus account (cf. Exod 16:31 and Num 11:8, in connection with the taste of the manna) and introduces an aspect unknown to Philo. The manna thus becomes the symbol of the gift of God who responds to every human aspiration (see the same theme sketched in 16:2-3) and, at the same time, manifests God's "sweetness" (v. 21a).[64] The idea expressed by our sage finds its counterpart in some midrashic texts (cf. Ex. Rab. on Exod 16:4). 16:20-23

Manna and Cosmos

In the philosophical and allegorical *relecture* carried out by Philo under the influence of Stoicism, the manna becomes an allegory of the divine *Logos* (*Leg.* 2.86; 3.175; *Det.* 118) which teaches that God can overturn the order of the elements by returning to the original act of creation (cf. *Mos.* 2.267).[65] Two of Philo's texts share common characteristics with Wisdom's texts relating to the manna: in *Mos.* 1.201, Philo writes that "the whole world, with its parts, is subjected to God, for every use that he wants to make of it, because they are like slaves who obey their master (ὡς δεσπότῃ δοῦλα ὑπηρετήσοντα)"; in 1.143, we read that "and the most surprising thing was that, under the same (blows), in the same place and at the same time, some perished and others were saved". These are ideas very close to Wis 16:17-19, 22-23, and 24-25: the creation is at the service of God to reward the just and to punish the wicked. For Philo, as for Wisdom, the gift of the manna presupposes a renewed cosmos.[66]

Our author shows that he also knows the Stoic reflection on the order and confusion of the elements that, according to the Stoics, can be transmuted into one another.[67] However, in these verses, the manna is rather the symbol of how the internal laws of the cosmos, although recognised as existing and comprehensible, are actually secondary in relation to the Creator who overrules and transcends them and who is the author of every change (cf. 16:22-23). For our sage, the manna is the sign of this extraordinary meeting point between creature and Creator, an outstanding synthesis between biblical revelation and Greek cosmology.[68]

---

63 Cf. Ginzberg, *The Legends of Jews*, 6:17 n. 99; Winston, *Wisdom*, 299; Dumoulin, *Entre la Manne et l'Eucharistie*, 59-60; cf. also Malina, Bruce J. *The Palestinian Manna Tradition*, Brill: Leiden 1968. For some patristic evidence, cf. Larcher, *Sagesse*, 2:926.

64 It is possible to think of a polemic against the use of particular drinks within some of the mystery cults, for example the consumption of the so-called κυκεών, a drink made with water, cereals and similar ingredients (and possibly some drugs), shared by the initiates of the Eleusinian mysteries. On this subject, cf. Dumoulin, *Entre la Manne et l'Eucharistie*, 136-143. On the drinks and food within the mystery cults, in addition to the bibliography cited by Dumoulin, cf. Delatte, Armand, *Le cycéon, breuvage rituel des mystères d'Eleusis*, Les Belles Lettres, Paris 1955; Burkert, *Ancient Mystery Cults*, 108, 110, and notes.

65 Cf. Dumoulin, *Entre la Manne et l'Eucharistie*, 79-85.

66 Cf. Beauchamp, "La cosmologie religieuse", 197.

67 Cf. Vílchez Líndez, "El libro de la Sabiduria y la doctrina de la transmutación".

68 Cf. Dumoulin *Entre la Manne et l'Eucharistie*, 95.

Part Two of the Diptych: Wis 16:24-29

24 For the creation, obeying you who made it,
becomes hard to punish the unjust
and softens in favour of those who trust in you.
25 At that time too, therefore, adapting itself to everything,
it was at the service of your gift, which nourishes all,
according to the desire of those who had need,
26 so that your sons, whom you love, o Lord, might learn
that it is not different kinds of fruits that nourish people,
but that your word protects those who trust in you.
27 For what was not destroyed by fire
melted, when simply heated by a fleeting ray of the sun,
28 so that it might be known that one must rise before the sun to give you thanks
and pray to you at the dawning of the light.
29 But the hope of the ungrateful will melt like the frost in winter
and seep away like useless water.

Notes on the Text and Translation

v. 25. According to Larcher (*Etudes*, 182), the participle μεταλλευομένη indicates a poor knowledge of Greek on the part of our author, denoting a confusion between μεταλλεύειν and μεταλλοιοῦν; cf. Scarpat, 1:486 in connection with 4:12. Reese, *Hellenistic Influence*, 29, is of a different opinion: he thinks of a use of μεταλλεύειν in the sense of being "subjected to a change".

The expression τῇ παντοτρόφῳ σου δωρεᾷ does not make for easy reading. *Παντοτρόφος is found only in a fragment of Aeschylus (frag. 192.4 Nauck), but Philo knows of πάντροφος as an attribute to wisdom (*Congr.* 174). If we take δωρεά in the sense of "gift" (so already Grimm, who translates with "Gabe"), we could understand "your gift which nourishes all" as the divine word which heals everyone (Wis 16:12). With τῶν δεομένων, it is possible to think (cf. 8:21c) of those who pray (cf. Job 8:5), who ask God for the gift of food. This is the understanding of some of the witnesses (cf. Ziegler, apparatus) who add the pronoun σου, referring clearly to God.

Synchronic Analysis

16:24: The Creation, Obedient to God

In the last part of the diptych, having returned to the theme of creation (v. 24), our author goes on to speak of the manna as a sign of the word of God (vv. 25-26) and of prayer (vv. 27-29).

Verse 24 returns to the idea, already seen in v. 21 and expressed, once again, with the verb ὑπηρετέω: the creation is at the service of God. To the two verbs ἐπιτείνω and ἀνίημι, "hardening" and "softening" (see below), our sage adds a double purpose: εἰς κόλασιν and εἰς εὐεργεσίαν; to punish the unjust and to favour those who trust in you. This is the sixth occasion of this antithesis in the book (cf. 3:4-5; 11:5, 13; 16:2, 9-11, 24).

Verse 25 returns to the theme of the manna. It is the proof that the creation adapts itself to everything (cf. v. 24). The sense is, probably, that the manna is able to acquire the most different of properties. The creation puts itself at the service of what is described here as "your gift which nourishes all". However, it is not the manna as such which nourishes all, but the generosity of God, God's gift, of which the manna is the tangible sign, coming to those who seek it. The manna thus becomes a lesson for Israel (cf. v. 26a, "so that they might learn..."), here described as "your sons whom you love" (cf. Hos 11:2; Mal 1:2). There is a return here of the "you" typical of the divine praise that characterises the third part of the book, and the language becomes especially warm and moving. 16:25-26: Manna and Word of God

Thus, the manna teaches Israel to trust in the word of the Lord, a theme already important in the previous diptych (16:7, 12b), first of all (vv. 25-26), because the manna is a concrete and tangible symbol of the efficacy of the word of God, who nourishes those who believe in God (v. 26c; cf. Deut 8:3). The manna teaches the sweetness of God (v. 21), the judgement of God on the ungodly (v. 22), the fact that the creation is at the service of God (v. 24), and that one must pray to and thank the Lord (v. 28). Philo's writings on the manna developed this didactic dimension more extensively; cf. the whole section of *Mos.* 1.200-299.

Taking their cue from a detail in Exod 16:21 (the manna had to be collected before the sun melted it), vv. 27-29 draw from the episode of the manna a final, important lesson: the prayer of thanksgiving. Verse 27 is a notable expansion of Exod 16:21: the manna resists the fire kindled to cook it (v. 27a) melts at the first rays of the sun. Thus (v. 28), the Israelites learn of the need to thank God and to pray to God before sunrise. 16:27-28: Manna and Prayer

Verse 28 also sees the appearance of the term εὐχαριστία, very rare in the LXX (Esth 8:12d [= Esth E,4]; Sir 27:11; 2 Macc 2:27), but one which will become a key word to express New Testament piety. Speaking of the ungrateful, v. 29 helps us to retain for εὐχαριστία the sense of "gratitude" towards God, who is invoked once again in the second person (σου). The parallel with ἐντυγχάνω (cf. 8:21, where χάρις and δέομαι also recur, which suggests a further relationship between the manna and wisdom, which is prayed for in Wisdom 9) also compels us to see in εὐχαριστία some form of prayer and not just a simple "thanksgiving". In Philo, one notes the tendency to replace the more typical verb of the LXX, εὐλογέω, with the verb εὐχαριστέω[69]. For Philo too, a continual "thanksgiving" is a duty for people (*Spec.* 1.297). However, unlike our sage, he never relates this theme to the manna.

As for v. 28b, it does not seem that our sage is thinking of forms of prayer in which the worshipper turns to the sun but simply of a prayer made before the rising of the sun (cf. the "waking the dawn" of Ps 56:9 LXX [57:9 MT]), something attested also by the Bible and by the ancient Jewish tradition.[70] Our sage emphasises the duty of this prayer, linking it – and this is the true novelty – to the gift of the manna.

By contrast, with two poetic comparisons, v. 29 sets out the opposite attitude, that of the ungrateful (ἀχάριστος). Exactly like the manna, their hope 16:29: The Useless Hope of the Ungrateful

69 Conzelmann, Hans, εὐχαριστέω, *TDNT* 9:407-415.

70 Cf. the discussion in Larcher, *Sagesse*, 3:941-942, and the texts cited by him.

"melts" away, at the rays of first light (27b). The explicit recalling of the winter (*χειμέριος) frost (πάχνη) is like a flashback to 5:14b, again in relation to the hope of the ungodly. In the second comparison, the hope of the ungodly, likened to useless water, highlights the alliteration which opens and closes the verse: ἀχάριστον ... ἄχρηστον. Without gratitude, the goods offered by God vanish into thin air. However, the link with 5:14 and the mention of hope causes the diptych on the manna to close with an allusion that is partly eschatological, which prepares and anticipates the development of 19:21c, on the manna as a food of incorruptibility.

Diachronic Analysis

16:24 The vocabulary of v. 24 is, again, of Stoic provenance: ἐπιτείνεται καὶ ἀνίεται ("it becomes hard and it softens"). Ἐπιτείνω and ἀνίημι are two verbs that literally refer to the string of the bow. In Stoic cosmology, the expression is connected with the idea of the cohesion of the elements and the harmony of the universe (cf. *SVF* II, 129 frag. 393 lines 37-38, in connection with the qualities of beings; III, 141 frag. 525, in connection with the virtues).

According to the Stoics, the concentration or hardening of energies in the cosmos ensures the stability of a substance and its essential properties; the softening, on the other hand, allows a nature to be subject to the action of other natures or to be penetrated by them.[71] We note again that the pair ἄνεσιν καὶ ἐπίτασιν appears also in Philo (*QG* 2.64), always in a cosmological context. In *Mos.* 1.201, the principle that the creation is at the service of God ([τὰ τοῦ κόσμου μέρη ὡς δεσπότῃ δοῦλα] ὑπηρετήσοντα) appears.[72] In fact, v. 24 remains rather vague and does not intend to put forward precise philosophical theories. Rather it restates the principle articulated right at the beginning of the book (1:14; 5:17-20) and taken up again in 11:5, 15-16, that the creation is the bearer of salvation for the just as it is of punishment for the ungodly.

The antithesis *punish / favour* (cf. the comment on Wis 16:11 for the connection with the Hellenistic treatises on kingship) is employed by Philo to describe God's dealings with people (*Deo* 80; *Sacr.* 131, 133). However, this is a God who is inclined more towards favouring than punishing (*Mut.* 129; *Fug.* 65-66). Philo's effort seems to be that of wishing to reconcile two opposing visions of God's actions: the idea, of Stoico-Hellenistic origin, of a god who does only good and the typically biblical idea of a God who punishes immorality. Both Philo and Wisdom are convinced that God is merciful because God is omnipotent and that this omnipotence is deployed in God's beneficent actions towards creation; towards people, in particular, the punishment is never an end in itself, but is always in the service of conversion. We note again that, in comparison with Philo, Wisdom puts more emphasis on the theme of history. He bases his own eschatological

---

71 Larcher, *Sagesse*, 3:935-936, speaks of a real *potentia oboedientialis* of the creation in relation to its Creator.

72 Cf. Larcher, *Sagesse*, 3:934-936; Winston, *Wisdom*, 300; and the texts cited there.

reflection on Israel's past and eschews allegory completely.[73] Thus, it is the background of history, with its wealth of accounts of both the salvific and punitive action of God, that sees to it that the author of Wisdom does not pass over the emphasis on punishment. He thus partly distances himself from Philo but also from Aristeas and the Hellenistic models which he also knows and utilises.[74]

Our sage takes his inspiration here from Deut 8:2-3, but takes up the text in 16:25-26
such a way as to make it address God in the second person and adds an explicit reference to God's love. The connection between Deut 8:2-3 and the manna is known to the Jewish tradition; cf. b. Yoma 76a.[75] Deut 8:3 is developed and put into a new context. Within the book of Wisdom as a whole, the word of God is much more than the word of the Mosaic law. Thus, the use of διατηρέω (cf. Wis 11:25b) refers to a divine word which preserves in being the entire creation and which, therefore, does much more than offer people salvation. The manna becomes as if it were the representation of the divine word on the level of the senses.[76]

The link between the gift of manna and the prayer of thanksgiving is another 16:28
of Wisdom's novelties. In Ps 105:40 MT, the manna is described as a response to the "request" of the Israelites,[77] and is included, as also in Ps 77:24-25 LXX [78:24-25 MT], in a broad context of praise. Sifre Num. 89 speaks of the collection of the manna which is to be done immediately after morning prayer and the recitation of the Shema'.[78] What is the object of this thanksgiving? Our sage does not say, but in the context of chapters 10-19 makes us think of the entire work of God in creation and in history.

Summary of Wis 16:15-29

The manna unites within itself the two main perspectives which animate the seven antitheses on the exodus: the soteriological perspective and the cosmological one, postponing to the conclusion of the book (cf. 19:21c) a final note on the eschatological aspect of the manna. In this diptych, everything is inserted in a profound atmosphere of praise and prayer.

A good part of the vocabulary of the fourth diptych reflects terms and concepts that belong to Hellenistic cosmology, particularly that of the Stoics. Yet, our author does not allow himself to be pressed into following a particular philosophical system, as happens in Philo, who constantly makes the manna into an allegory of the divine *Logos* and, also, of the laws which regulate the cosmos. For our sage,

---

73 On the contrary, "Philo's conception of the world historical process appears to be strictly impersonal. The sequence of world empires is determined by a cosmic principle of equality, a fundamental characteristic of the divine Logos", cf. Winston, "A Century of Research", 13-14.

74 Cf. Mazzinghi, "The antithetical pair 'to punish' and 'to benefit'", *passim.*

75 According to Malina, *The Palestinian Manna Tradition*, 76, Wis 16:26, Tg. Neof. on Deut 8:3 and the text of Deut 8:3 LXX depend on a common oral tradition on Deut 8:3.

76 Dumoulin, *Entre la Manne et l'Eucharistie*, 113.

77 It is necessary to read שׁאלו, "they asked", with the versions, instead of שׁאל.

78 Cf. Ginzberg, *The Legends*, 6:17 n. 101.

however, the manna is never an allegory but rather a symbol, a *sign*, like the bronze serpent in the previous diptych. It is within this work of actualisation that our author succeeds in making use of the Hellenistic culture and, at the same time, remaining faithful to the biblical texts and the Jewish traditions.

The richness of the theme of the manna presented in this diptych is found again in two texts of the New Testament: the discourse on the bread of life (John 6) and Paul's reflections on the exodus events in 1 Cor 10:1-6, where Paul mentions a "spiritual food" (πνευματικὸν βρῶμα). Both John and Paul could have been thinking of the text of Wis 16:20-29.[79] In any case, this passage has an important future in the interpretation of the Church Fathers and the liturgical traditions of the early church, read as an image and prophecy of the sacrament of the Eucharist.[80] In the light of the figure of the manna, as it is presented to us by Wisdom, the Eucharist too appears as a *sign* set by God in creation, a food that is simultaneously heavenly and earthly, which answers all human desires, food that is inseparable from the word of God and the culmination of every possible prayer of thanksgiving which people can raise to God for the gifts received from God.

---

79 Thus, according to Dumoulin, *Entre la Manne et l'Eucharistie,* 156-160.

80 Cf. Dumoulin, *Entre la Manne et l'Eucharistie,* 165-198. Cf. the usage, still alive in the Catholic liturgy of singing at the end of Eucharistic Benediction a text which corresponds almost exactly to the Latin version of Wis 16:20: "panem de coelo praestitisti eis: omne delectamentum in se habentem [You gave them bread from heaven: containing within itself all sweetness]".

Wis 17:1–18:4: The Fifth Diptych – The Darkness and the Light

The Literary Structure of Wis 17:1–18:4[1]

The fifth diptych presents a *relecture* of the plague of darkness recounted in Exod 10:21-23. In particular, Wisdom 17 develops three elements of the biblical narrative: the exceptional duration of the darkness; its extraordinary opacity; and the inability of the Egyptians to see one another and to move. Wis 18:1-4 develops a fourth element: the light which shines on the Israelites (cf. 17:20). Compared with the traditions about the plague of darkness known to us from the *targumim* and the most ancient *midrashim*, Wisdom shows itself to be undoubtedly original and offers an extensive reflection, characterised first and foremost by a strong psychological perspective. This is an interest found in texts like the Testaments of the Twelve Patriarchs, but not absent in Philo either.[2] The darkness falling on Egypt becomes a sign of the fear which has fallen on the Egyptians and their magicians. The attention to this psychological dimension is in the service of a precise theological message.[3]

Our sage makes use of the language of the Greek καταβάσεις, the accounts of the descent of a hero to the underworld.[4] Two other keys for understanding the diptych are the frequent use of a vocabulary drawn from the mysteries as well as constant allusions to the magical practices typical of Hellenised Egypt. In this way, our sage actualises the biblical account of the plague of darkness in the context of the addressees of his work.

The text of 17:1-18:4 does not make easy reading. In only 25 verses, there appear a good 44 *hapax* of the LXX. Many of these words are not found even in the NT. In some cases, it seems that our author is creating the terms he uses out of nothing (cf. *infra*). Moreover, the diptych is composed with the use of rare and poetic terms. The style too is poetic, making use of devices typical of the rhetoric of the time and not shying away from imitation of Alexandrian poetry.

Exceptionally for this book, the literary structure of the diptych is not very clear. On the basis of some inclusions and in relation to the different themes in the text, it is possible to identify five strophes:

The night of the Egyptians. Verse 1 constitutes a title proper, not without relation to the previous diptych (γάρ) but anticipating the themes of Wis 17:1-18:4: Wis 17:1-6

---

1 Cf. Mazzinghi, *Notte di paura e di luce*, XXXX-XXXII; 32-35; (89-90; 136-137; 179-181; 224-226, with further bibliography).

2 Cf. Mazzinghi, *Notte di paura e di luce*, 48-55.

3 Cf. Hay, David M., "The Psychology of Faith in Hellenistic Judaism", *ANRW* 20/2 (1987) 881-925.

4 Cf. Mazzinghi, *Notte di paura e di luce*, 42-43. Only fragmentary texts of these accounts exist. One notes the extremely high frequency in Wisdom 17 of words composed with the preposition κατά, the majority of which are LXX *hapax*; cf. *ibid.*, 27 n. 83.

the punitive and salvific judgements of the Lord (1a) and the sin of the Egyptians (1b). In v. 2, the terms σκότος and κατακλεισθέντες create an inclusion with 18:4 (σκότει... κατακλείστους); at the same time, κατακλεισθέντες points to the κατακλεισθείς which closes v. 16, at the centre of the development. The term νύξ returns, in an inclusio, at the end of v. 5 (νύκτα) and in particular again along with σκότους (2x) in v. 21, thus creating a further inclusio which closes the whole of chapter 17.

Verses 1-6 present a similar internal development: after the title of v. 1 (cf. above), vv. 2-3 describe the errors of the Egyptians from their point of view (2a, 3ab) and the consequences of these errors (2bc, 3cd); in 17:4a-6b, it is the author himself who describes the Egyptians' fear (ἀφόβους in 4a; φόβου in 6b). Two concluding stichs (17:6cd) highlight the connection between fear and terrifying visions.

Wis 17:7-11 *The magicians' fear.* This second strophe does not have a proper internal structure of its own and can be identified only from the clear existence of a strophe in 17:12-15 (cf. see below) in addition to the clear thematic caesura between v. 6 and v. 7, which introduces the magicians who are the protagonists of these verses. Verse 7 recounts the failure of the magic arts and the boasted cleverness of the magicians who fall prey to the sickness (v. 8) they are trying to cure. The centre (v. 9) tells of the baseless terror of the magicians. Verse 10 describes their absurd behaviour, further evidence of their failure, while v. 11 offers both the psychological and theological basis for it: the presence of an accusing conscience.

Wis 17:12-15 *A hellish fear.* This strophe is marked out by a clear inclusio: φόβος, προδοσία, προσδοκία (12-13a), and προδοσία, ἀπροσδόκητος φόβος (15,bc). The key term "night" (cf. the accusative νύκτα) is found in 14a, at the centre of the section. Verses 12-13 are devoted to a definition of fear. Verse 14ab describes the "hellish character" of that night. Verses 14c-15 return to the theme of fear, described this time from the point of view of its effects. The term μυχός (vv. 4 and 14) reappears from the first strophe, while the φαντασμάτων of 15a recalls the ἄσματα of v. 4.

Wis 17:16-21 *Prisoners of fear.* The beginning (κατακλεισθείς) and the end (νύξ and σκότους) of this strophe (v. 16b and v. 21) recall, in inclusion, the beginning of the diptych (17:2bc), and, at the same time, they anticipate its conclusion (18:4; see above: σκότει and κατακλείστους). Verses 16, 17 and 18b have a similar beginning: εἶθ' [οὕτως] – εἴ τε – εἴ τε. Verse 16 sees a change of subject: no longer only the magicians but all the Egyptians. Verse 17-18a expands v. 16 in four stichs: four classes of people are subject to fear. In eight stichs, vv. 18b-19 list seven natural realities which terrify the Egyptians (following the opening in 18b with εἴ τε, note the sixfold repetition of ἤ). The five concluding stichs (vv. 20-21) introduce, in antithesis to the night and the darkness (v. 21), the theme of light: the term φωτί (20a) points forward directly to φῶς in 18:1a. The theme of the κόσμος (20a) is also introduced.

Wis 18:1-4 *The light of the law.* The inclusio φῶς–φωτός (vv. 1a, 4a) governs the whole strophe. 18:1-4 is neatly connected with the conclusion of the fourth strophe (17:20a) and with the beginning of the diptych (17:2; cf. above). Verse 1a constitutes an introduction in which "your faithful" recalls the "holy people" of 17:2a and anticipates the "your sons" of 18:4b. Three stichs (18:1b-2) then describe the situation of the Egyptians with which is contrasted (v. 3) that of the Israelites. Both are then contrasted again in v. 4.

Wis 17:1-6: *A Night of Fear*

17:1 Indeed, great are your judgements and difficult to understand!
Therefore, uninstructed souls have been deceived.
2 For the lawless, having boasted of being able to oppress a holy people,
prisoners of darkness and enchained by a long night,
they lay, shut up under their roofs, in flight from eternal Providence.
3 Thinking also that they could remain hidden,
with regard to their sins committed in secret,
covered by the dull veil of forgetfulness,
they were scattered, terribly scared
and beside themselves on account of their hallucinations.
4 For the cavern that enclosed them did not protect them from fear,
but noises which reverberated rang out around them
and there appeared dismal spectres with gloomy faces.
5 The power of no fire was able to give light,
nor did the splendour of the brightest stars
succeed in lighting up that infernal night.
6 They were left with only the glimpse of
a funeral pyre, as if kindled by itself, full of fear.
Terrified by a sight which they did not understand,
they regarded as worse the real things put before their sight.

Notes on the Text and Translation

v. 1 The term *δυσδιήγητος seems to be a creation of our sage (Scarpat, "Ancora sull'autore", 177) and is probably to be understood with the nuance of "difficult to understand". God's actions escape the comprehension of "uninstructed souls", that is, those who lack the spirit of wisdom and παιδεία (1:6).

v. 3. The expression ἀφεγγεῖ λήθης παρακαλύμματι is particularly refined. *Παρακάλυμμα, a rare word, indicates a curtain or a veil, here described as *ἀφεγγής, "dull", another rare term, used by the tragedians (Euripides, *Phoen.* 543), which could recall, through antithesis and in a polemic key, that φέγγος which lit up the night of the initiates of the mysteries (cf. *Phaedr.* 250b3). The forgetfulness, λήθη, recalls the homonymous river of the underworld (Hesiod, *Theog.* 227; Virgil, *Aen.* 6.714), a place that was dark and gloomy (cf. *infra*). For Philo, forgetfulness is "the death of memory" (*Migr.* 206), "a sickess of the memory" (*Congr.* 40). It comes from outside and leads people to the loss of memory itself.

In 3c, codices A, C, and some minuscules with Sa, Aeth, read instead of ἐσκορπίσθησαν (S: διεσκορπίσθησαν) the reading ἐσκοτίσθησαν, already preferred by Grimm. However, the majority reading offers an acceptable meaning: the Egyptians are paradoxically "scattered" far from one another, separated by the darkness which also keeps them shut up in their own homes.

v. 4. The witnesses offer three different readings: καταράσσοντες, "booming downward", ταράσσοντες, "confusing", ἐκταράσσοτες, "terrifying" (Ziegler chooses the first,

Rahlfs the third; cf. Scarpat, *Sapienza*, 3:231). The choice is difficult. The reading καταράσσοντες, with the support of Lat (*sonitus descendens*), offers a better sense. The verb *περικομπέω is unknown before Wisdom (cf. Josephus, *B.J.* 1.502) and has here the etymological sense of "ring out around". The pair of adjectives *ἀμείδητος, "without a smile" (misunderstood by the versions; cf. Ziegler) and *κατηφής, "gloomy" indicates what is "dismal, dark" (with the meaning "gazing embarrassedly downwards" in *Od.* 24.432). The two adjectives refer to human life in Plutarch, *Tranq. an.* 20 (= 477E: τὸν δ' ἑαυτῶν βίον ἀμειδῆ καὶ κατηφῆ ... ὁρῶντες).

Synchronic Analysis

17:1: "Great Are Your Judgements!"

The diptych opens with an observation about the "great judgements" of God (cf. Exod 6:6; 7:4), that is, the divine actions, both punitive and salvific, performed at the time of the exodus. The "uninstructed souls" (the stress is placed on the soul, ψυχή, as subject of moral responsibility) cannot understand their meaning. These are those Jewish apostates, described in Wis 2:12, who have abandoned παιδεία, the education offered by the sages of Israel. In fact, only through the gift of wisdom (cf. Wis 1:6), is it possible to understand the meaning of the divine action.

17:2: Prisoners of Darkness

The ἄνομοι, the "ungodly", are described more precisely as men "without law", those who live without the Torah (cf. Wis 2:12). Right from the beginning of the diptych, the plague of darkness is being actualised thus: the Egyptians represent those Alexandrian Jews who have abandoned the Torah. As in Wis 2:10-20, this has given birth to violence. The ungodly think they can lord it over the "holy people", those who belong to God, according to the connotation ἅγιος has in Wisdom (cf. 1:5; 5:5; 7:22; etc.). The verb καταδυναστεύω is probably taken from Exod 1:13, but recalls again the attitude of the ungodly in Wis 2:10.

As a result of their actions, the ungodly discover that they are prisoners of darkness and night (cf. the *hyperbaton* in 2b, with "night" in emphatic position), shut up as if under roofs (*ὄροφος, rare word). With fine psychological intuition, our author links the immersion in darkness with the ungodly's desire to flee far from "eternal Providence" (with a new *hyperbaton*).

17:3: Fallen into Forgetfulness

Here we have another description typical of the guilty, the belief that they can remain hidden. But the secret acts of people cannot escape from God (Isa 29:15; 40:26 LXX; Pss 9:32 LXX [10:11 MT]; etc.; cf. Let. Aris. 132). Paradoxically, the ungodly have obtained the thing they desired: God has forgotten them, covering them with the veil of forgetfulness, a forgetfulness which undoubtedly has dimensions of the underworld (cf. the textual notes). The ungodly find themselves as if they were already in Hades, forgotten by God and wrapped in darkness. In some biblical texts, "secrecy" is characteristic of *she'ôl*: cf. Ps 138:15 LXX [139:15 MT]; Isa 45:19 LXX; the text of Ps 87:13 LXX [88:13 MT] speaks of a "land of forgetting" (MT) resp. of a "land forgotten" (LXX).

To this is added fear (θαμβούμενοι δεινῶς), another theme that runs through the whole chapter (cf. 18:17). Fear alters the perception of reality. The hallucinations (ἴνδαλμα, a rare term, with psychological value) which strike the ungodly are the fruit of their wickedness and anticipate the reality which awaits them in the underworld.

In v. 4, the houses in which the Egyptians are shut up during the plague of darkness are called μυχοί, "caves". Μυχός is a term already used by Hesiod to describe the dark recesses of Hades (*Theog.* 119; cf. also Sib. Or. 4.186); Philo speaks of μυχοὶ αἵδου in *Her.* 45; *Somn.* 1.151. The term returns in v. 14 in clear connection with Hades. Thus, the darkness that descends on Egypt has an eschatological value – see further on v. 21 – becoming an historical anticipation of the future punishment of the ungodly. To the two results of fear already seen, flight and hiding, another is now added: fear paralyses people and takes them prisoner.[5] 17:4: Enclosed in an Infernal Cave

The Egyptians believe that they can remain hidden in the darkness, but they do not perceive that they are immersed in a reality that is much more terrible: they are shut up in a real infernal cave in which strange noises echo around and monstrous spectres appear (cf. the textual notes). Φάσμα also indicates the inhabitants of Hades;[6] in this case too, the darkness which envelops the Egyptians is like something within the underworld.

Thus, this dark night, which no light – whether of fire or of particularly bright (ἔκλαμπροι) stars – can brighten, is called "infernal". The use of στυγνός, "hellish", recalls the other river of Hades, the Styx (*Od.* 5.185-187; *Il.* 8.369). Already in the biblical texts, *she'ôl* is seen as a dark place (Job 10:21; cf., also, 15:22; 17:13), like a prison (Ps 106:10, 14 LXX [107:10, 14 MT]); the idea returns also in Ps 17:6 MT ("the snares of the underworld"; Ps 18:6 LXX speaks of ὠδῖνες αἵδου, "pains of Hades"), while Job 18:9-11, 14, and 18 link the idea of the ungodly taken in a snare (v. 9) to that of death described as the "king of terrors" (v. 14); Job 18:18 adds the mention of darkness. 17:5: An Infernal Night

The only light visible to the Egyptians is the apparition, as in a nightmare, of a funeral pyre kindled without any human intervention, a further sign of death. In the gloomy light of this pyre, what they saw became the source of further fear. In fact, fear arises in people who, under the pressure of emotion, tend to consider everything as a possible danger (cf. 17:10, 18-19). Thus, the whole life of the ungodly is like a nightmare experienced by those who are awake, like finding oneself in hell before being dead. For Philo, moreover, Hades is none other than the actual life of the ungodly (*Congr.* 57). 17:6: A Terrifying Sight

Diachronic Analysis

The error of the Jewish apostates alluded to in v. 1 is described with the verb πλανάω which, as in 2:21 (cf. 5:6; 11:15; 12:24), has echoes of the mysteries and is used in this sense with a polemical point. The apostate Jews are those who have claimed to find in the mystery cults the right way not to wander into the darkness like the uninitiated (cf. *Phaedr.* 248ab, taken up in Plutarch, *De Anima* frag. 178 = Stobaeus 4.52.49) but obtain the opposite result: they themselves fall into darkness. 17:1

Above all in Stoicism, God is understood as πρόνοια, "Providence", who governs the cosmos benevolently (cf. 14:3). In using this type of vocabulary, v. 2 wishes to make it understood that, once they have abandoned wisdom and the law, people fall into violence and do not manage to discern the benevolent aspect 17:2

---

5 For the presence of these three elements in the Hebrew Bible, cf. Costacurta, *La vita minacciata*, 239-241 (flight); 426-427 (hiding); 224-225 (the paralysing effect of fear).

6 Cf. Larcher, *Sagesse*, 3:953.

of God's face and so wish to flee from God. For the "infernal" aspect of the idea of "prison", see below, in connection with v. 5.

17:3-5 Verses 3 and 5 are rich with allusions to the mystery rites. It is possible that, with κρυφαῖοις ἁμαρτήμασιν (17:3), our sage is also alluding to the κρύφια μυστήρια mentioned in 14:23, those mystery rites whose principal characteristic was secrecy.[7]

In the mystery rites, φάσματα (cf. 17:4) is used to describe the visions of the initiates during the *katabasis* ritual (Plutarch of Athens, *de anima,* frag. 178).[8]

In the case of v. 5 also, the allusion to the mystery cults seems clear. Recalling that the legislator (Moses) decided to banish the initiates from the city, Philo accuses them of hiding in caves in the ground and in deep darkness in order to hide their iniquity (καταδύσεις ἐπιζητοῦντες καὶ γῆς μυχοὺς καὶ βαθὺ σκότος ἐπικρυπτέσθωσαν; cf. *Spec.* 1.319-323 [321]).

The use of ἔκλαμπροι (cf. λαμπρός in 17:20) also recalls a mystery theme. In *Phaedr.* 250b, the light shines on the initiates, but here, the ungodly are in the deepest darkness.

Wis 17:7-11: The Magicians and Conscience

7 The childish games of their magic art showed themselves powerless
and the charge made against their boasted claim of intelligence, shameful.
8 Those who claimed to banish fears and worries from a sick soul,
were precisely the ones stricken by a ridiculous anxiety.
9 And even if nothing that could trouble them scared them,
made to flee from the passing of beasts and from the hissing of serpents,
10 they died, trembling with fear,
and refused to look even at the air which cannot be escaped anywhere.
11 For wickedness is something particularly vile
when it is condemned by its own testimony;
it always multiplies difficulties, oppressed by conscience.

Notes on the Text and Translation

v. 7. The expression *μαγικὴ τέχνη does not seem attested before Wisdom and is absent also from the *PGM* which prefers μαγικὴ ἐμπειρία (*PGM* 1:331); cf. Mazzinghi, *Notte di paura e di luce*, 65.

---

7 "The writer appears to attribute to the ancient Egyptians the mystery cults of his own time"; Holmes, *Wisdom*, 563.

8 For other allusions to the mystery cults in Wis 17:1-6, cf. Mazzinghi, *Notte di paura e di luce*, 35-41.

v. 9. To the reading μηδὲν ταραχῶδης, some witnesses (S[c], V, 613, 674; cf. Lat: *ex monstris*) prefer μηδὲν τερατῶδες, the reading preferred by Scarpat, *Sapienza*, 3:237 (cf. Philo, *Mos.* 1.118, who, in connection with the plagues, speaks of τερατωδεστάτην ὄψιν). The better-attested ταραχώδης (B, A *et alii*) recalls ταραχάς in 8a and creates a deliberate play on words: those who try to cure the troubles of others fall into even worse fears.

Here, and for the rest of chapter 17, we follow the numeration in Ziegler's edition.

v. 10. Τὸν *μηδαμόθεν *φευκτὸν ἀέρα. In Wis 13:2, the "air" is one of the elements of the world and by its nature cold and dark: *SVF* II, 141 frag. 430; Philo, *Opif.* 29; cf. Winston, *Wisdom*, 306-307. Scarpat thinks simply of the air in its various manifestations: cf. *Sapienza*, 3:238. Thus, our sage is affirming that the magicians have reached the peak of fear, refusing even to look at what they are enveloped in, the air – which, on the other hand, refers by its nature to the dark and infernal visions of which the Egyptians are the objects.

v. 11. Ziegler's text offers the reading: δειλὸν γὰρ ἰδίως πονηρία μαρτυρεῖ καταδικαζομένη, that is, "for weakness is particularly fearful and testifies to that when it is condemned", or else: "for wickedness testifies (to be something) particularly vile when it is condemned". Rahlfs proposes instead: δειλὸν γὰρ ἰδίῳ (with 248, 253[c]) πονηρία μάρτυρι (with S, A, *O* [253[c]], *L b c et alii*, Mal) καταδικαζομένη, which could be translated as "wickedness is weak when it is condemned by its own testimony". In addition to a secondary variant (δεινόν: V [δινον], 637, Syh; cf. Sir 2:12; cf. Kölner Pap: δεινός), we should note the reading of *O*-S[c], 766, Arm: δειλὸν γὰρ ἰδίῳ πονηρία ἰδίῳ μάρτυρι καταδικαζομένη. Finally, the Lat reads: *cum sit enim timida nequitia dat testimonium condemnationis (condemnationi, condemnata)*, that is, probably: δειλὸν γὰρ πονηρία μαρτυρεῖ καταδικαζομένη. It is difficult to remove ἰδίως, attested by the majority of witnesses, while the presence, in some witnesses, of the second ἰδίῳ is a signal which points to the well-attested μάρτυρι. It is, therefore, possible to read: δειλὸν γὰρ ἰδίως πονηρία [ἰδίῳ] μάρτυρι καταδικαζομένη, presupposing the removal of ἰδίῳ, which may appear inappropriate after ἰδίως. Thus, we have: "For wickedness is something particularly vile when it is condemned by its (own) testimony".[9]

In 11b, the reading προείληφε[ν] (S[c], V, 248 et alii), or "presumes", is *lectio facilior.* The majority of witnesses read προσείληφεν, from προσλαμβάνω, used in the sense of "add", here in relation to the difficulties (χαλεπά).

Synchronic Analysis

17:7-8: The Failure of the Magic Arts

As an example of fear, the book of Wisdom offers the figure of the magicians whose "arts" are only "childish games" (ἐμπαίγματα; cf. Isa 66:4) which are revealed to be completely powerless. The magicians boast (ἀλαζονεία)[10] of having superior "practical intelligence" (φρόνησις; cf. Wis 8:6),[11] like that boasted of by

9 Cf. Mazzinghi, *Notte di paura e di luce*, 76-77; Scarpat proposes the same reading (*Sapienza*, 3:238-240), but without citing Mazzinghi.

10 For Theophrastus (*Char.* 23,1), ἀλαζονεία is "the pretence of having specific goods which, in practice, do not exist"; cf. 4 Macc 2:15 which puts it among those passions which reason is able to dominate.

11 Wis 17:7 constitutes a real *flashback* to Wis 8:6 (Reese, *Hellenistic Influence*, 122-124): the magic arts and the claim to φρόνησις are not sufficient to bring about what only wisdom can realise. For φρόνησις understood as "Kenntnis geheimer Kräfte und Mittel", cf. Grimm, *Weisheit*, 276

the ungodly (5:8), whereas the boast of the just is that of having God as father (2:16). There is, therefore, a close link between the magicians and the ungodly of Wisdom 2. However, this boast is revealed to be, in fact, a shameful self-accusation (ἔλεγχος *ἐφύβριστος). The term ἔλεγχος which in Philo indicates the moral conscience (*Decal.* 87), could be alluding to the συνείδησις of v. 11, thus anticipating the theme of conscience and creating a sort of thematic inclusion in this strophe.

Moreover, the magicians boast of healing illnesses and removing every fear (*δεῖμα) and every worry from sick souls.[12] It was precisely the magicians, however, who were stricken by a "ridiculous anxiety" (καταγέλαστος εὐλάβεια, the latter term used in a different sense from that of the LXX); such "anxiety" contradicts the bravado with which they try to cure the fears of others.

17:9-10: A Baseless Fear

Verses 9-10 see the return of the motif of the "exaggerated disproportion" (cf. v. 6), typical of the psychology of fear.[13] The wicked live in terror of things which normally should not frighten them; they are slaves of their own fears. The magicians, who are used to dealing professionally with serpents and other animals, are now terrified of them and flee away like frightened birds (this is the sense of *ἐκσοβέω, a rare and late verb), dead with fear (διόλλυμαι; cf. Philo, *Ebr.* 223-224, in connection with the soul of the wicked person). Once again, flight appears as a reaction before fear, and this is translated into a refusal to face reality for what it is.[14]

The pair κνώδαλα καὶ ἑρπετά (cf. Let. Aris. 138 and 169) recalls the principle expressed in 11:15, and the beasts and reptiles are the applications of it. The Egyptians are punished with those beasts which they worshipped (cf. 15:18; 16:1); punishment and salvation come about through the creation. In Wis 12:23-27, the zoolatry of the Egyptians is compared to a game of foolish children (ὡς παισὶν ἀλογίστοις) and will be punished by God with a mocking judgement (τὴν κρίσιν εἰς ἐμπαιγμόν). Thus, in light of these links, magic in Wis 17:7-10 appears as one of the more absurd forms of idolatry.

17:11: Conscience

Accepting the reading proposed above (cf. the textual notes), v. 11 states that wickedness testifies to itself at the moment in which it is condemned, showing that it is something particularly vile. In fact, oppressed by conscience, wickedness has the effect of multiplying difficulties. Multiplying difficulties is another effect of fear, but the reference to conscience and the exodus context show that the psychological introspection which is typical of our sage is actually related to a theological vision of the facts.

The way in which Wis 17:11 employs συνείδησις is undoubtedly original (see below). Within a reflection on the divine "judgements" (Wis 17:1a) at work in Israel's past, the fear which conscience calls the ungodly to experience is the sign that he has not been able to recognise the action of God in history. The conscience thus acquires a highly theological value becoming the place where people can experience God's action. Moreover, it acquires an eschatological dimension: the darkness falling on the Egyptians has, in fact, an "infernal" value; it is the image (17:21) of that eternal darkness that awaits the ungodly. Deep down in their con-

---

12 The sick or troubled soul is a frequent *topos* among the tragedians; cf. Scarpat, *Sapienza*, 3:236.

13 Costacurta, *La vita minacciata*, 192-193.

14 Costacurta, *La vita minacciata*, 242.

sciences, however, during their lives, the wicked can already experience this fear which the ungodly will incur, full of terror (δειλοί) after their deaths (Wis 4:20). Conscience becomes a kind of warning bell much more than simple remorse for one's own wicked actions. It is the place where, anticipating the fear of the future judgement of God, people are called to conversion.

Diachronic Analysis

The Exodus account of the plagues mentions the magicians of Egypt several times (Exod 7:11). In the first two plagues, the magicians are successful (Exod 7:22; 8:3), but they are then forced to recognise the presence of God (Exod 8:14-15) and finally they are defeated (Exod 9:11). The reflection on the plague of darkness takes its cue from this failure of the Egyptian magicians but goes well beyond the biblical account. In Exod 10:21-23, the ninth plague, the magicians have disappeared. Also in the Greek-speaking literature, the traditions of the magicians are not as developed as in our text. 17:7-8

Why were the magicians chosen as an example of fear? Behind the magicians spoken of in the book of Exodus, our sage sees the magicians of his own time who claim to have an effective "art". As we have seen, however, these are "childish games" (ἐμπαίγματα).[15] The result hoped for by one who has recourse to magic is, therefore, the opposite of that expected: it is something truly laughable.[16]

17:11: History of "Conscience"

We find here the first biblical mention of the συνείδησις, understood as moral "conscience" (cf. the term in Qoh 10:20 LXX and Sir 42:18S, but not with this sense).[17] The idea of conscience is not foreign to the OT which utilises the metaphor of the "heart".[18] However, this is the first time that we find in Scripture an explicit term taken, for the most part, from the Greek world. The idea of συνείδησις, understood as the accusing moral conscience, begins to develop from the time of the third cent. BCE in the popular sphere before it was taken up by the philosophers. In the period in which our author was writing, the Hellenistic world and, above all, the Stoic currents widespread in Rome were well aware of the idea of the "moral accusing conscience", understood as the interior witness of one's own wicked actions (cf. Cicero, *Clu.* 58.159: ... illud est hominis magni, iudices, atque sapientis, ... maximi aestimare conscientiam mentis suae, quam ab dis immortalibus accepimus ...). "Bona conscientia turbam advocat, mala etiam in solitudine anxia atque sollicita est" (Seneca, *Ep.* 43.5); "hic consentiamus, mala facinora conscientia flagellari et plurimum illic tormentorum esse" (*Ep.* 97.15). Thus Polybius (*Hist.* 18.43.13): "no one in fact is such a terrible witness (μάρτυς) or such an implacable accuser as the conscience (ἡ σύνεσις) which dwells in each one's soul". In the Alexandrian sphere, the idea is also known to Philo (*Det.* 146; *Virt.* 124; *Spec.* 2.49). The conscience is like an interior witness which reveals to people their own wickedness

15 Ἐμπαίγματα is the title of a lost work by the magus, Bolos (Democritus) of Mende (200-190 BCE); cf. Wellmann Max, *Die ΦΥΣΙΚΑ des Bolos Demokritos und der Magier Anaxilaos aus Larissa*, (Akademie der Wissenschaften: Berlin 1928), 1:53-62.

16 For a possible background in the mysteries of the theme of "laughter", cf. Mazzinghi, *Notte di paura e di luce*, 97.

17 For a detailed analysis and a rich bibliography, cf. Mazzinghi, *Notte di paura e di luce*, 79-89.

18 Against Maurer, Christian, συνείδησις, *TDNT* 8:902-907.

and induces them to conversion (cf. *Praem.* 163-164); cf. T. Reu. 4:3: "till now my conscience oppresses me (συνέχει) because of my impiety ". Wis 17:11 presupposes such a moral accusing conscience which, with its interior witness, oppresses the wicked with fear and terror, making them aware of their own evil actions. The reflection in Wis 17:11 already prepares closely for that of Paul (cf. Rom 2:15).

Wis 17:12-15: An Infernal Fear

12 For fear is nothing other than betrayal on the part of the aids of reason;
13 inwardly, when the ability to foresee (evils) is vanquished,
it considers its own ignorance more grave than the cause which produces the torment.
14 But during that night which was really powerless,
coming upon them from the powerless caves of Hades,
falling into the same sleep,
15 on the one hand, they were pursued by monstrous phantasms,
on the other hand, paralysed by the soul's betrayal.
A sudden and unexpected fear fell upon them.

Notes on the Text and Translation

v. 13. The text of vv. 12-13 is often misunderstood by modern translations. Here, we are giving πλείονα a comparative value and consider ἥττων as an adjective in the positive degree to be translated by "vanquished (in war)" (Xenophon, *Anab.* 5.6.32; *Cyr.* 4.1.16): our translation is, therefore: "inwardly (ἔνδοθεν), when the ability to foresee (προσδοκία) evils is vanquished (ἥττων), it considers its ignorance more grave (πλείονα) than the cause which produces the torment".

v. 15. In 15c, it is difficult to choose between ἐπεχύθη (S, V, O, Arm; cf. Ziegler and Rahlfs) and ἐπῆλθεν (B, A, C, many minuscules, Lat). However, the latter can be judged a *lectio facilior* which arose on the basis of the participle ἐπελθοῦσαν in 14b. The verb ἐπιχέω is common in the LXX in the sense of "pour".
The pair αἰφνίδιος καὶ ἀπροσδόκητος is found in Thucydides 2.61.3, in Aeschylus (*Prom.* 680) and in Philo (*Ios.* 211: αἰφνίδιος καὶ ἀπροσδόκητος ταραχή), always in the sense of something which happens suddenly and unexpectedly; αἰφνιδίως is sometimes used in funerary inscriptions (Bernard, *Inscriptions métriques*, 84.11; 96.15-16).

Synchronic Analysis

17:12-13: A Definition of Fear

Verses 12-13 put forward the only definition of fear in the whole of Scripture.[19] Fear is described first of all as a "betrayal (προδοσία) on the part of the aids of

19 Cf. Scarpat, "Una singolare definizione della paura (Sap 17,11s)"; Id., *Sapienza*, 3:216-223.

reason". Wisdom is again making use of a vocabulary of philosophical and especially Platonic inspiration (cf. below). One of the consequences of sin, therefore, is the loss of the ability to reason. From this point of view, fear is also the defeat of the προσδοκία, the "ability to foresee evils".

Verses 12-13 utilise motifs well known to the Greek world (see below); yet the definition of fear here is inserted into a precise biblical context and presents aspects of striking originality. In fact, fear is not only a psychological factor. This definition follows immediately on from the reference to conscience in v. 11. Fear is, therefore, the consequence of the presence within people of a moral accusing conscience. Experiencing fear in it, as a sort of alarm bell, people undergo the terror of Hades in anticipation (v. 14): the fear which the ungodly experience in their life is already, in some ways, their own hell.[20] Moreover, it arises from ignorance of the cause which produces it (v. 13), from the ignorance of God, therefore, which according to Wis 14:22 is the root of all evils. The Egyptians are ignorant of the cause of their own fear because, in fact, they do not know God, and this is why they are plunged into darkness. The same connection between ignorance and darkness is found in Philo, *Ebr.* 155-166.[21] This theological dimension of fear – which, as we have seen, also assumes eschatological features – constitutes a further proof of our sage's originality. Fear is an enemy which renders people wholly incapable of reading history.

17:14-15: In the Heart of Hades

The magicians are again the subject of these two verses: the night in which they were immersed becomes more clearly the night which, in an unexpected way, comes (ἐπέρχομαι; cf. 1:5; 12:27; 16:4, 5) from the caves (μυχοί; cf. v. 4a) of Hades, which here has already acquired the characteristic of a place of punishment reserved only for the ungodly.[22] However, it is "powerless"; ἀδύνατος, repeated here twice, recalls the programmatic text of Wis 1:14: the underworld has no dominion over the earth. That means that the ungodly's fear is even more paradoxical. Hades has dominion only over those who want to be dominated. Thus, there exists a gap between appearance and reality: Hades, which in reality is totally impotent, becomes, ironically, very real for those who search for it. However, the use of ἀδύνατος also recalls, by contrast, the action of the true δυνατός, the Lord (Wis 10:12; 13:4).

The magicians sleep in the "same sleep", but they are really awake. It is as if they were living in a nightmare. There is nothing to fear, but for the ungodly everything is transformed into fearful visions of ghosts and monstrous spectres. The "same sleep", therefore, is the sleep of the inhabitants of Hades. The theme of sleep linked with Hades is already implicit in some biblical texts: cf. LXX-Pss 12:4 and 88:6 [MT-Pss 13:4 and 88:6].

The magicians' punishment consists of their being pursued by monstrous phantasms (cf. Job 20:8^{A}: ὥσπερ φάντασμα νυκτερινόν) which recall the same punishment as that already seen in v. 4c but which here seem to be, instead, mon-

---

20 This is an idea well known in Epicurean circles: "Hic Acherusia fit stultorum denique vita"; Lucretius, *Rer. Nat.* 3.2023 (cf. 981-982).

21 The texts of 4 Macc 1:5 and 2:24 connect ἄγνοια with forgetfulness (λήθη); cf. Wis 17:3b. For 4 Macc, having forgotten God goes hand in hand with the (culpable) ignorance of him; cf. Scarpat, *Quarto Libro dei Maccabei*, 70-72.

22 Cf. Mazzinghi, ""Non c'è regno dell'Ade"", 245-251.

strous images that are present only in the magicians' minds as a result of their fear. To these visions are added the "betrayal of the soul" which recalls the "betrayal of reason" in v. 12. In this case too, however, what happens to the magicians is a direct result of their fear, the total unexpectedness of which is emphasised here.

Diachronic Analysis

17:12-13 Fear is described here as an irrational element. It is the defeat of the λογισμός, which, according to Aristotle, is the highest human faculty (*Metaph.* 980b 28), the ἡγεμονικόν which is able to govern the passions (cf., also, *SVF* II, 227 frag. 836; cf. Philo, *Abr.* 256; 4 Macc 1:30, 35; 3:1-5); in 4 Macc, the concept of λογισμός appears more than seventy times.[23] Also in the text of *Ebr.* 160, the darkening of the rational faculty is compared to a besieged city, without any help (μηδὲν ... δυναμένη λαβεῖν ἔξωθεν βοήθημα).[24]

Already in the biblical world, fear is described as a failure of the reason which alters the perception of reality; cf. Exod 14:11-12; Isa 19:3, where fear leads people to consult magicians and diviners. In Sir 40:5-7, the altered perception of reason derives from the φόβος θανάτου.[25] According to Goodrick,[26] the definition offered in 17:12-13 comes from one of the Alexandrian philosophers, perhaps of Stoic provenance; cf. Philo in *Det.* 119: "the expectation of future evil (προσδοκία) generates fear (φόβον)"; cf. also *Mut.* 163: ἡ δὲ προσδοκία φόβον ἐγέννησεν. The προσδοκία μέλλοντος κακοῦ (thus, Plato, *Lach.* 198b; cf. *Tim.* 70c) is part of the classic Platonic definition of fear (cf. *Prot.* 358d): προσδοκία is precisely that expectation of future evils which produces fear (cf., in the LXX, Sir 40:2). Cf., also, *SVF* III, 98 frag. 407 (ὁ δὲ φόβος ἐστὶ προσδοκία κακοῦ); *SVF* III, 94 frag. 386; *De superstitione* (= *Mor.* 164E-167A), devoted to the theme of fear, Plutarch is surprisingly close to our passage.[27]

17:14-15 Recalling the powerlessness of Hades in v. 14, it is not improbable that our author is also polemicising against the world of the magicians who claim to possess a divine power: ἡ δύναμις τῆς θείας μαγείας (*PGM* 4.2448).[28]

In v. 15, the use of φάντασμα could be recalling a Stoic concept: in *SVF* II, 22 frag. 55, the φάντασμα "is an appearance of the mind, of the type one has in dreams (κατὰ τοὺς ὕπνους)".

---

23 In 4 Macc, λογισμός is reason as able to choose the life of wisdom and is opposed to the passions. The Stoic inspiration acquires a religious value. In fact, 4 Macc speaks more precisely of λογισμὸς εὐσεβής; cf. Scarpat, *Quarto libro dei Maccabei*, 66-70.

24 This type of military language probably derives from the Epicureans; cf. the texts of Philodemus cited in Mazzinghi, *Notte di paura e di luce*, 124.

25 Cf. Costacurta, *La vita minacciata*, 245-246.

26 Goodrick, *The Book of Wisdom*, 344-345.

27 Cf. Mazzinghi, *Notte di paura e di luce*, 122-123.

28 For the theme of the magicians' sleep in Jewish tradition, cf. Mazzinghi, *Notte di paura e di luce*, 144-146.

Wis 17:16-21: Prisoners of Fear

16 Thus, moreover, whoever fell there,
was imprisoned, enclosed in that prison that was not made of iron.
17 For whether he was a peasant or a shepherd
or someone who toiled in hard labours in desert places
(each one), taken by surprise, underwent a necessity which could not be avoided:
18 for all were bound by the same chain of darkness.
The whistling of the wind,
the melodious sound of the birds among the thick branches,
the rhythmic rushing of raging waters,
19 the harsh sound of falling rocks,
the invisible running of leaping animals,
the howl of ferocious beasts roaring,
the echoes reverberating from the hollows of the mountains,
(everything) paralysed them, filling them with fear.
20 But the whole world was illuminated by a bright light
and was occupied, without hindrance, on its (own) business:
21 only over those, by contrast, there stretched a heavy night,
image of the darkness that was to receive them;
but they were, for themselves, more heavy than darkness.

Notes on the Text and Translation

v. 17. The adjective *δυσάλυκτος, "difficult to escape", is attested before Wisdom only in Nicander of Colophon (second cent. BCE; *Alexipharmaca* 251, 537).

v. 19. In 19c, the better attested ἀπηνεστάτων is read, as *lectio facilior*, ἀπηνεστάτος, by A (- τατη by some minuscules) and so referred to φωνή; we would thus have another *hyperbaton*, "the ferocious howl of the beasts".
In 19e, the reading παρέλυσεν, although well attested (B S and many minuscules), seems secondary; the context requires the imperfect παρέλυεν.

Synchronic Analysis

17:16: A Prison of Darkness

Verses 16-21 shift the attention again on to the Egyptians and the effect the darkness has on them. Two themes return which were already seen at the beginning of the diptych (17:1-6): the darkness considered as a prison (vv. 16-18a) and fear (vv. 18b-19).

"Whoever fell there..."; the adverb ἐκεῖ refers to the caves of Hades (v. 14) and also the houses in which the Egyptians were shut up because of the darkness (17:2-4; cf. Qoh 9:10 LXX and Job 3:17-19 LXX, where ἐκεῖ actually refers to Hades). The idea of darkness as a prison (εἱρκτή, the prison reserved for serious criminals), a prison "not made of iron", that is, not a real, earthly prison, is another reference to the world of Hades (cf. the comment on 17:5).[29]

17:17-18a: The Inescapable Necessity

No one escapes this situation: neither the peasant nor the shepherd nor the workman who toils in the stone quarries of the desert.[30] The technique of "generalisation" is typical of the description of situations of fear (cf. Jer 4:9; 27:36-37 LXX [50:36-37 MT]).[31]

In this chapter, the darkness becomes increasingly a symbol of the situation of the ungodly who live as prisoners of their own sins (cf. 17:2), chained (ἅλυσις) by darkness, assailed by (*προλημφθείς; cf. Gal 6:1) "a necessity which cannot be avoided" (v. 17c; note the use of *hyperbaton*).

17:18b–19: Nature as the Source of Terror

Not only are the ungodly prisoners of darkness; rather, as we have already seen in connection with vv. 6 and 10, every reality, even the most harmless, becomes a further source of fear for them. In vv. 18b-19, with words that are rare and refined, our author lists seven elements of nature which, instead of becoming reasons for joy, are the source of paralysing terror (παρέλυεν αὐτούς, 19e).

17:20-21: Light for the World

Yet the rest of the world is lit up (λαμπρῷ κατελάμπετο φωτί) by a bright light, so that all can get on with their work without hindrance (*ἀνεμπόδιστος, a classical term). Thus, the darkness of that night is not something that really exists; it is, in fact, the "image" (εἰκών) of the darkness "bound to come", that is, of the darkness of Hades which will strike only the ungodly. As in Wis 2:23 and 7:26, the term εἰκών refers to the concrete representation of another reality. The causes of the fear are not so much external; rather, they are found in the conscience of the ungodly: "they were, for themselves, more heavy than darkness". This marks the return of an idea already seen (cf. n. 24) that hell already begins in the life of the ungodly: "maximum scelerum supplicium in ipsis est" (Seneca, *Ep*. 87.24). For the ungodly, the just man was a βαρύς, the very sight of him something heavy (2:14); now they discover that they are really "heavy" on themselves.

What is the light which, according to v. 20, illuminates the whole world? Through precise verbal cross-references, vv. 20-21, constitute a *flashback* to Wis 7:29-30,[32] a passage which exalts wisdom's superiority in compassion with the light of the sun. It is, therefore, the light of wisdom, which the ungodly are without, that illuminates the rest of the world. This is a further sign of the universalistic openness which goes well beyond the text of Exod 10:23 where the light is reserved for the Israelites alone. In the fifth diptych, therefore, despite its emphasis on darkness, there is no pessimistic vision of the world. The nature described in vv. 18b-19 becomes a source of terror only for the ungodly; for those who receive wisdom, on the other hand, the whole world is under a "bright light". As the ungodly were already in 5:6, the Egyptians are excluded from this light because they are without the light of wisdom. Finally, the theme of light reminds

---

29 We can also think of a classical reminiscence: the dark prison of Bacchus (Euripides, *Bacch.* 497: εἱρκταῖσί τ' ἔνδον σῶμα σὸν φυλάξομεν ("we will guard your body in prison"); *Bacch.* 549: σκοτίασι κρυπτὸν εἱρκαταῖς ("hidden in a dark prison").

30 For this interpretation of καθ' ἐρημίαν ἐργάτης μόχθων, cf. Mazzinghi, *Notte di paura e di luce*, 157-159.

31 Cf. Costacurta, *La vita minacciata*, 231.

32 Reese, *Hellenistic Influence*, 136. These are the only two occurrences of διαδέχομαι in the book of Wisdom, in both cases linked with "night" and "bright light".

us once more that the cosmos is an instrument in the hand of God (cf., again, 17:18b-19), and that it is precisely through creation that salvation takes place.

Diachronic Analysis

The expression *δυσάλυκτον ἀνάγκην is describing the God of Israel with vocabulary belonging to the Greek Fate, a vocabulary typical of Stoicism and not infrequently employed by Philo as well.[33] The action of that personal and caring God which our sage proclaims throughout his book acquires here the features of that unavoidability typical of the impersonal "Necessity" / "Fate" of the Greeks, but that happens only to those who reject the face of the biblical God. 17:17-18a

In the Hellenistic period, people lived with the feeling that they were crushed by destiny and sought a way to escape its power or to master it. This was something the mystery cults promised to their initiates as did the magicians to their own clients. However, in the face of the God of the power of the exodus, no mystery rite nor magic is efficacious. The ungodly cannot escape the Lord. The identical expression δυσάλυκτος ἀνάγκη is found in *PGM* 4.2858, in the context of a long magic prayer to Selene, invoked precisely as the "Necessity which cannot be avoided", but which the magician claims to dominate with his rites.[34] In relation to the mystery cults, those who are prisoners of fate are freed from it by calling on Isis: ὅσσοι δ' ἐμ' μοίραις θανάτου συνέχονται ἐν εἱρκτῇ... (Isidorus, *Hymns* 1.29); like the Egyptians, oppressed (πονηρία ... συνεχομένη) by their conscience (17:11) and prisoners (cf. εἰς ... εἱρκτὴν κατακλεισθείς; 17;16) but of an unavoidable fate. Escaping Destiny

For the underworld background of the prison theme, cf. the comment on v. 5; in the *Menippus* or *Nekyomantia* of Lucian of Samosata (v. 11), the damned appear ἁλύσει μακρᾷ δεδεμένοι; cf. Sib. Or. 2.188 (ἐν πυρίναις ἁλύσσεσι δεσμοῖς). The theme of Necessity also has echoes of the underworld; cf. the δύστλητον ἀνάγκη, the "intolerable necessity" mentioned in the *Katharmoi* of Empedocles of Agrigento, in the context of a descent into the underworld.[35] In 1 En. 103:8, the souls of the damned in Hades will be ἐν ἀνάγκῃ μεγάλῃ καὶ ἐν σκότει.

Wis 17:18b-19 is a good example of the book's "inculturated" style. The passage is constructed with great care and attention to the poetic aspect, following rhythmical models which imitate classical metre.[36] The text of 18c recalls a passage from Apollonius of Rhodes (*Argon.* 2.733, 741: the plane trees near the μυχός of Hades are called ἀμφιλαφεῖς) and one hears the echo [ἠχήεντος] of the sea). Rare and poetic terms are employed: *ἀμφιλαφής, *εὐμελής, *κτύπος, *ἀπηνής, *ἀθεώρητος, *ἀντανακλάω, *κοιλότης are all *hapax* of the LXX. However, Wisdom also takes its cue from the biblical texts concerning the fear of the ungodly, such as Job 4:13-16; 7:13-15; 33:14-18; cf. Lev 26:36. The description of the whistling wind, of the song of the birds on the branches of the trees, of the water which gushes with force, of the stones that fall, of the animals that leap, of the roaring beasts, of the echo reverberating from the mountain hollows is modelled on the classical descriptions of the *loci amoeni*, well known in Greek litera- 17:18b-19

---

33 Cf. Mazzinghi, *Notte di paura e di luce*, 160.

34 Cf. Mazzinghi, *Notte di paura e di luce*, 186.

35 Zunz, Günther, *Persephonae. Three Essays on Religion and Thought in Magna Graecia* (Clarendon: Oxford 1971), 247 frag. 10 (= 116 Diesel-Kranz).

36 Cf. also the use of anaphora and *accumulatio*; Mazzinghi, *Notte di paura e di luce*, 162-165.

ture (cf. Plato, *Phaedr.* 230b; Theocritus, *Thyrsis* 1-8; Plutarch, *Tranq. an.* 20 = *Mor.* 477CF). Instead of being a source of joy and peace, as in the Greek world, nature becomes for the Egyptians a real nightmare; a suitable punishment for those who have overturned the meaning of the creation with the sin of idolatry.

17:20-21 Ancient Jewish tradition reflected on this detail of the exodus narrative: the light that shines on Israel which, already, the Tg. Ps.-J. on Exod 10:23 links with the study of the law (Wis 18:4). However, there is no suggestion of a light that shines on the whole world during the plague of darkness. On the contrary, the rabbinic traditions comment on Exod 10:23 in the light of Isa 60:2: the whole world lies in darkness (Pesiq. Rab. 17.7; Pesiq. Rab. Kah. 7.12). Wis 17:20-21 too presents points of contact with Isa 60:1-3 LXX, but focuses particularly on Isa 60:3, reading it in a universalist sense (πορεύσονται βασιλεῖς τῷ φωτί σου καὶ ἔθνη τῇ λαμπρότητί σου). Here too, there is an anti-Isis polemical point: Isis, in fact, is φωτὸς κυρία (P. Oxy. XI, 1380, 248); λαμπρός is part of the vocabulary of the mysteries (cf. 17:5).

Wis 18:1-4: Wisdom and Law, Light for the World

18:1 But for your faithful there was a very great light.
The others, however, hearing their voice and not seeing their form,
proclaimed them blessed for not having suffered also.
2 They gave thanks because – although having undergone injustice at their hands – they did not do (them) evil
and prayed that they might be taken away.
3 By contrast, a flaming pillar,
guide for an unknown journey,
a harmless sun for a glorious emigration, you prepared.
4 Truly, those deserved to be deprived of light
and held prisoners of darkness,
they who had shut up and imprisoned your sons
through whom the incorruptible light of the law
would be given to the world.

Notes on the Text and Translation

v. 1. In 1c, the majority of witnesses read ὅτι μὲν οὖν, that is "(the Egyptians) proclaimed (the Israelites) blessed although they had also suffered". To what sufferings of the Israelites does this refer? Some commentators (Heinisch, followed by Feldmann, Fichtner, Fischer, Weber) think that, during the darkness, the Egyptians hear the groaning of the Israelites at their forced labour and proclaim them blessed because they themselves are suffering much more. With Grimm, instead of οὖν, we read the simple negation οὐ (attested by A, 248 *b*, 766, La, Sa, Mal). Our theory is that οὖν is a correction made subsequent to the false identification of ἐκεῖνοι with the Egyptians: "(the Egyptians) proclaimed them (the Israelites) happy because they (the Israelites) had not suffered like them (the Egyptians)".

v. 2. The sense of 2b is unclear: καὶ τοῦ διενεχθῆναι χάριν ἐδέοντο. The ancient versions understood διαφέρω in several different ways: Lat translates with *et ut esset differentia donum petebant*; SyrHex: "and they asked the grace to be changed"; Arm: "and because they went away, they prayed to them"; Arab: "they rejoiced in the favour done to them". Cornelius a Lapide translated "petebant ut Deus hoc discrimen differentis providentiae (...) continuaret et perpetuum faceret". In fact, διαφέρω can have the sense of "make a difference" only in the active, and, furthermore, the Israelites are not the subject of ἐδέοντο. Taking his cue from Exod 10:24 and Wis 19:2, Vílchez Líndez translates διαφέρω with "go away": "they asked the favour of going away"; so too Alonso Schökel and Winston, who adds possible references to Exod 11:8; Ps 104:38 LXX [105:38 MT]. This interpretation is ancient and already reflected in a gloss of Cantacuzeno; cf. Larcher, *Sagesse*, 3:987, but then one has to give διαφέρω a sense that is totally new. Many moderns follow Grimm: "inimicitiarum gratiam et veniam petebant" (Deane, Farrar, Cornely, Heinisch, Weber). Larcher has shown that, if διαφέρω can be understood in the sense of "be in discaccord", it is not possible to take χάρις in the sense of "pardon". In Wisdom, διαφέρω occurs only here and in 18:10 where, in the middle, it has the sense of "spread".

The verb δέομαι appears also in Wis 16:25 and 8:21, in all three cases in the sense of "pray, ask". In Wis 8:21, δέομαι appears together with χάρις in the sense of "gift" and refers to the wisdom for which Solomon is praying to the Lord. In fact, χάρις has not yet taken on in the LXX the theological sense that it will have in the NT and indicates in itself a "favour", a concession, a gift accorded in kindness and freely.[37] Thus, the expression χάριν ἐδέοντο could be translated with "they asked a favour, they prayed". Differently, Scarpat understands χάριν in an adverbial sense: "they prayed them not to take account of past enmities" (*Sapienza*, 3:280).

A passage which could throw light on this difficult expression is Pss. Sol. 16:3, a hymn entitled "for the succour of the saints (εἰς ἀντίληψιν ὁσίοις)". The soul of the worshipper lies asleep, far from the Lord, close to death and the gates of Hades: ἐν τῷ διενεχθῆναι ψυχήν μου ἀπὸ κυρίου θεοῦ Ἰσραήλ, "while my soul finds itself distant, separated from the Lord, God of Israel". Here, διαφέρω, from its meaning of "differ", takes on the less usual sense of "be carried away, be separated", a separation which is the result of a difference, in this case caused by the sin which has separated the soul from God. It is possible to read our text in this sense too: the Egyptians are praying that the Israelites go away, that is, depart ("um des Sich Entfernens willen"; Engel, "Weisheit", 2156).

Synchronic Analysis

18:1-2: A Light for Your Faithful.

With ὅσιοι, the same Israelites are intended as those who, in 17:2, were called ἅγιοι. If ἅγιος pertains to the theological sphere, ὅσιος relates to the moral sphere. In fact, Wisdom uses ὅσιος only for people, never for things. Classical usage employs ὅσιος to indicate what is prescribed or permitted by the divine law, and, when it refers to people, it represents somebody who is "pious", whose

37 Cf. Conzelmann, Hans, χάρις, *TDNT* 9:363-366 and 379; Spicq, *Notes*, 2:960-966. In Wisdom, χάρις occurs in 3:9, 14; 4:15; 8:21; 14:26; and 18:2.

behaviour conforms to this eternal ordinance.[38] In the LXX, out of 38 instances in which ὅσιος has a Hebrew equivalent, in 26 cases it corresponds to חסיד, the "faithful one", who has a special relationship with God.[39] This term assumes a special significance in Hellenistic Judaism where the ἀσιδαῖοι, those faithful to the law, become the model to be followed by the people (1 Macc 2:42; 7:13; 2 Macc 14:6).

In the use which Wisdom makes of the term,[40] two main lines emerge: the ὅσιοι are, first of all, the just who are faithful to the law; cf. Wis 3:9; 4:5; 6:10, compared with 6:4. In Wis 7:27; 10:15, 17; 18:5, 9, the term is employed to express the faithfulness and mercy of God towards God's people. In 18:5, as also in 18:9, both meanings clearly emerge: the ὅσιοι are those whom the Lord has favoured in the sight of the ungodly, guiding them through the desert (cf. v. 3); this belonging to the Lord is underlined by the possessive "your". At the same time, they are those who are "faithful" to the law which has been entrusted to them (v. 4). This thus completes the vision of the people offered in 17:2. Israel belongs to the Lord, is a ἅγιος people, but this "holiness" is not something magical. In fact, Israel is the people of faithful ones (ὅσιοι) who have experienced the goodness of the Lord and who keep his law. God's initiative and humanity's response are thus brought together in our text.

The "very great light" which shines for "your faithful" is the same light which illuminates the whole of the cosmos and was already mentioned in 17:20a (cf. Isa 9:1 LXX). Here, we are again faced with a midrashic expansion of Exod 10:23. However, the passage is open to a meaning which transcends the simple material level. If, in 17:20a, the light is that of the sun, here, the light is linked to God: it is for *God's* faithful ones that it shines. And v. 4a makes it clearer that this is about a gift coming from God, just as the darkness is the logical punishment for the ungodly. The inclusio with the beginning of chapter 17 makes all that still clearer: if the judgements of the Lord are "great" (μεγάλαι 17:1a), still greater, in fact, very great (μέγιστον), is his light (cf. 7:26).[41]

The two participles of 1b (ἀκούοντες and ὁρῶντες) refer to the Egyptians; they can hear the voice of the Lord's faithful ones (ὧν), but they cannot see their form (μορφή),[42] blinded as they are by the darkness. As already in 17:3d, 4c, 6ac, 10b, 15, and up to the mention of the light in 17:20a, there is a return to the theme of sight.

The Egyptians, therefore, proclaim the Israelites blessed for not having suffered like them. The verb which governs 1c is μακαρίζω, normally constructed

---

38 Cf. Motte André, "L'expression du sacré dans la religion grecque", in: Ries, Julien (ed.), *L'expression du sacré dans les grandes religions*, III (Homo religiosus: Louvain-la-Neuve 1986), 168.

39 Cf. Stoebe, Hans J., חסד *ḥesed*, *THAT* 1:618-620; Ringgren, Helmer – Fabry, Heinz-J., *hasîd*, *TDOT* 5:75-79.

40 Cf. Ziener, *Begriffsprache*, 60; Priotto, *La Prima Pasqua*, 32-34.

41 Cf. Hempel, Johannes, "Licht, Heil und Heilung im biblischen Denken", *Antaios* II/4 (1961), 375-388.

42 Μορφή is *hapax* in Wisdom and a term relatively rare in the LXX. Already from the time of Homer, μορφή indicates form, aspect, external appearance. In describing women, Plutarch uses the pair μορφή – φωνή, aspect and voice (cf. *Mor.* 769CD).

with ὅτι. This is not a true macarism as in Wis 3:13-15,[43] but the verb refers to the ὅσιοι of v. 1a and to God's action implied by the previous use of μακαρίζω in Wis 2:16 where the ungodly remember that the just man proclaimed his final destiny to be happy. Here, the Egyptians are proclaiming the Israelites blessed from a human point of view, but in reality they are blessed because they have experienced the salvific judgements of God (cf. 17:1a), and also because they are destined for immortality.

The verb πάσχω underlines the subjective aspect of suffering. The use is similar to that in Wis 12:27 and 18:11. The verb has the Israelites as its subject but refers to the sufferings of the Egyptians which they have not experienced. These sufferings ought to have been a lesson for the Egyptians, but the lesson was not learned, and their sufferings thus became the antechamber to death.

The second action of the Egyptians (18:2a) is their gratitude to the Israelites. The beginning of the stich refers to what goes before: to ὅτι δὲ, in fact, corresponds ὅτι μέν in 18:1c, just as the imperfect ηὐχαρίστουν is parallel to the previous ἐμακάριζον. The verb εὐχαριστέω does not yet have the strong sense that it will acquire in the New Testament. In the LXX, it is found only in Jdt 8:25; 2 Macc 1:11; 10:7; 12:31; and 3 Macc 7:16, always in the secular sphere with the meaning of "thank".[44] In this sense, our text could simply be translated with an expression like, "thanking heaven", or a similar expression. In Wisdom, the verb is present only here, but note also εὐχαριστία in 16:28. In Philo, under the influence of Hellenistic piety, both these terms mostly refer to God[45] and acquire a more poignant sense, coming to indicate a general attitude of praise and thanksgiving which people have to assume in their dealings with God.[46] The context of Wis 16:28 recalls our passage closely: in 16:25, we find δέομαι (elsewhere only in 8:20) and, in 16:28, we find ἥλιος and φῶς together (cf. 18:3). The gift of the manna arouses people to praise, "at the dawning of the light". Thus, the attitude of the Egyptians towards the Israelites is similar to that of the Israelites towards God! However, whereas the Israelites thank the Lord, recognising his historical interventions (the gift of manna), the Egyptians do not manage to detect the hand of God behind the plague of darkness, and their εὐχαριστία is a purely human act of thanks. This serves only to emphasise their distance from God and the benevolence towards them employed by the people of the "saints".

The motif of gratitude is expressed with the use of βλάπτω in the sense of "harm" (cf. Wis 10:8) and of *προαδικέω in the sense of "being the first to do evil" (cf. Aristotle, *Rhet. Alex.* 1452b 6; Philo, *Mos.* 1.303, where τῶν προηδικηκότων are "those who have done evil first"). The prefix προ- refers to a previous situa-

43 For the Greek world, cf. Gladigow, Burkhard, "Zum Makarismos des Weisen", *Hermes* 95 (1967), 404-413.

44 Cf. Polybius 16.25.1; Diodorus Siculus 20.34.5; Joüon, Paul, "Reconnaissance et action de grâces dans le Nouveau Testament", *RSR* 29 (1939): 112-114; Ledogar Robert J., *Acknowledgment, Praise-Verbs in the Early Greek Anaphora*, Rome 1968, 101-106.

45 So too in Josephus and in the pseudepigrapha: cf. T. Ab. 1.15.4; T. Gad 7:6; T. Iss. 5:3.

46 Cf. Laporte, Jean, *La doctrine eucharistique chez Philon d'Alexandrie*, Beauchesne: Paris 1972; Dumoulin, *Entre la Manne et l'Eucharistie*, 114-126; especially p. 118.

tion, further underlined by the use of the perfect participle with concessive value. It is the Egyptians who thank the Israelites for not taking their revenge and not having done them any evil, although they had undergone it first.

More difficult to interpret is the final action of the Egyptians described in 2b: καὶ τοῦ διενεχθῆναι χάριν ἐδέοντο. The translation is only probable (cf. see the textual notes): the Egyptians pray that the Israelites might be taken away, that they might go away. This passage could be considered a reflection on Exod 11:7-8: the distinction between Egypt and Israel, and the prayer of the Egyptians for Israel to depart; cf. Exod 12:33, 36[47]; Ps 104:38 LXX [105:38 MT] (εὐφράνθη Αἴγυπτος ἐν τῇ ἐξόδῳ αὐτῶν). The use of the aorist infinitive adds a tone of finality: the Egyptians seek a clear separation between Egypt and Israel, the departure of the Israelites once and for all. On the part of the Egyptians, there is the recognition of a "difference" between the Hebrews and them (cf. Exod 8:19). The use of δέομαι, χάρις and the passive of διαφέρω allude discreetly to this difference which, contrary to what the Egyptians think, becomes a reason for superiority. The Israelites are indeed different, but because of the presence of God, to whom the use of the passive could be alluding, a presence which, in the Exodus narrative, some of the Egyptians recognise (cf. Exod 9:20).

18:3: A Glorious Wandering

Verse 3 opens with the particle ἀντί which introduces the antithesis that concludes the whole of chapter 17: instead of darkness, the Israelites have the pillar of fire. The single verb refers to God: παρέσχες (cf. 17:13) thus acquires a notable importance which is reinforced by its position at the close of the stich. The object of the verb is the pillar of fire, described as "guide" and "sun"; for a similar construction, cf. Wis 16:20 (ἀνθ' ὧν... παρέσχες).

The principal role of the pillar of fire is that of being the "guide for an unknown journey". The term ὁδηγός seems relatively recent for it is not attested in the papyri before the third cent. BCE.[48] It is not frequent in the LXX (only in 2 Esdr 8:1; 1 Macc 4:2; 2 Macc 5:15, of people who know the country and act as guide). More frequent is ὁδηγέω, 42x, of which a good 27 are in Psalms, mostly with God as the subject. Israel experienced the ὁδηγεῖν of God in the exodus from Egypt: Exod 13:17; 15:13; Num 24:8; LXX-Pss 76:21; 77:53; 105:9 [MT-Pss 77:21; 78:53; 106:9]. Deut 1:33 refers the act of guiding (ὁδηγεῖν) explicitly to the pillar of fire (cf. 2 Esdr 19:12, 19; Ps 77:14 LXX [78:14 MT]). In Ps 42:3 LXX [43:3 MT], the ὁδηγεῖν is related to God's light. The use of ὁδηγός in our text is linked, therefore, to this Old Testament background: on the one hand, ὁδηγός refers to the cloud (so too in Philo, *Mos.* 1.178, ἡ ὁδηγὸς νεφέλη), and, on the other hand, to the action of God who is the true guide of Israel. In Wis 7:15, ὁδηγός is attributed to God himself. In Wis 9:11; 10:10, 17, the subject of ὁδηγέω is wisdom itself (with Isiac echoes; cf. the comment). In the light of these texts, and especially in the light of Wis 10:17, the pillar of fire assumes a symbolic aspect and seems to be alluding to the wisdom which is the true guide of the Israelites; cf. the *flashback* between

---

47 In Exod 12:36 LXX there appears the theme of the "grace", that is, the favour found by the Hebrews in the presence of the Egyptians: καὶ κύριος ἔδωκεν τὴν χάριν τῷ λαῷ αὐτοῦ ἐναντίον τῶν Αἰγυπτίων.

48 Cf. Preisigke, *Wörterbuch*, 2:150; Michaelis, Wilhelm, ὁδηγός, *TDNT* 5:97-102.

17:20-21 and 7:29-30.[49] In Wis 18:3 too, therefore, it is possible to discover an allusion to wisdom: by means of the pillar of fire, it is the same divine wisdom that is guiding Israel.

An Unknown Journey

The Israelites' journey is called ἄγνωστος ὁδοιπορία (cf. Herodotus, *Hist.* 2.29; 8.118; Xenophon, *Cyr.* 1.2.10). Rare in the LXX,[50] the term indicates a hard and difficult journey (Josephus, *A.J.* 2.321; 3.37; 11.159; cf. P. Oxy. 118,6). Philo uses this term in relation to Israel's march through the desert (cf. *Mos.* 1.215, 216; 2.73, 254). In *Mos.* 2.1, ὁδοιπορία indicates the crossing of the Red Sea, as in Wis 19:5. In 18:3, Wisdom is already alluding in some way to this crossing which the book of Exodus records as having taken place during the night (cf. Exod 14:20, 24, 27). This journey is called "unknown"[51] with reference to the fact that Israel is led by the Lord along another road (Exod 13:17-18), but also because it happens at night, under the guidance of God, and is a παράδοξος (cf. 19:5) journey, out of the ordinary, absolutely extraordinary, and difficult to understand, like the judgements of the Lord mentioned at the beginning of the diptych (17:1a).

For this extraordinary and unknown journey, the Lord provided the Israelites with a "harmless sun". The adjective *ἀβλαβής is absent from the LXX with the exception of Wis 19:6, where it has a passive sense ("unharmed"). Here, it can be translated with "harmless", following a classical usage.[52] The pillar of fire illuminates the night during which the Israelites come out of Egypt, but like a sun which does not harm and does not impede the journey with its heat, as the sun does in the desert (cf. Ps 120:6; Isa 49:10). In ἀβλαβῆς, one can discern a reference to v. 2a: οὐ βλάπτουσιν. Just as the Israelites do not take their revenge on the Egyptians by trying to hurt them, so the pillar of fire is a harmless sun for Israel.

The pillar of fire is guide and sun for a φιλότιμος *ξενιτεία. This last term is, again, a *hapax* of both the LXX and the NT. In the Hellenistic period, it has the sense of "live" or "travel in a foreign land" (Let. Aris. 257; cf. ξενιτεύω in Philo, *Ios.* 254, and Josephus, *A.J.* 16.401). Combining the sense of "travelling" with that of "foreign place", we could fittingly translate it in our passage with "emigrate"[53]. It is a φιλότιμος migration. This adjective normally has the sense of "lavish, famous, glorious"; cf. Let. Aris. 227; Plutarch, *Crass.* 544B and, in the LXX, φιλοτίμως in 2 Macc 2:21 with the sense of "courageously". In Philo, cf. *Virt.* 32 and *Prob.* 133; cf., also, Josephus, *A.J.* 15.194, where there is an *elogium* of Caesar, τὸν Καίσαρα φιλότιμον καὶ λαμπρόν. In a negative sense, φιλότιμος can indicate an ambitious

---

49 Cf. T. Gad 5:7, in connection with conversion: it "destroys ignorance (ἄγνοια), puts darkness to flight, illuminates (φωτίζει) the eyes, procures (παρέχει) knowledge for the soul and guides (ὁδηγεῖ) the intellect to salvation"; in fact, conversion is exactly what the Egyptians lack.

50 Cf. 1 Macc 6:41, in addition to Wis 13:18; 19:5 (in the NT: John 4:6; 2 Cor 11:26). Cf., also, ὁδοιπόρος in Gen 37:25; Judg 19:17; 2 Kgdms [2 Sam] 12:4; Prov 6:11; Sir 26:12; 42:3.

51 For ἄγνωστος, cf. Wis 11:18 and 2 Macc 1:19; 2:7; the term can mean both "unknown" and "unknowable".

52 Cf. Plato, *Resp.* 2.357b7, αἱ ἡδοναὶ ὅσαι ἀβλαβεῖς, "inoffensive/harmless pleasures"; *SVF* III, 154 frags. 587-588, and Josephus, *A.J.* 2.266, πῦρ ἀβλαβές.

53 Scarpat, "Ancora sull'autore", 180, claims that this is the first attestation of ξενιτεία in the sense of "emigrate".

man (3 Macc 4:15, the only other occurrence of the term in the LXX). Φιλοτιμία is a common *topos* to indicate ambition in Hellenistic morality (cf. Wis 14:18; Philo, *Praem.* 11; *Fug.* 28; etc. and, already, in Plato, *Resp.* 1.347b). In our passage, it seems preferable to understand the adjective in a positive sense: Wisdom speaks of a "glorious emigration", that is, of the exodus of Israel from Egypt.[54]

18:4: The Incorruptible Light of the Law

Verse 4 is the conclusion of the diptych and recapitulates its basic words and themes. There is a return of the main principle of 11:16 and the Egypt-Israel contrast: the ones who wanted to oppress those who had brought the world the *light* of the law are now deprived of *light* and immersed in darkness; cf. φῶς in an inclusio with 18:1a; also 18:4a, c, and, already, 17:20a; and σκότει in 4a. The play on words between φυλακισθῆναι and φυλάξαντες recalls the διεφύλασσεν of 17:4a, according to the logic of retribution: the Egyptians are stricken with what they had reserved for the Israelites: prison. At the same time, v. 4 appears to be constructed with words typical of the rest of the book and particularly of the first part but so far absent from our diptych: ἄξιος, φυλάσσω, υἱός, ἄφθαρτος (cf., also, ἀφθαρσία in Wis 2:23; 6:19), νόμος, αἰών, δίδωμι.

"Those", that is, the Egyptians (cf. 17:21a and 18:1c), "truly (γάρ) deserve" to be deprived (στερηθῆναι) of light and made prisoners of darkness. For ἄξιος used in a theological sense, cf. 1:16; the Egyptians deserved their punishment. The verb *φυλακίζω, *hapax* of the LXX, does not appear to have been attested before Wisdom, not even in the papyri;[55] the sense is that of "throw into prison" and, in the passive, "to be made a prisoner". This is the third appearance of κατακλείω (17:2, 16); in the first two cases, it refers to the imprisonment of the Egyptians in darkness while here it is applied to the Israelites.

The mention of "sons" brings us back to that of the "saints" expressed in 17:2a and 18:1a with different terms (ἔθνος ἅγιον, οἱ ὅσιοί σου). In this way, our author presents us with a threefold description of the Israelites.

The final stich opens with a δι' ὧν of instrumental value: "through whom". The people of Israel are the instrument employed by God to make the world know God's law. The grammatical subject of the whole statement is "the incorruptible light", but the logical subject is God, referred to by ἤμελλεν... δίδοσθαι. Out of 22 occurrences of δίδωμι in Wisdom, a good 21 times the subject is God or God's action.[56] The verb μέλλω recalls Wis 17:21b and adds an important nuance, leading to the thought not simply of something which is going to happen (that is, the gift of the law on Sinai), but rather of something that *ought* to happen, something which belongs to God's plan for the world.

In 17:20, Wisdom emphasises the fact that the plague of darkness struck Egypt alone while the rest of the κόσμος enjoyed the light of the sun. In 18:4, although it enjoys material light (cf. 17:20), the world is in need of another unifying principle, which is not the cosmic "eon" (cf. Wis 13:9), but a superior light, that of the

---

54 The link of the genitive with the previous ἥλιον ἀβλαβῆ leads to the thought of a genitive of scope or of relation (BDF § 166): "a harmless sun for their glorious emigration".

55 Cf. Scarpat, "Ancora sull'autore", 180.

56 Cf. Wis 3:14; 6:3; 7:7, 15, 17; 8:20; 9:4, 17; 10:2, 10, 14; 11:4, 7; 12:9, 10, 11, 19, 20, 21; 14:3; the only exception is Wis 4:3.

law. Αἰών is understood here both as "world" (cf. Wis 13:9) in the sense of "humanity" and in the sense of "temporal space", as in Wis 14:6.[57]

With τὸ ἄφθαρτον νόμου φῶς we understand "the incorruptible light which is the law" (νόμου is an epexegetical genitive). Only in Wis 2:12 does the law appear in the book in its regulatory character. In fact, our author prefers to speak of σοφία which assumes in itself both the revelatory (7:25) and the normative (6:18) character of the law. Here, the law is linked to the light and is being seen, therefore, in its revelatory aspect. We must think, therefore, of Israel as bearer not of a series of precepts but, rather, as the people who are to receive and transmit the divine revelation and the religious and moral truths that spring from it.

The law is described, metaphorically, as an "incorruptible light". For *ἄφθαρτος, cf. Wis 12:1, and ἀφθαρσία in 2:23 and 6:19. It is significant that Wisdom describes the law of the God of Israel with an adjective borrowed from Hellenistic philosophy, thus linking up with 2:23. That incorruptibility which the Epicureans reserved for the gods, God has given to people right from the beginning of the creation. The law is the means to obtain it and preserve it.

The law spoken of in 18:4, certainly the Mosaic law, is not introduced by our sage with categories that are directly philosophical. Yet his presentation does not contradict and does not exclude the Stoic concept of a universal law that is in harmony with reason, eternal and written in nature.[58] Rather than speaking of direct Stoic influences, therefore, it is preferable to talk of a description of the Mosaic law which is not opposed to the Stoic idea of νόμος but which recalls at least two of its basic elements : universality and harmony with reason. However, by contrast with Philo, in Wis 18:4 and in the whole of the rest of the book, our sage does not identify the Mosaic law with the natural law, despite employing ideas that are not too remote from the Stoic concept. In doing this, rather than appealing to obedience to a law of nature obligatory on everyone in the name of a reason that is divine and universal and which is embodied in the Mosaic law (as happens in Philo), Wisdom is convinced that the Mosaic Law does not contradict those universal values that lie at the base of the Hellenistic culture. It is precisely in this context that it becomes possible to accept it. Moreover, even before the law, there is wisdom which, in its turn, is the symbol of God's presence in the world and in people, that is, a figure of mediation. Rather than the law, wisdom is at work in the world before the revelation on Sinai (cf. Wisdom 10). This is perhaps precisely why the Mosaic law is never explicitly identified with reason or with nature.

Diachronic Analysis

In v. 18:1bc, there are two possible reminiscences of the book of Job. In 18:1b, one 18:1-2
can think of Job 4:16 LXX, a text already used on other occasions: in his nocturnal

57 On a possible background in the mysteries for the *Aion* connected with light, cf. Mazzinghi, *Notte di paura e di luce*, 221-222.

58 On the relationship between Wis 18:4 and the Stoic idea of "law of nature", cf. Mazzinghi, "Law of nature", *passim.*

vision, Eliphaz looks but does not see (εἶδον καὶ οὐκ ἦν μορφὴ πρὸ ὀφθαλμῶν μου); he only hears a voice (καὶ φωνὴν ἤκουον).

In 1c, the possible reminiscence is of Job 29:10-11 LXX: οἱ δὲ ἀκούσαντες καὶ ἐμακάρισάν με. Here, the theme of suffering as education appears together with the idea, frequent in Philo, that the ungodly encounter the same suffering which they prepared for others (cf. *Ios.* 156; *Mos.* 1.218).

In connection with 18:2b, (cf. above), in Exod 11:3 LXX, we read that "the Lord gave his people favour (χάρις) in the eyes of the Egyptians"; see also Exod 12:36 LXX. Wis 18:1b-2 makes no mention of the treasures which the Israelites extorted from the Egyptians. That is not surprising when one thinks of the difficulties which the spoiling of the Egyptians caused to ancient exegetes, both Jewish and Christian (cf. in connection with 10:17). The theme of "finding favour" with the Egyptians acquires a certain importance in the rabbinic commentaries.[59] The text of Wisdom seems close to these types of traditions when it speaks of the Egyptians thanking Israel for not taking revenge for the evil they had received. However, we find some significant new features here: Wisdom removes all references to the Israelites "finding favour" with the Egyptians; it is, rather, the Egyptians who seek "favour" from Israel, and who pray for it! Moreover, the Egyptians' gratitude, similarly motivated by Israel's correct behaviour, does not manifest itself in the giving of gifts to the Israelites but remains vague, perhaps because of the difficulties felt by our author in relation to the traditional motif of the "spoiling" of Egypt alluded to in 10:17. One can understand that, behind these modifications, emerges Wisdom's concern to promote a clear message to its Jewish readers: Israel has no need to "find favour" in the eyes of the Egyptians; it is, rather, Egypt which is in some way called to conversion. Seeking "favour" is typical of the language of the magicians of Hellenised Egypt: cf. *PGM* 3:575ff; *PGM* 4:477[60]; 739s; 9a:15; 13:704-708.

It remains to examine the theme of the Egyptians' prayer for Israel's departure. In the account of the final plague, Pharaoh urges Israel to depart (Exod 12:31-32), just as Moses had foretold in Exod 11:8. The targumic tradition transforms this request into a real prayer: in Tg. Ps.-J., the "bless me also" of Exod 12:32 MT becomes "I only ask that you pray for me that I do not die". So too, Tg. Neof. and Tg. Onq.: "pray [also] for me". Tg. Ps.-J. also modifies the previous verse, Exod 12:31, in this sense: "Pharaoh called Moses" becomes "Pharaoh prayed with a sad voice". Wisdom and Tg. Ps.-J. are, therefore, close to interpreting the Egyptians' request that the Israelites depart as a prayer. In later traditions, the same theme appears in a much more developed form; cf. the Mekilta of Rabbi Shim'on which actually seems to presuppose a kind of conversion of Pharaoh who forces his nobles to seek pardon from Israel for what its people have suffered.

---

59 Cf. Mekilta of Rabbi Shim'on which links the "finding favour" precisely with the plague of darkness; cf., also, the Mekilta of Rabbi Ishmael (*Pisha* 13) where "finding favour" is understood as obtaining objects from the Egyptians who recognise the Israelites' honesty in the three days of darkness; cf. Ex. Rab. 14:3 (Stein, "Ein jüdisch-hellenistischer Midrasch", 572).

60 This text invokes Providence (πρόνοια) to render the initiate worthy of immortality because of *his* own magic power (δύναμις); one notes again the complete reversal of Wisdom's perspective.

18:3: The Pillar of Cloud

When speaking of the pillar of fire, Wisdom is clearly referring to Exod 13:21-22: God led Israel by day ἐν στύλῳ νεφέλης and by night ἐν στύλῳ πυρός.[61] The pillar is described with the adjective πυριφλεγής, "flaming" (in the LXX, only in 3 Macc 3:29); cf. Pss 77:14 LXX [78:14 MT] and 104:39 LXX [105:39 MT], where, although the term "pillar" does not appear, there is mention of a fire that lights up the night. The Egyptians asked for the favour of being separated from Israel, that is, that Israel might leave; *by contrast,* God prepares the pillar of cloud as a guide for the journey: Israel does depart, but the separation sought by the Egyptians (cf. 19:2) is transformed into a "strange death" (cf. 19:5) precisely because of the pillar of cloud (cf. 19:7). Once again, the author's irony is apparent: the ungodly obtain only the opposite of what they had hoped.

As for ξενιτεία, the apologetic and polemical context which characterises the use of this term in Philo (*Flacc.* 172) suggests that Wisdom too is polemicising against the idea, widespread in Alexandria, that the Jews were "foreigners" (cf. Wis 19:13-17). The idea is well attested in the anti-Jewish versions of the exodus which tended to show the exodus as an inglorious expulsion of lepers (thus, Lysimachus, cited by Josephus, *C. Ap.* 1.304-320) or of the impure (so, Chaeremon, *ibid.*, 1.289-290). In these texts, the exodus becomes a journey of shame in which the Hebrews give themselves over to the worst vileness (*ibid.* 1.309-311; cf. Wis 18:2a) or appear as a rabble of the poor and weak (*C. Ap.* 2.15; cf. Wis 18:1c). On the contrary, according to our author, the exodus is a "glorious emigration": indeed, Israel appears "different", distant from Egypt (cf. 18:2b); but this diversity, far from being a mark of shame is, rather, a badge of honour.

18:4: A People of Sons and Daughters

The mention of "children" reminds us that, in the Old Testament, Israel's divine parentage is a fundamental feature of the description of the relationship between God and God's people, especially in connection with the exodus. Israel is YHWH's "firstborn" (Exod 4:22; Jer 38:9 LXX [31:9 MT]; cf. Deut 14:1), whom God has called out of Egypt (Hos 11:1) and considers his beloved child (Jer 38:20 LXX [31:20 MT]); God has marked Israel out from among the peoples, who are the other children (Jer 3:19). This relationship underlines, on the one hand, the distance (cf. Mal 1:6), but also the goodness and love of God (cf. Ps 102:13 LXX [103:13 MT]).[62]

At the time of Wisdom, the theme of Israel's divine parentage was very widespread: cf. Jos. Asen. (6:2, 6; 13:10; 21:3: Joseph is recognised as "son of God"), Jubilees 1:24-25, where the mention of the "sons of God" is connected with the observing of the commandments; cf. 1QM XVII, 8, "the sons of his covenant", and, again, Sib. Or. 3:702-703, where the theme of "sons" is linked to a promise for the future. Cf., also, Pss. Sol. 17:26-27 where the "sons of God" are set in relation to the "holy people" (λαὸς ἅγιος). In 3 Macc 6:28 and Esth E,16 [8:12q] (cf. Jdt 9:4), the theme of children appears, as in Wis 18:4, in connection with their oppression

---

61 Cf. Luzarraga, Jesus, *Las tradiciones de la nube en la Biblia y en el judaismo primitivo* (AnBib 54) PIB: Roma 1973; cf., also, Mazzinghi, *Notte di paura e di luce*, 235-236.

62 Cf. Haag, Ernst, *ben, TDOT* 2:147-159; Fohrer, Georg, υἱός, *TDNT* 8:340-353; Le Déaut, *La nuit pascale*, 84-87; for the theme in Wisdom, cf. Ziener, *Begriffssprache,* 75-81; Priotto, *La Prima Pasqua*, 112-116; Jimenez –Gonzalez, *"Si el justo es hijo de Dios"*, 271-306.

by the ungodly; thus, already, in 1 En. 62:11.[63] In the rabbinic tradition, the theme of Israel's divine parentage appears again in close connection with the observance of the law: thus, R. Aqiba in ʾAbot 3.21-22; cf. Deut. Rab. 7 on Deut 29:1: "God said to the Israelites: do you desire to be characterised as my children? Occupy yourselves with the Torah and the observance of the precepts, and so all will see that you are my children"; this tradition is attributed to R. Jehuda ben Shalom (c. 370 CE).

The book of Wisdom seems to be the text in which the theme of the divine parentage recurs most: the term υἱός alone appears in 2:18; 5:5; 9:7 (cf. the comment); 12:19, 21; 16:10, 26; 18:4, 13, with a thematic progression which goes from the individual just person (2:18; 5:5) to the whole of Israel: "The Israel of the exodus becomes type and model of contemporary Israel as well as of the individual!"[64] The third part of Wisdom shows that, in the story of the exodus, Israel can recognise its own divine parentage; God's patience (12:9, 21), mercy (16:10), miracles (16:26) to the point that the very enemies of God are compelled to recognise this relationship between God and Israel (18:13).[65] Wisdom's originality lies not so much in the presentation of Israel as God's child, and not even in the connection between "children" and "law" (cf. Wis 2:12-13), as, rather, framing the theme of parentage against the background of the story of Israel. If, in Wis 5:5, "sons of God" refers to the future and, in 2:18; 9:5, 6, 7, to the present (cf. 12:19, 21), in 18:4, Israel, as God's child, at one and the same time, refers to the past (the exodus), reminds the readers of Wisdom of their present reality, and establishes their hope in the future. The law is indeed "incorruptible".

Law and Mission of Israel

In connection with the final stich of 18:4, we shall discuss here whether our sage conceives or not of a mission of Israel to the world. Even in texts that display great openness to the Hellenistic world, such as Let. Aris. or the Testaments of the Twelve Patriarchs, there never appears an appeal to an explicit mission of Israel to the other peoples; not even in Joseph and Aseneth is there an appeal to active missionary practice. In Philo, Israel is sent to the world as priest and prophet (cf. *Abr.* 98 and *Mos.* 1.149; *Spec.* 1.96-97; Israel must pray for the world). Philo presupposes proselytism (cf. the idea of those who abandon their myths to turn to the truth: μετανασταὰς εἰς ἀλήθειαν; *Spec.* 4.178; cf., also, *Spec.* 1.309; 1.51f.; *Mos.* 1.244), but even he does not think of an explicit mission of Israel. Well distant from the particularism of the book of Jubilees, of Qumran and a good part of the rabbinic tradition, Wisdom highlights the universal destination of the law and a certain active role for Israel. The basis of its

63 Philo's usage is different: "sons of God" are those who possess the knowledge of the One (οἱ δὲ ἐπιστήμη κεχρημένοι τοῦ ἑνός; cf. *Conf.* 145) and seek to be sons of the divine *logos* (cf. *Conf.* 146-147); they are also those who perform what is virtuous (cf. *Spec.* I, 318). Again, Abraham is "son of God" as "friend of God" and sharer in his wisdom (cf. *Sobr.* 55-56, commenting on Gen 18:17). However, the theme of the divine sonship is not very common in Philo; cf Delling, Gerhard, "Die Bezeichnung 'Söhne Gottes' in der jüdischen Literatur der hellenistisch-römischen Zeit", in: Jervell, Jacob - Meeks Wayne A. (edd.), *God's Christ and His People*, Studies in Honour of Nils A. Dahl (Aarhus University Press: Aarhus 1977), 18-28 [23-24].

64 Priotto, *La Prima Pasqua*, 113.

65 In 12:21 and 18:6, 22, alongside the theme of parentage, there appears that of the covenant; the "children" are at the same time the "faithful". There is thus a direct link between Wis 18:1 and 18:4.

responsibility is the event of the exodus in which the particularist aspect is bound up with the universalist perspective. For Israel of the diaspora, it is a matter of reliving the exodus, not only as separation but as active testimony of the presence of God and so being "light" through a law which is incorporated in the offer of a broader wisdom that is available to everyone.[66]

Law as Light

The metaphor of the law as light has deep roots in the biblical tradition; cf. Prov 6:23 LXX, the "commandment of the law" (ἐντολὴ νόμου) is a lamp and a light (φῶς); cf., also, Ps 118:105 LXX [119:105 MT]: the word of the Lord is a "lamp" and a "light" for the path of the just; cf. Isa 2:1-5 and Mic 4:1-3. In these texts, the image of light refers in the first place to the idea of *guiding*; the law or the word are a light illuminating people's path. This underlines the strong ethical value of the law. A closer parallel to Wisdom seems to be offered by Sir 45:17(A): καὶ ἐν νόμῳ αὐτοῦ φωτίσαι Ισραηλ;[67] this is about the Mosaic law which has the task of guide illuminating people's moral path. Isa 2:3 does not lack a universalist perspective; cf. the "servant of the Lord" whom Isa 42:1-6; 49:1-6 describes as a "light of the nations"; cf. Tob 13:13-14^{S}. An interesting text is that of T. Levi 14:3-4: "the light of the law which has been given to you for the illumination of all people..."; but here the stress falls rather on Israel's failure to observe the law, even if, as in Wis 18:4, there is a universalist dimension. Wisdom's originality in presenting the law as light is its linking it with the plague of darkness and, at the same time, presenting it in relation to the incorruptibility, that is, the eternal life of the just. The ethical aspect which is very frequent in the Jewish traditions, and especially in the targumic and Qumran texts, is less important for our sage.[68]

Summary of Wis 17:1–18:4

From the very beginning of the diptych, it is clear that the book of Wisdom intends to present, here too, the antithetical actions of God, developing once again the principles laid down in Wis 11:5, 16. The face of God as revealed to us in the book of Wisdom as a whole is that of a merciful God. The emphasis on the punishment of the Egyptians in this diptych and, above all, in chapter 17 is to be understood, therefore, as a strong warning and an invitation to conversion addressed to the actual readers of the book. The Egyptians' sin is a form of idolatry; it is the same sin as that of the Alexandrian Jews, seduced by magic or the mystery cults, themes to which chapter 17 makes constant reference. The way to escape idolatry is indicated by the law (18:1-4), known through the gift of Wisdom and described,

66 On this text, cf. Mazzinghi, *Notte di paura e di luce*, 251-261, and the texts cited there.

67 Most manuscripts have, instead of φωτίσαι (A), the verbal form φωνῆσαι; the Hebrew text lacks an equivalent term for "illuminate". 4Q Test 17-18 presents a similar problem: the term יורו "they will teach [Jacob your laws]" in the text of Deut 33:10 appears in the Qumran text as ויאירו "and they will illuminate" (cf. Allegro, John M., *Discoveries in the Judean Desert*, V [Oxford 1968], 57-60). "The Qumran reading thus reflects a piece of Hellenistic Exegesis which was doubtless motivated not only by the superficial similarity of the Hebrew words, but also by the fact that φωτίζειν was a current *terminus technicus* of the mystery cults"; Gaster, Theodor H., "A Qumran reading of Deuteronomy XXXIII,10", *VT* 8 (1958): 217-219.

68 On these themes, cf. Mazzinghi, *Notte di paura e di luce*, 247-250, and the texts cited there.

in particular, by means of the two metaphors of the light (Wis 17:20-21) and the pillar of cloud (Wis 18:3), a law destined, at least in principle, for the whole world.

The darkness and the fear, images of the tragic situation of the ungodly, summarise the whole meaning of the diptych: darkness and fear have, first of all, a *psychological* value, relating to the very life of the ungodly who live precisely in darkness and as prisoners of fear (cf. 17:12-13). Darkness and fear have also an *ethical* value, as symbols of sins committed (cf. especially the first strophe, 17:1-6). Finally, they have a *theological* and *eschatological* value: that is, they are the image of what will happen to those who have abandoned God (cf., particularly, 17:21, but also 17:14). The infernal imagery employed in chapter 17 serves to underline with greater force this theological and eschatological character of the darkness and fear. The eternal punishment of the ungodly is contrasted with the light that awaits the just who accept wisdom and the law. The latter is an "incorruptible" light (18:4) which opens up to people the hope of a life without end. We observe that this same fourfold value, psychological, ethical, theological and eschatological is applied to the conscience mentioned in Wis 17:11 for the first time in Scripture.

The text of Wis 18:1-4 falls within a concentric structure formed by chapters 16-19. The author, therefore, does not place the emphasis of the final part of the book of Wisdom on the darkness but on the light. The light of wisdom and, at the same time, the light of the law become, together with the gift of the manna (cf. Wis 16:15-29) and that of the word of God (cf. the theme of the *Logos* in Wis 1:14-19), fundamental steps towards the renewed creation described in the last chapter of the book (cf., particularly, Wis 19:18-21). The emphasis on darkness and light in the fifth diptych reveals, once again, the salvific role of the cosmos in our author's mind.

The general tone of the entire diptych surely cannot be overlooked: both in Wis 17:1a, as in 18:1-4, God is addressed in the second person. Thus, the darkness diptych is not presented so much as a moral or theological reflection on the book of Exodus and on the traditions connected with it; rather, as has already been said, the diptych is a "hymnic anamnesis" of the exodus. The use of the divine "you" is the means by which our author transforms his text into something very like a prayer, into a hymn to the goodness of God who reveals himself through history and the cosmos, opening up for the faithful a future of hope.

Wis 18:5-25: The Sixth Diptych – The Night of the Passover

The Literary structure of Wis 18:5-25[1]

The text of the sixth antithesis is a reflection on the night of the Passover (Exod 12:1-13:16), contrasted with the episode of the death of the Egyptian firstborn (Exod 12:29-34). The theme of the "night" (cf. 18:6) binds this diptych to the previous one. As always, our sage does not use any proper names; the reader is invited to understand who is being spoken of only on the basis of his biblical "memory".

Until now the literary structure of the episode has been little studied. Verses 5-9 constitute a first unit; cf. the double inclusion ὁσίων – ὅσιοι (5a, 9a) and πατράσιν – πατέρων (6a – 9e). Verses 5-9 also contain clues to a concentric structure. The text of 7b is preceded and followed by seven stichs and summarises the theme of the whole section: "that night" (6a) is salvation for the just but destruction for their enemies (cf. σωθέντος, 5b, σωτηρία, 7b and ἀπώλεσας, 5d, ἀπώλεια, 7b).

Verses 10-13 make up a small unit more on the thematic than on the literary level and focused on the reaction of the Egyptians to the death of the firstborn. The prefix αντ- of ἀντήχει marks the beginning of the antithesis, the lament of the Egyptians for the death of the firstborn. Cf. in 13a ἀπιστοῦντες which takes up the ἐπιστεύσαν of 6b, thus emphasising the theme of faith.

Verses 14-19 follow, a third strophe in which there is an explicit appearance of the divine *Logos*. The pericope forms a thematic rather than a literary unit and is marked by the clear separation between 19b and 20a. The term ὀλεθρία in 15b acts as a hook-word with ἐπὶ τῷ ὀλέθρῳ in 13b. While vv. 14-16 describe the cosmic action of the *Logos*, vv. 17-19 focus on the psychological implications of its intervention.

> Verse 19 is constructed with a syntactic pattern parallel to that of v. 6. The foreknowledge of the fathers (προεγνώσθη πατράσιν ἡμῶν) matches the presentiment of the first born (οἱ ὄνειροι προεμήνυσαν); the awareness of the former (εἰδότες) compares with the ignorance of the latter (ἵνα μὴ ἀγνοοῦντες); the joy of the former (ἵνα ... ἐπευθυμήσωσιν) with the destruction of the latter (ἵνα... ἀπόλωνται; cf. ἀπώλεια in 7b).[2]

Verses 20-25 are characterised by a clear inclusion: πεῖρα (20a, 25b) and ὀργή (20c, 25b; for ὀργή, cf., also, vv. 23b). It is possible to identify a concentric structure: vv. 20-21 (eight stichs) are matched by vv. 23-25 (eight stichs). In particular, v. 20 corresponds to v. 25 (cf. the inclusion recorded above). The theme is the announcement of the plague and of its limited character. Verse 21bc recalls the

---

1 Cf. Wright, "The Structure", 183-184; Priotto, *La Prima Pasqua*, 28-29; Bizzeti, *Sapienza*, 96-97.

2 Cf. Priotto, *La Prima Pasqua*, 120.

liturgical role of Aaron, as does v. 24. With two aorists, vv. 21de and v. 23 recall the victorious action of Aaron (cf. ἀντέστη in 18:12d and στάς in 18:23b, with which the same term is taken up from 18:16b), which is, therefore, the theme of this last section. In the middle of the strophe, verse 18:22 is stressed: this verse describes Aaron's victory, that is, the theme of this final strophe in the diptych. In 18:22c the motif of the λόγος returns (cf. 18:15a). The motif of "death" (18:20a and 18:16b) constitutes a further link with the previous strophe.[3]

Later (cf. p. 455-456), we shall point out the concentric structure of chapters 16-19 and how the four strophes of this diptych correspond perfectly to the four strophes of Wisdom 17, thus centring the text on the light of the law in Wis 18:1-4.

Wis 18:5-9: Passover Night

5 Because they had decided to kill the new-born of your faithful ones
– and only one child who was exposed was saved –
for punishment you tore away from them a multitude of children
and destroyed them altogether in raging water.

6 That night was known in advance by our fathers,
so that, knowing with certainty the oaths in which they had put their trust,
they might be able to rejoice.
7 It was expected by your people:
the salvation of the just but the destruction of their enemies.
8 For you punished the adversaries with the same means
with which you made us glorious calling us to yourself.
9 For in secret, the faithful children of the good offered the sacrifice,
and agreed to the obligation of this divine covenant:
that the saints would share equally
the same blessings and the same dangers,
while already they were raising first the holy songs of the fathers.

Notes on the Text and Translation

v. 5. In 18:5c, αὐτῶν has a double function: it refers to the verb ἀφείλω ("you tore away *from them*") but also to τὸ... πλῆθος τέκνων ("the multitude of *their* children"), creating in both cases a *hyperbaton.*

3 Cf. the further links between this pericope and the texts of 18:6-9, 10-13 highlighted by Priotto, *La Prima Pasqua*, 175, links which demonstrate that 18:20-25 cannot be considered an isolated unit (against Wright, "The Structure", 183-184).

v. 6. The verb *ἐπευθυμέω is *hapax* in the LXX and does not occur elsewhere in Greek usage. It is, perhaps, a creation of our author. However, εὐθυμέω appears in the Greek text of Symmachus of Ps 31:11a LXX [32:11a MT] and Prov 15:15; cf. εὐθυμία in Ps 42:4 LXX [43:4 MT] and 50:10 LXX [51:10 MT]. Εὐθυμία is a term with a Hellenistic flavour (cf. εὔθυμοι in 2 Macc 11:6). In the Psalm texts, it is a joy which comes from God. This seems to be the sense in which Wisdom employs the compound verb (for the closeness of Wisdom to Symmachus, cf. Fichtner, *Der AT-Text der Sapientiae Salomonis*, 191-192).

v. 9. Scarpat (*Sapienza*, 3:284-285) devotes a long discussion to the problematic expression ἐθυσίαζον ὅσιοι παῖδες ἀγαθῶν, which he claims to be very unusual. He prefers to understand ἀγαθῶν as a neuter plural and to read "the sacrifice of goods offered"; but it is more consistent with Greek usage to consider the adjective ἀγαθός in its moral sense and refer it to the patriarchs ("fromme Söhne guter Väter": Grimm, *Weisheit*, 284).

In 9b, Scarpat (*Sapienza*, 3:285) prefers the *lectio facilior* ὁσιότητος (S, *O* and many minsucules; Lat, Sa, Syr, Arm; cf. Wis 2:22; 5:19; 9:3; 14:30), against the majority reading, *θειότητος, a rare word belonging to Hellenistic religious vocabulary (Let. Aris. 95; Rom 1:20; cf. Reese, *Hellenistic Influence*, 12).

In 9d again, Scarpat (*Sapienza*, 3:286) prefers to read τοὺς ἁγίους with reference to αἴνους (note, in this case, the *hyperbaton*) as object of the verbal form προαναμέλποντες, understood, in its turn, as *participium coniunctum* of διέθεντο; for *προαναμέλπω, absolute *hapax* in Greek, cf. Scarpat, *Sapienza*, 3:287; Engel, "Weisheit", 2156.

Synchronic Analysis

18:5: Introduction to the Sixth Diptych

The initial stich introduces the theme of the diptych by recalling, first of all, the narrative of Exod 1:16-22, the decree of Pharaoh who wanted to kill the male children of the Hebrews, here called, as shortly before, in Wis 18:1, the ὅσιοι, those "faithful" to God and God's law and, also, the object of the divine חסד. The Israelites are thus being idealised, following a typically midrashic process. The Hebrew babies are called νήπια; cf. Wis 12:24 and 15:14, in the classical sense of children without reason; Wis 10:21, with reference to the Hebrew "babes" in the context of the crossing of the sea. Here, νήπιος is being used in a context of persecution, as occurs regularly in Josephus.[4] The Egyptian children are called, more neutrally, τέκνα (5c; cf., also, Moses in 5b).

The parenthesis of 5b (in the form of a genitive absolute) recalls the episode of the birth of Moses who was saved from the waters (Exod 2:1-10). The mention of Moses's exposure recalls the text of Wis 11:14 which has ἔκθησις instead (τὸν ἐν ἐκθέσει πάλαι ῥιφέντα); cf. Acts 7:21.

As for the divine decision to destroy the Egyptians all together[5] in the waters of the Red Sea (ἐν ὕδατι σφοδρῷ, cf. Exod 15:10), that happens according to the

4 Cf. Bertram, Georg, νήπιος, *TDNT* 4:912-923.

5 Here, ὁμοθυμαδόν has a different sense from the more common one of "with one voice", as in Wis 10:20; cf., below, on 18:12. Priotto, *La Prima Pasqua*, 38-40, shows that, whereas the connection between Pharaoh's decree of infanticide and the death of the Egyptians in the Red Sea is present in the Jewish tradition (cf., for example, Jub. 48:14; Winston, *Wisdom*, 314-315), what is new is the connection with the birth of Moses.

principle laid down in Wis 11:5, 16 (cf. 18:8a). For the Egyptians, at the end of a story of their rejection of God, there is now only death which will pervade the whole diptych like a mournful refrain. Once again, another element of the cosmos, water, accompanies God's action.

For the combination εἰς ἔλεγχον, cf. 1:9; 2:14 and, especially, 11:7 where this combination introduces a punitive response by God which seems to be definitive here. As in 17:1, at the beginning of the previous diptych, and as in 18:1, we note the use of the "you" in relation to God whose constant presence beside his people is thus being recalled by our sage.

18:6-9: The Night of Salvation

Verses 6-9 describe the Passover night, "that night", as in Exod 12:42 LXX, the only time in which the expression ἐκείνη ἡ νύξ appears in the LXX. This is, thus, a "night" quite different from that of the fourth diptych and, especially, Wisdom 17, the night of fear that fell on the Egyptians. "That night", on the other hand, through antonomasia, is the night of salvation, just as it was already conceived of and celebrated by Israel in the time of our author.[6]

That night was known in anticipation by "our" fathers; probably, as later in v. 22, the text means to refer to the patriarchs (cf., also, 12:21).[7]

The joy mentioned by our author could be a positive interpretation of Abraham's laughter in Gen 17:17 in relation to the birth of Isaac (cf. Jub. 14:21; Philo, *QG* 3.55, and, on similar lines, John 8:56). It arises from having believed in the divine promises (ὅρκοι) of which the fathers had a sure and certain knowledge (ἀσφαλῶς εἰδότες); for the theme of faith, cf. Wis 12:2 and 16:26.

18:7-8: The Antithetical Actions of God

The expectation of the Passover (7a) refers to the whole story of the people of Israel but particularly to the people in Egypt who, according to Exod 11:4-8 and 12:21-27, had already been forewarned about what would happen. However, the pronoun ἡμᾶς in 8b betrays the thought of our author who is moving on to the historical situation in which he is living. This is all about "your people"; with a certain idealisation, a people of the just (7b), as appears already in 10:20 (cf. 11:14; 12:9; 16:17, 23; 18:20). As has already been said, these "just" ones recall the "just" protagonist of the first part of our book.

The author's thought is summarised in the second stich, which is structured concentrically (7b): "that night" is salvation for the just and destruction for their enemies. The term ἀπώλεια appears in the first part of the book in an eschatological context (see also below); cf. 1:13 (a programmatic passage in which our sage denies that God rejoices in the destruction of the living) and 5:7, a passage which reveals a further contact between our diptych and the ungodly-just antithesis of Wisdom 5.

Verse 8 takes up the principle of 11:5, applying it to the theme of the night in which some were saved but others punished. One can also think of the twofold action of the divine *Logos* described in 18:14-16 (the punishing *Logos*) and in 18:22 (the saving *Logos*). To the death of the enemies, alluded to in 8a, is counterposed the glorification of the Israelites. God called them to himself; the verb προσκαλέομαι, "call to oneself" (cf. Matt 18:32) is explicitly recalling Exod 3:18 LXX and 5:3 LXX, the only passages where the verb has God as the subject and Israel as the

---

6 One remembers the Targum Neofiti's famous "poem of the four nights written in the book of memories" (Tg. Neof. on Exod 12:42); cf. Le Déaut, *La nuit pascale, passim.*

7 Cf. the arguments adduced by Cheon, *Exodus Story*, 82.

object; with the rendering προσκέκληται ἡμᾶς "he called us to him" (MT: "he met us"), the LXX provides the text with an distinct sense (cf. Hos 11:1, μετεκάλεσα). The feast in the desert thus appears to be the aim of God's calling Israel. The glorification of the people consists in this call. On Passover night, the "glory" of God is manifested in relation to the historical salvation of God's people.

18:9: The Passover Feast

The Passover feast is described in v. 9: the Israelites become the "faithful" (cf. v. 5a, but here the emphasis is more on fidelity to the law), "sons of the good"; ἀγαθοί is probably referring to the "fathers" mentioned in 6a (cf. Philo, *Praem.* 67; *Abr.* 235). For the Passover viewed as a "sacrifice", cf. Exod 12:21, 27; Deut 16:5. Here, it is a question of a sacrifice offered by all the people which underlines their priestly character (cf. Philo in *Decal.* 159; *Mos.* 2.224; *Spec.* 2.145-146); for the theme of "secrecy", see below.

Passover and Covenant

Verse 9b is difficult to interpret.[8] The use of διατίθημαι, often linked with διάθηκη, with the covenant, in the LXX refers to the establishing of a covenant, and the aorist seems to point to a precise moment in the Passover celebration. With νόμος as object, the verb διατίθημαι is found only in Plato (*Leg.* 8.834a) and in Strabo (*Geogr.* 10.4.19). Thus, the verb points us in the direction of interpreting νόμος not so much in the sense of "law" as rather of "covenant", a ratified obligation, in this case with a proleptic allusion to the theme of the Sinai covenant (cf. νόμος in the context of the Passover narrative in Exod 12:49); and it is, in fact, a "divine" covenant. The covenant to which the Israelites agree becomes the response which they give to the divine call (cf. v. 8b), in the steps of the faith of the fathers (6b) and by contrast with the Egyptian ἀπιστία (v. 13).

The "faithful" (9a) are bound, particularly, to share the same blessings and the same dangers (9cd). The text is generic and could refer to the events of the exodus as also to the situation of the Jewish community of Alexandria.

The Holy Songs of the Fathers

The verse closes by evoking the "holy songs of the fathers" (cf. textual notes). The verb προαναμέλπω, "singing first", expresses the prior nature of the praise raised by the Israelites in relation to the funeral lament of the Egyptians (cf. v. 10). The particle ἤδη, "already", perhaps refers to a moment of celebration: the Israelites committed themselves to this divine covenant at the same time as they sang hymns. As for the "holy songs of the fathers", one can think of "traditional songs" handed down from the "fathers" understood as ancestors in the broad sense, beginning from the patriarchs mentioned in inclusio in v. 6. Our sage may be also thinking of the Passover *Hallel*, praise which, linked to the Passover, expresses the sibling communion evoked earlier and is translated into thanksgiving addressed to the Lord (cf. Jub. 49:6).

Diachronic Analysis

18:5

With regard to the baby who was "exposed", we observe that Philo uses ἐκτίθημι three times in a similar context (*Mos.* 1.10-12). The presentation of Moses here, and especially in Wis 11:14, as "exposed and thrown into the river" seems strange, as if his own parents had rejected him. Perhaps our sage is rereading Moses's story in a midrashic way in the light of the story of Joseph who was rejected by

8 Cf. the long, but inconclusive, discussion in Larcher, *Sagesse*, 3:1003-1006.

his brothers. In Philo too, Moses's exposure is presented as an act performed by the parents not with the direct intention of saving the baby. If that happens, it is, rather, because of the will of God (*Mos.* 1.12).[9]

In a single verse, our sage condenses an entire narrative arc: the text of Exodus 1-15, read in four movements: the decision to kill the Israelite babies; the birth and rescue of Moses; the death of the firstborn as retribution for the decision of the Egyptians (εἰς ἔλεγχον: 5c); and the divine decision to destroy the Egyptians in the waters of the sea. This combination is unique in the Jewish tradition.

18:6 As for the night "known in advance by our fathers", already the texts of Gen 15:13-14 and 46:3-4 lead to the thought that God had somehow let them anticipate the knowledge of the future Passover celebration. This could be the reference of the passive of *προγιγνώσκω (in the NT, cf. 1 Pet 1:20, along the same lines of thought). Cf. Wis 6:13; 8:8 with reference to wisdom's action in people, a wisdom to whose action our text could be discreetly alluding. More simply, the text could be alluding to Exod 12:21-23: God explains in advance to the ancestors what is going to happen, which means that the "fathers" could also be the exodus generation.[10]

18:7-8 The expectation of the Passover also discloses an eschatological dimension which is not absent from the rereadings of the exodus already made in the OT.[11] This is confirmed by the use of the verb προσδέχομαι which, in Wis 14:29, appears in an eschatological context, as also in Job 2:9 LXX and Ps 54:9 LXX; cf. Luke 2:25, 36. Also, the theme of "salvation", seen in connection with Wis 5:2, could lead to the thought of the future salvation of the just (here, in the plural) and not to a simple liberation from the danger of physical death.

For the glorification of the people (v. 8: ἐδόξασας), one could think of Isa 44:23 LXX where the subject of δοξάζω is indeed the people (Ἰσραὴλ δοξασθήσεται); cf. Wis 19:22, exactly at the end of the book. The mention of "glorification" has certainly also an eschatological shade (cf. the comment).[12]

18:9 In v. 9, the mention of a sacrifice "in secret" is puzzling. M. Priotto suggests a possible reference to Exod 11:2 LXX where the Greek translator actually adds an adverb, κρυφῇ, to the divine arrangements communicated to Moses. A more probable theory is the actualised rereading of the Passover sacrifice with (polemical?) reference to the mystery cults.[13] The literary connection with 17:1-6 sheds further light on the text.[14] The Egyptians think they can remain hidden with regard to

---

9 The act of exposing the new-born was common in the period (cf. Larcher, *Sagesse*, 3:669-670, and 995-996); indirectly, our sage could be intending to criticise this practice.

10 Cf. Hübner, *Weisheit*, 213, who thinks both of the patriarchs and of the exodus generation on the basis of the fact that our sage conceives of history in a single global vision.

11 A dimension grasped by Kuhn (*Beiträge*, 336) and developed by Priotto (*La Prima Pasqua*, 59-64). For the eschatological perspective assumed by the Passover in the biblical tradition, cf. Le Déaut, *La nuit pascale*, 119-121.

12 Hübner (*Weisheit*, 212, n. 163) notes a possible relationship between Wis 18:8 (προσκαλεσάμενος ἐδόξασας) and Rom 8:30 (ἐκάλεσεν... ἐδόξασεν).

13 Cf. Priotto, *La Prima Pasqua*, 73-75, who notes that this reference to the secrecy of the Passover sacrifice is wholly absent from the Jewish tradition; cf., also, Winston, *Wisdom*, 316.

14 Cf. Mazzinghi, *Notte di paura e di luce*, 292.

the sins they have committed in secret (17:3a); the Israelites too are shut up in their houses in secret but so as to encounter a God who saves.

In 9b, it remains to clear up what exactly is indicated by this "divine covenant" which, on the night of the Passover, the Israelites agree to ratify (cf. 4 Macc 3:21; for the Hellenistic background of ὁμόνοια, cf. the comment on 10:5). Thus, what does "divine covenant mean precisely? Our sage is probably referring to the laws on the Passover contained in Exod 12:43-48, unless he is referring to rituals unknown to us. In this way, the Passover expresses the brotherhood which characterises Israel; cf. Philo, *QE* 1.3 and the whole context of the Passover supper in John 13. The liturgical aspect which characterises the life of the Israelites is thus bound up with a concrete solidarity. This too is a response which our sage offers to the accusations of "misanthropy" brought against the Jews of his time. The connection between "covenant" and "Passover" is not infrequent in the most ancient Jewish traditions and reflects concern for the community's faith. In situations threatened by the risk of apostasy, the Passover celebration becomes a sign of unity for Israel and of fidelity to the covenant.[15]

Wis 18:10-13: The Egyptians' Dirge

10 This was echoed by the discordant cry of their enemies,
and the mournful sound of those who wept for their children spread far and wide.
11 With the same punishment, the slave was punished with his master
and the people suffered the same [punishments] as the king.
12 All of them together, under the one name of "death",
were found to have corpses without number.
For the living were not sufficient to bury them
because, in an instant, there perished the flower of their race.
13 They, who had not believed in anything, because they thought of their baleful gods,
in the face of the extermination of their firstborn,
confessed that this people is God's son.

Notes on the Text and Translation

v. 10. In the LXX, the term ἀσύμφωνος, "discord", is present only in Dan, Bel 15-17 LXX. It can indicate something that is "incomprehensible" in the light of Platonic texts (*Pol.* 262d; *Leg.* 777d); cf. Scarpat, *Sapienza*, 3:287.

15 Cf. the texts cited by Priotto, *La Prima Pasqua*, 79-84, and, in particular, the Targumim on Exod 12:42-49.

v. 11. The term δίκη can be understood as the punitive "justice" of God, personified as in 1:8; 11:20; 14:31 (cf. Priotto, *La Prima Pasqua*, 99 and the fn.). It is perhaps preferable, with the VL, to understand ὁμοίᾳ δίκῃ as a complement of means and to translate δίκη with "punishment": "with the same punishment they were punished..."; κολάζω, a verb dear to Wisdom, always has God as its subject, implicitly or explicitly.

v. 12. The expression in 12a is strange. Ἐν ἑνὶ ὀνόματι θανάτου is usually understood as "a single form of death". Larcher (*Sagesse*, 3:1010) thinks of a temporal sense: "they had scarcely the time to utter the word 'death'". One could also think of the Hellenistic custom of registering someone's title of property (Bietenhard, Hans, ὄνομα, *TDNT* 5:242-248); in this sense, the expression indicates that all the Egyptians were registered under a single name, that of "death".

Synchronic Analysis

18:10: The Egyptians' Lament

The Israelites' songs of joy (9a) are echoed, suddenly, by the dirge of the Egyptians (their "enemies") for the death of their firstborn. Our sage is constructing a powerfully dramatic scene, making us shift from one sphere to the other, from the joyous celebrations of the Israelites to the terrible laments of the Egyptians. The description culminates in the statement at the end of v. 13: the Egyptians were forced to confess that Israel is God's child.

The verb *ἀντηχέω recalls what the Egyptians heard during the plague of darkness (ἦχος, 17:4, 18; ἠχώ, 17:19). The Egyptians' "cry" (βοή) is ἀσύμφωνος, "discordant" (or "incomprehensible"; see above), and contrasts with the "agreement" of the Israelites (18:9b).

18:11-12: The One Name of "Death"

Verse 11 underlines that the death of the firstborn punishes with a single penalty (cf. the textual notes) every class of Egyptian (cf. 17:16-17a); here, slaves and masters, king (namely, Pharaoh) and common people (*δημότης). Both v. 11 and v. 12 open with words that indicate totality: ὁμοίᾳ [δίκῃ] and ὁμοθυμαδόν (cf. in v. 13, ὁμολογέω).

The expression of 12a, ἐν ἑνὶ ὀνόματι θανάτου, (cf. the textual notes) could refer to the fact that all the Egyptians have been registered under the one name of "death". Θάνατος appears here as personified.[16] In Ezekiel the Tragedian it appears in exactly this context, in Ezek. Trag. 187. This death is the cause of innumerable corpses (12b).

In 12cd, the dead are contrasted with the living who are not sufficient in number to bury the dead. This expansion concerning the extent of the plague is followed now (12d) by another concerning its suddenness ("in a single instant") which destroys the "flower of their race". On διαφθείρω as a typical verb for divine punishment, cf. Wis 16:5, 19, 27, in all three cases in connection with the word of God or with God's law, the observance of which guarantees ἀφθαρσία (cf. 18:4) to the one who accepts it.

18:13: This People Is God's Son!

Verse 13a emphasises the disbelief of the Egyptians (cf., by contrast, the faith of the Israelites in 6b). The verb ἀπιστέω appears in the LXX only in Wis 1:2; 10:7; 12:17; and 18:13, in addition to 2 Macc 8:13. The reason for this disbelief is bound up with φαρμακεία, a term which generally indicates magic and which refers to

16 Cf. Dodson, *The "Powers" of Personification*, 57-68 (but he does not cite this text).

the context of the polemic against the magicians in Wis 17:7-11 in particular. The term φαρμακεία is found in the exodus context in Exod 7:11, 22; 8:13, 14 (cf. Isa 47:9, 12, with a broader meaning).

The Egyptians' disbelief is extinguished in the face of the extermination of the firstborn, here called their ὄλεθρος, a term already present in Wis 1:12, 14 in connection with θάνατος and with a clear eschatological nuance, as will happen later in the NT (cf., for example, 1 Thess 5:3; 2 Thess 1:9). The physical death of the firstborn is thus being described as an anticipation of the eternal death of the ungodly. In the light of this experience, the Egyptians recognise that the people of Israel is God's son. This recognition is expressed with the verb ὁμολογέω. However, whereas, in 9b, the Israelites agree in celebrating the divine covenant, here, the Egyptians' recognition of the people's identity is not a genuine act of faith but something forced. Our sage is probably thinking of a recognition not in words but in deeds: the Egyptians, finally, allow the people to go.

The destruction (ὄλεθρος) of the firstborn, which is recorded explicitly only in 13b, is the occasion for the recognition of the people's divine parentage. Thus, 13b constitutes a real *flashback* to Wis 5:5.[17] At the moment of the divine judgement, the ungodly will have to recognise (ὁμολογεῖν) that the just are truly God's children (cf. Wis 2:13, 18); the same happened for the Egyptians with the people of Israel.

The meaning of this *flashback* is threefold. Israel's past serves to establish its eschatological hope; recognising that the people is the child of God thus signifies having faith in the destiny of *eternal* salvation which awaits each of these children.[18] Then, the text highlights a close relationship between the Israel of the exodus, the Israel of the author's time, and the ideal just figure spoken of in Wisdom 1-6; thus, being a people of children has already been realised and, at the same time, is still to be realised. Finally, linking 5:5 to our text, we find ourselves at one of the most solemn points in the book in relation to the definition of the identity of Israel.[19]

Diachronic Analysis

This little section reveals our sage's midrashic dimension: the Egyptians' "cry" (βοή; cf. v. 10) is the one mentioned in Exod 11:6 and 12:30 (κραυγὴ μεγάλη; cf., also, Philo, *Mos.* 1.136-137). This cry is "discordant", a detail particular to our author (but cf. Jub. 49:5-6). 18:10-13

The death which touches every class of the Egyptians (v. 11; cf. Exod 11:5; 12:29) and is the cause of innumerable corpses (12b) is a hyperbole that expands the already tragic Exodus account (Exod 12:30b), following a tendency not unknown to the rabbinic tradition.[20] The reference to the living not being sufficient

17 Cf. Reese, *Hellenistic Influence*, 137. For the theme of divine parentage, cf. the comment on 2:17-18.

18 Cf. Mazzinghi, "L'idea di "popolo" nel libro della Sapienza, 31-32.

19 Cf. Alonso Schökel, *Sabiduría*, 198-199.

20 Cf. the texts mentioned by Priotto, *La Prima Pasqua*, 104-105.

to bury the dead (12cd) is also an original detail which is not found elsewhere in the Jewish traditions. Perhaps it is a midrashic expansion of Num 33:4.

As for the Egyptians' disbelief and the allusion to the magicians in v. 13a, our sage knows well from the biblical account that the magicians have already been defeated (cf. Exod 8:14; 9:11), but he returns again to the idea that the Egyptians did not believe in the divine action, thinking of some kind of sorcery, until they saw God's word in action directly, as in this case. In 12:4, we have an indication that, with φαρμακεία, our sage means not only the works of the magicians of the exodus but, especially, the whole complex of magic common in the Alexandrian world of his time. Magic is a total worldview, and not just a question of magic techniques; cf. Philo's polemic in *Migr.* 83-85; Philo compares the Egyptian magicians to "sophists" who reject the true divine *Logos*.

The text of 13b elaborates the well-known exodus motif of the "recognition formula": "thus the Egyptians will know that I am the Lord" (cf. Exod 7:5; etc.). The Egyptians, and, through them, the ungodly of every age will discover, despite themselves, that the people of Israel, object of the divine favours, is really God's child, a development of the idea already contained in Exod 4:22.

Wis 18:14-19: The Punishing Logos

14 While a deep silence enfolded all things
and night was in the middle of its course,
15 your almighty word from heaven, from your royal throne,
a warrior implacable, leapt into the midst of that land of destruction,
16 bearing as a sharp sword your irrevocable decree.
He stood and filled everything with death;
he touched heaven and walked on the earth.
17 Then, suddenly, visions of terrible dreams threw them into confusion,
unexpected fears assailed them,
18 and, thrown here and there, half dead,
they showed the reason for which they were dying;
19 for their terrifying dreams had forewarned them,
so that they might not die in ignorance of the reason for their sufferings.

Synchronic Analysis

18:14-16: While a Deep Silence…

In these verses, we find the description of the death of the firstborn attributed directly to the divine *Logos*. The literary form is elevated, but the theological content even more so. With a poetic and very dramatic touch, the scene opens to a "deep silence" which enfolds everything – the whole universe. The adjective ἥσυχος (in the LXX only in Sir 25:20) could be recalling the text of Ps 75:9–10 LXX [76:9–10 MT]; the earth is fearful and silent (ἡσύχασεν) in the face of God's judicial intervention. We note that ἡσυχία in Ezek 38:11 and 1 Macc 9:58 indicates a calm preceding the enemy attack; cf. Euripides, *Alc.* 77-78, where the verb σιγάω appears in a pair precisely with ἡσυχία. Therefore, the "deep" silence is a silence laden with tension and dramatic expectation (σιγή is a very rare term; only in 3 Macc 3:23). Verse 14b specifies the time: midnight (cf. Exod 11:4; 12:29), described with a poetic circumlocution (μεσάζω, "to stay in the middle").

The Divine Logos

At this point, v. 15 introduces a "word" which breaks this silence: ὁ παντοδύναμός σου λόγος. This is the divine word, personified, which has already appeared in 9:1 (creative word in relation to σοφία); 12:9 (destroying word); and 16:12 (healing word).[21] Here, the word is "almighty" (παντοδύναμος), an adjective already used for the spirit (7:23) and for the punishing hand of God (11:17). The God in whom our author believes can do everything; cf. δύναμαι in 7:27; 11:23; 14:4, and δύναμις in 7:25; 11:20; 12:15, 17. It is a word that comes "from heaven", like wisdom (9:10, 16) or like the manna (16:20); and so from God, from God's royal throne, again, like wisdom (9:4, 10). What stands out clearly here is the parallel of the *Logos* with wisdom and, also, its divine origin. However, wisdom and word are not identical. In fact, wisdom encompasses within itself the functions of both the divine word and the divine spirit, assuming in the context of the book a role that is undoubtedly more important.

Verse 15b, together with 16a, continues the description of the *Logos* in military language which is to be understood in the sense of Wis 5:17-23 to which 18:14-16 constitute a further, clear *flashback* by means of the repetition of rare and significant words.[22] In light of this connection, the intervention of the divine word on Passover night appears as a sign and anticipation of the final judgement of God on the ungodly. Once again, the past is the basis of the future. Thus, the "death" mentioned in 16b cannot only be considered as physical death - that of the firstborn - but becomes an image of the eschatological death that awaits the ungodly.

Egypt, an unjust land (16:19) and land of destruction (18:15b), becomes here the symbolic antithesis of the land of Israel, a land holy (12:3) and honoured by God (12:7). As in 18:3, there again emerges our sage's awareness of being in the land of Egypt, but as foreigners.

In 16bc, the action of the *Logos* acquires a cosmic character. The participle στάς, which opens 16b, has a powerful dramatic value. The divine word stands and embraces heaven and earth (16c). The very presence of the *Logos* fills "everything" with death. As in 14a, with τὰ πάντα we must understand the entire creation (cf. "heaven" and "earth" in 18:15a–b.16c). The text expands to the utmost the significance of the plague of the firstborn, almost extending it to a whole world of wickedness. If, in 9:1, the divine word was creative, here it becomes punitive, an anticipation in history of the divine judgement already spoken of in Wis 5:17-23.

18:17-19: The Psychological Action of the Logos

A new theme is introduced in vv. 17-19: the dream visions which shock the Egyptian firstborn. The term φαντασία (17a), rare in the LXX (Hab 2:18, 19; 3:10; Zech 10:1), refers precisely to dream visions, a usage well attested by Philo (cf., for example, *Ios.* 100).

---

21 Cf. S. Pié y Ninot, Salvador, *La Palabra de Dios en los libros sapienciales* (Facultat de Teologia de Barcelona: Barcelona 1972), 193-228.

22 Cf. πολεμιστής (18:15b) and συνεκπολεμέω (5:20b); ἀπότομος (18:15b) and ἀποτόμως (5:22); ἅλλομαι in 18:15b and 5:21; ὀξύς (18:16a) and ὀξυνεῖ (5:20); ἀνυπόκριτος* as a description of the divine judgement or of its "irrevocable" decree in 18:16a and 5:18.

The Egyptians' Nightmares

Here, our sage uses the term ὄνειρος, more of Greek origin compared with the term more common in the LXX to indicate a dream: ἐνύπνιον. These dreams which suddenly disturb (ἐκταράσσω; cf. Wis 17:3) the firstborn are called "terrible". Δεινός recalls explicitly the fear of the ungodly in 5:2, on the occasion of the last judgement, but also the Egyptians' fear on the night described in Wis 17:3. Taking up the vocabulary of 17:15, v. 17 refers to the definition of fear already commented on in connection with Wis 17:12-13. There is a resultant emphasis on the psychological, theological and eschatological value of the Egyptians' fear.

Verse 18 pictures the Egyptian firstborn thrown down on their beds, "half dead" (*ἡμίθνητος). The action of the *Logos* seems to take place in two stages: first the fear, then the death. A similar tradition is found in the Pesiq. Rab. Kah. 7.5. In the light of 18b, the firstborn seem to have had time to acknowledge the reason for their death. In fact, v. 19 explains that it was precisely their premonitory dreams that served to manifest the reason for their sufferings (for πάσχω, cf. 12:27; 18:1, 11; 19:13). This also solves a theological problem: God cannot condemn the innocent (cf. Wis 12:15); so it was necessary for the Egyptian firstborn to admit their own responsibility.

Verses 17-19 witness again to our author's great interest in the psychological dimension. The vocabulary is very close to that of Wisdom 17 (cf. 17:1-6, but, in particular, 17:15[23]), but also recalls the *post mortem* fear of the ungodly described in Wisdom 5. The terrible visions and dreams of the Egyptians recorded here have no match in the Exodus narrative. Here, the visions and dreams are intended to make the Egyptians aware of the cause of their death. Already in life, therefore, it is possible to experience the severity of God's judgement which awaits the ungodly at the time of their death. In this sense, therefore, fear becomes an urging to conversion.

Diachronic Analysis

18:14-16 In 18:15, the book of Wisdom brings to its height an interesting theology of the word of God. What is the meaning of the personification of the *Logos* in these texts? As is clear from Wis 18:22, 25, our sage is well aware of the figure of the "destroyer" (cf. Exod 12:23) but avoids using it here, preferring to underline the direct role of the divine "word". The "word of God" is a well-known biblical figure which our author employs to illustrate the twofold nature and efficacy of the divine action, both salvific and punitive. The warrior image for the *Logos* could have been suggested by texts such as Exod 15:3; Josh 5:13-14; Habakkuk 3. For the image of the sharp sword, cf. Isa 49:2; Eph 6:17; Heb 4:12; Rev 1:16; etc. The emergence of the importance of the divine word is another sign of the great closeness of our text to the Jewish traditions of the period which we find reflected later, above all, in the targumic literature. In fact, the Targumim on the Exodus tend to replace the direct action of the Lord with the mediated action of God's word, and to attribute to the latter both the death of the firstborn and the salvation of Israel. The use of παντοδύναμος (cf. above) distinguishes the presentation

---

23 For the connection between 18:14-19 and 17:12-15, cf. Mazzinghi, *Notte di paura e di luce*, 293.

of the *Logos* in Wisdom from that in Philo. In fact, Philo distinguishes the *Logos* from the "powers" (cf. *Leg.* 2.86; *Somn.* 1.62).[24]

The image in 16b could have been inspired by *Il.* 4.443 (Discord whose face touches heaven while his feet rest on the earth; cf. *Il.* 1.44-47; Virgil, *Aen.* 4.177, about Pheme, Rumour: *ingrediturque solo et caput inter nubila condit*); but one could also think of the angel of 1 Chr 21:15, without the *Logos* described here assuming angelic features (see above).

In Hellenistic Judaism, nocturnal visions are often considered the result of human wickedness; cf. Sir 40:5-7 in relation to the dreams of the ungodly.[25] In Wis 18:17-19, the dream provides the ungodly with a kind of anticipated knowledge of reality; cf. the use of the verb προμηνύω* in 19a which returns in Philo; cf., especially, *Ios.* 107, where the verb indicates precisely the anticipated knowledge obtained in dreams (cf. Sophocles, *Ant.* 84). 18:17-19

Wis 18:20-25: The Trial of the Israelites and the Intercession of Aaron

20 Certainly, the trial of death struck the just also,
and in the desert there was a slaughter of a multitude,
but the wrath did not last for long;
21 for a blameless man rushed to the fight,
bearing the arms of his ministry,
the prayer and incense of expiation:
he opposed the wrath and put an end to the disaster,
showing himself your servant.
22 He conquered that host, not with physical power,
nor by force of arms,
but with the word he placated the one who was punishing,
calling to mind the oaths and covenants of the fathers.
23 When the bodies had already fallen in heaps, one on top of the other,
he, standing in the midst, caused the wrath to cease
and cut off the way that led to the living.
24 On his priestly robe was the entire universe

24 For further analysis, cf. the extensive reflection of Larcher, *Sagesse*, 3:1018-1022, and cf. Priotto, *La prima Pasqua*, 137-159, for a detailed analysis of the targumic texts. Scarpat, *Sapienza*, 3:264-272, claims that Wisdom knows Philo and is polemicising against his theory of the *Logos*. The Catholic liturgy applies these verses to the incarnation of Christ. In fact, the text of Rev 19:11-16 shows fairly clearly a dependence on these verses even if the context is that of judgement on the wicked rather than salvation. Cf. the *relecture* by Ignatius of Antioch in Ign. *Eph.* 19:1; Cabannis, Allen, "Wisdom 18:14f: An Early Christmas Text", *VC* 10 (1956), 97-102.

25 On the subject of dreams, cf. Mazzinghi, *Notte di paura e di luce*, 58-59, 144-146 and Priotto, *La Prima Pasqua*, 160-162.

and, engraved on the stones, arranged in four rows, the glories of the fathers,
and on the diadem of his head your majesty.
25 Before that, the destroyer yielded, of this he was fearful,
because this sole proof of his anger was sufficient.

Notes on the Text and Translation

v. 22. In 22a, almost all the mss, except for two minuscules (248, 157: ὀλοθρεύοντα; cf. 25a) read τὸν ὄχλον, "the host" (cf. Wis 6:2; 8:10); Ziegler accepts Bauermeister's conjecture of τὸν χόλον, "the wrath". This conjecture has its reasons (cf. ἀντέστη τῷ θυμῷ; 21d; ἀνέκοψεν τὴν ὀργήν; 23b; an easy confusion οχλ-χολ) but has no textual support. On the basis of a passage from Ezekiel, the Tragedian (Ezek. Trag. 210-214), Reese (*Hellenistic Influence*, 2; cf. Priotto, *La Prima Pasqua*, 175-178) interprets the well-supported τὸν ὄχλον in the sense of "confusion", "disorder". With more solid arguments, Scarpat (*Sapienza*, 3:294-296) understands ὄχλος in the sense of "army/host" (cf. Xenophon, *Cyr.* 5.5.4; cf. 1 Macc 1:17, 20, 29; 9:35; 2 Macc 14:23).

v. 23. In 23b, Ziegler proposes correcting the well-attested τὴν ὀργήν, "the wrath", and conjectures τὴν ὁρμὴν, "the attack" (cf. VL: *impetum*). This is unnecessary. In fact, ὀργή has an excellent parallel in θυμός in v. 21d; *impetum* could have arisen from a confusion between τὴν ὀργήν and τὴν ὁρμήν (cf. Num 11:11; etc.; Priotto, *La Prima Pasqua*, 178).

v. 24. The expression ἔνδυμα ποδῆρες is not found in the LXX. In Exod 28:4, ὁ ποδήρης translates the Hebrew מעיל, a term which indicates the priestly garment that reached to the feet (Exod 28:31-35; 39:22-26); cf. Aaron's ἔνδυμα cited in Ps 132:2 LXX [133:2 MT] and Josephus' description in *A.J.* 3.159-161. A similar expression returns in Philo, *Fug.* 185; cf. *Spec.* 1.85; cf., again, Josephus, *B.J.* 5.231–232.

In 24b, Ziegler chooses the reading λίθων, attested by A, C, V, Lat and some minuscules; B, S, 157, Aeth read, instead, the singular λίθου. In Exod 25:7; 28:21; and 35:9, the plural always appears, and this seems preferable. The expression ἐπὶ τετραστίχου λίθων γλυφῆς indicates "a fourfold engraving of stones"; cf. Exod 28:17; 36:17. For γλυφή, cf. Exod 25:7.

In 18:24c, διάδημα (cf. Wis 5:16) indicates the headgear of the high priest (μίτρα; in Hebrew מצנפת) which, according to Exod 28:36-38 had, at the front, a sheet of pure gold in floral form (πέταλον χρυσοῦν καθαρόν; in Hebrew, ציץ זהב טהור); this had the divine name (the Tetragrammaton) stamped on it. This name is alluded to by the expression μεγαλωσύνη σου (cf. Philo, *Fug.* 111; διάδημα, instead of μίτρα, emphasises Aaron's royal aspect).

v. 25. Various important manuscripts (B S* C and many minuscules) read ἐφοβήθησαν, "they were fearful", referring to the Israelites. This is a theological correction by scribes who, seeing in the destroyer an angelic figure, did not accept the reading that "he was fearful" (ἐφοβήθη).

Synchronic Analysis

18:20: The Plague in the Desert

In 20a, once again, the Israelites are called "just", as in v. 7. The expression πεῖρα θανάτου could be understood in a weak sense as "experience of death" or in a strong sense as "trial of death" (cf. πειράζω in 3:5 and 11:9). Here, the stress falls on θάνατος; the "death" experienced by the Israelites in the desert becomes a "trial/test", like that of the serpents (Wis 16:5-15), which, Israel, however, by contrast with the Egyptians, is able to overcome. This interpretation is confirmed by the use of θραῦσις, "damage", here, in the sense of "slaughter". The word is taken from the text of Num 17:6-15 LXX (vv. 12, 13, 14, 15), where it acquires a religious tone, as punishment sent by God (cf. 2 Sam 24:21, 25; Ps 105:23, 30 LXX). The reference to the "desert" and the slaughter of the "multitude" makes it clear that our sage is alluding to precisely this episode.

In Num 17:11, alongside the verb θραύω, our sage also finds the term ὀργή. However, as in Wis 16:5c, he is immediately concerned to emphasise the transitory character of the divine wrath and, thus, precisely in the light of 16:5c (see the comment), causes its educative and pedagogic value to emerge indirectly.

18:21: The Presentation of Aaron

According to the practice of our author, v. 21 introduces Aaron without naming him. He is a "blameless man" (ἀνὴρ ἄμεμπτος), like Job (cf. Job 1:8; 2:3); Abraham, especially (Gen 17:1) in the light of Wis 10:5; cf. Esther (Esth E,13 = 8:12n); all figures who took on the role of intercessors. It is not clear in what his "blamelessness" is supposed to consist. One might think, a little generically, of his faithfulness to God. In any case, Aaron emerges with a wholly positive valuation compared with the biblical tradition but well established in the Jewish sources (see below).[26] If Israel sins, there can always be found among the people an ἀνὴρ ἄμεμπτος able to intercede for them.

The portrait of Aaron is completed in 21e with the term θεράπων. His attitude shows Aaron to be truly "your servant" (see below).

Aaron "rushes" to fight with weapons typical of his priesthood. Σπεύδω recalls the role of the just in 4:14 with the same verb. For the motif of Aaron's "haste", cf. Num 17:11, 12 (καὶ ἔδραμεν). The weapons used by Aaron are those belonging to his ministry. With λειτουργία in 21b, we have a word which, in the LXX, begins to be used in a cultic sense (1 Chr 9:13; 23:24); cf., in particular, Sir 4:14 (those who serve wisdom render worship to God) and 24:10, the latter being especially important on account of the liturgical role Ben Sirach attributes to wisdom throughout the poem of Sirach 24. In Sir 45:15, it is Aaron who is the subject of the verb λειτουργέω. The priestly "ministry" of Aaron is explained here not as sacrifices but as prayer (προσευχή), a term typical of the LXX (cf. the Hebrew תפלה) which here, however, does not indicate, as almost always in Philo, the place of prayer but prayer in itself.[27]

In addition to the prayer, v. 21c mentions the θυμιάματος ἐξιλασμόν, an expression absent from the LXX but constructed on the basis of Num 17:11, 12. The incense burned by Aaron in the thurible is aimed at removing the plague of death from Israel. This is the sense of ἱλάσκομαι – ἐξιλάσκομαι. These words, in texts such as Exod 32:14; Num 25:13; and Sir 45:23 indicate "propitiating/placating", that is, the act of averting God's wrath, while, in Ezek 43:20, 22, 26; Lev 23:27, 28; etc., they indicate expiating, that is, performing a specific rite to restore a good relationship with God. This is the sense of the Hebrew root כפר which the LXX

---

26 Cf., particularly, the *Targumim* and Josephus; the texts in Priotto, *La Prima Pasqua*, 188-189.

27 Cf. Greeven, Heinrich, προσευχή, TDNT II, 807-808 and Hengel, Martin, "Proseuche und Synagoge", in: Gert, Jeremias (ed), Tradition und Glaube, das frühe Christentum in seiner Umwelt, FS K.G. Kuhn (Vandenhoeck & Ruprecht: Göttingen 1971), 157-184.

mostly translates precisely with ἐξιλάσκομαι.[28] In our text, the offering of the incense has probably both values: propitiation and expiation together.

Verse 21de interprets Aaron's actions as a real battle, anticipated by ὅπλον in 21b and, above all, by *προμαχέω in 21a; cf. 2 Esdr 15:7 [Neh 5:7]; 23:11, 17, 25 [Neh 13:11, 17, 25], always in a translated sense, as in our case where the meaning is that of "fighting on behalf of someone". In reality, Aaron is an instrument in God's hands, just as the cosmos is ὑπέρμαχος of God in Wis 16:17. Just as Moses resisted Pharaoh (10:16), so Aaron resists (ἀντέστη) the divine wrath, thanks to the "word" (v. 22c), and so puts an end to the "disaster" (συμφορά; 21d; cf. 2 Macc 6:12, 16).

18:22: A Spiritual Battle

At the centre of the development of vv. 20-25, v. 22 elaborates the idea of a battle that is spiritual, without weapons. In this connection, it is notable that Wisdom makes no explicit mention of another priestly figure, that of Phineas; cf. Num 25 (see, however, below for 18:23). Verse 22 opens with the verb νικάω which recalls again the context of Wis 16:5-15; cf. Wis 16:10 (the venomous serpents did not overcome...). The text of 22ab notes that Aaron's victory was obtained not by force of arms but owing to the λόγος who headed off the "destroyer" (τὸν κολάζοντα).

Taken on its own, it seems that, by λόγῳ, the text intends only Aaron's prayer mentioned above. However, the emphasis placed on the word in Wis 16:11-12 and 18:14-16 and the connection which we have highlighted precisely with 16:5-15 invite us to see in this "word" the same divine word which, from punisher (18:14-16), becomes saviour again, as in 16:11-12. We observe that Wisdom does not go as far as Philo's allegorical reading where Aaron becomes a symbol of the *Logos* (*Leg.* 1.76).

The final stich of v. 22 adds the memory of the oaths and covenants of the ancestors to Aaron's actions. Rare in the LXX (3 Kgdms 4:3; 4 Macc 8:14; cf. Wis 12:2), the verb ὑπομιμνήσκω is used in the same sense as ὑπόμνησις in 16:11 (cf. the comment) but here has God as the object of memory. Bound up with the prayer and liturgical action performed by Aaron, the verb indicates that worship is precisely the "memory of/calling to mind" the salvific acts of God. With "oaths and covenants of the fathers", Wisdom is referring to the covenants with Abraham, Isaac, and Jacob (cf. Gen 15:18; Gen 26:3-4; Exod 2:24; 6:4; Lev 26:42; Deut 4:31). For the only time in the book, the term διαθήκη is employed. In the LXX, it usually translates ברית, but in the plural it is found only in Sir 44:18.

18:23: Aaron's Victorious Action

This verse takes up v. 18:21de relating to the action of Aaron. Verse 23a alludes to Num 17:14 which speaks of a good 14,700 victims of the plague in the desert. Following Num 17:13, Wisdom describes here the action of Aaron who puts a stop to the plague (cf. 21de). The participle στάς in 23b associates Aaron's action with that of the *Logos* (cf. 16b).

18:24: Aaron's Clothing

Among the more powerful "weapons" available to Aaron, v. 24 lists some of his priestly vestments (cf. Sir 45:6-12). The symbolism of his clothing completes the description of Aaron's liturgical ministry in 21abc.

---

28 Cf. Hermann, Josef – Büchsel, Friedrich, ἱλάσκομαι, ἱλασμός, *TDNT* 3:301-323.

First mentioned is the priestly robe which represents the whole universe (ὅλος ὁ κόσμος).[29] It is as if the ministry of Aaron represents an aspect of that battle which the cosmos engages on behalf of the just (cf. 5:17-20; 16:17).

Next to be mentioned are the twelve stones engraved on the breastplate (cf Exod 28:17-21; 39:10-14) which represent "the glories of the fathers". Wis 10:14 already mentioned δόξα in connection with Joseph, the same divine δόξα shared by Solomon (8:10) from which Wisdom comes (7:25). The "glories" of the fathers (πατέρων δόξαι) engraved on Aaron's breastplate recall that he is in a close relationship with them and also recall those salvific acts of which the fathers were the object and so for that reason also in God's glory.

The description of Aaron's clothing is completed by the mention of the diadem. On it stands the symbol of "greatness" of the divine majesty (cf. LXX-Pss 78:11; 144:3, 6 [MT-Pss 79:11; 145:3, 6]; etc.; in the NT, Heb 1:3; 8:1; Jude 25; cf. T. Levi 3:9, where, as in our case, μεγαλωσύνη is a synonym of God himself). A well-attested tradition (Let. Aris. 98; cf. also 99 which mentions the extraordinary and terrible results of the vision of the high priest in his solemn vestments; Philo, *Mos.* 2.114-132; Josephus, *A.J.* 3.178) leads us to think that the inscription on the gold sheet (cf. textual note) was the Tetragrammaton itself. On this basis, Aaron represents not only the cosmos and the ancestors of Israel but God himself. He is really "holy to the Lord"; cf. Exod 28:36 and 39:30 which mention that it was this phrase which was inscribed on the gold sheet. The expiatory power of Aaron's action arises not from any magical rite but from that profound communion with God which makes his ministry authentic and the "word" of which he is the bearer efficacious (22c).[30]

18:25: The End of the Plague

Verse 25, which corresponds to v. 20 (cf. the literary structure) is also the close of the entire diptych. Verse 25a mentions the flight of the "destroyer" (Exod 12:23; cf. Wis 18:22c; cf. the mention of the "destroyer" in 1 Cor 10:10). Everything that Aaron represents (cf. the previous verse) is the cause of his fear. Thus, with φοβέομαι, there is a return to the theme of fear which ran through the previous diptych and reappeared in 18:16-19. Here, however, it is the "destroyer" who fears and is put to flight.

In 25b, returning in inclusion to v. 20 and precisely at the conclusion of the diptych, our sage underlines the limitation of the trial to which the Israelites were subjected (cf. 18:20c). If v. 12 said that the living were not sufficient (ἱκανοί) to bury the dead, for the Israelites, this one proof of the divine wrath was sufficient (ἱκανή). This marks a return to the idea of divine moderation which was the subject of the first digression (Wis 11:15-12:27).

Diachronic Analysis

These final verses intend to reply to an objection: how was it that Israel was also struck by death in the desert? The text of which our author is thinking is certainly that of Num 17:6-15, when, according to the biblical account, thousands of Israelite rebels

29 According to Winston (*Wisdom*, 321), there is an allusion to the idea, of Stoic provenance, that the whole of the cosmos is God's temple; cf. Philo, *Spec.* 1.66-97.

30 Cf. Priotto, *La Prima Pasqua*, 220-221.

died following the rebellion of Korah, Dathan, and Abiram against God and against Moses. As usual, Wisdom avoids speaking explicitly of Israel's sin. In fact, according to our author, what was going on here was a limited proof of God's anger (cf. v. 20c) from which Israel was freed through Aaron's intercession. What punished the Egyptians (vv. 14-19) now becomes (cf. 22c) an instrument of salvation for Israel.

18:21: Aaron In the texts of Exodus and Numbers, Aaron is not always presented in a very favourable light and not infrequently his faults are underlined (cf. Numbers 12). In Hellenistic Judaism, on the other hand, the increased importance of the priesthood led to a re-evaluation of his figure that is evident already in the *elogium* of Sir 45:6-22 which is four times longer than that devoted to Moses (Sir 45:1-5). Rooted in these more recent traditions, Wisdom presents Aaron here not only as a model of authentic worship able to obtain from God the lifting of his wrath but almost as a messianic figure, as Aaron would indeed become in some spheres of the Judaism of the period (cf. the expectation of a "Messiah [from/of?] Aaron", witnessed to in some Qumran texts: 1QS IX, 11; CD XII, 23 – XIII, 1).

As for calling Aaron "servant", we observe that, in the LXX, θεράπων is an appellative of Moses (Exod 4:10; Num 11:11; 12:7-8), of Joshua (Exod 33:11) and of Job (1:8^{A}; 2:3; 42:7, 8); never, however, of Aaron who, in our book, thus receives the same appellation as that used for Moses in Wis 10:16 (cf. also the use of the same verb ἀνθίσταμαι in 10:15-16 and 18:21) and for the patriarchs (Wis 10:9). However, although Moses is clearly present in Num 17:6-15, here he disappears from the scene.[31]
We note, in fact, that Numbers 17 does not mention Aaron's prayer which thus acquires here a very special value, following a tendency in the targumic tradition to read Aaron's action as an intercession proper. The Tg. Neof. on Num 17:13 mentions Aaron who "implores mercy", while the version of Tg. Ps.-J. speaks of an Aaron who "stood upright in prayer in their midst". It is clear that to attribute prayer to Aaron even before the use of the incense is particularly significant in a context where the Temple and its rituals are inaccessible.[32]

18:22 In v. 22, the participle τὸν κολάζοντα certainly refers to the "destroyer" of Exod 12:23 (ὁ ὀλεθρεύων) whom the tradition sometimes interprets as an "angel" (cf. 4 Macc 7:11 precisely in relation to Numbers 17). In connection with Numbers 17, the targumic tradition speaks of the destroyer (Tg. Neof. on Num 17:11, 12 in particular). Larcher thinks, rather, of an allusion to Satan, here linked (cf. 2:24) to the power of death.[33] The verb κολάζω is typical of our author, often in connection with εὐεργετέω (cf. the comment on 11:5; 16:11).

18:23 The vocabulary employed here in connection with Aaron's action recalls the action of Phineas which is described in Ps 105:30 LXX [106:30 MT]: καὶ ἔστη Φινεες καὶ ἐξιλάσατο καὶ ἐκόπασεν ἡ θραῦσις; cf. ἐξιλασμόν in 18:21c; θραῦσις in 18:20b. As v. 23c states poetically, Aaron cut off the "destroyer's" way to the living but without having recourse to the violence of Phineas.[34]

---

31 Larcher, *Sagesse*, 3:1031-1032, rightly excludes here a direct polemic against the claims of the Hasmoneans to the high priesthood.

32 Cf. the further texts mentioned in Priotto, *La Prima Pasqua*, 195-199.

33 Larcher, *Sagesse*, 3:1033-1034.

34 "*Aaron kämpft mit dem Gott der Versöhnung gegen den Gott der Todesstrafe und besiegt mit dem einen den anderen.* Noch anders gesagt: *Aarons Sieg ist der Sieg Gottes über Gott*"; Hübner, *Weisheit*, 218.

Compared with Wisdom, Philo elaborates much further the allegorical dimension 18:24
of Aaron's priestly garb (cf. the whole passage of *Mos.* 2.117-135). This is a typical tendency of Greek-speaking Judaism of which Wisdom seems to be the most ancient witness. If, for Philo, the stones of the breastplate are an allegory of the zodiac (*Mos.* 2.124-126), here, they become "the glories of the fathers" (see above).[35]

Summary of Wis 18:5-25

What is most striking in the sixth diptych is the emphasis on the terrible fate which falls on the Egyptians, namely, the death of the firstborn. Such harshness could antagonise the modern reader. However, it must always be remembered that Wisdom has not yet resolved the dichotomy between the mercy and wrath of God. Nor must we forget that the diptych is rereading the Exodus narrative which is certainly not gentle with Egypt. Moreover, particularly in the light of the references to Wis 11:15-12:27, the punishment that falls on the wicked is to be seen as a clear invitation to conversion. Finally, we must bear in mind that the whole text of Wis 18:5-25 has to be reread in the light of an eschatological perspective which the commentary has highlighted on several occasions. What happened to Egypt on the night of the Passover is a sign and anticipation of what will happen to the ungodly in the future judgement (cf., in this regard, the links with the first part of the book and, in particular, with Wis 5:17-20). The death of the Egyptians is thus the fruit of an obstinate refusal by the ungodly for which there is no longer any remedy. In this judgement, we should not undervalue the role of the cosmos which, in Wisdom 11-19, is presented once more as God's ally in punishing and favouring.

In this diptych, there emerge two particular ways in which the Lord carries out his salvation for God's people. First of all, there is the intervention of God's word (cf. vv. 14-16), and then, a theme never mentioned elsewhere in the book, the power of Aaron's priestly intercession (vv. 20-25). Thus, the significance of the theme of worship, which is little developed per se in the book of Wisdom, is heightened.

The salvific intervention of God is placed against the background of the exodus Passover which thus acquires for the Jewish community of Alexandria a strong dose of relevance and, at the same time, in this diptych, becomes almost a prophecy of future salvation. In fact, it was just at the time of our author that a real spirituality of the exodus was becoming widespread with the Passover celebration as its clear lynchpin. In this period, the Passover becomes a fundamental key with which Israel can interpret the whole history of the world and of the people themselves.[36]

---

35 "The *doxai* seem to have not only an ornamental value, but a "sacramental" one, as well: They cause and manifest the soteriological God's might"; Raurell, "The religious meaning", 382.

36 Cf. the fundamental work of Le Déaut, *La nuit pascale* (already quoted).

In the light of this diptych, for Israel, choosing to celebrate the Passover means believing in the effectiveness of the word of God and of prayer, in the presence of God and God's intervention in history, in the past as in the present and also in the future. Significantly, compared with the previous diptych, Wis 18:5-25 presents fewer contacts with the Hellenistic world and many more with the tradition of Israel. One of the responses which Israel is called to make in a cultural context which often presses it to forget if not exactly to betray its own faith is, in fact, to be found precisely in its own most authentic tradition: its liturgy, its prayer, and its Passover.

Wis 19: The Seventh Diptych and the Creation Renewed

The Literary Structure of Wis 19

Great confusion reigns over the internal structure of chapter 19 and its role at the conclusion of the entire book.[1] The main differences are concentrated on the literary structure of the first twelve verses for which there are no precise indications.[2] The majority of commentators agree in considering vv. 13-17 and vv. 18-21 as two small literary units. The problem is how to connect them with the rest of the chapter.

A first literary unit can be identified in 19:1-5, a pericope which proceeds from "anger" (θυμός, v. 1a) to "death" (θάνατος, v. 5b), and which has the Egyptians as its subject. From a temporal point of view, the sequence μέχρι τέλους (v. 1a) ... ἐπὶ τοῦτο τὸ πέρας (v. 4a) can be noted. In v. 5, we have the final contrast between the Israelites (ὁ μὲν λαός σου) and the Egyptians (ἐκεῖνοι δὲ). We could place the conclusion of the seventh diptych here.

Verse 6, which has the function of a title, sees the opening of a long pericope which constitutes the conclusion of the book as a whole, as far as v. 21; cf. the probable inclusion between γένει πάλιν (v. 6a) and ἀνάπαλιν... γένος (v. 21a.c). The term γένος appears in Wisdom only in 19:6a, 21c (cf. γένεσις in 10b, 11a). The whole text of Wis 19:6-21 is thus held together by the theme of the cosmos which runs through the entire passage.

Verses 6-12 make up a unitary pericope – note, in particular, the inclusion on θαλάσσης (vv. 7c and 12). This pericope is introduced by v. 6 which the initial γάρ connects with 19:1-5 and which introduces the theme of the renewed creation, thus forming a kind of title. The pericope revolves around v. 9, a verse which also has a capital importance in the overall structure of the third part of the book (see

---

1 Cf. Offerhaus, *Komposition und Intention*, 171-192; especially p. 335 n. 261; Bizzeti, *Sapienza*, 97-100; Gilbert, "Sagesse", 76-77; Priotto, "Il confronto Egitto-Sodoma", 370 n. 3; cf., also J. Marböck, "'Denn in allem, Herr, hast du dein Volk großgemacht': Weish 18,5–19,22 und die Botschaft der Sapientia Salomonis": G. Hentschel / E. Zenger (hrsg.), *Lehrerin der Gerechtigkeit*, (ETS 19), Leipzig: Benno 1991, 156-177; Engel, Weisheit, 291-312. Cheon (*The Exodus Story*, 89-93) has suggested considering 19:1-17 as a self-standing literary unit. However, we have to ask if it is legitimate to place vv. 18-21 on their own (see below).

2 Cf. a summary of the opinions of various authors in Vílchez Líndez, *Sapienza*, 526 n. 2.

also below).[3] The subject of this pericope is twofold: the holy people and the renewed creation. The praise of v. 9 binds together the theme of the crossing of the sea (vv. 7-8) with the recalling of the episode of the quails (vv. 10-12) and so constitutes the centre of this first section of the epilogue. At the same time, 19:9 recalls the beginning of the exodus antitheses in inclusio with 10:20.

Verses 10-12, therefore, represent a new section and already anticipate the conclusion of the book as a whole (vv. 18-21), but they cannot be separated from v. 6, of which they constitute a clear development, or from v. 9, since they have the same subject and serve to illustrate the reasons for the praise mentioned precisely in v. 9. Thus, vv. 7-8 form a first subsection of six stichs (cf. the inclusion ἐθεωρέθη – θεωρήσαντες), while vv. 10-12 form a second subsection, also of six stichs (note the term γένεσις in 10b and 11a), with precisely v. 9 at its centre.

The sections 19:13-17 and 19:18-21 are only superficially separated from the context: the historic judgement on the ungodly (19:1-5) is matched by the eschatological judgement, symbolised by the episode of the Egyptians and the Sodomites (19:13-17).[4] The historical salvation of the Hebrews, a salvation in which the creation plays an essential role (19:6-12), is matched by the eschatological salvation which consists of the renewed creation (19:18-21).

In its turn, the section of Wis 19:13-17 can be subdivided as follows, in particular, on the basis of the alternation of the subjects:

v. 13: punishment of the Egyptians
    v. 14: the Hebrews and the Egyptians
v. 15: (eschatological) punishment of the Egyptians
    v. 16: the Egyptians against the Hebrews
v. 17: punishment of the Egyptians and the Sodomites

Chapter 19 thus acquires its own internal coherence which can be highlighted by the following scheme:

vv. 1-5: seventh diptych.
vv. 6-21: epilogue of the whole book: the theme of the cosmos.
    vv. 6-12: the people and the renewed creation
        v. 6: introductory title: creation
        vv. 7-8: the crossing of the sea
        v. 9: hymn of praise (centre of vv. 6-12; inclusio with 10:20)
        vv. 10-12: development of the theme of creation

---

3 M. Gilbert has emphasised several times the importance of v. 9, considering it, however, as the conclusion of the diptych which he identifies in Wis 19:1-9. Nevertheless, it is true that Wis 19:9 forms an important inclusio with 10:20, thus setting the entire third part of the book under the theme of praise. In both cases – and only here in Wisdom – the verb αἰνέω occurs; in both cases, moreover, we find the vocative "o Lord" (κύριε). According to Gilbert, the entire section of 19:10-22 is separate from the rest of the chapter and forms the conclusion proper to the whole book, employing the literary form of the series or the list in a similar way to Wis 10:1-21, the introduction to the reconstruction of the events of the exodus (Wis 11:1-19:9) to which 19:10-22 would represent the conclusion. Cf. Gilbert, "Sagesse", 72-73, and "The Literary Structure" (= *Le livre de la Sagesse*), 20-25.

4 Cf. Priotto, "Il confronto Egitto-Sodoma", 371-377.

vv. 13-17: the Egyptians compared with the Sodomites (theme of punishment; cf. 19:1-5)
vv. 18-21: the renewed creation (cf. 19:6-12)
v. 22: conclusion of the whole book.

Concentric structure of chapters 16-19

In our examination of the literary structure of chapter 19, the close connection between this chapter and chapter 16 has emerged.[5] In particular, the following points of contact have appeared:

a. Wisdom 16 lays great importance on the theme of the "people": the mention of "your people" occurs twice, in vv. 2 and 20, two texts which reveal an identical construction. The same theme appears in 19:5 and in the conclusion of v. 22.

v. 2:	ἀνθ' ἧς κολάσεως	εὐεργέτησας	τὸν λαόν σου
v. 20:	ἀνθ' ὧν ἀγγέλων τροφὴν	ἐψώμισας	τὸν λαόν σου

b. The term κτίσις appears only four times in the book: Wis 2:6; 5:7; 16:24; 19:6: in the two latter cases in connection with the participle ὑπηρετοῦσα, so as to emphasise the theme of the creation obedient to the divine will; ὑπηρετέω appears in Wisdom only in these two texts.

c. A further correspondence is the underlining of the extraordinary aspect of the divine actions by means of the term παράδοξος which appears only in 5:7; 16:17; and 19:5.

d. Some key terms of chap. 16 appear again, in similar contexts, at the beginning of chap. 19:

- κολάζω (16:1) and κόλασις (19:4)
- ἀξίως (16:1) and ἄξιος (19:4)
- βασανίζω (16:1) and βάσανος (19:4)
- ἐπιθυμία (16:2 and 19:11; only here in Wisdom in the sense of "appetite").

e. A rare term, κρύσταλλος, appears in 16:22 and is taken up again by κρυσταλλοειδές with reference to the manna in 19:21.

f. The theme of God's wrath (ὀργή) which does not last "to the end" (μέχρι τέλους) links 16:5 and 19:1.

g. Finally, it is necessary to observe the close relationship between 16:22, 23 and 19:20 where the theme of the renewed creation emerges. Note the coincidence of the vocabulary: πῦρ, τῆς ἰδίας δυνάμεως, ἐπιλανθάνω.

Thus, at the level of literary structure and vocabulary, chap. 19 is taking up chap. 16; therefore, at the centre of the development of Wisdom 16-19, chapters 17-18 stand out, and they too are constructed in a concentric fashion.[6]

The first section of the fifth diptych, Wis 17:1-6, corresponds to 18:5-9 (ἐκείνη ἡ νύξ: 17:5c; 18:6); the night that fell on the Egyptians is balanced by Passover night; ruin for the ones, salvation for the others.

The second section of the fifth diptych, Wis 17:7-11, corresponds directly to Wis 18:10-13; in both cases, the theme of the magicians appears, but, in 18:10-13, the Egyptians are obliged to recognise that the people is the "son of God".

The third section, Wis 17:12-15, corresponds to Wis 18:14-19; the two sections are linked by the reference to dreams and fear. The mention of the *Logos* in Wis 18:14-16

---

5 Cf. Bizzeti, *Sapienza,* 100-104.

6 Cf. Mazzinghi, *Notte di paura e di luce*, 219-298.

allows us to understand that the fear described in Wis 17:12-13 is also the failure to accept the divine word which leads to a judgement that is not only historical but also eschatological.

Finally, the fourth section, Wis 17:16-21, corresponds to Wis 18:20-25 (ὅλος ὁ κόσμος; 17:20 and 18:24, the unique occurrences in the whole book). The whole creation is in alliance in terrifying the ungodly (17:16-21); the whole creation, symbolised by Aaron's vestments, is in alliance in saving the just (18:20-25).

Thus, the centre of chapters 17-18 is marked by Wis 18:1-4 where, with the metaphor of light, the theme of the "incorruptible law" is introduced, linked, as has been seen, to wisdom and the divine word, within a broad reflection on the role of Israel and on the destiny of eternal life which awaits those who do not close themselves off from the divine revelation in history.

In the final four chapters, therefore, everything revolves around the central passage of 18:1-4. Introducing the themes of food (16:1-4), of salvation from death (16:5-14) and of manna (16:15-29), chap. 16, prepares in particular for the conclusion of chap. 19 (vv. 18-21) where all these themes reprised within the frame of a renewed creation which offers people a "food of immortality" (Wis 19:21). Once again, in Wisdom, historical perspective and eschatological dimension are closely connected; and the point of contact is represented by the theology of creation. The emphasis on the role of the cosmos allows an openness to the future and a not forgetting of the past, and the discerning the roots of the history of salvation precisely in the creation.

Chapter 19 constitutes the true conclusion of the entire book. Already the "to the end" which opens v. 1 suggests that we are approaching a conclusion. The chapter then takes up, several times, expressions and themes already met with in the course of the book (cf. the comment): the praise begun in Wis 10:20 finds its correspondence in 19:9; in both cases – and only here in Wisdom – the verb αἰνέω (cf. above) occurs, thus justifying the idea that Wisdom 11-19 constitutes a real "hymnic anamnesis" of the exodus (M. Gilbert). Finally, v. 22 closes the whole book within this perspective of praise.

Wis 19:1-5:
The Seventh Diptych; the Crossing of the Sea

1 But the ungodly were pursued to the end by a merciless wrath:
for he already knew what they would do,
2 that is, that, having allowed them to depart
and having sent them away in haste,
after, having changed their mind, they would have pursued them.
3 For they had not yet finished celebrating the funeral rites
and mourning at the tombs of their dead
when they conceived another foolish plan
and set themselves to follow as if fugitives
those whom they had begged to leave.
4 To this extreme they were urged on by a just destiny
thus to throw [on themselves] the forgetfulness of what had happened,
in order to fill up the punishment which was lacking to their torments:

5 while your people experienced an astonishing journey,
they, on the other hand, encountered a strange death.

Notes on the Text and Translation

v. 2. Verse 2a presents two difficult textual problems: the alternation between ἐπιτρέψαντες and ἐπιστρέψαντες, and the double possibility of reading between ἀπεῖναι and ἀπιέναι. The reading ἐπιστρέψαντες is supported by B, S, C, many min., and by Lat (*cum reversi essent*); some authors understand this verb "change one's mind about" or "press someone to something". The reading ἐπιτρέψαντες is supported by A, S^{c}, V, *O* and some minuscules; followed by the infinitive, ἐπιτρέπω is to be understood in the sense of "allow".

The infinitive that follows also creates a problem. The best-attested reading is ἀπεῖναι, to be understood as "to be absent" (Ziegler). *O* and V, with some minuscules, have ἐπιτρέψαντες τοῦ ἀπιέναι (to be understood as "allow to go away"; thus, Rahlfs and Ziegler); in this case, the τοῦ would be considered as pleonastic (cf. BDF § 400.7 and Winston, *Wisdom*, 324). The use of the genitive (τοῦ) better validates the reading ἐπιστρέψαντες τοῦ ἀπεῖναι; the expression could then be translated with "being concerned that they go away". The translation remains hypothetical and the sense obscure (Larcher, *Sagesse*, 3:1048). Although with some hesitation, Scarpat (*Sapienza*, 3:312-313) proposes to reconstruct an hypothetical τοὺς υἱούς σου, speculating that this text fell out through a scribal error: "they allowed (your sons) to go away".

In 2b, P. Enns (*Exodus Retold*, 96-97) prefers to interpret προπέμπω in the sense of "accompany" ("to escort"), a sense that is technically possible for this verb. Thus, Wisdom would be the most ancient witness of an exegetical tradition reflected in the Mekilta (*Besh.* 1.1-3) and, again, in Exod. Rab. 20.3. The Hebrew verb שׁלח of Exod 13:17 (ויהי בשלח פרעה) is being interpreted in the sense of "escort" (לוה) rather than "send away", because only God can give this order.

v. 5. The witnesses alternate between πειράσῃ and περάσῃ (the latter reading being supported by A, B^{c}, V, Lat, Sah, Aeth, Arm). The verb περάω indicates "crossing". With extensive argument, Scarpat (*Sapienza*, 3:315) prefers it as *lectio difficilior* and translates "so that your people might carry out a wonderful journey". Larcher (*Sagesse*, 3:1053-1054) considers the two readings equivalent but prefers the first, understanding πειράζω in the sense of "experiencing" (cf. Wis 2:24; 12:26). The repeated presence of πειράζω in Wisdom (also in 1:2; 2:17; 3:5; 11:9) could be, *pace* Scarpat, an indication in favour of πειράσῃ in a pericope which deliberately takes up many terms already used in the rest of the book.

Synchronic Analysis

19:1a: A Merciless Wrath

The initial δέ matches up with the end of the previous episode which illustrated the salvation of the Israelites who were preserved from the "destroyer" because of Aaron's intercession (Wis 18:25). For the use of ἐφίσταμαι in the sense of "fall on someone, strike", cf. Wis 6:5; 16:8; and 18:17, in similar contexts. The clarification "to the end" (cf. 16:5), that is, to the point of complete destruction, causes the verb to assume a nuance of duration ("pursued"). The object of the verb is represented here by the ungodly. The author is thinking of the Egyptians, but, in calling them "ungodly", he is linking them to the characters who formed one of the subjects in the first part of the book.

The wrath of God is a frequent theme in Wisdom (cf. 16:5a). Here, a description of that wrath as "merciless" (the adjective is found again in Wis 12:5a; cf. Prov 27:4 LXX), points to an eschatological dimension: in recalling the episode of the sea, the author wishes to suggest the idea of the final judgement of the ungodly. The divine wrath is certainly not in contradiction with God's mercy. In fact, his anger is unleashed only when people refuse his mercy.

In this passage (except for v. 5a), God is mentioned only in the third person and indirectly. He is invoked again as "you", precisely with the mention of "your people" (5a), according to the distinctive style of Wisdom 10-19.

19:1b–2: The Divine Foreknowledge

The reason for God's implacable severity lies in the divine foreknowledge: God "already knew" what the Egyptians would do. We note the absence of the subject (clearly God), which is supplied by two codices with the reading in the second person singular.[7] The verb προοῖδα is rare and refined (in the LXX, only in 4 Macc 4:25); accompanied here by τὰ μέλλοντα (cf. Wis 8:8b), it refers to the foreknowledge of what is to happen. The reference is not to a generic future but rather to what the Egyptians would do to Israel. The text is referring to the well-known exodus theme of the hardening of the heart.

Prescinding from the textual problems, v. 2 refers to Pharaoh's permission for the Israelites to leave Egypt (cf. Exod 12:31-32). The second part of the verse is then inspired by Exod 12:33 (cf. the theme of haste: σπουδῇ). In this case, the author does not mention the information in Exod 12:35 (the gifts received by the Israelites) to which he had already alluded in Wis 10:17 (cf. Philo, *Mos.* 1.139).

The verb in the future in 2c (διώξουσιν) depends directly on the initial ὅτι and brings us into the account of the pursuit (Exod 14:6-9). In accordance with the information in Exod 14:5, not only does Pharaoh change his mind (μετεστράφη ἡ καρδία), but actually "repents of" his decision to escort the Israelites, if we wish to follow the proposal of Enns (see above). In this way, Pharaoh's decision appears sheer madness. Here, the author uses μεταμέλομαι which, for the most part in the LXX acquires the sense of "repent of something" (cf., for example, 1 Chr 21:15; 1 Macc 11:10 and, in the NT, Matt 21:29, 32; 27:3). In a mere three stichs, our sage thus summarises a substantial amount of information contained in the Exodus narrative in order to reach his main concern, the crossing of the sea.

19:3: Another Foolish Idea of the Egyptians…

"To have in the hands" is an idiomatic expression which acquires different shades of meaning according to the context. Here, the object is the plural τὰ πένθη which can be understood both as "grief" and as its external manifestation, that is, the funeral rites. The text does not seem to be alluding to the long time needed for embalming the corpses according to Egyptian practice.[8] The allusion to the dead refers, in fact, to Wis 18:12b-c (cf. Num 33:4a); but there is a certain contradiction: in 18:12c, the living are not sufficient to bury the dead; here, however, everyone seems occupied in these activities. This is one of the midrashic expansions typical of Wisdom where there is not always a concern to follow a cast-iron logic.

The text of 3b mentions the laments made at the tombs of the dead. One notes the use of *προσοδύρομαι, *hapax* in Greek, more common only its simpler form. Thus, Wisdom is playing on the contrast between the Egyptians' lament for

---

7 Cf. Ziegler's apparatus, *sub loco*.

8 Cf. Larcher, *Sagesse*, 3:1049.

those dead in the tenth plague and the, still more tragic, decision they take to chase after Israel. Their actions plunge the entire people dramatically into a bottomless abyss.

Verse 3c creates some problems of interpretation: the verb ἐπισπάομαι, as in Wis 1:12, a text which is probably being recalled here, has the sense of "took to themselves". Both the versions and modern authors understand it in the sense of "conceived another foolish plan", or "took another mad decision". Except for Wis 17:12, the use of λογισμός in Wisdom is always negative and refers to the plans, calculations and reasonings of mortals.[9] Here, as in 1:5, they are described as "foolish" (ἀσύνετοι), as "devious" (σκολιοί 1:3), or as "uncertain" (cf. δειλοί in 9:14). The term ἄνοια is very strong and recalls 15:18 where it is used in connection with Egyptian zoolatry. Here, the intention is to highlight the contradictory nature of the Egyptians' actions.

19:4-5: A Just Destiny – An Astonishing Journey

Verse 4 illustrates the deep reason for the Egyptians' foolish decision. They are urged to act in this way by a Necessity which forces them into error (4a). The purpose of this is double: for the Egyptians to receive the punishment they deserve (4c) and for the liberation of the people (5).

Another effect of the divine action (4b) is to have covered the Egyptians with forgetfulness (ἀμνηστία) of what had happened (τῶν συμβεβηκότων); cf. Wis 14,: 6 (χάριτος ἀμνηστία). God's action has done nothing other than to expose the Egyptians' attitude: they are not able to recognise God's presence in the events which they have witnessed. Our author chooses, perhaps deliberately, a term already used in a moral sense by Plato and later by Plutarch.[10] In introducing the theme of ἀμνηστία, he thus recalls, by contrast, the ἀνάμησις and the ὑπόμνησις of God's words and favours which have characterised the experience of Israel (cf. Wis 16:6, 11).

The first purpose of the Necessity which strikes the Egyptians is that they themselves fill up what is lacking in their punishment (κόλασις). The verb προσαναπληρόω* is *hapax* both in the LXX and in the NT, and is reserved to literary language. It is to be understood in the sense of "fill up to full measure". The idea expressed in 4c is close to that in 2 Macc 6:14.

Veres 5 closes the pericope relating to the seventh diptych by contrasting with the death encountered by the Egyptians the extraordinary salvation offered by God to God's people. Mention of the people (λαός) brings our author back immediately to the use of the second person: they are *your people*. The use of the same expression at the end of the book (19:22) highlights its importance and underlines its relevance; the people of whom the author speaks is not only that of the exodus but also the contemporary people of Israel, the public whom the sage of Alexandria is addressing.

This people experiences a journey that is unusual (for ὁδοιπορία, cf. Wis 18:3). The journey which the Israelites undertake on leaving Egypt is described as παράδοξος: astonishing, unexpected. Cf. Wis 5:2, in connection with the unexpected salvation of the just, and 16:17, with regard to the manna. All three cases underline the extraordinary nature and unexpected character of a salvific event brought about by God on behalf of God's people.

---

9 Cf. Wis 1:3; 1:5; 9:14; 11:15; and 12:10.

10 Cf. Reese, *Hellenistic Influence*, 20.

By contrast, the Egyptians experience a "strange death". Wherein lies the strangeness of this death? Clearly, in the miracle of the sea, to which the text alludes, but not just that. Right from the beginning, in fact, Wisdom has emphasised that God does not seek death (Wis 1:13). It something foreign which people seek but which does not correspond to God's plan (cf. the use of εὑρίσκω). Death is strange too in relation to what is stated in v. 6: the entire creation is lined up in the service of the just.

Diachronic Analysis

19:1b–2 In 1b, unlike some of the Exodus texts, (cf. Exod 7:3; 9:12; 10:1, 20, 27; 11:10; 14:4), our sage avoids speaking of the Lord's directly hardening Pharaoh's heart and limits himself to emphasising the divine foreknowledge, a thoroughly biblical idea (cf. Sus 35 LXX = Sus Th 42 [Dan 13:42]; the theme is common in Philo, cf., for example, *Deo* 29). Our sage could be depending on Exod 14:3-4a which contains the discourse in which God predicts what Pharaoh will do: ἐγὼ δὲ σκληρυνῶ τὴν καρδίαν Φαραω καὶ καταδιώξεται ὀπίσω αὐτῶν.

Larcher discusses the theological problem raised by this text,[11] claiming that our sage does not intend to enter into questions concerning God's action and human freewill but only to justify God's lasting state of unyielding wrath in the face of the obstinacy of the Egyptians. Probably a more correct way of reading this is to recall the eschatological background of this pericope (against Larcher who holds that the text here refers only to physical death). As happens to the ungodly of the first part of the book, so too the Egyptians receive from God the *extreme* punishment for their radical unbelief and thus meet with "a merciless wrath".

19:3 The information that the Egyptians want to follow those whom they have just sent away depends again on Exod 14:5-6. Here Wisdom is combining, in a really remarkable way, a double tradition from the book of Exodus. The Egyptians "beg" (ἱκετεύοντες; cf. Wis 13:18) the Israelites to leave (cf. Exod 12:31), and, at the same time, send them away (cf. Exod 12:33 LXX: καὶ κατεβιάζοντο οἱ Αἰγύπτιοι τὸν λαὸν σπουδῇ ἐκβαλεῖν αὐτοὺς ἐκ τῆς γῆς).

What is the reason for the Egyptians' decision? The fact that the text of Wisdom describes it as "foolish" leads to the thought that it was of a psychological nature. Verse 4 recalls the mystery of the hardening of Pharaoh's heart (cf. below). Here, the book of Wisdom shows itself profound and original, especially in comparison with the Jewish tradition which attempts to justify this decision.[12] The verbal link with Wis 1:12 appears even more significant at this point: foolish human reasoning is the cause of ruin. Death appears no longer as a punishment but as the direct consequence of human actions.

19:4-5 It is interesting how the author reformulates the idea of Exod 14:4 in the light of Greek thought. Verse 4 opens with the imperfect of ἕλκω, to be understood in the sense of "draw, urge", in a violent and irresistible way. On this verb depends the expression ἐπὶ τοῦτο τὸ πέρας, "to this extreme", which indicates the extreme

11 Cf. Larcher, *Sagesse*, 3:1046-1047.

12 According to the Tg. Ps.-J. on Exod 14:9, for example, Pharaoh believed that the god Baal-Zephon had barred the desert route to the Israelites; cf. Enns, *Exodus Retold*, 99-104.

point, the maximum limit of something, as in Wis 14:27. However, the closeness to ἀνάγκη, through the use of the rhetorical figure of *hyperbaton*, dear to Wisdom, makes it clear that this destiny (for ἀνάγκη, cf. the comment on 17:17) is not the blind or impersonal destiny or Necessity of the Greeks but the consequence of the Egyptians' own actions and so their just deserts. We note the use of ἄξιος which, in Wisdom, always has a theological significance; cf. 16:9. In fact, our sage is thinking of a story in which God's freedom is bound up with the free actions of people. Here, his thought is certainly biblical and not Greek.

The theme of forgetfulness introduced in 4b is wholly absent from the Exodus narrative. However, in Exod 14:17, we read that the Egyptian soldiers go into the sea because the Lord has hardened their heart. This is the explanation which the biblical text probably intends to provide for a very severe punishment which affects people who, at least apparently, are not guilty. However, in our sage's *midrashic* account, these people are considered guilty nonetheless because they should have remembered, as the Israelites did, the experiences which they had witnessed, but they did not do so.[13]

Here too, Larcher discusses the theological problem raised by the text of 19:4ab:[14] it seems as if the Egyptians were pressed into sinning by a mysterious force which urged them on to radical sins which could no longer be pardoned. We have already observed that the Necessity or destiny spoken of is not the impersonal Fate of the Greeks but can rather be linked to the biblical idea of the hardening of Pharaoh's heart. Some authors understand this Necessity as a relation of cause and effect. It would be something deriving from the actual deeds of the wicked, as a sort of vicious circle pressing them inexorably to evil. In reality, the Necessity spoken of by Wisdom embodies the will and action of God. Fichtner[15] emphasizes the apocalyptic orientation of the diptych; I prefer to speak, rather, of its eschatological orientation, as appears clearly from the use of the terms βάσανος and κόλασις, which have already been encountered (cf. Wis 16:3; 17:13; etc.). The perspective of the renewed creation which runs through the whole of chapter 19 helps us to see here an anticipation of God's future judgement on the ungodly. It is also possible to think of 4c as further evidence of the tension that exists in Wisdom between the theme of God's mercy and that of God's judgement, of the irrevocable condemnation of the ungodly.

Wis 19:6-12: The Crossing of the Sea and the Creation at the Service of God's Children

6 For the entire creation was fashioned anew, as at the beginning,
in its own elements,
obeying your commands,
so that your children might be preserved unharmed.

---

13 Cf. the observations of Enns, *Exodus Retold*, 109-110.

14 Cf. Larcher, *Sagesse*, 3:1051.

15 Cf. *Weisheit*, 67.

7 Now the cloud was seen covering the camp with its shadow
and the dry land rising up where previously there was water;
a path without obstacles in place of the Red Sea
and a verdant plain instead of billowing waves
8 through which they passed, like a single body, protected by your hand,
spectators of marvellous wonders.
9 They were like horses led to the meadow
and leapt like lambs,
praising you, o Lord, their deliverer.
10 For they still remembered what had happened to them
during their sojourn in a foreign land,
when the earth, instead of producing animals, brought forth gnats
and the river, instead of aquatic animals, vomited a multitude of frogs.
11 Later, they also saw a new production of birds
when, impelled by desire, they sought delicate foods:
12 to comfort them, there came up quails from the sea.

Notes on the Text and Translation

v. 6. In 6b, the reading ταῖς σαῖς ἐπιταγαῖς, chosen by Ziegler, alternates with ταῖς ἰδίαις ἐπιταγαῖς (B, C, some minuscules, Arab). With this reading, the text would be referring to the "particular" orders which God imparts to his creation. However, this reading contrasts with the idea that the creation is always ready to obey its Creator. The reading ἰδίαις could have arisen under the influence of ἐν ἰδίῳ γένει in 19:6a. The personal pronoun σαῖς refers directly to God who is again invoked in 6c in the second person (οἱ σοί παῖδες).

v. 9. Ἐνεμήθησαν: The mss 311 766 and Arm read ἐνεθυμήθησαν, "they took to heart", or "they reflected"; other mss have διενεμήθησαν, "manage", here in the sense of "lead". This variant is slightly attested but would correspond to the text of Isa 63:13 LXX: "the Lord led them (ἤγαγεν) ... like horses through the desert", which was certainly in the mind of our author. For other conjectures, cf. Larcher, *Sagesse*, 3:1061-1062. Here, we retain the better-attested ἐνεμήθησαν (from νέμω). However, the sense of "lead to the meadow" is not so certain.

In 9c, the apposition to κύριε is found in two different textual forms, τὸν ῥυόμενον (B, S, mss; Ziegler) and τὸν ῥυσάμενον (A,C, V, Lat *qui liberasti eos*, Arm, Syr, cf. Rahlfs) which seems *lectio facilior.* The first reading seems original; one does not see how it could have otherwise arisen. In this case, the present participle can be understood as an action in course ("the one who is delivering them") or as an action that has just happened ("the one who had just delivered them"); perhaps it is better to understand it as an adjective ("their deliverer").

Synchronic Analysis

19:6: A Renewed Creation

As already in Wis 16:24-25, our author introduces a reflection on the obedience of the creation to its Creator. With ὅλη ἡ κτίσις is intended nature in general, understood as "creation" (cf. Wis 5:17; 16:24). The qualification ἐν ἰδίῳ γένει creates some difficulties:[16] γένος could have been suggested by Gen 1 LXX where, ten times (vv. 11bis, 12bis, 21, 24bis, 25ter), κατὰ γένος indicates the "kinds" designated by the Creator. The verb *διατυπόω is to be understood in the sense of "stamp, carve". The two adverbs, πάλιν ἄνωθεν, are probably synonymous and could signify "again, once more", or else, as in Gal 4:9, assume a temporal nuance: "anew, as before".

The clear reference to the creation account in Genesis which runs through the entire pericope causes us rather to think of the second possibility, the temporal nuance: it is not a *new* creation so much as a creation *renewed*. The exodus is, as it were, a new beginning, a return to the origin of a creation that is definitively placed at the service of God (ὑπηρετοῦσα ταῖς σαῖς ἐπιταγαῖς), where every created element finally reveals what it really is.[17] The reference to the Genesis context is particularly important: the emphasis falls on the fact that the events of the exodus (cf. v. 7) involve, simultaneously, a recalling of the original creation and a modification of that creation (cf. vv. 10-12). One can appropriately speak, therefore, of a "renewed creation": that is, on the one hand, it is "as at the beginning" (ἄνωθεν), and, on the other hand, represents something new (πάλιν). Beyond the probable philosophical background (see below), the emphasis in Wis 19:6 is undoubtedly being placed on the *proclamation of the obedience of the creation to its Creator*. Thus, there is no question of the creation of new material but, rather of the divine action which permits the elements of the creation to be renewed by changing their very nature.

The verb ὑπηρετέω refers directly to Wis 16:24 (cf. the comment): contrary to the Stoic view, God is not present in the world in an immanent way but the creation is at God's service. God's aim in his action towards his creatures (ἵνα) is the preservation of "your children" (19:6c). As in Wis 12:7, 20, παῖς is to be understood as "child" rather than as "servant". The verb φυλάσσω, followed by a complement, is frequent in Wisdom; cf. Wis 18:4; for ἀβλαβής, cf. Wis 18:3. Thus, the miracles of the exodus have the aim of preserving the elect, the children of God, keeping them safe and sound. This is a reappearance of the concept of salvation typical of Wisdom; not "redemption" so much as "preservation" and keeping in life.

19:7-8: Spectators of Marvellous Wonders

The whole of v. 7 depends on ἐθεωρήθη at the end of the second stich. As elsewhere in the book (Wis 6:12; 13:5; 16:7; 19:8), the verb indicates a looking with attention, understanding (almost contemplating) the meaning of what is seen. The "marvellous wonders" seen by the people are four:

1. The cloud that covers the camp with its shadow (7a).

2. The emerging (*ἀνάδυσις) of the dry land in place of the water of the sea (7b). Here, the preposition ἐκ has the meaning of "in the place of". The verb *προϋφίσταμαι is rare even in Greek usage; according to Winston (*Wisdom*, 325), this is its first attestation; here, in the participle, it indicates "what was there before".

3. Instead of the Red Sea, there appears to the people a path without obstacles (7c). The adjective *ἀνεμπόδιστος already appeared in Wis 17:20 in the sense of "without hindrance"; here, it is to be understood as "without obstacles".

16 Cf. Larcher, *Sagesse*, 3:1054-1057.

17 Cf. Sweet, "The Theory of Miracles", especially p. 120.

4. The path through the sea is transformed into a verdant plain (7d). A rare and poetic word is employed to describe the waves, κλυδών, already used in Wis 14:5. This reference to the waves is interesting because it is an indication that our author was thinking of the Red Sea properly so called.[18]

Along this path created through the waters passes a whole people (v. 8). The expression "protected by your hand" recalls Isa 51:16 and links up with what was already stated in Wis 5:16.[19] This people are spectators of marvellous wonders; θεωρέω refers directly to the previous stich, 19:7b. The wonders referred to are precisely the four listed in the previous verse. The text speaks of θαυμαστὰ τέρατα. In 17:15, τέρας indicates phantasms, something monstrous which provokes terror, according to the normal use of the term in classical Greek. In the LXX, however, τέρας mostly translates the Hebrew מופת, often precisely in an exodus context, not infrequently in connection with σημεῖον, as in Wis 8:8 and 10:16 (cf. Exod 7:9; 11:9, 10; etc.). In these cases, the wonders refer to the extraordinary events which reveal a miraculous intervention by God. According to Wis 8:8, knowing how to discern the divine presence in the "signs and wonders" is a fruit of the gift of wisdom. The miracles of the crossing of the sea are "marvellous". Θαυμαστός has already been used in this connection in Wis 10:17 (cf. the verb in Wis 11:14). Everything that God does arouses the wonder of the believers (cf. Exod 34:10 LXX: ὅτι θαυμαστά ἐστιν ἃ ἐγὼ ποιήσω σοι) and leads them to contemplation (cf. the use of θεωρέω).

19:9: Like Leaping Lambs...

While crossing the sea, the Israelites are described with two very suggestive comparisons. The first is expressed through the aorist passive of the verb νέμω, "pasture" (cf. the textual notes). Larcher observes that, with a single exception (Sophocles, *Phil.* 709), the verb is always applied to animals.[20]

The second comparison is less difficult to understand (cf. below). The verb *διασκιρτάω does not appear before Wisdom and is to be translated with "leap here and there, frolic, gambol". As in the case of σκιρτάω in Wis 17:19a, the verb refers to animals rather than people.

In the third stich, the description of the outward demeanour of the Israelites is followed by the mention of the hymn of praise which they raised. The vocative κύριε brings us anew into an atmosphere of prayer.[21] The verb αἰνέω occurs only here and in 10:20[22] with which it creates a kind of *inclusio*, precisely on the theme of praise; cf. Ps 105:12 LXX [106:12 MT] about the same situation following the salvation at the sea: καὶ ᾖσαν τὴν αἴνεσιν αὐτοῦ: "and they sang your praise". We have already spoken of the importance of v. 9: its poetic dimension makes a fitting

18 Along with the name of the Pentapolis in Wis 10:6, this is the only mention (cf. also 10:18) of a proper name within Wisdom.

19 A flashback, according to Reese (cf. *Hellenistic influence*, 139): in 5:16, in relation to the eternal life of the just, here, in relation to the crossing of the sea; history and eschatology are intertwined; cf., above, the recalling of 1:12 in 19:3, with the same kind of link.

20 Cf. Larcher, *Sagesse*, 3:1061.

21 The invocation κύριε appears for the first time at the beginning of the prayer of "Solomon" in 9:1 and subsequently in strategic positions in the book's structure: Wis 10:20 and, successively, in Wis 12:2; 16:12, 26; 19:9 and, exactly at the end of the book, in 19:22.

22 We must add the presence of τοὺς ἁγίους πατέρων αἴνους in Wis 18:9.

match with the theme of praise which frames this whole great "hymnic anamnesis of the exodus".

19:10: The Memory of the Divine Actions

The beginning of v. 10 (ἐμέμνηντο γάρ) constitutes the immediate explanation of the hymn of praise in v. 9. Although introducing a theme that is apparently new, vv. 10-12 recapitulate a good part of the preceding diptychs and, alluding again to the Genesis context, are not separate from what we have seen in v. 7. Verse 10 returns to the theme of remembering and memory (cf. 19:4), thus completing the reflection that opened in 16:6, 11 and emphasising once again the pedagogic character of the exodus antitheses. The "things that had happened to them", which the Israelites remember, are the plagues which befell the Egyptians in which the same elements which saved Israel were used against their enemies. It is in the memory that these events acquire their real significance and become signs of the divine action which are actualised for the Jews of Alexandria, the addressees of the book, and become, in the light of Wis 19:9, a permanent source of prayer and praise.[23]

The first of these memories relates to the plague of gnats (Exod 8:12-15; cf. v. 14: ἐξαγαγεῖν τὸν σκνῖφα). On what grounds does Wisdom describe an abnormal origin for the gnats, who are seen as coming from the earth? Already employed in Wis 1:14b, the term γένεσις is to be understood here as "generation, production" (cf. also Wis 16:26 and, above all, γενεσιάρχης in 13:3 and γενεσιουργός in 13:5). The author would be doing nothing other than counterposing to the normal generation of animals an exceptional generation of gnats, or else, supported by Gen 1:20, 24 LXX (ἐξαγαγέτω), he would be thinking of an origin out of the ordinary of animals who ought to be heavenly (flying) beings, who ought to come not from the element "earth" but rather from the air.[24]

The latter explanation appears more probable, considering that, in the following stich, the element "water" appears with reference to the plague of frogs (Exod 7:26-8:11).[25] The verb ἐξερεύγομαι, "vomit", comes from Exod 7:28 LXX. The adjective *ἔνυδρος means "which lives in water", and the corresponding substantive indicates aquatic animals. The frogs would thus be terrestrial animals which come, in an anomalous manner, from the "water", here, more exactly, "the river", that is, the Nile. This is the basic point of both stichs: three of the four elements of the cosmos (air, water, earth) produce beings which are able to live in the opposite element: the gnats, animals of the air, come from the earth; the frogs, animals which live on the earth, originate in the water; the quails (v. 11), animals of the air (v. 11) come from the water.

19:11-12: The Wonders of the Creation

The third wonder brings us back to the diptych of Wis 16:1-4: the quails. The adverbial expression ἐφ' ὑστέρῳ is to be understood as "later", that is, once they have come out of Egypt. The quails are not a "new species", but a "new production" of birds, where "new" (preceded and reinforced by καί) is to be understood in the sense of "unexpected, strange". This strangeness is described better in the

23 "Die *memoria* der Exodus-Generation von 10 ist somit zugleich die *memoria* der in Alexandrien lebenden Diasporajuden"; Hübner, *Weisheit*, 225.

24 Cf. Larcher, *Sagesse*, 3:1064-1065, for discussion of further theories. He also seeks to describe the zoological species indicated by the term σκνίψ.

25 The term πλῆθος, "multitude", occurs also in Wis 11:15:17; 16:1; 18:5, 20, always with reference to the plagues sent by God (only exception 14:20).

two following stichs. The author wishes to highlight the unexpected way in which the birds come to life in order to illustrate further the principle expressed in 19:6 and taken up again in 19:18: the function of the elements and their properties change without, however, any alteration to their nature.

The verb προάγω is to be understood as "be impelled" (cf. Sir prologue 9); for ἐπιθυμία, cf. Wis 16:2. What the Israelites sought (αἰτέω was probably suggested by Ps 104:40 LXX [105:40 MT]) is described as ἐδέσματα τρυφῆς (cf. Num 11:4-6). The term ἐδέσματα (always in the plural) is found in the LXX in the sense of "food"; the substantive τρυφή indicates something delicate.

The quails come up from the sea (the expression goes back to Exod 16:13: καὶ ἀνέβη ὀρτογυμήτρα; cf. ἀπὸ τῆς θαλάσσης in Num 11:31). The substantive παραμυθία (only here and in Esth E, 5 = 8:12c, but with the meaning of "[bad] influence") indicates the aim of the sending of the quails: the comfort, the consolation of Israel.[26]

Diachronic Analysis

19:6 We cannot exclude the influence of the Greek theory of the elements in this verse. After all, it has been in our author's thought in the course of the seven diptychs;[27] the "elements" are thus those which make up the creation.

As for the verb διατυπόω, Philo employs it in the sense of "giving form" to the embryo (*Congr.* 136), or in connection with the person "formed" by God (*Opif.* 25); Scarpat refers also to Plato (*Prot.* 320d).[28]

19:7-8 The four miracles mentioned in Wis 19:7 are to be read against the background of the exodus traditions, but not only these:

– in 7a, the reference is to the text of Exod 14:19-20 (cf., also, Num 9:18 LXX: σκιάζει ἡ νεφέλη) and to the pillar of cloud which protects the Israelites by hiding them from the eyes of the Egyptians (cf. already 18:3). Here, the function of the cloud is not to give light but to protect, as in Ps 104:39 LXX [105:39 MT].[29] However, in the cloud which overshadows (σκιάζουσα), we can perhaps discern an allusion to Gen 1:1-2, namely, to the darkness and the deep covered by the waters, or even to the very Spirit of God which fluttered on the waters (cf. wisdom associated with the cloud in Sir 24:3).[30]

– in 7b, instead of emphasising the parting of the waters of the sea or the wind which drives them away, according to the traditions of Exodus 14, Wisdom

---

26 The term παραμυθία can also indicate "persuasion" or "exhortation", but that does not match the general tone. All the pejorative features have been taken away with the aim of highlighting only God's positive actions on behalf of Israel.

27 Cf. Van Rooden, "Die antike Elementarlehre und der Aufbau von Sapientia Salomonis 11-19". Winston, *Wisdom,* 324-325, thinks of an interchangeability among the elements according to very common Greek ideas which were well known to the Stoic philosophy.

28 Cf. Scarpat, *Sapienza,* 3:300 n. 2.

29 Wisdom would be the most ancient witness of this tradition which places the cloud as protection *before* the crossing of the sea or at the same time as it; cf. Luzarraga, *Las tradicciones de la nube*, 88-89; 133 n. 509; cf. also Beauchamp, "Le salut corporel", 504.

30 Cf. Winston, *Wisdom*, 325; Gilbert, "La rélecture de Gn 1-3", 339-341.

prefers to stress the emergence of the dry ground, a kind of platform emerging from the waters on which the Israelites can pass. Thus water and earth, both named in this stich, obey the orders of their creator. According to Larcher, the term ξηρός is borrowed from Exod 14:16, 22 LXX. With Winston, I think, rather, of Gen 1:9–10 LXX, the land which emerges from the waters (καὶ ὤφθη ἡ ξηρά ...). These links with Genesis 1 are important for the interpretation of the entire chapter.[31]

- as for 7c, prophetic texts describe the passage through the sea as a path: Isa 43:16 and, in particular, Isa 63:13 LXX which itself is referring to the salvation of the people delivered from Egypt; cf. Philo, *Mos.* 2.253-254.

- in 7d, the term "plain" (πεδίον) could have been suggested by Isa 63:14 LXX where it occurs precisely in a comparison linked to the crossing of the sea. The adjective "verdant" (*χλοηφόρος) is a literary and poetic term, taken perhaps from Euripides (*Phoen.* 647, 653), where it indicates the new vegetation which covers the earth in spring. It is a midrashic expansion which shows once again our author's link with these traditions, in particular those found in Midrash Exod. Rab. on Exod 14:16 (the Israelite women who gather fruit while they cross the sea); but cf., already, Tg. Ps.-J. on Exod 15:9: "there, therefore, streams of sweet water flowed and there were fruit trees, chosen vegetables, and fruits, at the bottom of the sea". However, the previous reference to Genesis 1 can better explain how it was possible for our sage to think of speaking of vegetation appearing on the dry land which he then describes as "verdant" (cf. Gen 1:13-14).[32]

In v. 8, the text employs an unusual adverb, *πανεθνεῖ.[33] As for 8b, it is possible that Wisdom is reflecting the seeds of those traditions which would go on to speak of the ten miracles performed by God at the Red Sea (Mek. Rab. Ism., Besh. 5.1-14; Midr. Tehillim 114,38; Pirqe R. El. 42; etc.).[34]

The comparison with the horses leads to the thought that the Israelites were 19:9
happy as horses led to the meadow, and this, perhaps, is the most likely sense.[35] Alonso Schökel suggests that the comparison with the horses could have arisen in our author's mind in an ironic sense, with reference to Pharaoh's cavalry

31 Cf. Larcher, *Sagesse*, 3:1059, and Winston, *Wisdom*, 325.

32 Cf., also, Bienaimé, Germain., "Un retour du Paradis dans le désert de l'Exode selon une tradition juive", in: Derousseaux, Louis – Blanquart, Fabien (edd.), *La Création dans l'Orient Ancien* (Cerf: Paris 1987) 447 n. 48; Enns, *Exodus Retold*, 119-121.

33 Enns (*Exodus Retold*, 123-128) proposes three interesting solutions to explain the presence of this term. The first is connected with the fact that, in the MT of Exod 14:30-31, there appears, for the first time in Exodus, the expression ישׂראל instead of the more usual בני ישׂראל. A second solution is linked to the interpretation of Exod 15:16 which – by comparison with Exod 12:38 – presupposes the crossing of the sea by the Israelites alone and not by the "multitude" which followed them. Wisdom, on the other hand, would be admitting the passage of *all* the fugitives from Egypt, *like a single body.* A third solution, which seems more practicable, arises from the fact that the Jewish tradition contains texts that speak of a lack of unity among the tribes at the Red Sea (Pseudo Philo, *Ant. Bibl.* 10.3; *Mek. Besh.* 3.128-136). Instead, the book of Wisdom is thinking of a unanimous decision of all the people who act like a single body (cf. a similar idea in Wis 18:9b).

34 Cf. Larcher, *Sagesse*, 3:1061 and, above all, Enns, *Exodus Retold*, 129-130.

35 Thus, already, Grimm, *Weisheit*, 295.

drowned in the sea.[36] More probably, however (see below), the comparison arises from having made use of Isa 63:13-14.

As for the comparison with the leaping lambs, the image is well known from Ps 113:4, 6 LXX [114:4, 6 MT], which uses the verb σκιρτάω (cf. also Mal 3:20 LXX); but Isa 63:14 already speaks of a "flock" (κτήνη) in connection with the departure from Egypt.

In the third stich, our sage is thinking of Exod 15:1ff.. For ῥυομαι, cf. Wis 16:8b; the verb was certainly suggested by Exod 14:30 LXX.

19:10: Being Strangers

The use of the term παροικία in v. 10 to indicate the sojourn in Egypt is interesting. Classical Greek knows the term πάροικος, mostly to indicate the foreigner resident in another country, one who, though dwelling in a specific land, does not enjoy its citizenship. Παροικία is a word proper to the LXX.[37] As in Acts 13:17, our author intends to indicate the sojourn of the Hebrews in Egypt by using a term which actually indicates being foreigners. It is one of the ways in which Wisdom intends to draw attention to the absence of rights for the Alexandrian Jews (cf. 19:13-17), while also referring to the biblical tradition which considers the patriarchs as "resident foreigners" (cf. Gen 12:10; 23:4; Lev 25:23; etc.).

19:12: The *Tryphê*

The τρυφή mentioned in v. 12, understood as luxury, abundance, wealth, could actually be described as the lifestyle of the Ptolemaic court; cf. the appellative of *Trypho* [Τρύφων] given to Ptolemy Euergetes I (246-222 BCE), Ptolemy Philopator (222-204 BCE), Ptolemy Euergetes II (169-164, 134-132/1, 126-116 BCE). Ptolemy XII Auletes (80-64 BCE) and, at the beginning of the Roman period, Mark Anthony, cultivated τρυφή, both considering themselves as νέος Διόνυσος.[38] The host of courtiers and servants, of banquets, rare animals and precious plants, delicate foods, wise men, the Library and the Museum, the journeys and the objects of luxury, the generous gifts granted to the people... all this is the τρυφή of the Ptolemaic court which is mirrored in the lifestyle of the ungodly as it is presented in Wisdom 2.

In the account of the historian Philarcus, Ptolemy II Philadelphus claimed to challenge death and to find immortality in his lifestyle which was characterised by τρυφή. Later, with Ptolemy XII Auletes and with Mark Anthony, this way of life is increasingly bound up with the Dionysiac cults and the appellative of *Neos Dionysos* assumed by the Ptolemaic monarch. Thus, towards the end of the Ptolemaic monarchy and the beginning of the Roman period, the search for τρυφή takes on a religious colour. The luxury and the pleasures of the court are an expression of the Dionysiac cults.

To Israel, however, the Lord offers a quite other type of τρυφή, through a gift that is unexpected and out of the ordinary. For Israel too, therefore, there is the possibility of living according to one of the commonest ideals of the Alexandrian nobility, but only within the perspective of the gift of God.

---

36 Cf. *Sabiduría*, 204.

37 Schmidt, Karl L. and Martin A., πάροικος κτλ., *TDNT* 5:841-853.

38 Cf. Tondriau, Julien, "La Tryphè, philosophie royale ptolémaïque", *Révue des Etudes Anciennes* 50 (1948): 49-54 [52-53].

Wis 19:13-17:
Egyptians and Sodomites – The Civil Rights of the Jews of Alexandria[39]

13 On the sinners, then, fell the chastisements,
not without having had, as warning signs, the power of thunderbolts.
For they justly suffered on account of their wickedness
because they had shown a really profound hatred
against foreigners [*or*: against guests].
14 The latter did not welcome the unbelievers who were present;
but the former enslaved guests who were benefactors.
15 And that is not all: certainly, there will be a visitation for them
because they received foreigners with hostility;
16 having given them a festive welcome,
when they already shared their rights,
they mistreated them with terrible labours.
17 Therefore, they were struck with blindness,
like those when, at the door of the just man,
shrouded in extreme darkness,
they each sought the entrance to his own door.

Notes on the Text and Translation

v. 14. As it is read by the majority of authors, v.14a would be a sudden allusion to the men of Sodom who did not welcome the strangers (τοὺς ἀγνοοῦντας) who arrived (παρόντας; cf. Gen 19:1-3; and, for the men of Sodom, Deut 29:23; Isa 1:9; 13:19; Jer 27:40 LXX [50:40 MT]; 30:12 LXX [49:18 MT]; Lam 4:6; Amos 4:11; Zeph 2:9).[40] Of the two sins for which the Sodomites are condemned, the sexual and the offence against hospitality, Wisdom would be referring here only to the second (cf. Josephus, *A.J.* 1.194), thus referring to the problem of the rights of the Alexandrian Jews.[41] However, Larcher[42] noted already that, in the expression τοὺς ἀγνοοῦντας, the active form presents a problem because we should expect a passive one. Thus, the text would not only be indicating the "unknown" but, in an active sense, "those who did not want to let themselves be recognised". Engel's reading is more consistent. He refers τοὺς ἀγνοοῦντας to "those who do not know", namely, the two men being entertained by Lot who do not yet know whether the Sodomites are good or evil. In any case, the Sodomites would be the subject of 19:14a.[43]

---

39 Cf., for this whole section, Mazzinghi, "Civil Rights", *passim.*

40 Along these lines, there is a gloss to SyrHex which refers to Gen 19:1-3; cf. Larcher, *Sagesse*, 3:1074.

41 Cf. Priotto, "Il confronto Egitto-Sodoma", 384-386.

42 *Sagesse*, 3:1074-1075.

43 *Weisheit*, 301-302: "Sie nahmen die nichtkennenden Angekommenen" (301).

Wholly different and undoubtedly stimulating is Scarpat's reading.[44] In attempting to solve the difficulties of v. 14a, he refers οἱ μέν to the Israelites previously mentioned and not to the Sodomites. With οὗτοι δέ, on the other hand, the text would be indicating the Egyptians. The Israelites avoided all contact with the unbelievers, called here precisely τοὺς ἀγνοοῦντας; cf. the theme of "ignorance" (ἀγνωσία, ἄγνοια) of God in connection with Wis 13:1 and 14:22. Consequently, Scarpat emends the accusative παρόντας to the nominative παρόντες, though without any textual support. In Scarpat's interpretation, on arriving in Egypt (παρόντες, with πάρειμι taken in its common sense of "arriving"), the Israelites restricted themselves to not mixing with the non-believers (τοὺς ἀγνοοῦντας), and that is why they were held to be haters of the human race; cf. Josephus, *C. Ap.* 2.210. Wisdom would thus be replying to this accusation of *misanthropy*, basing its reply on religious reasons. However, a grave difficulty with Scarpat's proposal is his emendation of παρόντας to παρόντες without any textual support.

An analysis of the use of πάρειμι in Wisdom shows that the verb is always used in the sense of "be present": cf. 4:2; 9:9; 11:11, 21; 12:19; 13:1; 14:17. Scarpat's reading would be the only case in which πάρειμι would be being used in the sense of "reach, arrive".

If, however, we accept the better-attested παρόντας,[45] and give to πάρειμι the, also well-attested, sense of "being present", we could understand that the Israelites (οἱ μέν) did not welcome the unbelievers (τοὺς ἀγνοοῦντας) who were present (παρόντας). Τοὺς ἀγνοοῦντας would thus be indicating the Egyptians, the inhabitants already present (παρόντας) in the country when the Israelites arrived. The latter would have separated themselves from the Egyptians only for religious reasons, without any hatred towards them (cf. Gen 43:32, for the Egyptians who do not eat with the Hebrews). The Egyptians, however, made slaves of the guests (ξένους) who were, instead, their benefactors.

v. 15. The text of v. 15a is problematic. Here, we accept the proposal of Scarpat, *Sapienza*, 3:323, who reads ἀλλ᾽ ἤ τις ἐπισκοπή, that is, "there will be for them a (certain) visitation". Cf. a *status quaestionis* in Priotto, "Il confronto Egitto-Sodoma", 377-380, who proposes reading ἄλλη τις ἐπισκοπή with the Vetus Latina (*et non solum, alius erit respectus illorum*), that is "there will be a different visitation for them".

Synchronic Analysis

19:13 A Profound Hatred for Foreigners

Establishing a connection with what goes before, the καί also underlines a climax. The understood subject of the whole verse is "the Egyptians", hidden under the term ἁμαρτωλοί, the sinners. On them "fell the chastisements"; τιμωρία (*hapax* in the book) indicates a punishment inflicted by the judiciary power (cf. the verb τιμωρέω in Wis 12:20 and 18:8) and thus refers to a judicial act of God against Egypt. The plural is emphatic. For ἐπέρχομαι, cf. Wis 12:27d, and, in 16:4, 5, in relation to a punishment sent by God on the guilty.

The second part of v. 13 emphasises God's justice in making the Egyptians suffer for their wickedness, especially for their hatred against foreigners.

The analysis of the use of πάσχω in the book reveals an interesting thematic: in 12:27 and in 18:11, πάσχω highlights a type of suffering which should bring the

44 *Sapienza*, 3:321-322.

45 The variant παριόντας ("the passers-by") is totally marginal.

Egyptians to conversion and to the abandonment of their persecution against the chosen people. Since that did not happen, their suffering becomes, in 18:19, the prelude to death; then, in 19:13, the final occurrence of the verb refers to the disaster at the Red Sea.

The rare verb ἐπιτηδεύω has the sense of "concern oneself with something". As complement, it often has a virtue or a vice. Here, the complement is represented by the term μισοξενία* which introduces a classic theme of anti-Jewish propaganda (cf. below). Verse 13 is evidence of the Jews' self-awareness of being ξένος in Alexandria (cf., below, on v. 14b): guests, yes, but foreigners. In Wisdom, ξένος also indicates something mysterious and out of the ordinary (cf. Wis 16:16, the extraordinary rain; 19:5, a strange death). Thus, on the one hand, through the words of the book, the Jews are claiming their right not to be hated, on the other hand, they are aware of their particularity, of being a ξενιτεία, as Wis 18:3 puts it.

Previously (cf. 12:19), Wisdom had claimed for the Alexandrian Jews the characteristic of φιλανθρωπία, a Hellenistic virtue through which the foreigner becomes the guest, even the benefactor (cf. Wis 19:14b). In this way, the message is clear: the Egyptians hated foreigners who were their guests (that is, they hated us, the Jews); we, on the other hand, by living to the full our φιλανθρωπία, a Greek virtue certainly, but consequence of our faith in the God of Israel, who loves everything that exists, have demonstrated that the true enemies of the human race are rather those who falsely accuse us. Above all, our sage is intending to polemicise with the Greek section of the population of Alexandria. However, the constant reference to the confrontation between the Egyptians and Israelites is meant to be an accusation launched against the Egyptian world in general which, already from the time of Manetho was characterised by a strong anti-semitic tendency.

19:14: Guests and Benefactors

For v. 14a, cf. the textual analysis. In 19:14b, the allusion to the Egyptians is clearer and the text combines the reference to the oppression at the time of the exodus (cf. Wis 17:1; 18:4) and the allusion to the story of Joseph, benefactor (εὐεργέτης) of Egypt, with the situation of the Alexandrian Jews.

19:15: A Visitation for Them

Apart from the textual difficulties (cf. above), v. 15a announces for the Egyptians an ἐπισκοπή, a visitation of God which, as elsewhere in the book, assumes a punitive aspect (cf. Wis 2:20; 3:7, 13; 4:15; 14:11). Given the explicit echo of the first part of the book, it is easy to think of a visitation of an eschatological character, perhaps a future punishment of the ungodly.[46]

Verse 15 refers entirely to the Egyptians.[47] In v. 15b, the eschatological visitation reserved for them is again accounted for by the theme of the oppression of foreigners, here called ἀλλοτρίοι, a very strong term which almost indicates an enemy. The adverb ἀπεχθῶς, "with hostility", is used here in a polemical sense. In fact, in the texts of 3 Maccabees, the terms drawn from this family (ἀπεχθάνεσθαι κτλ) are always used in connection with the hatred of the pagans for the Jews.[48] Through antithesis, the verb προσδέχομαι recalls Wis 18:7: the holy

---

46 So, Larcher, *Sagesse*, 3:1078-1079, but also Scarpat, *Sapienza*, 3:195-196.

47 There is a long discussion in Larcher, *Sagesse*, 3:1076-1078;

48 Cf. Scarpat, *Sapienza*, 3:323.

people waited for the salvation of the just and the punishment of the wicked. The wicked, on the other hand, "waited" for the strangers with hatred.[49]

19:16: Sharers of Their Rights

With οἱ δέ, the topic of the Egyptians is continued.[50] Verse 16a alludes again to the story of Joseph (cf. below), verse 16c, instead, to the oppression of the Hebrews in Egypt just as it is told in the first chapter of Exodus.

In 16b, the expression τῶν αὐτῶν μετεσχηκότας δικαίων stands out. In this case too, the biblical background is the story of Joseph (Gen 45:20). As for μετέχω, only the context can tell whether the verb is referring to things that are juridical, moral or more generic.[51] In *B.J.* 7.44, with regard to the rights of citizenship granted by the successors of Antiochus IV to the Jews of Antioch, Josephus writes: συνεχώρησαν αὐτοῖς ἐξ ἴσου τῆς πολέως τοῖς Ἕλλησι μετέχειν. This is exactly the sense which the verb has in our passage. What we have to ask is to what rights (τὰ δίκαια) our author is alluding. Unfortunately, both in Philo and in Josephus, expressions such as μετέχειν ἀξίων (*C. Ap.* 2.42) or τὰ πολιτικὰ δίκαια (*Flacc.* 53), close to that in our passage, do not have a uniform sense.[52] The text of v. 16 remains vague. Nonetheless, what stands out is the awareness of being "foreigners", except for being able to participate in the common rights (see also below).

19:17: Struck with Blindness

Only at this point is there a sudden mention of the punishment of the Sodomites who are recalled as a biblical model of inhospitality, here, towards the "just man", that is, Lot, who has already been mentioned in Wis 10:6-7 in relation to his flight from a city of ungodly people, considered as justly destroyed by God.

The blindness which, according to the account of Genesis 19, struck the Sodomites is placed in comparison with the blindness of the Egyptians recounted in 19:17a. When were they struck with blindness? The Exodus text does not speak of it, but our author certainly has in mind the blindness caused by the plague of darkness (Wis 17:1-18:4) which, as has already been said, presents notable links with our pericope. Thus, the condition of ἀορασία in which the Egyptians find themselves is much more than a material blindness, as was that of the Sodomites described in Genesis. Rather, it is the condition of those who have rejected the light of the law (cf. Wis 18:4) and so find themselves groping about in the darkness. In the end, therefore, our author's objective is not only that of criticising the Egyptians but also that of polemicising against the Jewish apostates, the ungodly of Wisdom 2, who are blind in the face of the light of the Mosaic law and justly struck by God's punishment.

Diachronic Analysis

19:13 The information in 13b, the thunderbolts as a warning sign of the punishment of the Egyptians, that is, their drowning in the Red Sea recounted in 19:1-5, is probably a midrashic re-elaboration of Exod 14:24, as already in Ps 76:15-20 LXX [77:15-

---

49 For the meaning of the verb, cf. Plato, *Leg.* 708a; Scarpat, *Sapienza*, 3:324.

50 Cf. Scarpat, *Sapienza*, 3:324.

51 Cf. Spicq, *Notes*, 2:555-560.

52 Cf. Pucci ben Zeev, Miriam, *Jewish Rights in the Roman World. The Greek and Roman Documents Quoted by Josephus Flavius*, Texts and Studies in Ancient Judaism, 74 (J.C.B. Mohr: Tübingen 1998), 481-482.

20 MT] and in Tg. Neof. on Exod 14:24.[53] The Egyptians' punishment was foretold by God. That is in harmony with Wisdom's theology which loves to underline the divine pedagogy in relation to the ungodly. On the one hand, they have to know who it is that is striking them, and, on the other, they must have the possibility of repenting. This is the point of the storm.

Hatred of Foreigners

The term *μισοξενία (19:13d) is found, as an adjective, in a text of Hecataeus of Abdera: the Jews live a life of hatred for all humanity: ἀπάνθρωπόν τινα καὶ μισόξενον βίον;[54] cf., also, some texts of Josephus such as *A.J.* 1.194, which uses a vocabulary very close to our passage, precisely in connection with the Sodomites, and, again, *A.J.* 8.117: "we are not misanthropic (ἀπάνθρωποι) by nature and do not behave as strangers (ἀλλοτρίως) towards those of another race". In both cases, Josephus is writing in the context of an anti-Jewish polemic. The accusation of being "haters of the human race" is one of the most repeated slogans of anti-Jewish propaganda; cf. Menon's letter to Hermocrates about a Jew who has not fulfilled his obligations, and the writing of a certain Heracles to an official called Ptolemy about the fact that the Jews are sickening (βδελύσσονται) the inhabitants of Memphis.[55] Here, the author of Wisdom is overturning against the Egyptians the charge normally made against the Jews. Μισοξενία has in itself a double shade of meaning: ξένος carries the sense both of "foreigner" and that of "guest". Wisdom lays weight especially on this second nuance. This was understood by the Latin version which translates 13d with *detestabiliorem inhospitalitatem instituerunt*. Thus the emphasis is laid on the Egyptians' hatred towards foreigners who are, at the same time, guests. This leads our author to think immediately of the comparison between the Egyptians and the Sodomites to which the following verse alludes.

19:14-16

Verse 14b sees the emergence of the term εὐεργέτης applied to the Hebrews. The biblical background is that of the story of Joseph as a whole, but the aim of our author in choosing this term is clearly apologetic. As already in Wis 16:2, 11, 24, εὐεργέτης and its derivatives are chosen polemically against the current use of this type of vocabulary. In the Alexandrian world, "benefactors" are the gods or else the civil authorities.[56] In describing themselves as "benefactors", the Jews are reclaiming their positive role in the society in which they are living. Here, Wisdom is reflecting a sincere intention to be integrated and to dialogue with Hellenistic culture as well as the awareness of a particular identity.

In v. 15, we also have the echo of anti-Jewish attitudes in Alexandria at the end of the first cent. BCE. Yet again, the background is the Exodus narrative, but, at the same time, the perspective is projected into the present of the Alexandrian Jews and into the future of God's eschatological judgement on the ungodly.

In 16a, there is an allusion to the positive welcome which the Egyptians gave to Israel within the story of Joseph (cf. Gen 45:17-20; 47:2-12). The Genesis text

---

53 Cf. also Philo, *Mos.* 2.254; Josephus, *A.J.* 2.343-344; Priotto, "Il confronto Egitto-Sodoma", 383-384; Vílchez Líndez, *Sapienza,* 536 n. 8; Winston, *Wisdom of Solomon,* 327.

54 Cited in Diod. Sic. 50.4 = FHG 2:392; 34.1 = FHG 3.256.

55 *CPJ* 1:135 and 1:141; cf. Winston, *Wisdom,* 327-329 and Stählin, Gustav, ξένος κτλ, *TDNT* 5:1-36. On the anti-Jewish currents in the Ptolemaic period, cf. Aziza, Claude, "L'utilisation polémique du récit de l'Exode chez les écrivains alexandrins (IVième siècle av. J.C. – Ier siècle ap. J.C.)", *ANRW* II, 20,1 (Berlin – New York 1987), 41-65; Mélèze Modrzejewski, Joseph, *Les Juifs d'Egypte de Ramses II à Hadrien* (Presses Universitaires de France: Paris 1997), 189-219.

56 Cf. Scarpat, *Sapienza,* 3:322 and Spicq, *Notes,* 1:307-314.

does not actually speak of feasts or banquets. Here, we have one of the midrashic techniques typical of our author, that of exaggeration.[57]

Wis 19:13-17 and the Civil Rights of the Jews of Alexandria

The third part of Wisdom reveals a very strong hostility to the Egyptians. It reaches a really dramatic peak in our pericope which is placed right at the end of the book. These are the Egyptians of the exodus but also the non-Jewish, Hellenistic, population of Alexandria who enjoyed full civil rights and had contributed to it. On account of the tax imposed by the Romans in 24/23 BCE, the λαογραφία (a tax aimed at a recalculation of the population, in other words, an increase in payments),[58] the Jews had lost their previous privileges and had been made equal to the native Egyptian population. It is against the latter that the great part of the book's anti-idolatrous polemic is directed.

However, in the light of the situation of the Jewish community in Alexandria at the beginning of the Roman period, it seems difficult to think that our author had in mind full civil rights, the equality of the Jews of Alexandria, pure and simple, with the Greek element of the population.[59] More probably, our author is seeking the confirmation of those rights that were bound up with the exercise of the "ancestral laws" (cf. the situation of the Jews of Berenice),[60] without forgetting the context created by the imposition of the *laographia*, which is certainly also an issue for our sage. Perhaps that is why he speaks not only of rights but of *their* rights, the rights of the same Egyptians – that is, we note once again, of the Greeks resident in Alexandria – rights which the Jews had enjoyed but which, with the institution of the *laographia*, they no longer shared. In fact, v. 16 seems to be presupposing a situation in the recent past in which the rights were recognised and shared, compared with the present situation where these rights have been infringed and the Jews are being oppressed. All that is referring to the situation created during the reign of Octavian Augustus. Our sage could certainly be thinking of that emperor's double policy. Referring to the privileges conferred by the Romans themselves on his community, our author, perhaps raising the tone a little, challenges the reduction of the Alexandrian Jews to a rabble deprived of the rights of citizenship. However, we are still far from the sad times of the emperor Caligula.

It remains to answer this question: why is this pericope precisely at the end of the book? Wisdom means to complete its rereading of the exodus with a note of great relevance, referring to the situation of the author's fellow Jews. The addressees of the book are not the Greeks of Alexandria, still less, the new Roman rulers. A pagan reader would really have understood very little. Rather, the book is directed at a Jewish community which must have known not a few internal problems. Our author puts himself clearly on the side of the "just poor ", oppressed by the ungodly (cf. Wis 2:10). We well know that, in the Jewish community of Alexandria, only the richest and most educated classes were struggling for full integration with the Greek element. Not even Philo achieved as much. However, the majority of Alexandrian Jews did not belong to the

---

57 Cf. Cheon, *Exodus Story*, 101.

58 For the *laographia*, cf. Tcherikover, *CPJ* 1:61; Smallwood, E. Mary, *The Jews under Roman Rule. From Pompeus to Diocletian* (Brill: Leiden 1976), 231.

59 Cf. Mazzinghi, "The Civil Rights", *passim*.

60 "The Jews seem in effect to have enjoyed both privileges and common rights of the kind of those usually enjoyed by many peoples who lived under Roman government": Pucci Ben Zeev; *Jewish Rights*, 481; cf. the list of rights on pp. 374-377; for Berenice, cf. Boffo, Laura, *Iscrizioni greche e latine per lo studio della Bibbia* (Brescia: Paideia 1994,) 204-216, especially, 208-209 and 209 n. 8.

upper classes.[61] Our author is an educated man, with a good knowledge of the Hellenistic cultural world, but he certainly does not line himself up with the rich and powerful who are constantly criticised in his book.

Over and against his community, our sage intends to put himself in a position between a polemical vision like that of the Third Book of the Maccabees, and the openness which will later mark Philo's thought. The attitude defended by Wisdom with regard to the problem of the rights of the Alexandrian Jews is that of a Judaism which is conscious of its own identity but which, at the same time, is seeking an amount of integration.[62]

As in the whole of the rest of the book, in this pericope too, our author never yields to the temptation to renounce his own faith. Even the Egyptians benefited from the presence of the Israelites, and if anyone hated guests and foreigners, it was they. The book of Wisdom undoubtedly tends to idealise reality: we would like to maintain our full religious identity, our sage seems to be saying, and, at the same time, to receive the recognition of common rights. For the Greeks, the Jews are hated for their privileges, as Josephus wrote, putting the words in the mouth of Apion: "why then, if they are citizens, do they not revere the same gods as the Alexandrians?" (*C. Ap.* 2.65). For Wisdom, on the other hand, it is a question of maintaining good relations with the Greeks while remaining faithful to the Jewish law. History has proved our sage wrong. Today, the problem is reproduced for believers in different but similar forms. Perhaps we could describe Wisdom's idealisation of reality as "faith".

Finally, by contrast with apocalyptic, in which eschatology appears profoundly dehistoricised, the book of Wisdom, which is more influenced by prophetic theology (above all, Isaiah 40-66), emphasises the coincidence of the historical with the eschatological moment. In this respect, our pericope is important because it offers an eschatological expansion to the theme of the historical judgement of God on Egypt recounted in 19:1-5. Inserted within chapter 19, the text of Wis 19:13-17 acquires a powerful theological value (see also below).

Wis 19:18-21 and 22: The Creation Renewed. The Book's Conclusion

18 For, among themselves, the elements were in harmony,
as on the harp certain notes change the name of the rhythm,
maintaining always the same sound.
This appeared precisely on a careful examination of what had happened:
19 for land animals were transformed into water creatures,
while those who swim walked on the earth.
20 Fire redoubled its strength in the water,

61 Cf. Tcherikover, *CPJ* 2:3-5.5; Pucci Ben Zeev, *New Perspectives on the Jewish-Greek Hostilities in Alexandria during the Reign of Emperor Caligula*, in *JST* 221 (2001): 227-235.

62 "To ask for the advantages of Greek citizenship and then to repudiate some of its obligations as incompatible with their national religion was to attempt to make the best of both worlds"; so, Smallwood, *The Jews under Roman Rule*, 14, in connection with the problem of civil rights.

while the water forgot its power to extinguish (the flames).
21 The flames, by contrast, were not able to consume
the flesh of frail animals that roamed among them,
nor could they melt what was similar to ice,
easy to melt, food of ambrosia.

22 In every way, o Lord, you have magnified your people and glorified it,
and have not neglected to come to its aid, at every time and in every place.

Notes on the Text and Translation

v. 21. The majority of witnesses read οὐδὲ τηκτόν, that is, "it (the manna) could not melt"; but that has to presuppose an ἦν or an ἐγένετο not attested by any manuscript. Ziegler, with Lat (*nec dissolvebant*), Arm, Syr, and some manuscripts, chooses to read οὐδ' ἔτηκον, "they did not dissolve / melt" (transitive), a reading adopted by many moderns which allows the retention of the parallelism with the previous verse, leaving the same subject, the "flames" (φλόγες); cf. the same verb in 16:22a, 27.

Synchronic Analysis

In rhetorical terms, these verses constitute the *anakephalaiosis*, the concluding recapitulation of the whole work. Our sage links up in particular with the diptych on the manna (16:5-15), taking on board its essential elements and emphasising the work of God who renews the creation by creating in it new relations, as in a musical composition. Thus, the theme of the cosmos, central in our sage's thought, reappears precisely at the end of the book and again confronts the readers with the theme of God's power over creation, but, this time, without the more severe aspects of the eschatological judgement. In this way, the musical allusion of v. 18 becomes the climax of a journey of praise which began in 10:20 with the song of joy for the crossing of the sea, and, after the mention of the songs of praise in 18:9, continued with the new reference to the song of the sea made a few verses later, in 19:9, praise which now involves the whole of creation.

19:18: Like a New Melody...

The difficulty caused by the musical comparison in verse 18abc has stumped the commentators for a long time.[63] Larcher notes the problem caused by the initial stich, a participial phrase without a finite verb.[64] The opening expression of the verse, διὰ ἑαυτῶν, is not to be understood in its normal sense, "by themselves"; in fact, the musical notes spoken of in the following stich do not change on their own! It is better to translate "among themselves". The verb *μεθαρμόζω signifies "change the arrangement of something", readapt; in musical contexts,

63 Cf. Larcher, *Sagesse*, 3:1082-1089.

64 For Larcher, *Sagesse*, 3:108, the text remains obscure and vague, and "cette indétermination peut résulter d'une réelle incompétence musicale chez l'auteur". Alonso Schökel comments that our author "does not appear to be too well versed in musical theory and does not seem to use the words with technical rigour"; quoted in Vílchez Líndez, *Sapienza*, 539.

transpose a melody, altering the key or else the rhythms (τοῦ ῥυθμοῦ τὸ ὄνομα διαλλάσσων).

The two following stichs introduce the musical comparison proper: the elements change their mutual relations; they exchange properties; like the notes (φθόγγοι) on the harp or some kind of stringed instrument (ψαλτήριον), they change (διαλλάσσω) the "name of the rhythm". The expression τοῦ ῥυθμοῦ τὸ ὄνομα is difficult. Our author is introducing the Greek notion of rhythm (cf. Wis 17:19), but it is not clear how the expression is joined to the verb and the rest of the stich.

The following stich creates further difficulties. The participle μένοντα refers grammatically to στοιχεῖα but logically to the musical comparison. The connection between the two terms becomes clearer if we also give στοιχεῖα a musical value. The elements of the cosmos agree among themselves like musical elements, that is, notes: they change their rhythm while retaining the same sound (μένοντα ἤχῳ).

For many authors, what our sage meant to say is simply related to a change of rhythm in the activity of the elements. They contract or expand (cf. Wis 16:24) beyond their own properties, just as, in music, the rhythm is determined by the variation in the length of the sounds. However, others think that God is being compared to a harpist who uses the same notes, that is, the elements of the creation, in a new way.[65] In any case, it is clear that, in the light of this text, the creation appears as a *renewed creation*. Our author emphasises that, while remaining themselves, the elements are interchangeable in their properties, as is seen from vv. 20-21. This is what normally happens in music with a simple change of rhythmical relations. The musical comparison transforms the exodus into a great symphonic poem which embraces the whole of creation:[66]

> "The concluding statements seem to be looking only at the positive aspect of the changes which have happened: animals which deploy their vital possibilities to the full, in water, on the earth and in the midst of fire. Fire and water are no longer in competition. Flames respect the weakness of tiny animals and light elements (manna = ice) so as to fulfil a precise plan of God. Each of these elements, however, retains its own recognisable characteristics while the new modes of operation are discernible only in relation to the other elements. What is new, therefore, is the relationship, the arrangement of the whole: in musical terms, the rhythm".[67]

The idea set out in the first three stichs arises not just from watching the things that are seen but from a penetrating reflection on what has happened, seeking to understand its profound causes (18d). This marks a return to the play on appearance and reality which we have already seen in Wisdom. The verb εἰκάζω is striking (Wis 8:8b; 9:16a; in the LXX, only in Jer 26:23 LXX [46:23 MT]). It is to be understood as "examining", scrutinising something in comparison with something else. It is linked here to the adverb ἀκριβῶς, "carefully".

---

65 Cf. the discussion of the various positions in Larcher, *Sagesse*, 3:1087-1088.

66 Cf. Alonso Schökel, *Sabiduría*, 206.

67 Pistone, "La lira e il creato", 228; cf. Passaro, "L'argomento cosmologico", 50 n. 14, for the interpretation of ῥυθμός. Scarpat proposes instead to understand ῥυθμός in the sense of "musical form"; cf. *Sapienza*, 3:304-308.

19:19-20: Some Exodus Examples

The exchange of the elements' properties is illustrated with some examples drawn from the exodus narrative. The land animals (χερσαῖα; cf. Lev 11:29 LXX with regard to the crocodileas a land animal) change (μεταβάλλω) into water creatures (ἔνυδρα*; cf. 19:10); the animals that swim (*νηκτά, a term that is rare and refined) walk instead on the earth. While this second example clearly refers to the frogs, mentioned previously in v. 10 (a similar idea appears in Philo, *Mos.* 1.103), it is more difficult to understand our author's intention in speaking of land animals which become water creatures. With many other authors, Larcher holds that the only possible explanation is to think of the Israelites themselves who – land animals as they are! – are able to cross the sea.[68]

Verse 20 refers more directly to the exchange of properties among the elements (cf. below).

19:21: The Manna, Food of Ambrosia

By contrast (*ἀνάπαλιν), the flames were not able to consume (ἐμάραναν, cf. 2:8) the flesh of animals that were frail or "easily corruptible": the adjective *εὔφθαρτος is rare, probably borrowed from Aristotle.[69] What are these animals which "roam" (ἐμπεριπατέω) among the flames? We could think, perhaps, of the locusts in the light of 16:18 where the flames could be those kindled by the Egyptians to drive them away. In this case too, however, the text remains obscure. Others think, instead, of an allusion to Dan 3:24Th which describes the three young men walking in the furnace (περιέπατουν ἐν μέσῳ τῆς φλογός). The easily corruptible flesh could then be that of human beings who do not fall into corruption thanks to the gift of the manna.

The second miraculous phenomenon clearly refers to the manna and links us directly to the fourth diptych. The structure of the third stich is very refined. So too its vocabulary: *κρυσταλλοειδής signifies "ice" and is deliberately recalling the term κρύσταλλος which is applied to the manna in 16:22a. The adjective is found only once, in Epicurus (*Epist.* 2.100); rare too is the other adjective, *εὔτηκτον, "easily melted", a technical term found in Aristotle.[70]

The manna is described as γένος ἀμβροσίας τροφῆς, with an adjective (*ἀμβρόσιος) which is *hapax* in the LXX and which refers to the Greek concept of *ambrosia*, that is, the nectar of the gods which guarantees their (physical) incorruption.[71] Talk of food links us again to the whole of chapter 16. The mention of ambrosia refers, then, to a food which guarantees eternal life to those who eat it. In this way, the end of the book brings us right back to the beginning, to 1:13-14 and, in particular, to 2:23, the plan of God for the life of the cosmos and humanity.

Our sage's last word is not an apocalyptic word of judgement but a promise of eternal life. Paraphrasing P. Beauchamp, we can state that if ever the last word of a book had weight, this is it.[72] If, in Wisdom 10-19, the exodus acquires clear

68 Larcher, *Sagesse*, 3:1089-1090.

69 Cf. *Cael.* 280b25; 305a6.

70 Cf. *De an.* 422a19; *Probl.* 865b1.

71 Cf. Dumoulin, *Entre la Manne et l'Eucharistie*, 133-136. The ancient versions paraphrase this expression with "divine food" (SyrHex); *bonam escam* (Lat); "incorruptible substance" (Arab). The term ἀμβρόσιος is to be understood in the sense of "not-mortal", that which is not part of being mortal (α-βροτοι).

72 "Le salut corporel", 509. "The argumentation of the author is brilliant"; Gilbert, "The Origins", 401.

eschatological features, here, this eschatology involves an element of the cosmos, the manna. Moreover, mention of the manna, food of incorruptibility, is a further indication that our author thinks of eternal life in terms of resurrection. In fact, the body too is involved in the life that awaits the just. Thus, the manna refers directly to the ἀφθαρσία of Wis 2:23.

19:22: The Book's Conclusion

This is the true conclusion of the whole book[73] in which our author reflects on the events he has recounted. The form is not that of a doxology but rather of a prayer in the form of a remembrance of the deeds of God in the style of the third part of Wisdom.

The verb δοξάζω occurs only three times in the book. In 8:3, it appears in the context of the *elogium* on wisdom and has the sense of "exalt". In 18:8, on the other hand, the context is similar to this one:[74] on Passover night, the glory of the Lord is manifested in the salvation of the Israelites. In both cases, δοξάζω is linked with λαός and acquires a soteriological value. In employing this verb, our author is reminding us once again of the reality of a salvation which concerns, first and foremost, "your people". The glorification is expressed through the continuous assistance of the Lord[75] "at every time and in every place". The verbs in the aorist show that the salvation awaited is already present in history. The past, the present and the future are bound together by the continuous presence of the Lord. Just as it had begun, the book ends with a note of hope. The concluding invocation, κύριε, sums up the final attitude which the author is seeking from his readers at the close of his book: do not forget the beneficial acts of God for God's people in time and space.

Diachronic Analysis

19:18

In this text, our author seems to be appealing to the Stoic doctrine of the elements (τὰ στοιχεῖα, a term present in the LXX only here, in Wis 7:18 and in 4 Macc 12:13) and to a musical comparison. In fact, of the four elements of the cosmos, he mentions only water, fire, and earth.[76]

19:19-20

In vv. 19-20, and in v. 20 in particular, the reference is to the text of Wis 16:17a, 22c-23. The reprise of the same expressions is certainly not accidental. In these verses, the use of the water/fire thematic reveals the knowledge of a cosmology that was characteristic of the period and well known in educated circles. To

---

73 Cf. the observations of Larcher in *Sagesse*, 3:1094: the author is aware of having concluded the communication of the message which he intended to pass on. Final doxologies are common in the Jewish writings of the time which, not infrequently, close with words of comfort (Winston, *Wisdom*, 333, who cites Ps 150; Sir 51:30; 3 Macc 7:23; 4 Macc 18:24; Tob^{S} 14:15; cf. Sifre Deut. 342).

74 Cf. Raurell, "The Religious Meaning", 382; in 19:22, "the author of the Book of Wisdom sees the history of Israel as the history of God who saves His people by manifesting Himself to them".

75 The expression "who does not neglect to come to its aid" is yet another, and final, *litotes*.

76 Larcher (*Sagesse*, 3:1088) observes that the sage of Alexandria does not claim to be employing the Greek doctrine of the four elements to its full extent but limits himself to retaining ordinary and common ideas to try to make the idea of a renewed creation accessible to the Greek mentality.

this we can add the concept of universal harmony, of Pythagorean provenance but well known to the post-Aristotelian schools.[77] Our author makes use of these concepts to underline the "paradox" (Wis 16:17) of water and fire which exchange their respective properties, but the whole appears here to be subject to the action of a singular and personal God who transcends the created world.[78]

A Possible Philosophical Background for Wis 19:18-21

From the time of Pythagoras, Greek thought elaborated the theory of the interchangeability of the elements. On top of this, Heraclitus, superimposed the idea of the *Logos*, rational norm and principle of becoming of the cosmos. In particular with Posidonius, Stoicism took up again a great part of the pre-Socratics' reflection – without forgetting the contributions of Plato and Aristotle – contributing to the creation of a precise vision of the world which was very diffused in educated circles.[79]

According to a widespread Stoic concept, the elements composing the universe consist of two active principles which form the world soul, fire and water, and two passive ones, earth and water (the world body). Air, water, fire and earth find their harmony precisely in the tension of opposites in a sort of *concordia discors*.[80] In the conception attributed to the Stoic philosopher, Cleanthes, "The true principles (are) god and matter. And the earth changes into water, the water into air, and the air is led upwards while the fire rotates around the earth. The soul is diffused throughout the body and we ourselves are animated to the extent that we share in it".[81]

Thus, the four elements of the cosmos can change themselves into one another because endowed with a *tonos*, a tension "of the substance of the All which never slackens", as Cleanthes claims again.[82] Thus, the cosmos exists on the basis of the principle of the harmony of opposites, by analogy with music. Death itself is nothing more than a transmutation of one element into another. From this point of view, the theory of the interchangeability of the elements and the musical analogy are a commonplace of Greek literature, frequent also in the medical sphere.

The Stoics, in particular, made use of the theory of the interchangeability of the elements to demonstrate how the gods can do everything that they want without, for this reason, violating the laws of nature. As Cicero writes:

"you are the first to repeat that the divinity can do anything whatsoever and do it without effort (...). And these affirmations of yours are not old wives' tales but physical truths supported by solid argument. In fact, the matter of reality in which everything exists and from which everything comes is able to be fashioned and changed completely since there is nothing that cannot suddenly be changed into it or come from it. However, it is divine providence which completely gives it form and harnesses it; and so this providence can do everything it wills wherever it turns its attention".[83]

---

77 Cf. Spitzer, Leo, "Classical and Christian Ideas of World Harmony", *Traditio* 2 (1944): 409-464; 3 (1945): 307-364.

78 Cf. Dumoulin, *Entre la Manne et l'Eucharistie*, 94-95.

79 Cf. Beauchamp, "Le salut corporel", 512-520; Cheon, *The Exodus Story*, 99; Passaro, "L'argomento cosmologico", a work which inspires me here; Mazzinghi, "La creazione rinnovata".

80 This expression (*discors concordia*) is found in Ovid, *Metamorphoses*, 1.430f.; Horace (*concordia discors*), *Epist.* I.12, 19; cf. Beauchamp, "Le salut corporel", 516 n. 4.

81 *SVF* I, 111 frag. 495. A not dissimilar idea is found in Philo, *de incorruptibilitate mundi*, 21.108-109; cf. Beauchamp, "Le salut corporel", 515-516.

82 *SVF* I, 111 frag. 497.

83 Cicero, *Nat. d.* 3.92; *SVF* II, 322 frag. 1107.

This philosophical principle leads Philo to reread the exodus miracles on the basis of a rationalistic explanation. We can conclude that "the miracles of the Exodus, described as a play of opposites, constituted a commonplace in Judaism".[84]

In fact, if our author shows himself aware of this kind of educated cosmology, the solution which he offers in 19:18-21 is undoubtedly original. For him, the cosmos does not exist *ad infinitum* in that continuous *concordia discors*, in a harmony of opposites typical of the Stoic conception. The creation is awaiting a renewal in which God himself will establish a new form of harmony allowing both the interchange of the elements and their mutual harmony. That will happen without anything being destroyed and will be possible only thanks to a miraculous and direct intervention of God. Both in Wis 16:24-25 and in 19:6, the use of the verb "to be at service" (ὑπηρετέω), used in connection with the cosmos, shows that, for our sage, the cosmos itself is not to be considered as an autonomous reality but precisely as a creature in the service of its Creator. Obedient to God, the creation believes that it is able to go beyond its own nature. This is the basic sense of vv. 10-12 and, in particular, of vv. 18-21, read in the light of v. 18:

"In Wis 19:18, then, in presenting the miracle of the crossing of the Red Sea as a parable for the future, the author is evoking the metamorphosis of what remains: the fire remains fire, the water remains water, the air remains air, and the earth remains earth; but, in a wonderful metamorphosis, they change their properties, their effects. These changes of function, without an alteration of the nature, do not destroy the harmony but change it. Thus, by contrast with the Stoics, from whom, however, he obtains his mode of explanation, the author of Wisdom does not reduce the miracle to a merely natural phenomenon, and affirms a continuous and total dependence of nature on God".[85]

Turning to the musical analogy of v. 18, for the world to change, there is no need for a new musical system; it is sufficient for the rhythm to be varied to attain a new harmony. Thus God does not need to destroy or replace the creation, as if it were somehow negative or evil in itself (cf., again, the programmatic text of Wis 1:12-15), but, with God's omnipotence, God is able to renew it continuously, without having to violate the laws which God himself has set:

"When, in hope, God's future, the eschatological future, is invoked, it is not necessary to repudiate the past, to divide history into periods on which to pass a judgment. Salvation is already there in the twists and turns of the past because all the history directed by almighty God, rooted in the creative act and understood as renewed creation, is already the history of salvation."[86]

In connection with this work of rereading and actualisation of the biblical texts, we can endorse the words of J.M. Reese: "his work is a practical example of how his ardent faith was able to contemplate the marvels of revelation and then use his insights as a means of integrating advances in human learning and culture into an apologia for the divine plan of salvation for mankind".[87] It is true that our author does not put Hellenistic culture on the same level as divine revelation. It is also true, however, that his constant attempt at actualisation of the latter could be fittingly described as "inculturation".

84 Beauchamp, "Le salut corporel", 521.
85 Passaro, "L'argomento cosmologico", 57.
86 Passaro, "L'argomento cosmologico", 61.
87 *Hellenistic influence*, 89; cf. Gilbert, "Inculturazione", *passim*.

Summary of Wis 19. The Theology of Chapter 19 and the Conclusion of the Book of Wisdom[88]

In Wis 19:18-21, as also throughout his work, the author makes use of typically Greek philosophical concepts to expound his thought to a public made up of Jews who were highly Hellenised. The tone of v. 18 reveals our sage's clear intention to reinterpret the exodus miracles in a rational key that was more comprehensible to his public and within a vision of the world that was typical of the educated circles of the time. As we have mentioned, he keeps in mind the Greek theory of the four elements of the cosmos:in Wis 19:13, 20-21, fire; in 19:10-12, water; in 19:10, earth; and in 19:13-17, air. According to a notion known also to Philo (cf. *Mos.* 1.143), the elements of the world are used by God now to punish, now to save.

A Biblical Background: Exodus and Creation

In addition to the philosophical background of which we have spoken, perhaps the most significant characteristic of chapter 19 is the author's capacity to use clear allusions to relate the events of the exodus to the event of the creation, in particular to Genesis 1. At the same time, references to the past become allusions to the future.

Take, for example, 19:7a, the cloud that covers the camp. The allusion to the account in Exod 14:19-20 is perhaps being combined with one to the Spirit of God hovering over the waters (Gen 1:2). Then, the dry land appears where before there was water (19:7b); cf. Exod 14:21-22 and Gen 1:9-10. A path in the sea is opened up for the Israelites and a verdant plain (19:7cd). This detail is not in Exodus but could refer to the production of the vegetables in Gen 1:11-12. Again: Wis 19:10 records that the land produced gnats: cf. Exod 8:12-15, and, in Gen 1:24, the account of the production of living beings. Wis 19:11 records the birds which recall the quails of Exod 16:13 and the birds created in Gen 1:20. The comparison between the Egyptians and the Sodomites (Wis 19:13-17) recalls the plague of darkness (Exod 10:21-23) and the creation of light which conquers the darkness at the beginning of creation (Gen 1:3-5). In this framework, vv. 18-21 close with the theme of the manna (Exodus 16) which recalls the food given by God to people at the end of the creation of the world (Gen 1:29-30). However, it is precisely the manna, at the end of the chapter, that permits us to reread the whole text in an eschatological key.

The essential point of such a process is the fact that, in composing his last chapter, our sage wished to follow a clear creational scheme while referring to the events of the exodus. At the same time, as we have noted, it is not to be forgotten that the language he uses is clearly influenced by the Greek theory of the four elements and by the medical ideas of the time. The conclusion of the chapter (19:18-21) is difficult to explain without taking account of this Hellenistic background (cf. above).

What conclusions can we draw from this distinctive way of proceeding? The link between the history of salvation (the exodus) and the eschatological salvation is represented precisely by the reference to the creation. It is, therefore, the centrality of the cosmos which reveals the profound theological unity of the book, and it is significant that the conclusion of Wis 19:21 closes by recalling the manna, an element both exodic and creational as well as being the source of incorruptibility.

---

88 Cf. Dell'Omo, "Creazione, storia della salvezza"; Gilbert, "Nouvelle création et expérience historique". Vílchez Líndez, "El libro de la Sabiduría y la teoría de la transmutación de los elementos".

> "The meaning of the cosmos is revealed: animated by the presence of the Spirit of God which is Wisdom, the cosmos seeks the life of God's friends. To contemplate it can lead to the recognition of the creator. Still more, it puts itself at God's service for punishing the guilty and saving the just. This last point is verified during the exodus, the foundational events of Israel, and it will be verified once again on the last day".[89]

For a long time, the profound link between the three parts into which the book seems to be subdivided escaped the attention of the readers of Wisdom. This has been particularly true of the relationship between the first and the third parts. From this point of view, chapter 19 acquires a fundamental importance. If we had only chapters 1-6, Wisdom's eschatology would appear somewhat vague. Moreover, if we were to add chapter 7-9, we could claim that eternal life is the reward for the one who has welcomed the gift of wisdom. However, the insertion of chapter 10, the hinge with the final part of the book (11-19), introduces the theme of history into the book in a powerful way. By contrast with the apocalyptic, in which eschatology appears profoundly dehistoricised, the book of Wisdom, more influenced in this regard by the prophetic theology (especially Isaiah 40-66), underlines the coincidence of the historical and eschatological moments. In Wisdom, therefore, there is no question of a dualistic vision of creation nor is there that sense of the imminence of judgement which is typical of apocalyptic literature.

Chapter 19 has the function of being, in its turn, a hinge between these two aspects (history and eschatology), read through the reprise of a theme common to the book as a whole, that of the cosmos. In Wis 1:13-15, our author announced his programmatic thesis: the creation is a salvific reality, and death does not form part of God's plan. On the contrary, God will make use of the creation to fight against the ungodly (5:17-20). Now, the exodus antitheses have shown that this plan of salvation takes place in reality through history: the God who creates is the same God who saves. Chapter 19 binds together both these claims through the splendid rereading in a Genesis key of the Exodus text of the crossing of the sea and the events connected with it.

Thus, we are struck by the importance of the contacts shown above with the exodus tradition and with Genesis 1: "At the moment of the exodus, the cosmos is organised in a kind of new creation to ensure life and the food of immortality to the just".[90] Chapter 19 is, therefore, replying to the question posed implicitly in the first part of the book: are the ungodly of Wisdom 2 right, perhaps, in their assertion that there is no hope beyond this life?[91] Furthermore, and on the con-

---

89 Gilbert, "Il cosmo secondo il libro della Sapienza", 199.

90 Gilbert, "La relecture de Gen 1-3" (= *La Sagesse de Salomon*), 426.

91 It is interesting to observe how chapter 19 takes up, even verbally, the objections of the ungodly in Wis 2:1-20: for them, death is only the dissolution of the body, a spark that is extinguished (cf. 2:3). In 19:20, we read that the water has lost its power to extinguish fire; fire and water are elements of the creation at God's service. In Wis 2:5b, the ungodly claim that there is no return (ἀναποδισμός) from Hades while the journey of the just through the sea is described as a path "without obstacles" (ἀνεμπόδιστος, cf. 19:7c). In Wis 2:8, the ungodly wish to celebrate the absurdity of life by crowning themselves with roses before they wither (2:8; μαραίνω), while, in 19:21, the flames do not consume (again, μαραίνω) the manna, food of incorruptibility.

trary, what is the foundation of the hope of the just which the reflection on the exodus in Wisdom 11-19 has already revealed to be well rooted in history?

The initial plan of the creator is matched in Wisdom 19 by the theme of the renewed creation. Salvation consists in bringing the world back to God's original plan. "The theme of creation thus becomes the hermeneutical criterion for showing that, although God's action is eschatological in its significance, it is carried out in history, not outside it or against it".[92] The theology of history is based on a solid theology of creation.

At this point, we must remember that, in Wisdom, the theology of creation has to take account of the role of wisdom and the spirit in the central part of the book (Wisdom 7-9): the whole cosmos will be renewed on behalf of the just because of the presence within it of the "spirit" of wisdom (cf. Wis 7:22-23; 8:1); and it is the mediatorial aspect of wisdom, bound up with God and with people precisely through the cosmos, which creates this profound link. In fact, wisdom, "mirror of the working of God" (7:26) "renews everything", "entering holy souls (...) it prepares friends of God and prophets" (7:27).

According to our sage (cf. Wisdom 10-19), history illustrates the structure of the cosmos and eschatology is part of this history. The future does not lie beyond creation or consist in denying it or transcending it but rather in meeting it in a new way. Not as the "end of the world", not even as a "new creation" which blots out the old, but – and we repeat – as a renewed creation. There is continuity between past, present and future. People are called to know how to read the presence of a personal God in the world and in history, and to live out this presence in the concrete details of their daily lives. This is the gift of wisdom that lies at the heart of the book (Wisdom 7-9).

Perhaps if we look at things from the aspect of the "why", and not so much of the "how", the book of Wisdom has still a message for our time. The big questions about the meaning of the cosmos remain the same for the people of today who certainly have a much deeper knowledge of it than our sage. For him, the attempt to understand the meaning of the universe is not necessarily a vain one. Rather, it leads to an encounter with the Creator; and it is this encounter that prevents the creation from falling headlong into dissolution and oblivion.

---

92 Passaro, "Escatologia, profezia e apocalittica", 111-112.

Bibliography[1]

1. Commentaries

ALONSO SCHÖKEL, Luis, Eclesiastes y Sabiduría, Madrid: Cristiandad 1974.

CLARCKE, Ernest George, The Wisdom of Solomon (CNEB), Cambridge: Cambridge University Press 1973.

CORNELY, Rudolph, Commentarius in Librum Sapientiae, Paris: Lethielleux 1910.

DEANE, William J., The Book of Wisdom: The Greek Text, the Latin Vulgate and the Authorised English Version, Oxford: Clarendon Press 1881.

ENGEL, Helmut, Das Buch der Weisheit (Neuer Stuttgarter Kommentar: Altes Testament 16), Stuttgart: Katholisches Biblelwerk 1998.

FELDMANN, Franz, Das Buch der Weisheit (Die Heilige Schrift des Alten Testaments 6:4) Bonn: Peter Hanstein 1926.

GEORGI, Dieter, Weisheit Salomos (Jüdische Schriften aus hellenistisch-römischen Zeit III/4) Gütersloh: Mohn, 1980.

GOODRICK, Alfred Thomas Scrope, The Book of Wisdom (The Oxford Church Biblical Commentary) London: Rivingtons 1913.

GREGG, John A.F., The Wisdom of Solomon: in the Revised Version with Introduction and Notes, Cambridge: Cambridge University Press 1909.

GRIMM, Carl L.W., Das Buch der Weisheit. Kurzgefasstes exegetisches Handbuch zu den Apokryphen des Alten Testamentes, Leipzig: S. Hirzel 1860.

HEINISCH, Paul, Das Buch der Weisheit (Exegetisches Handbuch zum Alten Testament 024), Münster in Westf.: Aschendorff 1912.

HOLMES, Samuel, The Wisdom of Solomon, in CHARLES, R.H (ed.)., Apocrypha and Pseudepigraphia of the Old Testament in English with Introductions and Critical and Explanatory Notes to the Several Books. Volume I, London: Clarendon Press 1913, 518-568.

HÜBNER, Hans, Die Weisheit Salomons (Das Alte Testament Deutsch. Apokryphen 4), Göttingen: Vandenhoeck & Ruprecht 1999.

LARCHER, Chrysostome, Le livre de la Sagesse ou la Sagesse de Salomon, I-III (Études Bibliques) Paris: Gabalda 1983-1985.

REIDER, Joseph, The Book of Wisdom, New York: Harper & Brothers 1957.

SCARPAT, Giuseppe, Il libro della Sapienza, I-III, Brescia: Paideia 1989-1999.

SCHMITT, Armin, Das Buch der Weisheit: Ein Kommentar, Würzburg: Echter 1986.

SISTI, Adalberto, Il libro della Sapienza, Assisi: Porziuncola 1992.

VÍLCHEZ LÍNDEZ, José, Sabiduría (Nueva Biblia Española, Sapienciales, V) Estella, Navarra: Verbo Divino; 1990); tr. it. Sapienza, Roma: Borla 1990.

WINSTON, David, The Wisdom of Solomon. A new Translation with Introduction and Commentary (Anchor Bible 43) New York: Doubleday 1979.

2. Secondary Literatur on the Book of Wisdom

ADINOLFI, Marco, Il messianismo di Sap 2,12-20: Atti XVIII Sett. Biblica It., Il messianismo, Queriniana: Brescia 1966, 205-217.

1 For literature on the book of Wisdom up to 1983, we commend the complete bibliography from M. Gilbert included in Ch. Larcher, Le Livre de la Sagesse, 1:11–48.

Adinolfi, Marco, Il senso dell'economia paleotestamentaria e il libro della Sapienza: Atti XX Sett. Biblica It., Dei Verbum, Queriniana: Brescia 1970, 320-342.

Adinolfi, Marco, La dicotomia antropologica e platonica e Sap 8,19-20: Cipriani, Settimio (ed.), Parola e Spirito, Brescia: Paideia 1982, 145-155.

Amir, Yehoshua, The Figure of Death in the Book of Wisdom: JJS 30 (1979) 154-178.

Backhaus, Franz J., 'Es wird schroffen Zorn zum Schwert schärfen (Weish 5,20)'. Beobachtungem zum Zorn und Grimm im Weisheitsbuch: F.-L. Hossfeld / L. Schwienhorst-Schönberger (eds.), Die Manna fällt auch heute noch. Beiträge zur Geschichte und Theologie des Alten, Ersten Testament (HBS 44), Herder: Freiburg 2004, 33-56.

Barucq, André, La gloire des justes (Sg 3,1-9), Ass. du Seigneur 96 (1967) 7-17.

Baslez, Françoise M., The Author of Wisdom and the Cultured Environment of Alexandria: Bellia, Giuseppe / Passaro, Angelo (eds.), The Book of Wisdom in Modern Research. Studies on Tradition, Redaction, Theology, Berlin – New York: De Gruyter 2005, 33-52.

Beauchamp, Paul, De libro Sapientiae Salomonis, cursus in P.I.B., Romae 1963 [handout].

Beauchamp, Paul, Le salut corporel des justes et la conclusion du livre de la Sagesse: Bib 45 (1964), 490-526.

Beauchamp, Paul, Epouser la Sagesse ou n'épouser qu'elle? Une énigme du livre de la Sagesse: Gilbert, Maurice (ed.), La Sagesse de l'Ancien Testament (BETL 51) Peeters: Leuven 1990, 347-369.

Beauchamp, Paul, Sagesse de Salomon: de l'argomentation médicale à la resurrection: Trublet, Jacques (ed.), La sagesse biblique, Paris: Cerf 1995, 175-186.

Beauchamp, Paul, La cosmologie religieuse de Philon et la lecture de l'Exode par le livre de la Sagesse: le thème de la manne: Arnaldez, Roger (ed.), Philon d'Alexandrie, Paris: Éditions du Centre National de la Recherche Scientifique (CNRS) 1967, 207-219.

Beentjes, Pancratius C., Wisdom of Solomon 3,1-4,19 and the Book of Isaiah: Beuken, Wilelm A.M. (ed.), Studies in the Book of Isaiah, Peeters: Leuven 1997, 413-420.

Beentjies, P.C., 'You Have Given a Road in the Sea': What Is Wisdom 14,3 Talking About?, ETL 68 (1992) 137-141.

Bellia, Giuseppe / Passaro, Angelo (eds.), The Book of Wisdom in modern Research. Studies on Tradition, Redaction, Theology, Berlin – New York: De Gruyter 2005.

Berruto, Anna Maria, Σοφία Σαλωμῶνος. Sapienza di Salomone: P. Sacchi – C. Martone (eds.), La Bibbia dei Settanta. III. Libri poetici, Morcelliana, Brescia 2013, 861-952.

Bizzeti, Paolo, Il libro della Sapienza. Struttura e genere letterario, Bologna: Dehoniane 1984.

Blischke, Mareike V., Die Eschatologie in der Sapientia Salomonis (FAT 2.26), Tübingen: Mohr Siebeck, 2007.

Blomqvist, Jerker, Interpretational problems in the Wisdom of Solomon, Classica et Mediaevalia 35 (1985) 87-114.

Bogaert P.M., Kurios, le nom incommunicable (Sg 14,21), in Calduch-Benages /Vermeylen, (eds.), Treasures of Wisdom, 387-394.

Bons, Eberhard, Conception, grossesse, naissance – Sagesse de Salomon 7,1-2 et son arrière-fond littéraire: Lehmann, Yves (ed.), Aristoteles Romanus. La réception de la science aristotélicienne dans l'Empire gréco-romain, Turhout: Brepols 2013, 71-83.

Bretón, Santiago, ¿Libro de la Sabiduría o libro de la justicia? El tema de la justicia en la interpretación del libro de la Sabiduría, Cuadernos Biblicos 1 (1978) 77-104.

Burrows, Eric, Wisdom X 10, Bib 20 (1939) 405-407.

Busto Saiz, José R., La intención del midrás del libro de la Sabiduría sobre el Exodo: Díez Macho Alejandro (ed.), Salvación en la Palabra, Madrid: Cristiandad, 1986, 65-77.

Busto Saíz, José R., The meaning of Wisdom 2,9a: Cox, Claude E. (ed.), VII Congress of the International Organization for Septuagint and Cognate Studies, Atlanta, Georgia: Scholars Press, 1991, 355-359.

Cabanis, Allen, Wisdom 18:14f: an Early Christmas Text, VC 10 (1956) 97-102.

Calduch Benages, Nuria / Vermeylen, Jacques (eds.), Treasures of Wisdom. Studies in Ben Sira and the Book of Wisdom. FS Maurice Gilbert (BETL 143), Leuven: Peeters 1999.

Calduch-Benages, Nuria (ed.), Wisdom for Life, FS Maurice Gilbert, Berlin / Boston: De Gruyter, 2014.

Camps, Guiu M., Midras sobre la història de les plagues: Díaz Carbonell (ed.), Miscellanea Biblica, Barcelone: Monasterii B.V.M. Montisserrati 1953, 97-113.

Cavedo, Romeo, Da una cultura all'altra: il libro della Sapienza, Parola, Spirito e Vita 15 (1987) 75-87.

Cheon, Samuel, The Exodus Story in the Wisdom of Solomon. A Study in the Biblical Interpretation, Journal for the Study of the Pseudepigrapha Supp. S. 23, Sheffield: Sheffield Academic Press 1997.

Cheon, Samuel, Anonimity in the Wisdom of Solomon, JSP 18 (1998) 111-119.

Cheon, Samuel, Three Characters in the Wisdom of Solomon 3-4, JSP 12 (2001) 105-113.

Clark, Dave K, Signs in Wisdom and John, CBQ 45 (1983) 201-209.

Clifford, Richard J., Proverbs as a source for the book of Wisdom: Calduch Benages / Vermeylen (eds.), Treasures of Wisdom, 256-263.

Collins, John J., Cosmos and Salvation: Jewish Wisdom and Apocalyptic in the Hellenistic Age, HR 17 (1977) 121-142.

Collins, John J., Jewish Wisdom in the Hellenistic Age, Louisville (KY): Westminster John Knox 1997.

Collins, John J., Apocalyptic Eschatology in Philosophical Dress in the Wisdom of Solomon: Kugel, James L. (ed.), Shem in the Tents of Japhet: Essays on the Encounter of Judaism and Hellenism, Leiden: Brill, 2002, 93-107.

Collins, John J., The Mysteries of God. Creation and Eschatology in 4Q Instruction and the Wisdom of Solomon: García Martínez, Florentino (ed.), Wisdom and Apocalypticism in the Dead Sea Scrolls and in the Biblical Tradition (BETL 168), Leuven: Peeters 2003, 287-307.

Collins, John J., The Reinterpretation of Apocalyptic Traditions in the Wisdom of Solomon: Bellia / Passaro (eds.), The Book of Wisdom, 143-158.

Colombo, Dalmazio, Πνευμα Σοφιας ejusque actio in mundo in libro Sapientiae, Studii Biblici Franciscani Liber Annuus 1 (1950) 107-160.

Colzani, Gianni, Il popolo di Dio fra tradizione giudaica e cultura greca: Ravasi, Gianfranco / Colzani, Gianni / Angelini, Giuseppe / Verga, Leonardo / Pozzoli, Luigi, Fede e cultura dal libro della Sapienza, Bologna: Dehoniane 1987, 35-54.

Conti, Marco, L'umanesimo ateo nel libro della Sapienza, Anton 49 (1974) 423-447.

Cox, Dermot, The new Writers. Wisdom's Response to a Changing Society, Studia Missionalia 42 (1993) 1-15.

D'Alario, Vittoria, La réflexion sur le sens de la vie en Sg 1-5. Une réponse aux questions de Job et de Qohélet: Calduch Benages / Vermeylen (eds.), Treasures of Wisdom, 313-330.

Dalla Corte, Ernesto, Il Dio vivente, Dio dei viventi. L'immortalità nel libro della Sapienza, Napoli: Pontificia Facoltà di Teologia 2003.

Dalla Corte, Ernesto, L'ἀφθαρσία nel libro della Sapienza. Analisi letteraria e semantica: Marcheselli-Casale, Cesare (ed.), Oltre il racconto. Esegesi ed ermeneutica alla ricerca del senso, Napoli: D'Auria 1994, 69-92.

Deane, William J., The Identification of the Serpent with Satan in the Book of Wisdom, The Expositor 2/6 (1883) 54-61.

De Carlo, Giuseppe, Ami, infatti, gli esistenti tutti. Studio di Sap 11,24, Laurentianum 36 (1995) 391-432.

De Bruyne, Donatien, Etude sur le texte latin de Sagesse, RBén 41 (1929) 100-133.

Dell'Omo, Mariano, Creazione, storia della salvezza e destino dell'uomo. Il significato e l'attualità spirituale del capitolo 19 della Sapienza, RivBib 37 (1989) 317-327.

Des Places, Edouard, Un emprunt de la Sagesse (11,10-21) aux Lois de Platon?, Bib 40 (1959) 1016-1017.

Des Places, Edouard, Epithétes et attributes de la "Sagesse" (Sg 7,22-23 et SVF I 557 Arnim), Bib 57 (1976) 414-419.

Di Lella, Alexander, Conservative and Progressive Theology: Sirach and Wisdom, CBQ 28 (1966) 139-154.

Dodson, Joseph R., Locked-Out Lovers. Wisdom of Solomon 1,16 in Light of the Paraklausithyron Motif, JSPE 17 (2007) 21-35.

Dodson, Joseph R., The "Powers" of Personification. Rhetorical Purpose in the Book of Wisdom and the Letter to the Romans (BZNW 161), Berlin-New York: De Gruyter 2008.

Dubarle, André-Marie, La tentation diabolique dans le Livre de la Sagesse (2,24): Mélanges Eugéne Tisserant, I (Studi e Testi, CCXXXI), Città del Vaticano: Biblioteca Apostolica Vaticana 1964, 187-195.

Dumoulin, Pierre, Entre la Manne et l'Eucharistie. Étude de Sg 16,15-17,1a (AnBib 132), Rom: Pontificio Istituto Biblico 1994.

Dupont – Sommer, André, Les "impies" du Livre de la Sagesse sont-ils des Epicuriens?, RHR CXI (1935) 90-112.

Engel, Helmut, Wem nimmt unrechtes Denken und Reden das Leben? Zur Deutung von Weish 1,11d: Hentschel, Georg / Zenger, Erich (eds.), Lehrerin der Gerechtigkeit, 62-66.

Engel, Helmut, "Was Weisheit ist und wie entstand, will ich verkünden". Weish 7,22-8,1 innerhalb des ἐγκώμιον τῆς σοφίας (6,22-11,1) als Stärkung der Plausibilität des Judentums angesichts hellenistischer Philosophie und Religiosität: Hentschel, Georg / Zenger, Erich (eds.), Lehrerin der Gerechtigkeit, 67-102.

Engel, Helmut, Weisheit Salomos: http://www.bibelwissenschaft.de/stichwort/12141 (2005)

Engel, Helmut, Sophia Salomonos / Sapientia Salomonis / Die Weisheit Salomos: Karrer Martin / Kraus Wolfgang (eds.), Septuaginta Deutsch. Erläuterungen und Kommentare zum griechischen Alten Testament, II, Stuttgart: Deutsche Bibelgesellschaft 2011, 2126-2157.

Engel, Helmut, Die Sapientia Salomonis als Buch. Die gedankliche Einheit im Buch der Weisheit: Kreuzer, Siegfried / Meiser, Martin / Sigmund, Marcus (eds.), Die Septuaginta – Entstehung, Sprache, Geschichte. 3. Internationale Fachtagung veranstaltet von Septuaginta Deutsch (LXX.D), Wuppertal 22.-25. Juli 2010, (WUNT 286), Tübingen: Mohr Siebeck 2012, 135-143.

Enns, Peter, Exodus Retold. Ancient Exegesis of the Departure from Egypt in Wis 10:15-21 and 19,1-9, Harvard Semitic Museum Monograph 57, Atlanta (GA): Scholar Press 1997.

Fabbri, Marco V., Creazione e salvezza nel libro della Sapienza. Esegesi di Sap 1,13-15 (Studi di Teologia 6), Rom: Armando 1998.

Fabbri, Marco V., Incorruttibilità e salvezza corporale. Il significato del termine ἀφθαρσία in Sap 2,23, Annales Theologici 24 (2010) 293-326.

Feldmann, Franz, Textkritische Materialien zum Buch der Weisheit gesammelt aus der sahidischen, syrohexaplarischen und armenischen Übersetzung, Freiburg im Brisgau: Herder 1902.

Festorazzi, Franco, La dimensione salvifica del binomio morte-vita (Qohelet e Sapienza), RivBiblt 30 (1982) 91-109.

Fichtner, Johannes, Die Stellung der Sapientia Salomonis in der Literatur- und Geistesgeschichte ihrer Zeit, ZNW 36 (1937) 113-132.

Fichtner, Johannes, Der AT-Text der Sapientia Salomonis, ZAW 57 (1939) 155-192.

Finan, Thomas, Hellenistic humanism in the Book of Wisdom, IThQ 27 (1960) 30-48.

Focke, Friedrich, Die Entstehung der Weisheit Salomos, Göttingen: Vandenhoeck & Ruprecht 1913.

Fornara, Roberto, Lo Spirito del Signore riempie l'universo (Sapienza 1,7): Calabrese, Gianfranco (ed.), Lo Spirito Santo teologo del popolo di Dio, Casale Monferrato (AL): Piemme 1997, 17-32.

GÄRTNER, Eugen, Komposition und Wortwahl des Buches der Weisheit, Berlin: Mayer & Müller 1912.

GAVENTA, Roberts Beverly, The Rhetoric of Death in the Wisdom of Solmon and the Letters of Paul: HOGLUND, Kenneth G. / HUWILER, Elizabeth F. / GLASS, Jonathan T. / LEE, Roger W. / MURPHY, Roland Edmund, The Listening Heart: Essays in Wisdom and the Psalms in honor of Roland E. Murphy (JSOT Supp. s. 58), Sheffield, JSOT Press 1987, 127-145.

GENZMER, Erich, Pondere, numero, mensura, RIDA 1 (1952) 469-494.

GEORGI, Dieter, Interpretation of Scriptures in Wisdom of Solomon: LICHTENBERGER, Hermann / OEGEMA, Gerbern S. (eds.), Jüdische Schriften in ihrem antik-jüdischen und urchristlichen Kontext, Gütersloh: Gütersloher Verlagshaus, 2002, 304-332.

GIGNAC, Alain, Quel sens donner à la morte prématurée du juste? La pédagogie éthique d'un texte biblique (Sg 4,7-20), EeT 27 (1996) 199-227.

GILBERT, Maurice, La structure de la prière de Salomon, Bib 51 (1970) 301-333 [= GILBERT, La Sagesse de Salomon, 167-202].

GILBERT, Maurice, Volonté de Dieu et don de la Sagesse, NRT 93 (1971) 145-164 [= GILBERT, La Sagesse de Salomon, 203-230].

GILBERT, Maurice, La critique des dieux dans le livre de la Sagesse (Sg 13-15), AnBib 53, Rom: Pontificio Istituto Biblico 1973.

GILBERT, Maurice, La conjecture μετριώτητι en Sg 12,22a, Bib 57 (1975) 550-553 [= GILBERT, La Sagesse de Salomon, 255-260].

GILBERT, Maurice, La connaissance de Dieu selon le Livre de la Sagesse: COPPENS, Joseph (ed.), La notion biblique de Dieu. Le Dieu de la Bible et le Dieu des philosophes, Leuven: University Press 1976, 191-210 [= GILBERT, La Sagesse de Salomon, 331-336].

GILBERT, Maurice (ed.), La Sagesse de l'Ancien Testament (BETL 51), Gembloux-Leuven: Peeters 1979.

GILBERT, Maurice, Spirito, Sapienza e Legge secondo Ben Sira e il libro della Sapienza, PSV 4 (1981) 65-73.

GILBERT, Maurice, Les raisons de la modération divine (Sagesse 11,21-12,2): CACQUOT, André (ed.), Mélanges bibliques et orientaux en l'honneur de M. Henri Cazelles (AOAT 212), Neukirchen-Vluyn: Neukirchener Vrl. 1981, 149-162 [= GILBERT, La Sagesse de Salomon, 241-255].

GILBERT, Maurice, Il cosmo secondo il libro della Sapienza: DE GENNARO, Giuseppe, Il cosmo nella Bibbia, Napoli: Dehoniane 1982, 189-199.

GILBERT, Maurice, La filantropia di Dio. Esegesi di Sap 11,15-12,27, Rom 1982-1983; dispense ad uso degli studenti del Pontificio Istituto Biblico.

GILBERT, Maurice, L'adresse à Dieu dans l'anamnèse hymnique de l'Exode (Sg 10-19): COLLADO BERTOMEU, Vicente / ZURRO RODRIGUEZ, Eduardo (eds.), El misterio de la Palabra. Homenaje de sus alumnos al Profesor D. Luis Alonso Schökel, Valencia – Madrid: Cristiandad 1983, 207-235 [= GILBERT, La Sagesse de Salomon, 277-300].

GILBERT, Maurice, La figure de Salomon en Sg 7-9: KUNTZMANN, Raymond / SCHLOSSER, Jacques (eds.), Etudes sur le judaïsme hellénistique: Congrés de Strasbourg (1983) (LeDiv 119), Paris: Cerf 1984, 335-349 [= GILBERT, La Sagesse de Salomon, 141-166].

GILBERT, Maurice, Il giusto perseguitato di Sap 2,12-20: figura messianica: DE GENNARO, Giuseppe (ed.), L'Antico Testamento interpretato dal Nuovo. Il Messia, Dehoniane: Napoli 1985, 193-215 [= Le juste persecuté de Sg 2,12-20: figure messianique: GILBERT, La Sagesse de Salomon, 65-88].

GILBERT, Maurice, "On est puni par où l'on pêche" (Sg 11,16): CACQUOT, André (ed.), Mélanges bibliques et orientaux en l'honneur de M. Mathias Delcor, AOAT 215, Münster: Butzon & Bercke 1985, 183-191 [= GILBERT, La Sagesse de Salomon, 231-241].

GILBERT, Maurice, L'Esprit Saint dans le livre de la Sagesse (ou Sagesse de Salomon), DBS XI, Paris: Letouzey & Ané 1986, 153-156.

Gilbert, Maurice, Sagesse de Salomon (ou le Livre de la Sagesse), DBS XI, Paris: Letouzey et Ané 1986, 58-119.

Gilbert, Maurice, La relecture de Genèse 1 à 3 dans le livre de la Sagesse: Derousseaux, Louis (ed.), La Création dans l'Orient Ancien; Congrès de l'ACFEB, Lille 1985 (LeDiv 127), Paris: Cerf 1987, 323-344 [= Gilbert, La Sagesse de Salomon, 405-431].

Gilbert, Maurice, La procréation: ce qu'en sait le livre de la Sagesse, NRT 111 (1989) 824-841 [= Gilbert, La Sagesse de Salomon, 337-356].

Gilbert, Maurice, Inculturazione: Id., La sapienza di Salomone, 2, ADP: Rom 1995, 9-22.

Gilbert, Maurice, The last pages of the Wisdom of Solomon, Proceedings of the Irish Biblical Association, 20 (1997) 48-61.

Gilbert, Maurice, Nouvelle création et expérience historique, in Id., Il a parlé pour les prophètes. Thèmes et figures bibliques, Bruxelles: Lessius 1998, 215-229.

Gilbert, Maurice, La Sagesse de Salomon et l'hellénisme, Hieros 4 (1999) 11-22 [= Gilbert, La Sagesse de Salomon, 27-45].

Gilbert, Maurice, La donna forte di Pr 31,10-31: ritratto o simbolo?: Bellia, Giuseppe / Passaro, Angelo (eds.), Il libro dei Proverbi. Tradizione, redazione, teologia, Piemme: Casale Monferrato (AL) 1999, 147-167.

Gilbert, Maurice, Wisdom of Solomon and Scripture: Sæbø, Magne (ed.), Hebrew Bible / Old Testament, The History of Its Interpretation, Volume I, From the Beginnings to the Middle Ages (Until 1300), Göttingen: Vandenhoeck & Ruprecht 2000, 606-617 [Gilbert, La Sagesse de Salomon, 45-64].

Gilbert, Maurice, Immortalité?, résurrection?, faut-il choisir?: témoignage du judaïsme ancien: Abadie, Philippe (ed.)., Le judaïsme à l'aube de l'ère chrétienne (LDiv 186), Paris: Cerf 2001, 271-297.

Gilbert, Maurice, Sagesse 3,7-9; 5,15-23 et l'apocalyptique: García Martínez, Florentino (ed.), Wisdom and Apocalypticism in the Dead Sea Scrolls and the Biblical Tradition (BETL 168), Leuven: Peeters, 2003, 307-322 [= Gilbert, La Sagesse de Salomon, 89-108].

Gilbert, Maurice, The Literary Structure of the Book of Wisdom. A Study of Various Views: Bellia - Passaro (eds.), The Book of Wisdom in Modern Research, 18-32 [= Gilbert, La Sagesse de Salomon, 9-27].

Gilbert, Maurice, "La vostra sovranità viene dal Signore (Sap 6,3)": ambivalenza del potere politico nella tradizione sapienziale: Manicardi, Ermenegildo / Mazzinghi, Luca (eds.), Il potere politico: bisogno e rifiuto dell'autorità, Atti della XXXVIII Settimana Biblica Nazionale (Roma, 6-10 settembre 2004), RicStoBib 18 (2006) 117-132 [= Your sovereignity comes from the Lord. Wis 6,4: Gilbert, La Sagesse de Salomon, 121-140].

Gilbert, Maurice, The Origins According to the Wisdom of Solomon: Calduch-Benages, Nuria – Liesen, Jan (eds.), History and Identity. How Israel's Latter Authors Viewed Its Earlier History (DCLY 2006), Berlin – New York: De Gruyter 2006, 171-185 [= Gilbert, La Sagesse de Salomon, 385-402].

Gilbert, Maurice, La Sagesse de Salomon – The Wisdom of Solomon. Recueil d'études – Collected Essays, Rome: GBP 2011.

Gilbert, Maurice, The Review of History in Ben Sira 44-50 and Wisdom 10-19: Corley, Jeremy – Van Grol, Harm (eds.), Rewriting Biblical History, FS P.C. Beentjies (DCLS 7), Berlin-New York: De Gruyter 2011, 319-334.

Gilbert, Maurice, The Fate of Impious and of their Families: Passaro, Angelo (ed.), Family and Kinship in Deuterocanonical and Cognate Literature. Yearbook 2012/2013, Berlin – Boston: De Gruyter 2013, 221-228.

Gill, David The Greek sources of Wisdom XII,3-7, VT 15 (1965) 383-386.

Gimenez Gonzales, Agustin, "Si el justo es hijo de dios, le soccorrerá" (Sab 2,18). Acercamiento canónico a la filiación divina del justo perseguido en Sab 1-6, Estella (Navarra): Verbo Divino 2009.

GLICKSMAN, Andrew T., Wisdom of Solomon 10. A Jewish Hellenistic Reinterpretation of Early Israelite History trough Sapiential Lenses, Berlin-Boston: De Gruyter 2011.

GLICKSMAN, Andrew T., "Set your desire on my words": authoritative traditions in the Wisdom of Solomon: KALIMI, Isaac / NICKLAS, Tobias / XERAVITS, Géza G., in collaboration with Heike HÖTZINGER (eds.), Scriptural authority in early Judaism and ancient Christianity, Berlin - Boston (Mass.): De Gruyter, 2013, 167-184.

GÖRG, Manfred, Die Religionskritik in Weish 13,1f: H. HÜBNER (ed.), Die Weisheit Salomos im Horizont Biblischer Theologie, 13-25.

GRABBE, Lester, Wisdom of Solomon, Sheffield: Sheffield Academic Press 1997.

GRABBE, Lester L., Intertextual connections between the Wisdom of Solomon and Qoheleth: DELL, Katharine / KYNES, Will (eds.), Reading Ecclesiastes intertextually, London - New York - New Delhi [etc.]: Bloomsbury, 2014, [201]-213.

GRANT, Robert McQueen, The Book of Wisdom at Alexandria: Reflections on the History of the Canon and Theology: CROSS, Frank Leslie (ed.), Studia Patristica, VII, Berlin: Akademie Verlag 1966, 462-472.

GREGG, John Allen Fitzgerald, The Identification of the Serpent with Satan in the Book of Wisdom, The International Journal of Apocrypha VI (1910) 77-78.

GRELOT, Pierre, Sagesse 10,21 et le Targum de l'Exode, Bib 42 (1961) 49-60.

GRELOT, Pierre, L'eschatologie de la Sagesse et les Apocalypses juives: ID., De la Mort à la résurrection. Etudes de théologie biblique (LeDiv 67), Cerf: Paris 1971, 187-199.

GRIBOMONT, Jean, L'édition Vaticane de la Vulgate et la Sagesse de Salomon dans sa recension italienne, RivStLetRel 4 (1968) 472-496.

HAAG, Ernst, "Die Weisheit ist nur eine und vermag doch alles". Weisheit und Heilsgeschichte nach Weish 11-12: HENTSCHEL, Georg / ZENGER, Erich (eds.), Lehrerin der Gerechtigkeit, 103-155.

HARL, Marguerite, A propos d'un passage du Contre Eunome de Grégoire de Nysse: απορροια et les titres du Christ en théologie trinitaire, RSR 55 (1967) 217-226.

HARRINGTON, Daniel J., "Saved by wisdom" (Wis. 9,18): soteriology in the Wisdom of Solomon: GURTNER, Daniel M. (ed.), This world and the world to come: soteriology in early Judaism, New York - London: T & T Clark, 2011, 181-190.

HAYMAN, A. Peter, The Survival of Mythology in the Wisdom of Solomon, JSJ 30 (1999) 125-139.

HEINEMANN, Joseph, Synkrisis oder äußere Analogie in der "Weisheit Salomos", TZ 4 (1948) 241-251.

HEINISCH, Paul, Das jüngste Gericht im Buche der Weisheit, TGl 2 (1910) 89-106.

HENTSCHEL, Georg / ZENGER, Erich (eds.), Lehrerin der Gerechtigkheit (EthS 19), Leipzig: Benno 1991.

HORBURY, William, The Wisdom of Solomon in the Muratorian Fragment, JTS 45 (1994) 149-159.

HORBURY, Wiiliam, The Christian Use and the Jewish Origins of Wisdom of Solomon: DAY, John / WILLIAMSON, Hugh Godfrey M, / GORDON, Robert P. (eds.), Wisdom in Ancient Israel. Essays in Honour of John A. Emerton, Cambridge: University Press 1995, 182-196.

HÜBNER, Hans, Zur Ethik der Sapientia Salomonis: SCHRAGE, Wolfang (ed.), Studien zum Text und zur Ethik des Neuen Testaments, Festschrift zum 80. Geburtstag von Heinrich Greeven (BZNW 47), Berlin-New York: De Gruyter 1986, 166-187.

HÜBNER Hans (ed.), Die Weisheit Salomos im Horizont Biblischer Theologie; BThSt 22, Neukirchen-Vluyn: Neukirchener Verlag, 1993.

JAUBERT, Annie, Echo du livre de la Sagesse en Barnabé 7,9, Recherches de Science Religieuse 60 (1972) 193-198.

HÜBNER, Hans, Die Sapientia Salomonis und die antike Philosophie: ID., Die Weisheit Salomos, 55-81.

Keller, Carl A., Glaube in der "Weisheit Salomos": Stoebe, Hans-Joachim (ed.), Wort – Gebot – Glaube, Beiträge zur Theologie des Alten Testaments Fs W. Eichrodt, ATANT 59, Zürich: Zwingli-Verlag 1970, 11-20.

Kepper, Martina, Hellenistische Bildung im Buch der Weisheit (BZAW 280) Berlin – New York: De Gruyter 1999.

Keyser, Paul-Gerhard, Sapientia Salomonis und Paulus: eine Analyse der Sapientia Salomonis und ein Vergleich ihrer theologischen und anthropologischen Probleme mit denen des Paulus im Römerbrief, Halle: [Diss.] 1971.

Kloppenborg, Verbin Johan S., Isis and Sophia in the Book of Wisdom, HTR 75 (1982) 57-84.

Koch, Stefan, Zur literarischen Bedeutung der Sapientia Salomonis im Neuen Testament: Tigchelaar, Eibert (ed.), Old Testament pseudepigrapha and the Scriptures, Leuven - Paris - Walpole (Mass.): Peeters, 2014, 183-194.

Kolarcik, Michael, The Ambiguity of Death in the Book of Wisdom 1-6. A study of literary structure and interpretation (AnBib 127), Rom: Pontificio Istituto Biblico 1991.

Kolarcik, Michael, Creation and Salvation in the Book of Wisdom: Clifford Richard J. / Collins John J. (eds.), Creation in the Biblical Tradition (CBQ Mon. Ser. 24), Washington: Catholic Biblical Association of America 1992, 97-107.

Kolarcik, Michael, Universalism and Justice in the Wisdom of Solomon: Calduch Benages / Vermeylen (eds.), Treasure of Wisdom, 289-302.

Kolarcik, Michael, The Sage behind the Wisdom of Solomon: Perdue, Leo G., (ed.), Scribes, Sages, Seers. The Sage in the Eastern Mediterranean World (FRLANT 219), Göttingen: Vandenhoeck & Ruprecht 2008, 189-217.

Kraus Reggiani, Clara, Il sorite di Sap 6,17-20: Vivian, Angelo (ed.), Biblische und judaistische Studien, FS Paolo Sacchi (Judentum und Umwelt 29) Frankfurt a.M – Bern – New York – Paris: Peter Lang 1990, 135-142.

Kuhn, Gottfried, Beiträge zur Erklärung des Buches der Weisheit. Die Beziehungen von Sap. Kap. XI-XIX zum Schema der Apokalyptik, ZNW 28 (1929) 334-338.

Kurzewitz, Christian, Weisheit und Tod. Die Ätiologie des Todes in der Sapientia Salomonis, (TANZ 50), Tübingen: Franck 2009.

Kutsch E., "Du sollst dir kein Gottesbild machen". Zu Weisheit Salomos 14,15: Hausmann, Jutta / Zobel Hans-Jürgen (eds.), Alttestamentlicher Glaube und Biblische Theologie: Festschrift für Horst Dietrich Preuss zum 65. Geburtstag, Stuttgart – Berlin – Köln: Kohlhammer 1992, 279-286.

La Bonnardière, Anne-Marie, Biblia augustiniana. A.T., Le livre de la Sagesse, Paris: Etudes Augustiniennes 1970.

La Bonnardière, Anne-Marie, Le livre de la Sagesse dans l'oeuvre de Saint Augustin, Rev. Et. August. 17 (1971) 171-175.

La Bonnardière, Anne-Marie, Le 'juste' défiée par les impies (Sap 2,12-21) dans la tradition patristique africaine: Benoît, André (ed.), La Bible et les Pères, Colloque de Strasbourg 1969, Paris: Presses Universitaires de France 1971, 161-186.

Lacoste, Nathalie, Solomon, the Exemplary Sage. Convergence of Hellenistic and Jewish Traditions in the Wisdom of Solomon, Journal of Jewish Thought 2013, http://cjs.utoronto.ca/tjjt/node/18#_ftn60.

Lagrange, Joseph-Marie, Le livre de la Sagesse: sa doctrine des fines dernières, RB 4 (1907) 85-104.

Larcher, Chrysostome, Etudes sur le livre de la Sagesse, Paris: Gabalda 1969.

Léonas, Alexis, The Poetics of Wisdom. Language and Style in the Book of Wisdom: Bons, Eberhard / Kraus, Thomas J. (eds.), Et sapienter et eloquenter. Studies on Rhetorical and Stylistic Features of the Septuagint (FRLANT 241) Göttingen: Vandenhoeck & Ruprecht 2011, 99-126.

LEPROUX, Alexis, Un discours de sagesse. Etude éxègetique de Sg 7-8 (AnBib 167), Rom: Pontificio Istituto Biblico, 2007.

LEPROUX, Alexis, Moïse, "conseiller de salut" en Sg 16,6? Une question de critique textuelle, RB 111 (2004) 161-192.

LEPROUX, Alexis, L'ἐπιεικεία divine ou la mesrue du jugement selon Sg 11,15-12,27: CALDUCH-BENAGES, Nuria (ed.), Wisdom for Life, FS Maurice Gilbert, Berlin / Boston: De Gruyter, 2014, 250-259.

LEPROUX, Alexis, La pieté du patriarche Jacob selon Sg 10,10-12, Bib 99 (2018) 189-201.

LINEBAUGH, Jonathan A., God, grace, and righteousness in Wisdom of Solomon and Paul's Letter to the Romans: texts in conversation, Leiden - Boston (MA): Brill, 2013.

LOADER, William, Wisdom of Solomon: ID.; The Pseudepigrapha on Sexuality, Gand Rapids (MI) - Cambridge (UK): Eerdmans, 398-426.

LUCIANI, Ferdinando, Il significato del verbo τελέω in Sap 4,16, BibOr 20 (1978) 183-188.

LYONNET, Stanislas, Le sens de ΠΕΙΡΑΖΕΙΝ en Sap 2,24 et la doctrine du péché originel, Biblica 39 (1958) 27-36.

MANESCHG, Hans, Die Erzählung von der ehernen Schlange (Num 21,4-9) in der Auslegung der frühen jüdischen Literatur: Eine traditionsgeschichtliche Studie, Bern: Peter Lang 1981.

MANESCHG, Hans, Gott. Erzieher, Retter und Heiland seines Volkes. Zur Interpretation von Num 21,4-9 in Weisheit 16,5-15, BZ 28 (1984) 214-229.

MARTIN HOGAN, Karina, The Exegetical Background of the "Ambiguity of Death" in the Wisdom of Solomon, JSJ 30 (1998) 1-24.

MATTIOLI, Anselmo, Felicità e virtù. La dottrina della Sapienza nel brano macarico per le sterili e gli eunuchi (Sap 3,13-4,6): REALI, Venanzio (ed.), Gesù Apostolo e Sommo Sacerdote. Studi biblici in memoria di P. Teodorico Ballarini, Casale Monferrato (AL): Marietti 1983, 23-49.

MAZZINGHI, Luca, Notte di paura e di luce. Esegesi di Sap 17,1-18,4 (AnBib 134), Rom: Pontificio Istituto Biblico 1995.

MAZZINGHI, Luca, "Non c'è regno dell'Ade sulla terra". L'inferno alla luce di alcuni testi del libro della Sapienza, VivHo 6/2 (1995) 229-256.

MAZZINGHI, Luca, "Dio non ha creato la morte" (Sap 1,13). Il tema della morte alla luce del libro della Sapienza, PSV 32 (1995) 62-75.

MAZZINGHI, Luca, "Un improvviso ed inatteso timore si era riversato su di loro". La paura dei malvagi in Sap 17, PSV 34 (1996) 81-92.

MAZZINGHI, Luca, Il giusto oppresso perché scomodo (Sap 2,10-20), PSV 34 (1996) 97-112.

MAZZINGHI, Luca, La barca della provvidenza: Sap 14,1-10 e la figura di Iside: MAZZINGHI, Luca / TAROCCHI, Stefano (eds.), Ecco l'uomo. Studi in memoria di Mons. Valerio Mannucci, VivHo 8/1 (1997) 61-90.

MAZZINGHI, Luca, Il cosmo nel libro della Sapienza: BONORA, Antonio / PRIOTTO, Michelangelo (eds.), Libri sapienziali ed altri scritti (Logos 4), Leumann (TO): ElleDiCi 1997, 381-398.

MAZZINGHI, Luca, Il libro della Sapienza: elementi culturali: FABRIS, Rinaldo (ed.), Il confronto tra le diverse culture nella Bibbia da Esdra a Paolo, XXXIV Settimana Biblica Nazionale, RStoBib 10/1-2 (1998) 179-197.

MAZZINGHI, Luca, La sapienza è uno spirito che ama l'uomo (cf. Sap 1,6 e 7,23), PSV 38 (1998) 103-115.

MAZZINGHI, Luca, La Sapienza, presente accanto a Dio e all'uomo: Sap 9,9b.10c e la figura di Iside: CALDUCH BENAGES / VERMEYLEN (eds.), Treasures of Wisdom, 357-367.

MAZZINGHI, Luca, Come nasce un idolo (Sap 14,11-22 e 15,7-13), PSV 46 (2002) 61-76.

MAZZINGHI, Luca, La memoria della legge nel libro della Sapienza: CARDELLINI, Innocenzo / MANICARDI, Ermenegildo, (eds.), Torah e Kerygma: dinamiche della tradizione nella Bibbia, Atti della XXXVII Settimana Biblica Nazionale, Roma 9-13 settembre 2002, RicStoBib 16/1-2 (2004) 153-176.

Mazzinghi, Luca, I misteri di Dio: dal libro della Sapienza all'Apocalisse: Bosetti, Elena / Colacrai, Angelo (eds.), Apokalypsis. Percorsi nell'Apocalisse in onore di Ugo Vanni, Assisi: Cittadella 2005, 147-182.

Mazzinghi, Luca, Wisdom 19:13-17 and the Civil Rights of the Jews of Alexandria: Passaro, Angelo / Bellia, Giuseppe (eds.), Yearbook 2005. The Book of Wisdom in Modern Research. Studies on Tradition, Redaction, Theology, Deuterocanonical and Cognate Literature, Berlin – New York: De Gruyter 2005, 53-82.

Mazzinghi, Luca, Morte e immortalità nel libro della Sapienza: alcune considerazioni su Sap 1,12-15; 2,21-24; 3,1-9, VivHo 17/2 (2006) 267-286.

Mazzinghi, Luca, Law of Nature and Light of the Law in the Book of Wisdom (Wis 18.4c): Xeravits, Géza G., / Zsengellér, Jozsef (eds.), Studies in the Book of Wisdom (JSJS 142), Leiden-Boston: Brill 2010, 37-60.

Mazzinghi, Luca, Aspetti della tradizione sapienziale nell'opera di Luca. Il caso di Atti 7,10.22: De Virgilio, Giuseppe / Ferrari, Pier Luigi (eds.), "Lingue come di fuoco" (At 2,3). Studi lucani in onore di mons. Carlo Ghidelli, Rom: Studium 2010, 91-102.

Mazzinghi, Luca. La figura di Abramo in Sap 10,5: una rilettura delle Scritture tra giudaismo e ellenismo: Bonney, Gillian / Vicent, Rafael, Sophia – Paideia. Sapienza e educazione (Sir 1,27), FS. Mario Cimosa, Rom: LAS 2012, 351-364.

Mazzinghi, Luca, L'idea di "popolo" nel libro della Sapienza. Spunti per una riflessione ecclesiologica: Noceti, Serena / Cioli, Gianni / Canobbio, Giacomo (eds.), Ecclesiam intelligere. Studi in onore di Severino Dianich, Bologna: EDB 2012, 17-34.

Mazzinghi, Luca, La creazione rinnovata (Sap 19,18-21), PSV 66 (2012) 63-80.

Mazzinghi, Luca, "I loved [Wisdom] and sought her from my youth: I desidered to take her for my Counsellor" (Wis 8,2a): Solomon and Wisdom: An Example of Closest Intimacy: Passaro, Angelo (ed.), Family and Kinship in the Deuterocanonical and Cognate Literature, Yearbook 2012-20123, Berlin: De Gruyter 2013, 229-252.

Mazzinghi, Luca, The antithetical pair "to punish" and "to benefit" (κολάζω - εὐεργετέω) in the book of Wisdom: Calduch-Benages, Nuria (ed.), Wisdom for Life, FS Maurice Gilbert, Berlin / Boston: De Gruyter, 2014, 237-249.

Mazzinghi, Luca, The figure of Moses in the Book of Wisdom: Xeravits, Géza G. / Zsengellér, Joszef / Szabó, Xavér (eds.), Canonicity, Setting, Wisdom in the Deuterocanonicals (DCLS 22) Berlin – Boston: De Gruyter, 183-206.

Mazzinghi, Luca, Testi autorevoli di epoca ellenistica in analogia con gli scritti biblici. Un esempio illustre: il libro della Sapienza: Prato, Gian Luigi (ed.), Israele fra le genti in epoca ellenistica: un popolo primogenito cittadino del mondo, RicStoBib 27/1 (2015) 157-176.

Mazzinghi, Luca, The Style of the Book of Wisdom: Bons, Eberhard / Joosten, Jan (eds.), Die Sprache der Septuaginta / The Language of the Septaugint (Handbuch zur Septuaginta / Handbook of the Septuagint, LXX.H Band / Volume 3), Gütersloh: Gütersolohe Vg. 2016, 386-392.

Mazzinghi, Luca Gli "empi" di Sap 2 e la polemica intragiudaica ad Alessandria: M. Crimíella / G.C. Pagazzi / S. Romanello (eds.), Extra ironiam nulla salus, Studi in onore di Roberto Vignolo nel suo LXX compleanno, Milano: Glossa 2016, 101-126.

Mazzinghi, Luca, Sap 4,10-14 e la figura di Enoch: un rapporto polemico: Ellen, Harold J. et al. (edd.), Wisdom Poured Out Like Water, FS G. Boccaccini (DCLS 38), Berlin, Boston: De Gruyter 2018, 302-320.

McGlynn, Moyna, Divine Judgement and Divine Benevolence in the Book of Wisdom (WUNT 139) Tübingen: Mohr Siebeck 2001.

McGlynn, Moyna, Authority and sacred space: concepts of the Jerusalem Temple in Aristeas, Wisdom, and Josephus, Biblische Notizen, 161 (2014), 115-140.

More, Jonathan, On Kingship in Philo and in the Wisdom of Solomon: Cook, Johann / Stipp, Hermann-Josef (eds.), Text-Critical and Hermeneutical Studies in the Septuagint, Leiden - Boston: Brill 2012, 409-426.

Morla Asensio, Victor, Vision de la historia en el libro de la Sabiduria, Reseña Biblica, Estella, Navarra 1998, 37-43.

Neher, Martin, Wesen und Wirken der Weisheit in der Sapientia Salomonis (BZAW 333), Berlin - New York: De Gruyter 2004.

Newman, Judith H., The Democratization of Kingship in Wisdom of Solomon: Najman, Hindi / Newman, Judith H. (eds.), The Ideal of Biblical Interpretation, FS James L. Kugel (JSJ Supp 83), Leiden: Brill 2004, 309-328.

Niccacci, Alviero, Wisdom as Woman, Wisdom and Man, Wisdom and God: Gilbert (ed.), Treasures of Wisdom, 369-385.

Niccacci, Alviero, The structure of the Book of Wisdom: two instructions (Chs. 1-5, 6-19) in line with Old Testament wisdom tradition: Liber Annuus, 58 (2008), 31-72.

Niebuhr Karl-Wilhelm (ed.), Sapientia Salomonis (Weisheit Salomos), eingeleitet, übersetzt und mit interpretierenden Essays versehen von Karl-Wilhelm Niebuhr, Walter Ameling, Folker Blischke, Mareike V. Blischke, Alfons Fürst, Rainer Hirsch-Luipold, Heinz-Günther Nesselrath, Maren R. Niehoff und Friedrich V. Reiterer (SAPERE 27) Tübingen: Mohr Siebeck 2015.

Nielsen, Donald A., La misura divina: creazione e retribuzione nel libro della Sapienza e in Filone: aspetti dell'incontro fra giudaismo ellenismo, Religioni e società 11 (1996) 9-21.

Niklas, Tobias, Food of Angels (Wis 16,20): G.G. Xeravits / J. Zsengellér, Studies in the Book of Wisdom, 83-100.

Nobile, Marco, The Hereafter in the Book of Wisdom (Wisdom 1-3): Calduch-Benages, Nuria (ed.), Wisdom for Life, FS Maurice Gilbert, Berlin / Boston: De Gruyter, 2014, 250-259.

Noël, Damien, Quelle sotériologie dans le livre de la Sagesse?: Trublet, Jacques (ed.), La Sagesse Biblique. De l'Ancien au Nouveau Testament, Actes du Congés de l'ACFEB (Paris 1993), (LDiv 160) Paris: Cerf 1995, 187-196.

Offerhaus, Ulrich, Komposition und Intention der Sapientia Salomonis, Bonn: Rheinische Friedrich-Wilhelms-Universität 1981.

Parisi, Serafino, Phronesis, phronein nel libro della Sapienza, Vivarium 3 (1993) 393-416.

Passaro, Angelo, The Serpent and the Manna or the Saving Word: Exegesis of Wis 16, in Bellia / Passaro, The Book of Wisdom, 179-194.

Passaro, Angelo, Escatologia, profezia e apocalittica. Indagine su Sap 19: Manfredi, Silvana / Passaro, Angelo (Hg), Abscondita in lucem, Fs. B. Rocco, Palermo: Sciascia 1998, 103-117.

Passaro, Angelo, L'argomento cosmologico di Sap 19,18 e la concezione della creazione nel libro della Sapienza, Armetta, Francesco / Naro, Massimo (eds.), In Charitate Pax. Studi in onore del Card. Salvatore De Giorgi, Palermo: Pontificia Facoltà Teologica di Sicilia 1999, 47-61.

Passoni Dell'Acqua, Anna, Alcune osservazioni sugli hapax legomena del libro della Sapienza, RivBibIt 40 (1992) 459-465.

Perdue, Leo G., Pseudonymity and Graeco-Roman rhetoric: mimesis and the Wisdom of Solomon: Frey, Jörg / Herzer, Jens / Janssen, Martina et al. (eds.), Pseudepigraphie und Verfasserfiktion in frühchristlichen Briefen, Tübingen: Mohr Siebeck, 2009, 27-59.

Perrenchio, Fausto, Struttura e analisi letteraria di Sap I,1-15 nel quadro del suo contesto letterario immediato, Salesianum 38 (1975) 289-325.

Pesce, Domenico, Numero, peso e misura (da Platone alla Sap. Sal.), Paideia 43 (1988) 203-209.

Philonenko, Marc, Le Maître de justice et la Sagesse de Salomon, TZ XIV (1958) 81-88.

Pistone, Rosario, The Lyre and the Creation. Music Theory and Persuasive Strategy in Wisdom 19: Bellia / Passaro, The Book of Wisdom, 195-218.

Pock, Johann Ignaz, Sapientia Salomonis. Hieronymus' Exegese des Weisheitsbuches im Licht der Tradition, Graz; Verlag für die Technische Universität Graz 1992.

Ponizy, Bogdan, Logos in the Book of wisdom 18:14-16: Augustin, Matthias / Schunk, Klaus Dietrich (eds.), "Dort ziehen Schiffe dahin..." (BEAT 28): Frankfurt am M.: Peter Lang 1996, 169-177.

Porter, Franck C., The Pre-existence of the Soul in the Book of Wisdom and in the Rabbinical Writings, American Journal of Theology 12 (1908) 53-118 [= Harper, William Rainey (ed.), Old Testament and Semitic Studies, Chicago: University of Chicago Press, 1908, 207-269]

Premstaller, Volkmar M., "Gericht" und "Strafe" im Buch der Weisheit. Alttestamentliche Vorstellungen und griechisch-hellenistische Terminologie, St. Georgen an der Gusen: St. Georgs Presse, 1996.

Priotto, Michelangelo, La Prima Pasqua in Sap 18,5-25: rilettura e attualizzazione (Supplementi alla Rivista Biblica 15); Bologna: EDB 1987.

Priotto, Michelangelo, Il significato del confronto Egitto-Sodoma in Sap 19,13-17, RivBibIt 32 (1984) 369-394.

Priotto, Michelangelo, Violenza e persecuzione contro il giusto (Sap 2,1b-20), RicStoBi 14 (2002) 137-146.

Priotto, Michelangelo, Building a Temple to Wisdom (Wis 9:8): Calduch-Benages, Nuria (ed.), Wisdom for Life, FS Maurice Gilbert, Berlin / Boston: De Gruyter, 2014, 250-259.

Puech, Émile, La conception de la vie future dans le livre de la Sagesse et les manuscrits de la mer morte: un aperçu, Revue de Qumrân, 21 (2003), 209-232.

Puech, Emile, The Book of Wisdom and the Dead Sea Scrolls: an Overview: Bellia / Passaro (eds.), The Book of Wisdom, 117-142.

Ramond, Sophie, La mort, thème critique dans l'effort de compréhension et d'actualisation de l'identité d'Israël dans le livre de la Sagesse?: Artus, Olivier / Ferry, Joëlle (eds.), L'identité dans l'écriture: hommage au professeur Jacques Briend, Paris: Cerf, 2009, 261-278.

Raurell, Fredric, The religious meaning of "Doxa" in the Book of Wisdom: Gilbert (ed.), La Sagesse de l'Ancien Testament, 370-383.

Raurell, Frederic, From δικαιοσύνη to ἀθανασία (Wisd 1,1.15): Calduch Benages / Vermeylen (eds.), Treasures of Wisdom, 331-350.

Reese, James M., Plan and Structure in the Book of Wisdom, CBQ 27 (1965) 391-399.

Reese, James M., Hellenistic Influence on the Book of Wisdom and Its Consequences (AnBib 43), Rome: Biblical Institute Press 1970.

Reese, James M, Can Paul Ricoeur's Method Contribute to Interpreting the Book of Wisdom?: Gilbert (ed.), La Sagesse de l'Ancien Testament, 384-396.

Reese, James M., A Semiotic Critique: With Emphasis on the Place of the Wisdom of Solomon in the Literature of Persuasion, Semeia 49 (1990) 229-242.

Reiterer, Friedrich V., Theologie im Proömium des Weisheitsbuches? Die poetische Struktur und Gestaltung als Mittel der Verkündigung in Weish 1,1-15: Moenikes, Ansgar (ed.), Schätze der Schrift. FS Fuhs, Hans F., (PaThSt 47), Paderborn: Schöning 2007, 43-68.

Reiterer, Friedrich V., Philosophische Lehre und deren Wirkung aus der Sicht eines Weisheitslehrers, Untersuchung von Weish 1:1,1-15: Xeravits / Zsengellér (eds.), Studies in the Book of Wisdom, 125-162.

Reiterer, Friedrich V., Die Macht und die Mächtigen im Buch der Weisheit, BN 161 (2014) 69-75.

Reiterer, Friedrich V., "In Fact his Life is Unlike that of Others" (Wisd 2:15), BN 164 (2015) 65-86.

Reiterer, Friedrich V., Emotionen, Gefühle und Affekte im Buch der Weisheit: ein Themenaufriss: Egger-Wenzel, Renate / Corley, Jeremy (eds.), Emotions from Ben Sira to Paul, Berlin - Boston (Mass.): De Gruyter, 2012, 281-315.

Ricken, Friedo, Gab es eine hellenistische Vorlage für Weisheit 13-15?, Bib 49 (1968) 54-86.

Risberg, Bernard, Textkritische und exegetische Anmerkungen zur Weisheit Salomos, ZAW 33 (1913) 206-221.

Rosa, Pietro, Note a Sap 2,6-9, Eikasmos 17 (2006) 202-209.

Rytel-Andrianik, Paweł, From the bread of angels to the food of immortality: manna in Wis 16:20-23, Warszawa: Wydawnictwo Sióstr Loretanek, 2012.

Ruppert, Lothar, Gerechte und Frevler (Gottlose) in Sap 1,1-6,21. Zum Neuverständnis und zur Aktualisierung alttestamentliche Traditionen in der Sapientia Salomonis: Hübner (ed.), Die Weisheit Solomos im Horizont Biblischer Theologie, 1-54.

Scarpat, Giuseppe, Un passo della Sapienza (2,9a), Tetraonyma, Miscellanea graeco-romana, (Pubblicazioni dell'Istituto di filologia classica dell'Università di Genova, 25), Genova: Istituto di filologia classica e medievale 1966, 247-249.

Scarpat, Giuseppe, Ancora sull'autore del libro della Sapienza, RivBiblt 15 (1967) 171-189.

Scarpat, Giuseppe, Note a tre passi della Sapienza (Sap 2,16; 2,24; 4,19): Testimonium Christi. Scritti in onore di Jacques Dupont, Brescia: Paideia 1985, 455-461.

Scarpat, Giuseppe, Una singolare definizione della paura (Sap 17,11s); in: Sapienza Antica. Studi in onore di Domenico Pesce, Parma: Franco Angeli 1985, 261-268.

Scarpat, Giuseppe, La morte seconda e la duplice morte dalla Sapienza a San Francesco, Paideia 42 (1987) 35-62.

Scarpat, Giuseppe, Osservazioni sul testo della Sapientia nella Nova Vulgata, RivBiblt 35 (1987) 187-194.

Scarpat, Giuseppe, Una speranza piena di immortalità (Sap 3,4), RivBiblt 36 (1988) 487-494.

Scarpat, Giuseppe, Ancora sulla data di composizione della Sapientia Salomonis. Il termine diágnôsis (Sap 3,18; At 25,21), RivBiblt 36 (1988) 363-375.

Scarpat, Giuseppe, Prologo di Giovanni e Sapienza di Salomone: Lingua e stile del vangelo di Giovanni: Ceresa Gastaldo, Aldo (ed.), Genova: Pubblicazioni del D.AR.FI.CL.ET 1991, 7-37.

Scarpat, Giuseppe, Un hapax assoluto: αἱρετίς (Sap 8,4): Curti, Carmelo / Crimi, Carmelo (eds.), Scritti classici e cristiani offerti a Francesco Corsaro, Catania: Università degli Studi di Catania: 1994, 643-647.

Scarpat, Giuseppe, Predisposizione naturale e preesistenza dell'anima (nota a Sap 8,19-20), RivBiblt 43 (1995) 93-100.

Schaberg, Jane, Major midrashic traditions in Wisdom 1,1-6,25, JSJ 13 (1982) 75-101.

Schaper, Joachim, ΝΟΜΟΣ and nomoi in the Wisdom of Solomon: Schipper, Bernd U. / Teeter, Andrew (eds.), Wisdom and Torah: the reception of "Torah" in the wisdom literature of the Second Temple period, Leiden - Boston (Mass.): Brill, 2013, 293-306.

Schenker, Adrian, Et comme le sacrifice de l'holocauste il les agréa (Sg 3,6): Calduch-Benages / Vermeylen (eds.), Treasures of Wisdom, 351-356.

Schmitt, Armin, Zur dramatischen Form von Weisheit 1,1-6,21, BZ ns 37 (1993) 236-258.

Schmitt, Armin, Der frühe Tod des Gerechten nach Weish 4,7-19: Ein Psalmenthema in weisheitlicher Fassung: Haag, Ernst / Hossfeld, Frank-Lothar (eds.), Freude an der Weisung des Herrn. Beiträge zur Theologie der Psalmen, Fs. H. Groß, SBB 13, Stuttgart: Verlag Katholisches Bibelwerk 1987, 325-347.

Schmitt, Armin, Skepsis, Bedrängnis und Hoffnung in Weish 1,16-2,24, Bibel un Kirche 52 (1997) 166-174.

Schmitt, Armin, Struktur, Herkunft und Bedeutung der Beispielreihe in Weish 10: Id., Der Gegenwart verpflichtet, Berlin: De Gruyter, 2000, 223-244.

Schmitt, Armin, Komposition, Tradition und zeitgeschlichter Hintergrund in Weish 1,16-2,24 und 4,20-5,23: Id., Der Gegenwart verpflichtet, Berlin: De Gruyter 2000, 164-184.

SCHMITT, Armin, Heilung und Leben nach Weish 16,5-14: JEREMIAS, Joachim (ed.), Gerechtigkeit und Leben in hellenistischer Zeitalter, FS O. Kaiser (BZAW 296) Berlin: De Gruyter 2001, 51-86.

SCHROER, Silvia, Die personifizierte Sophia im Buch der Weisheit: DIETRICH, Walter / KLOPFSTEIN, Martin A. (eds.), Ein Gott allein?, Ein Gott allein?: JHWH-Verehrung und biblischer Monotheismus im Kontext der israelitischen und altorientalischen Religionsgeschichte (OBO 139), Freiburg – Göttingen: Editions universitaires de Fribourg – Vandenhoeck & Ruprecht 1994, 543-558.

SCHWENK-BRESSLER, Udo, Sapientia Salomonis als ein Beispiel frühjüdischer Textauslegung. Die Auslegung des Buches Genesis, von Exodus 1-15 und Teilen der Wüstentradition in Sap 10-19, Frankfurt a.M.: Peter Lang 1993.

SCHWIENHORST – SCHÖNBERGER, Ludger, Weisheit und Gerechtigkeit in der Sapientia Salomonis – mit einem Ausblick auf die Politeia Platonis: REITERER, Friedrich V. / EGGER-WENZEL, Renate / ELSSNER, Thomas R. (eds.), Gesellschaft und Religion in der spätbiblischen und deuterokanonischen Literatur, Berlin – Boston: De Gruyter 2014, 129-159.

SCHWIENHORST – SCHÖNBERGER, Ludger „Die Welt in Heiligkeit und Gerechtigkeit leiten". Zur Auslegung von Gen 1,26-28 in Weish 9,1-3: FISCHER, Stephan / GROHMANN, Marianne (eds.), Weisheit und Schöpfung, FS Alfred Loader, Wien: Peter Lang 2010, 211-229.

SEELEY, David, Transumptive Narration and the Structure of Wisdom 1-5: LULL, David J., (ed.), Society of Biblical Literature 1988 Seminar Papers, One Hundred Twenty-Fourth Annual Meeting, 19-22 November 1988; Chicago (Seminar Papers 27), Atlanta, Georgia 1988, 245-248.

SEELEY, David, Narrative, the Righteous Man and the Philosopher: an Analysis of the Story of the Dikaios in Wisdom 1-5, JSP 7 (1990) 55-78.

SHEPPARD, Gerald T., The Relation of Solomon's Wisdom to Biblical Prayer, Toronto Journal of Theology 8 (1992) 7-27.

SISTI, Adalberto, La figura del giusto perseguitato in Sap 2,12-20, BibOr 19 (1977) 129-144.

SISTI, Adalberto, La morte prematura in Sap 4,7-17, RivBiblt 31 (1983) 129-146.

SISTI, Adalberto, La morte violenta del giusto nel libro della Sapienza: Gesù e la sua morte, Atti XXVII Sett. Biblica Italiana, Brescia: Paideia 1984, 239-309.

SISTI, Adalberto, L'ateismo di Sap 2, BibOr 28 (1986) 41-54.

SKEHAN, Patrick W., Isaiah and the teaching of the Book of Wisdom, CBQ 2 (1940) 288-299.

SKEHAN, Patrick W., Note on the latin text of the Book of Wisdom, CBQ 4 (1942) 230-243.

SKEHAN, Patrick W., Borrowings from the Psalms in the Book of Wisdom, CBQ 10 (1948) 384-397.

SKEHAN, Patrick W., The literary relationship of the Book of Wisdom to earlier Wisdom writings: ID., Studies in Israelite Poetry and Wisdom, CBQ Mon. S. 1, Washington D.C.: The Catholic Biblical Association of America, 1971, 172-236.

SKEHAN, Patrick W., The Text and Structure of the Book of Wisdom, Traditio 3 (1945) 1-12.

SUGGS, M. Jack, Wisdom of Solomon: a Homily based on the Fourth Servant Song, JBL 76 (1957) 26-33.

SWEET, John P.M, Miracles in the Wisdom of Solomon: MOULE, Charles F.D. (ed.), Miracles, London: A. R. Mowbray 1965, 113-126.

TAIT, Michael, Crudité à l'anglaise: MCCOSKER, Philip (ed.), What is it that the Scripture Says? Essays in biblical interpretation, translation and reception in honour of Henry Wansbrough OSB (LNTS 316), London-New York: T & T Clarck 2006, 74-88.

TAYLOR, Richard J., The eschatological meaning of life and death in the Book of Wisdom I-V, ETL 42 (1966) 72-137.

THACKERAY, Henry St. John, Rythm in the Book of Wisdom, JTS 6 (1905) 232-237.

THIELE, Walter, Vetus Latina XI,1, (Freiburg i.B.: Herder 1977-1985).

THOM, Johan C., Wisdom in the Wisdom of Solomon and Cleanthes' Hymn to Zeus: COOK, Johann (ed.), Septuagint and reception, Leiden - Boston: Brill, 2009, 195-207.

VANHOYE, Albert, Mesure ou demesure en Sag. XII,22?, RecSR 50 (1962) 530-537.
VAN IMSCHOOT, Paul, Sagesse et esprit dans l'Ancien Testament, RB 47 (1938) 23-49.
VAN ROODEN, Peter T., Die antike Elementarlehre und der Aufbau von Sapientia Salomonis 11-19: LEBRAM, Jürgen C.H. (ed.), Tradition and Re-Interpretation in Jewish and Early Christian Literature, Leiden: Brill 1986, 81-96.
VÍLCHEZ LÍNDEZ, José, El binomio justicia-injusticia en el libro de la Sabiduría, Cuadernos Biblicos 7 (1981) 1-16.
VÍLCHEZ LÍNDEZ, José, El libro de la Sabiduría y la teoría de la transmutación de los elementos: Miscelánea Augusto Segovia, Granada: Facultad de Teologia 1986, 37-49.
VOGELS, Walter, The God who Creates is the God who Saves: the Book of Wisdom's reversal of he Biblical Pattern, Eglise et Théologie 22 (1991) 315-335.
VIGNOLO, Roberto, Wisdom, prayer and kingly pattern: theology, anthropology, spirituality of Wis 9: BELLIA / PASSARO (eds.), The Book of Wisdom in modern research, 255-282.
VOLGGER, David, Die Adressaten des Weisheitsbuches, Bib 82 (2001) 153-177.
WEISENGHOFF, John P., Death and Immortality in the Book of Wisdom, CBQ 3 (1941), 104-133.
WEISENGOFF, John P., The Impious of Wisdom 2, CBQ 11 (1949) 40-65.
WINSTON, David, The Sage as Mystic in the Wisdom of Solomon: GAMMIE, John G. / L.G. PERDUE, Leo G. (eds.), The Sage in Israel and the Ancient Near East, Winona Lake: Eisenbrauns 1990, 383-397.
WINSTON, David, Wisdom in the Wisdom of Solomon: PERDUE, Leo G. / BRANDON SCOTT, Bernard / JOHNSTON WISEMAN, William, In Search of Wisdom, FS Gammie, Louisville (KY): Westminster John Knox 1993, 149-164.
WINSTON, David, Philo and the Wisdom of Solomon on Creation, Revelation, and Providence: The High-Water Mark of Jewish Hellenistic Fusion: KUGEL, James L. (ed.), Shem in the Tents of Japhet: Essays on the Encounter of Judaism and Hellenism, Leiden: Brill 2002, 109-130.
WINSTON, David, Theodicy in the Wisdom of Solomon: LAATO, Anti / DE MOOR Johannes C. (eds.), Theodicy in the world of the Bible, Leiden – Boston (Mass.): Brill 2003, 525-545.
WINSTON, David, A Century of Research on the Book of Wisdom, in: BELLIA / PASSARO, The Book of Wisdom, 1-18.
WOLFGANG, Werner, Denn Gerechtigkeit ist unsterblich; Schöpfung, Tod und Unvergänglichkeit nach Weish 1,11-15 und 2,21-24: HÜBNER (ed.), Die Weisheit Salomos im Horizont Biblischer Theologie, 26-61.
WRIGHT, Addison G, The Structure of the Book of Wisdom, Bib 48 (1967) 1665-184.
WRIGHT, Addison G., Numerical Patterns in the Book of Wisdom, CBQ 29 (1967) 524-538.
XERAVITS, Géza G. / ZSENGELLER, József (eds.), Studies in the Book of Wisdom (JSJS 142), Leiden: Brill 2010.
ZENGER, Erich, "Du liebst alles, was ist" (Weish 11,24). Biblische Perspektiven für einen erneuerten Umgang mit der Schöpfung, BK 44 (1989) 138-147.
ZENNER Johannes K., Der erste Theil des Buches der Weisheit, ZkTh 22 (1898) 417-431.
ZIENER, Georg, Die theologische Begriffssprache im Buche der Weisheit (BBB 11) Bonn: Peter Hanstein 1956.
ZIENER, Georg, Weisheitsbuch und Johannesevangelium, Biblica 38 (1957) 396-418.
ZIEGLER, Joseph, Sapientia Salomonis. Vetus Testamentum Graecum, XII,1, Göttingen: Vandenhoeck & Ruprecht 1962.
ZSENGELLER, Jószef, "The Taste of the Paradise". Interpretation of Exodus and Manna in the Book of Wisdom: XERAVITS / ZSENGELLER (eds.), Studies in the Book of Wisdom, 197-216.
ZURAWSKY, Jason, Separating the Devil from the Diabolos: A Fresh Reading of Wisdom of Solomon 2:24, JSP 21.4 (2012) 366-399.

Zurawsky, Jason, Hell on Earth: Corporeal Existence as the Ultimate Punishment of the Wicked in Philo of Alexandria and the Wisdom of Solomon: Ellens, Harold J. (ed.), Heaven, Hell, and the Afterlife: Eternity in Judaism, Christianity, and Islam, Santa Barbara: Praeger 2013, 193-226.

3. Other Literature

Aalen, Sverre, Die Begriffe "Licht" und "Finsternis" im Alten Testament, im Spätjudentum und im Rabbinismus, Oslo: Dybwad, 1951.

Barclay, John M.G., Jews in the Mediterranean Diaspora from Alexander to Trajan (323 BCE 117 CE), Edinburgh: T&T Clark 1996.

Baslez, Françoise-Marie, Bible et histoire. Judaïsme, hellénisme, christianisme, Paris: Fayard 1999.

Bernand, Etienne, Inscriptions métriques de l'Egypte gréco-romaine, recherches sur la poésie épigrammatique des Grecs en Égypte, Paris: Les Belles Lettres 1969.

Betz, Hans Dieter, The Greek Magical Papyri in Translation Inclunding the Demotic Spells: Including the Demotic Spells, Chicago: University of Chicago Press 1992.

Bickerman, Elias J. The Jews in the Greek Age, Cambridge, Massachusetts: Harvard University Press, 1988.

Blass, Friedrich / Debrunner, Albert, Grammatik des neutestamentlichen Griechisch (Bearbeitet von F. Rehkopf), Göttingen: Vandenhoeck & Ruprecht, [16]1984.

Boccaccini, Gabriele, Middle Judaism: Jewish thought, 300 B.C.E. to 200 C.E., Minneapolis: Fortress Press, 1991 [= Il Medio Giudaismo: Per una storia del pensiero giudaico tra il terzo secolo a.e.v. e il secondo secolo e.v., Genova: Marietti 1993].

Boffo, Laura, Iscrizioni greche e latine per lo studio della Bibbia, Brescia: Paideia 1994.

Botterweck, Johannes / Ringgren, Helmer / Fabry, Josef (eds.), Theologisches Wörterbuch zum Alten Testament, 1-10, Stuttgart: Kohlhammer, 1973-2016. = Theological Dictionary of the Old Testament, I-XV, Grand Rapids: Eerdmans, 1974-2006.

Burkert, Walter, Ancient Mystery Cults, Cambridge Mass.: Harvard University Press 1987.

Caird, George, Toward a Lexicon of the Septuagint, JTS 19 (1968) 453-475; 20 (1969) 21-40.

Calabi, Francesca, Storia del pensiero giudaico ellenistico, Brescia: Morcelliana 2010.

Cohn, Leopoldus / Wendland, Paul / Reiter, Siegfrid / Leisegang, Hans, Philonis Alexandrini Opera quae supersunt, 7 vol., Berolinii: Reimer 1896-1930.

Cohn, Leopold / Heinemann, Isaak / Adler, Maximillian / Theiler, Willy, Die Werke Philos von Alexandria: in deutscher Übersetzung, Berlin: Walter de Gruyter, 1962-1964.

Costacurta, Bruna, La vita minacciata. Il tema della paura nella Bibbia ebraica (AnBib 119), Rom: Pontificio Istituto Biblico 1988.

Cumont, Franz V.M., Lux Perpetua, Paris: Geuthner 1949.

Delatte, Louis, Les traités de la royauté d'Ecphante, Diotogène et Sthénidas, Liége: Faculté de Philsophie et Lettres, 1942.

Dimant, Devorah, Use and Interpretation of Mikra in the Apocrypha and Pseudepigrapha: Mulder, Martin Jan (ed.), Mikra: Text, Translation, Reading and Interpretation of the Holy Bible in Ancient Judaism and Early Christianity, Assen: Van Gorcum 1988, 379-419.

Festugière, André-Jean, L'idéal religieux des Grecs et l'Évangile, Paris: Librairie Lecoffre: J. Gabalda et Compagnie, 1932.

Feldman, Louis H., Jew and Gentile in the Ancient World. Attitudes and interactions from Alexander to Justinian Princeton (NJ): Princeton University Press 1993.

Fox, Michael V., Proverbs 1-9 (AB 18A), New York: Doubleday 2000.

Fraser, Peter Marshall, Ptolemaic Alexandria, I-III, Oxford: Clarendon Press 1972.

Gammie, John G. / Perdue Leo G. (eds.), The Sage in Israel and in the Ancient Near East, Winona Lake (Ind.): Eisenbrauns 1990.

Ginzberg, Louis, The Legends of the Jews, I-VII, Philadelphia: The Jewish Publication Society of America, 1909-1938.

Hengel, Martin, Judentum und Hellenismus, Tübingen: J.C.B. Mohr 1969.

Horbury, William / Noy, David, Jewish inscriptions of Graeco-Roman Egypt: with an index of the Jewish inscriptions of Egypt and Cyrenaica, Cambridge: University Press, 1992.

Kasher, Aryel, The Jews in Hellenistic and Roman Egypt (TSAJ 7), Tübingen: Mohr Siebeck 1985.

Kittel, Gerhard (ed.), Theologisches Wörterbuch zum Neuen Testament, 1-10, Stuttgart: Kohlhammer, 1933-1979. = Theological Dictionary of the New Testament, I-X, Grand Rapids: Eerdmans, 1964-1974.

Kuntzmann, Raymond / Schlosser, Jacques (eds.), Études sur le judaïsme ellénistique. Congrés de Strasbourg (1983), Paris: Cerf 1984.

Laporte, Jean, Philo in the Tradition of Biblical Wisdom Literatur: Wilken, Robert L. (ed.), Aspect of Wisdom in Judaism and Early Christianity, Notre Dame (IN): University of Notre Dame Press 1975, 103-143.

Le Déaut, Roger, La nuit pascale. Essai sur la signification de la. Pâque juive à partir du Targum d'Exode XII 42 (AnBib 22), Rom: Pontificio Istituto Biblico 1963.

Le Déaut, Roger, Targum du Pentateuque, I-V (SC 245.256.261.271.282) Paris: Cerf 1978-1981.

Liddell, Henry George / Scott, Robert, A Greek-English Lexicon, revised and augmented throughout by Henry Stuart Jones; with the assistance of Roderick McKenzie; and with the co-operation of many scholars, Oxford: Clarendon Press, 1985.

Maier Johann, Die Qumran-Essener: Die Texte vom Toten Meer Bd. I-III, München-Basel: Ernst Reinhard 1995-1996.

Mazzinghi, Luca, Il Pentateuco sapienziale. Proverbi, Giobbe, Qohelet, Siracide, Sapienza, EDB: Bologna 2012.

Nickelsburg, George, Resurrection, Immortality and eternal life in intertestamental Judaism, Cambridge: Harvard University Press, 1972.

Niehoff, Maren, Jewish Exegesis and Homeric Scholarship in Alexandria, Cambridge: Univ. Press 2011.

Perdue, Leo G., Wisdom and Creation. The Theology of Wisdom Literature, Nashville: Abingdon 1994.

Perdue, Leo G., The Sword and the Stylus: an introduction to wisdom in the age of empires, Grand Rapids (Mich.): Eerdmans, 2008.

Peek, Werner, Der Isishymnus von Andros und verwandte Texte, Berlin: Weidmannsche Buchhandlung 1930.

Preisendanz, Karl (ed.), Papyri Graecae Magicae: die griechischen Zauberpapyri, Leipzig: Teubner, 1928-1931.

Puech, Emile, La croyance des esséniens en la vie future: immortalité, résurrection, vie éternelle? Histoire d'une croyance dans le judaïsme ancien (EB ns 21-22), Paris: Gabalda, 1993.

Radice, Roberto, Stoici antichi. Tutti i frammenti, Milano: Rusconi 1999.

Scarpat, Giuseppe, Quarto libro dei Maccabei, Brescia: Paideia 2006.

Schürer, Emil, The History of the Jewish People in the Age of Jesus Christ (175 B.C.-A.D. 135); a new English version revised and edited by Geza Vermes and Fergus Millar, Edinburgh: T & T Clark, 1973-1987.

Siegert, Folker, Early Jewish Interpretation in a Hellenistic Style: Sæbø, Magne (ed.), Hebrew Bible / Old Testament. The History of His Intepretation. Volume I. From the Beginning to the Middle Ages (Until 1300), Vandenhoeck & Ruprecht, Göttingen 1996, 191-196.

Spicq, Ceslas, Agapé. Prolégomènes à une étude de théologie néo-testamentaire, Studia Hellenistica 10, Louvain: Presses Universitaires de Louvain 1955.

Spicq, Ceslas, Notes de lexicographie néo-testamentaire (OBO 22/1-3), Göttingen: Vandenhoeck & Ruprecht, 1978-1982.

Tcherikover, Victor A. / Fuks, Alexander (eds.), Corpus Papyrorum Judaicarum, I-III, Cambridge, Mass.: Harvard University Press 1957-1964.

Totti, Maria, Ausgewählte Texte der Isis- und Sarapis-Religion, Hildesheim: Georg Olms, 1985.

Vanderlip, Vera Frederika, The four Greek hymns of Isidorus and the cult of Isis, Toronto: A.M. Hakkert Ltd., 1972.

Verbeke, Gerard, L'évolution de la doctrine du Pneuma du Stoicisme à Saint Augustin. étude philosophique, Paris: Desclée de Brouwer, 1945.

Von Arnim, Iohannes, Stoicorum Veterum Fragmenta I–III, Lipsiae: Teubner 1921-1924.

West, Martin Litchfield, Iambi et elegi Graeci ante Alexandrum cantati: Volumen I: Archilocus; Hipponax; Theognidae; Oxonii: e Typographica Clarendoniana 1989.

Zerwick, Maximilian, Graecitas biblica, Rom: Pontificium Institutum Biblicum 1960.

Indexes

Index of Greek Words

Index of Key Words

Index of Biblical Citations

Index of Other Ancient Literature

Plan of volumes

Genesis
I (1–11): David Carr
II–III (12–50): Konrad Schmid

Exodus
I–II: Helmut Utzschneider / Wolfgang Oswald

Leviticus
Baruch Schwartz / Naphtali Meshel

Numbers
I–II: NN

Deuteronomy
I–II: Jeffrey Stackert / Joel S. Baden

Joshua
I–II: Michaël N. van der Meer / Cor de Vos

Judges
Andreas Scherer

Ruth
Shimon Gesundheit

1./2. Samuel
I (1. Sam 1–15): Regine Hunziker-Rodewald
II (1. Sam 16–2. Sam 5): Johannes Klein
III (2. Sam 6–24): Thomas Naumann

1./2. Kings
I (1 Kgs 1–15): NN
II (1 Kgs 16 – 2 Kgs 16): Steven L. McKenzie
III (2 Kgs 17–25): Shūichi Hasegawa

1./2. Chronicles
I–II: Ehud Ben Zvi

Ezra / Nehemia
I–II: Richard J. Bautch

Tobit
Beate Ego

Judith
Barbara Schmitz

Esther
Jean-Daniel Macchi

Job
Melanie Köhlmoos

Psalms
I–III: NN

Proverbs
I–II: Jutta Krispenz

Ecclesiastes
Katharine Dell / Tova Forti

Song of Songs
Martien A. Halvorson-Taylor

Wisdom
Luca Mazzinghi

Sirach
Frank Ueberschaer

Isaiah
I–III: NN

Jeremiah
I (1–25): Christl M. Maier
II (26–52): Carolyn J. Sharp

Baruch
NN

Lamentations
Andreas Michel

Ezekiel
Michael Konkel

Daniel
Devorah Dimant

Hosea
Eberhard Bons

Joel/Obadiah
Anselm Hagedorn

Amos
Rainer Kessler

Jonah
Irmtraud Fischer

Micah
Burkard M. Zapff

Nahum / Habakkuk / Zephaniah
Walter Dietrich

Haggai / Zechariah 1–8
Jakob Wöhrle

Zechariah 9–14
Paul L. Redditt

Malachi
Aaron Schart

1. Maccabees
Dov Gera / Jan Willem van Henten

2. Maccabees
Johannes Schnocks

1 Esdras
Dieter Böhler